Through Preservice Teachers' Eyes

Exploring Field Experiences Through Narrative and Inquiry

J. Gary Knowles
Ardra L. Cole
with
Colleen S. Presswood

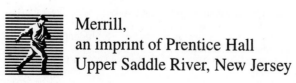
Merrill,
an imprint of Prentice Hall
Upper Saddle River, New Jersey   Columbus, Ohio

Editor: Debra A. Stollenwerk
Production Editor: Louise N. Sette
Cover Designer: Thomas Mack
Production Buyer: Corinne Folino
Electronic Text Management: Marilyn Wilson Phelps, Matthew Williams, Jane Lopez, Karen Bretz
Illustrations: Steve Botts

This book was set in Zapf Calligraphic by Macmillan College Publishing Company and was printed and bound by R.R. Donnelley & Sons Company. The cover was printed by Phoenix Color Corp.

Printed in the United States of America

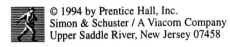 © 1994 by Prentice Hall, Inc.
Simon & Schuster / A Viacom Company
Upper Saddle River, New Jersey 07458

Library of Congress Cataloging-in-Publication Data
Knowles, J. Gary
    Through preservice teachers' eyes : exploring field experiences through
narrative and inquiry / J. Gary Knowles, Ardra L. Cole, with Colleen S. Presswood.
        p.   cm.
    Includes bibliographical references (p.   ) and index.
    ISBN 0-02-365371-X
    1. Student teaching—United States—Case studies.   2. Student teachers—
United States—Case studies.   I. Cole, Ardra L.
    II. Presswood, Colleen S.   III. Title.
    LB2157.A3K66   1994
    370'.7'330973—dc20   93-36349
                                                                    CIP

Printing: 6 7 8 9

To the preservice teachers whose stories of experience made this book possible

I like what one of my teachers said. He asked us if we had seen the full moon the week before and noticed its beauty. Most of us said "No, we had not." He said that he really could not describe it for us so that it would mean anything to us. He said the full moon would come around again and we should see it for ourselves. (Lynn Anderson)

Introduction

We offer a curriculum and pedagogy for preservice teacher education field experiences that is based on and heavily influenced by preservice teachers' perspectives and experiences. We write with a developmental perspective on the processes of learning to teach and becoming a teacher and with a focus on self-directed learning, facilitation of ongoing professional development, and inquiry.

To learn from and be informed by the experiences of peers in the learning to teach process is an important dimension of becoming a teacher. In the flurry and pressure of many preservice teacher education programs to attend to appropriate theory and practice, the perspectives of those learning to teach are often overlooked or not respected. A noticeable absence of preservice and beginning teachers' voices in most texts about learning to teach inspired us to write this book. Knowing from experience that beginning and preservice teachers have much to say about the topic and focus of their future profession we wanted to write a text that explores aspects of the early period of beginning to teach from that perspective.

Three books written by groups of beginning teachers were especially significant in our thinking prior to writing this book. *Don't Smile Until Christmas* (University of Chicago Press, 1970), *Biting the Apple* (Longman, 1980), and *The Roller Coaster Year* (HarperCollins, 1992) were edited or coauthored by Kevin Ryan and present actual experiences of first-year teachers—written by first-year teachers. Over the years we have used the first two books as supplementary texts in preservice teacher education course work. Because of positive responses from preservice teachers to these firsthand stories, we were encouraged to think about the format, structure, and usefulness of a book such as *Through Preservice Teachers' Eyes*. We were also encouraged to pursue this project by preservice teachers' positive responses to Robert Bullough's *First Year Teacher* (Teachers College Press, 1989), Bullough, Knowles, and Crow's *Emerging as a Teacher* (Routledge, 1991), and Rock Kane's edited *Real Stories by First Year Teachers* (Teachers College Press, 1991).

A large part of learning to teach involves grappling with and making sense of a broad range of experiences and circumstances in the field—in schools, classrooms, and other places where teaching and learning occur. Formalized opportunities to learn from experience and with experienced teachers come at various times during preservice teacher preparation. In some programs, field experiences are an ongoing and integral part of learning in coursework; in other settings, field experiences come at the end of programs and form the culminating and capstone experiences of preparation for teaching. Still other university programs represent formats, such as alternating periods of course work learning and intense field work, in which theoretical and practical pursuits are explicitly linked. This book is intended to address issues associated with a range of contexts and activities centered on field experiences within formal teacher education programs. We do not focus on or espouse any one configuration of course work and fieldwork, but we do advocate the substance of the book as a curriculum and pedagogy for field experiences.

Purposes and Perspectives of the Book

The primary purpose of the book is to provide preservice teachers and early practitioners realistic views of the prospects and problems associated with working in schools while providing a framework for discussion, critical reflection, and research into the practice of teaching. Our intentions are to tell about and discuss experiences, processes, tools, and practices associated with learning to teach in field settings, and to help early and more seasoned beginners develop a sense of the possibilities and opportunities for professional development in such settings.

In addition to writing for preservice teachers, especially student or practice teachers, and even those formally beginning their first full-time position in schools, we think that cooperating (also called facilitating or supervisory) teachers and principals, university supervisors and instructors, and those involved in teacher education in the broadest sense also will find this book useful. We also see value in the text for graduate students and others exploring elements of teacher development.

In the early stages of writing we struggled to establish a voice, tone, and audience for our work. Although we address readers as preservice teachers, we do not intend to exclude those more advanced on the path of professional development or who have facilitatory roles in the learning to teach process. We think the narrative accounts as well as the focal questions for discussion, reflection, and research at the end of each chapter, in addition to representations of formal research, will help make the book accessible to a wide variety of readers.

A word about what the book is *not* may be useful before we proceed further. We do *not* present, for example, topics covered in traditional teaching methods courses such as those focusing on learning theories, instructional strategies, and curriculum design and orientations. We also do not give much attention to classroom management and student discipline, not because we think these matters do not loom large in the minds of preservice teachers, or are not important, but because we think the topics are dealt with far more effectively by other authors in other texts. In addition, we chose not to emphasize these issues because we think that excessive focus on the behavioral elements of teaching—"How do I deal and cope with Betty's misbehavior today," for example—gets in the way of the development of coherent, consistent, compatible, and long-term professional perspectives grounded in *understanding* students, their behaviors, and preservice teachers' own responses.

Introduction

We do not delve into social, historical, racial, cultural, and political aspects of education and schools, either at the micro or macro levels, to the extent that other texts are likely to do. The narratives of the preservice teachers explore elements of these topics from the perspective of experience, although their attention to these matters is often less than optimum. Where possible, therefore, through research activities and presentations of formal research, we urge preservice teachers to place their experiences and understandings in the broader social context of teaching and schooling. We expect that readers' prior knowledge and experiences associated with all aspects of teaching will inform consideration of the topics raised for consideration.

The text focuses on the intensely human aspect of learning to teach and centers on preservice teachers' narratives about their experience; yet, it is far more than simply stories or vignettes of experience. Through the voices of preservice teachers we address a variety of issues and topics of interest and concern to most preservice teachers. For example, many preservice teachers experience considerable apprehension about returning to schools after an absence of anywhere from a few years to decades. Some even experience fears in anticipating the field experience aspect of their formal preparation to teach. We address these and other topics from a variety of perspectives. In so doing, we raise awareness of many of the common pitfalls and possibilities associated with learning to teach and learning to be a teacher. We do not cover *every* kind of scenario possible, but we do raise awareness of the kinds of issues that require attention when entering and learning in the field.

Throughout, we focus on discussion of experiences, strategies, processes, and contexts that may facilitate ongoing professional development through successful accomplishments in field experiences. There are three perspectives represented in the book. First and foremost are the views and experiences of preservice teachers themselves—the individuals who wrote about their experiences during and after periods of field experience activity. We see the representation of these perspectives as the central value of the book. We intend it, as we said earlier, to be a tool for developing educative field experiences and ongoing professional practice. Because the text invites personal involvement in stories about "learning to teach" we hope it will engender responses such as, "Yes, that's similar to my situation. I can learn from that person's experience," or, "I can see that these issues are probably really important to consider because . . ." And, within this framework, we consistently urge reflection on and critical analysis of field experiences and developing practice.

Second, as a kind of commentary, we present our perspectives as teacher educators, professors of education, and former classroom and cooperating teachers. At various times in our careers, we have taught all levels from preschool through senior high school students, as well as adults at various ages and stages of life, in traditional and alternative contexts, residential schools, and special education settings. Colleen Presswood was, until the last months of writing, a preservice teacher. Her perspective and experiences of teaching add yet another dimension to the text.

Third, we also draw on recent research about the early period of learning to teach. We include research perspectives especially because they provide us many additional insights into becoming a teacher. Also, linking the preservice teachers' narratives of experience with pertinent research makes explicit the theory-practice link; research and experience become mutually validating. Becoming both the facilitator and director of one's own professional development implies the need for a certain awareness of theoretical and research-based perspectives on which to hinge emerging exemplary practice.

Embodied in the three perspectives just noted are the central concepts of the book. We want to make them explicit. First, preservice teachers are themselves teacher educators. Their experiences are the starting points for reflection, discussion, and inquiry. Second, personal narrative is both the medium for presenting others' experiences and a vehicle for recording and exploring one's own thinking and practice. We advocate explorations of narratives as a way to invigorate personal, professional development. Third, inquiry is crucial to the overarching conception of professional development and the framework of the book. Based on the belief that inquiry fosters understanding, we highlight the role of ongoing inquiry into self, contexts, and relationships, as well as the role of formal research in beginning teacher development. Fourth, the notion of personal and professional empowerment is emphasized. We provide contexts for preservice teachers to become more fully aware of the programmatic and institutional orientations to teacher preparation and to the processes associated with becoming a professional. Not only do we validate self-directed professional development but, also, we honor individuals' past and present learnings about teachers and teaching and, in the process, point toward the notion of life-long and ongoing professional growth.

In summary, we are among those who believe that individuals who enter formal teacher education institutions—colleges, schools, or faculties of teacher education at universities—bring with them many perspectives and practices that represent long-held beliefs about teachers' roles and practices, and about classrooms and schools. These beliefs and other important personal insights into learning to teach are often overlooked in formal preparation programs. The book is written, therefore, to encourage reflection on past and current experiences that inform developing practice.

Organization of the Book

The overall organization of the book represents our pedagogy for field experiences and follows, chronologically, the typical kinds of issues, concerns, and foci of preservice teachers as they engage in the process of learning to teach and being a teacher. We intend to facilitate preservice teachers to extend their theoretical learning into the field, perhaps first as nonparticipant observers of practice and, then, as active participants developing emerging practice. We start, therefore, by focusing on appropriate tools of reflexive inquiry and explorations of self (particularly life history influences and professional role identity) in readiness for entering the field. We move on to explorations of contexts of practice and elements of those contexts, next to professional relationships and their nuances, and finally back to self as emerging professional.

There are four parts to the book. In Part 1, *Becoming an Inquiring Teacher,* we introduce the conceptual framework of the book and the notion of planning for professional growth. In Part 2, *Tools for Reflexivity and Inquiry,* we include approaches to make sense of field experiences and to facilitate and engage in professional development. In Part 3, *Narrative and Inquiry in Field Experience,* we present preservice teachers' perspectives on working and learning in formal education contexts. In Part 4, *Preparing for Future Teaching,* we focus on making sense of field experiences within the context of preparing for the first year of full-time or part-time teaching. Each chapter within the four parts ends with a list of recommended readings. Sometimes the list is extensive, other times it is not; we endeavor to provide examples of works that, in concert with each chapter, will extend readers' thinking and emerging practice.

Part 1 has only one chapter. In *Planning for Professional Growth* we consider the multiple forms of knowledge informing the processes of learning to teach and becoming a teacher. We discuss the interrelated nature of theory and practice, explore the meaning of becoming reflexive, and introduce the role of research in becoming a teacher. Our focus here is on ways of developing understanding about teaching and the work of teachers.

Part 2, Chapters 2 through 4, provides a foundation for developing sound strategies for ongoing professional development. We offer some tools for engaging in reflexive inquiry or research on practice. In Chapter 2, *Autobiographical Writing: Gathering Personal, Internal Information,* we focus on ways of gathering internal or autobiographical information as a means of exploring personal-professional understandings of practice through personal history accounts, journal writing, personal metaphors, and professional development records.

Chapter 3, *Looking and Listening: Gathering External Information Using Ethnographic Research Techniques* is intended to help preservice teachers look beyond themselves to understand educational contexts and the actions of those who work and learn within those contexts. We introduce tools for gathering external information. Observation, interviewing, and collecting documents or other artifacts form the basis for engaging in research activities within educational settings.

Chapter 4, *Professional Development Through Collaboration with Peers,* is based on relational learning. In it we suggest ways in which preservice teachers might work together to support and encourage professional growth, and develop their perspectives on teaching. We emphasize the sharing of autobiographical writing, the development of collective accounts of experience, group discussions, and peer observations as ways of prompting preservice teachers to think about practice in different ways.

Part 3, Chapters 5 through 11, is the heart of the book in that it intimately explores elements of field experiences. It represents glimpses of the learning to teach process from the formation of early, perhaps tentative, perspectives to more empirically informed thinking about the profession and the role of teachers. We begin by exploring issues associated with planning to teach and with early influences on personal perspectives on teaching and schooling. From there, we present thematic chapters, each consisting of several subsections that represent elements of field experiences and professional knowledge. Each subtheme or subsection is organized in a similar fashion. Following an introduction are

- *Narrative Accounts*
- *For Reflection and Discussion*
- *Links with Research*
- *Research Activities*

We see the *Narrative Accounts* or stories as the central part of each subsection. *For Reflection and Discussion, Links with Research,* and *Research Activities* serve to draw out elements that will give wider meaning to preservice teachers' experiences. Moreover, our intent is to provide examples of the range of perspectives that inform the development of thinking and practice over the long term. As we mentioned earlier, the *Narrative Accounts* are *not* intended to cover all the possible kinds of scenarios that preservice teachers may encounter or describe; nor do they represent the range of preservice teachers' thinking about particular topics. They simply serve as springboards for reflection, analysis, discussion, guidance, and decision-making. More than anything, we encourage the development of informed preservice teachers, individuals who can engage to the fullest the many resources, opportunities, and activities that make for optimum field experiences in a variety of contexts. Such engagement will realize the benefit of experiential learning, experiences grounded in careful and critical analysis of classrooms, schools, and emerging practices. The narratives also illustrate the use of many of the reflexive tools described in Part 2.

Chapter 5, *Exploring Images and Contexts of Teaching,* provides an opportunity to consider the role of prior experiences in schools in the development of personal conceptions of teaching. We discuss *teacher role models* and the relevance of *personal histories* in preservice teachers' thinking about the profession, recognizing that everyone coming to formal teacher preparation programs has preconceptions of teaching and what it means to be a teacher. The importance of understanding the roles of theory and practice in formal teacher education is raised in an attempt to coalesce newfound understandings of the profession of teaching. These subtopics lay the ground work for exploring contexts in which field experiences take place.

Chapter 6, *Expectations of Field Experiences and Fantasies and Fears About Teaching,* is almost self-explanatory. Understanding preservice teachers' expectations of and for field experiences is crucial for learning in the field and central to achieving educative field experiences. Fantasies and realities, as well as fears and emerging confidence, are elements of learning to teach in field settings that, without expression, can make for difficult experiences.

In Chapter 7, *Becoming Reacquainted with Schools,* we recognize the powerful influences of personal, past experiences in schools and other places where teaching and learning occur. We then move forward to explore the school as workplace and its relation to society and community and, from a broad perspective, student diversity and cultures.

Chapter 8, *Negotiating a Role and Developing Professional Relationships,* is an exploration of the preservice teacher-cooperating teacher relationship. In particular, we discuss negotiating a role and developing and maintaining productive working relationships with cooperating teachers, making sense of guidance and guidelines, and dealing with problems and differences. Each component is essential for productive experiential learning as guests in experienced teachers' classrooms.

Chapter 9, *Developing Professional Relationships with Supervisors and Others in the Learning Community,* focuses on learning from other professional and nonprofessional members of educational communities. We explore the role of university supervisors as influences on preservice teachers' development. School faculty (including principals, other teachers, counselors, and librarians), support staff (including teachers' aides, custodians, secretaries, cafeteria personnel, bus drivers, and others), the school district administration and school board members, parents, and members of the community may each and collectively influence preservice teachers' development. We explore ways to broaden experiences beyond cooperating teachers' classrooms.

Chapter 10, *Developing and Maintaining Relationships with Students,* centers on understanding students. We highlight the importance of and address issues associated with developing relationships with students, facilitating productive learning environments, and responding to student behavior and individual needs and differences.

Chapter 11, *Acknowledging the Complexity and Dealing with the Ups and Downs of Teaching,* focuses on a number of issues associated with understanding developing practice. We acknowledge and address the scope and complexity of teaching, the emotional highs and lows of teaching (particularly in the early period of developing practice), professional growth through successful and difficult experiences, and failure.

Part 4 has only one chapter. Its purpose is to offer readers the opportunity to focus on the various meanings of their field experiences in preparation for future professional roles. In Chapter 12, *Looking Back and Moving Forward,* we consider ways of pulling together the variety of experiences in field settings to determine what was learned. We explore how notions of teaching and learning are likely to be reconceptualized because of field experiences and then move forward to discuss preparation for the first year of teaching and the facilitation of ongoing professional growth.

Uses of the Book

We intend the book to be used in university-based course work as a main or supplementary text. It also may be used independently by preservice teachers. In addition, apart from being a resource for teacher educators and those exploring elements of practice from a distance, we also intend it to be a vehicle for facilitating the thinking and practice of teacher educators with responsibilities associated with field experiences. Therefore, we see it being used by cooperating or facilitating teachers, university supervisors and others. And, it may also inform the thinking and practice of beginning teachers, especially those who, retroactively, are struggling to make sense of field experiences.

As a main text we think the book is suited to a number of purposes. First, the book is designed for courses that prepare preservice teachers for participation in field settings. In such contexts we see the book as providing insights prior to actual experiences and, thereby, making for more informed, reflexive participation. Second, we see the book as significant for course work that involves participation in classrooms and schools, or places where teaching and learning occur. Such courses may include extended observation and/or practice, such as in student or practice teaching, or extensive and long-term tutoring activities. (In part, it was for this purpose that we first designed the text.) Third, the book is intended to be productive for course work that involves parallel and complementary attention to theory and practice such as in teaching methods courses that expect concurrent participation in the field. Fourth, we see the book being used in seminars associated with field placements. In this kind of context the book serves to enhance the principles and practices of experiential learning. Fifth, the text has a place in courses that explore the roles of cooperating or facilitating teachers, and other mentors, since it provides perspectives not commonly or readily available to professional teachers and school-based teacher educators, including school administrators. For example, we see the text as beneficial for facilitating the preparation of contexts for field experiences and the cooperating teachers and others who work therein.

As a supplementary text, we see major parts of it useful for seminars on beginning teaching and in aspects of preservice teacher education program development. We expect that university teacher educators will be informed by the perspectives in the book and will consequently bring them to bear on their own thinking and practice.

Represented in the book are perspectives of over one hundred preservice teachers at various points in teacher preparation programs. Thus, the book contributes to the knowledge base on learning to teach and, therefore, serves as a source of information for researchers studying processes related to teacher development.

Finally, we see the book being used independently of any kind of course work as a vehicle for helping potential preservice teachers and student or practice teachers become familiar with issues associated with field work in schools. As such, it will help preservice teachers become more informed participants in programs of teacher preparation. As a guide and companion to practice it will serve as a kind of reality check for preservice teachers.

Preservice Teachers' Narratives in the Book

The preservice teachers who contributed the narrative accounts in this book were, at the time of writing, either in field placements or had just completed them. For some, the field placement was their reintroduction to schools; for others, it was the culminating period of their student or practice teaching. They represent experiences had in a variety of settings and programs with different levels of intensity and commitment to learning in the field.

The preservice teachers used a variety of autobiographical tools to record and explore their experiences in written form. The accounts represent a range of comfort and experience with writing and reflect individual stylistic differences. They also represent individuals at different developmental levels. Most accounts were written while preservice teachers were in the field. We chose particular accounts for inclusion primarily because we saw their possibilities for informing others, especially other preservice teachers. For the most part, the narrative accounts of experience were only slightly edited by us. Some of the preservice teachers polished and edited their own work.

Some of the preservice teachers have narrative accounts threaded throughout the book; others are represented only once. Some wished to be identified by name and circumstance; others remain anonymous, with locations of their experiences camouflaged. We respect their various positions. The accounts were written by preservice teachers from the West Coast to the East Coast of the United States, as well as from Central Canada. Prominent racial minorities are represented, as are diverse socioeconomic groups within North American society. At the time of writing about their field experiences some of the preservice teachers were as young as nineteen years; others were well-seasoned adults, parents, and individuals entering either second or third careers. All of them display an enthusiasm for their intended professional life. After completing their preparation programs in either elementary or secondary education most chose to continue in their professional teaching pursuits although some elected to move on to other related fields or professions.

Without exception, the preservice teachers' experiences, partially captured in narrative accounts, have greatly informed our thinking. As university teacher educators, every time we engage preservice teachers in the learning to teach process, *our* practices are challenged. *They* are teacher educators themselves. Indeed, this is one of the premises on which we base this book. On one hand we view this book as an expression of our curricular and pedagogical thinking. On the other hand, it represents the aspirations, successes, and struggles of individuals grappling with the multiple purposes, tasks, and roles associated with becoming professional teachers. And, as such, it represents the notion of *preservice teachers as teacher educators*.

Acknowledgments

The preservice teachers who shared some of their hopes, fears, joys and frustrations about becoming teachers inspired this book. We thank them for enabling us to share their stories of experience with a wider audience. Although the narratives contained in the book were written and gathered over a five-year period, the book itself was written in a relatively short period of time. This was made possible by the assistance and support of several people.

Introduction

We extend our appreciation to Gary's colleagues in the cohort of the Master of Arts degree with teacher certification (MAC) program at The University of Michigan for their ongoing encouragement. Stella Clark provided helpful critiques through careful readings of our work as did Matt Schlein, a recent graduate of the program. The preservice and cooperating teachers of the 1992-1993 cohort inspired us to bring the work to completion.

Barry Arbreton, Maria Coolican, Rosebud Elijah, and Kerry Olson assisted us with reviews of pertinent literature and Priya Nagaraju provided both organizational assistance and helpful suggestions for the text. We thank Mary Beattie, University of Toronto, Mary Louise Holly, Kent State University, Greta Morine-Dershimer, University of Virginia, Richard Powell, University of Nevada, Las Vegas, Alfred V. Roman, Potsdam College, and Sandra Weber, Concordia University in Montreal for their thoughtful reviews. Reviews by Jennifer Krachtus and Bonita Dalton, formerly preservice teachers in Arizona and Alberta, helped us craft the manuscript. And, Helen Harrington of The University of Michigan also responded to an early draft.

Colleen's daughter, Leslie Aris, a junior high school student, provided insight and support throughout the writing process. Finally, we extend our utmost appreciation to Helen Candiotti, who continues in so many ways to help us maintain our sanity and get things done.

J. Gary Knowles
The University of Michigan

Ardra Cole
The Ontario Institute for Studies in Education

Colleen Presswood
The University of Michigan

Prologue

I brought a lot of unexamined baggage with me to the School of Education. I held tightly to my enthusiastic assumptions that not only would I learn everything there was to know about teaching elementary students but also that the process would be fun and painless. I was about to be relieved of some of that baggage.

During orientation to the first-term courses one of the professors remarked that at some time during the term our "lives would seem to go ka-plooey." She assured us that this was "normal." She hoped we would remember her statement when the event occurred. I was such an eager student of teaching that I took notes during the introductions and jotted down her remarks, even though I was very skeptical that the exciting curriculum about to be presented to us would have such a negative effect. But she was right. Much later in the term my life became a shambles. I remember sitting in my kitchen, pieces of course work assignments scattered all over the table, numbly asking "This is normal?" I remembered then a comment I had heard long ago, that "a person's desk resembles their state of mind." Well, my desk and my mind were both in flux.

I felt a panic and excitement when I learned that I would be in a classroom for three half days every week—panic because I was not "qualified" to teach. I had yet to encounter teaching methods course work, and I was acutely aware of my lack of knowledge in this area. But I did "know" about classrooms and teachers from my years of experience as a student. Initially, I thought this meant that I knew about teaching. When I first presented a lesson to a small group of students I was amazed to discover the multitude of elements that are routinely and simultaneously considered by teachers. It was not a comfortable experience to let go of the baggage of "knowing" about teaching. It was a bit like losing a purse or a wallet—anxiety followed by a period of vulnerability. Disoriented, because my identity had been temporarily misplaced, I began to move from identifying with a student's role to that of a teacher.

Part of the course work involved keeping a journal of my experiences in an elementary school classroom. My early entries closely resemble the diary entries that I made as a child: "Woke up. Went to school. Had math and language arts. Came home and ate lunch." The only difference was that as a preservice teacher I didn't go home for lunch. With time, the blur of activity came into sharper focus, and my journal entries became much more detailed. I found writing to be very helpful in sorting through the multitude of activities and exchanges that daily occurred in the classroom.

The journal entries reflected the wide range of emotions I experienced and in combinations that I had not thought possible: variations of calm observer, acid critic, and shrill reformer; as well as evidence of resignation, searing personal doubts, and jubilant successes. The emotional impact of my experiences surprised me.

I do not easily share feelings of self-doubt, so I began to feel *very* alone. Later, I discovered that many of my peers shared similar feelings, and I regretted not being forewarned about the potential impact of them. Although I was fortunate to have a friend who had preceded me in the teacher preparation program, she too was silent about this aspect of her experience. All along, her pragmatic support had been invaluable. When I encountered frustrating aspects of the program and expressed some anxiety she would calmly reply that I was "right on track." When the term ended I told her about my surprise at the emotional impact and asked her how she had appeared to remain so calm. Only after time had provided distance could she safely examine that period of her learning and share with me her habit of "reserving weekends for tears." I told her that I wished I had known that it was "normal" to feel so shaken. She confided that at the time she experienced such feelings she worried that admitting them might indicate that she was unsuited for the field of teaching or unable to present "professional detachment." She also did not want others to interpret her reactions as an indication that she should pursue a different career. We decided to interpret our reactions to our experiences as evidence of depth of caring and agreed that the taboo against admitting self-doubt compounded feelings of isolation and caused unnecessary discomfort.

But whose voice would we have listened to? I was skeptical when one of my professors offered a forewarning about the disorientation that would occur. Yet, I listened with rapt attention when my friend discussed her experiences in the classroom and her frustration with the short amount of time that she had to complete assignments. I also came to value the opinions and experiences of my peers as we shared concerns about theory and practice.

Fortunately, I did not experience the same things at the same time as fellow preservice teachers. Because of this we alternately supported and comforted one another. Sharing our experiences provided a wonderful opportunity to accept and offer suggestions, and to notice that a problem can have multiple solutions. The source of the solutions to most problems was ultimately found in ourselves, and that realization was as sobering as it was empowering.

I experienced tremendous growth during that first term and first field experience, and I did some of it in an adolescent fashion, kicking and screaming internally all the way. I came to understand that I would not learn everything there was to know about teaching in the university classes—only enough to get me started on the learning course that would continue throughout my professional career. At first, that realization felt as if I had just opened a beautifully wrapped package to discover an empty tool box. How could I be expected to teach with an empty tool box? That feeling of chagrin was only gradually replaced by excitement as I realized that tool selection depended upon the craftsperson. I would make my own choices as I learned about my chosen craft. This meant that I also needed to learn about myself. How did I view myself as a teacher? How had prior experiences influenced my decision to become a teacher? What were my assumptions about teaching and being a teacher?

The first term spent in the School of Education was an intense experience. In retrospect, my shifting perspectives resulted in the development of a kaleidoscopic array of theories, feelings, and experiences. Journal entries and written assignments now provide snapshots of my growth. The honest voices of the preservice teachers in this book provide snapshots of *their* development, glimpses of *their* growth. Captured in the book are the moments and fragments of experience that comprise the kaleidoscopic experience of learning about a multidimensional career.

Reading the narrative accounts of experience in this book reminds me of conversations that occurred in classes before the professors arrived. Some of the issues raised and feelings expressed resemble my own, and I recognize my concerns in the voices of others. Identifying areas of concern is a first step. But how do you proceed to the second? How do you come to recognize potential conflict? Or, how do you move toward some resolution of the problem you have identified for yourself? How do you know what questions to pose for yourself that will lead to helpful answers?

Peers provide camaraderie and a "safe" place to examine and even complain about practices and theories in an effort to achieve new levels of understanding. Talking and working with peers allow you to articulate concerns and formulate some questions for yourself. University professors provide support for your inquiry by posing questions that further refine your concerns and relate them to the development of sound practice—*your* practice. Professors also pose questions for you to consider that challenge your assumptions and stimulate your growth.

This book offers both the perspective of peers engaged in preservice practice and the generous support of two insightful and compassionate educators. Their focus has always been on what would be most helpful and supportive for preservice teachers. They answered this by turning to and learning from preservice teachers. As a result of their learning, they represent preservice teachers as teacher educators.

I first saw a proposed outline for this book when I was asked if some of my writing could be included in it. I was flattered to be asked to contribute and curious about the proposed format of the book. I thought it would have been nice to have such a text when I first began to study. I was privileged to watch the book grow and change in response to the preservice teachers and the concerns that they presented. I was invited to take a greater role in writing and shaping the final form of the text. As my participation increased so did my excitement about the book. Implicit questions and concerns that can feel overwhelming to a preservice teacher have been made explicit and are presented in a way that allows readers to examine the issues that are of most importance to them. The book is infused with a level of caring and compassion that provides direction for the passion that beginners bring to teaching.

The book took shape as a result of an interactive process. Engage yourself with it in the same spirit. Personal and professional growth and change are not easy, but the way can be made smoother by sharing in the process with others and listening to those who have gone before.

Colleen Presswood
Ann Arbor, Michigan

Contents

CHAPTER 10
Developing and Maintaining
Relationships with Students   224

CHAPTER 11
Acknowledging the Complexity and Dealing
with the Ups and Downs of Teaching   273

▼ PART IV
Preparing for Future Teaching   311

CHAPTER 12
Looking Back and Moving Forward   312

Contents

PART I

Becoming an Inquiring Teacher

Becoming an inquiring teacher is a central concept in this book. To inquire about self-as-teacher, the profession of teaching, the places where professional practice takes place, and the individuals and groups associated with that practice is essential in the process of becoming a teacher. To begin to be an inquiring teacher is to begin to plan for professional growth. Inquiry begins when we first ask ourselves questions such as, "Why teaching? What do I know about teaching and schools? What have I learned about being a teacher by being a student?" Through personal inquiry, by seeking to understand the complex arenas where teaching and learning take place, by asking questions, and by seeking to understand the practice of others as well as your own emerging practice you are establishing the foundation and developing the framework for lifelong learning about the work and roles of teachers, schools, classrooms and other learning environments, and the students and others who move through those places.

CHAPTER 1

Planning for Professional Growth

I started out thinking that teaching was like following a formula. My formal teacher education courses would give me that formula, and I would then apply it in the classroom. I found out that this procedure is not true. Teaching is a process of discovering yourself; picking through the theories and methods that work for you; developing some theories and methods of your own and going out into the field and using them; and taking the curriculum and putting some of yourself into it. In short, teaching is a process of giving your classroom its own personal character that fosters students' learning. You cannot expect to teach others until you know yourself. With this in mind, learning about teaching is a never-ending process. (Angele Doucette)

As this preservice teacher, Angele, discovered, teaching is a complex and personal endeavor. Becoming a teacher is a career-long, perhaps lifelong, process of continuing professional growth.

Although we cannot delineate for you exactly what you need to know as you engage in the process of becoming a teacher, we can point you in several appropriate directions and offer you some tools for gaining access to and making sense of the various forms of knowledge that will inform your teaching and professional development. Our focus in this book is on exploring ways of developing understanding about teaching. In this chapter, we invite you to consider

- the distinct but interconnected processes of learning to teach and learning to be a teacher
- the interrelated nature of theory and practice
- the process associated with becoming inquiring or reflexive teachers
- the role of research in becoming a teacher (including exploring ways to access the seemingly vast research literature and developing your own research questions)

Learning to Teach and Learning to Be a Teacher

Because of its complexity, teaching is informed by multiple forms of knowledge and is representative of a variety of ways of knowing. To give you an idea of just how complex teaching is, coming up with a definitive knowledge base of teaching is a challenge that has yet to be met in the education community—and for good reason as you will discover. We know, for example, that teachers draw on knowledge about subject matter of various kinds, as well as general and content- or subject-specific pedagogical knowledge; look to research and relevant professional literature; rely on the wisdom of experience and practice; make use of personal leanings and intuitions; are mindful of how to operate within the bureaucratic structures of state or provincial departments of education, school boards and districts, individual schools and other educational institutions, and even local community and government bodies; and, situate themselves and their work within the larger historical, political, and social forces within local, regional, and national communities. The list goes on and on. The knowledge teachers draw on in the run of a normal teaching day is so varied and abundant that the question, "What do I need to know to be a teacher?" is unanswerable, at least in a definitive and discrete sense.

To complicate matters even more, we suggest that learning about teaching involves the study of two distinct but obviously interconnected phenomena and processes: (1) learning about *how to teach* and (2) learning about *how to be a teacher*. The first process involves developing an understanding of self, students, subject matter, pedagogy, curriculum development and subsequent activities, strategies, and techniques associated with facilitating students' learning. The second process has to do with coming to grips with the scope of roles, responsibilities, and ways of acting and thinking as emerging professionals. One has to do with matters largely associated with the activities of students and teachers in classrooms and other places of learning. The other is broader in scope, since being a teacher does not cease as you walk out the classroom door. It is not only associated with classroom roles but participation in the school, local and professional communities, and beyond. If, for example, in developing your professional practice as a preservice teacher, you were located in field placements that only placed you inside particular classrooms with experienced teachers, the chances of your learning how to teach are fairly good given other appropriate conditions. If, however, you had little opportunity to extensively explore the workings of schools[1] and the work of teachers outside their classrooms, you might have some difficulty formulating informed and contemporary notions about *how to be a teacher*. In saying this, we wish to emphasize the importance of stepping beyond classrooms to explore the complex workings of educational institutions. Part of this broadening perspective also involves taking responsibility for exploring the overt and covert social and political

---

[1]   For convenience, we refer to fieldwork as taking place in schools and classrooms. Nevertheless, we think of it as potentially taking place in a variety of settings. Chapter 5 discusses alternatives for field experiences.

influences that have an impact on the thinking of school administrators and teachers. Although it is essential that opportunities to explore practice in field experiences involve educational institutions of various kinds, both inside and outside classrooms, not all preservice programs facilitate such experiences. You may have to take it upon yourself to find ways of exploring the complexity of diverse educational contexts.

To extend our position, teaching and being a teacher require proactive rather than reactive responses to students and classroom learning contexts. *Inquiring* or *reflexive* teachers are more able to take such a stance. Reflexive teachers are more able to influence and mold the contexts, environments, and decision making associated with various teacher-related roles. We, therefore, place emphasis on the importance of your becoming teachers who engage in critical analyses of teaching practices, the contexts of those practices, and the complex roles of teachers. The topics we address in this chapter provide a foundation for thinking about and assessing your developing practice in schools or other places of learning and instruction.

One of the crucial things to recognize about learning to teach and becoming a teacher is that it is not a passive affair. Despite what some people (including guidance counselors, classroom teachers, teacher educators, friends, family members, and other apparently knowledgeable individuals who have "words of wisdom" about the profession) say, preservice teacher education is *not* a trivial pursuit. Sound, progressive programs of preparation do not merely present a set of hoops for you to pass through (although at times it may seem so). Even if only regarded as a series of prescribed courses within a program, preservice teacher education commands your full involvement as you reflect upon and make meaning of the various and varied experiences of practice associated with becoming qualified teachers. This kind of response implies taking a stance other than that of a passive and subservient learner. It means taking a position, despite potential institutional constraints, in which you ask yourself, "What are some ways in which I can take control of my own learning, my professional development, to insure that the activities I engage in as a preservice teacher will serve my needs as an emergent new teacher and professional?"

From our experience teaching in preservice teacher education programs we know that some individuals enter the formal process of "becoming a teacher" believing that they have nothing to learn. Their purpose, they maintain, is merely to obtain provisional teacher certification. In their minds they are already teachers—a position that we respect, by the way, although would pose alternative perspectives for them to consider. As such, however, these individuals maintain a passive presence, attending only to the minimal requirements for passing programs and courses. The contrary position to take is one where you help craft the direction of your own learning and development in significant ways. Ultimately, your heightened professional development will serve the welfare and learning of those future students under your guidance. The process of facilitating your own learning as a professional will also serve as a template for working with students who, all too frequently, are not encouraged to take responsibility in the crafting of their own learning and education.

Your teacher preparation program will no doubt create numerous opportunities for you, in other than relatively superficial ways, to get started on your career path as an inquiring professional. How might you begin to do this? Throughout the book you will catch glimpses of how other preservice teachers started and maintained the process. As you continue reading, keep central in your thinking the notion that becoming a teacher is a process *not* an event!

The Interrelated Nature of Theory and Practice[2]

Many new teachers tell stories of becoming overwhelmed with the demands and scope of their responsibilities in the first months—even years—of teaching. A good proportion of these individuals are likely to tell you that their teacher preparation programs did nothing, or very little, to help them manage the day-to-day routines and exigencies of full-time teaching. They say, for example, that the theory learned in university classrooms was next to useless. What is needed, they typically maintain, is plenty of hands-on or practical experiences coupled with being told *what* works in particular situations and *how* to do it. You may also hear experienced teachers echo such sentiments. You may even hear university teacher educators place similar emphasis on practice at the expense of theory, or conversely, on theory at the expense of practice. Such positions are evidence of a serious, yet common, misconception that claims that the theory and practice of teaching are distinct entities bearing little relationship to one another. In other words, it is often said that theory resides and is learned within the context of the university or college; the real world of teaching practice is embodied in the field. Theory and practice, however, are not distinct entities—they are inextricably linked.

The traditional view of theory developed "out there" under controlled conditions and then "applied" to practice holds for scientifically controlled contexts; however, in the complex human realm of teaching and learning, applying principles of pure science to classroom teaching is not always straightforward. In the context of teaching and learning, there are no completely generalizable rules, laws, or theories. Human behavior is far too idiosyncratic, complex, and unpredictable. In education, the classroom *is* the "laboratory." Theory and practice, therefore, are interdependent. To think otherwise is to set up inappropriate frameworks for understanding teaching, guiding your introductory, full-time, professional experiences, and facilitating your ongoing, career-long development as a teacher.

In exploring your understandings of theory and practice, it may be helpful to think about two kinds of theory informing teacher education: (1) *formal* theories such as those typically studied in teacher education programs and courses and that are usually built on the work of academic researchers; and (2) *personal* theories that are comprised of the beliefs, values, perspectives, attitudes, and ideas devel-

---

[2] This topic is widely addressed in the literature on teacher education and development. See, for example, Clandinin (1986), Connelly and Clandinin (1988), Hunt (1987, 1991), Louden (1991), Ross, Cornett, and McCutcheon (1992), and Schön (1983, 1987, 1991).

oped through professional and nonprofessional experience. Formal theory is generated by researchers studying classroom practices, contexts, and phenomena; personal theory is developed and understood by examining one's own experience of and ideas about practice. Formal theory is developed at a distance through the use of systems of externally-derived constructs or frameworks for understanding, and may be derived from formal observation of collective contexts and phenomena. Personal theory is an explication of one's own implicit understandings. Reflexive practice comes about by melding the two forms of theory and processes of theory generation, that is, by considering elements of formal theories in the context of one's own personal theories. As such, teachers can be both theory generators and theory users. Integrating elements or principles of both personal and formal theories is the essence of reflexive or inquiring practice.

Making links between theory and practice—and, for that matter, between the two forms of theories—represents a significant challenge to preservice and experienced teachers alike. We encourage you to challenge the misconception about the theory-practice relationship. Try thinking about theory and practice as inextricably linked and mutually dependent, and finding different forms of expression and interpretation in different contexts. The university typically offers a setting for systematic, intensive inquiry, reflection, and discussion of theories, concepts, and issues embedded in practical action; field settings provide contexts for identification and practical exploration of key concepts, issues, and topics, places to explore the evidence of inquiry, and to examine whole or parts of theories in practice.

At this period in your preparation it may not be readily apparent to you that theory and practice enjoy a symbiotic relationship. We encourage you, however, to approach both initial teacher preparation and ongoing teacher education with the intention of developing a clearer understanding of how the various and equally important forms of knowledge inform each other and, in turn, contribute to *your* knowledge of teaching theory and practice. In the following, Jeanne, Molly, and Freida have begun to come to understandings of the roles and relationship of theory and practice in preservice teacher education. Note the implicit reference to *both* forms of theory.

▼

Trying to encapsulate all of the information that I have gathered or been exposed to is a difficult task. With lectures, readings, and discussions, I have been exposed to many new theories and philosophies concerning teaching and instructional methods. Experience in classrooms has helped me formulate and formalize my thoughts concerning these different issues. The classroom was an excellent "testing ground" for these new ideas and helped me apply the more formal information from courses. (Jeanne Worthen)

Combining opportunities for learning from field experience with opportunities for learning theory has worked quite well for me. One experience without the other would leave an inexcusable void in my preparation. The field experience has allowed me to see how theory can come into practice. It has also shown me that some of the theory is very difficult to follow through on and to do. Even though educational theory and the reality of school settings can be drastically different, having a solid foundation in the theory is crucial so that, as a teacher, I am able to evaluate the learning environment, my role as a teacher, and subsequently strive to make improvements [in my practice]. (Molly Jacobs)

I have really valued the opportunity to actively participate and observe in a school setting while enrolled in teacher education courses. I feel that this is a crucial component of my learning. I had previously spent a year as a teacher aide in a kindergarten class, and although the experience was very valuable, I think that I learned more about myself and my philosophy of teaching in these three months [of field experience] than in that whole year as an aide. I was able to directly apply theories and methods that I learned in my education classes to my classroom placement. Also, I was able to discuss the things, as I learned about them, with veterans in the field—which often gave me a much broader perspective. Based on these experiences, I began to formulate some concrete plans for my own classroom and methods of teaching. (Freida Pierce)

▲

On one level the meaning of the experience behind these statements may seem quite obvious. These statements are, however, very typical of individuals striving to make connections between the relatively static events and foci at the university and the dynamic settings and practices of schools and classrooms.

The process of beginning to make links between theory and practice often creates a dilemma for some preservice teachers. Knowing the weight to place on opportunities for practice or observation in the field and opportunities for more formal learning in the university is often difficult. This is especially so if you have extensive responsibilities for formal course work at the same time as you actively engage in experiential learning in the field. This was a problem for Jean.

▼

Finding balance between university courses and my placement in the field was something that I needed to work out at first. When I recognized how the topics in the courses could be applied in the field, however, I was on my way up the ladder. Actually implementing elements of course work in the classroom through lessons was my first step. My cooperating teacher showed me again and again how it was done, and then acted as a safety net when I tried it on my own. I also recognized my limitations. (Jean Holden)

▲

These brief statements about the theory-practice link illustrate how some preservice teachers grappled with the issue. For the most part, these particular individuals wrote these accounts relatively early in the period of formal preparation. Their struggles may be similar to those you may experience. In this regard, teachers are little different from other professionals who also must regard both theory and practice. The main difference, however, is that teaching acts are performed under more complex circumstances than those of, say, engineers or architects.

Even those in other helping professions (for example, health care and social work) have less complex contexts in which to work—and they often work one-on-one.

It is all too easy to disregard theory because it does not seem to work in practice. We have listened, for example, to many preservice and beginning teachers tell stories about how "trying out" ideas from, or implementing elements of, formal theory "did not work" in *their* practice. On questioning these teachers we often find out that the conditions or contexts for facilitating learning, for example, were not appropriate for the theory or its implementation; yet, all too readily, the theory itself was disregarded as being of "little value." Such conclusions about formal theory are likely to be erroneous.

In one case, for example, a new teacher wanted to introduce Whole Language principles and practice into his classroom. Without any serious heed to developing the kind of classroom climate and levels of student responsibility essential for this approach, after only one week he decided that it was a "fruitless endeavor" and that Whole Language was "totally unsuited to reality." This decision was contrary to his initial belief but, after "trying it out," he determined that "energetic pre-adolescents cannot be given great amounts of academic freedom." The practice of Whole Language did not work for him, in fact, because of poor conceptions of theory *and* practice, and a short-lived focus and implementation time. Examples like this help to explain why so many individuals in the field place a lesser value on formal theory. As a way of counteracting the tendency for practitioners to place lesser value on what are commonly called "theoretical aspects of teaching," perspectives that embody principles of reflexivity and inquiry are particularly useful.

Becoming a Reflexive or Inquiring Teacher

Accepting a perspective that stresses the interrelated nature of the theory-practice relationship demands a commitment to ongoing exploration of that relationship. Contemporary literature on teacher education and development points to the importance of becoming an inquiring teacher. Inquiring teachers are those who actively explore aspects of their own practice within both the narrow confines (classrooms) and broad boundaries (schools, communities, regions—national and international) of formal education. John Dewey, often referred to as "the father of progressive education," advocated the notion of teacher-inquirer.[3] More recently, Duckworth (1986), among others, encouraged the idea of "teachers-as-researchers," implying that, under certain conditions, the act of teaching is an act of researching. In the last decade, a whole teacher-researcher movement has sprung up. (We refer to this movement again later on.) Such inquiry involves teachers making the focus of study their day-to-day interactions with children, their curricular decisions and the relationship between that curricula and social and political influences, their instructional techniques, or the contexts that facili-

---

[3]   You may have already explored some of Dewey's work. Some useful sections of his writings associated with the notion of teacher as researcher can be found in *How We Think* (Dewey, 1933), *Experience and Education* (Dewey, 1938), and in a book of selected writings, *John Dewey on Education* (Archambault, 1964).

tate or hinder their ongoing professional development. Studying one's professional practice, therefore, promotes ongoing improvement of those practices and associated contexts for learning and teaching. Through systematic reflection and analysis of emerging practice, new teachers like you can take charge of their professional development. The reflexive process is illustrated in Figure 1.1.

Due to recent popularity and acceptance of the notion of reflection in the context of teaching, the terms *reflective practitioner* and *reflection-on-* and *-in-practice* (Schön, 1983, 1987) are now part of the teacher education vernacular. Within the contemporary contexts of teacher education and the teaching profession, however, there are many nuances to the term *reflection*.

What Does It Mean to Become Reflexive?

One way to think about the meaning of *reflexive* is in terms of the properties of mirrors and prisms. The analogy is as follows. Mirrors and transparent prisms reflect and refract light, they change the direction that light rays travel, sometimes even "bending" them back on themselves, causing them to move in directions opposite to that in which they originally traveled. Reflexive practices associated with teaching and being a professional have somewhat similar qualities and may induce similar outcomes. Being reflexive is like having a mirror and a transparent prism with which to view your practice. Reflexive activities are also like windows. They are vehicles that help you to stand back and view your work, enabling you to analyze the substance, direction, and intent of your own practice. (Recognize that at this point you have already established parameters of practice even though you may not have stepped inside school classrooms since you were a student, a point to which we will return in Chapter 2.) When you examine practice with an eye to modifying or improving it, or even questioning the assumptions underlying it, the results sometimes witness complete turnabouts in thinking. Mirrors and prisms also separate light rays into component wavelengths, making visible the colors of the spectrum. Similarly, reflexive practices allow you to analyze the various components or elements of your teaching and work as a teacher. In making these assertions we do not wish to stretch the meanings of the metaphors too much but, from the vantage point of both exploring your own practice and observing others doing the same, outcomes of reflexive practices can sometimes be quite surprising and illuminating.

The ideas and thoughts you "bend back" will derive from a range of interactions and experiences both prior to and during your period of preservice preparation. In a reflexive stance, as you think about and make sense of those prior experiences you likely will begin to see things under different, probably brighter, lights. And, chances are, you will begin to question or wonder about some of the previous conclusions you have drawn and insights you have gained. You may also wonder, for example, about how your understandings compare with other preservice teachers in different contexts; about what kinds of things you have to look forward to as a beginning teacher; or, knowing your strengths and less developed

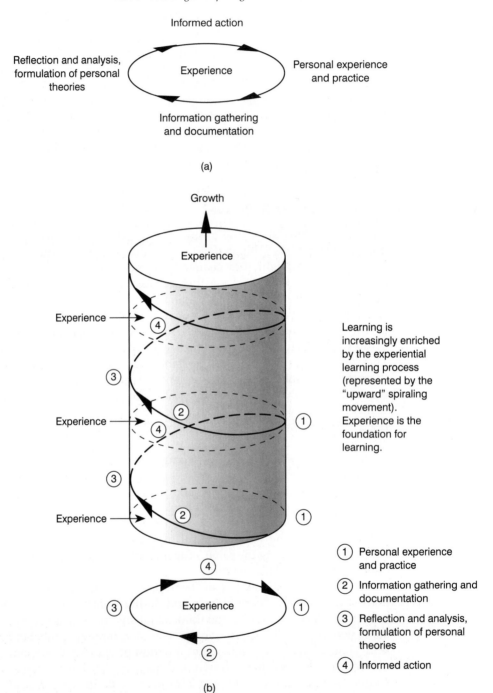

Informed action

Reflection and analysis, formulation of personal theories

Experience

Personal experience and practice

Information gathering and documentation

(a)

Growth

Experience

Experience

④

③

Experience

②

④

③

Experience

②

①

①

Learning is increasingly enriched by the experiential learning process (represented by the "upward" spiraling movement). Experience is the foundation for learning.

④

③

Experience

①

②

(b)

① Personal experience and practice

② Information gathering and documentation

③ Reflection and analysis, formulation of personal theories

④ Informed action

Figure 1.1   Experiential Learning Cycle/Spiral

areas of expertise may inspire you to extend the boundaries of your thinking by actively engaging in activities beyond those with which you are familiar. For these and other reasons we point to the value of pertinent research or inquiry, a claim we substantiate throughout the book as well.

Educators and researchers have struggled to define *reflection*. The underlying theme running through the various definitions and interpretations characterizes reflection as an intrapersonal process (Canning, 1990) through which personal and professional knowing can occur (Connelly & Clandinin, 1988; Sikes & Aspinwall, 1990). Reflection is seen as a process and method of giving reason to action or practice (Grimmett & Erickson, 1988; Russell & Munby, 1991; Schön, 1988, 1991; Witherell & Makler, 1989; Zeichner & Liston, 1987), as a dynamic process with action implicit in its meaning (Schön, 1983; Noffke & Brennan, 1988). It is seen as a vehicle for promoting changed behaviors and practice (Boyd & Fales, 1983; Cruick- shank, 1987) and as a means of improving foresight (Buchmann, 1990; Schön, 1983), thereby lessening the chances of taking inappropriate lines of action. Some, such as Kemmis (1985) and Zeichner and Teitelbaum (1982) insist that reflection is broader than simply an examination of personal considerations, that it encom- passes a consideration of ideological positions as well as contemporary contexts encompassing socio-political factors.

Louden (1991) offers a comprehensive conceptual framework for understand- ing the many interpretations of reflection. He characterizes reflection along the complementary dimensions of *forms* and *interests*. Along the dimension of forms are *introspection, rehearse and replay, enquiry,* and *spontaneity,* which he identifies as characteristics of various acts of reflection. Along the interests dimension are the various goals of reflection, which he identifies as *technical, personal, problematic,* and *critical.* Louden's framework is helpful in making sense of the myriad ways in which reflection is talked about in the context of teaching and teacher education.

We take the stand that, within the profession of teaching, reflection refers to the ongoing process of critically examining and refining practice, taking into care- ful consideration the personal, pedagogical, curricular, intellectual, societal (including social, political, historical, and economic), and ethical contexts associ- ated with schools, classrooms, and the multiple roles of teachers. A key question for teacher educators such as ourselves is, "How can we foster a climate of critical inquiry into practice?" And, for you as preservice teachers, "How do I become an inquiring, reflective (or to use the term we prefer) *reflexive* teacher?"

The Role of Research in Becoming a Reflexive Teacher

Besides being central to the development of instructional and learning theories, research plays an important role in the learning-to-teach process. On one hand formal research informs and becomes part of the practice of teacher educators but, on the other hand, a more intimate and personal level, informal research is crucial to your growth as a burgeoning professional. John Elliott, a pioneer in the "action research" movement in the United Kingdom, distinguishes between these two kinds of research. The former, he says, is conducted with the intention of knowledge production; the latter with improving practice while integrating practice, development, research, self-assessment, and reflection (Elliott, 1991).

One way to more fully understand your own practice is to engage in action research or reflexive inquiry on an ongoing basis. You will also be greatly informed about elements of your own practice, however, as you become familiar with the findings of inquiries conducted in other educational settings by both professional classroom teachers and professional researchers or professors. You may even begin to find formal research on teacher education to be quite informative. As it becomes more readily available and accessible the research of classroom teachers, in the form of action research accounts, may also be highly informative. Your pursuit of research will help to break down some of the barriers between formal theory and practice. Dwayne and Colleen articulate thoughts on this matter. Dwayne had just read a series of case studies of beginning teachers that focused on the context and conditions of practice. Colleen worked through a classroom problem by consulting research and considering it in the context of her practice.

Exploring the experiences of beginning teachers caused me to think very carefully about the work I was doing in the classroom. More specifically, accounts of their experiences helped me anticipate some of the changes in my own practice that I might need to make—both now and in the future. I will certainly need to be more flexible than I have been to date. Knowing the difficulties that other beginners have had encourages me to more carefully think through my planned work. (Dwayne McAuslin)

The weekly spelling test scores were pretty low for the whole class, so I decided to offer treats to those who scored 100 percent. The rewards seemed to work well at first, but the good effect of increased scores only lasted a short while. This puzzled me. I remembered reading about Daniel Berlyne's theory of intrinsic and extrinsic motivation, so I decided to do some further reading. I discovered studies by Lepper that indicated that my action may have replaced the intrinsic motivation of the students with an extrinsic motivation that might result in lower performance. I decided to suspend treats and try an approach that would increase intrinsic motivation instead. This experience resulted in my determination to think carefully about my practice. I had acted with the assumption that the students would be positively affected. When this did not occur I realized that my assumptions had a pretty weak base—"kids like candy." (Colleen Presswood)

Exploring the Practice of Others: Gaining Insights from Formal Research

Throughout the book, part of every topic discussed is devoted to *Links with Research.* Our purpose is to provide a glimpse of the scope of the formal research literature on the topic and, in particular, to point out some potentially useful research reports for you to examine. These *Links with Research* are not meant to be exhaustive reviews of relevant research; they are intended to provide for you a brief introduction to the place of research in the process of *your* becoming a teacher. They also present an opportunity for you to begin thinking about infusing formal theories and understandings into your practice. Most of the cited journal articles, chapters, or books were selected because of their relevance to professional development or improved practice within formal teacher preparation programs. We tried also to make selections based on their readability. In the bibliographies or reference lists of the research reports are many relevant citations, some of which you may wish to locate and read. In an attempt to demystify research and to counter the claim that reading research reports requires specialized knowledge of theoretical underpinnings, statistical research methods, or research jargon, we emphasize reports that are in the form of descriptive case studies, teachers' narratives, and in-depth accounts of practice.

The purpose and benefits of exploring research reports are threefold. First, by accessing literature on "learning to teach" you take a step forward in facilitating your own professional development. You begin to become "intelligent consumers" of preservice teacher education activities, courses, and programs, not in the sense that you will come to know definitive answers to questions but that you will begin to know the definitive questions to ask about teacher education in general and, specifically, regarding the program in which you are enrolled. You will become knowledgeable in a general way about issues associated with the initial period of teacher education and teaching. In the process of doing this you will take charge of an aspect of your professional education.

Second, these research-based accounts about the process of learning to teach may provide insights into specific ways in which you can act, develop your practice, and focus specific attention on matters that interest or concern you. These accounts may help you do this because they relate to similar situations or contexts in which you find yourself, or they simply may make inherently good sense to you. We draw more heavily from those research reports that present work grounded in the qualitative or interpretive paradigm, many of which, as we just noted, present in-depth case studies of individuals learning to teach. These kinds of reports tend to represent "real" preservice or beginning teachers' experiences in descriptive, in-depth, and intensely personal ways. Because of this, on reading these reports you may find yourself making statements such as, "I thought I was the only one with that problem," or "I can relate to that," or "Maybe that approach would work in my situation."

Third, reading research reports may help you become more familiar with the various ways that others have explored both their own practice and the practice of others. In other words, familiarity with the research foci in the work of other teachers and researchers may help you more clearly define points of interest, issues, or concerns important for your own research. You even may find yourself coming into contact with other "teacher-researchers."

In response to the question "How do I explore the research base on learning to teach and beginning teaching?" we encourage you to begin by checking out some of the research reports we cite; read them and note their reference lists, locate those citations relevant to your interest or foci, and build up a bibliography of your own. You will soon have plenty of reading material, so skim and read judiciously. Of course, there are also several computer data bases in North America, such as those of the Educational Research Information Center (ERIC) and Canadian Education Index (CEI), which you can usually readily explore at university reference libraries. At some institutions these data bases may be available on CD ROM or through computer networks. Get into the habit of reading or reviewing professional and research periodicals or journals. Your university librarian can help you locate pertinent ones. At the end of this chapter we list some research periodicals that often focus on the early period of learning to teach and tackle the subject from individual and institutional perspectives as well as those that typically present teachers' research and accounts or are solely devoted to the work of teachers. We do not list subject-specific journals because we think it more useful at this time to focus on research about the process of learning to teach.

Developing Questions About Teaching: Beginning the Research Process

The format of each chapter in Part 3 of the book is intended to mirror the reflexive inquiry or research process. Each chapter, as we mentioned in the Introduction, has several sections.

The first section, *Narrative Accounts,* provides an experiential grounding for the research process. We hope you consider the accounts we present along with your own experiences, and those you hear about from peers.

The second section, *For Reflection and Discussion,* models the process of developing questions (and, ultimately, a focus for further inquiry) from practice. More than anything we hope you will develop a critical perspective on that which you observe and experience. Reflexive teachers are questioning teachers, ones who take little for granted.

The third section, *Links with Research,* provides a foundation—a research base—on which to situate the experiential framework. It may also provide substantive and technical directions for the inquiry by giving you some clues as to how to proceed, perhaps by raising questions or making comparisons.

The fourth section, *Research Activities,* presents ideas and questions for potential research projects, not as isolated, discrete activities that can be pigeonholed from our experiences to yours or that serve as busy, unrelated assignments but, rather, as examples of directions and ways in which you might proceed in the process of inquiry. We focus on raising questions, seeking to pique your interest in researchable topics rather than laying out prescriptive tasks.

Finally, we present *Recommended Readings,* sometimes a relatively short, pertinent list of works that may extend your thinking as a researcher and teacher. They may present either complementary or opposing perspectives that are likely to extend your thinking in some way.

The inquiry process and how it is mirrored in each chapter is depicted in Figure 1.2. Notice that the spiraling, conceptual representation of experiential learning places primacy on one's experience as it informs future actions. The model of

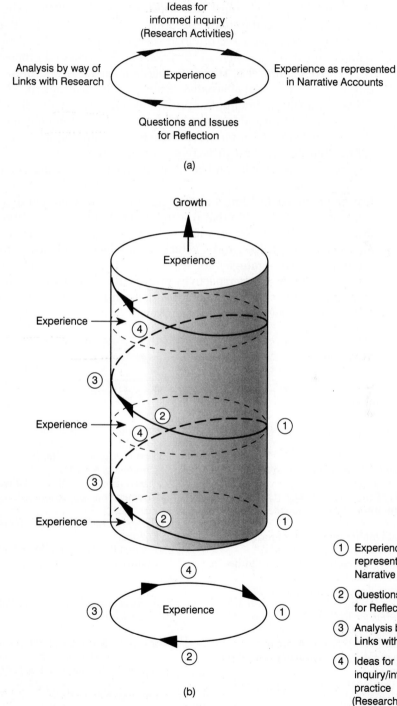

Figure 1.2   Reflexive Inquiry Cycle/Spiral

experiential learning, inquiry into experience, has parallels in the formal research process as well, and the chapter sections are designed to reflect that.

If the process we have outlined seems a little formal and rigid this is partly because research is a systematic process. Experience-based problems, questions, or issues drive inquiry; they stimulate collection, analysis, and presentation or laying out of evidence so that alternative actions can be determined. Also, we have been deliberate about describing the process in hopes that you will recognize its commonsensical nature and integrate it into your way of thinking and working. As we said earlier, *teaching is inquiry*. Reflexive teachers are inquiring teachers, ones critical of their actions and proactive about change. In other words, engaging in research on your practice and becoming reflexive are one and the same.

We conclude this chapter with a list of further readings for those interested in learning more about being a teacher-researcher. The common theme in all of these publications is the notion that research is a tool for personal professional empowerment, as well as an opportunity to forge critical evaluations of present teaching and schooling practices, and a vehicle from which to advocate change and implement alternative strategies for working and teaching in schools. Although we espouse many of the perspectives presented in these various books, space constraints prevent us from pursuing the matter further. We encourage you to explore this relatively new arena of teachers' work on your own. If you do so, we think you will benefit greatly.

Recommended Readings

Periodicals (available in most university education libraries):

Action in Teacher Education (Association of Teacher Educators, Reston, VA)

Alberta Journal of Educational Research (University of Alberta, Edmonton, Alberta, Canada)

Among Teachers (University of Calgary, Calgary, Alberta, and Ontario Institute for Studies in Education, Toronto, Ontario, Canada)

Curriculum Inquiry (Ontario Institute for Studies in Education, Toronto, Ontario, Canada)

International Journal of Qualitative Studies in Education, The (Taylor & Francis, London, UK)

Journal of Education for Teaching, The (Carfax, Abingdon, UK)

Journal of Teacher Education, The (American Association of Colleges for Teacher Education, Washington, DC)

Language Arts (National Council of Teachers of English, Urbana, IL)

Orbit (Ontario Institute for Studies in Education, Toronto, Ontario, Canada)

Teachers College Record (Teachers College, Columbia University, New York, NY)

Teachers' Journal, The (Brown University in Cooperation with Rhode Island Public Schools, Providence, RI)

Teaching and Teacher Education (Pergamon Press, Oxford, UK)

Theory into Practice (Ohio State University, Columbus, OH))

Books about classroom research including accounts by classroom teachers:

Bissex, G. L., & Bullock, R. H. (1987). *Seeing for ourselves.* Portsmouth, NH: Heinemann.

Brause, R. S., & Smayher, J. S. (1991). *Search and research: What the inquiring teacher needs to know.* London: Falmer Press.

Bullough, R. V., Jr. (1989). *First year teacher: A case study*. New York: Teachers College Press.

Bullough, R. V., Jr., Knowles, J. G., & Crow, N. A. (1991). *Emerging as a teacher*. London and New York: Routledge, Chapman, & Hall.

Clandinin, D. J. (1986). *Classroom practice: Teacher images in action*. East Sussex, UK: Falmer Press.

Clift, R. T., & Evertson, C. M. (1992). *Focal points: Qualitative inquiries into teaching and teacher education*. Washington, DC: ERIC Clearinghouse on Teacher Education.

Daiker, D. A., & Morenberg, M. (1990). *The writing teacher as researcher: Essays in the theory and practice of class-based research*. Portsmouth, NH: Boynton Cook.

Fosnot, C. T. (1989). *Enquiring teachers enquiring learners: A constructivist approach for teaching*. New York: Teachers College Press.

Goswami, D., & Stillman, P. R. (1987). *Reclaiming the classroom*. Upper Montclair, NJ: Boynton Cook.

Hargreaves, A., & Fullan, M. G. (Eds.). (1992). *Understanding teacher development*. New York: Teachers College Press.

Jersild, A. T. (1955). *When teachers face themselves*. New York: Teachers College Press.

Kincheloe, J. L. (1991). *Teachers as researchers: Qualitative inquiry as a path to empowerment*. London: Falmer Press.

Kohl, H. (1984). *Growing minds: On becoming a teacher*. New York: Harper & Row.

Louden, W. (1991). *Understanding teaching: Continuity and change in teachers' knowledge*. New York: Teachers College Press.

Mohr, M. M., & Maclean, M. S. (1987). *Working together: A guide for teacher-researchers*. Urbana, IL: National Council of Teachers of English.

Newman, J. M. (1989). *Finding our own way: Teachers exploring their assumptions*. Portsmouth, NH: Heinemann.

Nias J., & Groundwater-Smith, S. (1988). *The enquiring teacher*. London: Falmer Press.

Perrone, V. (1991). *A letter to teachers*. San Francisco, CA: Jossey-Bass.

Ross, E. W., Cornett, J. W., & McCutcheon, G. (1992). Albany, NY: State University of New York Press.

Russell, T., & Munby, H. (Eds.). (1992). *Teachers and teaching: From classroom to reflection*. Bristol, PA: Falmer Press.

Schubert, W. H., & Ayers, W. C. (1992). *Teacher lore: Learning from our own experience*. New York: Longman.

Steffy, B. E. (1989). *Career stages of classroom teachers*. Lancaster, PA: Technomic.

Van Manen, M. (1986). *The tone of teaching*. Richmond Hill, Ontario: Scholastic–TAB.

PART II

Tools for Reflexivity and Inquiry

"How can I become more reflexive?" "What are some tools to help me become a reflexive teacher?" "What do I need to do to become reflexive?" These are some of the questions we often hear preservice teachers ask. There are many ways to promote reflexive inquiry. Here we offer some suggestions for facilitating the process and engaging in activities that provide both evidence and method for thinking about experiences. In a sense, the tools we advocate can only promote the process; they do not, in themselves, insure quality to that reflection. Indeed, they do not even ensure reflection at all; that is up to you. And, although we make no judgments about the quality of reflection, we do advocate a focus that is clearly more comprehensive and critical than narrow and technical. We explore internal information gathering or autobiographical writing, and external information gathering, especially through participant observation, interviewing, and collaboration with peers and mentors.

Notice the distinction we make between *internal* and *external* information gathering. By beginning with an exploration of self, you may be more able to engage in an exploration of those phenomena around you. In fact, as you may have noticed, the organization of the book reflects that view. We move from developing understandings of self, to contexts and people, to self in relation to contexts and people, and back to self again. Figure 2.1 captures our thinking. That is, once you have a reasonably clear view of yourself as teacher you may more usefully understand the contexts in which you are situated and yourself in those contexts. We return full circle as you focus on elements of self in preparation for full-time professional work, by which time you are engaging in internal explorations of self and external investigations of contexts and people. By focusing on both *internal* and *external* inquiry you will have an enhanced opportunity to understand self-in-context and self-in-relationship-to-others, both important for promoting holistic professional development.

19

Part II   Tools for Reflexivity And Inquiry

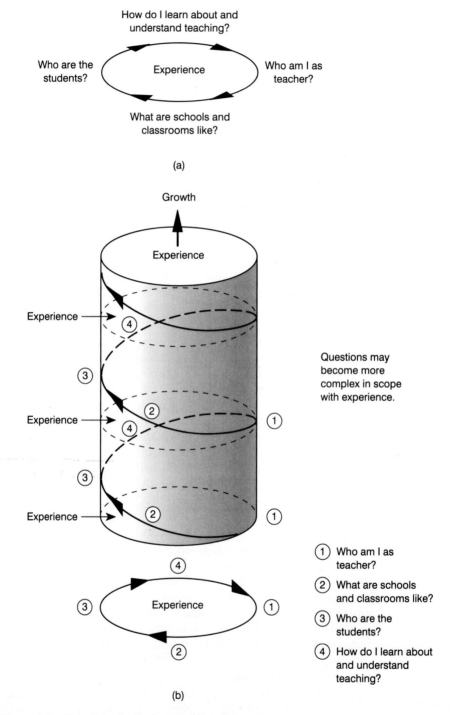

(a)

(b)

Figure 2.1   Questions for Professional Development

CHAPTER 2

Autobiographical Writing: Gathering Personal, Internal Information[1]

The value of autobiographical writing during the period of learning to teach is rooted in the process of coming to terms with what it means to be a teacher. Some forms of autobiographical writing having particular value include

- personal or life history accounts
- journal keeping
- explorations of personal metaphors
- reflective accounts of practice or professional development summaries and records

We see the primary value of autobiographical writing as "rooted in the process of coming to terms with oneself" (Knowles & Holt-Reynolds, 1991, p. 106). In the process of becoming aware of self, we recognize the often circumlocutory trails taken in the process of becoming preservice teachers. In so doing, we acknowledge the primacy of experience in developing perceptions and beliefs about practice and conceptions about what it means to be a teacher.

Autobiographical writing in the period of formal learning about teaching is valuable for several reasons. First, and perhaps foremost, is the value of record keeping. Its value rests on the premise that you come to formal teacher preparation programs with a whole array of experiences in schools and other places of learning and instruction, a matter we discuss in Chapter 5. Having a written record of your thinking about the influence of schools, learning and being in classrooms as a student is a useful place to begin to frame your present orientations.

---

[1] In this chapter, we draw extensively on Knowles' earlier work with Diane Holt-Reynolds, particularly an article, "Shaping pedagogies through personal histories in preservice teacher education," published in 1991 in Teachers College Record, 93(1), and on Knowles (1993), "Life history accounts as mirrors: A practical avenue for the conceptualization of reflection in teacher education," in J. Calderhead and P. Gates (Eds.). *Conceptualizing reflection in teacher education.* London: Falmer Press.

Moreover, such a record will enable you to trace your developing thinking, important in forging your ongoing professional development.

Second, autobiographical writing is a powerful vehicle for enhancing learning, especially if you think about writing as a problem-solving or thinking-through process. You probably have discovered the strong relationship between writing and the development of subject matter expertise in courses that focus on learning through the writing process. A focus on making clear, in writing, your philosophies, theories, principles, and skills related to teaching and education in general may help you to reveal the extent of your learning. Autobiographical writing is a very useful pedagogical tool, as evidenced in many elementary and secondary school classrooms.

Third, autobiographical writing, if shared with others, provides a window into your thinking. In particular, it may help the teacher educators with whom you work to better meet your learning needs. They may gain insights into your thinking, your reactions to learning contexts, your responses to their guidance, instruction, and to the program and field placements. We have found the medium of autobiographical writing a useful way for some preservice teachers to alert us to the difficulties they faced in field placements and with other matters associated with their preparation programs.[2]

Fourth, teachers are expected by parents and other members of the community to be good, if not exemplary, writers. Autobiographical writing seems to be particularly useful for improving writing because it is less formal than many other kinds of writing assignments and, therefore, presents fewer barriers to writing. Autobiographical writing helps writers to focus on the creative processes as much as the products of writing.

Fifth, other values of autobiographical writing in the context of preservice teacher education have to do with its usefulness for personal inquiry and formal research. In the first case it presents opportunities for generation of internal information for your own use; in the second case, and when permission to do so is granted, as data for other researchers. It is also a mechanism and medium for sharing experiences with others and for learning from others.

Personal History Accounts

Each of us possesses personal histories that are rich and intensely interesting. By personal or life history accounts we mean stories of your experiences of learning in formal and informal settings—in families with parents and others, in schools and other institutions with teachers in classrooms, and so on—and the meanings you attribute to those experiences. Personal history accounts represent, in a sense,

---

[2]   There are, of course, other ways to achieve this, but for those who seldom venture to the office of a professor uninvited this may indeed be crucial. In the article entitled "The student teacher who wouldn't go away: Learning from failure" (Knowles & Hoefler, 1989), you will find an account of a student teacher's experience. There, the professor was first alerted to the serious difficulties of the student teacher by her journal writing.

the informal reflection that occurs as you recollect, ponder, and interpret various education-related experiences. Like formal or published autobiographies, diaries and journals, and artistic expressions of various kinds (such as poetry and creative writing, painting, and sculpture, as well as crafts), personal history accounts are a ✓ distinct form of personal documents.

For the most part, our personal histories are private, mental constructs; however, most individuals possess observable evidence of elements of their personal histories: photographs, report cards, the outcomes or products of school assignments, creative writing efforts, artworks, craft works, old textbooks and readers, trophies, school yearbooks, even scars. These artifacts of experience may serve to jog your memory about experiences and perspectives that have shaped your thinking about becoming a school and classroom teacher. You may have even been a classroom teacher, an assistant teacher or aide, a camp counselor, a church school teacher, or someone else with instructional responsibilities. These experiences also have shaped your thinking about teaching. And, as you already know, education-related life experiences have contributed to your thinking about teaching. Although writing a personal history account may, for some individuals, be a difficult and perplexing task—especially if elements of prior experiences are confronted that are contradictory to elements of present lives, career directions, or philosophical orientations of teacher education programs and school placements—writing a personal history account will greatly assist your professional development.

One of the reasons we make the claim that writing a personal history account may facilitate your professional development is because, in writing about your experiences associated with learning, schools, classrooms, and teachers, you can make known the implicit theories, values, and beliefs that underpin your thinking about being a teacher. Another purpose for encouraging you to construct a personal history account is to develop a basis for a continuing conversation with others about the nature and substance of your thinking about becoming a teacher.

A Preservice Teacher's Personal History Account

Rather than talk more about the value of personal history accounts, reading one may prove useful. Colleen wrote a personal history account in the early part of her formal preparation to teach. At the beginning of her third year as an undergraduate student, she entered an elementary preservice teacher education program and was immediately placed in a field setting associated with a general teaching methods course. This was the immediate context in which she wrote. This is part of Colleen's personal history account.

▼

Most of my neighborhood friends were older than I was, and I benefitted from their positive experiences in school. My best friend loved school and told me all about her wonderful teachers. My earliest attitudes toward school were entirely positive, and my expectation was that school would be a wonderful place to be.

My kindergarten teacher made that expectation come true. We learned a lot of things about the world and used many different materials to explore. When my mom asked me what I had learned in school that day, I always had something to say. Nap time was a trial for me because I was a chatterbox. It seemed like the perfect time to get better acquainted with my classmates, especially because the teacher kept moving me next to children I had not played with much. I made many mistakes in behavior that year, but Miss Clancy never compromised my self-esteem when she corrected me. She was an affectionate, warm, and sensitive person. I loved her so much that I cried when I found out that I had been promoted to first grade. Like many kindergartners, I decided (while hugging Miss Clancy) that I would be a teacher when I grew up.

Fortunately for me, my first grade teacher was also a wonderful person. Mrs. Rice did not demonstrate the physical warmth of Miss Clancy, but she was unfailingly supportive and had expectations that we were eager to meet. This was a teacher who impressed my parents as well. I will never forget my mother's pleased response when I asked for a section of the newspaper to read as my homework. We learned about Hawaiian culture by rehearsing and performing an interpretive hula dance. I am sure we looked very cute to our parents that night, but the experience served to broaden our perceptions of other people and their customs, heighten our awareness of communication styles, and was fun, too. When we learned about nutrition and the value of peanut butter, she passed a mortar and pestle around the class and we took turns grinding peanuts into butter. We then ate our product, spread on a banana. She thoughtfully gave us the option of tossing it into the trash if we did not like it after tasting it.

Off to a happy "well-adjusted" start, firm in the belief that teachers were wonderful, loving creatures, I entered second grade in a brand-new school building. It was very different from my previous experiences in school because we moved to different classrooms to learn different subjects from different teachers. Our desks were arranged in traditional rows, which differed a great deal from kindergarten's round tables and first grade's horseshoe arrangement. There is something about regimented rows that contributes to a sense of alienation; many people become faceless voices in that situation. I realize now that class crowding was a real problem in those baby-boom years, perhaps the horseshoe arrangement of desks could not accommodate the large numbers of students. Perhaps the feeling of being lost in the crowd made students a bit easier to manage. Whatever the reason, that particular configuration was the dominant one for several years. I remember feeling both vulnerable and liberated when the seating arrangement was changed in middle school. So, second grade was a year of many adjustments: to a new school building, new teachers, and a new approach called "team teaching." I liked learning about dinosaurs and then building one from clay in art class. I enjoyed the exposure to different teachers in my grade too. The good thing about changing classes was that a negative relationship with a teacher was diluted by contact with other teachers. The major drawback was that no teacher knew you really well.

Third grade was the first year that I was exposed to some questionable characters. My reading teacher seemed more interested in her ability to balance the pointing stick on her shoulder than in listening to us read. She had an odd habit of "bragging" about herself that did not serve to endear her to her students. When she fumbled her pointing stick and it fell to the floor, some children reacted with outright glee. She used competitive games and utilized the bulletin board to publicly display our progress in reading a series of basal stories. Her intention may have been to provide an incentive for us to continue but the effect was to cause highly self-conscious behaviors. I can remember making deliberate mistakes to spare the feelings of a classmate who quietly cried each week because she had yet to receive a score of 100. Another teacher came in to view that bulletin board, and it disappeared a short time later. My teacher disappeared too, after that year.

The lesson I learned best from my fourth grade teacher was distrust. I was predisposed to feel respect toward my teachers, but my faith was badly shaken after a year in her class. She, too, left after that one year in my school; I often hoped that someone asked her to leave. She was a young, fairly attractive woman with the meanest spirit that I have ever encountered. Her demeanor was drastically different whenever there was another adult present. When she was in charge of the classroom she was petty, sarcastic, and indiscriminate in her criticisms. Although I was spared most of her wrath, the classroom atmosphere was poisoned with her harsh criticisms. For the first time I felt afraid to participate in class. She repeated questions asked of her in a snide, mocking tone, and I learned very quickly not to ask her anything. I suppose I was an eternal optimist because I felt certain that fifth grade would be much better.

I began fifth grade with some caution. Never again did I leave myself open to a new teacher. It may be that my skepticism correlated with my age; as I matured, I lost some innocence. Fourth grade had been a painful experience. My fifth grade teacher was much better than the previous teacher, yet she taught entirely from textbooks and managed to transform the most exciting subjects into exercises of boredom. She often stared out the window with a blank daydreamy gaze. It seemed a little unfair that she should indulge in that fine sport after chastising us for engaging in it.

Sixth grade may have been the best year I ever spent in school. I was a little worried at first because my previous experience with a male teacher was not very positive. My sixth grade science teacher, although academically challenging, was a genuine grouch. Mr. Millet started out like a "toughie," but that rough exterior simply protected a heart of gold. He challenged us in our thinking, gave us assignments that were relevant, and caused us to stretch. He also addressed us as budding adults. His approach was different from any I had encountered. His behavior remained the same whether he was talking to a colleague or a student. He listened respectfully, as he required us to listen to him. I began to feel better about myself in school because Mr. Millet expressed a sincere interest in me. He did so much for me personally that I will always regard him as a "standard of excellence." He took pains to prepare us for the different academic demands of junior high school. Some homework assignments were actually more difficult than those we encountered in seventh grade.

Mr. Millet addressed our pubescence. I have since realized that his willingness to tackle such a tender subject was an act of sheer bravery. He spoke to us about hygiene, and as I remember it, this was an impromptu discussion brought about by a very warm day and his proximity to two very large, mature boys. He opened the discussion with directions for using deodorant. When the initial giggles subsided, he sensitively, yet firmly, explained that some of us were more than ready to use it regularly. He wove the principle of self-control and responsibility into this discussion. He also touched upon the issue of respect toward each other—one of the boys was grossly overweight and often cruelly teased by classmates. His anger was evident when he discussed how hurtful this could be to another person, and he gave us examples of many other differences to which we should be sensitive. He used my freckles as an example of something over which I had no control and might feel sensitive about, and expanded on that to discuss different skin color.

It seems to me now that Mr. Millet realized fully the influence that a teacher has, and he exhibited a holistic attitude toward his pupils. We were people, not skin bags to stuff with facts. Under his regard, we all grew toward the realization that *we* were responsible for what we learned and that all of us had the tools to learn.

I maintained a correspondence with Mr. Millet that lasted almost three years. I have since discovered that several students from various classes also wrote to him. I am now amazed that he made the time to respond to us. He was a husband and father of two children who continued his formal education and became principal of an elementary school—and held another administrative position for a time. The correspondence ended because I ceased to write to him. He made himself available to his students as long as his students continued to need him.

Junior high school was initially exciting, even though it was frightening to find my way around such a big place. It seemed as though I spent as much time in the halls going to class as I did in class. Seventh grade was a very busy year. There were so many new people to meet from other elementary schools and so many things to learn about what was "cool" and what was not. I was not cool. I did not even know it until later. There was an adjustment to a different grading system—I used to get "excellent" or "superior" on my report cards, and now I was an "A" sometimes "B" student. I did not like those "B" grades. I later found out that they were not cool either; "C" grades were acceptable but grades of "A" and "B" were viewed with suspicion. Having spent seventh grade adjusting to the fragmentation of my daily schedule, feeling lost in the crowd, and learning that there was no apparent relationship between any of my classes, I got busy in eighth grade acting a little tougher.

My seventh grade physical education teacher was a horror that I would not have believed if I had not experienced her myself. There was a pool that was used for swimming lessons, and I was quite pleased that I would be going swimming. There was one catch for girls though—if you had your period, you had to dress in gym shorts and sit out. I had problems with frequent and irregular periods when I was twelve. Some girls did not like swimming and would stay out using that as an excuse. One day she angrily told us that she would check our clothing herself to confirm if we were telling the truth. I was terrified. I begged my mother to let me stay home on days we had swimming, but since that was out of the question, my mother (who always expressed support for teachers) wrote her a letter. My teacher did not threaten me after that, but I never learned what was in the letter. Unfortunately, this teacher stayed tough, hard, and mean. Two years later, in my ninth grade class, she pushed a black girl a little too hard and was physically assaulted. This incident marked a turning point for me. A year earlier, I would have run to the principal's office for help. I should be ashamed to admit it, but I cheered for the black girl.

There was a great deal of racial tension in that particular school. Girls were afraid to go to the bathroom without two or three friends with them. Some people began smoking pot at school too. In my ninth grade English class with students coming to class after lunch period either stoned or ready for a fight, it really is a wonder that we got through *The Old Man and the Sea*. But "Wacky Wilson" would sing "Onward Christian Soldiers" while marching in place to start class—and we all paid attention. I have often thought of her wacky classroom management techniques. She was most certainly loony, but also effective. She had plans for us, and we carried them out. Amidst the drugs and the fights between blacks and whites, she taught us the structure of literature. It seems strange to me now that no one in authority addressed the issue of racial tension. It was truly a crisis situation. I was never assaulted—and I went to the bathroom alone—but I was in the minority. Perhaps it was because I defended the girl who assaulted our teacher, who knows?

The first year I attended high school, riots in the halls caused the school to close for a few days. The building already possessed the personality of a prison; after the damage was repaired, we experienced "lock-up." The office was inaccessible, all classroom doors were locked after the bell rang and would not be opened to you if you were late and without a note from the principal's office. It was a pretty grim first year. Black students demanded a black student union and were repeatedly refused. They remained persistent and eventually were allowed to form a black student group.

Meanwhile, some hippie-type kids and sympathetic teachers tried to start an alternative high school. Some of my elementary and junior high school friends were in that group. They were very insistent that I join them in their effort and were quite surprised when I declined. I had already given up. I was disillusioned by the hypocrisy of the whole disjointed system of education. I could not appreciate the wisdom of trading one system for another. Teachers would still be teaching there. The teachers closest to my experience at that time were primarily concerned with maintaining the status quo and ignoring the reality of drugs in the bathroom and blood on someone's shirt. I could hardly wait to leave school.

I stayed far away from school for a very long time. I gave college a halfhearted try a year after I graduated, but I was not ready at that time.

Although I stayed away from school, I did not stay away from learning. I read voraciously and without any guidance. I acquired a rather eclectic assortment of information, some of which has been useful, some not. John Holt, Abraham Maslow, Erik Erikson, Carl Jung, and Rollo May are a few of the people whose work I admire and know a little about. For a time, I considered teaching as a profession to stay away from because there are enough white women involved in it. But, there is nothing that comes close to teaching in terms of the positive contribution that can be made in someone's life by your own active intellectual involvement.

The influences that my earliest teachers had on my development were profound. When I think of my sixth grade teacher, I get an urge to be the best that I can be. I left sixth grade almost a quarter of a century ago. Can the teacher imagine that I still think of him? I wonder where Miss Clancy is today and if she could possibly understand the strength she built into my early approaches to learning. I think an apt metaphor for teaching is planting seeds. Some of them will sprout quickly like radishes, and you will have the satisfaction of seeing your success. Some of those seeds will turn out to be oaks. You may never personally see the extent of your efforts. (Colleen Presswood)

As you can imagine, there are many ways in which Colleen could have written her personal history account. She chose this chronological format to present her story. Other preservice teachers have centered their narratives on very detailed accounts of particular and critical experiences. Audra had another approach in mind as she prefaced her personal history account.

▼

This is an interesting task—to write a personal history account. I like the idea because for a few years I have wanted to write down the experiences of my life. This way, I can get to know myself better and also allow those who read this work to get an inside perspective on who I am and what I am about. I will write this personal history account in conversation form because I enjoy talking and because I feel that this will make it easier to describe myself and what I perceive to be my role in life. Questions appear throughout the text—questions I ask myself as an interviewer and interviewee. So here goes. . . . Hope you enjoy listening in! (Audra Green)

▲

Back to Colleen's account. Notice, that despite the fact that she did not directly and concisely make clear her preconceptions of teaching, her implicit beliefs about good teachers, appropriate learning contexts, and that which inspired her own learning, for example, are very evident. It may have been very useful for Colleen to have explored other aspects as well, but she chose not to do so—and that was appropriate. For instance, she mentioned little about values of her family and their encouragement to learn; nor did she talk about her decision to teach. These and other topics are potential chapters, as it were, in personal history accounts.

In preparation for writing, Colleen and other preservice teachers in her cohort were given some guidelines and suggestions to get started. These guidelines consisted of a list of topics and questions designed to promote responses and thinking about the substance and influence of prior experiences and the suggestion to address how these prior experiences might play out in emerging practice. Colleen decided not to do the latter, although in subsequent conversations with her instructors, many aspects of her experiences were related to her teaching practices.

Finally, as Debbie reveals, the act of beginning to write her personal history account revealed two characteristics about herself as potential teacher.

▼

As I sat down to write this personal history account, I thought to myself, "I wonder, what is the correct way to write a personal history account? Perhaps I could go to the library and find a book that would tell me how to write it, important things to include, good tips for writing." Perhaps this is a good way to introduce my personal history pertaining to teaching. Two significant characteristics about me emerge—an inherent need to find the "correct" way to do something and that my first inclination was to find the answer in a book. (Debbie Martinez)

▲

Developing a personal history account is an opportunity to acknowledge significant characteristics about yourself as an emerging teacher.

Writing Personal History Accounts: Getting Started

There is no definitive way to get started writing. Personal history accounts are not intended to be exclusively chronological records of events but, rather, to be examinations of your efforts to become a teacher within the context of your educational life. Although you may write a chronological personal history account that focuses on early memorable experiences as they relate to your present thinking about teaching (as Colleen did), there are other approaches you could take. For example: you may revolve your story around critical, memorable incidents related to your early experiences; you may organize your account in themes, focusing on broad meanings of your experiences; you may write about your biases, strengths, and less developed areas as a prospective teacher, focusing on those experiences that have helped shape your perceptions and positions. Some potentially useful topics to explore and to start you writing include

- your decision to become a teacher
- teachers' work
- visions of teachers and teaching
- outstanding teachers and their influence on you
- metaphors for teaching and working with students in classrooms (more about this later)
- learning styles and opportunities
- conflicts about the nature of schools and their organization
- doubts about self-as-teacher
- the influence of class, race, society, and location on educational experiences
- relationships with teachers and students
- your relationships with specific groups of society such as persons of different ethnicities and races, and persons with special needs

Within the context in which you find yourself and in which you write, it is important for you, your peers, and preservice teacher educators, together, to be very mindful of the importance of developing a learning community. In developing a climate conducive to writing and discussing elements of and understandings associated with personal histories, it is important to

- create open, safe, and respectful learning environments within small peer groups
- accept and openly acknowledge personal experiences as valuable for informing theories and practices of teaching
- acknowledge and model the value of discussing shared experiences of classrooms and schools
- share elements of each other's personal history accounts—in written and oral forms

- discuss the process, nature, substance, and value of constructing life history accounts
- acknowledge, when it occurs, the difficulty of writing (and some of you may need to think about alternative structures, topics, or questions if you are hesitant writers)

Also, if this kind of writing activity becomes a formal assignment in your course work, negotiate the manner of its completion and format with the intent that the process of its construction promotes the growth of your professional knowledge and skills, and *your* satisfaction with the completed account and process.

Journal Accounts

Not only has journal writing gained popularity as a pedagogical tool in school classrooms over the last decade or so, it has also become central to many university courses. Fulwiler's (1987) edited book, *The Journal Book,* for example, includes chapters representing journal use across the school and university curricula. You probably have encountered numerous courses in your university career that relied on journal writing. Some of the numerous purposes behind teachers' use of journal writing with students include: aiding creative story telling and writing; serving as a vehicle for recording responses to readings, texts, performances, movies, observations, interviews, and the like; as a chronological log of activities; and, as a vehicle for articulating and making sense of issues affecting their personal lives. This list is not exhaustive, and you may add to it other purposes for writing.

Some useful sources for understanding aspects of journal writing are to be found in Staton, Shuy, Peyton, and Reed's (1988) *Dialogue Journal Communication,* Fulwiler's (1987) *The Journal Book,* Holly's (1989) *Writing to Grow: Keeping a Personal Professional Journal,* and Progoff's (1975) *At a Journal Workshop.* Each of these publications provides a different slant to the writing process. Staton, Shuy, Peyton, and Reed, for example, focus on interactive journal writing, whereas Fulwiler provides a broad overview and gives numerous examples of journal use across the curriculum. Holly's work is highly pertinent to teacher education and development in the broadest sense, and a careful reading may prove to be very helpful to you. In our view, it is one of the most useful explorations of the subject and will serve you well into your career.

Teachers' journals have formed the basis for a number of autobiographical accounts about teaching. *Spearpoint* and *Teacher* by Sylvia Ashton-Warner (1972, 1963), *A Schoolman's Odyssey* by Harold Disbrowe (1984), *Two Years: A Teacher's Memoir* by Mary Kenner Glover (1992), *Crocus Hill Notebook* by Gary Jones (1991), *The Real Me is Gonna be a Shock* by Jill Solnicki (1992), *Armed with a Primer* by Sybill Shack (1965), and *The Thread that Runs So True* by Jesse Stuart (1949) are some examples. Journals also figure prominently in literature, and there is much published nonfiction based on journal accounts. You probably know of some. Also, a number of personal journals or diaries published in the twentieth century stand out as representing unique accounts of experiences and times. Journals provide unique historical accounts and records of personal growth, development, and life and career histories.[3] Exploration of the card or computer catalogue at most libraries will reveal an interesting array of published journals.

The power in journal writing within the context of learning to teach is primarily located in its usefulness for recording your reactions to schools, classrooms, teachers, and students. Also, it offers a place to explore the planning and outcomes of your curricular, instructional, relational, and classroom management activities. It is a particularly good place to record your reactions to some of the pervasive and central issues surrounding education, such as racial and gender inequities, financial and resources inequities, political and social influences and demands, issues of empowerment, authority, and autonomy, roles and influences of teachers' unions on learning, and so on. The scope of your journal writing is *only* limited by the contexts in which you are working, the time you have available, your foci, and your energies. At this point, it may be more helpful to hear what some preservice teachers have to say about journal keeping. First, Jean again.

Writing in a journal was one of the most valuable things I did this semester. It helped me to explore my beliefs and philosophies about teaching in an honest and open way. The journal also provided me with a way of recording and formally reflecting on my own development as a teacher. Acknowledging that my beliefs do not have to be congruent with others in order to be "correct" was also something that was cemented for me this semester. Previously, I incorrectly assumed that all professors and teachers are experts, and I should take what they have to say at face value and accept it as the truth, or at least as an enlightened opinion. I also used to be more likely to accept the opinions of my peers, assuming that they somehow knew something I did not. I have grown in this respect. (Jean Holden)

Leila, Gene, Claudia, John, and Steve had other perspectives.

Because this is the last page in this journal, I will write about how journal writing has been helpful to me in the past few months. This did not hit me until today—I only came to notice its effect. Through writing, I have begun to think more clearly and, furthermore, expand my original reflections or thinking about topics. *I have begun thinking on paper.* (Leila Muniroui)

---

[3] A good place, we think, to begin exploring published journal accounts is with compilations. For example: *Our Private Lives: Journals, Notebooks and Diaries* (edited by Daniel Halpern, 1988) is a collection of excerpts from a spectrum of writers; *The Pleasures of Diaries: Four Centuries of Private Writing* (edited by Ronald Blythe, 1989) witnesses writers experiencing the range of human emotions and life events, and represents writers spanning the range of occupations and stations in life; *Family Portraits: Remembrances by Twenty Distinguished Writers* (edited by Carolyn Anthony, 1989) focuses on life in families during the twentieth century; *An American Childhood* by Annie Dillard (1987) represents another kind of account, a childhood reflected upon as an adult.

When I was assigned to keep a journal as a part of the [graduate teacher preparation] program, I treated the entries just like an assignment. Though we were assured no one would read our journals unless we so desired, I was still cautious at first. I was uncomfortable writing in a journal because I had not kept a journal or diary in years. We were to write about our observations at the school [to which we were assigned for the full year]. My deep thoughts, feelings, or opinions were not included in my observation entries. I wrote mechanically, trying to be "objective" in my accounts: "The students have a lot of energy, but ask good questions and are challenging. My mentor teacher is confident and has excellent control of the class (not over the class)" (September 5). As the semester continued, I began to include more personal thoughts. The journal became therapeutic. In it I could share thoughts and emotions that I could share with no one else. I began a personal section in the back of my notebook that I use for my journal. I am not sure if this change related to my being more comfortable with journal writing (my first conclusion) or because I had begun to interact with the students. (Gene Seen)

I have found keeping a journal of my preservice teaching experiences invaluable for several reasons. The obvious is that it has helped me to remember those experiences in a vivid way. As I read over my entries, I am immediately aware of the many different emotions I felt at particular times. I can also look at particular actions teachers did that I liked or disliked. This is critical for me as a preservice teacher. I am constantly looking for new techniques I can try to be more effective as a teacher. I can also look at my own actions as a teacher in a more objective light. Observations of my peers are interspersed with my journal entries. As I focus on how I perceive them as preservice teachers, I am forced to reflect on my own actions in the classroom. Am I similar or dissimilar to this particular person? How might I teach the same lesson in a different way? What techniques would I like to adopt as my own? (Claudia Conners)

I came to enjoy and appreciate keeping a journal. Journal writing was beneficial because it forced me to consider what I was doing with my time in relation to working in the classroom. I found myself more concerned about wanting to be productive and accountable for the time I spent on the [university] cohort class once I began to appreciate the time spent writing in my journal. Journal writing was also beneficial in prodding me to think about my experiences. I found myself less concerned or anxious about the next period of student teaching, and I came to enjoy pondering about what had passed. I wrote in my journal those things that seemed most important to me but often found the time short—still, it caused me to reflect a lot. It helped me set aside time to ponder [areas of concern] and this was beneficial. (John Corporan)

I would now like to make some comments upon the evolution of this journal. Although I had often been told of the reflective value of such musings, I would never have had the discipline to do so. Now that I must, I am indeed finding it of value to put my thoughts into writing even if only a fragment of my mental wanderings can be recorded. I also notice an anticipatory and interpersonal slant to my writings. I dwell on what I might do instead of what has actually happened. Furthermore, the mechanics of lesson plans tend to take second place to the interpersonal aspects of teaching. That is only natural because it is in my personal dealings with the students that I am experiencing my greatest challenge. As a bachelor, with little recent exposure to this age group, I have much to learn. Well-formulated lessons are necessary but will come to naught unless implemented with a human common touch. It is an empathy I have yet to develop. (Steve Bruno)

About the process of writing, Robert airs some concerns.

I have never kept a journal or diary before, and I commence this assignment with some trepidation. My worries are: 1) I write like a second grader—my penmanship is legible, but it would lead anyone who saw it to think I am retarded or palsied; 2) I do not write well in rough drafts. My finished papers are of pretty good quality, but I have never produced a first draft of which I am proud; 3) I am scared that I may write the wrong things that may upset or antagonize the unseen reader. I do not want to screw up my future due to some injudicious scribblings in a journal; 4) a journal's value to a journal writer is in the rereading. Feelings that otherwise might have flown from the writer's mind are recaptured when the journal is read again. My reservation on this point is that I doubt I will ever find time to reread this journal. But, I guess, because I have to write a journal, I should try to convince myself that it is a good idea and put forth some conscientious effort to record my real thoughts and feelings and trust in the discretion of [the professor] not to judge me harshly or to hold grudges over anything that may be found objectionable. (Robert Marigold)

Actually, Robert did *not* "have to" keep a journal. In order for journals to be meaningful vehicles for exploring emerging practice, their use and the purposes they serve have to be open to negotiation.

One form of journal writing—dialogue or interactive journals—is, for many individuals, especially suited to the purposes of teacher preparation. We make this claim because the notion of a dialogue or ongoing conversation and interaction with a more experienced colleague or peer seems to naturally follow the process of writing about prior experiences and preconceptions of teaching—as one might focus on in writing a personal history account. If a dialogue journal format is used, therefore, the writing process becomes the vehicle for extending the conversation to others about the perspectives you hold. The interactive component of the journal writing process comes about when you present your writing for another person or persons to read and respond. The interaction or dialogue that ensues is initiated by the intersection of *their* experiences with *yours* as they question, ponder, and comment upon your narrative. In one sense such a close relationship with a reader is a risky business, but if you agree to a format, focus, or range of topics for discussion, and address issues of confidentiality and trust, you may be able to proceed in a very productive and agreeable fashion. Leila, who kept a traditional journal, as we have described, talks about the potential of developing a dialogue with another person, especially during student teaching.

▼

Journals could be used to start a dialogue between the supervisor and the student teacher. The same way supervisors make comments when they observe us, they can do in journals also. Each of us can question the parts we do not understand, make comments, look at events in different lights, or simply share emotional responses and similar experiences. Such journals could help to establish rapport between student teachers and supervisors. The trust relationship builds up between both people through sharing experiences. The key thing is that the other, more experienced reader can gradually make comments and remarks that will guide the preservice teacher into thinking critically and analyzing their own actions rather than reacting defensively to any remarks (as students in the cohort often did). (Leila Muniroui)

▲

We also know, however, that some individuals, like Robert, find journal writing particularly difficult. A few have even suggested that it is a waste of time. If you are one of those people we can only suggest that you really persevere with the writing process. Keeping a journal as a course requirement may prove problematic for some. (Being a personal document it ought to defy formal evaluation and grading by an instructor.) If you are not just maintaining a journal for yourself, it may place an element of artificiality on the task and the writing. And, there are some who find it perhaps inconsistent with their learning or life styles. Nevertheless, many preservice teachers who, for various reasons, did not keep a written record of their activities through teacher preparation programs have expressed their regret to us.

Before you too hastily reject the idea of keeping a journal, be prepared to try other alternatives for recording your experiences. For example, one preservice teacher we have worked with had been, as a younger person, coerced to keep a journal for religious purposes and found the process highly repugnant. Together we devised an alternative strategy for keeping track of her responses to the field experience site—she dictated her responses into an audio tape recorder and had another person transcribe the narrative. (This is the preferred method that one of us uses to maintain a journal.) Others have used video cameras to record, whereas yet another wrote poetry rather than narrative. Still others have interspersed narrative text with copious diagrams and sketches, finding the writing and drawing reciprocal and mutually responsive. One particularly interesting journal we have been privileged to read was written by a preservice art teacher who used a combination of narrative, poetry, sketches, and more polished artistic renderings. These were recorded in a relatively small unlined book.

Journal Keeping: Getting Started

To get you started writing, the following are some suggestions. Regarding format, use a form that feels appropriate to you—lined loose-leaf, small lined pocketbook, blank field book, or computer generated text. Considering that the journal may be either read by others or that you will want to reread it and explore it as though it were a "source of research information," wide margins of about two or three inches (or 50 to 75mm), perhaps on the left, may be useful for notations.

Some questions and ongoing themes to consider beginning and maintaining in your writing include the following:

- the most valuable thing about teaching that you have learned so far
- previous beliefs that have been changed or challenged as a result of your experiences in the school and classroom
- previous ideas or beliefs about teaching that have been most reinforced as a result of these new field experiences
- the most difficult idea, position, or concept about teaching you have encountered so far
- positive and negative teaching experiences you have had (consider teaching to mean your school experiences in toto). Try to come to an understanding about the origins of your thinking about the experiences
- schools as places to teach and work
- your perceptions of teachers as professionals
- students as learners
- perceptions (yours and others) of your role as preservice teacher
- your concerns about addressing issues of student diversity
- your concerns about addressing students with special needs in classrooms
- technology in classrooms and how it can be used to facilitate student learning
- the intersections between schools and issues of race, class and gender
- the interactions between yourself and students, cooperating teacher(s), supervisor(s), others working in the school, parents, and peer preservice teachers
- various periods of your experience during the term, such as first day observations, first lessons, particularly positive or negative days of teaching, crises, highlights, and interactions with peers, as in observations of your teaching

Finally, the best way to get started is to begin to write and to talk about your writing with others. In particular, sharing the various ways in which you and your peers began writing, the formats you each use and why, and the foci will probably propel you further in a successful experience. And, with growing confidence you may even come to share excerpts from your writing or engage in a journal dialogue.

Explorations of Personal Metaphors

Teaching and learning are things you *do*, not things you typically talk about; consequently, attaching language to or finding appropriate ways to communicate about teaching is often difficult. We, and many others, have found the use of figurative or metaphoric language helpful both as a way of communicating about teaching and as a way of enhancing personal understanding of teaching. The idea is a relatively simple one.

In everyday life we use analogies and images to help us clarify or make ideas more meaningful. We try to see one thing *as* another. The word "metaphor" is derived from the Greek "to carry across." Metaphors provide a way of carrying ideas and understandings from one context to another so that both the ideas and the new context become transformed in the process. When we apply this notion to teaching we have a way of understanding and representing teaching that is more personally meaningful. Personally generated metaphors of teaching give meaning to the abstract and elusive aspects of classroom practice. They can capture and communicate the very essence of one's perspective. As vehicles of thinking, metaphors are coherent ways of succinctly organizing and representing thoughts about particular subject matters, activities, or theories. At another level, metaphors are linguistic representations of mental images that reflect personal perspectives; therefore, one of the ways in which you can explore some of your perspectives on teaching is through metaphor. And, as you expand your thinking about being teachers and working in schools, your metaphors may change to reflect your moving mental landscape of practice.

There are several ways to generate or discover existing metaphors or images of teaching:

- through analysis of the language *you* use to talk about teaching
- through analysis of the language *experienced* teachers and others use to talk about teaching
- through exercises involving guided imagery
- through free association exercises such as, "Teaching is . . ."
- through observation of practice

Some examples of teaching metaphors we have heard expressed by preservice teachers include teacher as: parent, nurturer, police officer, professor, tour guide, gardener, ringleader, and actor. These examples are all associated with roles of adults or occupations. Other examples might be couched in terms of a process, such as teaching as: gardening, conducting, acting, helping, nursing, playing football, traveling, and knitting. It is important that the metaphor you generate has meaning and relevance for you. The whole idea is to enhance *your* self-understanding. In the following examples, Lena describes her image of teaching in a musical context, and Sandra and Gail illustrate how metaphors can be used as constructs for analyzing teaching.

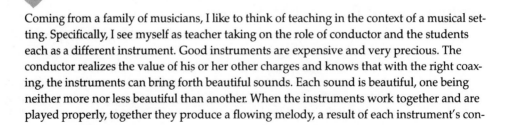

Coming from a family of musicians, I like to think of teaching in the context of a musical setting. Specifically, I see myself as teacher taking on the role of conductor and the students each as a different instrument. Good instruments are expensive and very precious. The conductor realizes the value of his or her other charges and knows that with the right coaxing, the instruments can bring forth beautiful sounds. Each sound is beautiful, one being neither more nor less beautiful than another. When the instruments work together and are played properly, together they produce a flowing melody, a result of each instrument's contribution. When the total sound lacks even one instrument the absence does not go unnoticed. Although others may attempt to perform as a substitute, none can fully replace the missing one, as it is unique. The conductor has an idea of what he or she wants the orchestra to sound like—and the sheet music provides some order. From there the conductor works with each instrument to ensure its preparedness and to develop the orchestral sound to its full potential, always mindful that each sound is different, bringing its special characteristics, which are vital to the fluidity of the performance. (Lena Bolin)

The following is Sandra's account. Her metaphor for teaching is embedded in her experience in the field.

A teacher of art is like a jeweler who has an intimate one-to-one relationship with each stone. Each student is as a stone. Because of her experience, the teacher can see "the diamond in the rough."

Classes were in their second week when I arrived in the school as a student teacher. My mentor teacher decided I should initiate the Grade 11 unit on clay head making. I introduced the project, incorporating a film, a series of slides that illustrated the step-by-step process, along with actual clay head examples and mini-demonstrations. The class activities also included several drawing exercises related to the study of facial structure and proportions. The students' project required them to produce half life-size self-portraits (sculptures) in a naturalistic way, using their facial measurements along with a mirror. Students worked slowly with the clay because it was a new medium for most of them.

Since it was close to the beginning of the new term, the students were not yet entirely comfortable and at ease in the new environment, with new subject matter, and a new teacher. Nor were they comfortable with the other students whom they did not know. Requiring them to look observantly at their faces in a mirror during class time and in front of the other students caused unique problems. I was challenged when I discovered that several students using mirrors were involved in producing fantastical characters instead of naturalistic portraits of themselves. Also, when questioned about clay sculptures as a class, students were insecure about answering—even though they may have known the answers. Most classes began with a brief refresher or introduction to a particular technique, and the bulk of my time was spent encouraging individual students with their creative projects. This experience, though only a fragment of the challenges that confronted me as teacher, relates well to my metaphor of the jeweler.

A jeweler puts forth a lot of hard work with caring and focused attention because she sees the potential for the stone to become polished. When the student becomes aware of this interest, she begins to "shine." No matter how many stones the jeweler has to work with, she does not assume that they are all the same, regardless of however similar they may first appear to be. An experienced jeweler can see the subtle differences in each gem. Similarly, a graded, advanced art class does not imply that each student is at the same level. In fact, all students are of differing abilities, interests, backgrounds, strengths, and weaknesses. It would be an error to assume otherwise. There are flaws, yet an inclusion in a diamond may have a positive outcome because it often aids in providing more brilliance—it is more reflective. The art class affords an environment where students are expected to express their feelings, ideas, and opinions (keeping in mind of course, that students are affected by layers of such conditioning as societal, cultural, and political influences). The job of the sensitive teacher is to understand the pressures placed on students and to draw out their hidden beauty by directing questions or providing guidance—just as a dull stone can be made to shine and sparkle given the appropriate effort and skill. Hence, a teacher must be aware of the varying needs within the class.

Frank was an overweight student of Eastern European origin. He was regularly late purposefully, so that no mirrors were left by the time he arrived. He disliked looking at himself. His clay sculpture, a thin long face, was unlike his small round one. He seemed to be in need of constant reassurance. I tried to make him aware of just how interesting his face really was. We looked at his face together in the mirror and described it. Then, together, we decided on the changes and made adjustments to his sculpture. Slowly during the process, I asked him questions about himself and was genuinely thrilled by some of his stories and his keen sense of humor. Basically, I was trying to draw him out of what I thought was a negative self-image and to make him feel good about himself. Like an inclusion in a precious stone, imperfections can add extra brilliance and character.

Mark was a Native North American student who religiously wore a black leather jacket along with a cap over the top of his long, black hair. During class, he was very quiet and withdrawn. Upon observation of his sculpture I was immediately struck by the sensitive treatment of his clay head portrait. Although this was his first experience with clay, Mark worked in a self-assured manner. He, too, would not use a mirror and produced instead a rather interesting stylized portrait. When I expressed praise at the quality of his work, his brown eyes looked shyly up at me for acceptance. Like a jeweler, I tried to cut away the unnecessary parts of the stone so as to expose the real gem hidden behind his long hair, cap, and jacket.

Students like Frank and Mark can easily be overlooked. They are phantom students and theirs is a silent voice. As a teacher, I worked at making them feel comfortable—first about themselves, and then as members of the class. As a jeweler, I used my experience, skill, and intuition to see the potential luster and was able to catch a beginning "sparkle." Such are the elements for a positive experience. Like a precious stone, the relationship between teacher and student is multifaceted. (Sandra Crisante)

Gail's metaphor, also told with reference to her field placement experience, reveals some of the roots of her thinking about teaching.

I am a teacher. I am a tree. I have roots that reach deep into the ground and branches stretching high to the sky. My body is strong against the elements yet usually flexible enough to withstand breaking. I change with the seasons; change is an integral part of my existence. I provide shade, shelter, renewable resources, recreation, and beauty.

My last teaching placement was in an elementary school, teaching music at all grade levels. There, the Board of Education shows much encouragement for young people's musical skills, providing instrumental programs beginning in Grade 5.

Erin is in Grade 5 and had been playing the flute for only a few months. The flute is one of the more difficult instruments and requires much lung capacity. Erin is a petite person. She must breathe deeply and reach far with her fingers to achieve success, but she works hard and is advancing beyond the level of expectation. Erin, however, claims not to enjoy the flute and wants to switch to the clarinet. (One of her best friends is an excellent clarinet player and is willing to spend the time helping her after school.)

Erin has mentioned to my cooperating teacher, Mr. Gordon, her desire to switch instruments. Mr. Gordon asked if I would listen to Erin's work and coach her. Afterward, we both talked to Erin and discussed her natural ability and success with the flute. We talked about her accomplishments and the possibility of giving up those accomplishments for, perhaps, a struggle with a new instrument. We eventually discovered that the root of Erin's problem was not her dislike of the instrument but rather her dissatisfaction with her progress. She felt that for the amount of effort she was giving she should be a much better player. Mr. Gordon asked her to take the flute home and practice again and, if she still felt dissatisfied, she could switch instruments.

Erin was eventually allowed to switch to the clarinet. Mr. Gordon helped her with the new instrument, as did her friend. Erin was also permitted to switch back to the flute a few days later.

We are all trees—all teachers. Erin is a sapling. She was given the opportunity to branch out further, discover her resources and beauty. She was permitted to change with the season and grow. Fortunately, unlike many trees today, her resources were not considered expendable. Her teachers, older fellows of the forest, provided limbs for climbing, room for growth, and nutrients.

Erin is a strong young tree. Her strength was recognized and trusted. Her teacher did not convince her that she needed to be clipped in order to grow, nor that she might break if trying to branch out. A strong, older tree must: recognize and facilitate a sapling's growth at the root stage and throughout the stages of branching out; recognize potential resources and beauty; be aware of natural, ever-occurring changes; be strong, and hopefully bend but not break; provide shade, shelter, renewable resources, recreation, and beauty; give nutrients and recognize those received; and, recognize that if roots are damaged, growth will be impaired.

All educators have roots of knowledge from which they may draw, and many-faceted branches of experience. Their bark and trunk develop strength, yet must remain flexible in their ever-changing environment. Through knowledge and guidance, young people can be given the ability to see things in different light (shade), learn about commitment (shelter), recognize potential (renewable resources), enjoy life (recreation), and hopefully, love themselves, others, and their surroundings (beauty). (Gail Sheridan)

Although the idea of personal metaphors of teaching is relatively straightforward, finding a metaphor that "fits" and working with it to enhance self-understanding is slightly more complex. You may need to try on several for size before you find a "best fit." But that process, too, may be a useful exercise because it will allow you to explore different assumptions underlying images of teaching. In any case, if you are interested in finding out more about metaphor and its use in teacher education and development, there is a list of recommended readings at the end of the chapter. Especially, you may want to explore Connelly and Clandinin's (1988) *Teachers as Curriculum Planners,* Diamond's (1991) *Teacher Education as Transformation,* Hunt's (1987) *Beginning With Ourselves: In Theory, Practice and Human Affairs* and (1991) *The Renewal of Personal Energy.*

As we and the above authors suggest, metaphors and images of teaching are vehicles for professional development when they are generated and examined for purposes of gaining insight into thinking and practice. Metaphors used in this way are quite different from those used in casual conversations and writing, the point of difference resting in the degree to which the concept is examined. For example, "teaching is nurturing" or "teaching is mothering" are commonly touted notions associated with lower elementary school work, but the assumptions behind these concepts are rarely examined. There are also great gulfs between the kinds of personal metaphors for teaching that we have encouraged you to think about and some of the public clichés that we often hear tired teachers, the press, politicians, and the public using. For example, "teaching is a battle" and "schools are battlefields" are acceptable concepts for those who believe that "teachers are in the trenches." These kinds of public metaphors—and their origins—deserve careful examination, something we urge you to do by comparing them with your own private metaphors.

Professional Development Summaries and Records

Making sense of your immediate, formal teacher preparation experiences is as important as understanding the influence of prior experiences on your current thinking about being a teacher. To be sure, you engage in such practices on a daily basis as you informally reflect, ponder, question, and work away at formal assignments, making meaning from your field experiences. Our thinking here is that there is particular value in writing about your experiences within a critical, analytical framework. In a sense we see this kind of activity as one which employs the information or data that you, as an emerging teacher, compile about yourself. One way to think about this kind of activity is that it is like writing a formal research paper. In preparing a research paper you use data of some kind—usually text or book information as in an historical analysis or review of a body of research literature, or results from some laboratory experiments—to support the expression of a coherent, cogent argument or point of view.

Instead of the data on which you build your professional development summaries being those which a social or physical scientist, historian, or some other researcher produced, the foundation of your professional development summaries are *your* records of *your* emerging and developing thinking about being a teacher. The journal records, personal history account, class assignments, practice teaching plans or logs, videos and perhaps photographic accounts, and other recorded activities provide the evidence and, in turn, the substance of your professional development summaries. In a sense, these summaries are the continuation of your personal history account. They represent ongoing analyses of the professional experiences associated with participation in a formal program of teacher education and *data* for future professional development summaries. Therefore, presuming you develop these summaries at various points along the continuum of your formal preparation to teach, these summary narratives build upon each other into a coherent critique and record of your professional development which you can take with you and extend throughout your professional practice.

How might you proceed? How might you analyze your professional development summaries? We will talk in more depth about the topic of information analysis in the next chapter but, for the moment, consider the following as *one of several* ways to begin.

1. Read all your records (that is, the different kinds of autobiographical writing you have engaged in, as well as observation notes, and so on) for the period of your development you are exploring.
2. Jot down the repeating or common topics, themes, problems, concerns, and other issues.
3. Reorganize these notes into a meaningful list of categories.
4. Reread your records with the express purpose of identifying passages in your records that provide examples of the topic, theme, problem, concern, or issue.
5. Organize your narrative examples of these categories so that they evidence some kind of progression.
6. Then, try writing a summary analysis using these passages from your "data records" as the substance around which you build a discussion of your professional growth.

The outcomes of these activities (at various points in your preparation) are the professional development summaries. These, put together, represent a professional development record.

For a more focused analysis of your records you could use the strategy we have outlined to explore a given topic. For example, you could focus on

- your participation in the various contexts of learning
- your ability to relate to theory and practice in some kind of balanced way and your translation of educational theories and principles into practice
- assessment of your strengths in the field and areas that need to be developed
- formulation of goals for continuing professional development
- relationships with the various participants and contributors to your learning to be a teacher

Professional development summaries (and taken together, records), therefore, are reflective statements about your professional development. Here are some portions of preservice teachers' summaries. Note the different points of emphasis and analysis on which these individuals focus. For example, Gene struggled with the matter of keeping a substantive record of her development and with the issue of developing her own teaching style. Of particular concern to her was the degree to which she should or should not adopt the teaching style of her cooperating teacher (whom she refers to as her mentor). Josephine's summary statement is a retrospective analysis of how some of her thinking about teaching changed over the course of the year.

My mentor teacher appeared to have command over the subject matter and the students. I remember it being difficult to include everything that my mentor teacher did in my notes. Information about how he addressed and responded to the students, where he moved in the classroom during recitation, and how he treated inattentive students was included. I described how he patiently waits for students to answer questions and how he goes over to a disruptive student, talks quietly and privately to the student in order to get the student to settle down. What I was not able to express in my writing was the personality of my mentor teacher. I could not capture it on paper, though it was important. This led me to consider my future role as a student teacher. I recall being aware of my own insecurities. I wrote: "Can I fill his shoes?" (September 5).

In addition, observation notes contained information about what the students were doing in the classroom. "Student is putting on lipstick, appears restless at first but settles down" (October 1). At this point entries included notes about which students were called on, what students said in response to the questions, what the disruptive or inattentive students were doing. I recorded notes on the actively participating students and disruptive students, and not much on the quiet, attentive students. "One . . . student is really responding. The teacher calls on her. Another student is talking. The teacher stands near him and he settles down" (September 24).

By observing and recording information about my mentor's teaching, I wondered how the observing and writing would affect my own teaching. Did I copy his techniques and behaviors as a result of observing them? As I taught during my internship, I recall being aware of my mentor's teaching style and techniques and attempting to emulate them. I remember finding myself consciously thinking about his approach as I stood teaching, in front of the class. At first I was not successful at imitating his techniques. It felt very uncomfortable, like wearing someone else's shoes. During about the middle of the second semester, I had acquired some of his techniques and approaches to teaching. Students were even saying I sounded like my mentor. I took this as a compliment. By this time, I had switched from observing my mentor to teaching the class. This allowed me to practice some of my mentor's techniques and helped me adopt many aspects of his teaching style.

I still struggled, though, to be even more like my mentor teacher. A teacher's teaching style reflects that teacher's personality and, because I could not comfortably acquire my mentor's personality, my struggle continued. I finally came to realize that one can acquire some of another teacher's techniques by watching and recording information about that teacher's behavior and then practicing that behavior, but because a teacher's teaching style is unique, a student teacher will have to develop his or her own teaching style. (Gene Seen)

Looking back over my notes I realize that if I had taught a class at the beginning of the quarter, I would have been a "Textbook Teacher" simply because I did not know how to do the kinds of things I wanted to do. I would have been following the example of teachers who taught me even though that is not what I would have wanted to do. I was not sure what to do in the classroom or how to do what I think is a better way. Now that I have learned some options and have had some experience applying them, I find myself looking in different ways at the material to be presented, to see which philosophical orientation suits it best. I also look at my objectives from different perspectives to see if there isn't something I am missing or something more important. I try (but do not always succeed) to match my methods to my aims. Now, I can see why they did not coincide or why they were successful.

I am better able to look at what I do objectively in order to improve it for the next time and improve myself for the next lesson. I am also better prepared when I go into the classroom because I have direction, purpose, and meaning for the material I am going to present. I also feel like I have direction, purpose, and meaning for (my) being in the classroom. I can justify to myself and the students why we are there and what they can expect to get from the various learning experiences. (Josephine Figueroa)

Summary

In this chapter we have suggested and illustrated some ways in which you might become reflexive through autobiographical writing. Throughout the text, particularly in Part 3, there are hundreds more illustrations of preservice teachers' autobiographical writing. In fact, the narrative accounts, which make up most of the book, were generated using the very methods we describe in these first few chapters. In the next chapter we suggest ways of gathering external information about the people, contexts, and materials that will also inform your thinking and developing practice. We conclude this chapter with a list of suggestions for further reading that will provide you with additional information about personal history accounts, journals and journal keeping, metaphors, and other forms of autobiographical writing.

Recommended Readings

Ashton-Warner, S. (1963). *Teacher*. New York: Simon & Schuster.

Ashton-Warner, S. (1972). *Spearpoint*. New York: Knopf.

Ball, S. J., & Goodson, I. F. (1985). *Teachers' lives and careers*. London: Falmer Press.

Bullough, R. V., Jr., Knowles, J. G., & Crow, N. A. (1991). *Emerging as a teacher*. London: Routledge, Chapman, & Hall.

Clandinin, D. J. (1986). *Classroom practice: Teacher images in action*. East Sussex, UK: Falmer Press.

Clandinin, D. J., Davies, A., Hogan, P., & Kennard, B. (1993). *Learning to teach, teaching to learn*. New York: Teachers College Press.

Connelly, F. M., & Clandinin, D. J. (1988). *Teachers as curriculum planners*. New York: Teachers College Press.

Daiker, D. A., & Morenberg, M. (1990). *The writing teacher as researcher: Essays in the theory and practice of class-based research*. Portsmouth, NH: Boynton Cook.

Diamond, C. T. P. (1991). *Teacher education as transformation*. Milton Keynes, UK: Open University Press.

Dillard, A. (1987). *An American childhood*. New York: Harper & Row.

Disbrowe, H. B. (1984). *A schoolman's odyssey.* London, Ontario: University of Western Ontario.

Eddy, E. M. (1969). *Becoming a teacher.* New York: Teachers College Press.

Ferri, B., & Aglio, M. (1990). *I'm not alone: Teacher talk, teacher buddying.* Mississauga, Ontario: Peel Board of Education.

Fulwiler, T. (1987). *The Journal Book.* Portsmouth, NH: Boynton Cook.

Glover, M. K. (1992). *Two years: A teacher's memoir.* Portsmouth, NH: Heinemann.

Goodson, I. F., & Walker, R. (1991). *Biography, identity and schooling episodes in educational research.* London: Falmer Press.

Goswami, D., & Stillman, P. R. (1987). *Reclaiming the classroom.* Upper Montclair, NJ: Boynton Cook.

Greenstein, J. (1983). *What the children taught me.* Chicago: University of Chicago Press.

Hunt, D. E. (1987). *Beginning with ourselves: In theory, practice and human affairs.* Cambridge, MA/Toronto, Ontario: Brookline Books/OISE Press.

Hunt, D. E. (1991). *The renewal of personal energy.* Toronto, Ontario: OISE Press.

Jones, G. (1991). *Crocus Hill notebook.* London, Ontario: Althouse Press.

Keizer, G. (1988). *No place but here: A teacher's vocation in a rural community.* New York: Penguin Books.

Kincheloe, J. L. (1991). *Teachers as researchers: Qualitative inquiry as a path to empowerment.* London: Falmer Press.

Kohl, H. (1984). *Growing minds: On becoming a teacher.* New York: Harper & Row.

Newman, J. M. (1989). *Finding our own way: Teachers exploring their assumptions.* Portsmouth, NH: Heinemann.

Perl, S., & Wilson, N. (1986). *Through teachers' eyes: Portraits of writing teachers at work.* Portsmouth, NH: Heinemann Educational Books.

Progoff, I. (1975). *At a journal workshop.* New York: Dialogue House Library.

Ryan, K., Newman, K. K., Mager, G., Applegate, J., Lasley, T., Flora, R., & Johnston, J. (1980). *Biting the apple.* New York: Longman.

Ryan, K. (Ed.). (1970). *Don't smile until Christmas.* Chicago: University of Chicago Press.

Ryan, K. (Ed.). (1992). *The roller coaster year: Essays by and for beginning teachers.* Boston, MA: HarperCollins.

Shack, S. (1965). *Armed with a primer: A Canadian teacher looks at children, schools, and parents.* Toronto, Ontario: McClelland & Stewart.

Solnicki, J. (1992). *The real me is gonna be a shock.* Toronto, Ontario: Lester.

Staton, J., Shuy, R. W., Peyton, J. K., & Reed, L. (1988). *Dialogue journal communication: Classroom, linguistic, social and cognitive views.* Norwood, NJ: Ablex.

Stuart, J. (1949). *The thread that runs so true.* New York: Charles Scribner's Sons.

Witherell, C., Noddings N. (1991). *Stories lives tell: Narrative and dialogue in education.* New York: Teachers College Press.

CHAPTER 3

Looking and Listening: Gathering External Information Using Ethnographic[1] Research Techniques

We turn to ways of gathering information in response to questions you may have developed about the contexts, processes, or actions of people associated with teaching and learning. We refer to some of the ways you may gather *external* information to inform your thinking about teaching roles or practices. Having referred to autobiographical writing and explorations that place you and your experiences at the center of inquiry as *internal* information gathering, we turn to accessing information that originates from the outside, from *external* sources. We explore the major characteristics and usefulness of being an observer (especially a participant observer), an interviewer, and a collector of documentary or artifact information—doing "ethnographic" research. Remember that library research is included in these active processes of gathering information. Reviews of literature pertinent to the inquiry or research topic on which you focus are developed after extensive library work. Throughout the book, the *Links with Research* serve to highlight the usefulness of library research and provide jumping off places for you to begin such explorations.

In this chapter, as a way of gathering information and developing sensitivity to the educational contexts in which you find yourself, we explore

- participant observation
- interviewing

---

[1] We use the term *ethnographic* broadly. Anthropologists may dispute the use of "ethnography" to characterize the kind of research we encourage in this chapter; the essential elements of a lengthy period and a focus on understanding "culture" in a comprehensive sense are likely not to be present in this kind of activity. Although ethnographic research is often conducted within educational contexts, here we are simply borrowing the research tools of the ethnographer.

- collecting documents or artifacts
- analyzing information and using ethnographic research techniques

All of these activities demand a sensitivity to the ethical implications of your actions. For example, if you maintain a personal journal or make field notes about observations or conversations, then it is important to keep these confidential and, perhaps, not use any identifying information such as proper names. You may want to keep them on your person or in a safe place. Also, it is a good idea to gain permission to conduct formal observations or listen in on conversations, such as you might do in the faculty lounge. One key point to remember is to protect the confidentiality of all persons in your inquiries, particularly students. Because the scope of this book does not allow us to delve deeply into the topic of ethics in field work or the various ways of gathering information we strongly suggest that you explore some of the *Recommended Readings* at the end of the chapter. As you may suspect, there are many books and other publications on the topic of gathering external information, analyzing it, and "doing ethnography" (see *Recommended Readings*). Another way of learning how to engage in research using ethnographic tools is to read accounts of ethnographic research. Many such accounts are listed in the *Recommended Readings* throughout the book. Several examples are also included at the end of this chapter.

Participant Observations

Participant observation is the hallmark research method of anthropologists. Think of coming to understand schools and classrooms as being similar to the task of an anthropologist who wants to understand a foreign culture. But you want to understand more fully the context and cultures of teaching. When engaging in the activities of your field experience within the culture of schools and classrooms you are at the same time both a participant in the culture and an observer of that culture and its participants. Keep in mind, however, that in some ways your situation is distinctly different from that of the anthropologist. Unlike most anthropologists who explore "foreign cultures," you have had a long "apprenticeship of observation" within the culture—you have spent upwards of 12 years in schools and have much knowledge of the school cultures. Although this can be advantageous, you are likely to make assumptions about what you observe and experience based on prior knowledge.

Think about this for a moment. Perhaps recollect our discussion in Chapter 1 where we introduced the notions of *informal* and *formal* theories. You already have considerable knowledge about schools and classrooms, at least the schools that you attended as a student, and this represents, in a sense, informal theories about the way schools operate and teachers and students behave. (If you were educated by your parents at home you may well enter schools with fresh eyes.) When you see and hear events and circumstances in educational contexts, how can you be sure that you are *not* "seeing what you want to see" or that you are blind to certain behaviors and situations? Here is one example of what we mean. Dwayne came to have "fresh eyes" as a result of an opportunity to observe, but the new perspective did not come easily.

When I went into the school I was intent on continuing my interest in football. I wanted to begin coaching. As an observational assignment a group of us decided to focus our interest on the gymnasium and locker room talk of male students. (We were actually trying to understand students' views of school and the place of extracurricular activities in their lives.) I was, of course, very comfortable in the locker rooms as I listened to the familiar bantering among students and the loud, jovial, competitive, and often sexually-explicit talk. I had considered this to be all in good spirits—"fun" if you like. We collected quite a bit of information over several weeks.

At first I recorded only those parts of the conversations that were directly related to extracurricular sports. As time progressed, I recorded conversations much more faithfully, I think. Even at the time, however, I did not think much about them. But, as I began to expand my notes and talk with the other preservice teachers in the group, I became increasingly aware of the nature of the talk. Not only was the talk biased against boys who were not seen as being masculine, but it was *highly* biased against girls. More than that, it was directly related to the sexual harassment that I began to see these students engaging in outside of the locker room. This experience brought me up short. I had been blind to these offensive behaviors. (Dwayne McAuslin)

One way to partially counteract tendencies to make assumptions about what you see and hear in educational contexts, especially schools and classrooms, is to become a keen observer and systematic recorder of contexts and situations within your field experiences. (In Chapter 5 we deal extensively with the preconceptions that you bring to formal teacher preparation, and that discussion may help you think further about this matter.) The key to being successful in this endeavor is to strive to describe in detail that which you see and hear.

In the following accounts, preservice teachers talk about the place of observations in their learning. First, Jeannie talks about the relationship between observations and journal writing and then John mentions the development of his skills associated with observation.

In learning to become an observer I have gained a greater awareness of the happenings in a classroom. Recording observations in the classroom during my field placement was complemented by writing journal entries. In writing my journal, I have consistently reflected on what I observed. In writing, I defined for myself what I felt [about particular practices which] helped me think about what I would do in similar situations in my own classroom. This ongoing process of analyzing and rethinking my observations has emphasized the importance of reflecting [on my work] as a teacher. When I reread parts of my journal I found that I had biases toward particular students at the beginning of the term—I had formed ideas about their personalities based on their academic performance and comparisons with people from my past. Many times I found my initial judgments were quite unfair. In the future I hope to treat each student with equal respect and explore their personalities by interacting with them. To do this, I will need to be aware of my own actions and be able to analyze whether or not I am carrying out my intentions. To do this, observation is central. (Jeannie Gore)

I found the observations the most helpful and rewarding experiences during the Fall Quarter. Observing was helpful in many ways. Most significant was the time spent making descriptive observations of the classroom. Never before have I recorded observations without [immediately injecting] my own values. I have always analyzed my experiences based on values and norms that I have been taught and that appeal to me. It was tough to approach classroom observations like an anthropologist approaches people of another culture. One takes descriptive notes of what occurs and only after much time and many observations are interpretations made on what seems to be the meaning of what is happening. I think if you are not taught some principles on how to observe classrooms it is extremely easy to only use your past experiences to interpret the meaning of what you are observing.

   With an introduction on how to be an "ethnographer," we were sent out to observe life at the high school. It was exciting and enjoyable to sit back in a classroom and observe the proceedings, writing down what I saw; it allowed me to focus on the students and listen to what they had to say. I found myself more concerned about how students reacted to the teacher, and my observation skills developed considerably. One of the most important concepts that developed out of my observations was learning how to notice patterns of behavior, analyzing these patterns, and developing an interpretation.

   I originally had no plans on observing any certain aspect of classroom life in my cooperating teacher's mathematics class but was drawn to the discipline tactics he employed. I found the observations particularly rewarding because there was very little discussion on discipline between me and the cooperating teacher. I figured out the major tactics he used in classroom management by spending time in his classroom seeing the patterns occur over and over again. (John Corporan)

Getting Started

Many preservice teachers need some suggestions about what to focus on when they first begin to make observations in classrooms and schools. "How might I get started on making observations?" "How might I begin to develop expertise in making observations and taking notes?" "What should I look at?" These are some of the questions we often hear. We suggest that you think about less complex foci for your first observations. For example, you may want to work with a peer and select two or three students who may be talking or "hanging out" in the hall, or two or three teachers talking over lunch in the faculty room. (Keep in mind the ethical implications of your activities.) One useful strategy to develop observation skills is to agree on a focus for observations and then observe and take notes for a short time (five to ten minutes or less). Aim to describe in note form what you see and hear. Soon afterwards, take time to enlarge or "thicken" your notes. By thickening your notes we mean enlarging them from words, phrases, incomplete sentences, sketches, or diagrams to a descriptive narrative. Try not to make judgments or inferences about what you observed. Once each of you has developed separate narratives of your observations, compare them and talk about where you agreed and where you differed in both the recording and the narrative or expanded notes. Repeat the process, each time exploring the differences in your observations and the strengths, weaknesses, and differences within your descriptions.

Observing is not a skill that always comes easily. Some references that may help you develop understandings of this process include the chapter on observation in *Inside Schools* by Woods (1986) and the chapter on data collection strategies in *Ethnography and Qualitative Design in Educational Research* by Goetz and LeCompte (1984).

As you feel comfortable observing, move into more complex situations, but remember that classrooms and schools are very complex environments; therefore you will need to focus many of your observations. The following are some areas where you might begin making useful observations:

- teachers' strategies and approaches to classroom organization, management, and discipline
- student-teacher relationships, including rapport and ways of interacting
- how teachers address diversity in their classrooms (consider decor, displays, teaching and learning materials, techniques, relationships, and so on)
- use of technology in the classroom
- how a teacher handles the paperwork and other administrative affairs of the classroom
- how teachers go about planning, including how they select instructional methods and how these plans play out in practice
- various teachers' philosophies of teaching as they are expressed in classrooms
- teachers' individual lesson structures and patterns of instruction

You also might want to operate from a broader perspective (as an ethnographer initially would do) and attempt to answer the more general question, "What is going on here?" Shadowing a teacher in her or his full responsibilities, both in and out of the classroom, to explore the questions, "What is a teacher?" and "What is teachers' work?" is one example of this approach.

In the lists we have just provided, we mainly suggested observation of teachers and their actions, practices, and so on. We have done this intentionally, primarily as a way to help you to get started. Observations of teachers may at first be more easily accomplished than observations of students and their cultures. Chapters 7 and 10 (which focus on schools and students respectively) suggest potentially useful questions with which to frame further observations if you are most interested in observing students in context.

Well-developed observation skills will enable you to become "kid and teacher watchers" and will afford considerable opportunities to develop insights about students and educational contexts. We see this as being essential for your ongoing professional development. Throughout the book the *For Reflection and Discussion* subsections of each chapter may give you some ideas for developing productive observations. In addition, the *Research Activities* sections raise specific questions, many of which could also be the focus of your observations.

Interviewing

There are many people from whom you may gain useful perspectives about a whole range of topics pertinent to your professional development. Interviewing is one potentially rewarding and informative activity. Think of this process as having conversations with "informants," as these individuals are often called by anthropologists or sociologists. Informants in schools—people who have "insider" knowledge that will help you learn and understand the group or culture—could include students, teachers, administrators, professional and non-professional support staff, parents, and representatives of special interest groups.

There are basically two ways of conducting interviews, and both may serve your purposes at different times. One is as a formal process, relying on interview protocols usually consisting of a fairly structured set of predetermined questions and probes. The other technique is informal and less structured, where the interviewer relies more on intuition and the course of events within the interview or conversation to ask pertinent questions and seek clarification of responses. The formal process may be best when you are approaching someone with whom you are unfamiliar or when you are unsure of being able to conduct a focused conversation (perhaps because of the questions you wish to ask or because of being unsure of the subject matter). The informal process may yield the best quality of information, particularly if you know the person with whom you are talking or the subject matter, or if you are confident in your abilities as an interviewer.

As you begin to think about having casual and more formal conversations (interviews) with people within educational contexts, you may wish to refer to some of the references in *Recommended Readings*. Woods' (1986) *Inside Schools*, Goetz and LeCompte's (1984) *Ethnography and Qualitative Design in Educational Research*, and Spradley's (1979) *The Ethnographic Interview* have useful sections dealing with the interview process.

Collecting Documents or Artifacts

As you participate in field experiences and explore aspects of the school and student cultures, various kinds of documents may prove useful. School district offices, school administrators, teachers, students, parents, and the community including the news media produce voluminous amounts of printed matter (policies, rules, guidelines and forms of various kinds, statements of core curriculum, curriculum materials, school newspapers and newsletters, community newspaper articles, stories, and photographs) that may provide additional insight into the school community. After collecting some of these artifacts, you can use a process of analysis similar to that used in preparing your professional development summaries and records (see Chapter 2), that is, looking for patterns and themes, or consistently presented topics, issues, or concerns. It is likely that the documentary evidence will help "fill in the blanks" or explain some of the findings from the other forms of information gathering. Bogdan and Biklen (1992), in *Qualitative Research for Education,* offer some useful ways to think about accessing and analyzing school and classroom artifacts. Similarly, Woods' (1986) *Inside Schools,* among other books in *Recommended Readings,* has a useful chapter for exploring documents of various kinds.

Analyzing Information and Using Ethnographic Research Techniques

If you combine the three external data gathering techniques we have introduced into a study of some aspect of teaching and schooling, then you are engaging in a form of *ethnographic research.* There is much you can learn by employing the techniques of ethnographic research. We encourage you to try them out with an eye to incorporating them into your inquiry-based practice.

The account below is drawn from a report of one preservice teacher's attempt to understand school through the eyes of one student. It illustrates how observations and informal conversations (interviews) were used as information gathering tools, and the insights gained as a result of gathering information in this way. Matt describes these two elements both in his thinking about research and in the actual account of his research activities. The following account is his story of Barnaby.

▼

As I spent more time with Barnaby, I decided that it was crucial to determine how much of his apathy was self-manufactured. In our discussions over the next few weeks, Barnaby revealed to me that he had been in the "accelerated classes," designed for college-bound students, until he was in the tenth grade. He said he had to leave that track because the work load did not give him any opportunity to pursue his own interests. When I asked what some of his outside interests included, he responded, without a moment's hesitation, "Chess."

I must confess that at this point I was startled by Barnaby's response. Although the increased time I spent with him was showing me a student who was clearly capable of insightful and careful thinking, I erroneously projected the level of apathy that he brought to the classroom onto his whole outlook on any activity that applied the exertion of cerebral clarity.

Several days later I decided to follow Barnaby for a day and get a sense of his "total experience of school." Barnaby said that it would be no problem if I tagged along with him. So, I met Barnaby the next day at 7:40 A.M. at his typing class. When I arrived, I was immediately struck by the absence of any social interaction among the students. They simply walked into the classroom and turned on their machines. The teacher made some comment about how far along each student should be, and then went behind her desk and began reading. The students, meanwhile, busily worked on activities from their typing books, avoiding any interaction with their peers. The teacher did not say another word until the end of the hour when she asked students to close their books to do some timed typing. The students did just this, and turned in their work. Barnaby made several good-natured attempts to socially engage himself with some of the other students; however, the mood of the class was not conducive to interaction, and Barnaby soon gave up his attempts. When the period ended, Barnaby explained to me that this was fairly typical of the typing class. He told me that the next class on his schedule was gym, where they were playing basketball. He said that he did not like basketball and expressed little enthusiasm about this next class.

When we got to the gymnasium the teacher did not greet the students. Sitting in the bleachers, she took attendance and then threw several basketballs to some of the students. The students divided themselves into teams and played basketball for the duration of the period. Apparently, Barnaby was not one of the better players in the class and, as is wont to happen when students divide themselves into teams, the stigma of being the last picked was placed on him. Barnaby seemed fairly indifferent about his dubious distinction. Still, he participated in the game and tried to cooperate with his teammates. A fairly interesting anecdote occurred at this point.

Midway through the class the teacher approached me and asked me a little bit about what I was doing. When I explained to her that I was following Barnaby around to get a sense of what his experience of school is like, she responded by saying that if I had any questions about Barnaby she could give me an in-depth answer. I politely declined, saying that I was trying to let the experience of his day speak for itself. She accepted this statement and soon added that she knew Barnaby well, and if I had any questions about him later that I should come see her. I thanked her and continued to observe Barnaby in class.

When class was over, I began to ask Barnaby a little bit about his experience in gym. For reference purposes, I asked him the name of his teacher. He did not know it. I thought to myself how ironic this situation was. Here was a teacher who was certain that she knew everything relevant that there was to know about a student, convinced that she had some insight into his life. But the student did not even know the teacher's name and clearly felt that her influence on his life was parenthetical at best.

During Barnaby's third and fourth period classes, Modern Readings and American History, he walked into the classes and was immediately handed a worksheet. Although the teachers were friendly to Barnaby, at no point was he given the opportunity to interact with them or any of the students. As I looked at each of these worksheets, I noticed that both assignments called on him to repeat information supplied in the reading assignment. At no point was he given an opportunity to apply his own knowledge of the subject.

During the course of the fourth hour period I began to get physically uncomfortable sitting at the desk. The absence of any vibrant activity also left me craving some sort of human interaction. It was much to my chagrin when I discovered that the short lunch break was not any real break from the day's monotony. As Barnaby interacted with a couple of his friends I asked them questions about why so many of the students seemed both bored and withdrawn. They explained to me that because they were required to stay within the confines of the cafeteria and were not allowed to bring any diversions with them, such as playing cards, lunch could get boring. After I finished eating lunch, Barnaby challenged me to a game of chess, which he told me was one of the activities that was allowed in the cafeteria. His high skill level was apparent, and he beat me in two games that lasted no longer than fifteen minutes.

When the lunch period ended, I found myself getting antsy. Clearly, I was not the only person feeling this way. Perhaps the greatest testimony to the penned-up feeling I experienced in the lunchroom was the large number of students who pushed out of the cafeteria to get to class early rather than extend their break from the rigors of their daily academic routine.

According to Barnaby, the final period of the day was his favorite class. He told me that the history class worked for two reasons. The first reason was that the students in this class were more committed to learning than those in the other classes. This apparently made a big difference. The second reason was the way the teacher engaged the students. My experience in this class soon supported his conclusions. Not only was this the first class where the students actually interacted with one another, but the students really seemed to get a sense that the teacher was invested in the success of the class.

The teacher raised for discussion some of the problems associated with establishing Affirmative Action programs by dividing the students up into various members of the community who had different levels of interest in seeing the successful implementation of these programs. The exercise was effective and seemed to induce some investment by the students in the topic of study. For the first time during the day, the students were given the opportunity to think and establish some connection between what went on inside and outside the classroom. As I looked around the classroom I noticed, for the first time, a large number of students who had smiles on their faces. I was also aware that this was the first class that left me stimulated instead of relieved upon the ringing of the bell. After thanking Barnaby for letting me spend the day with him, I went home feeling completely drained, both physically and mentally.

The overwhelming impression, which still vividly occupies my thoughts on Barnaby's experience in school, is that he had few opportunities to do anything more than learn by rote means. Moreover, it was not until sixth period that he had any type of quality interaction with his teachers. Although I do not doubt the sincerity of the teachers in his first five hours of classes or their commitment to educating their students, at no point in the day was this commitment a working reality from Barnaby's perspective. Instead, I detected that for Barnaby school was seen as an exercise of survival in a place that was essentially meaningless in relation to his experience of the world. In talking to Barnaby, it is clear that he is an intelligent and capable individual. He, however, is given no opportunity to hone his intelligence and develop his own potentials.

When I examine my initial notes, which characterize Barnaby as "a quiet student who seems apathetic about school, suspicious of his peers, and unwilling to engage in any creative activities that require some investment in the subject matter," I feel somehow guilty. These impressions seem to me largely a function of his environment. Although on some level Barnaby is responsible for his selection of courses, the options presented at Kennedy High do not give him many opportunities to find a schedule that will give him the chance to develop his abilities.

If I was so exhausted after participating in Barnaby's schedule for one day, what was going on inside him after doing this day in, day out? People observing classes similar to those that Barnaby takes would be quick to point out how the students are not motivated and do not seem to exercise critical thinking skills. But perhaps what is going on in the schools serves to deaden the students' enthusiasm so that being numb to the experience is the only way to survive. (Matt Schlein)

Like most ethnographies and ethnographic-like accounts, Matt's brief story of Barnaby represents hours of information gathering and interpretation, and numerous pages of field notes of observations, interviews, and ongoing reflections. Upon completion of the information gathering part of his study with Barnaby, Matt faced questions that you, too, will face: "Now what?" "What do I do with all this information?" "How do I make sense of it all?" "How can I determine what I learned?" As with most things, there is no one best or easiest way to interpret the rich data gathered with the tools of the ethnographer; therefore, we will provide some general guidelines and refer you once again to the texts on ethnography and qualitative inquiry listed in the *Recommended Readings* at the end of the chapter.

Interpreting observational, interview, and artifactual data is similar to the process outlined in Chapter 2 for analyzing personal data and compiling professional development records and summaries. Begin by reading through all the information you have gathered (that is, observation and interview notes, narrative and expanded descriptions developed from your notes, documents, and any reflective comments you may have made along the way in your journal). As you proceed, highlight key words, phrases, or statements that stand out for some reason. Look back over this preliminary analysis and reorganize your notations into a meaningful list of categories or clusters that represent repeating topics, themes, patterns, consistencies, and so on. Also, note inconsistencies or anomalies in the data (information that does not seem to fit the scheme you are constructing from the evidence). Some of these anomalies may suggest a need to get more information, perhaps by asking clarifying questions or by doing more observations. Then, reread the data with the express purpose of identifying passages that exemplify the topics, themes, or patterns you have identified. Also, try to explain the inconsistencies you find. By systematically analyzing the information in this way, you are trying to make large amounts of data sufficiently manageable so that you can learn about the phenomenon you have studied. Your next challenge is to represent the analysis in an account like the one written by Matt.

Summary

We conclude this chapter with Sean's reflection on doing a group ethnographic research project and with some suggestions for further reading for those who would like to learn more about ethnographic research.

As our group began compiling information for our inquiry project, I began to explore the school and to become acquainted with teachers, librarians, and administrators. This was a positive experience for me. I probably would have been less inclined to explore and search out aspects of the school and student interactions without this specific assignment to do so. When I had time, I enjoyed poking my nose into classrooms, gyms, lunchrooms, the media center, the ESL [English as a Second Language] office, the counseling center, administration offices, art rooms, and the auditorium. I was surprised that, while at the school, I met five people I had known in the past, three of them fairly well. Renewing these friendships and knowing I had friends at the school was encouraging. Getting to know the school and people better was a valuable experience. I feel much more comfortable at the school now. I have met more teachers, and they have been sympathetic, encouraging, helpful, and great to work with. (Sean McCabe)

Again, throughout the next part of the book, you will see further examples of insights gained through the various forms of gathering external information described in this chapter. We encourage you to try out some or all of the methods either by beginning with some of the activities we have outlined here or by engaging in some of the various research activities we suggest in Chapters 5 through 12. The following *Recommended Readings* will provide you with additional information and ideas. In the next chapter, we invite you to consider ways in which you can become reflexive teachers through collaboration with peers.

Recommended Readings

Agar, M. H. (1980). *The professional stranger: An informal introduction to ethnography.* Orlando, FL: Academic Press.

Barker, R. G., & Gump, P. V. (1964). *Big school, small school.* Stanford, CA: Stanford University Press.

Bissex, G. L., & Bullock, R. H. (1987). *Seeing for ourselves.* Portsmouth, NH: Heinemann.

Bogdan, R. C., & Biklen, S. K. (1992). *Qualitative research for education: An introduction to theory and methods.* Needham Heights, MA: Allyn & Bacon.

Brause, R. S., & Smayher, J. S. (1991). *Search and research: What the inquiring teacher needs to know.* London: Falmer Press.

Bruckerhoff, C. E. (1991). *Between classes: Faculty life at Truman High.* New York: Teachers College Press.

Bullough, R. V., Jr. (1989). *First year teacher: A case study.* New York: Teachers College Press.

Bullough, R. V., Jr., Knowles, J. G., & Crow, N. A. (1991). *Emerging as a teacher.* London: Routledge, Chapman, & Hall.

Carini, P. F. (1979). *The art of seeing and the visibility of the person.* Grand Forks, ND: University of North Dakota Press.

Carini, P. F. (1982). *The school lives of seven children: A five year study.* Grand Forks, ND: University of North Dakota Press.

Clift, R. T., & Evertson, C. M. (1992). *Focal points: Qualitative inquiries into teaching and teacher education.* Washington, DC: ERIC Clearinghouse on Teacher Education.

Coles, R. (1986). *The moral life of children: How children struggle with questions of moral choice in the United States and elsewhere.* Boston: Houghton Mifflin.

Connelly, F. M., & Clandinin, D. J. (1988). *Teachers as curriculum planners.* New York: Teachers College Press.

Daiker, D. A., & Morenberg, M. (1990). *The writing teacher as researcher: Essays in the theory and practice of class-based research.* Portsmouth, NH: Boynton Cook.

Eckert, P. (1989). *Jocks & burnouts: Social categories and identity in the high school.* New York: Teachers College Press.

Freedman S. G. (1990). *Small victories: The real world of a teacher, her students and their high school.* New York: Harper & Row.

Gannett, C. (1992). *Gender and the journal: Diaries and academic discourse.* Albany, NY: State University of New York Press.

Gitlin, A. (1992). *Teachers' voices for school change.* New York: Teachers College Press.

Goetz, J. P., & LeCompte, M. D. (1984). *Ethnography and qualitative design in educational research.* Orlando, FL: Academic Press.

Good, T. L., & Brophy, J. E. (1991). *Looking in classrooms.* (5th ed.). New York: HarperCollins.

Goswami, D., & Stillman, P. R. (1987). *Reclaiming the classroom.* Upper Montclair, NJ: Boynton Cook.

Hammersley, M. (1990). *Classroom ethnography.* Toronto, Ontario: OISE Press.

Kidder, T. (1989). *Among schoolchildren.* Boston, MA: Houghton Mifflin.

Kincheloe, J. L. (1991). *Teachers as researchers: Qualitative inquiry as a path to empowerment.* London: Falmer Press.

Kottak, C. P. (Ed.). (1982). *Researching American culture: A guide for student anthropologists.* Ann Arbor, MI.: University of Michigan Press.

Lubeck, S. (1985). *Sandbox society: Early education in black & white America.* London: Falmer Press.

Mohr, M. M., & Maclean, M. S. (1987). *Working together: A guide for teacher-researchers.* Urbana, IL: National Council of Teachers of English.

Nias J., & Groundwater-Smith, S. (1988). *The enquiring teacher.* London: Falmer Press.

Palonsky, S. B. (1986). *900 shows a year.* New York: Random House.

Perl, S., & Wilson, N. (1986). *Through teachers' eyes: Portraits of writing teachers at work.* Portsmouth, NH: Heinemann.

Peshkin, A. (1986). *God's choice: The total world of a fundamentalist Christian school.* Chicago: University of Chicago Press.

Peshkin, A. (1991). *The color of strangers, the color of friends: The play of ethnicity in school and community.* Chicago: University of Chicago Press.

Spindler, G. (1982). *Doing the ethnography of schooling: Educational anthropology in action.* New York: CBS College.

Spindler, G., & Spindler, L. (Eds.). (1987). *Interpretive ethnography of education: At home and abroad.* Hillsdale, NJ: Lawrence Erlbaum.

Spradley, J. P. (1979). *The ethnographic interview.* New York: Holt, Rinehart, & Winston.

Spradley, J. P. (1980). *Participant observation.* New York: Holt, Rinehart, & Winston.

Woods, P. (1986). *Inside schools.* London: Routledge & Kegan Paul.

CHAPTER 4

Professional Development Through Collaboration with Peers

Working in isolation has been a norm of academic culture and a norm that traditionally has characterized teachers' work. Increasingly, however, efforts are being made in schools to challenge the isolationist mode of teaching through providing opportunities for teachers to engage in collaborative or joint work. In many schools, teacher development and school improvement efforts are linked to notions of collaboration and collegiality. It may be helpful to do some collaborative work in your preparation program as a way of familiarizing yourself with the idea. Depending on the kind of teacher preparation program in which you are enrolled, you will have varying degrees of opportunity to work closely with peers.

Learning from peers is a basic premise on which this text was founded. Your peers are extremely important in the professional development equation. They are sounding boards *and* mirrors on your emerging practices. They can create a safety net as you try out new things in the classroom. One of the most beneficial outcomes of working closely with peers has to do with making sense of your participation in classrooms. We suggest that you develop close professional relationships with a number of other preservice teachers—and not just those who hold similar perspectives to your own. Seek out individuals whose views are contrary to yours but who can commit to close collegial relationships. Among the many ways in which you might begin to work together are through

- sharing autobiographical writing
- developing collective accounts
- group discussions
- peer observation

We recognize that engaging in joint or group work is not always as easy as it sounds. As with any relationship, working together is a process of ongoing negotiation. Roles, responsibilities, expectations, and goals need to be mutually decided upon, and a working process, once identified, needs to be periodically assessed and modified if necessary. In other words, working together requires as much, if not more, attention to process than to the product or purpose that brings you together. We know, however, that working together and sharing ideas and perspectives is invaluable. We agree with Baum's (1971) assertion that "The important role of dialogue continues through the whole of a person's life. We come to be who we are through conversations with others. We are created through ongoing communication with others" (p. 41). We urge you, therefore, to invest some time and effort in working together and learning from one another.

Being so accustomed to a product rather than a process orientation many are likely to echo Tony's response to group work (as presented in the following narrative). We suggest, however, that a preoccupation with product (getting the job done) can take away from or undervalue the process (doing the job). In other words, working together may be an occasion when the journey is more important than the destination. As Colleen points out, however, such a journey requires preparation and, in some cases, dogged determination. There is always the risk of following dead-end paths but, given proper attention to conditions, working (or traveling) together can be a rewarding learning experience.

Yesterday, I went to the library to prepare some questions for our inquiry project. Our group has been having some problems getting started on this project. I have some real questions that I would like to research at the school so I am excited about this. That is why it is so hard to work in groups on the project. I have always hated working in groups. I do much better on my own. It will be hard to make myself do group work in my classes. I have always had the feeling that group work and simulation games are just kids' stuff. Even in high school when a teacher made us work together, or we did some type of game, I felt we were wasting time. I wanted to learn the required content "quick and dirty." Lectures were always my favorite. Anyway, I do have problems working in groups. I want to go at my speed. I do not want my weaknesses to pull others down (or labor under that fear), or have others slow me down.

With the group project I felt I was being slowed down on developing and stating the questions I wanted to research. I was the only one in the group who really put forth a topic to research, and some were only critical and offered no alternatives. So yesterday, when I went into the library, I decided to type out all my ideas and make copies for everyone in the group. This would give us something to work on. I also thought this would cement the chance of our group working on my questions. (Tony Dehyle)

Working in groups can be a frustrating aspect of college course work. It can top the anxiety experienced during final exams. Thrown together with strangers, the chances are you are given an assignment with little or no instruction in *how* to collaborate. If the group is dysfunctional and you are courageous enough to complain about it you risk appearing dysfunctional yourself.

I did complain once when members of a group I worked with began fabricating data during the final stages of a school-based inquiry project. I had trusted them when they told me that their work was on computer diskette. They eventually brought their diskette to a meeting to copy my work. Sharing work doesn't bother me but, later, when they said that they were fabricating the substance of the interview data (that they were supposed to have collected) I became upset. My partners were confident that no one would check their sources; they did not seem to understand why I was concerned. I did not know what to do. How could I withdraw from the project after they had modeled their contributions on my work? I hesitated about talking to the professor because I didn't know how to talk about the circumstances without incriminating anyone, and I felt so foolish that I hadn't discovered the extent of the problem earlier. It also seemed too late in the term for me to find alternatives to working with the group. I felt as though I was in a burning building with no exit. Say nothing and receive a poor grade for a poor assignment; say something and receive a poor grade for failing to make the group work! Finally, I approached a teaching assistant who turned to the professor for advice about my problem, and the suggestion was made that I turn in my work separately. A friend (not in school) suggested that it appeared that my reward for complaining was doing the assignment twice.

After this first nightmarish experience a college friend assured me that it was a bizarre aberration. I wanted to believe that. Despite my experience with nonsupportive group members, a similar situation occurred again. I began to wonder what I was doing wrong. I had always been evaluated very highly for peer cooperation and teamwork. But what was going on here at the university was different. I began to think that for people to be involved in group work they need to evidence a similar level of care about the assignment, or one of them would end up doing a disproportionate amount of work. It seemed that some preservice teachers realized that the lack of evaluation or feedback about individual contributions constituted a free ride.

The third time I was assigned a major project to be done within a group I was simply grateful to realize early on that the workload would be a large one. It was much easier for me to plan, knowing in advance that my partner was disaffected or uncaring. He said that he did not like to work in groups because his grade was dependent upon the effort of the whole group. He preferred having his work evaluated individually. We spent a lot of time discussing issues related to the assignment. We met in the library for one five-hour block of time and met twice at my house for three or four hours each time. I really gave it my best shot! I didn't hope to change his mind about working in teams but, as a senior, it was the "last chance" I had to change my own thinking about group work. I worked hard to create a positive working atmosphere for both of us. It would be a shame if our negative experiences with collaboration in college classes impaired our ability to be collaborators in a professional teaching context because it seems that collaboration can yield great benefits for both students and teachers.

I came to appreciate some of the benefits during minor group work assignments. The strangest thing is that the most negative experiences involved projects that were major course requirements. In class, spontaneous group experiences were far more positive. It may be that the time constraint imposed facilitated the negotiation of roles and tasks. It was fascinating to listen to ideas, share my own, and to consider aspects that would never have occurred to me. The result had an element of surprise to it as well. It would have been difficult to predict the final outcome based only on the initial ideas presented because the ideas became transformed, synthesized, and expanded upon (or rejected) based on conversation and discussion within the group. (Colleen Presswood)

Sharing Autobiographical Writing

Autobiographical writing such as personal history accounts or interactive journals provides a vehicle for you to begin sharing your experiences as learners and future teachers. Share portions of your personal accounts with those with whom you are comfortable. Alternately, talk about elements or themes present in your writing. Focus on the meaning of each other's experiences in the development of pedagogical thinking. Mutually held, similar, or even contrasting stories from these documents may serve as catalysts for developing professional relationships. As you become comfortable with others you may want to regularly share the products of your autobiographical writing and, certainly, work on making sense of your developing practice as well as resolving common problems together. *Learning to Teach: Teaching to Learn* (Clandinin, Davies, Hogan, & Kennard, 1993) illustrates the sharing process in a way that might help you get started.

Collective Accounts of Experience

Getting together with other preservice teachers in small groups to develop collective accounts of experience—for example, of learning together at a field site, developing as teachers, teaching specific lessons or using particular teaching strategies, conducting research—allows you to reach different understandings than you may have reached on your own. How might this process work?

Again, think of developing collective accounts as a variation on the experiential learning cycle theme (Figure 4.1). That is, begin by sharing individual accounts of experience, thoughts, or ideas and, instead of engaging in individual reflection and analysis, look for patterns and themes among the shared accounts. Bringing the collective wisdom of the group to bear on issues and concerns will enhance understanding and broaden perspective. In this way, future action is informed by a rich diversity of ideas and experience.

Group Activities and Discussions

By engaging in conversations with your peers, working on assignments together, and otherwise exploring each other's assumptions, theories, and practices you will help to extend each other's thinking through reflexive practices. Group activities and discussions may occur naturally in some of your courses; if not, and depending on your situation, it may be appropriate to suggest the idea to one or more of your instructors. It might also, or instead, be useful to form a peer support or discussion group to meet informally but regularly according to a mutually defined schedule and agenda. The following is what Keri says about this matter.

Chapter 4   Professional Development Through Collaboration with Peers

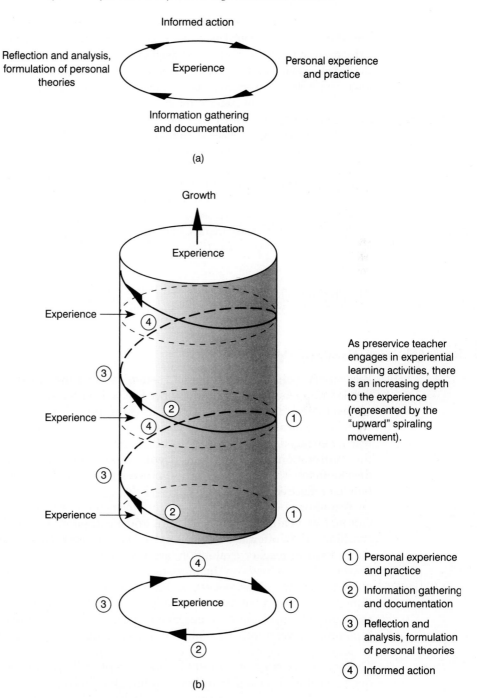

Figure 4.1   Experiential Learning Cycle/Spiral

The relationships I developed in the university have been important to me. They have provided me with a support group that I thought I would never have. The group discussions on the various readings proved to be very worthwhile. They provided an arena in which I could discuss my feelings and opinions about a certain topic, as well as listen to others, and revamp my previous thinking. For example, the group discussions about textbooks and the prejudices that might be expressed in them gave me new insights into how other people think. Some things that I thought were offensive were viewed as harmless by others and vice versa.

Teaching the lessons forced us to get together, discuss our intentions, observe each other, and discuss what happened. This was helpful to me because it made me get together with and learn about the other people in my cohort. It compelled me to look at what I was about to do, voice my fears and concerns, and then discuss what I did that was effective or ineffective. It increased the camaraderie between us. All of the activities gave me the opportunity to make friends, learn from them, and to know that I am not alone with my feelings and concerns. (Keri Hong)

Also, recall Colleen's reflection on in-class group work and how, for her, ideas were extended and transformed through group discussion.

Peer Observations of Practice

Peer observations of practice in field settings extend the function of peer tutoring and learning. As a new teacher you need reliable and formative (constructive and nonevaluative) feedback about your teaching practices to help you refine your work. Reciprocal observation of classroom practices, at any one time, with one teacher engaged in practice and the other engaged in observing, can contribute to the information you amass about your classroom practices and professional development. The peer observation process is yet another variation on the now familiar reflective cycle (Figure 4.2).

Variations on the reflective process form the basis of many formative and summative evaluation, supervision, and professional growth models. "Peer coaching," most often used by in-service teachers, and "clinical supervision," regularly used in teacher evaluation, are widely known variations. These models, however, tend to focus on the more technical and overt aspects of teaching, often overlooking the values, beliefs, and attitudes underlying teaching practice. It is difficult to develop habits and attitudes of critical reflexivity if you do not allow these underlying elements to enter conversations about your teaching. We, therefore, propose yet another variation of the reflective model but with an emphasis on intentions, values, and assumptions rather than on techniques and strategies. The process we suggest is most like the concept of "horizontal evaluation" developed by Gitlin and Goldstein (1987). Although we shy away from the term *evaluation,* the following statement, which underlies horizontal evaluation, also underlies our thinking about peer reflection and professional development.

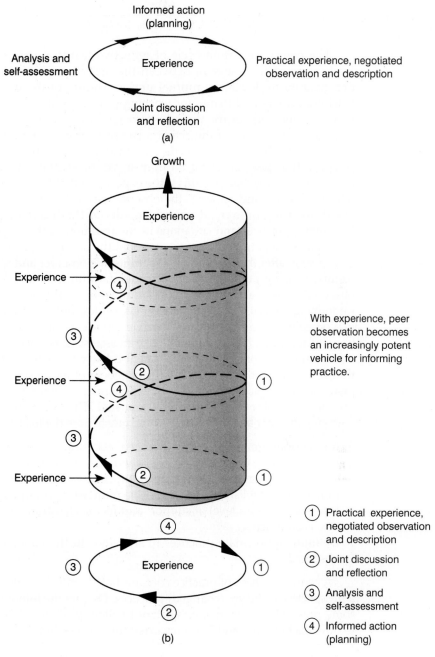

Figure 4.2 Peer Observation Process

A good teacher is not one who simply demonstrates an ability to restrain classroom chaos and produce high academic results, but one who thoughtfully and consistently engages in a dialogical process of trying to understand what links choices among various means, purposes, and aims in teaching (Gitlin & Smyth, 1989, p. 75).

The peer observation cycle of reflective learning goes something like this. First, a preteaching session between the observer and the teacher provides an opportunity to develop a mutual understanding of the intent of the lesson or teaching activity and venue for teaching practice. Within this discussion the normative framework, or the underlying perspective, of the teacher is made clear as well as the intentions of the activity. The teacher may identify a specific focus for observation. The teacher's needs for constructive feedback supersede any other purpose that peer observation may serve. Next, the teacher teaches and the observer observes. Because this is the experience that will form the basis for subsequent reflection and analysis, the observer strives for a meaningful record of the event, focusing on agreed-upon elements of the teaching context or practice. Describing practices and situations in the tradition of the ethnographer is preferable to making judgment statements about the observed practices.

As soon after the lesson as time permits, the observer and teacher meet together to talk, sharing perspectives and understandings about what was taught and observed. This is a time for critical examination of the observed practice and the underlying implicit and explicit intentions, values, and assumptions. Using the information gained as a result of the observer's presence and the subsequent conversation, the teacher is in a position to make an assessment of his or her practice that will inform future action. Such an assessment is likely to result in plans to change some things, maintain others, and think further about other aspects and issues. This completes the first spiral of the cycle of experiential learning, which is extended each time the peer observation process is repeated. The key points to remember when engaging in peer observation of teaching practice are the following:

1. It is a nonjudgmental activity (the feedback is descriptive not evaluative).
2. Its purpose is to uncover and understand intentions underlying teaching action.
3. The process provides a structure and focus for you and others to observe your practice by establishing the normative framework your practice is based on.
4. It provides a high level of support and feedback during and after the period of observed practice.
5. Defining appropriate practices to change is in the hands of the person being observed.

A central analysis of practice contains both a critique of observed practices and a prospectus for future (changed) practices. Despite the intent of peer observation, some preservice teachers are reluctant to allow peers to observe them. But, listen to how Rachel, Sara, and Tracy regarded the process and the benefits.

▼

The actual teaching, peer observation, and ensuing reflection provide a means by which I can gauge my performance in the classroom. Because, for example, one's perception of reality is not always reliable or because things can go unnoticed while the actual lesson is taking place, it is helpful to receive feedback from colleagues. By observing fellow preservice teachers I not only developed a critical eye toward teaching but I also learned from the [outcomes of the] teaching methods and strategies used. The process of observing and being observed, and of actually teaching in a real classroom, provided the necessary interactions that allowed me to thoroughly [think about] myself as teacher. (Rachel Baab)

[The opportunity] for peer observation was greatly appreciated. Having a peer along to observe and record [my teaching practice] gave me [an opportunity to make] an analysis based on their observations, and not [exclusively] on my feelings. They did not fill my head with great details about my lesson and my teaching style. They did give me a most realistic look. Their observations [developed into] constructive criticisms. [They] gave me insight into my role in the front of the classroom that I had not realized on my own. I think one even said that I was "laid back" in front of the students. She thought the students responded in a relaxed fashion as well. Because I felt nervous and tense, her words were a great source of encouragement. As I observed peers, [the process] reciprocated its effectiveness for me.

Seeing peers in action was another step in my formulation of more realistic conclusions about my abilities to teach. They appeared equally as nervous and, from comparing styles, appeared equally as willing to [reveal] their personalities to the students. My observations were also appreciated . . . as some of my peers saw much less satisfaction in their work than my notes suggested. (Sara Field)

Peer observations helped me tremendously. Having a peer watch a lesson and watching a lesson for a peer are both learning experiences we would not have known otherwise. We are still learning [to be a teacher], and by watching one another, we can see how others [at our point of development] choose to run their classrooms. Sometimes it is easier to relate to feedback we receive from peers than it is from someone who is already experienced in the field. These sessions helped me to reevaluate what I may or may not do in the future. (Tracy Dell)

▲

Katarina was one not initially comfortable with the idea of peer observation. If you share Katarina's sentiments, we invite you to listen to her concluding comment.

▼

The whole issue of approval is why I probably get so uptight over people observing me teach. It is very scary. What I have generally done in the past to get out of this panic is to downgrade or devalue the opinion of whoever is in a position to hurt me or disapprove. This, of course, is very dumb. I will never get anywhere until I change this. (Katarina Burquart)

▲

Summary

Working with peers can enhance your professional development, broaden your perspectives, and provide encouragement and support. We have suggested a variety of ways in which you might engage in collaborative work with other preservice teachers. Facility with these methods and the attitudes that necessarily accompany them will serve you well as you move into classrooms, schools, and other educational contexts. Those interested in further exploring collaborative work will find useful the readings at the end of this chapter. We call your attention to the publication, *I'm Not Alone: Teacher Talk, Teacher Buddying* (Ferri & Aglio, 1990), an account of a dialogue journal written by a beginning and an experienced teacher. You may also find several chapters of *Learning to Teach: Teaching to Learn* (Clandinin, Davies, Hogan, & Kennard, 1993) to be of value.

Recommended Readings

Clandinin, D. J., Davies, A., Hogan, P., & Kennard, B. (1993). *Learning to teach: Teaching to learn*. New York: Teachers College Press.

Connelly, F. M., & Clandinin, D. J. (1988). *Teachers as curriculum planners*. New York: Teachers College Press.

Ferri, B., & Aglio, M. (1990). *I'm not alone: Teacher talk, teacher buddying*. Mississauga, Ontario: The Peel Board of Education.

Gitlin, A. (1992). *Teachers' voices for school change*. New York: Teachers College Press.

Gitlin, A., & Goldstein, S., (1987). A dialogical approach to understanding: Horizontal evaluation. *Educational Theory, 37*(1), 17–27.

Gitlin, A., & Smyth. J. (1989). *Teacher evaluation: Educative alternatives*. Barcombe, Lewes, East Sussex: Falmer Press.

Lytle, S. L., & Cochran-Smith, M. (1992). Teacher research as a way of knowing. *Harvard Educational Research, 62*(4), 447–474.

Newman, J. M. (1989). *Finding our own way: Teachers exploring their assumptions*. Portsmouth, NH: Heinemann.

Oja, S. N., & Smulyan, L. (1989). *Collaborative action research: A developmental approach*. Philadelphia, PA: Falmer Press.

Perl, S., & Wilson, N. (1986). *Through teachers' eyes: Portraits of writing teachers at work*. Portsmouth, NH: Heinemann Educational Books.

Shulman, J. H., & Colbert, J. A. (1987). *The mentor teacher casebook*. Oregon and California: ERIC Clearinghouse on Educational Management and Far West Laboratory for Educational Research and Development.

Shulman, J. H., & Colbert, J. A. (1988). *The intern teacher casebook*. Oregon/California/Washington, DC: ERIC Clearinghouse on Educational Management, Far West Laboratory for Educational Research and Development, and ERIC Clearinghouse on Teacher Education.

Staton, J., Shuy, R. W., Peyton, J. K., & Reed, L. (1988). *Dialogue journal communication: Classroom, linguistic, social and cognitive views*. Norwood, NJ: Ablex.

Wood, D. R. (1992). Teaching narratives: A source for faculty development and evaluation. *Harvard Educational Review, 62*(4), 535–550.

PART III

Narrative and Inquiry in Field Experience

We could not have written this book without understanding field experiences from the perspectives of preservice teachers. Much of our understanding has come from engaging with written and spoken narrative accounts of preservice teachers' experiences. These accounts witness their struggles to understand themselves as teachers both in concert and in collision with students and other adults within the vibrant contexts of schools, classrooms, and university settings.

In the following chapters you will see the interaction between the meanings we attribute to field experiences—as derived from our own experiences as students, teachers, and teacher educators—and the meanings of experiences expressed by preservice teachers. Sometimes these perspectives are at odds, but mostly they complement one another. The guiding and central purpose is to gain insight into learning to teach and learning to be a teacher by considering the perspectives represented and the opportunities for inquiry. As you continue to inquire about becoming a teacher, there are seven clusters of facilitating questions that you will want to answer. They include the following:

1. Who am I as teacher? What does it mean to be a teacher? What are the roles of teachers?
2. What are schools and classrooms like? Who works in schools and why? What goes on in schools and why?
3. How do I forge relationships with individuals in learning communities? How do I develop relationships with the various groups of people who comprise a learning community?
4. Who are the students? What are their needs as learners? What do they already know? How do I come to know them as persons and as learners?
5. How do I focus my teaching? How do I think about teaching?
6. How do I teach? What teaching methods are most appropriate?
7. How can I forge my professional development as a new teacher?

Versions of these questions essentially form the focus of the following seven chapters. They are vehicles to make explicit the various elements of a curriculum and pedagogy of field experience. They can guide the progression of your professional development. They do not represent stages of your development, nor do they represent a linear development or progression. Rather, they represent some semblance of ordering the complex task of becoming a teacher. They are places to begin your professional inquiry. Starting with yourselves is useful because it presents opportunities to assess the preconceptions and beliefs with which you enter teacher preparation and opportunities for field experience. The questions represent an intentional moving away from self to understanding contexts, the other central players, relationships, and the experiences of teaching.

The remainder of the book, therefore, builds on Parts I and II in that there are many suggestions about ways to utilize the various tools for inquiry and numerous points for beginning the inquiry process. The narrative accounts provide examples of how other preservice teachers used the tools to make sense of their emerging practice.

CHAPTER 5

Exploring Images and Contexts of Teaching

Already, you have had years of experience in classrooms and school settings. You have learned alongside professional and nonprofessional teachers alike. You know much about teaching and learning, and have some clear ideas on what it means to be a teacher. For the most part, though, your experience of teaching has been from the other side of the teacher's desk where you have spent countless hours, days, and years engaged in what has been called "the apprenticeship of observation" (Lortie, 1975). Even if you may have previously spent time in various teaching roles and have a clear sense of what teaching is all about, there is a massive difference between assuming some teaching responsibilities and being a fully responsible, certificated classroom teacher.

As a participant in a formal teacher preparation program you will have opportunities to begin to develop a fuller understanding of what it means to be a teacher. If you have not done so already, two of the first things you will discover are that the role of a teacher is complex and demanding, and that learning to teach is a career-long, perhaps lifelong, process. As we pointed out in Chapter 1, the processes of learning to teach and learning to be a teacher are distinct and are each informed by multiple and diverse knowledge sources. Tapping into and making sense of the knowledge that informs teaching and teachers are challenging tasks made easier if placed in the context of experience. Because we think experience is the best teacher, we invite you to consider the many aspects of learning to teach and learning to be a teacher within the context of experience—past, present, and future.

In this chapter we look at

- the influences of your own past experiences of schools, teaching, classrooms, and learning, and the understandings about the profession you bring to your formal teacher education program
- the profession of teaching as the broad context within which you will work and experience teaching
- various field contexts in which learning to teach takes place

We begin with a retrospective look at past experiences and their influences on current understandings and career plans.

Reflecting on Personal Histories: Influences of Prior Experiences on the Development of Conceptions of Teaching and Learning

When you began formal preservice teacher preparation you brought with you beliefs, attitudes, ideals, influences, and expectations developed over years of life experience as family members, public or private school and university students, in some cases as parents, in other cases as community leaders or youth workers, or as persons in successful business, professional, or technical careers, and in *all* cases as persons involved in human affairs. The thoughts and ideas about education, schools, classrooms, and teaching that derive from your past experiences are potent influences that will form the foundations of your emerging practice. Some of you have well-formed images of teaching constructed from positive prior experiences of schooling and learning; others may have images resulting from negative experiences that may inappropriately influence your developing practice. Your images and expectations of students are also rooted in your own experiences. Many of the students you will encounter will have had different experiences than yours, and some of the meanings they derive from being students may be in direct conflict with your perspectives. It is important for you to reflect on and make sense of some of your prior experiences and to understand their influence on your current thinking and practice. Through field experiences you will have the first formalized opportunities to verify, challenge, and modify some of these preconceptions.

Narrative Accounts and Questions for Reflection and Discussion

In the following accounts, several preservice teachers reflect on what *they* identified as particularly influential prior experiences. Covering a time span from early childhood to adult life, they recall significant teachers and school-related experiences, as well as individuals and events outside of school learning. The questions that follow each subsection are intended to encourage you to be reflexive about similar kinds of past experiences.

INFLUENCES OF TEACHERS

Leslie, Trisha, Janet, Kinsey, Gini, Melody, and Miranda remember teachers who had significant influences on them as learners and developing individuals.

Narrative Accounts

One of the greatest learning experiences I ever had was in a nontraditional teaching context. I was fortunate that the school district [in which I was a student] strongly believed in providing opportunities for outdoor education experiences—and so did my sixth and eighth grade teachers. Their willingness to provide a residential outdoor education experience brought the world into perspective. Suddenly, the various topics I had spent so much time studying became real. They were not just in textbooks and tests. These experiences began my understanding of what learning and school was all about.

The concept of self-motivation was introduced in my eighth grade math class and again in my freshman year high school English class. If I wanted to learn, I had to take on that responsibility myself. I had to recognize my resources, teach myself from written texts, struggle on my own, and know when to ask for help. I was no longer the bored child I had been in the lower elementary school grades. I was suddenly challenged to learn because I wanted to grow in understanding. There was no limit to what I could accomplish, but I was given guidelines as to what should be accomplished in a given period of time.

These teachers taught me more than what is in textbooks or course descriptions. They taught me to inquire, to question why, and how to find information. They taught me how to think for myself and how knowledge fits into the scheme of life. They truly put the world at my feet, and left me to decide what to do with it. (Leslie Aris)

I had teachers who were great friends and listeners. I had teachers who couldn't relate to anything current no matter how hard they tried and who didn't know students' names on the day of the final exam. There were some who sent us for doughnuts and coffee every day and others in whose classroom chewing gum was forbidden. Certain teachers reveled in giving trick questions on exams and pop quizzes on the year's hardest reading assignment, but others gave all the questions and answers to a test in advance and only memorization was required [to pass].

Every teacher has strengths and weaknesses as well as methods and strategies that work well and some that fail. A great teacher (or a poor one) can't be defined within a framework of characteristics. What was good for [one of the teachers], for example, would have never worked for [the other], but both were great teachers. (Trisha LaPorte)

My seventh grade social studies teacher . . . didn't inspire any excitement for the subject in our young impressionable minds. Lessons dealt with memorizing information and reciting it back to him. We never had the chance to think about why events happened or their implications for society. As a result, I never learned anything substantial in his class [and since then] I have always approached history by memorizing dates and events. I never developed a real grasp of or love for the subject, perhaps because during a growth period of my knowledge base I had negative learning experiences. By using that class as an example, I now remind myself that rote memorization of facts is not the best way to learn or retain important ideas. (Janet Black)

When faced with the dilemma of whether to teach chemistry or physics in high school, or to change my plans altogether, I thought of my calculus teacher. We loved her, not because she was fun, caring, and exciting, but because she was incredibly [adroit] with numbers and words. I will never forget the clarity with which she explained derivatives to us. I was in absolute awe as I left that particular class period. When I faced college calculus, I was really happy to have already heard her explanations. She never gave us "free days" or smiled too often, but we loved her. As a teacher, I want to reach kids like she did, and I know if I cannot be a downright excellent teacher, I will be unhappy with my performance and myself. (Kinsey Milhone)

When I reached Grade 10 in high school, I finally had a teacher who made a lasting impression on me. He taught me about art and about life. He was the first person to seriously challenge my world view; he caused me to seriously examine myself, both as an artist and as a member of society. He saw enough value in me to set aside some of his time to give me individualized instruction and to provide me with individualized assignments. This was finally a classroom where I felt as if I belonged. I know that the quality of my life is richer because of the time I spent in his classes. (Gini Angelotti)

At the end of elementary school I rediscovered creativity and [personal] exploration. I was put in a gifted program for part of the school day and Mrs. Dungan, my teacher, told us about the Galapagos Islands she had visited. She showed us slides of the wild water and the giant turtles in danger of extinction.

How many pupils can remember lessons more than ten years later? I can remember hers. We combed wool as they do in Peru; we built a "habitat," a little wooden building of several rooms within our classroom; we were the "root children," and hung paper roots from the ceiling above the habitat; we went to the genealogical library and drew our family tree, and to the cemetery to make gravestone rubbings that we pasted on the walls. And I used to curl up in the habitat in a beanbag chair and write in my journal. That was school! School unlike anything I had called school before. On the wall above the habitat, a sign was drawn in fiery wings and dark roots: "There are two things that we may bequeath to our children—roots and wings." When children have the roots of knowledge, they still need the wings of creativity and exploration to fly.

Bonnie Williams, my high school creative writing teacher, is one of my models for bringing out what is in the student instead of stuffing things in. She taught us to be creative. She taught us to trust ourselves, to love words, and to explore the world we could express in words. She taught us not to expect the expected, to return where we had been before and find it the same yet not the same, to come full circle back to the beginning and find the beginning beautiful for also being the end. She taught us to be ourselves when everyone else was asking us what we were going to become. Bonnie has been an important role model and support system for me since I was her student in high school creative writing, and continues to be so now that we are both teaching French. As Bonnie impacted my life, I hope to impact my students and to look back from the ending to the beginning and find that some things were worthwhile. (Melody Potter)

I took a literature course from a professor who had a great effect on my life. He had gained a major teaching award and was described as creating "an atmosphere that integrates passion for scholarship with compassion for students." That statement sums up his teaching approach as he managed to demand academic excellence while being personally warm and involved. When I asked him yesterday why he teaches, he said "because I like people and I like ideas, in that order." When I asked what he thought made him effective as a teacher, he became wistful, as if he wished he knew, or even wished he were: "I think good teaching is a different matter for every teacher. For me, it is crucial to care intensely about what is going on in the classroom. I try to ask real questions as opposed to Socratic or leading questions, questions I wonder about, questions at the frontier of what I know. And I listen to the answers."

Steve was not only a superb teacher but has become a close personal friend. We traded books and discussed, or argued, ideas. Our conversations were full of thoughts and thoughtfulness. Steve and my husband became friends and eventually wrote and published a book together. We were lucky to be close to the same age so we did not have the usual barriers to personal friendship between teachers and students. The friendship gave me a chance to see Steve as a great and interesting teacher because he is a great and interesting person. Teachers can't continuously act out some part they have decided is the best role for a teacher. The authentic person eventually shows through. Seeing a teacher like Steve in action influenced me to want to teach (I was also influenced to want to teach when I saw bad teaching).

Once, in an adolescent literature class, I ended up in a hostile encounter with the teacher. Her arrogant, authoritarian attitude was startling and unnecessary in a college setting. Being an older adult made it impossible for me to accept her imperious demands for childlike obedience. This was not to deny her abilities as related to literature, but her methods of dealing with people were condescending and destructive. Students deserve better. (Miranda Carter)

For Reflection and Discussion

In thinking about the statements we have just presented, several questions come to mind. Some of these questions focus on the relationship of thinking to practice and others explore aspects of the place of experience.

1. Leslie vividly recalls the positive impact of a nontraditional education experience. She states that outdoor education experiences allowed her to relate topics to the world rather than just to textbooks and tests. Leslie was inspired to learn through alternative contexts to traditional classrooms and textbook learning. She also remembers the quality of learning opportunities offered by favorably remembered teachers. She felt challenged and excited by classes that were guided by the notion of self-motivation.
   a. How do teachers encourage students who seem reluctant to learn in school? Is a self-motivated learning environment effective for most students? How can teachers facilitate learners making connections between texts and the world?
   b. To what extent are you comfortable with providing alternative contexts to traditional classroom learning? Are you comfortable learning in such environments? To what extent do you have expectations for learning about becoming a teacher that are bound by concepts of traditional or nontraditional classroom learning? What do you see as the relationship between self-directed and authority-directed (as in a teacher or traditional textbook) learning?
2. Trisha does not believe that a good teacher can be defined within a framework of particular characteristics. Her experience of great teachers suggests that what worked for one of them may not have worked for the other. She also noted a variety of interpersonal styles among teachers she enjoyed.
   a. If a "good" teacher cannot be defined within a framework of characteristics, how can we define a "good" teacher? How do *you* define a "good" teacher? How does *your* definition compare with that of your peers?

   b. To what extent, if any, do you think your definitions of "good" teaching have molded your expectations for yourself as you enter into extensive field experiences? Are there ways in which these definitions can be helpful, or not helpful, as you develop your professional perspectives?
3. Kinsey remembers that she "loved" her high school calculus teacher because the woman was incredibly good with numbers and words. Kinsey left this teacher's classroom in awe and writes "I want to reach kids like she did and I know that, if I cannot be a downright excellent teacher, I will be unhappy with my performance and myself."
   a. How useful is it for beginning teachers, ones early in their professional development, to compare themselves with experienced teachers?
   b. Is trial and error the only approach to excellence for beginning teachers? What are some alternative strategies for your learning about teaching and the role of teachers?
   c. How can the elements of excellent teaching and the characteristics of such teaching be identified and adopted by beginning teachers like yourself?
4. Extra time and personal attention from Gini's high school art teacher gave her a sense of belonging and challenged her in important ways. She states, "I know that the quality of my life is richer because of the time I spent in his classes."
   a. How can teachers increase the opportunities for individualized instruction and attention? How can you take advantage of these kinds of opportunities as a prospective new teacher?
   b. Is it possible for teachers to reach every student in such a personal way? If not, how are students in need of such attention identified? How does individual attention differ from favoritism?

INFLUENCES OF FAMILY

Tracy, Angele, and Morris reflect on the impact of family members on their thinking about teaching.

Narrative Accounts

▼

Having a mother who is a teacher I got the chance throughout high school, when I had an afternoon free or a day off from school, to go into my mother's school and help her with classes. From this time spent in her classroom I began to consciously realize how important the education of our children is to the future of the nation and the world. I observed her methods of teaching and assisted her with some lessons. I read students' stories and compositions that she brought home to grade. I was so interested in everything she did with her students that I knew I would enjoy teaching as much as she does. (Tracy Dell)

Going into my mother's classroom to observe and discuss teaching with her greatly influenced me. When I had her as a teacher I learned a lot and enjoyed it, but I never really appreciated what she did until, as an adult, I observed her in the classroom. She seems to get a real sense of accomplishment from teaching and really enjoys what she is doing. After working at a daycare program, and observing her teach, I decided that I wanted to become a teacher. She is one of the best teachers I have had.

My mother has many of the qualities I consider to be "good" in a teacher: she is creative; she has good classroom management; her students seem to be really motivated; she knows her students and how best to explain the subject material; and, she learns just as much from the children as they learn from her. I only hope that I am as good a teacher as my mother. (Angele Doucette)

I remember the way in which my father taught me many everyday kinds of things about the house, the car, the yard, and even the natural life of the countryside—the native flora and fauna. He almost never answered my questions directly but, rather, sent me to explore, figure out the answers, and then talk about them with him. Often I went directly to books and then to the actual object I was inquisitive about. Many times I was right on target in my "figuring it out."

The garage was an especially great place because he had all kinds of tools and equipment there and, after we showed aptitude, he taught us to use the various tools, instruments, and machines, and they were especially helpful in learning. Much later I discovered that he used, very ably, the principles of what is known as discovery learning. He must have spent a great deal of time organizing opportunities for me and my brothers and sisters to learn from because, almost no matter what the question, he would suggest a process by which we could uncover some new understandings. (Morris Swartz)

For Reflection and Discussion

1. Tracy and Angele were influenced in their career decision by their mothers who are teachers.
   a. What are the advantages of following the career path of a parent? What are the disadvantages? How might their experiences inform or misinform you?
   b. In what ways may children of teachers face greater challenges than others in developing their own thinking about teaching?
   c. What part might gender role modeling play in choice of career and in receiving support for that choice? What problems might be encountered in attempts to emulate a parent as a teacher role model?
2. Morris was encouraged by his father to investigate his environment to find answers to questions that he posed for himself. Morris recognizes that his father facilitated his learning by ably using principles of discovery learning.
   a. Might gender be a factor in the teaching style of Morris' father?
   b. Morris was deeply influenced by the discovery process of learning. What challenges may he face in evaluating other approaches to teaching?
   c. What problems might Morris encounter if his field experience is located in a traditional classroom?
   d. In what ways can Morris' experiences be seen as especially advantageous for a future teacher?

INFLUENCES OF SCHOOL

Experiences of schools and schooling in a variety of contexts left their mark on Stacy, Trish, Jodi, and Katarina.

Narrative Accounts

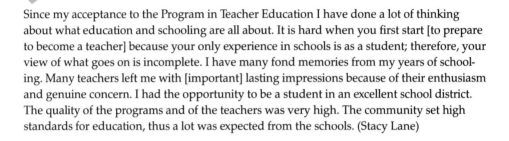

Since my acceptance to the Program in Teacher Education I have done a lot of thinking about what education and schooling are all about. It is hard when you first start [to prepare to become a teacher] because your only experience in schools is as a student; therefore, your view of what goes on is incomplete. I have many fond memories from my years of schooling. Many teachers left me with [important] lasting impressions because of their enthusiasm and genuine concern. I had the opportunity to be a student in an excellent school district. The quality of the programs and of the teachers was very high. The community set high standards for education, thus a lot was expected from the schools. (Stacy Lane)

Much of my childhood was spent moving from one school to another as my family followed my father's work all over the country and the world. I remember being delighted by the excitement of learning new things and experiencing new situations. In a sense, the whole world was my classroom just waiting to be explored. I continue to be fascinated by learning new things (perhaps to the extreme of not enjoying learning about "old things" in depth), and love to share the excitement of exploring the world with other people. Mobility had its costs, however, in relationships and roots. As a result, I am now very interested in social interactions in the classroom, particularly in how much responsibility the teacher has for helping children learn social (as well as academic) skills and for fostering a respect for diversity in the classroom.

As we moved around, I was fascinated by superficial differences between people and between cultures, but I was also impressed by what appeared to be many underlying similarities. I became very interested in the issue of assumptions: What are a person's implicit assumptions about the world and how it operates? How different are these assumptions depending on family background or culture? These questions have continued to interest me as I have tried to communicate with children whose racial or ethnic backgrounds differ from mine. Clearly, some assumptions about the way the world operates are not universally held, and some ways of communicating are not universally understood.

I spent much of my junior high and high school years in a school system that had just implemented a comprehensive tracking system. I saw firsthand some of the ill effects of ability grouping on those labeled "most intelligent" and also on the group labeled "least intelligent." Because the organization of the student body was based on ability groupings, "intelligence" became a very important commodity. One person had more worth than another simply because his or her IQ test score was higher. Intelligence was assumed to be a good predictor of performance in school and also of success in later life. I remember being surprised when a good friend, a "B" and "C" [grade] student in school, became a very happy and successful professional later in life. (Trish London)

I was not a very popular child, nor was I a very beautiful child; I could not play sports well, and I had no special talents. But, there was one thing that I could do well—school work. I behaved in such a way as to be "teachers' favorite," and I got good grades. My parents rewarded me for such accomplishments and, over the years, my self-worth was built on my ability to master the explicit and implicit curriculum. I was considered a "good student." Unfortunately, as I grew, my goal became stationed on getting the "A." Learning for learning's sake was never the focus, nor was it the focus of any of my friends or of my parents. "What did you get on your report card?" and "What's your grade point average?" were the questions asked, not "What did you learn today?" or "What did you learn this year?" Consequently, my attitude has been very grade oriented instead of learning oriented. As a learner, I see myself as quite dysfunctional, but I plan to change that. The curiosity to discover and learn things was long ago killed. Whether this is the fault of my teachers, my parents, society, or me, I do not know. I am sure each had a part.

I have come to realize this past year that my attitude must change so that I can become an effective teacher. I want to teach kids how to learn—not to get grades or to please me as teacher—and to learn in substantial ways. If I want my students to be curious and to explore things in order to learn, I also must do so. (Jodi Johnson)

When I was in kindergarten, the teacher asked each of us what we wanted to be when we grew up. Being a master of flattery and manipulation I answered "a teacher, just like you," and immediately won her over. When adults asked me this question over and over again, as adults have a habit of doing, I answered by mentioning over time a variety of occupations, from writer, restaurant owner, and librarian, to lab technician, interior decorator, and hermit. One answer that kept cropping up over and over again, however, was "teacher."

Probably the reason I kept saying I wanted to be a teacher is because I am very comfortable in academic and classroom settings, and this may be because in such places I know what is expected of me and I can meet these expectations. School was and is a place where I can succeed. School was not only my occupation as a child but also my hobby. My parents never had the money or the interest to give me piano lessons, skiing lessons, or dance lessons, but I always had lots of books to read. Up until I was about fifteen years old, I always got good grades and was often "teacher's pet." I was often teacher's pet because I always came to school, was never late, did not talk in class, and was basically more interested in the teacher than in my peers. Teachers always liked me. I cannot figure it out sometimes. I am doomed to be a "good kid" in everybody's eyes. I remember going out of my way to do things to make the teacher dislike me, but it never worked. They always dismissed my actions with the phrase, "Are you having a bad day today?" Sometimes they did not even notice my ill behavior. (Katarina Burquart)

▲

For Reflection and Discussion

1. The experience of a tracking program left a lasting impression on Trish, and she recalls being surprised to discover that a fellow student who received "B" and "C" grades became a successful professional.

a. To what extent were Trish's assumptions about the future success of her classmate influenced by her socialization as a student within the culture of that particular school?

b. What part do teachers and schools play in promoting the development of academic stereotypes? How do teachers' assumptions about students' academic abilities affect student performance?

2. Moving through many different schools caused Trish to reflect on cultural differences and to develop an interest in fostering respect for diversity in the classroom. She writes, "Clearly some assumptions about the way the world operates. . . and some ways of communicating are not universally understood."

a. In what ways may stereotypical assumptions be grounded in experiences of homogeneous schools? For those of you educated in heterogeneous schools, how has that experience influenced your thinking about working in schools and being teachers?

b. How can students be assisted in developing a recognition of stereotypical assumptions?

c. How can you learn to be sensitive and responsive to students in classrooms exhibiting cultural diversity?

3. Jodi writes that her focus on being an "A" student killed her curiosity. She recognizes the importance of this trait and hopes to encourage her students to use their own curiosity to learn rather than earn grades.

a. Is it possible to teach well without modeling curiosity? How might assigning letter grades squelch curiosity? What other practices might influence student curiosity?

b. How did her experience as a successful student influence Jodi's vision of teaching?

c. To what extent might negative schooling experiences provide motivation toward a teaching career choice? Why? How can negative experiences as a student be reflected upon to inform positive teaching practices?

INFLUENCES OF LIFE EXPERIENCES

And, finally, Marta, Renee, Kevin, and Steve stand back and reflect on various life experiences that influenced their perspectives on teaching and education.

Narrative Accounts

Starting as young as fifth grade, my sister and I created our own summer day camp for preschool children in our neighborhood. We prepared a two-week session of activities, arts and crafts, games, and entertainment. We invited all the young children, freeing their mothers for some time to themselves. We organized the allotted time for each activity, bought the materials, and drew up plans for every day. In retrospect, it was an impressive curriculum for two young girls to have put together. All of the mothers praised us for our preparation. Seeing the children get pleasure out of something I taught them gave me such an incredible feeling. I loved that experience and have never forgotten it. As I grew up I gained some other opportunities in teaching-type settings that eventually influenced my career plans. (Marta Willeims)

As a camp counselor, I had my first opportunity to make connections with young children. After twelve summers of being a camper I switched roles. Over the years, my "warehouse" of songs, art projects, games, dances, and stories increased. I was excited to share all that I had collected with my campers. I remember how much I appreciated counselors for all they had taught me. After that first summer as a counselor I swelled with personal satisfaction from watching campers do much growing under my tutelage. My efforts as a counselor brought further rewards when I was asked to be the director of the day camp. It was a camp that met in an elementary school, and we had use only of the classrooms, the nearby field, and the playground. It was up to me to design the program and prepare staff to keep the kids entertained for five hours every day. I also took my own group of campers because working directly with children is what I love best. Because I am the youngest child in my family, my experience as a counselor and director was my first opportunity as a formal role model, and I valued this opportunity. (Renee Buscho)

I taught for two years as a Spanish instructor at an elementary school. I joined just after the program was initiated. The language immersion program had some general guidelines, but much of the curriculum was developed by the instructors. I had classes of about 10 to 15 students. The classes met four days each week for a half hour before school. I learned a lot about lesson preparation and about using materials and visual aids in a classroom. Perhaps one of the most powerful lessons was that learning is not passive. A child quietly sitting in his or her seat behaving in a passive manner may not learn as much as a student who is actively engaged in the learning process.

I recently taught one class for six months at a private high school. I had to develop a curriculum using a textbook and other material I scrounged from various sources. I was treated as an equal by faculty members and given "regular responsibilities" and the academic freedom of a professional and specialist in my field. From what I have heard, I proved worthy of their trust. I worked in several capacities with an established teacher in my field for over a year. I started by teaching a few sessions of his class in conjunction with a teaching methods class. He liked my teaching and background enough that I found myself substitute teaching in his classes for two weeks. Later, I helped chaperon 45 students on a five-day field trip. (Kevin Queen)

Much of my education that I really value took place outside the classroom. Maybe this is due to the rather exotic circumstances of my upbringing. Perhaps one learns more out of rather than in school. The varied exposure to people and places over years of travel have been worth more than any geography class. I've always been fascinated by maps and learned to read them through years of traveling hither and yon. I've been to Europe at least six times—the last three times on my own as an adult. I've "thumbed around" southern Africa and made the trip from Luanda to Cape Town five times. I've been to sea, crossing the Atlantic and making the Lisbon to Cape Town run a number of times. From all of this has come my education. (Steve Bruno)

For Reflection and Discussion

1. Providing pleasant experiences to younger children had a powerful impact on Marta's decision to become a teacher.
   a. Have your experiences with younger siblings or involvement with child care influenced your perspectives on education? If so, in what ways were the influences positive or negative?
2. Renee spent many years as a summer camper and came to value her position as counselor because, as the youngest child in her family, it represented the first time that she had been viewed as a role model.
   a. How have you been influenced by birth order (or family relationships) in developing your concept of self as teacher?
3. Exotic circumstances provided Steve with an enriching education.
   a. In what ways may Steve's thinking about education differ from his peers? His professors?
   b. To what extent does your concept of education include experiences like Steve's ?
   c. How will the challenges he faces as a new teacher differ from those preservice teachers with more traditional educational backgrounds?

Links with Research

As you have probably gathered by our emphasis, there is a small but increasing amount of attention paid in research literature to the role of personal histories in the learning-to-teach process. Some of it relates to the kinds of influence that personal histories have on views of teachers and decisions to become members of the teaching profession. Other reports focus on the influence of personal histories on the ways in which new teachers think about professional practice.

Lortie (1975) was one of the first to recognize the importance of understanding the role of biography or personal history in the developing practice of teachers. The phrase "apprenticeship of observation" acknowledges the influence on teachers' thinking and practice of the time they themselves spent as students with teachers in many and diverse educational contexts. Since Lortie proclaimed a need for attention to the role of prior experiences in the process of becoming a teacher, a field of investigation on the topic has grown. Now, it is widely accepted that formal teacher education has an important but secondary influence on teachers' thinking and practice. Perspectives and practices are indelibly imprinted by life, school, and career experiences prior to entry to formal programs of teacher preparation. To get a comprehensive sense of the work conducted in this area we refer you to literature reviews conducted by Zeichner and Gore (1990) and Kagan (1992), and to ongoing work by Clandinin and Connelly (that is, Clandinin, 1986; Connelly & Clandinin, 1988), Butt and Raymond (for example, Butt & Raymond, 1987; Butt, Raymond, McCue, & Yamagashi, 1992), and Goodson (for example, Ball & Goodson, 1985; Goodson & Walker, 1991; Goodson, 1992). Here, we provide only a glimpse into this literature by drawing on some examples of studies investigating the role of biography or personal history in teacher development. We urge you to read some of these studies yourself because it is impossible for us, in a few sentences, to communicate the richness of this work.

Wright (1959) and Wright and Tuska (1967, 1968) advanced a "childhood romance theory of teacher development" that suggests a strong influence of significant others (usually adults) during childhood on teachers' self-image and practice. Role identity was further explored by Ross (1987) and Crow (1987a, 1987b). Ross argues that preservice teachers select attributes and practices of their own former teachers and synthesize them into an idealized image or model of the teacher they want to become. Crow's case study of four preservice teachers provides additional evidence of the biographical influence on individuals' beliefs about teaching, education, and practice. The ways in which the preservice teachers in Crow's study viewed themselves—their "role identities"—were strongly linked to their biographies. Their personal role identities became tools for evaluating and making sense of theory and practice in the preparation program.

Building on Crow's study, Knowles (1992) worked with five preservice and beginning teachers and developed a model that characterizes the influence of personal histories on teaching practice by considering the interaction between biography and school context. He linked success and failure in beginning teaching practices to early field settings and to role identities and images of teaching formed over years of prior experience in education and school settings. In his study, preservice and beginning teachers with strong role identities (rooted in positive formative life and school experiences) had less difficulty coping with challenging situations and contexts and experienced more success than did those with weak role identities (rooted in negative formative life and school experiences). Another study conducted by Aitken and Mildon (1991) reports similar findings.

The influence of personal histories on preservice teachers' images of effective and ineffective teaching, conceptions of appropriate student and teacher behaviors and attributes, and pedagogical decision making are also illustrated by Knowles and Holt-Reynolds (1991). Holt-Reynolds (1992) explored the relationship between the personal history-based beliefs preservice teachers brought to formal teacher preparation and the pedagogical principles advocated and practiced by one of their professors. Her study points out the potency of prior experience in the formation of personal definitions and interpretations of appropriate pedagogy:

> [Preservice teachers'] conclusions—their beliefs about what actions, states of mind, attitudes, and intentions combine to personify a "good" teacher—work behind the scenes as invisible, often tacitly known criteria for evaluating the potential efficacy of ideas, theories, and strategies of instruction they encounter as they formally study teaching (p. 343).

Britzman's (1991) ethnographic study of two preservice teachers is a description and analysis of the interaction between biography and the social structure of the school settings. Preservice teachers' conceptions of the roles of students and teachers and their understandings of school structures and curriculum were firmly rooted in biography and, as such, needed to be uncovered and examined so that they might facilitate, not constrain, innovative practice and development.

We are each products of our life-long personal experiences and these come to represent powerful arguments that, in many different and complex ways, influence the way we conceptualize teaching and the role of teachers. We cannot deny the power differential between the influences of experiences prior to and during preservice programs. The challenge is to find ways of *understanding* early influences on developing and emerging practices. As Feiman-Nemser (1983) states:

> The likelihood that professional study will affect what powerful early experiences have inscribed on the mind and emotions will depend on its power to cultivate images of the possible and desirable and to forge commitments to make those images a reality (p. 154).

Research Activities

1. The influence of personal histories on our thinking about being teachers is as complex as we are as individuals. We do not live our lives as sequences of disconnected events or in purely systematic and methodical ways. Most of the decisions we make are in some way influenced by past experiences. Past experience is *not* the only influence on and predictor of future actions and practice; however, prior experiences as represented in personal histories exert a complex and complicated influence on your development as a teacher. More than anything, therefore, we encourage you to explore your personal history through understanding the connections between your past experiences and your current thinking about teaching. More specifically, consider the following:

   a. What or who have been some of the major influences on your personal and emerging professional lives? How have these persons or events influenced you and, more specifically, your thinking about life?

   b. Can you be explicit about the way in which these persons, events or circumstances, or these prior experiences, have influenced your thinking and actions about working in educational settings? The term *critical incidents* is often used to describe significant events in teachers' lives and careers; these are incidents that stand out as milestones, beacons, turning points, decision points, times and places in one's life that introduce significant change in thinking and practice.

2. Using your personal history account as a basis, outline or list some of the significant experiences of schools, teachers, classrooms, and learnings that have influenced your thinking about being a teacher. Some questions to consider may include:

   a. What assumptions have you made as a result of these experiences? In what ways are your assumptions contradictory or internally consistent with each other? Do you have any explanations for any of these inconsistencies?

   b. What might be some potentially negative ways inconsistencies might play out in your field experiences and first year of full-time teaching?

   c. How have assumptions about the *meaning* of your experiences played out in your *practice* in classrooms and schools as a preservice teacher?

   d. To what extent have commonplace experiences among your peers resulted in divergent assumptions about learning, teaching, and classrooms? Why?

   e. In the process of asking these and other questions share your thinking and writing with one or two peers as you are comfortable. Try to extend each other's thinking by asking each other to clarify assumptions and the relationships between assumptions and emerging practice.

3. To help you think again about the processes associated with developing personal history accounts refer to Chapter 2. Recollect that personal histories influence a whole range of issues connected to your professional development. Extend your personal history account by drawing on elements of your personal history that illuminate in specific ways your orientations and decisions in the following areas:

   • your decision to become a teacher
   • your orientations about teaching and being a teacher
   • your beliefs about how children learn
   • your beliefs about how teachers teach
   • your decisions about subject matter focus and interests

   a. Do these personal history influences make good sense as bases for practice in light of what you have learned in your teacher preparation program? What are their strengths? What are their weaknesses? When are they appropriate or inappropriate foundations for practice?

4. There are others whose personal histories are also worthy of consideration, perhaps even exploration. Acknowledge, for example, that the teachers with whom you work in field experiences also have personal and career histories that have greatly influenced *their* orientations to practice. Sometimes you may be at odds with your mentor or cooperating teachers; however, consider the impropriety of criticizing their practices without exploring the underlying thinking and experiences that have shaped those practices. Thus, exploring teachers' careers is one way of understanding their practice. Talk with your cooperating teacher and explore some of the following questions, making sure not to cause discomfort.

   a. What are some of the critical incidents (see exercise 2) in your cooperating teacher's career? How have personal history influences shaped experienced teachers' past, present, and future practices in the classroom and in the school?

5. Explore some of the questions in exercise 3 with others working in education: those in public and private institutions; other teachers besides your cooperating or mentor teacher, teacher educators and professors of education; librarians and other support staff; principals, superintendents and other administrators; teachers in other than formal schools; and so on. Recognize that some people are going to be more forthright than others, depending on many factors including the context of the conversations and their familiarity with you. Check out published biographical, autobiographical, and ethnographic explorations of the lives and careers of teachers. (See *Recommended Readings*.)

6. This exercise will help you explore your implicit thinking about teaching as a career and profession. Imagine that you have recently received a letter from a good friend with whom you had lost contact. Write a response to your friend's inquiry about how and what you are doing. Include your decision about choosing teaching as a career and your reasons for making the choice. Mention your expectations and ambitions as well as areas of concern to you.

7. Knowing, acknowledging, and recognizing that you and your peers, along with the professional teachers with whom you work as well as the students you teach, all have personal histories is an important realization. Although this statement may seem trite, from experience we know that many teachers in preparation often fail to acknowledge that students grow up with perspectives that are idiosyncratic and beyond stereotype. Explore with your cooperating or mentor teacher ways of uncovering the idiosyncratic backgrounds of students with whom you work. For example:

   a. Who are your students? What are their various backgrounds, beliefs, values? What are their families like?

   b. How do you distinguish between information about students that may be formative in your teaching of those students and that which serves little meaningful purpose in your roles and responsibilities? What are your ethical and moral responsibilities regarding personal information to which you may be privy?

Recognizing Preconceptions of Teaching

To every encounter or engagement, whether it is with a person, text, or situation, we take with us preconceived ideas or images that serve as foundation blocks on which we build new understandings. These preconceptions, developed through past experiences or associations, have powerful influences on the way we approach new situations, or revisit familiar ones, and on how we respond within those situations. Often, in part because they are so much a part of our thinking and way of knowing, we remain unaware of our preconceived ideas. Their influence, however, makes itself known in our thoughts and subsequent actions.

Because you have had an opportunity to think about your early experiences of schooling, classrooms, teachers, and learning, you have become more aware of some of the preconceptions you bring to teaching. In this section, we want to further explore the importance of recognizing preconceptions of teaching for they are the lenses through which you will first view all aspects of your role as teacher. First, listen as Matt, Gabrielle, Jane, and Leila tell about some of their perspectives on teachers and teaching. Through reflection on his own experiences of learning in schools, Matt articulates some of his preconceived beliefs about teaching and learning. You will notice a common theme in the final three accounts. Gabrielle and Jane struggle with issues of prejudice, stereotyping, and ethnocentricity related to different cultural groups. Leila, as a recent immigrant speaking from the perspective of an "outsider," reminds us how easy it is to assume an ethnocentric stance and be governed in our thinking by views representative of dominant societal groups. Each of these perspectives illustrates some of the preconceptions that shape our thinking.

We all have preconceived ideas about issues of race, ethnicity, gender, and class. Like any other preconceptions, these thoughts and attitudes will play out in your actions and practice as teachers. It is essential, therefore, to make explicit and examine your hitherto implicit beliefs, values, and ideas about critical social and political issues. It is important for teachers to develop sound, coherent, consistent, and proactive perspectives on these and many other topics related to being a professional.

Narrative Accounts

At the outset of the [practicum] term, the issue of what it means to teach seemed fairly simple. During my own secondary schooling I went through trying times. As I reflected on the various transitions that took place in this time period I remembered the solace I found in literature. Being able to formulate connections between the adventures of characters such as Odysseus with my own rites of passage seemed to supply meaning to a turbulent and chaotic period. My aesthetic appreciation of literature blossomed during this period. Consequently, I conceived of English teachers as people who facilitated this appreciation while offering students opportunities to make sense of their individual experience amidst transitions into adulthood. While I still adhere to the importance of the teacher as a catalyst for individuals' development, in order to give depth to this belief, a variety of factors have impacted my thoughts on how this is achieved.

The first crucial hinge for me was understanding how I conceived learning taking place. In addressing this issue, I began to contemplate my own experiences; I recollected moments where I truly learned. In considering these experiences, I noted that the only knowledge that I took away from a class well beyond the final exam was that which had required that I be invested in the material. In other words, [usually] the subject I was studying was not something that existed outside of me. It was intrinsically linked to my own interests and thinking at the time. Effective teachers convinced me that there was some link between my understanding of a situation that appeared in a text and my own growth and experience as an individual. Such teachers did not look at me as a tabula rasa waiting to be filled with the proper moral and aesthetic fiber. Instead, emphasis was placed on looking at the various disciplines as a means to awaken some understanding of the truths that are dormant within me.

In the Jewish treatises known as the Kabbalah, there is a passage that states that when every child is an infant, an angel comes down to teach him or her the Torah (or Law). After the child learns this, the angel puts his finger on the child's lips and says, "Forget it." The point of recounting this story is that when learning takes place, it is a reawakening. Good teachers recognize that this reawakening does not take place in a vacuum. Such teachers acknowledge that they are catalysts for students' understandings and do not maintain illusions about imparting some vague body of information known as "knowledge" (to students). (Matt Schlein)

I grew up in a culturally diverse neighborhood. My family lived in a town house in an upper-middle-class neighborhood in the heart of downtown; it was a melting pot of all races, religions, and nationalities. My friends were black, white, oriental, Indian, Christian, and Jewish. This did not seem unusual. I never thought about the backgrounds of my friends; they were just my friends. They were from varied socio-economic backgrounds, a fact that I did not realize until about a year ago when my mother and I were reminiscing. My elementary school was part of a busing program to integrate underprivileged children into better schools, so I had friends who lived in the housing projects. The beauty of this is that issues of class, race, and religion did not mean anything to our friendship. Such matters are not salient to a five-year-old and should not be to an adult. My background has given me valuable insights into the lives of some people who have dissimilar backgrounds to myself.

The shock of my life came at age eight, when I was in the third grade. My parents moved our family from the friendly urban community to a wealthy, all-white neighborhood. I hated it. I was viewed as an outcast, and I did not understand why. My values were completely different from those of my new peers. The values of the new neighborhood were based on appearances and material possessions. I heard for the first time the word "nigger" and it infuriated me. Not only were these kids insulting some of my closest friends, they had never even met a black person! I tried for five years to fit into my new environment, but I never did. (Gabrielle Tuchow)

One must be careful about the information presented to young people. [Presentation of] absolutes about a culture or people creates stereotypes. Children are not born with prejudices. They slowly acquire them through life. It is my job [as a new teacher] to make sure that children's experiences in my classroom do not contribute to the perpetuation of stereotypes.

The schools I attended as a child had fairly homogeneous populations. Until I was in high school, I had never had any personal interaction with individuals representing minority groups. On entering high school I became more aware of the many things to which I had not been exposed. Up until that point, my learnings about other cultures, races, and religions were, apart from a few token pages in history texts, from television and newspapers. The implications of such a narrow knowledge base upon which children grow are horrifying. (Jane Atman)

I grew up and was educated outside North America; my knowledge of the education system here was limited. In North America when professors or preservice teachers talked about elements of school curriculum, I did not understand specifically the meaning of that curriculum. When I entered North American schools, where students were kept busy with worksheets all the time, I did not know what worksheets really were. The hardest thing was not having a background similar to my peers. They had [these similar experiences] from which to draw and teach. These other preservice teachers, my peers, could at least follow models of teaching based on their experience with North American high school teachers, but I could not.

Not only did I not have any idea of how to teach in a North American classroom, but I was totally unaware of the students' expectations of teachers. Moreover, I had no clue as to what I can or cannot expect from students. The hardest part is simply that a lack of prior experience as a student in the school system here made everything so much more difficult. Whereas other preservice teachers made comments such as, "What's to learn about teaching? I have gone to school, I know how to teach, I know how it's done," I was silent. After having spent some time in the school [where I was placed for one practica] I was amazed by elements of the system. For example, it was beyond me how technology in education could have advanced so far. (Leila Muniroui)

For Reflection and Discussion

1. Matt's conception of teachers acting as a catalyst is confirmed for him through a cultural reference.
    a. How has your own culture influenced your conception of teachers and teachers' work?
    b. How do teachers respond to the various culturally defined values of education?
2. Gabrielle's early youth was spent in a multicultural neighborhood. She attributes to this experience her own lack of prejudices and her understanding of multicultural contexts.
    a. How has Gabrielle defined prejudice? What are the elements that comprise prejudicial thinking?
    b. What impact did her attendance at a heterogeneous and then a homogenous school have upon her own development of prejudices?
3. Stereotyping is an issue that concerns Jane and she feels that her job as an educator is to prevent the further accumulation of stereotypes by her students.
    a. How could Jane's experience in school have promoted the production of stereotypes? How did her reflection upon her experience influence her sensitivity to the issue of stereotypes?
    b. Are you aware of character representations that may be offensive to others? How has your exposure to stereotypical representations affected your opinions of others?
4. Jane had limited experience with people of differing cultures and Gabrielle formed close cross-cultural friendships.
    a. What effect did these disparate experiences have upon the development of teaching perspectives?
5. With a different cultural background than her fellow students, Leila notices that she does not share the same preconceptions about teaching. In many ways her experience was similar to that of an anthropologist studying a foreign culture.
    a. In what ways did Leila's lack of knowledge of North American cultures and system of education enhance her learning? How was it disadvantageous?
    b. How can the reliance upon previous experience be detrimental for students of teaching?
    c. How can previous experience be used to extend understanding of teaching?

Links with Research

Teaching is a complex and personal phenomenon. As we act and interact within professional contexts we engage in an ongoing reorganization and reconstruction of the foundational knowledge and conceptions that have evolved in our thinking. Interest in understanding teachers' personal, usually implicit, theories, beliefs, and attitudes has spawned considerable research. This work is related to but distinct from studies of teachers' personal histories primarily in that it takes for granted but does not focus on the role of biography in teaching. Like the personal history research, however, studies of preservice teachers' beliefs, attitudes, and implicit theories provide considerable evidence to support the idea that the preconceptions preservice teachers bring with them to preparation programs have powerful influences on developing thinking and practice. These preconceptions, left unchallenged, remain relatively stable and intact.

In a study of 38 preservice teachers, Weinstein (1990) found that the teachers' self-image and beliefs about teaching resisted the influence of course work and field experience, and remained relatively unchanged throughout the semester during which they were studied. Similarly, Pigge and Marso (1989), who examined attitudinal change of 133 preservice teachers, discovered that throughout the program of teacher preparation, and despite some challenging experiences, preservice teachers maintained their high ideals, aspirations, and optimism for their future work as teachers.

Calderhead and Robson (1991) and McDaniel (1991) found that preservice teachers' beliefs and images, remained relatively stable and inflexible at least through the early stages of formal teacher preparation. And, despite the potentially influential experiences and interactions of the programs, the preservice teachers in these studies relied on their own prior experiences as interpretive lenses and reference points for decision making about teaching. Likewise, Goodman (1988), reporting on a study of preservice teachers' perspectives, observed that no matter how logical or sound a new or intriguing idea seemed, it was rejected unless it was congruous with an existing perspective. According to Goodman, the teachers in that study tended to act on an intuitive rather than on an intellectual level when introduced to new ideas or experiences.

Other studies report more flexibility and conceptual change depending on personal, programmatic, and contextual factors and influences. For example, in a study of prior beliefs and conceptual change conducted by Hollingsworth (1989), 5 of 14 preservice teachers were able to modify some of their preconceived ideas about classroom instruction in part because they were encouraged by their cooperating teachers to confront their beliefs. In another study in which opportunities for examination of and reflection on prior beliefs about teaching writing were provided to preservice teachers within the context of their field experience, those teachers also were able to reconstruct their preconceived ideas (Florio-Ruane & Lensmire, 1990).

Some preparation programs have been redesigned to take into account and build upon prospective teachers' preconceptions or personal theories of teaching and learning. These programs, based on constructivist views of education, acknowledge that:

> The well developed views of teaching and learning [that preservice teachers bring to the program] are very persistent and often at odds with the views we hope to cultivate. Hence the views need to be identified, discussed and evaluated by student teachers in light of carefully managed teaching/learning experiences (Gunstone & Northfield, 1987, p. 3).

Research specifically designed to explore programmatic attempts to influence preservice teachers' thinking and practice (for example, programs based on constructivist views or with a reflection and inquiry orientation) reports varying degrees of "success" in facilitating conceptual change. What is noteworthy in these studies and programs is *not* the identification of observed change but rather the recognition of the importance of attention to contextual factors in promoting teacher development (for example, the role of the cooperating teacher, and the practicum context) as well as the critical role of the reflective process (usually facilitated by journal keeping, observations, and reflective activities and discussions).

Erickson and MacKinnon, for example, in a program of research focused on the development of a reflective practicum in science teaching (Erickson & MacKinnon, 1991), describe how, with guided supervision, preservice science teachers reconstructed their understandings about science teaching. Zeichner and Liston (1987) discuss personal and contextual factors that facilitate and constrain the realization of goals in a reflective teacher education program intended to "help student teachers become more aware of themselves and their environments in a way that changes their perceptions of what is possible" (p. 25).

Over the course of one year, Labosky (1991) observed preservice teachers become more reflective and more able to challenge their prior beliefs and knowledge through journal keeping. Similarly, preservice teachers in a study conducted by Cole (1989) attached high value to self-examination of personal theories of teaching. They viewed reflection and theory articulation as opportunities to

> . . . understand themselves and open their understanding to others; . . . evaluate convictions and personal values; . . . review beliefs and values about teaching; . . . clarify perspectives on teaching in order to reconceptualize what teaching is all about; critically assess approaches to teaching by reflecting on experience both as students and student teachers; and to see change over the year (pp. 11–12).

The ideas and images about teaching that preservice teachers bring to formal teacher education programs are deeply etched on their perceptual lenses. But, because such preconceptions were formed based on limited experience and understanding of what teaching is all about, it is important for preservice teachers to, as Buchmann (1989) says, "break from experience," that is, to go beyond habitual interpretations of persons and events to make more open and informed educational judgments and decisions.

Research Activities

As you have no doubt detected, there is only a subtle difference between the preceding section (Influences of Prior Experiences on the Development of Conceptions of Teaching and Learning) and this one. The former is slanted toward the influences of teachers, family, school, and life experiences on your thinking; the latter is intended to go a step further and explore in a general way the preconceptions of teaching that you bring to the classroom. In other words, these preconceptions are the articulated meanings associated with your professional development that you have derived from your (personal history-based) experiences. It is to these meanings that we wish to draw your attention.

1. In thinking about your preconceptions of teachers and teachers' work try exploring the following, first on your own and then in group discussion with your peers.
   a. Identify specific perspectives, beliefs, or attitudes about the role of teachers and their work that are directly related to some of your pivotal life experiences. What are these direct links, and how do you anticipate they will play out in the development of classroom practice? Is there congruence or consistency across these beliefs?
   b. Try to connect these preconceptions into a personal philosophy of education and teaching.

2. A personal philosophy of teaching is a set of unified beliefs, practical arguments, and (pre)conceptions of teaching that lays the foundation for practice in classrooms and places where learning is facilitated. One way of gaining access to and making explicit some of your preconceptions and beliefs about teaching is through metaphor. Refer to the section on metaphor in Chapter 2 and try to generate a personal metaphor (or metaphors) of teaching that captures and communicates your image of teaching and how you see yourself as a teacher.

3. You have probably read several books about teaching and education. Were you able to discern the various authors' philosophies of education and teaching as expressed in the different writings? Try reading, for example, *Teacher* or *Spearpoint* by Sylvia Ashton-Warner (1963, 1972) or *Summerhill* by A. S. Neill (1960) and writing a coherent statement that represents what these authors believe about teachers' instructional activities and roles.

   a. What kinds of personal history influences do you imagine might have influenced these authors' thinking? How do their early perspectives evidence themselves? On what points would you challenge their philosophies, and why?

   b. It might be interesting to try out the same activity with this book; that is, identify our philosophies of teaching and education and think about where and why you would challenge our thinking.

4. As in the *Research Activities* of the previous subsection, refer to Chapter 2, which focused on making meaning through autobiographical writing. Some of the questions associated with developing autobiographical writing practices may be more meaningful now. Try responding to these questions, perhaps by enlarging or extending your personal history account, or through attending to them in your journal writing, or in discussions with close peers.

Understanding the Profession of Teaching

Teaching was my dream as a small child. I used to go home from school and imitate my teacher, using the small blackboard in our basement. The desire to become a teacher remained with me through high school but, as soon as I got to college, something changed. I still loved the thought of teaching, but the attitudes of others around me were very discouraging. I heard many stereotypical statements such as, "The only reason people go into teaching is because they want an easy job with good vacations." I also heard that teachers were people who were not smart enough to have "real" jobs. Although I explored other avenues first, I eventually decided to pursue my dream. (Stacy Lane)

Contrary to the understanding of most "outsiders"—like those who criticized Stacy's career choice—teaching is a tough and significant job, an occupation that contributes much to others. Think about it, though. What do you *really* know about the teaching profession and what do you know about teaching in classrooms? If you are like the preservice teachers whose stories follow, you will have

Teacher - one who teaches, especially one hired to teach. } American
Teach - to impart knowledge or skill to :   } Heritage.
                 one
Teach - to give some knowledge, to instruct, to train

91

Chapter 5   Exploring Images and Contexts of Teaching

entered a formal preservice teacher education program with a fairly narrow view of teaching as a profession. And, like them, you will be surprised to discover how complex and demanding are the roles and responsibilities a teacher must assume and carry out. The "delivery of subject matter content" is but a small part of what teachers do and comprises only a portion of their many responsibilities within and outside the classroom, school, and community. Indeed, the impact of teachers can be far ranging, as one cooperating teacher maintained:

> I sincerely believe that teaching is probably the most important profession in the world. . . . I try to hold the banner high for education and teaching. I try to tell [preservice teachers] who work with me that it's a very important job, a gratifying job, but it's not an easy job. . . . Let's face it, you have a lot of kids looking up to you. If you do it "right" you can leave a positive impression; if you do it "wrong" you can have a really bad influence on kids.

That so many of the preservice teachers with whom we have worked have made career decisions because of the effectiveness and influence of particular teachers is evidence of the powerful potential of teachers to influence for good. You probably know of many accounts by friends and others that speak to this point.

Considering the public's views, as often portrayed in the mass media, it is easy to fathom the pervasive lack of understanding about teaching and how responsibilities as great as those of teachers are allowed to bear down with little or no assistance and support. Some say the reasons are gender-related. Traditionally known as "women's work," teaching, like parenting, has a low occupational status in some parts of North America, especially the United States. (In many parts of the world, teachers are afforded high status.) So, like parenting, although it may be an extremely demanding and encompassing enterprise, teaching is, for the most part, a taken-for-granted profession. In other words, public demands continue to increase on par with societal changes, yet, there is little apparent need to know what it means to teach or be a teacher. One of our favorite depictions of the public's perception of teaching was written almost 30 years ago by a retired schoolteacher, Sybil Shack.

> All of us who teach, young or old, those who stay and those who leave, have found ourselves irritated by the attitudes of other adults toward us. I am not really surprised, though often annoyed, that teachers are reluctant to admit to their profession, and that women particularly are flattered when they are told that they "do not look like teachers," whatever that may mean. Because the moment it becomes known in a social gathering that I am a teacher, . . . the very atmosphere around me begins to change. Mothers and fathers want to talk to me about everything from their children's bed-wetting to the difficulties of learning algebra. I am harangued about the shortcomings of my dinner partner's stenographer's spelling, and put on the defensive about the failure of my new acquaintance's little boy to learn to read fluently. . . . [And I must listen to] my host's victories over his teachers during his own distant school career. . . . We [teachers] smile politely the first hundred times we hear the joke about the three sexes—male, female, and teacher. We respond politely the first hundred times we are jocularly poked in the

ribs with the joke about the nine-to-four day and the two-month vacation. The hundred and first time we are likely to be either bored or surly (Shack, 1965, pp. 4–5).

Despite many societal changes in the intervening period, not much has changed about the perception of teachers and their work.

It is likely that some of the early and later understandings of teaching and teachers, as recounted below by Stacy, Jeanne, and Brad will strike a familiar chord with you. After reading them, we invite you to think back to what being a teacher *used* to mean to you and consider that in light of what you *now* know. Have your conceptions changed? (We presume they have.) How have they changed? As you gain further insights and experience being a teacher your understanding of the profession will continue to change and grow. We encourage you to continue to challenge your early assumptions, particularly as your view of the profession opens to an ever-broadening perspective of the educational landscape, a panorama of contexts, roles, and responsibilities.

Narrative Accounts

I had not really thought of the great importance of teachers and the heavy responsibility they hold because of their profession until this summer [prior to entering the teacher preparation program]. Faced with the thought of being in a classroom answering children's questions and monitoring their behavior, I started seriously reflecting on what my images of teachers were when I was young. When I was in school, I thought Mrs. Duncus, Mr. McNichols, and Mrs. Ford knew everything. I thought they never made a mistake, and I was sure that school was all they had in their lives. I once saw one of my teachers in a shopping mall and could not figure out what she was doing there. Of course I know now that teachers are "regular" people who don't know everything, who do make mistakes, and, even occasionally, go to the shopping mall. (Stacy Lane)

Teachers are expected to be *so* dynamic, meaning that they have to keep so many things under control, bring interesting material to students, be effective in using a variety of teaching methods, understand differences between students, incorporate different resources, consider diverse perspectives and the diversity of students' backgrounds and ethnicities, construct curriculum, and be understanding and flexible. And this list barely begins to cover what people expect. The prospect of being a teacher is at once exciting and frightening. (Jeanne Worthen)

Whenever I talked to some of the better teachers I had about becoming a teacher, almost all of them told me that I was not really smart to go into education [at this time]. They said that the pay was not worth the effort, that teachers were not well respected in society, and that parents, in many cases, were not supportive of teachers' efforts to help children do better in schools. This was really depressing to me; it blew away the visions I had of teaching. I had seen nothing but smiles and fun on the teachers' faces behind their desks. But, what I could not see was the fact that they had to cope with a lot more than just 35 kids per class period. That was an eye opener to me.

My experience in schools, except for some difficult ones in the [lower] elementary [grades], had given me faith in the education system as a whole. I feel that if there are enough dedicated people in the field of education that it will eventually improve. Society will sooner or later see how thousands of dedicated people each day deal with millions of students and try their best to teach things that society thinks their children should know. This thought alone keeps me thinking that if I teach long enough and am an effective teacher, I will see these changes.

My mother has had a dramatic impact in my decision to be a teacher. For years I have watched her correct papers, talk to parents, complain about pay, and talk about how many great kids she has observed grow up. I have spent many hours with her in the classroom, helping, and watching her work. I have assisted her with everything from bulletin boards to actually teaching. She has never said that I should not become a teacher. She has said that, if she were to do it all again, she would not go through all of the bullshit to get where she is now. She has repeatedly said, however, that the teaching profession [especially regarding the kinds of relations teachers have with kids] is by far the most rewarding profession she can think of. (Brad Church)

For Reflection and Discussion

1. Stacy and Brad discovered that their years of observing teachers from a student perspective was dimensionally limited.
   a. In what ways might such pervasive observations contribute to the misconception that teaching is an easy job?
   b. In what ways is your concept of teachers' work influenced by excellent teachers who made it look easy?
2. Jeanne came to recognize that a teacher's tasks are multidimensional and discovered that the prospect of teaching is at once exciting and frightening.
   a. To what extent were Jeanne's initial understandings of teaching based upon the explicit and observable acts of teachers?

Links with Research

"Schooling is long on prescription, short on description" (Lortie, 1975, vii). Descriptions of schools and teaching that do exist have generally, until recently, represented a simplistic and rather superficial view of teaching. As Lasley and Watras (1991) observe:

> The preoccupation with the knowledge base and with accountability has encouraged the adoption of simplified pedagogy and educational reductionism. . . . Teaching is emerging in the popular educational literature as a linear process. . . . Preservice teachers learn the steps, and then during . . . field practices they are evaluated on those skills. The linear approach is reinforced by the reliance school districts place on . . . packaged approaches. . . . Even in teacher education pro-

grams . . . students [for the most part] go into field placements and work with teachers who possess the "right" method (p. 6).

Thus, they go on to argue, preservice teachers have little opportunity to understand and appreciate the complexity of teaching and schooling, and to treat teaching as more than a narrow, applied field. Such a confining perspective focuses exclusively on the technical and procedural elements of teaching and forgoes developing understandings of the complex nature of the profession and its context.

The recent shift to a qualitative approach to research on teaching has resulted in an increase in descriptive research that more accurately depicts the complexity of teaching and life in schools and classrooms. (See the lists of recommended readings at the end of each chapter.) Also, awareness of the complexity of teaching has been raised through studies such as *Schoolteacher* (Lortie, 1975), a sociological study of the teaching profession in the United States, and *Teachers at Work* (Johnson, 1990), an examination of teachers' work with a focus on the context of teaching as it is experienced by teachers. And, in an analysis of "the cultures of teaching," Feiman-Nemser and Floden (1986) make a helpful distinction between the job of teaching and the work of teaching. But, because educational literature is not widely read by those not already in the profession, few preservice teachers enter formal preparation programs with either comprehensive or realistic understandings about the teaching profession.

Past personal experiences of schools and teaching, combined with simplified or stereotypical depictions of the profession in the mass media, contribute to the formation of inappropriate images and inadequate expectations of teaching as a career and profession. For example, in the United States teacher education is seen as easy to gain admittance to and intellectually weak (Lanier & Little, 1986). (This perception about easy admittance is not widely held in Canada where, in many universities, the admissions standards are so high that only a small percentage of applicants is accepted.) And, as Book, Beyers, and Freeman (1983) assert, about a quarter of those entering teacher preparation programs in the United States maintain that there is little they need to learn to become successful teachers because they already have pedagogies in place in their thinking. The prominent view held by preservice teachers is that teaching is learned through experience (Lortie, 1975) and that formal preparation programs do not prepare individuals for the challenges of classrooms. This view is also represented, for example, by the research findings of Eisenhart, Behm, and Romagnano (1991).

Preservice teachers often experience surprised confusion upon discovering the multifaceted and multi-layered nature of teaching, especially when teaching is simplistically represented in teacher preparation programs and in the popular press. And, it is only recently that the complexities inherent in the teaching profession have been acknowledged.

Research Activities

1. Think about your perceptions of teachers and teaching over the last 20 years or so. No doubt you can see through your mind's eye some of the many teachers you have encountered. Try the following questions as foci for further inquiry:

   a. Can you identify your changing conceptions of teachers? For example, what was your perception of the work and role of your first-grade teacher? And, . . . your fourth-grade teacher, and those you had in seventh, tenth, and twelfth grades? How have your perceptions changed? How have they not changed? (How might your memories change over time?)

b. What are the conditions or elements of your ongoing experience that have induced you to change or not change your preconceptions of teachers' work and roles? How would you characterize the unfolding nature of your thinking about the teaching profession? Do you have a metaphor to describe this process? What is it, and why?

c. In what ways are your conceptions shaped by work experiences and experiences of formal and informal learning opportunities? To what extent has participation in a formal program of teacher preparation challenged or reinforced your conceptions of teaching and the role of teachers?

2. Probably the best places to go to find out about the profession of teaching are schools or other places where teachers work. Try exploring with experienced professionals their conceptions of their work and roles.

a. What do teachers think about their work? How does the reality of teaching differ from their expectations as beginning professionals? (Why are there gaps between expectations and realities?) In what ways does the system within which individuals work (including society) shape these expectations and realities?

b. How have their conceptions changed over time? How has society changed in its perspective on teachers, and how has this affected these practicing professionals?

c. To what extent are the views of younger, less-experienced teachers different from long-tenured individuals?

3. Refer to the video list located at the back of the book. Some titles on this list will probably be familiar to you. Think about the images of teachers as they are portrayed in popular media.

a. Make a list of the dominant characteristics (themes, routines) portrayed by the teacher in your favorite film about teaching. Develop a composite list of several characters (collaborate with someone if needed). Give some thought to your increased knowledge about the roles and responsibilities of teachers as you examine your list to discover what is missing. Think about the facets of teaching that are underrepresented in videos about schools, classrooms, and teachers. What are the possible reasons for portraying the profession in this way? To what extent do media depictions of teaching reinforce culturally bound stereotypes of teaching? To what extent do the films accurately portray the profession? Does your favorite film provide motivation for considering teaching as a career?

b. Think about the personality of the teachers presented. To what extent are the characters of the teachers shaped by the type of student or the teaching context (elementary/secondary, rural/urban, public/private)? Do you think the shaping of teacher character by context, as represented in the media, authentically represents the phenomenon of developing a teacher persona? Is teacher development dependent upon context? To what extent?

4. Imagine that you have accepted your first teaching position. Visualize yourself as a teacher engaged in daily classroom routines. You are required to arrive earlier than your students and to remain in the building for some time after they leave. Think about the

tasks you perform when your students are not present. Think too about the amount and kinds of paperwork that you process during the day as well as the nonteaching interactions you may have engaged in with students. Use brief descriptive phrases to make a list of the roles and responsibilities you have assumed. Examine your list to discover themes. Note the tasks and responsibilities that are related by theme. What patterns emerge?

5. A research technique that may be helpful to you at this point is the "I search" (Macrorie, 1981). Doing one for yourself will allow you to experience an alternative way of learning how to learn. In contrast to more formal research an "I search" is an informal first person account of a student's search for information about a particular topic. It includes the story of that search as well as a report of what was discovered. The following steps outline the process; feel free to adapt them to your own needs.

- Select a topic of interest to you, for example, roles adopted by teachers.
- Ask questions about the topic and reflect upon them.
- Think about what kinds of information you seek as well as the most appropriate sources.
- Follow leads.
- Talk to people who might know about your topic.
- Find out what *you* want to know regardless of where the search takes you.

To write about your "I search," first explain your interest in the topic and then tell the story of your search. Include successful and unsuccessful efforts. Your account should answer the following questions: What did you want to know? Why? How did you find out? What did you learn?

Exploring Different Contexts for Field Experiences

Structured experiences in the field—in places where teachers and students gather to learn—are a vital part of learning to teach. Many say that the field experience component is the most meaningful part of formal preservice teacher preparation. We would qualify that assertion. We would also want to stress, as we have done before, that there is a delicate balance and a relationship to be developed between theory and practice. And, further, that the balance and relationship are not achieved exclusively by attention to the field component of preparation programs. As Dewey (1938) reminds us, it is not enough to just have an experience or engage in activities; everything depends on the *quality* of the experience that is had, not only how agreeable it is but also how it influences later experiences. A primary influence on the quality of an experience is the context in which the experience takes place. We, therefore, invite you to consider the range of options available for learning in field contexts.

Although most structured field experiences are situated in traditional public or private school settings, opportunities for experiences in alternative settings are also available. When we think about other successful learning experiences we have had, they are not always (perhaps seldom) confined to formal classrooms as we know them. Education and life itself enjoy a reciprocal relationship, and to think of teachers owning the "domain of learning" is ludicrous. The acts of teaching and learning are not confined to formal school or structured settings.

In thinking about becoming a teacher and learning to teach, professional development can be enhanced by attention to the possibilities afforded by different contexts of field experience: community recreation centers; tutoring and remedial learning centers; outdoor education sites; recreation sites; vacation, special interest, and sports camps; cross-cultural settings in other countries or other regions of your country (including urban or rural settings, whichever you are *least* familiar with); churches and religion classes; child care facilities; community volunteer or action sites; and individual and group instruction in classes for fine and performing arts. These are but some of the myriad possibilities for structured field experiences. You may need to explore such options on your own and negotiate alternative placements as part of your program's field experience component, or you may want to participate in additional field experiences at other times to enhance and enrich your learning. (There are even institutions that specialize in providing additional field experiences, especially international ones.) No matter what path your formal teacher education program takes, we invite you to carefully consider the usefulness of engaging in practice in a variety of different, contrasting sites.

In the narrative account that follows, Priya reflects on her field experience in an alternative context. The key to thinking about engaging in field experiences is to explore your own preconceptions about teaching and teachers, analyze your potential strengths as well as your less developed areas. In light of these reflections on your professional development, try to place yourself in appropriate contexts with the view to extending those areas of knowledge, skills, and understandings that are in most need of development or challenge.

Intent on exploring culturally different contexts in North America, many suburban preservice teachers we know have placed themselves for an extended period in an inner-city school. Others have sought international experiences. Priya was interested in seeking international contexts to expand her emerging professional growth. Without much input from those with whom she worked in the program (in which she gained a provisional teacher certificate), she struck out on her own to discover vehicles through which she could extend the grounding of her experience to another country.

Narrative Account

New Zealand, a country so far and away "down under," was a place I had longed to see. With only an obscure knowledge of this nation's background, I envisioned it to be an environmentally rich, remote and peaceful country, green, and with lots of sheep. In fact, this is what I did see, along with culturally diverse people and a unique education system. I learned a great deal from my adventure abroad, a result of traveling and teaching in this country. But, the best lesson from this experience was the value of understanding and appreciating cultural traditions and practices of people outside my own little world.

Along with a chance to travel and see this exotic land, my main purpose in New Zealand was to have an alternative student teaching experience while gaining exposure to a different educational practice and styles of teaching. I had high expectations. I wanted to develop my teaching skills and broaden my interests in the field of education. I was optimistic and ready to face challenges set before me in this new cultural setting.

The small elementary school (or primary school as it is called there) in which I was placed had nearly 150 children; it presented a cohesive and warm atmosphere. I felt a part of this family-school in the 10 weeks I spent with the faculty and students. Although the class sizes were fairly large with between 28 and 33 students, the school's integrated nature and activities seemed to alleviate some of the teachers' responsibilities. Working in a small school setting was an interesting change from the larger schools I had become familiar with in North America. It did not take long to get acquainted with the faculty, the students, the surroundings, the procedures and expectations—the "ins and outs" of the school. Most of the students were aware of all the happenings within the school, and very eager to share their knowledge with newcomers like myself. I was impressed when my curiosities and questions about the school were eagerly and easily answered by whomever I approached—students and teachers alike.

Each member of the faculty had a significant role in the school besides being a classroom teacher. In a small school setting, each person tends to wear several hats, because the school may not be able to afford hiring a different person for every need or role existing in the school. Further, the school faculty depended on one another to carry out the various roles and responsibilities.

Team teaching was a common practice at the school. It was a pleasure to see how harmoniously and effectively the ten-member teaching faculty seemed to work. For the most part, the teachers were aware of each others' classroom successes and problems as they all shared and consulted each other with personal accounts of their work. They were very supportive of one another and very flexible when called upon for any type of assistance in another classroom.

Teachers worked in two separate syndicates to plan their lessons and activities for each week. Two teams of three teachers each were established—one for the Junior Block of students and one for the Senior Block. The whole school often studied the same theme for a certain period of time. Thus, the syndicate teachers worked together to decide upon appropriate teaching activities for their respective classes, and they shared teaching ideas, materials, resources, and activities. In some cases, one teacher might decide to focus on a certain part of the theme and teach a lesson to all the classes.

A team teaching approach was taken in the preparation and presentation of all subjects, academic and nonacademic. Thus, the responsibility and load of planning, preparing, and teaching a topic or unit was shared among the syndicate teachers. Consequently, each teacher was able to provide a more thorough and concentrated lesson by focusing on a smaller portion of the content area. Team teaching as I observed it seems to provide a richer learning experience for the students as they gain a more diverse understanding of the subject matter at hand.

The open-plan system and Whole Language learning, which I became better acquainted with during my experience in New Zealand, gave me a clearer account of some of the programs and methods currently being implemented in North American schools. In particular, the Whole Language system is based on a philosophy that stresses that, in learning to read and write, language should be kept whole and uncontrived, and that children should use language in ways that relate to their own lives and cultures. Whole Language advocates that children read material that makes sense to them and has personal meaning, as opposed to books that entail a repetitive format and engage them in rote learning. Content and process are integrated and taught holistically in the Whole Language system, providing a rich and meaningful reading and learning experience for students. Further, this system allows each child to focus their learning on what is important and interesting to them. I was impressed with the school's philosophy of working with children at their individual levels of understanding and helping them to develop a self-interest in learning.

One of the most fascinating programs instituted in the school was the Maori Bilingual Unit. The Maori are the indigenous people of New Zealand. I was excited to learn about this group of Polynesians and their contribution to New Zealand's history. Maori children made up nearly 15 percent of the student body, so I felt fortunate to be involved in some of their teachings and cultural traditions. The Maori Bilingual Unit, present in most of the elementary schools in New Zealand, gives students the opportunity to be immersed in academic learning through their language and traditions, and it exposes all the children in the school to the practices of this indigenous culture.

I am very fortunate to have had an opportunity of an alternative student teaching field experience. It broadened my interest in the field of education and my desire to work with children. Further, it enhanced my curiosity about other cultures of our world. Immersion in a culture or society different from mine was valuable in that it helped me to be more open-minded and develop respect for traditions and values that are quite distinct from my own. (Priya Nagaraju)

For Reflection and Discussion

1. Priya went to considerable lengths to seek alternative field placements.
   a. What might be the disadvantages and advantages for you to do the same?
   b. What advice do you think Priya might give to persons considering seeking alternative placements? To what extent might the experience cause Priya new challenges as she seeks a position in North American schools? To what extent might the experience strengthen Priya's ability to meet the challenges found in North American schools?
   c. What might be the limitations of international field placement experiences? What might be the advantages of alternative placements within North America (say, teaching in a different state)?

Links with Research

Earlier in the chapter we referred to research that points out the influence of contextual factors on preservice teacher development. Here, we focus on some of the work that deals specifically with issues related to contexts for field experiences. We make a brief reference to research embedded in traditional field experience contexts and go on to highlight some of the available research on alternative field settings.

As researchers point out (for example, Guyton & McIntyre, 1990; Feiman-Nemser & Buchmann, 1987; Zeichner, 1990), in spite of the significance of field experience, little attention has been given to the contexts in which preservice teachers are placed. Classrooms and schools generally not conducive to facilitating preservice teachers' growth (Copeland, 1981, 1986; Watts, 1987) or at odds with the goals and orientations of particular preservice teacher preparation programs (Goodman, 1983; Zeichner and Liston, 1987) are, for a variety of reasons, not uncommon field placement sites. Zeichner (1992) identifies the following as conceptual and structural obstacles to preservice teacher learning in the practicum: inappropriate conceptions of reflective practice; neglect of teachers' practical theories, values underlying educational practice, and the social conditions of schools; placements in individual classrooms rather than whole schools; inadequate supervisory practices; and a lack of placement in multicultural settings. Taken together, contextual factors represent a large proportion of these obstacles to educative field experiences.

In mis-educative settings preservice teachers are likely to experience confusion, disillusionment, difficulty, and even failure (see, for example, Knowles & Hoefler, 1989, a case study of failure) and, in most cases, practice compliance to achieve a passing grade (see, for example, the cases of Susan and Molly reported by Feiman-Nemser & Buchmann, 1987). More attention is now being paid by teacher educators to selection and preparation of field placement sites and to the activities comprising field experiences.

The professional development school concept, enjoying recent popularity, holds promise for improving field experiences. Studies of various professional development school models (for example, Beynon, 1991; Clark & LaLonde, 1992; Cole, 1991; McNay & Cole, 1993) highlight opportunities for preservice teachers to develop affinity, affiliation, and professional identity; to get a better sense of the complexities of schools, teaching, and being a teacher; to "come close" to the realities of teaching; and to develop a more solid foundation for ongoing development. In some cases, schools reflecting the real complexity and diversity of modern day classrooms and society as a whole are designated as teacher education sites. Not only do these contexts more accurately represent the reality of classroom life, they also provide opportunities for preservice teachers to engage in reflection and discussion organized around critical social issues in education. Thus, such contexts will help to overcome the kinds of obstacles noted by Zeichner (1992). In a study of the impact of two types of field experiences on 52 prospective teachers, findings indicate benefits of an immersion-type field experience that provides a variety of diverse experiences. Working within an inner-city school was important, for example, for those who came to the teacher preparation program with a limited view of cultural diversity (Gipe, Duffy, & Richards, 1987).

Other opportunities for broadening perspectives and learning through field experiences are available through international exchange or international student teaching programs, and many directors of such programs operate with missionarylike zeal in promoting them. Unfortunately, the research literature on student teacher exchange programs and their benefit is fairly limited. In a longitudinal study, Canadian preservice teachers who participated in an overseas practicum in England perceived the experience as an overall positive influence on their personal and professional lives (Kelleher & Williams, 1986). Booth, Fox, and Tubbs (1992) conducted a small scale survey (N = 45) and investigated four case studies of Australian preservice teachers who completed practicum experiences in Fiji, Thailand, and Malaysia. In general, but varying among individuals, the experience positively influenced the preservice teachers in personal and professional development and in awareness and understanding of issues related to cultural diversity. Similar outcomes are reported in an analysis of a United States-United Kingdom student teaching program (Schnur, Kersh, & Slick, 1992). There do not appear to be research reports that explore the usefulness of other than school contexts for teacher preparation field experiences.

Research Activities

1. On entering schools as a new teacher, one engaged in professional preparation, you are likely to run across two major groups of people: those who have been employed in only one school district, perhaps even one school; and those who have moved around. Of the latter group there are bound to be at least two subgroups: those who have taught predominantly in one culture; and those who have experienced multiple cultural contexts of practice. Try identifying some teachers who represent each of these groups. Plan to talk with them about their experiences.

   a. How does continued work in one context influence one's approach to teaching? How does work in multiple contexts inform one's thinking about practice? How have these teachers been enriched by their experiences?

2. Some teachers may have participated in exchange visits to other states, provinces, or nations. Some may have moved from urban to suburban or rural settings or vice versa. For those who worked in international settings, some may have done so on numerous occasions, either as exchange teachers or as temporary residents of those countries. Try talking to these people.

   a. How have exchange visits influenced their thinking about practice as well as their theories? What are the pros and cons of exchange visits, to other cultures or ethnic settings or to other kinds of schools and communities? What kinds of experiences are highly formative for those people who make exchanges to other cultures, countries, or settings?

3. As you have found out in the narrative accounts above, experienced teachers are not the only ones to experience a variety of cultural contexts. You can try writing to universities that have such programs, inquiring as to the experiences of emerging teachers who place themselves in different settings. Better still, try locating such people, asking them the same kinds of questions. But, given the plight of urban schools:

   a. How might you benefit in your preparation to teach by seeking out experiences in urban schools? How might these kinds of experiences shape your future? In what way is the kind of school in which you do the major amount of fieldwork likely to shape your thinking and your future?

Summary

In this chapter, we invited you to consider some of the broader dimensions related to your planning to be a teacher. We introduced some stories and ideas related to the influences of prior experiences on decisions and perspectives associated with becoming a teacher. We glanced at your developing understandings of the role complexity and multiplistic demands placed on those in the profession. In the next chapter, we keep a trained eye on the ideas you bring to teaching. We narrow our lens, however, and invite you to begin preparing for your field experiences by articulating some of the expectations, fantasies, and fears inspired by the thought of teaching real-life students in actual classrooms.

Recommended Readings

Aptekar, L. (1988). *Street children of Cali*. Durham: Duke University Press.

Ayers, W. (1989). *The good preschool teacher*. New York: Teachers College Press.

Britzman, D. P. (1991). *Practice makes practice: A critical study of learning to teach*. Albany, NY: State University of New York Press.

Clark, R. M. (1983). *Family life and school achievement: Why poor black children succeed or fail*. Chicago: University of Chicago Press.

Connelly, F. M., & Clandinin, D. J. (1988). *Teachers as curriculum planners*. New York: Teachers College Press.

Disbrowe, H. B. (1984). *A schoolman's odyssey*. London, Ontario: University of Western Ontario.

Eddy, E. M. (1969). *Becoming a teacher*. New York: Teachers College Press.

Freedman S. G. (1990). *Small victories: The real world of a teacher, her students and their high school*. New York: Harper & Row.

Goodlad, J. (Ed.). (1987). *Ecology of school renewal*. Chicago: University of Chicago Press.

Heck, S. F., & Williams, C. R. (1984). *The complex roles of the teacher*. New York: Teachers College Press.

Jackson, P. W. (1990). *Life in classrooms*. New York: Teachers College Press.

Kidder, T. (1989). *Among schoolchildren*. Boston, MA: Houghton Mifflin.

Kohl, H. (1982). *Insight: The substance and rewards of teaching*. Menlo Park, CA: Addison-Wesley.

Nehring, J. (1992). *The schools we have, the schools we want*. San Francisco, CA: Jossey-Bass.

Peshkin, A. (1986). *God's choice: The total world of a fundamentalist Christian school*. Chicago: University of Chicago Press.

Peshkin, A. (1991). *The color of strangers, the color of friends: The play of ethnicity in school and community*. Chicago: University of Chicago Press.

Ross, E. W., Cornett, J. W. & McCutcheon, G. (1992). *Teacher personal theorizing: Connecting curriculum practice theory and research*. Albany, NY: State University of New York Press.

Russell, T., & Munby, H. (Eds.). (1992). *Teachers and teaching: From classroom to reflection*. Bristol, PA: Falmer Press.

Schubert, W. H., & Ayers, W. C. (1992). *Teacher lore: Learning from our own experience*. New York: Longman.

Shack, S. (1965). *Armed with a primer: A Canadian teacher looks at children, schools, and parents*. Toronto, Ontario: McClelland & Stewart.

Sizer, T. (1984). *Horace's compromise: The dilemma of the American high school*. Boston, MA: Houghton Mifflin.

Sizer, T. (1992). *Horace's school: Redesigning the American high school*. Boston, MA: Houghton Mifflin.

Witherell, C., & Noddings N. (1991). *Stories lives tell: Narrative and dialogue in education*. New York: Teachers College Press.

CHAPTER 6

Expectations of Field Experiences and Dealing with Fantasies and Fears About Teaching

Uncertainty, doubt, anxiety, apprehension, curiosity, and excitement are but a few of the emotions that seem to take up residence in our very being as we prepare to enter new contexts or situations. These kinds of feelings are likely to be strong as you prepare for field experiences.

> *What can I expect? What do I expect? What do others expect of me? Are these various expectations realistic? What challenges will I face? Will I be able to overcome them? Will I experience success? Will I enjoy myself? Will others like me? Will I enjoy working in classrooms? How do I relate to the teachers (and other professionals) in the school? How will I learn from the experienced teachers? Will they expect me to be successful at everything I do? How long will it take to become an expert? Can I experiment with doing things differently? What will my friends think? What will my family think? Are my motivations to teach sound? Will students want to test me to the limits? How do I make sense of the many new experiences that I will have? Will I want to continue?*

Either privately or in conversation you probably have entertained these and other similar questions as you prepare for your reentry into classrooms and schools for your field experiences. Your perspective of learning environments is no longer that of a young school-aged person, and much is different.

Many preservice teachers experience considerable apprehension about returning to elementary and secondary schools after an absence of anywhere from a few years to a few decades. Some of you may have particular fears or anxieties rooted in your own experiences with teachers and students or of schools. Perhaps those fears are related to feelings of self-doubt or uncertainty. Chances are you also have certain hopes or images of what your field experience will be like. Rest assured that you are not alone. In this chapter we consider

- expectations of and for field experiences

- the ways various expectations of field experiences are realized or find resolution
- some of the fantasies and fears about teaching that are part of many preservice teachers' expectations of field experiences
- the realities of field experiences as they supersede fantasies and fears
- negotiating opportunities for practice and developing confidence in the field experience learning environment

Expectations, Fantasies, and Realities

Like most preservice teachers you entered a preservice teacher preparation program with high ideals and aspirations, impatient to become a full-fledged teacher. And you probably have waited eagerly with anticipation and enthusiasm for the opportunity to be part of "the real world" of classrooms and schools. As many may have told you, "Being in classrooms is where you will *really* learn about teaching." Having had years of experience in schools and having spent considerable time deliberating over your career choice, it is likely that you have formed a fairly clear image of the experience and contexts that await you. Once in the field, however, you may soon discover that what you *thought* it would be like, and what it *is* like, are quite different.

Shattered images and mild to severe shocks of reality often characterize preservice teachers' experiences of reentry to schools. It is not uncommon to hear comments from preservice teachers such as: "I don't remember the classroom being so . . . ;" "I thought it would be easy;" "I never realized how much was involved;" "I thought I knew what students were like;" "I thought all the kids would be like I was in school;" "I didn't realize schools were such busy places;" and "I assumed that . . ." We do not intend to frighten or deter you. Nor do we mean for you to be unprepared for the scope of emotional and rational responses that you or your peers may have on moving to the "other side of the teacher's desk." We do think it is important, however, to recognize the phenomenon of "shattered images." In so doing, you may better prepare yourself to resolve dilemmas associated with any discrepancies you may encounter between your fantasies about teaching and yourself as teacher, and the realities of classroom and school life. Often, such discrepancies can interfere with experiential learning. And, because you may have such limited time in the field as a preservice teacher, it is important that your experiences be as educative as possible.

Articulating your expectations and images prior to your reentry to schools, classrooms, and other places where learning takes place is one way to help prepare for the experience. In the following accounts, we are privy to the detailed, idealized images of working in classrooms that Priya, Deja, and Kevin articulated prior to their field experiences. Sandra thinks through one of her foremost concerns—how she will establish herself as a teacher. Patricia and Sadie illustrate how their images of classrooms and themselves as teachers clashed with the reality they experienced in the field. And, Colleen expresses her disillusionment with public school education after spending some time in classrooms. After reading their accounts we invite you to engage in further reflection and discussion by considering the questions that follow.

Narrative Accounts

As I envision myself as a teacher, I see myself standing in front of the classroom where the seats are arranged in a semicircle, allowing for the students to have a clear view of the chalkboard, and discussing with students the lesson I had prepared for the day. I see myself using plenty of visual aids, writing important points on the board, repeating myself several times, and waiting to receive responses or questions from the class. The classroom atmosphere is very comfortable; the room is full of bright objects, posters, and bulletin board ideas. The learning environment is, in many ways, created by the students, since they are the ones who need to have a pleasing atmosphere in which to learn and study. It is bright but not distracting, cozy enough so that the students do not feel that they are in a strange place, and intellectually stimulating so that they are always being exposed to something "educational."

There are several important ways in which I present myself. For instance, I do not want to be the type of teacher who stands in front of the classroom monotonously lecturing; rather, I want to be one who shares interesting knowledge with my students by providing many examples and stories, and encouraging as much student interaction as possible. As a teacher, I intend to be approachable and open-minded so that students are not afraid to ask questions or afraid that I may reject their thoughts. Being prepared and appearing confident are crucial. I am appropriately prepared and ready to present material in an organized manner, and able to respond to questions or doubts students may have about the material. I give my students the 100 per cent effort that I also expect from them. (Priya Nagaraju)

My aspiration is to take all the knowledge and experience I have compiled as a learner and utilize it so that I will fit my definition of a superior educator. As an elementary school teacher, I want to provide my students with a strong foundation that they can build on for the rest of their lives. I would like the students' experiences in my classroom to be so positive that they will come to love learning as much as I do. I want my students to feel my sincerity so they will be able to trust me to stimulate their intellectual growth and allow them to "take flight." I want to be an inspirational teacher who challenges children while giving them confidence in their ability to meet those challenges and find success. It is also important to me to create a relaxed, yet disciplined, atmosphere where the children can feel free to attempt to reach their full capacity. I want to avoid attaching a negative stigma to slower learners while allowing accelerated learners to advance at their pace. (Deja Dominguez)

Ideally, I see teaching as a variety of activities that convey to eager students an understanding of their universe. Attendance is not taken because the students enjoy class so much. Administrative details never take more than a moment. Disruptions and discipline problems are nonexistent because all of the students really want to learn. Frequent exploration activities are noisy and full of discussion, action, and interest. Lectures are quiet and filled with subdued anticipation but frequented with relevant, in-depth questions. Lively discussions and debates bring up intense ethical questions; and open, sensitive dialogue is common. The students see the teacher as a mentor, one helping them learn and learning along with them. The administration is super-supportive and takes an active interest in the teacher's programs. Supplies are readily available and materials virtually unlimited. Finally, at the end of the day, the teacher is tired from truly appreciated effort, happy with the day's accomplishments, enriched in knowledge, and emotionally uplifted by the enrichment of others and self. (Kevin Queen)

Regarding classroom management and discipline, I have my work cut out for me. I have never worried much about whether or not my students will like me. I am basically a friendly person. I do not think I could cover that up if I tried. So the difficulty will be in letting students know that I mean business about [establishing] an orderly classroom. I know from my own high school experiences how little can be accomplished in a rowdy class. I intend to start off my classes with a strict attitude and possibly a formal topic (such as grammar) to set a controlled tone. As the kids and I get to know each other, I hope that I will be able to loosen the reins but, in the meantime, it will be important to follow through with any threats and to isolate the kids who are attention grabbers.

Ideally, I will keep the students busy and interested so that they will have neither the time nor the inclination to misbehave. I cannot pretend that I know that any of my ideas will work in the classroom or that my approach is a good one. At this stage of my teaching career, virtually everything is a theory. I do know that I like kids and I like my subject areas. I have an open mind, and I want to work at improving myself—my teaching methods and knowledge of my subject areas. If there is one thing that I wish I knew now, it is how to enhance curiosity or a desire to learn. If I can [help students] want to learn and do their best in any situation, I will be one happy teacher. (Sandra Rene)

Back in September, when most of us were still starry-eyed with excitement, we all dreamed of changing the lives of hundreds of youngsters through our teaching techniques. We knew that if we only tried hard enough, we could make everyone learn everything they were supposed to learn in the time allotted for them to learn it in, and make all the children love us at the same time. We knew that we were going to stand in front of classrooms and silence the masses with our brilliant and creative ideas for learning how to count to ten, and that the cooperating teachers were going to break their arms patting us on the back, and the principals were going to offer us jobs the day after we graduated because there had never been a teacher like us before. (Patricia Long)

I always thought that teaching would be like a fairy tale. All the children would have nothing but respect for their teacher. They would sit there and listen when the teacher was talking. There would only be a few children who were troublemakers; the rest would be angels. They would want to be at school and they would really enjoy learning. I guess I was assuming that all the kids would be like I was in elementary school. I do not remember classrooms being as chaotic when I was younger. I thought it would be so easy to plan what you were going to do each day. I never realized how much would be involved in getting students motivated and keeping their attention. Obviously I was misled by my assumptions. (Sadie Rabinowitz)

At such an early age, school serves to shut down the finest qualities. Creativity and imagination are thwarted and controlled to fit into an adult's conception of appropriateness. It seems that children are naturally curious and delighted to make discoveries and be creative. Many adults end up striving to recreate or search for the very qualities that all of us have intuitively as children, and learn so early to hide. I have been surprised (shocked is better) to see what the implicit curriculum contains: "Don't help a classmate;" "Cover your work;" "Don't cry if you are hurt." I am hesitant about entering the field as a full-time teacher and continuing that process while thinking (hoping) that it doesn't have to be that way. (Colleen Presswood)

For Reflection and Discussion

1. The power of detailed visualization can be seen in Priya's expectations for her field experiences and roles in the classroom.
   a. How might having such a clear image of her classroom and teaching facilitate and constrain Priya's professional development through field experience?
2. Deja reveals many high ideals in thinking about herself as a teacher.
   a. When you reread Deja's account did you notice conflicting ideals? What problems might this cause Deja as she begins student teaching?
3. Kevin's idealized vision of teaching reveals some understanding of the challenges to be faced in the classroom.
   a. What problems might this cause Kevin when he encounters the reality of classrooms?
4. Sandra expresses common concerns about management and has formulated a "be tough" plan for the beginning of the school year.
   a. What atmosphere is likely to be established as a result of her decision? To what extent are silence and compliant behavior indicators of effective teaching? of learning?
   b. How might the commonly held perspective of "Don't smile until Christmas" play out in actual classroom pedagogy? How might the admonition be potentially dysfunctional for students and teachers? Will students respond with trust, for example, when the reins are loosened?
   c. Sandra writes that she is a "friendly person." Do her plans for teaching appear to conflict with her personality? What effect might this have on her success in carrying them out?
   d. How have your experiences with classroom discipline (or apparent lack of it) as a student informed your thinking about establishing your own authority as a teacher?
5. Patricia's account reveals the tempering quality that experience has upon idealism.
   a. Is it important for teachers like Patricia to retain their idealism? Why?
6. As Sadie discovered, memory of your own youthful experiences in a classroom can be misleading.
   a. Why might experience be a limited guide for individuals reentering classrooms as teachers?

Links with Research

Comparatively speaking, the research literature that examines expectations, fantasies, and realities associated with field experiences is scant. Most of the literature from which we draw focuses on general expectations for field experiences, reentry to schools, and influences of field experiences on preservice teachers' conceptual development. As such, it does not fit neatly into the sections within this chapter. Thus, because the work to which we refer comes from diverse areas of study, there is less obvious congruity between the text and the findings as presented here (and in the following *Links with Research*) than is found in most other chapters. Much more research needs to be done to better understand issues related to preservice teachers' expectations and the phenomenon we call "shattered images."

It is probably fair to assert that the research literature is not in agreement about the matter of expectations of the field experience triad—that is, the preservice teacher, cooperating teacher, and university supervisor. (See *Links with Research* in Chapters 8 and 9 for further research associated with the field experience triad.)

Research on expectations for field experiences reveals that preservice teachers' expectations are often different from university administrators and supervisory teacher educators. Whereas university teacher educators are seen to focus more on expectations related to applications of theory, cooperating and preservice teachers are more concerned with, for example, the development of self-confidence (Tittle, 1974; see also Brown & Hoover, 1990). Other studies, however, suggest there is not the same degree of coherence between cooperating teachers' and student teachers' perspectives (for example, Martin & Wood, 1984).

Frequently, preservice teachers have inappropriate or unrealistic expectations about the students they are to teach (Gomez & Comeaux, 1990; Kagan, 1992), perhaps a result of limited knowledge of those students (Florio-Ruane & Lensmire, 1990). For many, therefore, reentry to schools delivers a mild to severe "reality shock" (Gaede, 1978)—when preservice teachers find that their images of students, teachers, and schools are inappropriate. Some of these discrepancies rest in a commonly held perception that the students they will encounter will be like *they* were as students (Hollingsworth, 1989; Knowles & Holt-Reynolds, 1991). Coupled with entering viewpoints about what is needed to become a teacher, distorted perspectives about students have some bearing on the wide gap between expectations and reality that many preservice teachers encounter as they enter schools again.

Preservice teachers experience bouts of low self-confidence or even fluctuations in mood (Goldhammer, 1969). They anticipate failure or feel like they are failing in their teaching efforts despite initially high expectations. A student teacher who anticipates failure will have more difficulty noticing his or her accomplishments; one who is tired, facing crises in the classroom, or anxious is less likely to notice the motivational needs of students (see also, Knowles & Skrobola, 1992).

For some preservice teachers reality shock is terminal; they end their teaching careers before they have a chance to begin (Knowles & Hoefler, 1989; Knowles & Sudzina, 1991); therefore, as Weinstein (1988) points out, there is a need to help preservice teachers bridge this reality gap. Although discrepancies between expectations and realities do not necessarily lead to failure or career exit, they do impede the learning to teach process. Because such discrepancies create barriers to seeing things in new or different ways, this often leads to less than optimum outcomes from field experiences (see Kagan, 1992).

Related to reality shock, disillusionment with the profession probably comes about as individuals become cognizant about the state of affairs in schools. Disillusionment can be caused by events within field experiences (see Poirier, 1992) or developed from perspectives gained at more general levels of experience (Cole, 1985; Kagan, 1992). In Cole's study preservice teachers' disillusionment was not so much grounded in unsuccessful teaching practice as it was in discoveries about teachers' work. Some student teachers found that they were at odds with the reality of the work and role of teacher—they did not like elements of the profession they were about to enter.

Poirier (1992), reflecting on her own practicum experience, highlights another source of disillusionment—the experience of loss of power:

> My new-found empowerment and power in my life (created by a congealing vision of teaching, its value and hope), was contrary to this practicum experience which told me I was merely naive and unrealistic. My journal entries pondered the distorted realism of established teachers as I struggled to understand and felt my power (my ability to act) slipping away (p. 87).

In making sense of their research into preservice teachers' knowledge growth, Mcneely and Mertz (1990) suggest that, for preservice teachers in their study, disillusionment could be related to idealized notions of students and classrooms communicated during course work. Whether preservice teachers' misconceptions of the work of teachers and students and their cultures rest in personal experience or university course work, or both, the outcomes are potentially dysfunctional and can lead to mis-educative experiences in field experiences, representing something akin to the "pitfalls of experience" that Feiman-Nemser and Buchmann (1983) talk about.

In summary, going into their field experiences (either student teaching or various forms of practica) most preservice teachers have hopes, images, and expectations that all too often are quickly shattered by exposure to certain realities of schools, classrooms, and teaching. Dilemmas and difficulties often arise, sometimes leading to failure, when preservice teachers' preconceived ideals or internalized images of teachers, teaching, and schools do not match what they encounter. Repercussions less extreme than failure serve to dampen enthusiasm or wipe the sheen from the looking glass.

Research Activities

1. Expectations of field experiences are usually of two kinds: those that are placed on us by others and those we place on ourselves. Both are important to understand, but sometimes those not of our own making are the easiest to get a handle on. We will start with expectations placed on us by others because often they are in written form (although their most important meanings may be implicit) as in a prepared "Handbook for Field Experiences." The following are some questions that may suggest to you some explicit activities and help clarify some of your thinking about expectations associated with your field experience placement.

a. Who is responsible for developing external expectations for your activities in schools and other learning communities? What are those expectations, and are they communicated directly to you? What are the underlying assumptions associated with those expectations?

b. Who is responsible for assisting you to successfully negotiate and complete your field experiences? What is their role? Do they evaluate you? What kinds of evaluation practices are used by others for making sense of and gauging the success of your field placement experiences?

c. How do other student teachers, your immediate peers, and those ahead of you in the teacher certification program in which you are participating, talk about the expectations of professors, university supervisors, and cooperating teachers? Are there discrepancies between explicitly and implicitly stated expectations of these teacher educators, and, where are they centered? To what extent, if at all, have other preservice teachers been confused by the expectations of others? Why?

2. Having clarified some of the expectations that others place on you as you prepare to enter the site of your field experiences puts you in a good position to turn the lens on yourself.

a. What are *your* expectations in terms of: relationships with students and teachers, with university supervisors, with other learning community faculty and staff, and with parents and the community; teaching and instructional opportunities; broader learning community involvement; developing socio-political perspectives about schools; and, in terms of opportunities for general professional development and growth through reflexive practice and inquiry?

b. Try writing a summary of *your* expectations and then ask yourself whether these expectations are reasonable, given the time and energy you have available. You may want to talk in detail about your expectations to university- and school-based teacher educators to gauge their reactions to your thinking.

c. Knowing the purposes of field experiences and their place within a teacher education program also will help you put your expectations into perspective. What is the link between *your* expectations for field experience and the purposes of field experiences as articulated by your professional preparation program?

3. Think back to the short time ago when you entered the formal preparation program.

a. What were your initial intentions and expectations? Now that you are much more informed about becoming a teacher, in what ways have your expectations changed? Why have they changed? Where do your expectations for field experiences overlap with those who guide your teacher education program? Where do they not overlap? Why? Are *your* expectations reasonable? How do your expectations match those of the teacher educators with whom you work?

4. One other side to the question of expectations is worth checking out. Sometimes we find that preservice teachers working in schools are constrained by the expectations of family and friends.

a. Consider the following questions in light of any new understandings about programmatic and self expectations. What expectations do family and friends have for you in relation to your preparation program? Are *their* expectations useful in framing *your* professional development? To what extent are these expectations at odds with those based on programmatic and individual needs?

b. Given that there are bound to be discrepancies among the various expectations you are trying to meet, try talking frankly to family and friends explaining the expressed programmatic expectations for field experiences as well as your own expectations, even your phobias and fears. In doing so, give attention to matters of time, energy, and commitment. (For many, if not most, preservice teachers the period in the field exceeds their imagination in terms of energy required. This is difficult to predict and plan for.)

5. Although we have endeavored to address aspects of the reality of field experiences, so far we have not addressed the fantasies associated with entering schools and becoming a teacher. Like the preservice teachers whose accounts you have just read, chances are that you also have idealized images of teaching and being a teacher. And, like them, it is likely that the fantasies you hold rest in the way you conceptualize yourself as teacher. Making explicit your idealized image about your teaching and field experience will help you prepare for and understand your classroom experiences.

a. Picture yourself as a teacher in a classroom setting or other educational context. Let the image fill out and take shape until you can pick out details of the experience including sights, sounds, and smells. Take a few minutes to record your image on paper through words and/or pictures. Be as detailed as you can. Look back over your description. What did you discover?

6. As you are probably beginning to realize, there is a fine line between fantasies and phobias when planning to reenter the classroom. Perhaps you are one of those who manages to hold an array of fears and fantasies about entering classrooms. Here, then, are some issues to consider:

a. Does your image of yourself as teacher match the way others see you? Why? Where are the discrepancies?

b. To what extent is your image grounded in realistic conceptions of your roles as teacher or of the state of schools and classrooms?

c. In what ways is your image either exaggerated, unrealistic, or based upon incomplete or inadequate information? Identify the origins that have led you to think the way you do. To help you with this you may want to reread Chapters 2 and 3.

Fears and Emerging Confidence

Fear of the unknown is as commonplace within the teaching profession as it is anywhere else. And, as with any new challenge we face, thoughts of beginning teaching are, not surprisingly, replete with self-doubt and uncertainties. It is natural to be hesitant. After all, you have made a decision to make the profession of teaching your career. You have a lot invested—money, time, energy, commitment, and emotions. In your personal investment, you have probably taken some steps in faith based on the belief that you can be a teacher. Further, you are about to undertake a major responsibility—the education of tomorrow's citizens. No doubt, bubbling below the surface of your consciousness are several hidden doubts and fears. As you will discover on reading the narrative accounts that follow, concerns and questions like yours are fairly typical.

Robert begins by disclosing some of his hidden fears and apprehensions about teaching, and revealing a sense of how his expectations were and were not realized when he entered the classroom for the first time in many years. Self-doubt and uncertainty imbue Steve's thoughts as he worries over what it will be like to be a teacher. Sara and Patricia present us with a lengthy list that reflects some of their fears and uncertainties. As Sara demonstrates, it is often the case that anxieties and self-doubt are soon alleviated once you are in the situation. For her, confidence emerged with experiences of success in the classroom. As Patricia acknowledges, "a good deal more time in front of the classroom" is likely to help resolve some of the dilemmas. Perhaps you better relate to Madeleine's situation. It may be that you have no qualms about beginning teaching. You will just have to wait and see what emerges from experience and in the meantime, consider others' experiences.

Dealing with diversity in the classroom, having sufficient knowledge of subject matter, getting to know and understand the students, establishing oneself as a teacher—in short, feeling successful—are some of the many preoccupying concerns of preservice and beginning teachers. Tracy worries about her ability to understand students from cultural groups different from her own and recognizes her need for assistance in this area. Three entries from Leila's journal depict other commonly held concerns. As Leila and Keri recognize, with time and appropriate experience, worries dissolve as confidence and comfort level increase.

Narrative Accounts

When it was mentioned at the beginning of the year that we would be out in the schools in two weeks, I was petrified. Why? This first appearance in a class had been postponed so long that I had come to view its approach with ever-increasing dread. As I was thinking about becoming a teacher, I envisioned a gradual introduction to actual teaching practice but, for the last 18 months of teacher preparation, I have functioned as a student the entire time and never once as a teacher. Now, all of a sudden, I am supposed to teach. Nothing I have studied the last 18 months has prepared me to teach; instead, it has trained me to sit and take notes, which is very different from teaching. I looked forward to teaching but the 18 months of "studenting" kind of dulled that desire.

In studying teaching, you become aware of more and more ways of doing it wrong, which is hardly conducive to building the confidence necessary to stand in front of a group and perform. If I am convinced that I am scared of student teaching then, when the time rolls around to do it, I will be scared. If I am convinced that people do not like me and that they are unfriendly, then I will act in ways that will turn my expectations into reality. What was the basis of my fear of student teaching? Why was I so scared to do it? One, I did not want to do it—it was someone else's idea and I was being forced to do it against my will. I was being victimized. Two, I felt inadequate to the task—I was questioning my abilities, and

I was sure I would feel uncomfortable, would stumble, and would feel humiliated. Three, I felt the students would not like me.

How do these items relate to my fear of teaching? I had unrealistically high expectations. If you see yourself in your mind's eye as a great orator casting one pearl of wisdom after another at the feet of eager students, you have set the stage for FEAR. Why? One, your role will shrink in the real situation and you will feel inadequate. Two, when the students act bored instead of enthralled, you will be mad at yourself and at them.

Well, tomorrow is my forty-second birthday, September 18. What a way to celebrate—by going into the alien environment of Glen View for the first time. Can you believe it, we are supposed to meet there at 7:15 A.M.—what a god-awful time! I wonder if I will get lost. I wonder if my cooperating teachers will like me.

Like so many things in life, my first experience at Glen View was: not as frightening as I anticipated; not as big a deal as I anticipated; and, not as demanding as anticipated. So, as with almost everything that we look forward to in life, my first day at Glen View was both a relief and a disappointment. Almost all events that loom large on the horizon turn out the same way. What is it they say? "Expectation always exceeds realization." (Robert Marigold)

Until the show begins, I can simply mull over my doubts and hopes—of which I have ample amounts. Although I am very conscious of a great and impending task, I am not dwelling on it much. Either that is because I am avoiding the unpleasant or because I simply cannot project into the unknown. The latter is probably the case, as I feel basically confident that I will succeed at my new career. With time, I will certainly gain proficiency and control—the lack of which now worries me—but will I enjoy teaching? I know I can cope with the academic demands of the job, but what of the social aspects? I am a very solitary person entering a people-oriented career. But much more to the point is the extent to which my own very checkered schooling will help or hinder me. It has been 20 years [since I was in schools], yet I still stumble around with the emotional baggage from those years. Will it help me empathize with kids "at risk," or will I rebelliously butt my head against the bureaucratic structures of the job? Well, time will tell.

After some thought, I realized part of my confusion stems from taking university ideals too literally. After years of being told to never use worksheets, eschew the test, and be novel, innovative, and fascinating at all times, I concluded that my planning paralysis was self-induced. If I am feeling overwhelmed, it is with good reason. I have never taught a day in my life. It has been 20 years since I studied geography, history, and reading in school. I am worried about management, puzzled by grading, and confused by the working of schools. And then, being the perfectionist that I am, I expect to stand up and dazzle their little minds with original thoughts. It is time to be realistic—just playing it by the book will be a feat at first. Take it a step at a time. Make it manageable. The texts come with a full set of teacher aids, activities, and tests. Use them. I know that is called "being spoon fed." For a veteran there would be no excuse but, for a novice, accept the help. I can deviate a little at a time as I learn my subject and ropes of classroom teaching. (Steve Bruno)

There was a period in the semester when I was as sure that teaching was not for me as I was sure, not two months earlier, that it was the only thing for me. I thought myself too passive to lead a functional discussion, let alone a functional classroom. I thought myself too quiet to make keeping control feasible. I thought myself too afraid to take the challenge and see, but I thought myself too concerned about the students and our system of education to flee on account of the other personal factors. I wanted so badly for my compassion and insight about the students to compensate for my lack of verbal confidence. I was in a state of utter question and confusion about my own capabilities and felt pressed to make conclusions for the sake of my sanity and future plans.

I suppose a common element of fear is lack of knowledge in areas that students may question, as well as simply the fear of failing. I had such high expectations in the beginning that these insecurities would be magically cured. I later realized that I was convinced that I had failed before I had even attempted. It must have been my first lesson that heightened my outlook and brought back a little hope. The lesson did not go extremely smoothly, and it was not unbelievably enriching. But there was a lot of discussion between the group and me. I felt excited to be exposing them to a style with which I am comfortable, and they showed enthusiasm and interest in my approach. (Sara Field)

I am not so sure that I am comfortable with the role of teacher yet. I think I will have to spend a good deal more time in front of the classroom before I feel totally at ease. I have some very big faults that I hope I will be able to overcome. First and foremost is my inability to direct the students. I would much rather let the children go their chosen ways than force them to sit quietly and work on something that does not interest them. I have problems coming up with creative ideas on how to teach the children. I am almost afraid my ideas will not be acceptable. Another thing I sometimes wonder about is how teachers stay uninvolved with their students on an emotional level. I know that teachers do not remove themselves totally and that they must feel something when they hear of a difficult home situation or a tragedy in a student's family, but when I hear of something tragic (like when I found out that one of my little boys had been sexually abused) I just want to throw my arms around them and take them home with me at night. (Patricia Long)

When I think of teaching, I get worried. Before this semester, I was full of confidence; I had no qualms about teaching. I felt I could do it and be good at it. Now, however, after a semester in an elementary school, I get a little uneasy at the thought of teaching. I never became comfortable in Ms. Samson's class. I never felt at ease or like I belonged. I began to worry that it might be like that in my own classroom. I realized this feeling of discomfort probably stemmed from the fact that it was not my class; yet, even with this rationalization, the worry remained. Perhaps it could be the fact that I am not as far away from [being a member of] the teaching profession as I was last September, and I am starting to get a little scared. I just hope I can shake this feeling. (Madeleine Lamb)

After deciding how I want to act as a teacher, I realize that something is holding me back from having full confidence in my teaching. [I am wondering about] the issue of diversity in the classroom. I grew up in a very racially homogeneous suburb where I was rarely exposed to races other than my own. My teachers dealt with students who were all from fairly similar backgrounds. I don't remember the topic of race ever being discussed in any of my classes. Unfortunately, I don't believe I know how to go about understanding people from other races. I think I would be very scared going into a school to teach where the students were not from the same kind of background as my own. I don't mean that I would be scared of what they might do to me. I worry that I would not be able to relate to their needs and abilities. At this point I don't have the knowledge base to do so. I am very glad that this issue is one of importance in our teacher education program because I hope to gain some new insight that would help me teach those not like myself. I am fairly certain that some time in my future the situation will come up that I will teach in a racially diverse classroom, and I know that I need to prepare for that time. (Tracy Dell)

I gave my first lesson today. I taught third and fourth periods. I was anxious because I did not have any idea of how it was going to go. Although I did not do too badly, there is a lot of room for improvement. I was so much concerned with having control over the class, I did not cover the subject as well as I wanted to. I was not concentrating on the subject matter as much as I was focusing on the kids and their reactions. I did much better the second period, giving the same lesson to another group of students. I think I was more relaxed and the novelty of standing in front of a class was to some extent gone.

I think it will take me a little while to get used to the school scene and to relax. When I reach that stage I will be more capable of creating an environment in which students can really learn. Then, I can be more creative and make the subject matter more relevant to students' lives, more interesting, and more challenging. I was perhaps too strict today. I just felt like I had to establish myself as a teacher and not just a teacher's helper. . . .

I gave three lessons today in biology and Spanish. I felt good about them. I think I did better than the first lesson I gave last week. I was more relaxed. I now know that I will be okay. I did not have any discipline problems even though in all classes there were some rowdy kids. They are nice kids; they were just noisy. I must be getting used to the level of noise in schools too. Basically, I did not have any problems. . . .

Now that I have gotten over the fear of getting in front of a class, or the anxiety of how they might react, the big question is how to get students interested. Because I have only been in the school for two days, it is hard to figure out what their interests are or how they think and what they think about. It will be easier, I think, in January when I have the class to myself every day. Then, I can plan the whole thing myself and not just have to fit in individual lessons within the teacher's curriculum. (Leila Muniroui)

I was terribly frightened to start this practicum. I thought that maybe I should not have gone into teaching. Or, I thought that I would be devoured by my students, or that I was not knowledgeable in my subject areas. All of these thoughts plagued me at the beginning of the term. Reading [about beginning teaching] helped me understand that all first year teachers have fears like these to some degree. Besides that, it gave me ideas about teaching strategies so that I could feel more secure about that. Discussions about the beginning teacher readings reassured me that I have a lot of the same beliefs as others. Class observations provided me with the advantage of getting to know some of the students and assured me that they are not as frightful as I supposed them to be. In fact, they seemed to accept me and respect me.

Teaching a cluster of six lessons was the best ego booster of all. The students loved my newfound techniques and the subjects I wanted them to explore. I know that a lot of the excitement was just because of the change of pace, but it made me feel good nevertheless. It ultimately comforted me that I was in the "right place"—that I did want to be a teacher after all. As long as I do not let up on my standards for myself and what I want to do, I do not see why I cannot have an overall successful experience student teaching even when I have a few bad experiences. I am confident now. (Keri Hong)

For Reflection and Discussion

1. Robert expresses several fears and anxieties common to many preservice teachers.
    a. How did he manage those anxieties? How and to what extent did he use writing to help manage his anxieties? What are other ways he may have worked through his feelings?
    b. How did making his implicit fears explicit help Robert prepare for his first day as a preservice teacher? Why did it appear that making his fears explicit restored some confidence?
2. Steve acknowledges that teaching involves a lot of work. He writes that he will "accept the help" that comes with textbooks. Planning to rely on sources other than himself reduces some of the fears associated with managing the workload of lesson planning and presentation.
    a. What other approaches could Steve have taken to address the fear of an overwhelming workload?
    b. What are the advantages of tapping into material that has already been "tested?" Are there disadvantages inherent in Steve's developing a reliance upon "packaged" curriculum, units of work, and lessons?
    c. To what extent should beginning teachers like Steve seek support from commercial texts and other resources in developing their practice?
3. Sara and Patricia express concern about their lack of assertiveness. Sara feels that she is too passive and quiet to control a classroom, and Patricia would rather let students direct themselves "than force them to sit quietly and work on something that does not interest them." Also, they express an awareness of their emotional commitment to students.
    a. To what extent might there be gender issues at play in their thinking? For example, to what extent is an urge to nurture and care a feminine trait? Is it a strength or potential problem?
    b. Assuming that the basis of their thinking is rooted in particular pedagogies, what might be their pedagogies?
4. Sara and Patricia assert that more practice will help them gain confidence. Sara recalls that the first lesson she taught was not smooth or "unbelievably enriching," but it restored her hope and improved her outlook about herself as a teacher.
    a. How did their adjustment of expectations influence their perceptions of failure or success?
5. Tracy recognizes that her background had ill-prepared her to teach culturally diverse students.

  a. How might Tracy have prepared herself to address the lack of experience or familiarity with minority groups?

  b. To what extent might Tracy's fears be the result of her increased understanding about schools and students?

Links with Research

Like the previous discussion of research pertaining to the expectations, fantasies, and realities of teaching there is not a large body of literature on fears and emerging confidence of preservice teachers. That preservice teachers in field placements feel considerable pressure to perform to the satisfaction of those around them (such as mentors or cooperating teachers, and university supervisors) is well documented (see for example, Guyton & McIntyre, 1990; Zeichner & Gore, 1990). And this, being one of the most powerful socialization factors in preservice teacher preparation, can be disconcerting to preservice teachers.

Field experiences can be sufficiently stressful to lead individuals to rethink their suitability for the profession. A small percentage of prospective teachers counsel themselves out of preparation programs for a variety of reasons, including their perceived potential for and actual poor performance in field placements (Guyton & McIntyre, 1990; Knowles & Sudzina, 1991; see also, Knowles & Hoefler, 1989). Even the anticipation of teaching a particular subject matter may cause high levels of anxiety, as was evident in a study of elementary preservice teachers about to teach science (Westerback, 1982). Further, insecurities about subject matter knowledge (and its translation into pedagogical subject matter knowledge) are likely to result in compensatory approaches to teaching such as over-reliance on textbooks and on memories of their own schooling—teaching as they were taught (see Feiman-Nemser & Buchmann, 1983, 1987). Preservice teachers like this are likely to lack confidence in their teaching (Borko, 1989).

Borko (1985) and her colleagues (for example, Borko, Lalik, & Tomchin, 1987) have noticed that student teachers considered to be "weak" have relatively narrow conceptions of planning and developing curriculum. When teaching, preservice teachers with less developed notions of planning are less able to adjust to changing needs within the classroom. As a result, these individuals perceive their lessons as unsuccessful and incongruous with their conceptions of "good" teaching. (This perspective is also supported by research into student teachers who fail to meet institutional expectations for their period of practice. [See, Knowles & Skrobola, 1992; Knowles & Sudzina, 1991]). As Aitken and Mildon (1991) and Knowles (1992) report, personal histories or biographies have an important influence on the outcomes of practica experiences. Aitken and Mildon note that those who entered field experiences with images of teaching and teachers more congruent with the realities of classrooms were able to adjust and learn from the problems they encountered.

Student teachers typically witness a growing confidence in their perceived abilities to teach as they become less concerned about themselves and more aware of the complex influences of the classroom (for example, Pigge & Marso, 1989; see also, Caruso, 1977; Sacks & Harrington, 1982). As this happens, and as they begin to make sense of their experiences, conceptual changes are likely to occur, particularly about views of themselves as teachers, and their notions of curriculum and instruction (Shapiro, 1991). Moreover, there is typically an ebb and flow to those perceptions (McIntyre, 1983).

One downside to this emerging confidence is that often it is accompanied with shifts towards more custodial, controlling practices (Hoy & Woolfolk, 1990; Lacey, 1977). Nevertheless, as Applegate (1986) notes, many preservice teachers "perceive field experiences as an opportunity to learn about themselves, to explore career decisions, to test their confidence, and to assess their skill levels" (p. 29). Although Applegate notes the tentative relationship between notions of confidence and performance, preservice teachers seem to relate success in their teaching to feelings of confidence.

Because beginning and experienced teachers alike tend to regard the capstone field experience of student teaching as the most valuable component of their professional preparation to teach (Appleberry, 1976; Guyton & McIntyre, 1990), the probability is that most view the experience as successful. Statistics also give evidence that, for a variety of reasons, few preservice teachers fail to succeed in the final practicum (Johnson & Yates, 1982; Koehler, 1984), a point to which we will return in Chapter 11, *Links with Research.*

Research Activities

1. Exploration of the elements of your emotions engendered in anticipation of working in schools is energy well spent. A degree of apprehension is probably useful because it may urge you to pay careful attention to the field experience journey on which you are about to embark. But, sometimes, that apprehension can weigh down on you. Consider the following scenarios and questions as a basis for some personal explorations and research activities into your apprehensions and fears.

   a. Think about the times you are a little tentative or even fearful about anticipated responsibilities within any kind of public or private setting connected to family, school, or work contexts. What is at the heart of your emotions? Where do these apprehensions or fears rest? Are they imbedded, for example, in the newness of the context, in the role or roles you may play, or in the response of other individuals within the context?

   b. How do you typically work through such emotions? When, after your initial exposure to these kinds of emotional situations, do you begin to feel more relaxed and less fearful or apprehensive? Is there a recognizable pattern or time frame to the cycle of these emotions and their dissipation?

   c. What have you learned about yourself and feelings of fear and apprehension?

2. You may want to explore your fears or apprehensions a step further. Are they imbedded in general or specific concerns?

   a. General concerns may not be directly related to the field placements you are about to enter. They are likely to be located in more general or relatively undefined apprehensions about becoming a teacher. For example, you may be concerned about whether teaching is for you or whether your motives for teaching are grounded in sound reasoning. Perhaps you are concerned about your "suitability for teaching" or have worries about your personality being accepted by students. If you have some broad and deep-seated concerns, try exploring your underlying intentions and purposes for becoming a teacher. Some useful activities and tools to help you resolve these kinds of feelings are found in the previous chapters, especially Chapters 2 and 3.

b. Specific concerns are those which emerge directly from elements of your proposed placement and its resulting responsibilities. Such concerns may rest in: your ability to handle the subject matter; some aspect of your physical appearance or the quality, style, and care of your clothing; the relationship you are about to develop with your mentor or cooperating teacher; your ability to navigate the route to the school and the school itself; your financial resources and ability to make ends meet when you have reduced opportunities to work; and, aspects associated with the physical site of the placement itself. It may be helpful to take a few minutes to create a list of everything that is causing you concern at this point in your preparation. Because it is likely that you are not alone in your concerns, compare your list and discuss these concerns with one or more of your colleagues or peers.

c. It also may be helpful to consider the roots of your concerns. Some may be deep-seated; others may be due to "anticipation anxiety." Some may be alleviated easily; others may require further explanation. Here are some questions for you to consider.

d. In what are your fears and apprehensions grounded? What is the place of previous experiences in your concerns? Do others around you share the same apprehensions? Have these fears and apprehensions in your thinking been observed by teacher educators or mentors with whom you work? If so, how have they suggested you try to resolve these feelings? Do your peers have similar concerns? If so, how have they tried to resolve those concerns? Is resolution of your feelings necessary for you to proceed successfully?

3. The chances are that some of your peers, or certainly preservice teachers preceding you in the same program, have previously participated in the site of your field placement. Perhaps they have even worked in the same classroom with the same cooperating teacher. Because of their knowledge of the setting you are about to enter they are a valuable resource for you. Seek them out. Also, talk with several people who work at the learning site to which you are assigned. Talk with others who have been involved there in some capacity—as preservice or student teachers, parents, or past teachers, administrators, or staff. Follow up on any potentially useful leads. Given the concerns mentioned in the previous activity and those raised in the narrative accounts written by the preservice teachers in anticipation of their reentering schools as professionals, the following questions deserve serious and perhaps even sustained attention as you prepare for your field placement.

a. What do you know and what do you not know about the placement? How can you understand more about what is presently unknown? Who are the key personnel associated with your placement, and what do they expect of you? What beliefs or practices are they renowned for holding? How can you find out about the roles and responsibilities of these key personnel? What are their responsibilities to you and to their institutions—school and university? Who is responsible for making summary assessments of your performance?

b. What are some of the qualities for which the learning environment is renowned? What have others who have visited the site said about the classroom and institutional climates? What are some typical daily activities within the institution as a whole and of the teachers who teach there?

4. How do you see yourself as a teacher? You have probably envisioned yourself in a teaching role many times. Try the following activity to bring your vision into sharper focus and to apply your understanding of teaching to yourself.

   a. Take some time and visualize yourself in a teaching situation as an idealized self. Allow your ideals to become reality within your vision of yourself as a future teacher. Include such detail as your clothing, hairstyle, gestures, and facial expressions to clarify the image. Envision yourself performing various teacher tasks as this best self. While the image is fresh commit it to paper by writing about it in a descriptive fashion.

   b. Use the same technique to think about a dreaded outcome. Think about behaviors that you dread adopting for yourself and hope to avoid. Write about this worst case scenario in a descriptive fashion.

Your development as a teacher can be self directed as you encounter elements of your "possible selves" and decide to either accept or reject them.

Summary

In this chapter, we began with a discussion of the expectations, fantasies, and realities associated with entering field experiences. We encouraged you to think about articulating your expectations as you reentered schools and classrooms to work with experienced teachers because, by so doing, you will likely develop appropriate and empowering perspectives on your emerging practice. We also invited you to consider ways to deal with any fears associated with moving into schools while encouraging you to find ways to acknowledge your emerging confidence. Having raised for discussion the potential of reality shock as you move into a period of practice in school, in the following chapter we offer ways to counteract the possibility of such shock. We lay open some avenues by which you can begin to understand the nature and complexity of schools as places of work and learning from a new perspective—the other side of the teacher's desk. We invite you to explore the many facets of schools and classrooms as a way of understanding more completely teachers' work and institutional environments.

Recommended Readings

Clandinin, D. J. (1986). *Classroom practice: Teacher images in action.* East Sussex, UK: Falmer Press.

Fedullo, M. (1992). *Light of the feather.* New York: William Morrow.

Ferri, B., & Aglio, M. (1990). *I'm not alone: Teacher talk, teacher buddying.* Mississauga, Ontario: Peel Board of Education.

Hunt, D. E. (1987). *Beginning with ourselves: In theory, practice and human affairs.* Cambridge, MA/Toronto, Ontario: Brookline Books/OISE Press.

Jersild, A. T. (1955). *When teachers face themselves.* New York: Teachers College Press.

Kobrin, D. (1992). *In there with the kids: Teaching in today's classrooms.* Boston: Houghton Mifflin.

Kohl, H. (1984). *Growing minds: On becoming a teacher.* New York: Harper & Row.

Troyna, B., & Hatcher, R. (1992). *Racism in children's lives: A study of mainly-white primary schools.* London, UK: Routledge.

CHAPTER 7

Becoming Reacquainted with Schools

Anthropologists who immerse themselves in the study of people and cultural groups have a rule of thumb that guides their work. As they enter a "new" context, intending to come to know it in a comprehensive way, they strive to "make the familiar strange." This phrase describes their attempts to see even common, everyday things as if for the first time. Such a perspective is based on the recognition and understanding that humans view situations through personal lenses that provide a shortsighted perspective and that we need to break free from those myopic tendencies. An explicit effort to see things more broadly and clearly aids in understanding a particular context in its complexity. It also helps us recognize that for every event and circumstance there are multiple perspectives. Making the familiar strange, or seeing things through new lenses, is no easy task; the more familiar, the more difficult it is to accomplish. For anthropologists, and for yourself as a preservice teacher, it may well be easier to tackle the task of understanding a foreign culture than it is to understand that which is familiar.

Regardless of where in the world your familiarity with schools is rooted, schools *are* familiar places. Collectively we have worked in or visited many schools in North America as well as in developing countries. Schools, regardless of location, tend to look more similar than different. When you walk into a building called "school," no matter where you are in the world, you instantly know that it is a place where teachers teach and students learn. There are certain qualities and forms that are instantly recognizable: large numbers of children in a room or rooms with usually one adult; dialogue between adults and children, especially questioning and directing of children by adults; rooms configured with arrangements of seats or desks; a place for teachers and students to write on the wall, usually a chalkboard; perhaps a place called "Principal's Office" or "Head Teacher's Office;" and a central congregating area or an outside space where children play. Most schools give evidence of the value placed on book learning, and textbook usage is usually visible, as may be a book storeroom or library.

For most of us, school played a central role in our lives throughout our formative years and beyond. As a child and adolescent you probably devoted more of your waking hours to school, either in attendance or engaged in school-related activities, than to anything else (although we are often told that television occupies a greater amount of children's time). Chances are you spent more time with your teachers, collectively, than with most of your family members. If you have or have had parental responsibilities you know schools in another way. You have conversed with teachers, watched your children in extracurricular activities, and attended parent-teacher meetings of various kinds. Perhaps you have even volunteered to participate in parent committees or other groups, helped out on field trips, or spent time assisting in classrooms or libraries. You are likely to know that school has a large place in your children's daily activities and thinking. Those who have spent time in teaching-related roles have yet another insider's view of students and their learning; you may have spent time tutoring or talking to students in your child's class.

We all know schools. Although some of you have viewed schools through many different lenses at different times in your lives, mainly you know schools from a student's perspective. Your field experiences will provide opportunities to see schools in a different way—through a preservice teacher's eyes. You will become reacquainted with contexts that may seem at once familiar and strange. For some of you, the faintest hint of an aroma will release a flood of memories, tumbling you back in time; cafeterias and special purpose rooms like those for various art media, crafts, vocational preparation, family studies or home economics, music, science laboratories, and gymnasia (with their change facilities) may trigger your olfactory nerve. For others, the sights and sounds of gymnasia and changing facilities, "ordinary" classrooms, cafeterias, principals' offices, corridors and lockers will spark "instant replays" of events from school days. Some of you may even trip into the past at the sight of a student being reprimanded by a teacher or principal. Perhaps recognizing places where students "hang out" or noticing the playing fields and play equipment will spark memories. You may even feel apprehensive about some aspects of schools. For example, for those of you who attended large high schools, noisy, writhing, and sweaty bodies shoving in crowded corridors may be intimidating places where, as students, you treaded cautiously. Or, perhaps you attended a small school and large institutions are beyond your realm of experience. How will you view these various places, smells, sights, and sounds? Whatever your reaction, one thing is certain—schools are places where memories and experiences are brought to the fore again.

Not everyone becoming a teacher in North America has experienced North American schools as a student. The school or other place of learning you are about to enter, therefore, may have new and powerful meanings for some of you. It may be, for example, that nothing immediately obvious about the culture of the school or the teachers is consistent with your experience, and it is the blatant lack of familiarity that draws your attention. Regardless, as preservice teachers, you all have one thing in common. For the first time, as emerging professionals, you will experience schools and classrooms from the teacher's side of the desk. The view from there is quite different.

In this chapter we focus on some of the new perspectives from which you will view schools. Beginning once again with a reflection on past experiences, we invite you to think about

- the perspectives with which you will reenter school contexts
- the school as a place of work, a place having a central role in the community, and whose influence is felt in various societal contexts
- students, especially the diversity comprising today's classrooms and the related demands placed on classroom teachers

Acknowledging the Influences of Personal Past Experiences of Schooling

George Kelly, a noted American psychologist and proponent of individualism, coined a phrase to describe the sometimes rigid nature of our perceptual boundaries. He diagnosed those unable or unwilling to break out of established conceptual molds to develop new perspectives as having "hardening of the categories" (Kelly, 1955) Conceptual molds are formed over time and with experience, and it is not always easy to recast or acquire new perspectives. We know, however, that to continually broaden our perspectives—to learn—we need to do just that; we need to soften the boundaries of our thinking. In the accounts that follow, Cynthia, Louise, Gabrielle, Kari, Matt, and Trica demonstrate elements of that process.

As each preservice teacher admits, recognition of the influence of personal past experiences in schools is the first step toward opening one's mind to the development of new perspectives. Cynthia starts out by reminding us that anything that takes us outside the familiarity of our own experience can be initially bewildering. She then tells us about the powerful impact of her past experience on her reentry to school—a vivid portrayal of how the familiar, too, can at first be anxiety-producing. Louise and Gabrielle show how preconceptions grounded in one's own experience can sometimes create rigid boundaries that inhibit the understanding and acceptance of alternative ways of doing things. They explain how they allowed those boundaries to gradually break down and, as a result, how a new horizon of alternatives was revealed to them. Faced with the prospect of teaching a class of adolescents, Kari and Matt travel back in time to their own high school experiences. Finally, we experience some of Trica's mounting enthusiasm as she resolves issues left over in memory from her high school days. After reading their accounts we invite you to think about the perspectives with which you will reenter schools and learning contexts, and to consider how you might prepare yourself to be open to new ideas and alternative ways of doing things.

Narrative Accounts

[This is my] first visit to the assigned school. This is hard. Not only do I have to become acquainted with a foreign environment (the junior high school) but also to a new city and driving on the freeway. I have lived in rural areas for so long that city traffic and freeways make me nervous. . . .

I arrived at the school early. I am awed by the numbers and the size of students. The map of the school is confusing. I have trouble finding where I am supposed to be. . . .

The first time I set foot in the school I was terrified. I was transported back 25 years to my own junior high school days. I was suddenly shocked into reliving all the things I had hated about school—all the frustration, loneliness, injustice, boredom, and resentment. For a while I thought there was no way I could be part of that system. What I saw and sensed was so contrary to everything in which I believed.

The school I was assigned was not what I had wanted it to be. I felt that the structure of the classes, classrooms, and rules were too restrictive, too narrow. The kids were forced into a mold that too often did not fit. As I became familiar [with the place I] felt the physical and administrative structures were counterproductive. I felt that the school was really wasting students' time. I resented the inability [of teachers] to give students individual attention and the necessity of constant attention to discipline problems.

At first I felt awkward and ill at ease in the school. I was trespassing in someone else's world. I was not quite sure what was expected of me. And, having never been in front of a classroom or having had any sort of substitute teaching experience, the assignment to actually teach a practice lesson was intimidating. It was not something I was ready to jump right into. Even though I was apprehensive, I gathered together my nerve and prepared a lesson to teach. That first class was even harder to manage than I expected—but the students did the assignment. I was happy when several of them asked interesting questions. After I had actually taught, I found it was not so hard after all. I felt more comfortable doing something with the class than I had felt observing them. I found that teaching can be an exhilarating experience as well as a frustrating one.

I feel more comfortable in the school now that I have been around there awhile. I am more familiar with the environment. I have met and talked with more of the teachers and students. I know the kids better. When some of the kids started talking to me about things that interest them, I suddenly felt much better. (Cynthia Hohnke)

I was placed in an "open school." After envisioning the typical Catholic school environment, [the kind of school I had been in] all my life, I could not even begin to conceptualize what an open school might be like. After the first few days in a kindergarten–grade 2 classroom, I was very skeptical and wary about how much I would get out of a full semester in this "open" environment. I was intrigued by the freedom students were given and yet unsure of how a child could learn in that kind of dynamic environment. I was thoroughly confused on my first day in the class. Unfortunately, first impressions of an open school classroom can be so deceiving.

Week after week I realized that there was so much learning going on that I could not hope to see it all. The students initiated their own projects. Math, reading, and writing were "done" through baking, book making, and even the construction of a science "museum." These were only some of the many activities I never expected to see or encounter and probably would not have done so in a more traditional school. These [kinds of integrated] activities encouraged students to want to learn and taught them to be independent in the learning process. As I saw my hopes and beliefs for students being fulfilled in front of my eyes, all the conceptions associated with the classrooms that I grew up with went right out the window.

Before I acquired any type of [formal] understandings about teaching, I assumed the role of teachers and the style of classrooms were much like the kind of classrooms I grew to know as a student. I figured that the teacher was mainly the disciplinarian behind the big desk who came out from behind to pass out materials or teach a lesson to the class. Now, as I look at myself becoming a teacher, I find that I want to incorporate many of the structures and methods I have seen this semester in the open school while maintaining a style of organization that is most comfortable to me. (Louise Martin)

When I first walked into Mrs. Hindman's room, I hated it. I thought it was very dirty and disorganized. I felt that because Mrs. Hindman was not organized, she did not have a clear sense of her goals and objectives, nor of the capabilities of her students. Now I know that this was a false assumption. At the beginning of my preservice teaching, I was too uptight, too rigid. I had certain ideas of how I thought a classroom should be run, and Mrs. Hindman did not fit my expectations. Because of the discrepancy between her classroom and my expectations, I was forced to step back and reevaluate exactly what teaching is all about.

Through observing the students' interactions with Mrs. Hindman and [by exploring the operation of] the classroom, I found that her room was an effective setting for children to learn. Her methods seemed to work well with the students. It took me half of the semester, however, to come to this realization. I was so set on my personal way of doing things that I was blinded to all of the good things going on around me. I spent the first half of the semester focusing on what was going wrong in the classroom. In retrospect, this was not an entirely detrimental perspective. Since it took me so long to appreciate the open school setting I am more sure now of its pros and cons. I see particular benefits of open school settings resting in [opportunities for initiating] hands-on experiences with students. Indeed, I feel very fortunate to have been placed in an open school. [In contrast to my earlier position], . . . the active learning environment of the open classroom is probably better for encouraging students to learn. (Gabrielle Tuchow)

The room would be somewhat depressing if not for the Garfield posters that paper the yellow concrete walls. The hardwood floors echo as I walk up and down the aisles. This was "my room"—at least for two hours, Monday through Friday, for six months. . . . I'd be willing to wager that most teachers have vivid memories of the room in which they first embarked on the journey of teaching. Room 222, John Kennedy High School. It used to be a gallery to display student work, and the track lights on the ceiling attest to the fact that room space is at a premium and art must be put aside for the sake of academics. There are no windows to the outside, but there are two windows at the back of the room that frame the movements of students up and down the hallway. These windows are shrouded with butcher paper to keep wandering eyes focused on what is happening in the classroom. The blackboard was affixed improperly to the yellow walls, and it moves back and forth against the wall when I write upon its surface.

The students who enter this room of mine move rather reluctantly to their seats. It is just after lunch and most of them are too sleepy to concentrate on algebra. These are "my" kids, mostly seniors and a few juniors—sixteen- and seventeen-year-old teenagers who have so much more to do than math. I was afraid of them at first, afraid of their teasing and potential brightness, afraid that they would not like me, afraid because they were not that much younger than I. I can remember what it was like to be seventeen. It was only a few years ago I was sitting in their seats, thinking the same sorts of thoughts, feeling the same passions. Their lives are filled with monumental happenings and vivid emotions, and there is little room left for me and my demands. How I dreaded the time I was forced to spend with them. (Kari Ralph)

As I walked into Kennedy High School for the first time this year, I remember the sensation of feeling as if I had entered a different culture. Walking up to the classroom that was to be my home for the next eight months, I quickly became lost in the frantic rush that seemed to accompany the two thousand adolescents eagerly looking to reach their destinations, clearly intent on the impression they were making as they navigated the halls. Over the next few weeks as the disorientation settled, I found that even though it had been many years since I had been in a high school, I relived the various emotions and feelings that accompanied my own journey through high school.

Although the superficial uniforms of the cliques had undergone some transition, the artificial boundaries still seemed alive and well. I soon discovered that beneath these "clique costumes" were individuals who each were going through their own personal struggle to come to terms with their identities. (Matt Schlein)

My first experiences in the classroom as a college student observing and helping out were intimidating and confusing. I felt my cooperating teacher's enthusiastic and flattering introduction of me to the students helped create a very confident shell that hid a wealth of fears and desires for more knowledge and competence. To my dismay, I found myself identifying more with the students than the faculty. My cooperating teacher emitted an air of confidence and always seemed to know the right technique to show individual students while they worked. I was haunted frequently by an episode in my own high school experience when an art teacher invalidated a student teacher's instructional methods.

One day, as I walked among the Hookland High students at their desks, I stopped to help a boy working on an "op-art" project. His composition lead the viewer's eye off the paper. As I explained the disadvantage of a one-way direction in his work, I felt I had validity in so doing. What I told him represented sound compositional concepts. He seemed to understand, and I sensed a spark of enthusiasm in his understanding. This was very exciting to me. I realized I did have authority in my subject matter. I dismissed my high school teacher's poor handling of the student teacher as a mistake in diplomacy.

As my intimidation began to melt, enjoyment immediately grew in its place. I found the classroom experience to be outright fun, and as I participated in teaching my first lesson plans, I frequently had to be reminded to tell students when it was time to clean up because I was so absorbed in what they were doing. Of course, I recognize the presence of a teacher who has already established order in his well-cared-for classroom as a tremendous help—training wheels of sorts. My excitement over the students' work deepened. Their abilities were so impressive. Such potential!

I found myself enjoying some of the environmental elements of the school. I am attracted to the idea of having my own space (classroom) to perform a job the way I choose. I enjoy an environment that allows me to dress nicely—vain thing that I am. How many artists get to do that? I began to notice near the end of the term that, mingled with the scornful expressions of acquaintances when hearing my career direction, there were many envious and pleasantly surprised expressions from friends. Some of those looks may have been flashes of high school nostalgia, but I could not help wonder how many people contemplate a teaching career only to shelve the idea because of economic reasons. (Trica Donald)

For Reflection and Discussion

1. Cynthia felt shocked, Gabrielle recalls being "forced" to reevaluate, and Louise confesses confusion at entering classrooms and schools.
   a. Is disorientation or confusion a necessary precursor to adjustment to new contexts? If so, what implications do their experiences hold for you as you prepare to reenter and learn about schools?
2. Cynthia recalls that the school in which she did her preservice teaching was not what she "wanted it to be." She initially felt that the classroom structures and rules were too narrow and restrictive. When she taught she discovered that the classroom was harder to manage than she had anticipated.
   a. Reread Cynthia's account and identify some of the preconceptions influencing her experience.
   b. How do you think the change of roles, from observer to participant, influenced Cynthia's perceptions?
3. Although Cynthia felt terrified and apprehensive about teaching a lesson, she discovered more comfort in practicing than observing.
   a. How does Cynthia's assessment of her lesson reveal her changing perspectives?
   b. What problems might occur from "jumping in" to teach too soon? What problems might result from waiting too long to "jump in?" How do you know when to "jump in?"
4. Louise and Gabrielle observed classrooms that were different from those they experienced as students.
   a. How did their preconceptions influence their observations, initially and eventually?
5. Gabrielle writes, "I was so set on my personal way of doing things that I was blinded to all of the good things going on around me." She states that this recognition came only after she had spent half a term in the classroom.
   a. How could Gabrielle have recognized sooner that it was her preconceptions that were causing her difficulty in seeing the "good things" and not the structure of the classroom or the practices of the teacher?
6. Trica and Kari identify with their students. Trica relates more closely to the students than to faculty, and Kari feels that the full lives of her students leave little room for her and the demands of her teaching.
   a. How might Trica have used her prior experience as a student to empower her teaching?

b. How might identifying with students influence Kari's teaching in negative ways? Positive ways?

Links with Research

In Chapter 5 we highlighted some literature on the influence of prior experiences on learning to teach, focusing in one section on biographical or personal history influences and in another on preservice teachers' preconceptions of teaching. This section is closely connected to those topics. We, therefore, suggest that you revisit those sections of Chapter 5 because we will be drawing on some of the same work to address the topic, Acknowledging the Influences of Personal Past Experiences of Schooling

Case studies of preservice teachers' experiences upon reentry to schools (for example, Britzman, 1991; Crow, 1987a, 1987b; Knowles, 1992) evidence how firmly grounded in personal history are preservice teachers' expectations and understandings of schools, teachers, teaching, and students. Because such understandings form the foundation for developing practice and because they usually are incomplete and often derive from negative experiences, these and other similar studies stress the importance of helping preservice teachers make explicit for examination both their personal histories and preconceptions of teaching (see also, Knowles & Holt-Reynolds, 1991; Zeichner & Grant, 1981). The idea behind this argument is that unexamined constructs are likely to remain unchallenged and therefore static. And, when preconceived images are at odds with realities presented in field experiences, difficulties are likely to arise (Aitken & Mildon, 1991; Knowles, 1990; Knowles & Hoefler, 1989).

In an attempt to assess the influence of biography on preservice teachers' attitudes towards student control, Zeichner and Grant (1981) studied the effects of the student teaching experience on preservice teachers' beliefs about pupil control. At the end of their student teaching experience all of the 40 preservice teachers retained the high custodial attitudes toward students they expressed prior to reentering schools. Even those who worked with cooperating teachers having significantly more humanistic views did not alter their beliefs about pupil control. This study led the authors to conclude, among other things, that "Although it is probably incorrect to assume that biography is the sole determiner of socialization outcomes, . . . what student [teachers] bring into the experiences cannot be ignored" (pp. 307–308). Similarly, in Knowles' (1992) study, Mora's student teaching practices mirrored her own recollections of schools, which she remembered as serious places characterized by strict discipline and organization, firm expectations of students, respect for teachers, an emphasis on academics, and little time for the "frivolities" of extracurricular activities.

Another clear illustration of this concept is presented in a study of 20 preservice English teachers (Zitlow, 1986). Reflecting on their reentry to schools, they described teachers, students, and classrooms as "real eye openers" when viewed in comparison with their own experiences as students. Preservice teachers who, in their field experiences, gave limited priority to learning or who felt constrained by pressures and demands of the school organization and culture, had themselves attended dysfunctional high schools or felt that they were not "winners" in competitive high schools. One person who had attended a challenging high school found the "apathetic, sleeping" students to be a rude awakening. On the other hand, preservice teachers who reported having repeated chances to make decisions about their own learning, often because of individual outstanding teachers, held more comprehensive learning priorities for their future students. Other examples of difficulties encountered as a result of preservice teachers' expecting students to be like they were are found in Hollingsworth (1989), Knowles and Hoefler (1989), and Knowles and Holt-Reynolds (1991).

With a slightly different focus, Bullough (1991) worked with 15 preservice teachers in the student teaching segment of their preservice program to explore the development of professional self-image. Upon reentry to classrooms all of the teachers initially interpreted their experiences through the foggy lenses of their own experiences as students and persisted in seeking confirmation of those images.

Research Activities

A sizable portion of the book thus far has focused on making meaning from your personal experiences in schools. You may find it useful at this point to quickly review Chapter 2 where we talk about the usefulness of autobiographical writing, particularly personal history accounts, as a way of accessing and recollecting some of your prior experiences in schools. Those experiences will influence both your thinking about practice and your reentry to schools as places where your future professional work will be located.

1. Recollect an elementary or secondary school you attended as a student. What features come immediately to mind? Try recreating a map of the school, identifying on it the various locations where different functions took place and places that are memorable because of the event that took place there.
   a. What were the circumstances of your most memorable and satisfying experiences in schools? How might that influence your reentry to schools? Consider also memories to the contrary. What were the circumstances of your least satisfying, frustrating, or hurtful experiences in schools? How have they shaped your thinking as you move back into schools?
2. As you are becoming increasingly aware, schools and the work of teachers are incredibly complex.
   a. Thinking back to your experiences as a student, what do you recall about the ways in which the school worked? What were your images of principals and office staff? How did you think about the principal and other school administrators? To what extent did you understand the role and functions of principals and administrators? What were your conceptions of principals' work? What did principals and other administrators do on a typical day? How did principals relate to teachers? How are your conceptions of principals and administrators shaped by your experiences as a student and, perhaps, as a parent?
3. Artifacts are powerful devices for stimulating recall. Locate some artifacts or memorabilia from your own school days and use them to reconstruct stories of your experience as a student. From these stories extract some of the preconceptions with which you will reenter school contexts. You may find this an interesting activity to engage in with other preservice teacher peers.

Developing New Understandings of the School

By their function and responsibility schools are different from most other institutions within society. As you enter a school for the first time as a prospective teacher you will wonder how that new status will feel and how you will be received by the students and other community members. As you don and adjust to your new "teacher lenses" the school will look different. It will take on new dimensions and significance as a workplace, as an organization that figuratively and literally has a central role in the local neighborhood and community, and as an institution that has a pivotal place in society. It is likely that you will more closely attend to understanding the bureaucratic structure of the school as workplace, its system of administration, and how it operates on a day-to-day basis. As never before, you will become awakened to the covert and overt rules and norms that govern the ways in which people regularly interact personally and professionally within the institution.

Learning about the micro-politics of the school, coming to some understandings about where the authority is located, is probably one of the first and most important things you ought to do as you begin your placement. Having said this, however, we recognize that for most preservice teachers the individual and programmatic focus on becoming a professional rests in the anticipated experiences of the classroom. In earlier chapters, particularly the Introduction and Chapter 1, we made the point that becoming a teacher involves two distinct yet integrally connected areas of professional development. The first rests in becoming aware of the tasks associated with developing competency in the classroom; the second is immersed in the knowledge and understandings associated with the complexity of being a teacher. Most prospective teachers with whom we have worked want to focus their complete energies on the classroom at the expense of understanding the complexity of teachers' roles and the school itself. Many of these understandings are to be found in the socio-political arena. It is also true, however, that for outsiders like yourself, learning about the domain of the school micro-politics is one of the most difficult and potentially messy chores, perhaps the reason why some teacher educators tend to overlook this task.

Every school is different, each having its own set of defining characteristics. And people who work in a school or other learning community habitually do things in a certain way. There are stated rules, guidelines, and procedures by which the school formally operates and, then, there are the implicit or unspoken rules. Although getting a handle on the expressed rules and regulations is potentially useful, it is learning about the latter kind that is likely to more strongly influence the kind of experience you will have in the school. Sometimes these implicit rules seem to be about trivial matters but, nevertheless, they may have far-reaching consequences. For example, one preservice teacher got off to an embarrassing start when he parked his car in the principal's usual spot. There was no indication of designated parking areas; however, as he soon discovered, everyone else in the school "just knew" not to park there.

Another preservice teacher walked unknowingly into a feud between two teachers over their room assignments. One of the teachers was displaced by the other from a room in which she had worked for many years. Until the preservice teacher realized the cause of the personal disagreement he was at a total loss to understand why his cooperating teacher was so against the other's curriculum and was uncooperative in departmental planning meetings. In the meantime, this preservice teacher had been denied access to the other teacher's classroom by the cooperating teacher.

In Chapters 1 through 4 we raised the issue of reflexive practice. The notion of inquiry is central to becoming a teacher, not just because it provides an opportunity and vehicle to explore your own practice but also because it enables, in the context of the present discussion, the exploration of micro-politics and other educational issues. The key to understanding elements of the political environment associated with your placement, we assert, is *not* to place all of your energies in classrooms but to spend considerable time examining these other elements of schools. School-based inquiry projects, of the kind discussed in Chapter 3 and in the Research Activities of other chapters, are one way to gain these new understandings.

In the following, Ellen, Leila, Gary, Mary, Angele, Eva, Renata, Steve, and Sandra share with us some of their perceptions, observations, and learnings as they experienced school for the first time through preservice teachers' eyes. As these teachers experienced, everything you discover about schools will not necessarily be positive. Some things that take place in schools may disappoint or surprise you. There is much for which public schools are criticized, and on these matters you would be well advised to be informed. Nevertheless, as Eva and Angele admit, observing the workplace context and gaining insights into the role of schools in society is time well spent. Ellen points out the value of surveying the community context of the school. Renata and Sandra comment on the important role of "the other" in the development process as they reflect on their relationships with other preservice teachers.

Narrative Accounts

The first day, I looked at the neighborhood. The homes are well kept, and those nearest the school are quite new. On the drive across town, I crossed the downtown area and several blocks of railroad tracks, all of which are within the school boundaries. There are seven or eight blocks of old, older, and oldest homes. Some are well kept and attractive; some are decaying. There are some apartment buildings but no really large complexes. Many of the yards have gardens and a few even have animals: chickens, ducks, and rabbits. It gives an almost rural tone but probably reflects attempts to stretch the food dollar. It is obviously not a high income area, but there are some nice homes. The residential areas are bordered by businesses and some industry. A popular park is only a few blocks from the school. Another nice feature is the nearby Botanical Gardens, which cover several square blocks. In spite of the pollution and close proximity to the railway tracks and downtown, the area has a certain charm.

What I saw in the neighborhood is echoed in the school and its students. Most are nicely dressed and clean. There is a mix of ethnic groups. Some of the [junior high] girls are much bigger than I am, and some of the students look like they just popped in from the elementary school next door. The halls and lockers are exceptionally neat and clean. Having had a chance to visit several local high schools, the students here seem to be cleaner, make less litter, and are less rowdy in the halls. I'm developing a sense of loyalty to the school and students, and a sense of camaraderie with the staff. (Ellen Findlay)

Here I go. It is my first, no, my second day at North Central. I am here early. It is 7:30 A.M. I enter the building through the west side door with a couple of other students. There are some students already in the building standing by their lockers in groups of two or three, talking and laughing. They notice me and point at me to one another. I can hear what they whisper as I pass them to go to the faculty rest room across from the office. "It's the new teacher. Boy, she's short. Is she really a teacher?" I smile. I am glad they have noticed me. That way they will get used to my being here sooner. (Leila Muniroui)

I thought I knew what schools were like. Well, I just wasn't prepared for the demands of working in schools. Actually, there were two levels of unpreparedness: [the first] had to do with my preparedness to work with kids only a few years younger than I; [the second] had to do with understanding the various ways that I could act and interact in the school and classroom so as to benefit my [own professional development]. Really, the second [one] is much more important, and it was the one to which I did not attend. (Gary Purdue)

Teachers (especially beginning teachers) must realize that they are entering more than just a building. They are entering a place with a set of established roles, relationships, rules, and ways of behaving and understanding that give each particular school its own unique character. [On one level] the principal establishes and maintains the academic tone of the school and is extremely important for faculty morale, but it is primarily the teachers who set the tone of the school and encourage students to perform to their abilities.

During field experiences I observed that a school is more than a building. It consists of many different people, all with their own set of values and own curriculum. Often, people within the school actually do not know what other staff members really do. For example, I discovered that the classroom teachers in the school did not know what the resource teachers did or the exact procedure for referring a child to Special [Education] Services. I also found that certain matters are somewhat secretive, at least in a bureaucratic sense, and it is important not to appear intrusive. I also noticed that it is a lot easier to introduce new topics and ideas when both the school [administration] and society support the teacher. If people like what a teacher is doing, they are more willing to help the teacher cut through the red tape in order to get necessary materials or assistance. This relationship between school and community is important, not only so that teachers will be better able to try new methods but also so that the field of education can continue to grow with our everchanging society. (Mary Mac)

I was not surprised to find out that kindergarten and first grade children are excited to come to school and learn. Learning is viewed as fun; therefore, school is basically fun. I was disappointed, however, to realize that somewhere between first grade and fourth grade, school becomes a chore, a means to an end, something to help students get jobs and earn money. It is sad that learning is valued for its material worth instead of being valued for learning itself. I think that this simple discovery offers some very interesting implications for me as a teacher. (Angele Doucette)

When I started, Ms. Ledbetter thought it would be a good idea for me to sit in the teachers' lounge in the morning to get a taste of "what some teachers have to put up with." Unfortunately, this experience was a disturbing one. The very behavior I was hoping to leave behind in high school, and which made it to the university, I also saw at the professional level. I'm talking about cliques. I noticed so much defaming of colleagues' characters—so much back stabbing. I also witnessed an outcome of all this gossip; several faculty members were so hurt by what was said about them that a "cold war" started. The faculty seemed divided into three groups: the gossiping clique who were avid "lounge-goers"; the "fair weather" clique; and, the group of faculty members who rarely have anything to do with [the events and discussions of the faculty] lounge. Although it was very disturbing to sit in the lounge and listen to the gossip and back stabbing, I am glad for the time I spent there. It was a valuable learning experience. (Eva Sendele)

I often thankfully consider my friendship and trust in my fellow student teachers, especially when I think of them in comparison with the high school faculty. I have observed the faculty. The words catty, fearful, uncooperative, and downright mean often come into play when I think of them. Various cliques and individuals vie for power and prestige by making others look bad or inefficient. Some teachers in the school hate this atmosphere and avoid contact with [opposing] fellow faculty members whenever possible. The net result is rather unwholesome and unproductive for promoting the best academic and educational atmosphere. So much for the idea of professional people working together to improve the quality of education. "Career ladders" seem to have added to the competition between teachers. Is this the best approach to developing career professionals? (Renata Lalonde)

The focus of staff meetings and staff room discussions are twofold: in the staff meetings, faculty inevitably center on school functions; in the staff room they focus on student control. The purpose for which teachers ostensibly are hired—instruction—is glaringly absent in conversations. Staff room gripe sessions might serve the purpose of letting off steam—allowing teachers to stay sane—but something seems amiss at staff meetings. Maybe I am still too idealistic and would like to concentrate on teaching and not "dress-up day" or whether boys should wear earrings—Christ, isn't that one battle we could avoid? Let the boys make their statement. That is what growing up is all about. Is this stress on order and appearance common to all schools and all principals? In this school there are expensive planter boxes in the foyer, and other fancy equipment, while some classes lack textbooks. (Steve Bruno)

I remember my first impressions of North Central Junior High—it was very clean and had great student artwork displayed openly in the halls. Despite the fact that anyone could have torn it down or defaced the posters and paintings very easily (which surely would have happened at the junior high school I attended), they remained intact until this week when they were taken down by teachers. That first impression of an orderly, well-disciplined school has held up. The teachers and the vice principal want quiet, obedient students and, for the most part, that is what I saw. Although I must admit that this made my teaching easier, I believe that it stifles some of the creativity and initiative in the kids.

For the most part, the teachers at North Central are conservative, and many actually attended the school as students. I have rarely had the opportunity to meet a nicer, more helpful and encouraging group of people but have been surprised on more than one occasion by attention to the status quo. Lunch time, for example, is a time for gender separation. The men eat in one part of the teacher's workroom and the women in the other. I had fifth period with Bill (my cooperating teacher) and initially walked with him to lunch every day. I was well into my second week of teaching before I realized I was always the only female in that part of the workroom. For whatever reasons (convention? discomfort? not wishing to unsettle things?) I tended to eat in the other end of the room from then on.

Something I have really enjoyed and that has made my student teaching much easier is the contact that I have had with the other student teachers, particularly those at North Central with me. At times, I have wondered about the wisdom of having so many student teachers in one school (or at least having them concentrated in ninth grade classrooms) because I have discovered that many students have two or three student teachers a day—and one girl has five classes a day with a student teacher. I suppose I should have more confidence in our ability to teach. At any rate, I have no doubts as to our ability to support each other. I enjoyed getting feedback and ideas from those in the same content area as me as well as from those in other disciplines, and by generally comparing how we all handled similar situations. (Sandra Rene)

For Reflection and Discussion

1. Ellen describes detailed observations of the neighborhoods surrounding her school.
   a. How might such observations help Ellen understand the culture of the school?
2. Mary's careful observations reveal that a school is a complex establishment with explicit as well as implicit values and procedures.
   a. How might Mary have discovered the covert rules?
3. Angele notices that the "fun of learning" apparently decreases as grade level increases.
   a. To what extent might Angele's opinions be dependent upon the school she observed?
   b. To what extent can observations from one school be applied generally to all schools?
4. Eva and Renata discovered disturbing relationships among the faculty when they spent time in the teachers' lounge.
   a. Should Eva and Renata plan to create positive alliances among the faculty? If so, with whom?
5. Renata noticed conflict between teachers and administrators. She observed that feelings of animosity between the two groups do not result in productive outcomes.

     a. How do the goals of teachers and administrators differ?

     b. What might Renata do when facing such a situation?

     c. How are workplace conflicts escalated? conciliated? initiated?

6. Steve expresses some disappointment with the content of discussion at staff meetings. He recognizes that "staff gripe sessions" let off steam but wonders why the subject of instruction is absent.

     a. What might have happened if Steve had introduced the topic of instruction? Would that have been appropriate? Why? Why not?

Links with Research

Schools are complex organizations, each defined by and imbued with a set of shared characteristics, values, beliefs, and ways of interacting and operating that guide behavior and give meaning, support, and identity to teachers and their work. Although widespread recognition in educational literature of the uniqueness and complexity of schools as workplaces has only come about recently, there is a fairly substantial body of work dealing with the social organization of schools and school culture (including teacher and student cultures). As Rosenholtz (1989) notes in an analysis of 78 elementary schools in 8 school districts of one southern state, the manner in which teaching is defined, performed, and changed is inextricably linked to the social organization in which it occurs. Similarly, Johnson (1990), working with 115 teachers in one eastern state, points out that teachers' perceptions and experience of the school as workplace—the physical features, organizational structures, socio-political aspects, economic conditions, and psychological dimensions—strongly influence their career choices and attitudes toward work.

In Canada, Hargreaves has extensively explored the phenomenon of school culture and its influence on workplace interactions (see, for example, Hargreaves, 1990; Hargreaves & Dawe, 1991). In *The Cultures of Teaching,* Hargreaves (1990) identifies four types of school culture, each influencing patterns of workplace interaction in a different way. "Fragmented individualism" is the predominant culture of schools characterized by norms of privacy, isolationism, conservatism, and a general lack of enthusiasm for substantive growth and change. In schools characterized by a "balkanized" culture, teachers separate themselves into sometimes competing groups or cliques defined and identified by certain attitudes or perspectives, subject matter orientation, professional goals, or personal interests. In schools where a "collaborative culture" prevails there is a broad agreement on educational values and shared commitment to the attainment of mutually agreed upon goals. Teachers (and staff) work together and interact with a natural warmth and sincerity and with the support and encouragement of the school administration. "Contrived collegiality" defines a recently adopted pattern of interaction. Teachers in schools characterized by this type of culture work together largely by fiat of administration. Examples of contrived collegiality are peer coaching, mentoring, and team teaching initiatives that are externally imposed by district or school administration usually without the will and commitment of the teachers involved.

The significance of this and other similar research on school culture for preservice and beginning teachers is noted in Rosenholtz' (1989) reference to what she called "isolated" schools, where working together is an uncharacteristic norm:

[New teachers'] capacity for growth is limited almost entirely to trial and error learning. With little access to role models among their peers, they rely on memories of good teachers as they recall from their own student experiences instead of gaining substantive knowledge from their more experienced colleagues (Rosenholtz, 1987, p. 23).

A contrasting image is presented in an exploration of workplace relationships and teacher development conducted by Cole (1991). Fourteen teachers who began their teaching careers in a school characterized as a "helping and caring community" or, in Hargreaves' (1990) terms, a collaborative culture, experienced professional growth and personal satisfaction during their first year of teaching. The influence of staff relationships on teachers' work and development was also examined in an ethnographic study of three British primary schools (Nias, Southworth, & Yeomans, 1989).

The common thread weaving together all of these studies is the conceptualization of teachers' work as an integral part of a complex system of interdependent components, not merely as a discrete, classroom-based enterprise. Traditionally, preservice teachers have not been exposed to this view either in theory or in practice; consequently, as Goodlad (1990) argues, they have been ill prepared to assume the full range of responsibilities of a full-fledged teacher. (For a comprehensive discussion of schools as workplaces and how preservice teachers are socialized into such cultures, see Zeichner & Gore, 1990.)

Preservice programs do little to help preservice teachers expand the relatively narrow conceptions of teachers' work they hold on entering formal teacher preparation. Placing preservice teachers in individual classrooms and keeping their attention focused almost exclusively within the walls of that classroom and on the more technical aspects of teaching, reinforces those narrow conceptions of teachers' work, fosters the perpetuation of norms of isolation, and contributes to the reality shock often experienced by beginning teachers. Also, lack of attention to understanding the community within which the school is situated and the role of the school within the community does little to help preservice teachers understand and appreciate the contextual and cultural makeup of the students (Comer, 1988; Cummins, 1986; Zeichner, 1992).

To conclude this section, we call your attention, once again, to the recommended readings at the end of the chapter. For the most part, they are rich and readable accounts of life in schools.

Research Activities

The preceding narrative accounts focus on preservice teachers' responses to reentering schools. Several preservice teachers evidenced considerable surprise at some of their early observations and newfound knowledge of schools. To alleviate this "culture shock," or as others have named it, "reality shock," we suggest that you try a variety of research activities aimed at making you more cognizant of the situations and contexts found in schools. It may be helpful to review the methods for gathering external information described in Chapter 3. As your explorations will point out, students and teachers see everyday school experiences differently. (On another level, as you aspire to be a successful teacher, bridging this gap of perspective may be of great value.) Try to be far-ranging in your explorations. Following are some ideas to get you started.

1. Try and find out the perspectives of teachers and students on everyday events and situations in schools.

    a. Conduct an interview (see Chapter 3) with one or more teachers. Start with broad questions about how teachers view the roles and purposes of education and schools, for example, and move on to more specific and locally imbedded contextual questions. You also may want to raise for discussion some contemporary issues about schools and the public education system (for example, the "back to basics" movement; destreaming of high schools; the "overcrowded curriculum"; and, mainstreaming of special needs students). The following questions could form the basis for beginning interviews or conversations: What do teachers think is the purpose of education? schools? teaching? What is the most important function of and in the school? What do they think is *their* most important function in the school? in the classroom? How do teachers account for the changing landscape of schools over the last 20 years, for example? How do teachers view students? How do teachers categorize students? What are the characteristics of students that teachers identify most readily? Who or what shapes teachers' perspectives of students? How are these perspectives shaped?

    b. Using appropriately modified versions of the above questions, conduct an interview with one or more students (that is, ask the same questions of students).

    c. How do teachers' and students' views about schools, teaching, and learning compare? How do they differ? Presuming there is a large discrepancy in perspectives, why do you think it is so? Take, for example, the teaching tasks of the faculty. How do teachers view their responsibility to teach specific subject matter? How do students view participation in course work with particular subject matter? Why are there discrepancies in these views?

2. The place of schools within communities is central. Yet, despite the centrality and importance of formal education within society and communities, there are often gulfs between some of the thinking of the most creative educators, actual practice in schools, and the aims and aspirations that business people and local communities have for schools. This is a complex issue that deserves considerable attention. As either a prospective school faculty member or an educator in some other kind of learning community, try to become more cognizant about the sometimes delicate link between communities and schools. You can gain some insight into this through local media reports (newspaper, radio, and television), talking with members of various lobbying groups (especially those who put pressure on school board members and schools), school board members, parents, retail and commercial business owners and employees, manufacturing or business executives and their company's employees, and various other community members.

    a. Find out when the local school board meets and attend one of the meetings. (Most boards have public meetings, and some may be televised for local cable networks.)

    b. Over a period of a month or term, for example, closely watch the local newspapers for any education- or school-related items. An analysis of these clippings will reveal important information about educational issues of concern in the community, public and political positions on such issues, and the general nature of the relationship between local schools and the community. They will also give insights into the level of educational discourse within the community. Sometimes, university or school/faculty of education libraries keep a current file on popular press coverage of education issues. The school library may also do likewise. A browse through this material may be informative.

c. You will have some sense of the community perspectives on the following questions and issues if you completed the preceding two groups of research activities. You can gather additional information by talking with members of the local community. Periodically, engage in conversations with people in public places, retailers, and business people. Try to find out various responses to these questions and others like them: How do community members view schools and their roles and functions? What are their substantive criticisms of schools and teachers? How would they change schools? What is their view of teachers' work? What roles do they see for schools in resolving the massive urban and societal problems that have placed children at risk on issues related to crime and justice, health and welfare, and educational achievement? What place do they give academic learning, for example, in comparison to the more humanistic, sensitive, and democratic processes and attitudes that many educators would respect?

3. Having made some inroads into a small aspect of reacquainting yourself with schools, understanding some perspectives of teachers is likely to underscore the importance of coming to grips with some of the more pervasive bureaucratic, structural features of schools. As students you were aware of some of these features (for example, the rules and regulations affecting students) but unaware of others. Structural issues run the gamut from concerns and practices embedded in unions, legal systems, families, communities, society, governments, economics, social welfare, and business to a whole range of elements such as personal and professional relationships and development, administrative needs and pressures, students' vocations and tracking, textbook selections and usage, parental participation, athletic programs, and so on. Perhaps one of the first tasks in reacquainting yourself further with schools is to uncover the incredible range of issues that regularly surface in the daily operation of schools. If you can arrange to "shadow" or spend a good part of a day with a school administrator you will gain tremendous insight into the bureaucratic structure of schools as organizations. The following questions will help to get you started: What are the functions of schools as they operate today? Who appears to be in control of the school in which you are assigned? What are the roles of administrators and teachers within the school as far as its organizational structure and functions are concerned? Who makes the decisions about organization, curriculum, timetable, work assignments, rules and regulations, and so on? Why? When? Who is responsible for the day-to-day decisions? How are governance and managerial responsibilities shared? Who among the faculty and staff are responsible for facilitating extracurricular activities and organizations? Why? How are budgetary decisions made, and who shares in the process?

4. Focusing on some other, often unspoken, issues about teachers may also be beneficial to your thinking and professional growth. For example, legal constraints, parental lobbying,

faculty relationships, legislative and administrative mandates, and teachers' unions and collective bargaining all contribute to a workplace climate within schools and a whole set of complex relationships, political maneuverings, and oppositional and cross-purpose activities and practices. Schools are often far from being smooth-running, and intellectually and academically coherent places. You will probably recognize that there are many voices in schools, all competing for a slice of the pie of control, authority, curriculum, budget and space resources, even students. Probably the best way to access this information is through participant observation methods described in Chapter 3. Spending time in nonteaching areas within the school (for example, counseling and attendance offices, general office areas, meeting places, supply rooms, staff rooms, work rooms, foyers), carefully watching and listening, will help you find answers to some of the following questions about the unspoken or less spoken of relations and dynamics within schools.

a. What are the functions of the various faculty "representatives," those elected as union representatives, for example? How do unions function within the school?

b. Who are the most influential faculty on the staff of the school and why? Is there a hierarchy of informal leadership that is discernible within the school?

c. What are the foci of teacher and staff conversations in faculty meetings, departmental meetings, faculty lounges and lunchrooms, in the halls, in the faculty rest rooms, and at social and athletic functions?

d. What do teachers think are the most important dynamics of the school? How does this perception about school dynamics differ from the perceptions of school administrators and board or district administrators?

e. What are the explicit and implicit messages that teachers give you when discussing *your* future career? And, how does this influence your thinking about being a teacher? Do you ever get the sense that answers to these and other questions are being "whitewashed" by the professionals with whom you talk? If so, why?

Understanding Student Diversity and Cultures

Whether in junior or senior high school or lower or upper elementary school, the most predictable thing that can be said about students as individuals is that they are all different and, for the most part, unpredictable. Add social context and factor in peer interactions and group dynamics, and the diversity becomes greater and behavior less predictable.

As you are aware, the demographics of school-age students is changing rapidly in North America. Grant and Secada (1990), in presenting a comprehensive review of the research on diversity within schools in the United States, draw on some revealing statistics. Students belonging to groups referred to as minorities will be in the majority in many more school districts by the year 2000, representing between 30 and 40 percent in the national school population. Projections suggest this trend will continue well beyond the turn of the century. At the same time children of poverty are likely to occupy a greater place within schools—and they will represent all racial and cultural groups. Yet, in the face of student population changes, the teachers of these children are likely to become an ever more homogeneous group. The percentage of minority teachers is projected to drop, and the teaching force is extrapolated to have more white women than represented now. In the face of these demographic changes is the need for teachers to be more informed, reflexive, responsive, and understanding about their work with diverse student populations. Grant and Secada present formidable challenges to the teacher education community to change the way in which teachers are prepared for handling a diverse student group. We take up their challenge and present a challenge to you. Who are your students, both now, and in the future? (We will revisit this topic in Chapter 10.)

While stereotypes of students abound, so do contradictions to the various categorizations placed on students and their cultures. In the narrative accounts that follow, several preservice teachers recount that all students are different and have characteristic needs and uniqueness. In various combinations and permutations, age, gender, religion, ethnicity, socio-economic status, background experiences and opportunities, and other special challenges and needs are among the many factors contributing to the complexity and diversity within classrooms. Experience in one setting with one group will not necessarily prepare you for any other group in any other setting. Nevertheless, you can develop some strategies for understanding students and their various cultures.

Many secondary preservice teachers, because of their proximity in age to those whom they are about to teach in high schools, think they know students. Often they are mistaken. Another factor that often confuses and confounds the development of new teachers' practices is that some pattern their practices on their *own* experiences as students, a point you have heard us make before. As you may appreciate, although this perspective has some value, it has real disadvantages when the students you teach represent diverse perspectives and backgrounds.

From child and adolescent development courses you may have learned about aspects of human intellectual, psycho-social, and moral development. And, those of you who are parents will know firsthand about child development, to some extent. As teachers, however, we have relatively limited knowledge about and control over the social and environmental factors influencing the development of the students we teach—and this can be frustrating. Some students knowingly or unknowingly choose detrimental paths, and some have to struggle against odds. It is difficult to watch human potential go unchallenged or unrealized. Teachers vicariously experience pain felt by their students and struggle to deal with difficult issues placed at the doorways of their classrooms. Anxious to right all wrongs and repair possible damage to a child's healthy development, teachers can sometimes, too quickly, resort to missionary-like zeal and attitudes by responding with excessive nurturing or condemnation of student behavior and parenting practices.

All teachers face challenges with respect to understanding and relating to students' needs, interests, and backgrounds. Leila, in the account following, being a recent immigrant, faced a special challenge related to her exposure to and understanding of North American culture. Whether it is responding to differences inherent in religious or cultural heritage, or teaching students who live with adversity in the home, it is a challenge to accept and celebrate differences and demonstrate an appropriate level of sensitivity to individual needs. As is suggested in the following accounts, knowing how and when to respond, and determining what are "appropriate" responses and levels of sensitivity are issues that teachers daily grapple with.

Rebecca is surprised by the contrast between students in two field experience placements. Ellen and Noelle encounter some of the realities of adolescence. Stacey is concerned over her students' awareness of and attitudes toward socioeconomic differences. Amanda is faced with the issue of alcoholism, and Cynthia and Eileen wonder how to deal with the diversity they encounter. And Allen reflects more generally on issues of race and diversity. As in other chapters and sections the questions in *For Reflection and Discussion* at the end of the accounts are intended to offer you an opportunity to begin to examine your perspectives on some of the critical dimensions of classroom complexity. In Chapter 10 we will deal in more detail with issues of individual needs and differences.

Narrative Accounts

Kids are moody in junior high. They have different moods on different days. I notice that their moods affect my teaching, especially if I am not considerate of those moods. You have to be aware of what kind of moods the students are in and adjust the activities of the day somewhat. It has taken me awhile to recognize that. . . .

It was not until I realized that the perception of public school education is different here [than in the Eastern European country in which I grew up] that I understood why I had to make a case for the worth of the subject matter to the class and that I needed to do more than just present facts. I discovered that I needed to present lessons in a way that was not only novel and challenging to students but also relevant to their lives and interests. The problem was that I did not have a clue about the background of American children or their interests. Having been a teenager myself was of no help because the period in which I was that age was not spent in North America, and it was quite different. Being from a different culture made this all the more challenging. Not only do I not share their background but the value systems under which I grew up differ markedly.

To resolve this dilemma I tried two things: first, I tried to get to know the students through observing and talking to them; then, I had them get involved and take responsibility for planning activities of interest to them. I saw their participation and involvement as the only solution [to the problem I faced]. By listening to the kids I learned about their experiences in the family and about the social classes in the school community. Developing my listening skills has done wonders for me. I think if we are all open to learning and recognize that everybody has something of value to teach us, we will maximize our learning potential. (Leila Muniroui)

I was in a fourth grade classroom for one field placement. The school consisted of predominantly white, upper middle class students. We had no discipline problems, no deviant behavior. Everyone was a "perfect, high achiever" and class time was almost never wasted on management problems. My experiences with this group of students were great. The site afforded me the opportunity to work with the "cream of the crop." Working with these kids, however, did not prepare me for life in a diverse and challenging classroom.

When I went to my second placement, I was uneasy. It was not easy for me to adjust to the energy, activity, high noise levels, and the ethnic diversity of the student body. These kids did not all come in the same size and attitude. Some of the eighth graders were bigger than I; some of the sixth graders were under four feet tall. The one thing these kids had in common was their energy level. They were all hyperactive! After four months in this school I was finally more at ease and more comfortable with the general population of the school. (Rebecca Buono)

Junior high school students are so volatile. You can have a perfectly controlled class and lose them to an ill-timed interruption or an ill-turned phrase. They are newly aware of their changing bodies and are very charged with becoming young men and women. The art teacher, Gwen, told me during a visit in the faculty room of "losing a class" and not being able to regain them, even though she is an accomplished teacher and recognized "disciplinarian." It seems that her honors art class was working on individually selected projects. One girl decided to create a rug. The rug was to have a tropical island with sandy beachfront supporting a large palm tree complete with coconuts. As the day's projects were passed out, someone noticed that the student's rug was only partially finished. The beach was there and the trunk of a palm tree, but it was topped only with two large round coconuts. The resemblance to the male anatomy was too much for them. The giggling soon became a roar. Gwen took part of the blame herself for when the art project was shown to her she also smiled, even laughed a little, and the die was cast. For the rest of the hour, there were giggles and references to the palm tree. I will have to remember not to laugh even a little bit when we get down to brass tacks in sex education. "Do not smile until sex education is over" shall be my motto. (Ellen Findlay)

Tanya is a student who is capable of getting an "A" in every subject if she so wanted. She picks up on concepts extremely fast and could be one of the best students in the class. Her mother agrees that she could do really well. In fact, she was on the list of "high honor" in intermediate school. This year she has not done very well. Sometime during the year Tanya decided she did not care about school anymore and became involved with a group of students who had the same attitude. Now she thinks that it is not her responsibility to keep up with the class; that it is the teacher's job to keep her informed if she is failing. She has been given the same rules as all the other students but wants exceptions made. It is sad to see a student become involved with new friends who do not positively reinforce participation in school and learning activities. (Noelle Frandsen)

I encountered [students with] a wide range of socio-economic backgrounds. About one half of the students in the class walk to school from homes in the "nice" subdivision that surrounds the school; the other half are bused to school from various places, one being a low-income housing complex. Even though the students are only in the first grade, they know where their classmates are from and the "status" of their different living situations. So many of the students who walk to school have a negative attitude toward the students who are bused to school. The extreme range of economic backgrounds is a touchy subject that needs to be handled with sensitivity. (Stacey Chin)

After experiencing a classroom setting and the many "traumas" that happen in second graders' lives I understand how essential it is to be sensitive to their problems. For example, the class I worked in attended a school assembly on drug abuse after which a little boy talked about how his mother drinks a lot of alcohol. My cooperating teacher simply said that it was all right for grown-ups to drink as long as they did not do it all the time. Apparently, the social worker of the school just found out that this boy's mother is possibly an alcoholic. It seems that, nowadays, with single-parent homes, working-parent homes, less time for development and maintenance of parent-child relations, and increased public demands for an expanded "social" curriculum catering to sex education, drug abuse awareness, AIDS education, to name a few areas, the teacher's job has increased tenfold. (Amanda Luckey)

There are many children in my room who are victims of divorce. Others have been abandoned by one or both parents and have to deal with this rejection. There was even one girl in the class who had to deal with her mother being in and out of jail and who had two relatives shot in the past three months. It is easy to say that the personal lives of the students should not affect their academic performance, but I found out firsthand that this is not the case and feel very strongly that, as a teacher, I must address these concerns to have the students work effectively in a classroom setting.

I have encountered many issues that do not seem to have any specific or easy answers. For instance, in my classroom there were two Jehovah's Witness children who did not celebrate holidays; therefore, it was very hard to incorporate these children into various class activities that had to do with celebrations of one kind or another. Do you make the whole class miss out because not everyone wants to participate? Do you make up alternate activities for these children and run the risk of them feeling ostracized? It is not an easy situation, and this matter must be handled sensitively. This issue also needs to be examined in the context of other religious groups. For example, the Jewish parents do not want their children to have to deal with the celebration of Christmas. Does this mean that I, as a teacher, should overlook [the celebrations of] another [religious] culture? This will be a tough issue to deal with when I have my own classroom—to keep an even balance while trying to educate students about multiculturalism. (Cynthia Jackson)

When evaluating and helping students, I learned to consider many different issues. The behavior and performance of students in the classroom can be affected by illness, religion, or family background, for example. A student in our class, who was a very slow learner, had chronic asthma and was hospitalized several times. As a result, he was absent quite a few days and was required to take large doses of medication. Missing school set him back in his work. His performance may also have been affected by the medication that he was required to take.

Another student was from a Jehovah's Witness family. Because of her religious beliefs, she was not allowed to participate in some classroom activities, such as celebrating birthdays and working at learning centers on activities teaching celebrations around the world. It became difficult to explain to the students why she could not participate because her religion was not a reason they could understand.

Another important consideration when evaluating and understanding a student is family background. Almost half of the students in this class are from single parent families. One girl, in particular, is having a very difficult time dealing with her parents' divorce. (Eileen Katz)

Over the course of the semester I wrestled with the issues of race and diversity, and with my role as a white male in the changing society. I worked in an ethnically diverse school. We, as educators, need to be more explicit in stating curriculum objectives that encourage students to become aware of the diversity of their school, community, nation, and world. I am very aware of the need for this. By the end of the twentieth century—only a few years away—fewer than half of the people in the United States will be European-Americans. A majority of the population will be "minorities." What will be my role as a white male teacher or administrator in relation to these demographic changes? This is one question with which I will continually wrestle. (Allen Montgomery)

The accounts you have just read touch only a fraction of the many questions that are likely to be raised as you begin to understand your students. As you may recall from Chapter 3, Matt was interested in understanding the students with whom he worked. In Chapter 3 we presented Matt's account of beginning to understand school through the eyes of Barnaby. It began when he came to the realization that students, like Barnaby, were involved in struggles of identity and purpose and that he could understand more about those struggles by spending time with them. We invite you to revisit Matt's account of Barnaby, this time in the context of understanding students' diversity and cultures. (You will come across accounts by other preservice teachers in other chapters that will also reflect the struggle to understand students and their cultures.)

You may have noticed that many of the preservice teachers who wrote about students, in this chapter and others, did so with little reference to the larger contexts in which students exist. We wondered about this. One explanation is that many of these preservice teachers were placed in traditional (classroom-based) contexts for their field experiences. Many simply did not have the opportunity to explore contexts and people beyond individual classrooms.

For Reflection and Discussion

1. Leila met the challenge of teaching in a school and student culture different from her own. She involved students in designing projects of interest to them.
   a. What other ways might she have used to get to know the students as a group?

b. To what extent should preservice teachers design instruction to cater to students' current interests and to what extent should they aim to create new interests?

2. Rebecca observed vast differences in behavior between a fourth grade homogeneous classroom and an eighth grade heterogeneous classroom.

   a. Rebecca noted that age and ethnicity influence classroom culture. What are some of the other elements that comprise the culture of students?

   b. To what extent would it be possible for Rebecca to predict behavior based on age? Socio-economic level? Ethnicity? Family structure? In what ways would making such predictions be helpful when preparing to teach a new group of students? How might these kinds of predictions have a negative influence on developing rapport with students? At what point do such predictions become stereotypes?

   c. To what extent, if at all, should Rebecca have examined her own preconceptions and, subsequently, her expectations, and adjusted those expectations according to student culture?

3. Noelle observes a bright student succumb to peer pressure against academic achievement.

   a. What was Noelle's responsibility in that situation? What may have been some alternative course of action?

4. The disparity in the socio-economic status of her students concerns Stacey. She notices that young children hold negative attitudes toward the poorer students.

   a. How could Stacey begin to address the problem of economic differences as it appears in her classroom? What are the more subtle ways in which these differences may be reinforced and replicated in schools and classrooms?

5. Amanda views the visible outcomes of changing family (demographic) patterns as a contributor to teachers' workloads. She believes that an increase in single parent families and dual career households have placed greater burdens on schools.

   a. How have such changes in family demographics affected what students need from schools? To what extent are Amanda's perspectives stereotyping particular families? Why? How is this useful? Dysfunctional?

   b. What are some of the problems that children from such families bring to school? How can these problems be addressed?

   c. Is there evidence to support or contradict Amanda's perspective? What is it?

6. Cynthia's encounter with diverse cultures in the classroom caused her to question how she will handle multicultural concerns.

   a. If class time is spent on various cultural observances how should those cultures be selected for presentation? How can you respect all cultures if a few are singled out?

   b. To what extent should various cultural holidays be presented in classrooms that lack diversity?

   c. Should presentation of celebratory customs be determined by the cultural composition of the classroom?

7. An awareness of demographic changes has led Allen to believe that multicultural education should have an explicit and central place in the curriculum.

   a. Do you think that an increased emphasis on a multicultural curriculum will contribute to greater understanding and unification among students, or will it increase alienation and divisiveness? Why? What challenges will Allen face as he attempts to maintain a responsive, empathic, informed attitude toward those of ethnic minorities?

   b. How realistic is Allen's concern about being a white male educator in a culturally diverse society?

Links with Research

Student diversity and culture is a broad topic. In an effort to provide a glimpse of some of the research that explores these topics, we draw on only a few sources and, in the process, omit reference to many of the topics raised in the narratives. The following references to research are intended to challenge you to explore further. Several major journals in teacher education, and education more generally, have published special issues on student and cultural diversity. *Teaching Education* (Vol. 4, No. 1), *Harvard Educational Review* (Vol. 58, No. 3), and *Journal of Teacher Education* (Vol. 43, No. 2) are three publications that may be useful, especially the first and second because they have several firsthand accounts by minority students.

Understanding the diversity of a student body is a formidable task. As a way of beginning to think about appropriate understandings, the work of Ross and Smith (1992) provides insight into how a group of six preservice teachers thought about the issue of diversity. Using categories of orientation to diversity to organize the extensive data gathered, they discovered that the preservice teachers had rather simplistic notions about the diversity of students. These preservice teachers did not, for example, see that the educational welfare of minority students had any connection to broader societal conditions—they saw issues of diversity and their consequences resting largely at the individual level. Ross and Smith note that Weinstein (1988) has suggested that unrealistic optimism may hamper preservice teachers from engaging in a serious study of educational issues. This is, perhaps, an explanation for the relative shallowness of understandings exhibited by these individuals. As a way of gaining further access to a small part of the research on student diversity and cultures we turn to studies that explore students' experiences of school. At the outset, however, understand that these studies are context-specific illustrations. It is difficult to make generalizations appropriate for the diverse cultural and locational contexts that exist in North America.

Researchers, investigating either the larger context of schools or individual schools as learning communities, throw some light on students and their diversity. For example, Coleman and Hoffer (1987), in a large-scale statistical study of the impact of communities on public and private high schools, verified the connections between the dropout rate of students and the economic well-being of their families. Coleman and Hoffer found that even in communities in which high dropout rates might be expected, those rates were tempered by the support available to students within the immediate community. Clark's (1983) analysis suggests that the extent to which impoverished black children succeed or fail in school rests on their family life. This work, along with Coleman and Hoffer's research, is useful in beginning to think about student diversity. Still, Clark, and Coleman and Hoffer do not directly illuminate the students themselves; other studies like these have limited value for furthering your understandings of student diversity and culture. They do, however, alert us to the powerful links between social class, race, gender, and school achievement, and understandings about students (see for example, Bowles & Gintis, 1976; McLaren, 1989.

Several researchers have explored school communities in detail. For example, social categories and identities in high school were the focus of Eckert's (1989) ethnographic case study research at one institution. In uncovering the cultures of students, Eckert provides insights into the ways society, the community, and the school structure shape students' identities. Similarly, Steinitz and Soloman (1986) explored the identity-formation process of working class youth in three communities. Although their account is not so powerful in the evidence it presents and the conclusions about identity drawn, it provides penetrating glimpses of working class students.

Chang's (1992) ethnographic study of one semi-rural high school focused on the overall culture and adolescent life of the students, as well as the ethos of the school. The portrayal of students' daily lives identifies the tension between their ideals and realities with those of school and society. Similarly, but with a different agenda and purpose, Grant and Sleeter (1986) investigated a school within one community using a theoretical construct that suggests that institutions are shaped by the conflicting interests within communities. In coming to understandings about the quality of schooling and teaching in relationship to the cultural backgrounds of the students, portraits of students and their cultures are presented.

Schofield (1989) studied an urban middle school with the intent of understanding how desegregation affects students and teachers. This work sheds light on the development of peer relations between black and white students and reveals the context-sensitive nature of relationships and the pervasive problem of fear. It also sheds light on the erosion of innovation within the school community. Likewise, Peshkin (1991) explored peer relations through the roles of play and ethnicity in a school and community renowned for its record of ethnic discord. For the Sicilian, Mexican, Black, and Filipino students in the school, along with the few Whites, the division of color was not the barrier to relationships that Peshkin had expected. Break dancing turned out to be a vehicle for Deyhle (1986) to begin to understand the social identification and interaction between Navajo, Anglo, and Ute students in a New Mexico school community. A study of a fundamentalist Christian school, also by Peshkin (1986), contains portraits of students and presents a different picture than that represented in studies of urban public schools.

Accounts by teacher-researchers of their students are particularly illuminating. Paley (1981, 1986a, 1986b, 1988, 1990), for example, reminds us of the value in closely observing children within the classroom as a way of informing practice. Her accounts, set within the context of an elementary school classroom, are compelling in that they draw attention to the kaleidoscope of individual differences among students, even in one small laboratory school classroom in Chicago. From a different perspective, Palonsky (1986), a researcher turned teacher, tells of his experience working in a high school. He provides glimpses of the students (who are not a focus of the study) and their cultures. In making a case for a critical pedagogy, McLaren (1989) presents numerous student narratives through an autobiographical account of his experiences teaching in Toronto, Canada. In so doing, class, gender, and race become center points in McLaren's effort to articulate a more equitable schooling for students.

Laycock's (1991) experience as a student teacher-researcher, observing a student as a means of gaining access to understanding "life as a student," is reminiscent of Matt's exploration of Barnaby in Chapter 3. Central to Laycock's experience, however, was the realization that institutional pressures bear heavily on the affairs and well-being of minority students and, in this case, to the child's detriment. (Perhaps more disturbing were the constraints placed on Laycock by those who wielded power over her— primarily a university teacher educator who insisted she not report disturbing observations.)

Researchers and others exploring lives and work of teachers reveal much about students. Kidder (1989) and Freedman (1990), for example, represent journalistic accounts of teaching, teachers, and classrooms. Others, such as Jervis (1986), illustrate the processes and outcomes of a teacher who places great value on understanding students.

Personal accounts by students are powerful and useful for understanding student diversity and cultures in schools. For example, Saunders (1991), a teacher educator and researcher, reflected on her own experiences as an African-American student. What is particularly prominent in the account of her experience is the notion and reality of "support" and "acceptance" as concepts from which to begin to understand the culture of others. Being educated primarily in schools with large white populations magnified the importance of being connected to her own culture for support of various kinds and for learning to live with the relative ignorance of African-American culture by those around her. In a remotely similar way Neira (1988) straddled two cultures. But, in his case they represented extremes, that of a poverty stricken inner-city neighborhood and an elite preparatory school. What is particularly powerful in his story is the confrontation with degradation on the one hand and racial stereotypes on the other—he was a foreigner in both cultures.

Anger at the way others denied them their visions of the future is a common theme in the life stories of 14 university undergraduate students. In a publication edited by Schoem (1991), these young Blacks, Jews, and Latinos focus a great deal in their accounts on their experiences in schools and as school-aged children and adolescents growing up in hostile worlds. They proclaim they are ready for a society that accepts their different backgrounds—their individual differences as the persons they are—and provides those like them equal opportunities.

More revealing of the experiences of students, perhaps because the authors were high school students themselves at the time of writing, are two accounts by African-Americans: a fifteen-year-old high school student (Perry, 1988) and a twelve-year-old junior high student (Hunter, 1992). Like Saunders (1991) and Neira (1988), Perry tells of being caught between two worlds—in her case those of private and public school. In the private school she felt isolated; in the public school she felt her identity as a human being was denied. This work is penetrating in its interpretation of her experience and in presenting potential solutions to some of the associated dilemmas. Hunter, however, presents a journal of her experiences that is a far different record than those previously mentioned. It is a depiction of day-to-day life in the Bronx—a compelling portrayal of a young life, one in which school does not figure prominently.

In sum, the research and accounts presented here are intended to provide a sense of process and method rather than characterize student diversity and cultures. Although we have concentrated more on presenting research that focuses on the experiences of minority students, there are many other research reports that explore the experiences of students more generally.

Research Activities

Of the various strategies for beginning to understand students and their cultures within the school, engaging students in a variety of ways will give you the most useful insights. This, together with information from other sources, is likely to aid you in amassing a fairly comprehensive and realistic picture of students. Despite its limitations, your own experiences as a student may be a useful place to start accruing information. In thinking about how to begin to get a handle on understanding students and the cultures of students within schools, there are at least six lines of action you might consider.

1. Check the statistical data that the school, school district, or school board has on the student body. This information is likely to provide only superficial measures of students, but you may find it helpful. This data set is likely to include demographic information about student performance on national and local standardized tests; records of past performance; comparisons of performance within age, ethnic, and racial groups, and subject areas; comparisons between and within schools; and other similar information. There may be restrictions on the availability of these data, but some form of them are often available as appendices to annual school board reports. Once you have studied this information consider the following questions.

    a. What is the scope of statistical information available to school faculty about the student body and about individuals? What are the limitations of this information? How do administrators and faculty use statistical data about students? How are they most useful? What forms of statistical data can inform teachers' work with individual students and groups of students? How? To what extent do statistical data inform teachers about the varied learning needs of a diverse student body? Do statistical data serve a valuable purpose in understanding students and their school cultures? How? Why? Why not?

    b. What are the costs associated with collection of statistical data that measure students' performance? Is data collection, for instance, highly intrusive and disruptive to everyday work with students? What are teachers' views about their participation in various mandated testing programs?

2. Talk to faculty and administrators in one-on-one conversations about how they perceive students as a group and as individuals. They may give you insights into individual and group behavior, places where students hang out, student interests inside and outside school, student participation in school activities, and individual and group performance in a general and specific subject matter sense. Now, stand back and consider the information you have gathered.

    a. How do faculty and administrators view students? What kinds of generalizations or stereotypes do they present when talking about students and the student body? What are some of the experiences behind administrators' and teachers' stereotypes? How does their knowledge of students inform their work and interactions with students?

    b. To what extent are students able to define their own spaces, activities, learning, and so on within the school? What substantial voice do students have in the affairs of classrooms and the whole school?

3. Listening to faculty talk is likely to reveal different information from that elicited through engaging in conversations with faculty. The rhetoric of teachers, that which they say to outsiders like yourself, may be different from the realities in which they and their colleagues are immersed and talk about in faculty lounges and other "safe" places within the school. We, therefore, suggest that you listen to faculty conversing in staff lounges and lunch rooms as a way of accessing how those within the culture of teachers regard students and their cultures.

   a. How do teachers describe students? What are some of the stories about students that they tell? What are some of the metaphors faculty use to describe students' actions and behaviors? What appear to be the assumptions behind the stories?

   b. What are some ways in which students are categorized and in which their exploits or actions are told and retold to other teachers? Are there students whose names regularly surface in conversations between teachers? Why? How are these students categorized by teachers?

   c. How do you think teachers regard their faculty room talk? What do teachers actually think about their faculty room talk? Are there teachers who seem to regularly talk disparagingly about students? Why do you think this is so? Are there teachers who seem to keep aloof or refuse to participate in disparaging talk? Why might this be?

4. Talk to parents and community members, those not directly involved in teaching students, to get their perspectives about the student body. (Those who work with students in extracurricular activities—recreation specialists, youth workers, guidance counselors, school volunteers—are likely to have some different perceptions about students.) From their perspectives

   a. Who are the students? For what are they renowned? What are the differences among student groups? What do the various student groups stand for?

   b. How do parents, youth workers, and other community members view students differently than school administrators and teachers? Why might this be so? What are the multiple contexts in which parents and community members view students, and how may this affect perceptions?

   c. What kinds of insights can these adults provide into students' cultures that are not available from those adults involved in schools? What might be the limitations of these people's perspectives on students?

5. Spend considerable time with students in various capacities, perhaps during extracurricular activities, tutoring activities, or merely being at places where they hang out. Participating in activities with students, simply "being yourself" around them, and being genuinely interested in them may yield all kinds of insights. Being a keen observer and an attentive listener will help you understand students and their culture. Like Matt, as illustrated in Chapter 3, you could listen and observe by spending time "shadowing" one or more students as they participate in the daily affairs of the school. Experiencing a day in the life of a student is likely to have a strong impact on your teaching practice. Unfortunately, few teachers take the time to see schools through the eyes of students.

6. Select and view some of the movies on the Video List, most of which aim to depict a slice of life in schools often highlighting student culture. As you watch, consider the portray-

als of student life in light of the kinds of questions posed in Research Activities 2, 3, and 5. Think about how such depictions might positively and negatively influence your preparation for reentering schools.

Summary

In this chapter we have underscored the importance of unpacking the ideas and images you have brought to the preservice program in preparation for your reentry to schools. We hope we have not belabored the point that who you are as a teacher is strongly influenced by who you were as a student and how you experienced teaching, learning, and educational contexts. Shifting the lens outward, we took a wide-angle look at school contexts and student populations. We introduced the concept of school culture and encouraged you to think about the micro-political and socializing influences on teaching and teachers' work. Finally, and in a broad sense, we addressed the topic of student diversity and cultures. In subsequent chapters (particularly Chapters 9 and 10) we will sharpen the focus on these areas.

Now that you have had opportunities to think about and prepare for your reentry to schools, we shift the camera once again and zoom in on an elemental, yet ever so delicate, feature of humankind—the negotiation, development, and nurturance of relationships. We begin with an exploration of the role of the cooperating teacher and the preservice teacher–cooperating teacher relationship.

Recommended Readings

Aptekar, L. (1988). *Street children of Cali.* Durham: Duke University Press.

Barker, R. G., & Gump, P. V. (1964). *Big school, small school.* Stanford, CA: Stanford University Press.

Clark, R. M. (1983). *Family life and school achievement: Why poor black children succeed or fail.* Chicago: University of Chicago Press.

Coleman, J. S. (1961). *The adolescent society.* New York: Free Press.

Cottle, T. (1973). *The voices of school: Educational issues through personal accounts.* Boston: Little Brown.

Cusick, P. (1972). *Inside high school.* New York: Holt, Rinehart, & Winston.

Davies, B. (1982). *Life in the classroom and playground.* Boston: Routledge & Kegan Paul.

Dennison, G. (1969). *The lives of children: The story of the first street school.* New York: Random House.

Dichter, S. (1989). *Teachers: Straight talk from the trenches.* Los Angeles: Contemporary Books.

Dworkin, A. G. (1987). *Teacher burnout in the public schools: Structural causes and consequences for children.* Albany, NY: State University of New York Press.

Eckert, P. (1989). *Jocks & burnouts: Social categories and identity in the high school.* New York: Teachers College Press.

Fletcher, R. (1990). *Walking trees: Teaching teachers in the New York City schools.* Portsmouth, NH: Heinemann.

Freedman S. G. (1990). *Small victories: The real world of a teacher, her students and their high school.* New York: Harper & Row.

Giroux, H.A., & Simon, R.I. (1989). *Popular culture, schooling, and everyday life.* Toronto, Ontario: OISE Press.

Greenstein, J. (1983). *What the children taught me.* Chicago: University of Chicago Press.

Hunter, L. (1992). *The diary of Latoya Hunter: My first year in junior high.* New York: Crown.

Johnson, S. M. (1990). *Teachers at work: Achieving success in our schools.* New York: Basic Books/HarperCollins.

Jones, G. (1991). *Crocus Hill notebook.* London, Ontario: Althouse Press.

Kidder, T. (1989). *Among schoolchildren.* Boston, MA: Houghton Mifflin.

Kotlowitz, A. (1991). *There are no children here: The story of two boys growing up in the other America.* New York: Doubleday.

Kozol, J. (1967). *Death at an early age.* New York: New American Library.

Kozol, J. (1988). *Rachel and her children: Homeless families in America.* New York: Crown.

Lieberman, A., & Miller, L. (1992). *Teachers—Their world and their work.* New York: Teachers College Press.

Lortie, Dan C. (1975). *Schoolteacher: A sociological study.* Chicago: University of Chicago Press.

Mathews, J. (1988). *Escalante: The best teacher in the world.* New York: Henry Holt.

McLaren, P. (1989). *Life in schools: An introduction to critical pedagogy in the foundations of education.* New York: Longman.

Nehring, J. (1989). *Why do we gotta do this stuff, Mr. Nehring?: Notes from a teacher's day in school.* New York: Fawcett.

Neill, A. S. (1960). *Summerhill: A radical approach to child rearing.* New York: Simon & Schuster

Palonsky, S. B. (1986). *900 shows a year.* New York: Random House.

Perrone, V. (1991). *A letter to teachers: Reflections on schooling and the art of teaching.* San Francisco: Jossey-Bass.

Peshkin, A. (1986). *God's choice: The total world of a fundamentalist Christian school.* Chicago: Chicago University Press.

Peshkin, A. (1991). *The color of strangers, the color of friends: The play of ethnicity in school and community.* Chicago: University of Chicago Press.

Rosenholtz, S. J. (1989). *Teachers' workplace: The social organization of schools.* White Plains, NY: Longman.

Schofield, J. W. (1989). *Black and white in school: Trust, tension, or tolerance?* New York: Teachers College Press.

Sizer, T. (1984). *Horace's compromise: The dilemma of the American high school.* Boston, MA: Houghton Mifflin.

Sizer, T. (1992). *Horace's school: Redesigning the American high school.* Boston, MA: Houghton Mifflin.

Sleeter, C. (1992). *Keepers of the American dream: A study of staff development and multicultural education.* London: Falmer Press.

Solnicki, J. (1992). *The real me is gonna be a shock: A year in the life of a front-line teacher.* Toronto, Ontario: Lester.

Yee, S. M. (1990). *Careers in the classroom: When teaching is more than a job.* New York: Teachers College Press.

CHAPTER 8

Negotiating a Role and Developing Professional Relationships with Cooperating Teachers

Teaching is commonly referred to as an "isolated" profession. This is because, other than hallway or staff room conversations and occasional group planning or faculty meetings, teachers' work is characterized by little regular, substantive adult interaction. Most teachers spend a good portion of their professional time alone with groups of students behind the closed doors of classrooms. They also spend time in extracurricular activities and contexts supervising, teaching or coaching, or working alone on pre- or post-instruction activities in classrooms or at home.

Despite the picture of solitude, it is important to realize that some teaching contexts encourage mutual planning and teaching more than others. Many preservice teachers, for example, have found that "open schools," "special purpose" schools, and schools implementing vigorous reform initiatives often witness more collaborative work than traditional environments. Despite the tendency for teachers to work behind closed doors, the formation and development of professional relationships is a significant part of becoming a teacher and a member of a professional community. And, despite personality and ideological conflicts that you may encounter, you will benefit from beginning to work intensively, cooperatively, collaboratively, and in partnership with peers and more experienced teachers. Having said this, however, we recognize that for many preservice teachers this may be a foreign notion because many new teachers express fantasies that place them behind closed doors working on their own with pupils. Having your own classroom or teaching space and feeling autonomous are important for developing a sense of professional identity; establishing productive working relationships with others is also vital for contributing to your development.

Beginning now and continuing over the next few years, you will be engaged in a process of socialization to the profession and to contexts in which you teach. As you act and interact within those institutional contexts, you will be influenced both personally and professionally by those who comprise those professional communities:

- parents, students, administrators, support staff, experienced teachers and other beginning teachers within the school
- administrators, support staff, and other colleagues from outside the school but within the school board or district
- associates from the institution of your formal preparation, other universities with which you may be associated, and other professional associations

Your field experiences are, in a sense, entry points to the professional community. Thus, you will have some unique opportunities that will not be so easily afforded once you are employed as a full-time beginning teacher. Now, you have opportunities to become familiar with one or more educational contexts and meet, observe, and interact with some of the various people in those contexts. And, because you will be initiating your membership to both a particularistic local community and a larger professional community, you also will be sorting out and defining your own role as a teacher and emerging professional. We now turn to this latter point.

You can expect variation in the way in which you are received by experienced teachers and others in your field placement sites. Some will welcome you and your fresh perspectives and enthusiasm, and see you as a new colleague; others may respond to you with patronizing remarks and attitudes. Because you are a neophyte teacher, experienced teachers are likely to give you more leeway, show more understanding and empathy, and be more forthright with you; however, some may labor under the difficulty of knowing how to identify with you. Are you their student or their colleague?

As a preservice teacher entering a field placement you are in an ambivalent position. At the crossroads of being a student of teaching and a teacher of students, you have responsibilities related to *both* roles. You will, no doubt, have differing levels of comfort with each. At times you are likely to feel like a student; at times like a teacher. And, the degree of ease with those feelings will vary, even within short spans of time. Sometimes you are likely to feel as though you are already an accomplished, full-fledged teacher; at other times you may well feel like an awkward newcomer, inept in dealing with multiple roles and affairs of schools, classrooms, teachers, and students.

As you struggle through this early period in your development as a teacher you will interact with individuals who will have a significant influence on your immediate and emerging thinking and practice, and on your career development. In this chapter we look at professional relationships with cooperating teachers and how certain roles and relationships are defined, negotiated, and developed. Because you will be assigned to work with cooperating teachers during your field experiences we specifically consider

- negotiating a role and developing and maintaining productive working relationships

- dealing with and learning from differences in perspectives and styles of working and interacting
- negotiating and making sense of guidance and guidelines

Within this framework we seek to make clear some of the crucial issues that will facilitate your ongoing work in learning communities such as schools. In Chapters 9 and 10 we consider the development of relationships with others in the school and education community.

Negotiating a Role and Developing Productive Working Relationships

Cooperating teachers, as "on-site teacher educators" and "practitioners of theory," have a significant role in preservice teacher education. And, for a number of reasons, their influence usually extends beyond the bounds of the field experience period. The first reason is that cooperating teachers usually have a major role in the evaluation of your performance. They also have a major role in the evaluation of your potential for future practice—they usually write recommendations for you. Principals hiring new teachers place considerable weight on the assessments of cooperating teachers.

A second reason is that, even after your graduation, cooperating teachers may prove to be an important source of support, particularly if you worked well with them. For those of you who choose to remain near your cooperating teacher for the first year of teaching, the experienced teacher may prove to be helpful. Most teachers feel a bond with those who assisted them in the early period of professional development.

A third reason rests on the models of instruction and classroom management and modes of professional interaction that cooperating teachers provide. Even if you have contrasting or conflicting viewpoints about teaching, spending anywhere from a few weeks to a year in someone else's classroom is usually an experience that is not easily erased from your early professional thinking about teaching.

The role of cooperating teacher is a challenging one, particularly when considered amid the complexity of a teacher's day-to-day roles and responsibilities. Even with the hectic pace of classroom and school life, however, most experienced teachers who assume the role of cooperating teachers do so for the many benefits it offers *them* and *their students*. For example, two cooperating teachers had this to say in a recent conversation:

I always look forward to having preservice teachers in my classroom. They come with such fresh, new perspectives, and even though they are feeling their way in the classroom, I feel that my teaching is greatly enlightened [by their presence]. I grow as these new teachers ask me about my practice, as they seek clarification of my actions, and as they begin to interact with students and inquire into the goings-on of the school and classroom. Of course, I take particular care to make my teaching first rate. Actually, they also greatly enrich the learning of my students. (Cooperating Teacher)

At first I perceived the job [of being a cooperating teacher] as one in which I was offering something to the student teachers. Then I realized it was a two-way street. Student teachers provide fresh blood, new faces, new ideas. They keep me up to date with current trends. It's [an opportunity for] adult contact—a team approach in a sometimes solitary profession. It also provides time for me to observe my class. But, most of all, it's a challenge that can be fun! (Cooperating Teacher)

Having given two examples of the positive ways some cooperating teachers are likely to view your presence in their classrooms and schools, there is another side to the picture. For a variety of reasons, not all cooperating teachers display this kind of attitude. Not all field experiences are as educative as you might hope. Educative field experiences rest on a complex interplay of human actions and institutional contexts.

The reality is that, in many preservice teacher education programs, the least developed element of preparation to teach may rest in the field experience. And, there are many reasons why this may be so. One of them lies in the fact that some universities have been slow to develop reciprocal, cooperative partnerships with schools and school districts. Consequently, often times there is not a strong degree of philosophical compatibility between preparation institutions and the field. A shared, coherent, congruent philosophical base is important because when widely opposing and often unarticulated perspectives are present, teacher educators in the field and those in the academy are likely to work at cross purposes and cause confusion in the minds of preservice teachers. Imagine being in such a tug of war.

To add further complexity, as we have said before, many school personnel view the university as an institution with little regard for the rigors of practice and for developing long term, mutually beneficial arrangements and relationships. In some cases this perspective may be accurate; however, many teacher educators and their institutions are trying to forge vastly different relational climates with schools than have been commonly evidenced over the last 30 years or so. Suffice it to say that the way cooperating teachers are coopted, selected, and prepared for preservice teachers' presence in classrooms is often less than optimal. This is an area about which many teacher educators are concerned and, coupled with the issue of placement sites, is one in which prominent teacher education researchers urge drastic changes. Many teacher preparation programs and schools are trying to take corrective actions.

We know of a range of reasons why cooperating teachers may elect to work with you. Most times it is because of the reasons stated by the two cooperating teachers whose statements you just read; professionals genuinely want to share their expertise and want, in turn, to be enriched by your experiences, perspectives, insights, and ideas. Nevertheless, the circumstance of your assignment can often occur in haphazard ways, such as when principals assign preservice teachers to cooperating teachers according to their seniority or with regard to some cyclical, chronological order. And, some local teachers' unions demand that all senior teachers have equal access to preservice teachers with little regard to their members' suitability to mentor or to their professional status, competencies, and philosophical suitability or match with preparation programs.

Other times cooperating teachers are assigned to work with preservice teachers because of the pressure of their full-time assignments or duties; the principal or other administrator, or even the teachers themselves, believe that you will be able to help out, acting as a kind of unpaid aide. According to this perspective, you are seen as giving a tired or overworked teacher, even one who may be ineffective, an infusion of contagious enthusiasm. We have even known cooperating teachers to schedule surgery or personal leave, leaving preservice teachers with a major role in helping to keep together the affairs of the teachers' classrooms. Too often we hear of stories where cooperating teachers "simply disappear" once student teachers have assumed full responsibilities for teaching.

Despite these kinds of less than satisfactory circumstances, the vast majority of university teacher educators, principals, and other on-site teacher educators work hard to establish productive placements for preservice teachers. The issue of pairing new teachers with experienced teachers is difficult, however, and the methods for matching preservice teachers with cooperating teachers often leave much to be desired. Sometimes cooperating teachers have opportunities to select people like you through interviews or some assessment of your suitability through examination of your resume, transcript, and other submitted materials. Less often, preservice teachers and cooperating teachers interview each other. And, more often, placements are made purely on matters of convenience—teachers and schools are close by for ease of university supervisor visitations, or there is a subject matter or grade level congruity (sometimes at the expense of other professional or personal attributes of both parties).

We raise these matters not because we wish to induce doubts in your mind about your future placements but because we want to facilitate your thinking and encourage you to be proactive as you enter this new phase of your professional development. We believe that this kind of information can only help you forge a productive experience. In other words, we want you to be informed of the realities of field placements so that you can influence the decision making associated with your assignment. We think it is extremely important to begin to think early on, well before your placements, about all of the aspects and ramifications associated with developing what is probably one of the more important professional relationships of your preservice teaching career.

For many reasons related to contexts and persons, the quality of field experiences varies. For some preservice teachers, all the time spent in field experiences will be meaningful and educative; for others, that may be true only some of the time; still others may have several difficult or frustrating field experiences. There are no guarantees. There is no magic formula for a successful field experience even if the best of planning and preparation take place. Like all human endeavors involving relationships, the cooperating teacher–preservice teacher relationship is fraught with complexity and idiosyncrasies. For example, there may be differences in how you and your cooperating teacher perceive your roles; you may have differing expectations for the time you are together; you may differ in teaching styles, philosophies, and approaches to education; and there are personality factors and contexts in which you may find yourselves at odds.

Prior to your first meeting with your cooperating teacher, you should think about how you wish to define your role, establish yourself as a teacher, and prepare yourself to learn from your field experiences. This kind of preliminary attention may make it easier for you to negotiate these things with your cooperating teacher. Negotiating a role with your cooperating teacher may be the most important act associated with your beginning work in schools. We suggest you quickly review the early chapters of the book. Recollect that we placed considerable focus on the issue of *your* definition of your professional self.

The narrative accounts that follow provide a starting point for discussion and lead into some potentially useful research activities. Leila describes the process by which she became aware of how preconceived expectations and negative attitudes toward her cooperating teacher could interfere with her learning. She also describes how she was able to change the course of her thinking and prepare herself to learn from the field experiences. Kevin raises questions about his own attitude toward working with cooperating teachers. The stress and anxiety Kinsey experienced over unrealistic expectations and standards she had set for herself illustrate the need to address such issues with cooperating teachers.

Linda and Melissa recognize differences in cooperating teachers' attitudes toward their own teaching and professional development. They comment on the importance of reciprocity in the cooperating teacher–preservice teacher relationship. Related to this, Julia presents her view on the preservice teacher's role in developing an agenda for field experiences. She is aware of the need for sensitivity to existing classroom practices and procedures. Opinions vary as to whether the field experience is a time for preservice teachers to experiment with various methods and begin to develop personal teaching styles or a time to follow in the footsteps of more experienced teachers. We think this is a matter for you to think about as you prepare for and work in schools with more experienced others. For instance, as a preservice teacher, do you see yourself as an apprentice learning the craft from a master or as one forging new ground, trying out various practices and theories as a developing professional? One central question encapsulates these alternatives: Is the field experience in its current state an appropriate context for either of these conceptions?

Louise and Brian share some of the joys of their relationships with cooperating teachers. They reflect on some of the qualities of these relationships that contributed to their having educative field experiences. Nina describes how she established and strengthened her relationship with the cooperating teacher through informal conversation in between parent conferences. Finally, Trica provides a retrospective account of her learning through experience, mentioning the importance of negotiating a productive working relationship with her cooperating teacher. Following the accounts, we pose several questions to stimulate thinking and conversation related to defining and negotiating the cooperating teacher–preservice teacher relationship. First, we gain some insights into the diversity that awaits you in the field as we hear Robert describe his introduction to his two cooperating teachers.

Narrative Accounts

Following our tour of the school, I went off to meet my cooperating teachers. Ms. Olson, my cooperating English teacher, is about forty years old, friendly, has a nice smile, talks rapidly and loudly, and is extremely enthusiastic. She immediately gave me about seven texts and a whole bunch of papers to refer to. She seems to have the whole year planned out already. I like her, but I cannot tell what she thinks of me. I am glad we are about the same age; otherwise, I would have been more intimidated by her mile-a-minute approach to communication. I wonder why I was put with such a tense, rapid person when I am so thorough and methodical. I would have thought that my friend Joanne would have been a more logical choice—same sex, more similar dispositions, both mothers, both married, both very enthusiastic. Oh well, I guess I can be happy with Ms. Olson. The only question is, "Will she be happy with me?"

My other cooperating teacher is a man, and his personality and rate of speech seem to be more compatible with my own. He seems to be more callous to teaching and to student teachers than Ms. Olson. He is more concerned with *when* I am going to start teaching, *how many* of his classes I will teach, and for *how long*. My first impression is that he is a little less concerned with the students as individuals than Ms. Olson, but I am not sure whether that is good or bad. He allows quite a bit of noise in his classroom, and he informs me that it is conducive to learning. His third period class is "one of the noisiest he has ever had but also one of the brightest." I guess I am an old "fuddy duddy" to expect high school students to behave the same way today as they did when I was in high school over twenty years ago. I am worried about teaching his classes. I do not know if I will be able to keep my train of thought in the face of so much verbal competition. I asked him about this and he said:

> You're not me. You cannot teach the same way I do. The students will see you are
> a different person, and they will respond to you differently. Let's see how they act
> when you teach them. They may be quiet and you may not have anything to
> worry about.

Sounds like good advice. (Robert Marigold)

I think I judged Diane, my new cooperating teacher, too early and unfairly. I believe I walked into her classroom wanting to find problems with her teaching methods. I wanted to believe that knowing the subject better does not necessarily make one a better teacher. So, rather than focusing on what I liked about Diane's teaching and what I could learn from her, I focused on what I didn't like about her teaching. I recognized this after the first week, though, and reasoned that somehow I needed to turn this into a better [more positive] learning experience since I would be with her until the end of the year. Consequently, I began to open my mind to what I could learn from her. I started noticing a lot of techniques that I liked, as well as others that I did not agree with, but I turned my attention to those techniques I could use. The whole thing started me thinking more analytically about teaching. For example, I asked myself, "Why is it that I don't like a certain technique? How can I improve it? Do I have any alternatives to offer? Why is it that my alternatives will work better?" (Leila Muniroui)

Both of my cooperating teachers have been very supportive of me, but certain things about my French cooperating teacher's teaching have bothered me all year long. One first-year student came to hand in his book and told me that French class had been much more pleasant since I came. Of course this pleased me, but it also reminded me that I have been measuring myself against my cooperating teacher. I wish I had not felt like I was trying to "better" her all year long. We have not had an antagonistic relationship; we have gotten along very well, except that I have tried to prove to myself that I was doing better than she was. Without saying as much to her, although perhaps showing it, I have had a very competitive attitude that may not have been professional. (Kevin Queen)

It is about 12:30 A.M. I lie awake in bed fighting not to think about my worries, which flutter around in my head a million miles an hour. I think about going to school tomorrow and my heart begins to race as I feel the adrenaline rush into my arteries. Why? I am beginning my second week of school—I should not feel like I did last Sunday night. Once I get to school tomorrow morning, I will be okay but, then, when I walk out the doors tomorrow afternoon, I will sing with relief. What's going on with me? Last week I would come home and refuse to write in my journal (something I really do enjoy) because I wanted to forget about the day. Last Thursday night I had a long talk with myself, and Friday I was better able to be myself. I reminded myself that to strive to be a perfectionist is to waste my time, energy, and happiness. I believed last week that my latent perfectionist—"I must-be-the-best"—characteristic, which I thought had been dismissed from my person, had returned.

Being an awesome teacher is something I take seriously and Petrocelli (the cooperating teacher) is the one whom I aspire to be like. She intimidated me badly last week. When I observed her, I studied hard to see what she could improve on, but she is almost infallible. She is not only an excellent communicator and instructor, she is an expert in organization, time management, and a "nicest-person-of-all-time" kind of woman. I love her and know I will learn a lot, but this sense of inferiority is new and uncomfortable to me. (Kinsey Milhone)

I had a cooperating teacher who was fairly new herself. She was very open to new ideas. It was nice to know that I was giving her ideas as well as taking them [from her]. Some cooperating teachers are really rigid about how they do things and are not interested in new ideas; whereas, others are very interested in what we've been learning at the university and want to know how they can get more information and perhaps try out some of the ideas in their teaching. (Linda Sampson)

It really makes you feel good when you've come up with something unique or even a little different, something that your cooperating teacher may not have thought about before. If the class really enjoyed [your teaching] and the lesson went over well it makes you feel not only that you are accomplishing what you set out to do but also that you are not just taking [from the cooperating teacher] and not giving anything in return. (Melissa Piercy)

Having student teachers is hard on cooperating teachers. They've made their long-range or unit plans and then we come in and they have to reschedule all their planning. They feel like they should let us do what we want to do, but I felt terrible interfering with their plans. When they asked me what I wanted to do I usually just went with the plans they had made. It didn't bother me; I was still learning. But I think they felt they were restricting me. If they're in the middle of a unit you can't always say, "I don't want to do that. I want to do this." (Julia Candiotti)

My cooperating teacher constantly had methods, theories, and advice to offer me—even when I did not ask. I soaked up everything like a sponge and always had my ears open. Since the first day that I set foot in the classroom, she seemed immediately interested in my desires and interests and made sure that I would be a part of the classroom. Not only did she offer her methods of teaching and classroom management but she also encouraged me in my own teaching, telling me when she thought my lessons went very well and taking the time to tell me that I have the enthusiasm one needs to be a teacher. (Louise Martin)

Donna and I went over her evaluation of me for the first part of the term. It was a real ego trip for me. She had said so many times before that I was doing a great job, but I did not know if I should take her seriously or not. I knew I had been doing at least an okay job, but I wondered if all her encouragement and praise were just the product of a nice person trying to set up a comfortable environment for me. In our discussion of the evaluation she really made me feel like I was growing a lot, had a lot of natural ability, and was doing an excellent job. It really motivated me and made me feel good about what I am doing. She said that one of my strong points is my relationship with the kids, that they really seem to connect to me and depend on me. I like that. I have always found that it is difficult and takes a long time to build relationships with anyone. It does seem easier to do this with children, and this is a comforting thought. Our discussion was a good basis for me to try some other ways of doing things and to feel comfortable in taking some risks. (Brian Forbes)

I attended parent-teacher conferences with Cheryl [my cooperating teacher]. At first I was not excited to go but, afterwards, I was glad that I had gone. A couple of good things came out of this night. First, it gave me a chance to talk with the parents and make associations with the students as to their home life. And second, it gave me a chance to converse with Cheryl on things other than the classes. Talking with the parents was interesting. It amazed me that, for the most part, only the parents of the quiet well-behaved students attended. Cheryl and I both wanted to talk with a few specific parents (parents of the problem students) but not many of them came.

In between the parent sessions, Cheryl and I talked about many things, which gave us a chance to get to know each other better. She is an open person, and I, for the most part, am a private person. Many people have told me that I am hard to really get to know. I have tried to be open with her, but my mind is usually racing one hundred miles an hour so that not a lot of small talk comes to mind. Anyway, during this night, we shared many things: she asked me to play on her softball team this summer; we set up a game of basketball against a few students who wanted to play us; and, we chatted about home lives and all, which was really fun.

This occasion was a good stepping-stone to a better working relationship, one in which I am not as afraid of asking advice or taking ideas. I have a hard time asking someone I do not feel comfortable with for help or advice. I feel that spending this extra time together without pressures of the next class coming in will help me to get more out of my student teaching. (Nina Mines)

I am now in the process of being placed with a second cooperating teacher because of some problems I had with the first one. Most of the problems were instigated by me. I greatly underestimated the time commitment required for good teaching. I did not plan far enough in advance. When some minor emergencies hit in the middle of a two-week teaching unit I was left giving a rushed, frazzled, lower than desired teaching performance. Also, not having taken pains to ensure a good relationship for good communication with my cooperating teacher, I was also left without feedback from him.

The cooperating teacher interpreted my actions as lack of commitment and even questioned my desire to become a teacher. A simple five minute talk to communicate his doubts would have been most beneficial and would have helped me to resolve any misunderstandings about what I should be doing. When I stopped in to speak with him about some of these realizations I had arrived at on my own, I discovered that he had made arrangements the previous day for my withdrawal from his classroom to another placement. I was shocked and devastated. At first I pleaded with him to allow me another chance, but after careful reflection, and concern about the lack of feedback I had received from him, I felt it best to be placed with another cooperating teacher.

This experience left me with a very bitter taste. I was frustrated at my inadequate performance and misjudgments but also angry at my cooperating teacher's nonconfrontational handling of the situation. His behavior indicated to me that he did not feel I was important enough to spend five minutes telling me how he felt or that he was [planning to have me removed from the classroom].

When the assignment for my new cooperating teacher is attained, I intend to correct my past self-defeating behaviors. I will create the time needed to do better. I will concentrate on better time management. I will take the responsibility to develop a good communicating relationship with my cooperating teacher. I will not wait for feedback; I will ask specifically for it. I will tell him or her of the seriousness of my desire to become a teacher. I will plan further ahead. I will evaluate my lesson plans every day after teaching. I will be careful to project a more dedicated attitude. In the future, if I am ever a cooperating teacher, I intend to give prompt feedback to student teachers before making assumptions and to deal ethically and honestly with them. I believe when a teacher makes a commitment to take on a student teacher, he or she accepts a stewardship. Responsibility of the student teaching experience should be felt by both participants. (Trica Donald)

For Reflection and Discussion

1. Robert recognized the differences in personality between himself and one of his cooperating teachers. He decided that he could be happy with her but wondered if she would be happy with him. He discovered a closer personality match with another cooperating teacher only to find that their teaching styles differed.
   a. To what extent should Robert have been expected to emulate his cooperating teacher?
   b. What issues of matching preservice teachers with cooperating teachers arise from Robert's account?
   c. How might Robert have discovered and responded to his cooperating teachers' expectations?
2. Initially feeling critical of her cooperating teacher, Leila began to question herself in a way that expanded her analysis of teaching techniques. Leila writes that she decided to open her mind.
   a. How did she do this? How do you feel about this issue?
3. Kevin regrets feeling that he had to "better" his cooperating teacher. He questions whether his competitive attitude represents "professionalism."
   a. Reread Kevin's account. Can you find clues in his writings that help explain his thinking?
   b. How might he have addressed what "bothered" him about his cooperating teacher without becoming competitive?
   c. What other issues besides that of "professionalism" might be involved in being competitive with a cooperating teacher?
4. Kinsey describes being intimidated by her cooperating teacher (whom she sees as a model of her own aspirations). She attributes her anxiety about this to her own latent, perfectionist streak.
   a. How might Kinsey's experience be revealing of the problems associated with a match that is, perhaps, too close?
   b. How could Kinsey begin a dialogue with the cooperating teacher to ease such feelings? How might the cooperating teacher respond to the ideas you have for Kinsey?
5. Linda notices differences among cooperating teachers in their acceptance of new ideas.
   a. To what extent might this difference toward ideas among teachers be attributed to the expectations of the building principal or the community within which the school is located?
6. Linda and Melissa were pleased that their cooperating teachers welcomed their new ideas about teaching. Consider the relationships that Linda and Melissa seem to have developed with their cooperating teachers.
   a. How might the relationships have come about?
7. Julia expresses much respect and empathy for cooperating teachers. She felt hesitant about interfering with her cooperating teacher's plans. She writes that it did not bother her to follow their plans because she was still learning herself.
   a. What, according the Julia, are the advantages and disadvantages of following cooperating teachers' plans?

    b. How could Julia maintain respect for her cooperating teacher that would not restrict her learning?

8. Louise describes her cooperating teacher as providing support and feedback.

    a. What actions or behaviors do you think Louise adopted to facilitate a positive and supportive relationship with her cooperating teacher?

9. Brian was not sure if he should take seriously the praise offered by his cooperating teacher. The discussion that originated with the midterm evaluation gave him a "good basis" to feel comfortable taking risks.

    a. In what ways might the relationship that Brian enjoys with the cooperating teacher parallel that of the students and the cooperating teacher? Himself and the students?

10. Nina, a private person, experienced some difficulty conveying openness to her cooperating teacher. Small talk was elusive because her mind was "usually racing one hundred miles an hour." During an evening of parent conferences she and the cooperating teacher chatted about their home lives. Nina viewed this conversation as a "stepping-stone" to a better working relationship and felt more comfortable asking for help and advice as a result.

    a. What affect might the setting have had upon Nina's ability to be more "open"?

    b. What steps might Nina have taken to deliberately achieve this level of communication?

11. Trica's account vividly illustrates the importance of becoming proactive in establishing communication with cooperating teachers. Planning for a new placement, Trica vows to take the responsibility to develop good communication with the new cooperating teacher.

    a. How should Trica begin to establish effective communication?

    b. Might Trica have overlooked some warning signs from her cooperating teacher? What might be some of the warning signs?

Links with Research

There is a plethora of literature on the field experience component of preservice teacher education. In almost all of the studies, the cooperating teacher is involved or implicated in some way, which points to a need for more and better attention to the role of the cooperating teacher. These studies are about

- cooperating and preservice teacher relationships
- preservice teachers' concerns
- supervisory practices
- the role of the cooperating teacher as teacher educator
- influences of cooperating teachers on preservice teachers' development
- issues related to selection, preparation, and support of cooperating teachers

As Feiman-Nemser and Buchmann (1987) observe in an exploration of the question, "When is student teaching teacher education?"

    The job of cooperating teachers is to talk aloud about what they do and why, to demonstrate how to probe and extend student thinking, to alert student teachers to interpret signs of understanding and confusion in pupils, to stimulate student teachers to talk about their reasons for decisions and actions and the difficulties inherent to finding out what pupils know and what they need to learn (p. 272).

But, as they and many other researchers admit, for cooperating teachers to take seriously their role as teacher educators there has to be an emphasis on preparation and support for these individuals. It is perhaps hard to believe, but with few exceptions, cooperating teachers receive little or no preparation for their role in field experiences and little or no recognition and support for their involvement. Nevertheless, as logic and any study of field experiences point out, the cooperating teacher has a vital role in the field-based component of teacher preparation.

The role of cooperating teacher is demanding and multidimensional. One cooperating teacher described her experience of the role in this way:

> My experience as a [cooperating] teacher was perhaps one of the most challenging experiences of my life. It called into question the confidence that I had in myself as a person, my ability to communicate with others and above all, it tested my beliefs about teaching, and my ability to be a professional (Beynon, 1991, p. 20).

Given the inadequate conditions under which most cooperating teachers are expected to carry out their responsibilities, one wonders why they elect to do so. Stout (1982) explored that question with 40 secondary school cooperating teachers. Whereas 73 percent became cooperating teachers because of an interest in making a positive contribution to the profession, 50 percent cited the opportunities such work provided for examining their own practice and keeping abreast of new ideas. Only 28 percent viewed preservice teachers as "an extra pair of hands," and a mere 5 percent mentioned a monetary incentive. These findings are corroborated in a Canadian study conducted by Cole and Sorrill (1992).

Stout (1982) also asked the cooperating teachers to identify qualities characterizing "successful" student teachers. While considering the views reported, keep in mind that they are the views of secondary school cooperating teachers, a factor that is likely to explain heavy emphasis on subject matter knowledge and a relatively low importance given to some of the other qualities. Enthusiasm for the subject and teaching, and subject matter knowledge were identified as the most important qualities associated with success (78 percent and 72 percent, respectively). Interest in and commitment to students, and demonstration of initiative, creativity, and willingness to experiment with new ideas were the second most frequently identified qualities (both by 38 percent of the cooperating teachers). Whereas 20 percent cited strong rapport with students as a quality related to success, 13 percent attached importance to exhibiting a sense of humor.

Obviously, cooperating teachers' perceptions of "success" in student teaching and conceptions of what constitutes "good" teaching overall differ enormously. That is why it is so critical at the outset and throughout the development of working relationships to address such matters with cooperating teachers. Morris and Morris (1980) report that the supervisory aspect of relationships with cooperating teachers is one of the main sources of stress for preservice teachers. Numerous studies of the practicum (for example, Beynon, 1991; Campbell & Williamson, 1983; MacKinnon, 1989a) report that the development of a positive and productive working relationship between cooperating and preservice teachers is the most significant factor in determining a successful practicum. And, in turn, the key to developing a significant relationship is communication (Beynon, 1991; Guyton & McIntyre, 1990). "What is said, what is meant, and how it is understood constitute the key issues in the development of relationships between the cooperating teacher and the student teacher" (Beynon, 1991, p. 17).

MacKinnon (1989a) explored relationships in the student teaching triad (cooperating teacher–preservice teacher–university supervisor) with four preservice teachers. Although each preservice teacher felt that the development of a healthy relationship with the cooperating teacher was most critical for ensuring a successful field experience, in each case the relationship was quite different. The way the cooperating teacher defined her role, which in turn influenced the relationship that developed, had a significant impact on how the preservice teachers experienced the practicum. Relationships that were more collegial, characterized as a "team approach," were perceived by the preservice teachers as more positive and less stressful than those based on a novice-expert or master-apprentice model.

Issues of role definition and expectations are integral to any discussion about relationships in the practicum. There is general agreement, in the literature and in the field, that the role of the cooperating teacher is poorly defined and that expectations related to the role are diverse, ambiguous, and often overlapping or at odds (Grimmett & Ratzlaff, 1986; Applegate & Lasley, 1982, 1984). Expectations for the cooperating teachers' role in facilitating preservice teachers' learning through field experiences are determined both at an individual and institutional level, and it is little wonder that so much discrepancy exists.

Beynon (1991), for instance, working with preservice teachers, cooperating teachers, principals, and university supervisors discovered that expectations for the role of cooperating teacher reflected ambiguity, inconsistency, and lack of clarity, and that the cooperating teachers were not always comfortable with others' expectations of them. For example, the preservice teachers in the study expected their cooperating teachers to be models of exemplary practice, to be knowledgeable about current methods, curriculum, and philosophies of teaching, and to be able to espouse their philosophies of education in light of school board and government policies. The cooperating teachers, however, were not comfortable with these high expectations. They were in favor of communicating to preservice teachers that they, too, were still engaged in a process of learning as developing professionals, a position the preservice teachers found difficult to understand and accept.

Griffin, Barnes, Hughes, O'Neal, Defino, Edwards, and Hukill (1983) observe that university- and school-based educators rarely agree on or even articulate policies and practices to guide student teaching. According to Feiman-Nemser and Buchmann (1987), and Guyton and McIntyre (1990), what results is a less productive and less educative field experience than is possible. We will further address the field experience triad in Chapter 9 when we look at the role of the university supervisor in field experiences. For now, suffice it to say that negotiating a role and developing a productive working relationship with cooperating teachers are keys to a successful and fulfilling field experience. As the research literature points out, differences in expectations and poor communication account for most of the problems encountered by preservice teachers (Applegate & Lasley, 1982; O'Neal, 1983; Griffin, et al., 1983).

Research Activities

Negotiating a role with cooperating teachers is a complex process. The research activities that follow are intended to facilitate your comfort with the process because you have enhanced information about the role and responsibilities of cooperating teachers and your own purpose for working with such professionals. In thinking about these things refer to earlier chapters, especially Chapters 1 and 5.

1. Negotiating a role with a cooperating teacher presupposes two things: first, you know and recognize the benefits of working with a cooperating teacher; and, second, you have some notion about what you want to negotiate. Given the importance of these two conditions, the questions that follow imply certain lines of research action to be taken by you. Talking with cooperating teachers is a good start to your inquiry. A group discussion with your peers based on these questions and the information you gather is a useful follow-up activity.

    a. What are the benefits of working with an experienced teacher? What do you expect from such a relationship? How do you expect the experienced teacher to benefit from your presence in the classroom? What are your expectations for field experiences?

    b. What kinds of demands and expectations does the program in which you are enrolled place on the cooperating teachers with whom you are likely to work? Are they remunerated for their work? How? What are the limitations on cooperating teachers' time and energies, and how might these affect your presence in their classrooms? What expectations, if any, do principals and other administrators have of cooperating teachers? How are cooperating teachers expected to evaluate your participation in their classrooms?

    c. What do you expect to learn from working with the cooperating teacher? Are these expectations realistic given the various constraints placed upon you (and them)?

2. You are likely to know someone who has already participated in field experiences of different kinds—perhaps periods of observation, tutoring, and longer periods of practice. Explore with them elements of their experience with cooperating teachers.

    a. To what extent did these preservice teachers put sustained energy into negotiating roles and relationships with their cooperating teachers? In retrospect, what are their views about negotiating roles? What kinds of conditions and roles do they wish they had negotiated differently?

    b. What is their advice about negotiation? What can you learn from their experience? How does their advice complement or contradict the discussion within this book? Why?

    c. What do other preservice teachers say are the important or crucial elements to developing a relationship with cooperating teachers? To what extent are these views compatible with your perspectives or the perspectives presented in this book?

3. Uncovering cooperating teachers' personal theories about teaching is also likely to be useful to you because it will enable you to make decisions about the potential for productive, mutually beneficial relationships. You may want to inquire of cooperating teach-

ers about their backgrounds and philosophies of teaching. Also, because teaching beliefs are played out in classroom practice, a period of observation focused on discerning your cooperating teachers' beliefs and personal theories about teaching will be useful. The following are some questions to guide your observations and conversations so that you can get a handle on their philosophies.

    a. What are the cooperating teacher's prominent beliefs about good teaching? How does the cooperating teacher view the role of teachers? What does a typical day in the cooperating teacher's classroom look like? How does the cooperating teacher describe a typical day in the classroom? What is the central value the cooperating teacher holds? What are the prominent instructional strategies used by the cooperating teacher? What are the cooperating teacher's views of classroom management and disciplining students?

4. The stories cooperating teachers tell about "good" and "bad" preservice or student teachers may be revealing—they may help you understand cooperating teachers' perspectives about processes associated with negotiating roles and relationships.

    a. Do cooperating teachers tell stories about other preservice teachers? What stories do they tell? What roles are seen to be most advantageous for preservice teachers? How might these roles be either empowering or disempowering, depending on the contexts? What were the "blunders" of the less well thought of preservice teachers? What qualities seem to epitomize "good" preservice teachers? What are the kinds of roles that cooperating teachers seem to like of preservice teachers? To what extent are these desired roles compatible or incompatible with your thinking?

    b. How might the stories of cooperating teachers inform your thinking and assist you in forging roles and relationships? To what extent may such stories be helpful and less than helpful in your endeavors?

5. Even though it may be beyond the realm of your direct experience, try to imagine that you have become a cooperating teacher and are about to have a preservice teacher come into your classroom.

    a. What preparation do you need to assume such a responsibility? Is that preparation or guidance available? Where? How do you feel about fully sharing your professional life with a stranger? Do you view the newcomer as a much needed pair of extra hands or as a student of teaching with extra needs? How comfortable do you feel about having your teaching closely observed and analyzed? What would you most like to know about your preservice teacher's subject area preferences or expertise, grade level preferences, and goals for working in the classroom? Do you plan to guide or observe her or his development? What kind of feedback do you plan to provide? How do you think the preservice teacher may best learn in your classroom and school?

Dealing with and Learning from Differences in Perspective and Style

As you are aware, teaching practice reflects human diversity. Each teacher's practice is an individual expression of knowing, being, and interacting. Throughout your career you will encounter colleagues with values, beliefs, attitudes, perspectives, and pedagogical practices varying in similarity to your own; and you will decide about how you will respond to such diversity. Chances are you will choose to work in closer association with like-minded teachers rather than with those with fundamentally different perspectives. That is not to say that productive working relationships are confined to like-minded individuals. On the contrary, interactions with those of contrasting orientations can be intellectually challenging and can invigorate practice. (We suggested in Chapter 4 that you form collegial relationships with peers having different perspectives.)

In the situations we have just described there is an element of choice in the relationship. In some field placements you may have little control over selecting the teachers with whom you will work; consequently, it is important to prepare for situations in which style, personality, and philosophical differences are apparent. We believe that there is strength in diversity; however, we also recognize that in field experience situations where there is a clear power differential, appreciating and learning from diversity can be trying. In many ways, the cooperating teacher–preservice teacher relationship is like an arranged marriage. In some cases the relationship develops more easily and productively than in others.

There is no easy way to resolve differences with those with whom you work. We have no prescriptions other than to urge you to explore the meanings of those differences, discuss them openly, and decide accordingly. We know of too many cases in which either preservice teachers or cooperating teachers opted out of situations where they perceived differences in perspective or style to be too great to handle. In most of those cases individuals were unwilling to explore beneath the superficial representations of the other person. We think this is a great mistake and urge you to make considerate, thoughtful decisions when faced with working with someone holding perspectives unlike yours. One of the keys to tapping into differences is to first look for the powerful and potentially uniting similarities, building upon them while coming to an understanding of the differences and the reasons behind them.

In the following accounts, preservice teachers reflect on field experiences in which they were challenged to deal with and try to learn from incompatible and sometimes difficult situations. Issues of selection and matching arise from Audra's and Debbie's accounts. Renee compares field experience placements and identifies some of the constraints or limitations of incompatible placements. For Shawna, Mary, Allen, and Stacey, observing and experiencing difference helped make obvious and strengthen some of their own convictions about teaching and learning. Colleen and Dendi illustrate a coming to terms with issues of difference and how they resolved to learn from them.

Narrative Accounts

I expected that the teacher with whom I was placed with would be worthy of university approval as a cooperating teacher, but I did not feel that in reality this was true. In fact, I felt she was a good example of what a teacher should not be—a nonplanner, a ditto-maker, somebody ignorant of most of the recent theories I had learned about in courses. I was placed with a teacher I thought was lazy, and the experience was very disillusioning—I felt it was a very expensive loss in terms of experience. (Audra Green)

Communication skills are incredibly important to have as a teacher, and I do not feel that there is the potential for a lot of communication between Ms. Sorenson and the people with whom she works. In the last week, I have heard how difficult it is for others to get along with her, not only her students but the other faculty members and administrators as well. She is very demanding, yet she does not have a clear picture of what it is she is requiring. She has a real flair for acting out of pure spontaneity without thinking about the implications of what she says or does. She really does not have a sense of the big picture or, if she does, she does not know how to achieve it. I think that if she would listen to people a little more, it would help her immensely and possibly bring her to the reality of a situation.

In order for me to deal with this situation for the next little while, I feel like there has to be a lot of open communication. I need to go in knowing exactly what I want and stand up for myself completely and not give in to her suggestions. This may be very hard for me because I usually just go with the flow rather than be assertive. I guess this will be something I will have to practice over the holiday. Also, I will have to be extremely clear and succinct and really know what to tell her and ask of her. (Debbie Martinez)

Ms. Hannah and I have different styles, which can be frustrating, but I just don't think it is my place to reorganize things. Although I am not even sure what I would do differently, I just don't look at Ms. Hannah and think, "Yes, that's how I am going to do things." I guess I got depressed today because I wished to be working with someone who was more like me. Sometimes I feel that I am not getting all the ideas and insights that I need. In my earlier field experience I appreciated everything my teacher did. Sometimes I kick myself for not going back to her. At the same time, I realize it is pointless to get depressed about something I have no control over. I know that I am learning; I am just feeling aggravated. I hope that tomorrow I will have a better day and my outlook will be brighter. (Renee Buscho)

Just this week, after doing a lesson at Hookland High, I talked to my cooperating teacher. She said something like, "How funny it is that we will be working together because we are very opposite in our personalities and also in our approaches to teaching and our classroom demeanors." She is kind of the "rigid, strict type" who keeps a very tight rein on her classes. She lectures quite a bit and says she "really hates group work and learning games." The extent of student involvement in the class seems to be when they read something in class and each student [reads] a few paragraphs as they move up and down the rows. From most of my observations it seems that a lot of kids just tune her out. Her classes are always quiet and well behaved, but it seems like a lot of that is because the kids put their heads down and go to sleep. She told me she prefers them sleeping and being quiet to being loud and disruptive. I think sleeping kids would bother me enormously if I were teaching. I know we are not supposed to take students' actions personally, but when a student puts his or her head down and goes to sleep, it makes me feel like a sign is going up that says, "You, teacher, are boring me." (Shawna McCabe)

In my field experiences, I have observed two different teachers and how they give feedback to their classes. Ms. Lionel, my cooperating teacher, gives very little feedback to the children and, when she does, it often dwells on the negative rather than the positive. Students are fearful to ask her to help because they feel they will be yelled at for not knowing how to do an assignment or for not following directions. I feel this manner of teaching is very inappropriate. No child should dislike their teacher or be fearful of asking for help. Children should feel comfortable asking questions; otherwise, how will they ever clarify confusing facts and learn? Teachers have an obligation to be supportive of every child in their class. Often Ms. Lionel's students do not enjoy lessons because of the negative manner in which they are presented.

Ms. White, another fourth grade teacher, is a very optimistic person, and it is seen in her classroom atmosphere. She is always enthusiastic and interested in what the class is doing. From observing in her class, it appears that her students are more willing to attempt new projects than students in Ms. Lionel's room. Ms. White's students know she is their friend and she always encourages them to do their best. (Mary Mac)

Richie was one of the kids that my cooperating teacher had me work with early in the semester. Richie did not know the multiplication tables above the "fours" and needed some extra help or, at least, some extra time. Richie could and did learn the tables. He mastered multiplication. It may have taken him a little longer to do it, but he did it. Here is where I almost got into my first argument with my cooperating teacher. Last week, the kids did a worksheet to review for the test they were to have at the end of the week. I commented to my cooperating teacher the next day on how well Richie was doing on the worksheet. She grunted and made the comment that he had not even finished half of the sheet. On that half of the sheet, though, he had every one of them right and in such detail that it was easy to see that he knew how to do the stuff. It just took him more time to do it. Kids like Richie can master the material. They might just need some extra time or instruction, or maybe just different instruction. (Allen Montgomery)

One day, the student teacher [in the class I was observing] told a child "Not to color a duck blue since it is not the real color of ducks." I asked the student teacher why she tells them what colors to use and not to use, to which she replied, "Students should color objects their realistic colors." I thought to myself, "Why?" Another time, my cooperating teacher told the students exactly what they could draw for an "art activity." The activity was to draw a tree trunk on a piece of paper and later to use paints to add fall-colored leaves. She showed them an example of a drawing that they could use as a guide, which included a brown tree trunk, green grass, and two flowers. She emphasized to the students that they should not add more than two flowers, to ensure that they would leave room to paint the leaves on the tree. One morning, I helped the teacher with a project and did not insist that the children follow her directive. The teacher either did not notice or just did not say anything to me about it. Prior to my field experience, the issue of how to promote children's creativity had not entered my mind. (Stacey Chin)

My cooperating teacher conducted her classroom in a cool, detached, business-like manner. This caused me some discomfort during the term because I could not behave in the same way. I regarded her initially as *the* model of professionalism. I heard (unsolicited) praise about her from her peers as well as from the parents of her students. I "tried on" her teaching style, and it did not fit. At first, I confused style with ability and felt worried that I could not perform as she did. Later, some things began to bother me; her voice was consistently loud, she preferred using a teacher-centered style, and she was quite strict about student noise and movement. She was completely professional but just not a model for me to follow. Her style was familiar to my own learning experiences but not representative of the goals I had for myself as a teacher. It took me a long time to realize that the things that bothered me about her classroom did not have to take place in mine. (Colleen Presswood)

This term [the second of a two-term sequence] has not resolved some of the problems that I have had with my cooperating teacher. In the first term I identified the differences between me and Mr. Mack. That set me at ease because I understood that it is "okay to be myself." I have accepted that our dissimilarities exist and that all I can do is deal with them one day at a time. That realization came very hard to me because I would dwell on the complexity of our differences. It has been helpful to not worry until a conflict arises and then deal with it quickly. I know that I will be a stronger person after this experience. Mr. Mack is not as bad as I made him out to be. He is very supportive, kind, complimentary, and eager to come to agreement. It is just that I struggle quite a bit with our contrasting opinions. (Dendi Birchum)

For Reflection and Discussion

1. Audra felt that she was placed with a grossly inferior educator.
    a. What is an appropriate way for Audra to think about her placement? Should she renegotiate the placement? Why or why not?
2. Debbie hears that her cooperating teacher is difficult to work with. Careful observations reveal some of the reasons for the reputation this teacher has earned. Concerned about establishing the communication necessary to meet her needs as a learner, Debbie developed a plan of action that includes asserting herself to address this situation. She admits that the plan will be hard to carry out because, in contrast to her cooperating teacher, she usually "goes with the flow" rather than make demands.
    a. In what ways might it be advantageous for Debbie's growth to closely interact with someone so temperamentally different than herself? How might it be disadvantageous?
    b. Think about Debbie's description of her cooperating teacher. What are the strengths in Debbie's plan to address the problem? What are the weaknesses? Can you think of other options that Debbie might employ to negotiate their differences?
    c. How might Debbie's cooperating teacher react when Debbie addresses the problem?
3. Renee realizes that the differing style presented by her cooperating teacher is causing some frustrations. She feels depressed because she would rather work with someone

more like herself—an experience she enjoyed in an earlier placement where she appreciated *everything* about her cooperating teacher.

   a. What might Renee do to increase her satisfaction with her present placement?
   b. To what extent might Renee's acute awareness of differences be the result of her own continued study about teaching?
   c. How might the awareness of differences indicate a more refined sense of self-as-teacher?
4. Shawna's cooperating teacher openly addressed their differences during a conversation. Shawna writes that her cooperating teacher presented lackluster lessons that students slept through and preferred that kind of quiet to the noise generated by group work.
   a. How did the open acknowledgment of differences influence the learning environment for Shawna?
   b. How might working with "her opposite" afford Shawna the opportunity to identify and strengthen her personal vision of teaching?
   c. How might the restraints implicitly imposed upon her own developing practice negatively influence her professional growth?
5. Mary observed two teachers whose practice differed a great deal. She noted the response of the students to the differing styles and made some conclusions about each situation. One cooperating teacher's style was controlling and critical, and Mary noted a negative impact upon the students. A different teacher of the same grade level had a more positive and supportive approach, and she observed that students of the second teacher were more willing to take risks.
   a. How might Mary's observations clarify her own values about teaching?
   b. Why do you suppose Mary sought out another classroom to observe?
6. Stacey observed a student teacher tell a child not to color a duck blue. She also observed a teacher give explicit instructions about how to complete an art activity. She writes that prior to these observations the "issue of how to promote children's creativity had not entered my mind."
   a. In what ways did Stacey 's observations allow her implicit beliefs about teaching to become explicit?
   b. How did Stacey use these observations to reflect upon and discover differences that helped define her own style?
   c. To what extent might the student teacher's approach to creative tasks have been influenced by the classroom teacher?
7. Colleen and Dendi perceive differences between themselves and their cooperating teachers. Colleen acknowledges some discomfort with this difference, and Dendi writes that the realization to deal with it one day at a time came hard to her because she dwelt upon the complexity of those differences.
   a. How might the recognition and acknowledgment of differences within an ongoing working relationship facilitate professional growth?
   b. In what ways might Dendi's struggle over their differences be reduced by discussing them with her cooperating teacher?
   c. Both preservice teachers acknowledge respect for their cooperating teachers. To what extent might this aspect of their relationship have contributed to their feelings of discomfort about the differences?

Links with Research

It is unfortunate that the selection of cooperating teachers is based more on issues of collective bargaining and politics than on guidance of preservice teachers (Cole & Sorrill, 1992; Howey, 1977). And, generally, not much attention is paid to matching preservice and cooperating teachers along any lines other than grade level, subject matter (in secondary schools), and convenience of location. As a result, the quality of field experiences is wide-ranging. Considerable research has been done in attempts to determine the influence of cooperating teachers on preservice teachers' thinking and practice and on the quality of preservice teachers' field experiences. Although the *potential* influence of cooperating teachers is great, there is too much controversy and disagreement about the extent of their influence to make any unequivocal claims. Such influence seems to be context-specific and particularistic.

Student teaching can have negative as well as positive influences (Hull, Baker, Kyle, & Good, 1982; Zeichner, 1980). Some studies suggest that the cooperating teacher, and student teaching experience in general, have little, if any, lasting influence on preservice teachers' thinking and practice (Copeland, 1978; Lortie, 1975; Zeichner, 1980; Zeichner & Grant, 1981; Zeichner & Tabachnick, 1981). (Recall the discussion of personal history influences in Chapter 5.) Several researchers investigating the influence of cooperating teachers on preservice teachers' thinking and practice report that preservice teachers conform to behavior and expectations of cooperating teachers perhaps because of the evaluative role of the cooperating teacher (Barrows, 1979; Boschee, Prescott, & Hein, 1978; Brodbelt & Wall, 1985; Griffin et al., 1983; Mahan & Lacefield, 1976; MacKinnon, 1989b; Pritchard, 1974).

Whether or not matching preservice and cooperating teachers along lines of perspective has any significant influence on the quality of field experiences has been investigated. Bunting (1988) measured views on student-centered and teacher-directed learning of 17 randomly paired cooperating and preservice teachers. Preservice teachers paired with cooperating teachers holding extreme (that is, more flexible and adaptable) views on student- and teacher-centered learning experienced no change in their perspectives; preservice teachers paired with cooperating teachers with less extreme views developed more flexibility in thinking about student-centered and teacher-directed learning. Preservice teachers who were involved in decision making about various aspects of their field experiences, including selecting cooperating teachers and defining goals for their field experience, were inclined to place themselves with cooperating teachers with views and practices congruous with their own. During their field experience, the preservice teachers confirmed their preconceived ideas about teaching and increased their levels of confidence (Tabachnick & Zeichner, 1984). These findings are also supported by Schumer and Knowles (1991).

Other studies suggest that significant learning occurs when preservice teachers are placed with cooperating teachers with perspectives and practices markedly different from their own. Placed in a situation engendering cognitive dissonance and presenting challenge, preservice teachers may respond by working harder to overcome the disequilibrium they experience (Leslie, 1969; Pritchard, 1974; Griffin et al., 1983). Hollingsworth (1988), in a study of the impact of the cooperating teacher on preservice teachers' conceptual change, reports that preservice teachers placed with cooperating teachers with opposing views and practices demonstrated significant conceptual change and growth, particularly when the cooperating teacher explicitly challenged the preservice teacher's ideas. Together, these studies point out the learning value inherent in exposure to diverse perspectives.

Research Activities

1. Learning from difference is often more difficult than it sounds, and it requires a perseverance on all fronts. How do people within any context come to work successfully with those of vastly different perspectives and styles? Explore experiences of others within the framework of this question, drawing on media stories and reports, book accounts, and personal experiences.

   a. What are some of the common elements of these stories? How can these elements be applied to the context you are about to enter or have already entered?

2. As you become acquainted with your cooperating teachers and observe their practice it may happen that the stylistic or philosophical differences are immediately apparent. Be aware that your initial impressions may distort your perceptions. Initially, your view may be either too rosy or too dark. It is up to you to refocus and adjust the lens for a more accurate assessment of the situation. The following activities may help you recognize the reasons for the differences, and this understanding may make it easier for you to learn from them.

   a. You have probably taken some observation notes that focused upon the actions of your cooperating teacher. Review these notes and use one or two descriptive words to create a list of differences (for example, lenient, loud voice, and so forth). Examine this list and create categories such as, "style," "methods," and "personality" from the differences you listed. Make a separate list to describe yourself according to the same categories. Look for patterns and degrees of differences.

   b. Repeat the preceding activity, but this time seek out similarities. Compare the two lists. Have you discovered categories that are in agreement or perhaps neutral? If so, this may indicate an area that could be used to open dialogue about mutual expectations in other areas.

3. For your own "perspective development" you might find it useful to think through a technique used to talk about differences. This approach is adapted from the "pillow education" technique taught to Japanese children to solve problems (see, Adler & Towne, 1987). A problem or difference, like a pillow, is seen to have four "sides" and a "middle." Choose a viewpoint with which you strongly disagree. This is the "problem" that you will attempt to approach from different perspectives. As your position around the "pillow" moves, place yourself in it as if the thinking and feeling were your own. The first position (and easiest) is to assert that you are right and the other is wrong. The second position reverses the first position; you are wrong and the other is right. (Most of us get stuck vacillating between the first two positions.) The third position merges the first two; both of your positions are right and both of your positions are wrong. The fourth position asserts that it is not important which side is right or wrong; all positions are true. Finally each position is affirmed—each springs from the center.

   It is difficult to be accepting of positions two, three, and four, especially if the problem is important to you. This process will be effective only if you can suspend your judgment and imagine how it would feel to hold the other positions. You can see that position three is a rich place to begin to achieve some consensus about complex issues. You can measure your success with this technique by assessing the degree to which you can understand, though not necessarily accept, another perspective. After reaching this understanding do you notice a change in how you feel about the other position?

4. Field experience and practice teaching can represent a period of considerable growth for you. If you are comfortable in the relationship with your cooperating teacher it may be illuminating for you to engage in conversation with the teacher about his or her growth. After all, the methods and approaches you are presently observing were developed only after much practice. The following questions may be helpful in initiating conversations about professional growth. (Remain sensitive to issues of privacy as you think about questions of your own.)

   a. What was your biggest surprise about teaching? Did you discover unknown strengths during your student teaching? How did you first handle classroom management?

   b. How has your practice changed since your first teaching year? How did those changes come about? How did you decide upon the present management strategy? Does your teaching continue to change and evolve or are you comfortable with your present style?

Negotiating and Making Sense of Guidance and Guidelines

In thinking about working closely with one or more cooperating teachers there are several issues to consider as you negotiate and renegotiate daily and weekly. Notice that we specifically said "renegotiate." Perhaps we should also say "Renegotiate, again." The first point we want to make here is that modes of cooperating teachers' guidance, and their guidelines, are *not* set in stone, nor are they usefully unilaterally established.

Consider the guidance that cooperating teachers can provide you as being like the guidance a parent can offer a child learning to ride a bicycle. There are many ways for parents to assist the child. Fixing "training wheels" on the bike is one option. Parents are sometimes seen walking or jogging, rope in hand, child and bicycle in tow, as they provide both the direction and motive power. Sometimes the child is guided and assisted by parents grasping the handle bars; other times parents clutch on to the child. Or, you might see a parent gently guiding by fingertip, lightly holding the back of the seat; there, the parent can provide balance and a little motive power without the child feeling that the task of learning to ride has been taken away from her or him. This last scenario is how we prefer to think of the mode of guidance offered by cooperating teachers. In using this analogy we are not suggesting that learning to teach is a child's endeavor; nor are we suggesting that it is like learning to ride a bicycle; nor is it a unilaterally directed endeavor.

In describing the "learning to ride a bike" scenario we have omitted one important element: the child's perspective. How did the child want the parent to assist and guide? What kind of assistance did the child request? For how long did the child want the assistance? And, When? How much? These kinds of questions may be implicit, conveyed by gesture, actions, or subtle looks of impatience. Or, more often than not, the child is likely to be explicit in requests to parents. Turned around, these questions are similar to the kinds of questions other learners might ask when in various contexts and situations. They illustrate core issues in the preservice teacher–cooperating teacher relationship.

Within the context of this book the analogy of learning to ride fails unless we mention one other part of the child's experience. Undoubtedly, the child behind the handle bars thinks a great deal about being like "a big person"—able to ride alone down the sidewalk and on to the road. Perhaps such thoughts are more dreamlike. Lying on the bed or the bedroom floor, for instance, the child reflects on the experience, reliving swooping into the corner, braking hard at the curb, and steering clear of the toys on the sidewalk. The experiences are relived as the child balances in his or her mind the multiple skills involved in riding a bike. "When I did . . . this happened." Or "I crashed into Dad's leg because I wasn't looking out. . . ." And, "When you balance and steer around corners you do. . . ." And so on. The analogy has its limitations, and we certainly do not want to give you the impression that learning to teach is the mere mastery of skills. What we do want to point out is the importance of reflection. Through it, you are able to rethink practice, refine, and change it into something more contextually progressive and responsive to roles and needs.

We have regularly observed preservice teachers act in ways with cooperating teachers that imply that *all* of the decisions about guidance and the establishment of guidelines are cooperating teachers' responsibilities and, as such, are beyond their control. This suggests that as emerging professionals these preservice teachers have little idea about how to ask for and shape guidance. We have also found some preservice teachers to be intimidated by many of the professionals in schools, especially principals. Having been students much of their lives, some preservice teachers are unfamiliar with the collegial role they are about to enter; "feeling intimidated" is how some preservice teachers have described their emotions during the task of negotiating roles and guidance from cooperating teachers and others. Rest assured that, contrary to common practice, learners have a right to negotiate the guidance they receive from teachers such as, in your case, cooperating teachers and teacher educators. For your work in schools to be mutually benefiting, you and your cooperating teacher need to take responsibility for developing the foundation and structure of the working arrangement and professional relationship.

A second point for you to consider is that the relationships you establish with cooperating teachers ought to facilitate guidance and feedback. This is, of course, one of the roles of *any* teacher. The reasons you are in a particular cooperating teacher's classroom may be varied. The primary reason, however, is to advance *your* professional development. Without appropriate guidance and feedback the chances are that the purposes of the field experiences will be significantly lost and the opportunities considerably reduced. As a way of facilitating feedback about specific teaching activities, we suggest that you use "peer observation" (see Chapter 4) as a point of discussion with cooperating teachers and as a way to shape your developing practice. Feel free to talk directly about the kind of guidance that is most useful for you.

A related issue bears mention. We have worked with preservice teachers whose attitude is that it is a sign of weakness to ask for and accept guidance. To the contrary, learning from others about *their* perceptions of *your* actions or practices is a powerful way to facilitate learning and professional growth. View these observers of your work within classrooms and learning communities as providing you with another set of eyes with which to examine your emerging professional practice.

The third point we raise for your consideration is acknowledging and dealing with different approaches to guidance and feedback. Each teacher has a different pattern and personal style of working and interacting. In addition, external elements are likely to influence the manner in which the cooperating teacher works and interacts with you. These external influences include

- the school timetable
- workloads and responsibilities
- commitments to specific activities with the school board or district
- commuting patterns
- family responsibilities
- mentoring experiences
- philosophical perspectives
- personalities
- career stage
- other professional responsibilities (such as office in a professional organization)
- other pressures that may be unknown to you

You may be able to influence some of these elements, but the chances are this will be minimal. You can, however, facilitate communication and feedback by structuring opportunities that are mutually beneficial and considerate of each person's responsibilities. Considerations of time constraints, sequence and timing, place, and moods of each person are essential if opportunities for optimum feedback and guidance are to be realized.

As you have probably anticipated, heard from others, or read in anecdotal accounts or formal research reports the role of evaluator clouds the relationship between preservice teachers and cooperating teachers. Our view is that there are a variety of conditions that have the potential to facilitate the process of evaluation and make it relatively painless. A model of evaluation that honors the growth and integrity of each person is desirable, if not essential. If such evaluation is open, formative, constructive, and considerately conveyed, much of the fear and pressure associated with the evaluation process may be avoided. Of course, this presupposes that both preservice teachers and cooperating teachers discuss the scope, focus, and form of the evaluation *before* the process begins and that both have a clear sense of their responsibilities. There are likely, however, to be constraints placed on the evaluation process—enter the role of the university supervisor and the official documentation of the preparation institution—but for the moment we will place these elements in the background.

Your relationship with cooperating teachers in the field is bound, at some time, to be framed by tensions. These tensions may mold your relationship and the kind and degree of guidance you seek and receive. Two sets of questions capture and frame these tensions. First, an internal tension, one that may largely rest in your thinking and articulation of that thinking: Do you want to learn deductively or inductively from your field experience? How much specific direction do you want cooperating teachers to provide? To what degree do you want to be left alone to try things out?

A second tension emerges from cooperating teachers' perspectives: How much guidance do they give you? Do they tell you what to do or let you discover pitfalls and prospects for practice? How do they know when to step in and offer assistance? How do they best facilitate your professional growth? To what extent do they encourage you to emulate their practice? These kinds of questions, representing the dichotomies of internally- and externally-induced tensions, will shape the relationship you establish with cooperating teachers and the degree of guidance they give and you accept. We urge you to think carefully about these kinds of issues as you move forward in your field experience.

Leila discovered the importance of being open to constructive criticism when she realized that stylistic differences between her and the cooperating teacher were not going to interfere with her learning from experience. Melanie also learned to trust the cooperating teacher's judgments once she recognized that her own lack of self-confidence was at the heart of her perceived difficulties. Jane shares excerpts from her journal in which she reflects on aspects of her relationship with the cooperating teacher pertaining to guidance and evaluation. She struggles with the dilemma of wanting to be independent and learn through experience, and receiving more explicit direction; reflects on her attitude toward asking for and accepting guidance; and describes the influence the evaluative role of her cooperating teachers had on her performance and practice. Noelle feels pressured by the cooperating teacher's directive approach to guidance. Paulo and Miranda analyze and try to work through difficult (potentially harmful) relationships with their cooperating teachers. Issues of selection, placement, and preparation of cooperating teachers also arise from these accounts.

Narrative Accounts

I gave two German lessons last week. They did not go very well at all. Having been in the classroom for only a short time, I was nervous. What made me somewhat nervous was the statement the teacher made before giving me the floor. I really did not appreciate it when she said, "Will you guys be quiet for Leila?" I can quiet a classroom myself if I want to or it needs it. And besides, it does not give a good impression of me to the students. I do not believe, however, that Ms. Sommers did this on purpose. She was very nice to me after I gave the lessons. She made a few comments that I felt were to the point and helpful. She mentioned that I had not stated my objectives clearly and had not demonstrated an example and, since my method of teaching is very different from hers, students were a little confused. She also mentioned that I tried to cover too many things at one time, which I guess was true. I had not noticed those things myself. I believe that some of the things I did were out of anxiety and some things I just had not noticed fully. It really made me loosen up when her comments on my lessons were so objective. I did not know what to expect because her methods are so different from mine. She merely said, "Well, it's good for students to be exposed to other methods." I was surprised. (Leila Muniroui)

Sometimes I needed to ask about rules in the classroom. I wish Ms. Simpson would have told me the rules before I met the students because I learned most of the rules as the semester progressed. I understand that it is nearly impossible to tell me all the rules I need to know before experiences arise that call for them, but it would have made me look more confident in front of the children. If I am supposed to discipline them, I should know the rules before I let them do something they are not allowed to do. Maybe Ms. Simpson felt that I was confident enough to handle most situations that come up. For my lessons, usually she did not look over the specific details of my lesson plans, especially for small groups; she trusted my judgment. At first, this made me feel nervous because I was not that confident in my own teaching skills. But now, it makes me feel good that she had confidence in me and my teaching abilities. She knew that I would make mistakes; everyone does. But she was sure that they would not be major ones. (Melanie Colander)

During the past weeks, I have become frustrated by Paula's lack of guidance. Often, I feel hurt that she does not approach me and offer to help or ask how I am doing; however, after thinking about it for quite a while, I have realized that this dilemma has been created by my desire to be independent. For example, when I discuss teaching with Paula, I always mention how I need to do as many things as possible on my own. My feeling is that by struggling, I will learn what type of planning and teaching works best for me. The impression that this leaves with Paula is that I need little or no guidance unless I seek it. Although I am responsible for setting this tone, at times it is frustrating. A result of this desired independence is a lack of communication between Paula and me. For some reason, I am finding it very difficult to ask for help; therefore, I try to predict what Paula is looking for. I do not know if I am being stubborn or really trying to grow as a teacher. I imagine it is a combination of both.

There is also another element involved in our lack of communication—fear. I am fearful that bombarding Paula with questions will lead her to see me as weak and incapable of being a teacher. I am fearful that she will begin to resent me being in her classroom. I am fearful that she will give me a poor evaluation. Let's face it, the cooperating teacher's evaluation is either a gift of employment or the kiss of death. With one person having so much power, one can become obsessed with pleasing him or her.

This combination of fear, stubbornness, and desire to learn has resulted in a number of embarrassing situations. For example, in mathematics I decided to introduce a five-step process for solving word problems, part of which involved the students in creating their own story problems. Without consulting Paula I proceeded to teach this lesson. I quickly realized that many of the students had had little or no exposure to verbal or written story problems. They had only encountered procedural work. After realizing that my lesson was entirely too advanced for these students, I quickly changed my focus and geared the lesson to the decoding of the word problems. Later, Paula approached me and commented that my lesson seemed too difficult for the students. Once again, I was embarrassed that I had not consulted her and had overestimated the students. What I need is a better balance between trying things on my own and knowing when to ask my cooperating teacher for guidance.

At this time [several weeks later], I feel comfortable sharing my opinions with Paula. In turn, she has begun to confide in me and share her struggles as a teacher. Still, there exists a communication problem. I am still struggling with Paula's lack of guidance. I am an insecure person when it comes to my teaching practices. Although I try to be reflective about my teaching, I know that there are crucial things I am missing. I often wish she would give me more guidance about what I am doing. In the last three weeks, she has said only one thing to me concerning my teaching and this was after I asked. After one of my reading group sessions, I was concerned with the class's general tension level. I mentioned it to Paula. She said, "Don't worry about it. It takes time." So, I walked away and thought about it. Twenty minutes later, I walked up to her and said, "My hour with the students is rushed because I try to do too much. I need to do less and relax more. This will help the students relax." Paula looked at me and said, "I think you are right." I suddenly realized what she had done. I said, "You knew exactly what I should do 20 minutes ago when I first mentioned it to you. You wanted me to figure it out for myself." She smiled and said, "I knew you could." Although I appreciate her confidence, I am often worried that she is not being critical enough. I realize that when I teach in my own class, there will no one to guide me. And, I would like to take advantage of my cooperating teacher's expertise as much as possible. (Jane Atman)

One thing I am generally frustrated about right now is my relationship with Carol. I think our basic problems amount to having different philosophies about students. Sometimes I feel that she does not think that I reason things out before I do them in class. I appreciate Carol's help and suggestions but, right now, it is hard to constantly defend everything I do and not have any time to put her suggestions to work before another ten [suggestions] come the next day. I am feeling pressured by constant criticisms and suggestions when I am trying to figure out how I want to be as a teacher. (Noelle Frandsen)

Ms. Mulcahey expects me to have "100 percent control 100 percent of the time." She will not give an inch and has given me very negative feedback and evaluations. I have talked to her about it at various times, and she always insists that I do things her way. I tried a system I thought would work. I cannot seem to do anything to please her. I have been worried that, no matter what I do, I will get a bad evaluation from Ms. Mulcahey. I do not think that I have problems taking criticism or advice from a woman but, if that is the problem, I need time to work it out before my future as a teacher is ruined by a bad evaluation before it gets started. That is a real fear. I realize that in the past I have not paid enough attention to advice given to me, but I am now overcoming that.

I feel the level of discipline is satisfactory in the class. I have devised a system where the students have rules and a chart that plots their "citizenship grade." I feel I have good control of the class. There are a couple of problem kids I will need to work on, but I am confident I can handle them. And my lesson planning has been a little weak and not detailed enough.

Tomorrow I will have to talk with Ms. Mulcahey and let her know that I will not be able to stay with her anymore. I will tell her that I have tried and she has seen no progress, so I do not believe I will ever be able to live up to her expectations. I know I have problems, but it is not only me. I am doing very well in my other cooperating teacher's class doing the same things. I do not think I could do enough in the time remaining to please her and get an acceptable evaluation. It may be a personality conflict or just my inability to adapt to her personally. Whatever the case, I do not feel good about the present situation and am afraid it may be too late to remedy it.

I believe I did a satisfactory job teaching, even though I was weak in discipline, but Ms. Mulcahey pounced on me. I wanted to work it out myself, but she would not have it. I should have been more open and diplomatic. She should have been more understanding and loosened the reins. I should have used some of her examples. She should have let me use some of mine. I should have spent more time learning classroom management. She should have allowed me to use some of the ideas without telling me what would work and what would not. I have found that she is far from an expert in classroom management. Maybe that is why it concerns her so much. (Paulo Antonios)

After reading this stuff I just wrote, I feel the urge to kick myself for feeling that it is somehow my fault whenever things are not going perfectly. In truth, I did my best with all this. I worked harder day in, day out to meet all those demands than I had worked in seven years of higher education. (At least with that I have the comfort of graduating magna cum laude with a GPA of 3.9.) It is like painting a picture that, brilliant or not, exists regardless of whether or not it is appreciated. Maybe that is it. Maybe I feel unappreciated after putting so much into it.

It was a real pain to spend hours preparing lessons that did go well 90 percent of the time and have Ms. Trotsky focus on the 10 percent that went wrong—90 percent of the time. I am sure she felt this was constructive criticism, but sometimes it amounted to merely an insistence on doing things her way. At first I was too eager to prove myself and would strive to do things exactly as she wanted them done. I was amazed when she said (in a conference) that I had not pushed the students hard enough and that there was grammar curriculum that she had not made me teach. How ironic when she wrote out exactly what and when she wanted me to cover on those exact grammar requirements. I followed her instructions as closely as possible—too closely, perhaps.

Also, Ms. Trotsky said I was "too nice" with the students at first. And, to some extent, she was right about that. I have always had a kind of easy camaraderie with my own children and their adolescent friends. So, I assumed that this was appropriate classroom behavior. At our midterm evaluation conference, she made it clear that the "Don't smile until

Christmas" demeanor and consistently strict disciplinary measures were the only way to fly. At that point I became overly concerned with always being in charge of the students' behavior. I wrote demerits for any possible infraction partly because I knew she would give me a comprehensive list of students who deserved them in any class she had observed. In no time I had quiet classes and less friendly students. This seemed more acceptable to her and was certainly easier for me. But, one day when classes had gone especially well, she wrote up a list of petty student infractions and negative comments that angered me.

Ms. Trotsky had been moody and touchy all day and I felt she was taking it out on me for no real reason. We had a verbal confrontation at the time. I am sure she felt I was moody also, but I had simply reached the point where I was tired of being in a position where someone—anyone—had that kind of control over what I did. Maybe she had a "teacherly" experience I needed to learn from, but I am experienced and strong enough in what I have done and who I am as well. She could learn some things from me too. That, no doubt, seemed competitive and wrong-headed to her. But while I was doing "*her* thing" I got little credit for the effort; so, I decided to do it "*my* way" even if that did not suit anyone else.

I wish I could say that my way was an unqualified success. It did create meaningful interactions and "breakthrough" learning moments, but it also brought some frustrations, not the least of which was that by the time I knew *how* I wanted to teach, I was caught in a time-bind situation that made it a struggle to "cover the material"—let alone do it in innovative or time-consuming ways. That is not offered as an "I could have done better if. . ." excuse. I did okay. I taught at a slower pace—she felt I was "losing the bright kids." When I quickened the pace and geared the lessons to interest the more advanced students she felt I was "losing the slower students." I can teach to either level but could not seem to find the magic methods where I could get past being "damned if you do and damned if you don't."

In short, I think Ms. Trotsky might have been fine with someone who might benefit from "being taken down a notch or two" or who would take her ongoing comments with a grain of salt. I was too vulnerable and took her ideas too much to heart. She is the kind of person from whom much can be learned once you begin to understand something of her need to control and be "in charge." (Miranda Carter)

For Reflection and Discussion

1. Leila's cooperating teacher gave specific and impartial feedback about a lesson she taught. Their methods were different, and Leila did not know what feedback to expect. Leila was pleasantly surprised when the cooperating teacher said, "It's good for students to be exposed to other methods."
   a. Why do you think the feedback from the cooperating teacher allowed Leila to "loosen" up?
   b. To what extent could Leila have negotiated with the cooperating teacher about the type of feedback desired before teaching her lesson? How might she have done this?
2. Melanie felt a need for more structure and guidance early in her classroom experience. She notes that her nervousness about a perceived lack of guidance came about "because I was not that confident in my own teaching skills."

    a. How did Melanie seek to create a more secure environment for herself?

    b. What effect did the freedom to make mistakes (allowed by her cooperating teacher) have upon Melanie's developing sense of herself as a teacher?

3. Jane interprets the lack of guidance she received from the cooperating teacher as evidence that the teacher has confidence in her. Yet, she worries that the cooperating teacher is not critical enough and that she will have no one to guide her when she has her own class.

    a. In what ways are Jane's concerns (about lack of criticism) substantiated by educational research?

    b. Jane is aware of the paradox involved in asking for help from the person whose letter of recommendation can be "the kiss of death." How might Jane untangle her apparently conflicting needs to both learn from and impress the cooperating teacher (so that she can better meet her needs as a learner)?

4. The guidance offered to Noelle by the cooperating teacher caused her to feel pressured. She writes about "not having time to put her suggestions to work before another ten [suggestions] come the next day." She also writes that she is "trying to figure out how I want to be as a teacher."

    a. What steps might Noelle take to reduce the pressures of the field placement?

    b. How could Noelle use her developing teacher identity to focus on the suggestions that would be of most help to her?

5. Paulo decides to tell his cooperating teacher that he cannot stay with her anymore. He feels he cannot live up to her expectations during the remainder of the term. He is also fearful that no matter what he does she will remain displeased and write a negative evaluation.

    a. Did Paulo have other options? What might they have been?

    b. Did Paulo view the purpose of practice or student teaching as a place to develop his own practice or as an apprenticeship?

    c. Paulo mentions having two cooperating teachers. How might each of the cooperating teachers have viewed Paulo's role within the classrooms? How do you suppose they viewed their own roles?

6. Miranda and Noelle mention the difficulty of simultaneously accepting criticism while discovering their own teaching styles.

    a. How might the active acceptance of guidance facilitate the development of a personal teaching style?

    b. To what extent might acceptance and utilization of critique be made easier when some sense of personal teaching style is formulated?

7. Miranda worked hard to accommodate herself to the critiques of the cooperating teacher. She understood (too late) that it was the need of her cooperating teacher to be in charge and controlling that resulted in feeling "damned if you do and damned if you don't."

    a. Recognizing, as Miranda did, the powerlessness of her position, what might she have done to improve the situation?

    b. Should Miranda have sought a different placement? Why or why not?

Links with Research

> For student teaching to be teacher education, it must go beyond survival or extend practice in the outward forms of teaching to sort out appropriate from inappropriate lessons of experience. Well-meaning praises from cooperating teachers, coupled with a focus on management, fixes the attention of student teachers in the wrong direction (Feiman-Nemser & Buchmann, 1987, p. 272).

The extent and quality of learning from field experiences depend in large part on attitudes and practices related to guidance and supervision. The way in which cooperating teachers and preservice teachers work together to facilitate learning is influenced by factors such as goals, attitudes, expectations, role perceptions, and preparation for providing and accepting guidance and direction.

As was indicated in the two previous *Links with Research* sections in this chapter, for the most part, cooperating teachers are not adequately prepared for their roles. Cooperating teachers in one study admitted that, due to lack of preparation, they rely heavily on their own experiences as student teachers and attempt to model themselves on what they consider to be "good" cooperating teachers (Cole & Sorrill, 1992). Guyton and McIntyre (1990), in their comprehensive review and discussion of literature on student teaching and school experiences, cite lack of preparation for supervision as one of the three main problems of field experiences (lack of interpersonal and inter-institutional communication, and issues related to preservice teachers' skills, behavior, and attitudes were the other two main areas identified).

It is not surprising, then, that student teaching does not always turn out to be the learning opportunity it is intended or expected to be. Preservice teachers often experience confusion and frustration as a result of receiving inadequate or unhelpful feedback on their teaching (Feiman-Nemser & Buchmann, 1987; Griffin et al., 1983; Richardson-Koehler, 1988) or dissatisfaction with the cooperating teachers' approach to supervision (MacKinnon, 1989a). Recall from the discussion on preservice teacher–cooperating teacher relationships that the preservice teachers in MacKinnon's study who experienced the least stress and frustration, and most overall satisfaction with their field experience, worked in partnership with their cooperating teachers.

The "team approach" to supervision is one way of characterizing the way cooperating and preservice teachers can work together. Horwood (1981) studied the interactions and working relationships including supervision conferences of eleven pairs of cooperating and preservice teachers and used three models to describe those relationships. Most common was the "master-apprentice" model where the cooperating teacher as "expert" assigns, models, oversees, and evaluates student teachers' work. The "idiosyncratic" model was characterized by less guidance and focused observation and discussion of student teachers' work. This model was based on the idea that teaching is best learned through independent discovery. The third, the "brewmaster" model, was characterized primarily by advice-giving about "tried and true" techniques and strategies. The emphasis in this recipe approach was on "what works" with little or no reference to theories or philosophies underlying any of the pedagogical practices.

In their review of literature on field experiences, Guyton and McIntyre (1990) summarize the research on the conference element of formal supervision in this way:

> [Preservice teacher–cooperating teacher] conferences are dominated by cooperating teachers and student teachers take a passive role. Conferences involve low levels of thinking: descriptions and direction-giving interactions predominate. Analysis and reflection on teaching are not common; the substantive issues of conferences tend to focus on teaching techniques, classroom management, and pupil characteristics. Craft and experiential knowledge and efficiency are rationales for most recommendations (p. 525).

Attitudinal factors were cited by Campbell and Williamson (1983) as creating obstacles to cooperating and preservice teachers working together to facilitate learning through experience. Some preservice teachers perceived a sense of competition with their cooperating teachers; others an unwillingness of cooperating teachers to give up control of their classrooms. Some cooperating teachers believed that preservice teachers should strictly model their own teaching. Clearly, these and any other obstacles to a productive working relationship can be removed through communication.

The quality of field experiences hinges on ongoing communication and negotiation and, as is apparent by now, the responsibility for initiating and maintaining that process *does not* and *should not* lie solely with the cooperating teacher. We conclude this section with reference to a study involving 172 cooperating teachers and the problems they confront as they work with preservice teachers. We invite you to consider them as you prepare for and participate in your own field experiences. The following are six factors describing cooperating teachers' most significant problems:

- student teachers' lack of preparation for field experiences—lack of understanding of student behavior and lack of curiosity about becoming a teacher
- feelings of isolation and sole responsibility for preservice teachers' field experiences
- preservice teachers' and university supervisors' lack of interest in school norms and professional responsibilities
- preservice teachers who do not display a commitment to teaching or to doing certain tasks related to teachers' work
- preservice teachers' lack of initiative and enthusiasm for teaching
- planning, organization, and management abilities of preservice teachers (Applegate & Lasley, 1982)

Research Activities

1. Given the potential for you and cooperating teachers to experience tensions as you mutually forge relationships and make sense of their guidance, developing a sense of *their* understandings about the purpose of field experiences, particularly student teaching, may be useful. In focusing on developing your thinking about making sense of guidance and guidelines, the following are questions to consider. (You may also want to

explore these questions [and similar ones] with others who are becoming or are teachers. You may find it useful to talk with relatively new teachers to find out their perspectives.)

    a. How do cooperating teachers perceive the role of practice and the role of theory in learning to teach? What do they see as the important elements of field experiences— ones which shape experiential learning opportunities? How do they define their role in facilitating your growth? To what extent does that role mesh with your perspectives?

    b. What were the circumstances of the cooperating teachers' own field experiences as students of teaching? When and where did they engage in field experiences? In what ways do these cooperating teachers view contemporary opportunities for field experiences being similar or different from the opportunities they experienced as preservice teachers? What were the high and low points of their own field experiences? What elements of those experiences would they want to change should they have the opportunity to relive their experiences? What elements of those experiences do they desire to replicate with you?

    c. What "stories" do cooperating teachers tell about their own field experiences? On what elements do these stories focus? What elements of experience do they omit?

2. Understanding the experiences of other preservice teachers in the program before you— about negotiating and accepting guidance and guidelines from cooperating teachers— may also be helpful. Potential questions of these individuals include the following:

    a. How did they go about negotiating guidance and guidelines? What were some of the high points in these processes? What were some of the pitfalls? What elements of their experiences stand out most vividly in reflections on the experience? What are the stories they tell about working with cooperating teachers?

    b. What advice do other "more experienced" preservice teachers freely, or without invitation, give you about negotiating guidance and guidelines from cooperating teachers?

3. In reading the *Links with Research,* what points piqued your interest? How have the outcomes of research informed your thinking? Check out some of the research reports cited. Consider using appropriate examples of these research findings as foci for discussion with cooperating teachers. Questions that might promote discussion, for example, include: To what extent do cooperating teachers agree or disagree with the research findings in general and in specific cases? What is the basis of these opinions and perspectives? Why might it be difficult or inappropriate to apply such findings to your immediate situation?

4. Teaching is a complex endeavor and teachers are expected to demonstrate leadership while following guidelines established by mandated and school board (or district) curriculum, the building principal or administration, and teacher groups. They are expected to work well independently as well as collaboratively. It is likely that you will begin to feel some of these apparently contradictory expectations when you begin to teach. The activities that follow may be helpful for you to begin to anticipate and articulate areas of the practicum that may be comfortable for you as well areas that may present difficulties.

    a. Make a list of ten adjectives to describe yourself. Ask someone who knows you well, such as a parent, to do the same. Also ask a close friend and an acquaintance, perhaps a classmate, and then examine the lists closely and note the similarities and differences. What adjectives are repeated most often? How might the quality most often noted influence your experience as a student teacher? If you notice descriptors such as "pleasant," "friendly," "complacent," "quiet," and "easygoing" you may have to stretch a bit to assert yourself and make your learning needs known to your cooperating teacher. If terms such as "independent," "assertive," "willful," and "headstrong" appear frequently you may need to stretch a bit to ask for help and feedback and to adopt a collaborative attitude. The point is that you can use your knowledge about yourself to anticipate and mitigate the difficulties often associated with accepting and negotiating guidelines.

b. Think about the learning situation you are in or about to enter. In what ways is it similar to engaging in university coursework? In what ways is it different? It may be helpful to brainstorm a generic list of course requirements that you have become familiar with as a student. Think about issues of syllabi, feedback, task assignment, reading and writing requirements, and the criteria used for evaluation. Use this list to discover items that you expect will appear in your student teaching practicum. What are the similarities? How might they be addressed during the practicum? How might you address the differences?

Summary

In this chapter we focused on the cooperating teacher. We introduced topics associated with establishing yourself alongside such experienced teachers in the field in readiness to learn from engaging in opportunities for practice. We opened the discussion with the subject of negotiating a role and developing and maintaining productive professional relationships with cooperating teachers. In order to maximize the opportunities for experiential learning we invited you to think about how you can deal with and learn from those with perspectives different from your own. Finally, we explored the issue of negotiating and making sense of guidance and guidelines. In all of these topics the underlying implication—and suggestion—is that you be proactive in shaping the roles, relationships, guidance, and guidelines that determine the boundaries and scope of your experiential learning in the field.

In the following chapter we invite you to think about other professional relationships that are important for optimizing field experiences (in Chapter 10 we center on students). In particular, we focus on the university supervisor and others—faculty and staff—with whom you will regularly interact. The university supervisor and some school-based faculty may be directly involved in facilitating some aspect of your field experience, whereas others may only be involved as you interact with them or at your invitation. Nevertheless, you are entering a community of learners, and your sphere of influence will move beyond the confines of the classroom. We, therefore, invite you to consider not only your developing relationships with professionals within learning communities but also the relationships with parents, the predominant partners in students' learnings and growth.

Recommended Readings

Britzman, D. P. (1991). *Practice makes practice: A critical study of learning to teach*. Albany, NY: State University of New York Press.

Bruckerhoff, C. E. (1991). *Between classes: Faculty life at Truman High*. New York: Teachers College Press.

Clandinin, D. J., Davies, A., Hogan, P., & Kennard, B. (Eds.). (1993). *Learning to teach, teaching to learn*. New York: Teachers College Press.

Cohen, R. M. (1991). *A lifetime of teaching: Portraits of five veteran high school teachers*. New York: Teachers College Press.

Cohn, M. M. (1993). *Teachers: The missing voice in education*. New York: State University of New York Press.

Macrorie, K. (1984). *20 teachers*. New York: Oxford University Press.

Posner, G. J. (1989). *Field experience: Methods of reflective teaching*. New York: Longman.

Roe, B. D., Ross, E. P., & Burns, P. C. (1989). *Student teaching and field experiences handbook*. New York: Macmillan. (Chapters 2 & 3)

Shulman, J. H., & Colbert, J. A. (1987). *The mentor teacher casebook*. Oregon: ERIC Clearinghouse on Educational Management and Far West Laboratory for Educational Research and Development.

Shulman, J. H., & Colbert, J. A. (1988). *The intern teacher casebook*. Oregon: ERIC Clearinghouse on Educational Management, Far West Laboratory for Educational Research and Development, and ERIC Clearinghouse on Teacher Education.

Wood, D. R. (1992). Teaching narratives: A source for faculty development and evaluation. *Harvard Educational Review, 62*(4), 535–550.

CHAPTER 9

Developing Professional Relationships with Supervisors and Others in the Learning Community

In the preceding chapter we explored elements of relationships with cooperating teachers, the persons most able to help you negotiate your field work and capitalize on your immediate experiences. There are others, also, who will influence your development through field experience and who play significant roles within learning communities.

Within most contexts, the university supervisor is the most important of these other people, especially when it comes to facilitating your development through conversations, observations, and perhaps formal course work or seminar activity. More than the others, however, university supervisors are usually transient within the school or learning community. They come and go and usually have no fixed or transcending responsibility in the setting apart from working with people like yourself and perhaps the cooperating teachers. The other professional members of the learning community, although usually not overtly interested in your development as an emerging professional, are very interested in your general performance within the school and/or classrooms. In this chapter, therefore, we explore ways to develop relationships with

- university supervisors or school-based representatives of the teacher preparation program
- administrators and teachers not working directly with you as well as nonteaching support staff
- parents and the community

We assert that new teachers in contemporary schools have to be cognizant of the many supportive relationships that are possible and potentially productive. Developing productive relationships within the school or learning community will advance your work in the classroom with students because you will be able to draw on more resources.

Establishing Relationships with University Supervisors

University supervisors (or school-based representatives of the university program) complete the triadic relationship that typically characterizes the field experience component of preservice teacher preparation. In some situations, such as a major or culminating field experience, the university supervisor may be someone with a distinct supervisory role. In other cases, such as in any course with a field component, the university supervisor may be a professor or instructor who is simply facilitating opportunities for field experiences. Although much of this section applies more directly to the first kind of situation, it is also applicable to situations where elements of the supervisory role are not highly emphasized.

Among other things, the university supervisor acts as a conceptual link and liaison between the university faculty and the field. Perhaps surprising to you, university supervisors sometimes struggle with the ambivalent nature of their role, particularly with respect to evaluating preservice teachers' success in field experiences. The clearly defined role they often have at the university becomes cloudy as they move into the field where their presence and actions are less central and less integrated with the general affairs of schools and classrooms. They, like you, are guests in cooperating teachers' classrooms and schools, although sometimes they are more closely affiliated with schools than the picture we have drawn. You, too, are likely to experience some of this ambivalence as you attempt to sort out your relationships with cooperating teachers and university supervisors. Some university supervisors describe the process as "switching loyalties." By that they mean that you will make a change from being primarily grounded in relationships and theories associated with the academy to being primarily embedded in the practice of the classroom and relationships associated with schools.

How do preservice teacher education programs usually conceive the role of university supervisor? As you might expect, there are a multitude of ways in which university supervisors' work is conceptualized. One role often attributed to supervisors is a public relations role. The job of supervisors may be to make clear to those in the field, particularly cooperating teachers, the intents of the preparation program in general and the field experience in particular. At the same time they are likely to take responsibility for field placements and moves within placements (although in many institutions a Field Experiences Director may be in charge of this latter aspect).

A second role of university supervisors is usually to provide formative feedback about your emerging practice in the classroom. In this regard, supervisors are likely to observe your work as teacher—perhaps even work or teach alongside you in the classroom—and provide frequent opportunities for you to talk about theory and practice, as well as problems and prospects associated with your placement. They may also be responsible for running a seminar that operates parallel to your work in the school. Such work is geared to help you refine both your thinking about practice and the practice itself.

A third role of supervisors may be to provide summative evaluations of your work. In many cases, both the supervisor and the cooperating teacher are required to assess your performance and progress. It may be that others such as principals or other professionals (or even lay persons) of your mutual choosing may be involved in the process.

Given these complex, multiple, and sometimes contradictory roles (not unlike those of principals), you can see how there may be some hesitancy about some of the supervisor's actions. To make a difficult task even more complex, however, recognize that in some institutions of teacher preparation supervisors are graduate students—most likely successful classroom teachers now attending graduate school to further their own careers and professional development. Individually and collectively, they have considerable expertise to offer you; however, they do tend to have heavy workloads as well as a commitment both to your development and the immediate and pressing needs of their own development. This can induce many dilemmas and instances of ambivalence. In addition, they often have less decision-making power within programs and, like most cooperating teachers, may be reluctant to take a stand on problematic issues such as relocating your placement if all is not working well or making difficult judgment calls. (One of the criticisms of preservice teacher education, for example, is that few program participants are denied teaching certificates because university supervisors, among others, tend to give only passing grades.) Having said this, let us move on.

Thus far we have talked as though the university supervisor is likely to be wholly responsible to the university and on the payroll of the university, either as a faculty member, a seconded teacher (a classroom teacher on temporary assignment), or a graduate student. Some supervisors may be totally field-based and may be practicing teachers assigned to the specific tasks required for guidance of practice such as, for example, in settings where universities and school districts have collaborative teacher preparation programs. "Professional development schools" (see, Holmes Group, 1990) may also be sites where supervisors have full-time responsibilities that span both supervision of emerging practice and the work of experienced colleagues. In these kinds of contexts there may be a different perspective on practice and its relationship to theory. The point we wish to make, however, is not that one is superior to the other or that one has advantages but that there is a variety of models of supervision and frameworks within which supervisors work.

You undoubtedly will conceptualize the role of your university or school-based supervisor differently than that of your cooperating teacher; thus, you will have different expectations for your relationship with that person. It may be helpful to articulate some of your expectations prior to your field experiences so that you and your university supervisor can more easily negotiate your relationship. The experiences of other preservice teachers may offer some guidance. In the following narrative accounts, Cynthia expresses her initial disappointment with the university supervisor. She had an initial image of his role that did not entirely play out, and it was only after a period of discussion that she felt more comfortable with their relationship. Jody, too, reflects on the difficulty of accepting and responding to different conceptualizations of roles and relationships. Leila reflects on a matter of concern to many preservice teachers: working with more than one supervisor; understanding and dealing with evaluation; and finding enough time to realistically and productively meet the demands of the field experience. Kevin also raises the issue of evaluation. This is a pervasive concern among preservice teachers; it is also a concern to cooperating teachers and university supervisors. Colleen concludes this section with a candid depiction of the kind of emotional trauma often experienced as preservice teachers question and worry over their teaching competence and performance, especially as seen through the eyes of their university supervisors.

Narrative Accounts

John, my supervisor, came by "checking up" on me. I was angry that he dropped in for the last five minutes of the two hours I had been teaching and started saying, "Do this. Do that. Have you done this yet?" I guess I felt threatened because I wanted to think he was on my side and was not somebody else I had to impress.

Later I talked with John about the school setting and some of the problems I have with classrooms and schools, and my feelings about education. He listened to me and did not say that my ideas were wrong. He gave me the impression that he wanted to listen and encourage me. He has a diverse background in many of the same areas of my experience. He is not a stereotypical college teacher but a person with many interests and some controversial opinions to which I can relate. I feel more comfortable talking to him now that I know more about him. (Cynthia Hohnke)

I have come to appreciate my supervisor's emphasis on personal learning. I have felt uncertain about what he wants on assignments and the amount of teaching we are expected to do, but I appreciate the fact that he has oriented assignments and teaching to help us gain as much as possible from the program and also to help us secure a position next year. He seems to be committed to helping preservice teachers. He is very flexible, and some of us have had difficulty dealing with this. We are in the program because we have learned to function well within fairly rigid, standard classrooms; and it can be unnerving to have so much freedom. The ironic aspect is that his approach is probably truer to life. There is a difference between "the halls of ivy" and "the real world." In the real world, people are expected to be self-directed with a minimum of supervision. (Jody Metzker)

It has been hard being supervised by so many people at the same time. I have appreciated and needed the advice and suggestions given, but at times it has been quite difficult, especially because of the time it all takes. I have had four supervisors altogether, and it has been hard to accommodate pre-teaching conferences and post-teaching conferences with everybody. Dr. Hayden visited me twice each week for the first three weeks and each visit was followed by us having a talk; the same with one of my other supervisors, an hour before and after each visit.

Between the classes at the university, the classes I have to teach, and all these conferences there is not much time left for me. At times, I am really exhausted by the time I get home because I have been running around nonstop from 7:30 in the morning until 7:30 at night.

Dr. Missick stopped by my German class the other day. I did not get much of a chance to talk to him before or after the visit. He just left his notes for me and talked to me for about five minutes after he observed me. I would have liked more time to talk to him so I could hear what he thought rather than just reading his observations. But there was no time. What really bothered me about his observation was a simple sentence he put at the beginning of the page. He wrote: "Leila was nicely attired." This was his first sentence. I guess I did not expect to be evaluated by my supervisors for my clothing. I know that student teachers need to be aware of their appearance in school, but it hardly seems like an issue university supervisors should be concerned about. I know that Dr. Missick meant well, but it is disturbing how much emphasis is put on appearance. (Leila Muniroui)

The evaluation process troubled me midway through student teaching. I got annoyed when supervisors came unannounced at a few routine and uninspired moments. I wanted them to see me at the times when I thought I was doing my best. The other student teachers complained about it too. "Does a supervisor ever come when I am doing this and this and this? No, they come when I am doing this." Then one of the group pointed out, "But why should they only see us when we are at our best?" He was right, but it is a feeling that is hard to avoid. (Kevin Queen)

When I first discovered who my student teaching supervisor was I had mixed feelings. I had worked with him in two other classes and felt that he had supported me in one class and harshly criticized me in the other. Initially I wondered if a new "objective" observer would be better for me, but I was so relieved that his would be a familiar face that I decided to focus on the positive aspects of the situation. Thinking positively, I realized that his criticism of my past work was valid and my feelings were hurt because of his accuracy not his unfairness. I had also come to like him in a "warts and all" way that accepted his eccentricities and valued his accomplishments.

His first observation of my teaching was a personal disaster. He had to reschedule with short notice and his visit took place about five weeks into the term. It seemed that another student teacher had an urgent need for him. My nervousness increased to a level that I had never experienced before. I taught the lesson, leaving out the important conclusion in my haste to simply be done with it. The lesson that preceded this (the one he missed) was so much better that I felt like a failure. I'd failed myself, but more importantly, my students. They deserved better than that stammering disjointed nonsense when they and I had done so much better before.

The supervisor made it a point to meet immediately after the lesson to share his notes. He began by asking me to list the strengths about the lesson, and I muttered through the rapidly growing lump in my throat, "I can't think of any." He gently asked if it would be easier to start with weaknesses. I tried so hard to swallow the lump in my throat that I choked, and the tears just flowed. I apologized and realized that his notes would make sense only after my emotional storm had subsided. When I was much calmer I reread what he had written and thought that he had lied. He had managed to see something positive in a situation that had left me a shaken shadow of myself. I will never forget the kind way that he handled my fragility.

He used the same pattern for subsequent observations. I usually began with weaknesses instead of strengths. He would return to weaknesses and ask me what I would change. I had many small successes, but my perceived failings seemed to cancel them out. The supervisor's style of encouraging me to re-examine the weaknesses for future planning prevented the sense of gloom from descending upon me completely. He reminded me to focus on one aspect at a time, and I remembered this advice when I began feeling overwhelmed.

Tears seemed to be a big secret. By the end of the term I discovered that most of my peers had felt upset enough to cry. My cooperating teacher recalled her own student teaching twenty years ago as a tearful experience. A substitute teacher commented upon this topic as well. I wish I would have known earlier that student teaching could have such an emotional impact.

The supervisor rearranged scheduled observations another time or two during the term, and I began to feel neglected. I complained to a friend that the supervisor spent more time observing and responding to the other student teachers. My friend thought that this meant he had confidence in me, but I turned nasty and snapped, "I might be older but I'm still a beginner too."

Student teaching is not an experience I would wish to repeat. I have never felt so needy in my life. I had never cried so often before either. I am usually independent, self-sufficient, and extremely private about expressing the blues, and the experience turned me inside out. Life as a teacher was a whirl of questions. My only criticism of the supervisor was his tendency to answer a question with a question. I needed some firm ground. Unfortunately I was so enmeshed in the immediate needs of the classroom, and adrenalized, that I did not know what I needed or how to ask for it. I felt certain that I was failing in my placement and was overwhelmed by not knowing what to do.

The supervisor called me at home a few times and patiently listened as I tried to express the inexpressible. I always felt better after our conversations. I cannot imagine that he felt good, though, because sometimes I was quite rude. I realized early in the term that the supervisor intended to provide support and guidance in a nonthreatening manner, and I appreciated that. I also recognized that no individual could meet my multiplying needs.

I viewed student teaching not as a place for me to practice and develop but as a final exam—if I were judged unfit, I would fail. The irony of that fear is that it resulted in my being stiff and anxious and muted the joy and excitement that is inherent in teaching. (Colleen Presswood)

For Reflection and Discussion

1. Cynthia recalls feeling threatened initially by her supervisor's presence because he did not appear to be "on her side." After talking with him she felt encouraged by him.
    a. In what way might Cynthia's expectations have contributed to her reaction to the supervisor?

  b. How might Cynthia have been more proactive in relating to the supervisor, thereby precluding some of her distress?
2. Jody describes feeling uncertain about her supervisor's expectations and recalls that the flexibility and freedom he allowed her were unnerving.
  a. To what degree can such feelings of insecurity be attributed to the change of role from student to teacher?
3. Kevin writes about the universal phenomenon of university supervisors witnessing the mundane rather than the inspired moments of teaching. His concern is that evaluations are based upon such visits.
  a. What is the function of supervisors' observations?
  b. How does evaluation anxiety influence performance?
  c. Should Kevin have negotiated scheduled visits to ensure that an adequate lesson would be presented and observed? Why? or Why not?
4. Colleen's supervisor provided feedback in a supportive, predictable manner. Despite this support, Colleen's underlying fear of failure interfered with her ability to recognize her own success and amplified her anxiety about being observed.
  a. How did Colleen's implicit belief about the purpose of student teaching affect her experience?
  b. How could Colleen have anticipated the anxiety producers inherent in student teaching before she became busy with classroom needs?
  c. What steps could she have taken to reduce the anxiety she felt? In what ways might she have utilized the assistance of the university supervisor to do this?

Links with Research

Unlike the plethora of literature on the cooperating teacher, research on the role of the university supervisor in field experiences is relatively scant. As in the research on the cooperating teacher, however, there is considerable ambiguity surrounding what we know about the roles, practices, and influences of university supervisors. A large portion of the pertinent research focuses on the field experience triad (that is, the preservice or student teacher, cooperating teacher, and university supervisor). Recall from *Links with Research* in Chapter 8 that there is considerable confusion and inconsistency associated with the roles and expectations of cooperating teachers and university supervisors in field experiences (Applegate & Lasley, 1982, 1984; Beynon, 1991; Grimmett & Ratzlaff, 1986; Guyton & McIntyre, 1990; MacKinnon, 1989). Although Grimmett and Ratzlaff (1986) point out that there is little evidence in the literature that the triad members work together toward common goals, experience of success in the practicum is increased when there is agreement among the triad members in philosophy, expectations, and teaching approaches. Such agreement also increases chances that preservice teachers will experiment with ideas and approaches, and engage in reflection and analysis (McIntyre & Morris, 1980; Zevin, 1974).

The question of the nature and extent of the influence of the university supervisor on preservice teachers' classroom practice has been explored. Some suggest a questionable influence (Emans, 1983; Koehler, 1984; Zeichner, 1980) primarily because of structural barriers such as the amount of time university supervisors actually spend in field placement sites

(Richardson-Koehler, 1988; Zimpher, deVoss, & Nott, 1980). Nevertheless, university supervisors are seen as an important complement to cooperating teachers (Alverman, 1981; Becher & Ade, 1982; Friebus, 1977; Zimpher, deVoss, & Nott, 1980). Several factors are identified as limiting the potential of university supervisors to influence classroom practice. Time is a central factor according to Zimpher, deVoss, & Nott (1980). The limited amount of time university supervisors are able to spend in classrooms and schools with student and cooperating teachers may reduce their practical credibility, thus limiting their potential influence. Also, because the preservice and cooperating teacher spend so much time together, a bond may be created that, in effect, often places the university supervisor at a distance, again reducing his or her potential to influence.

Similar findings were reported in an ethnographic study conducted by Richardson-Koehler (1988). She identified several barriers to improving the student teaching process faced by university supervisors: limited amount of time in field sites; lack of time to build trust and establish rapport; awkwardness associated with discussing anything that may seem like a criticism of cooperating teachers' practices; and, perceived lack of reciprocity in effort on the part of cooperating and student teachers (that is, a perceived imbalance in time devoted to field experiences by triad members). In light of these findings Richardson-Koehler suggests a reconceptualization of the university supervisor's role from that of supervising preservice or student teachers in the classroom to supervising the *process* of student teaching. In other words, Richardson-Koehler calls for a role that goes beyond supervision of practice to involve attention to preparation of context and ongoing facilitation of professional development.

Studies have been conducted to examine the roles university supervisors assume in field experiences. As might be expected, supervisors perform a variety of roles and functions including

- setting goals and expectations for field experiences
- orienting student teachers to field placement sites
- acting as a liaison between the university and the field and reinforcing university perspectives
- reducing conflict in field settings and serving as mediators when necessary
- observing and providing constructive feedback and assessment
- supporting student teachers and facilitating their development in ways not necessarily directly related to classroom practice (Alverman, 1981; Koehler, 1984; Zimpher, deVoss, & Nott, 1980)

This last function is akin to Richardson-Koehler's (1988) suggestion about reconceptualization of the role.

The practices of university supervisors were studied by Zahorik (1988). He identified three main types of supervisory practice characterized by the goals set for student teachers and the style of interaction used by supervisors. Those using the "behavior prescriptive" style of supervision concentrated on giving advice and suggestions to student teachers about effective and appropriate teaching behaviors. The "idea interpretation" style of supervision consisted of pointing out perceived injustices in classrooms and schools, particularly with respect to power, authority, and humanity, and suggesting ways to bring about change. The "person support" style of supervision focused on facilitating student teachers' thinking and practice by encouraging independent thinking and decision making. Because of the variation in approaches to supervision, Zahorik notes, some student teachers receive extensive exposure to pedagogical skills, some to human relations sensitivity, and some to critical thinking and decision-making skills. Therefore, "what is emphasized, and presumably learned, in a student teacher's student teaching program is, in large part, a function of his or her relationship with a university supervisor" (p. 14).

In a related study, O'Connell Rust (1988) analyzed journal entries of six university supervisors to examine how they think about teaching and approach supervision. As might be expected, each supervisor's approach to supervision and the emphasis each placed on different aspects of classroom practice reflected each one's own image of "good" teaching and supervision. In other words, student teachers were encouraged to think about teaching and their own development, and attend to matters of practice differently, depending on their supervisor's beliefs and practice. This underscores the importance of negotiating roles and expectations. Also in the study, supervisors revealed many supervising strategies that again reflect individual styles and preferences. Among those identified are: leading seminars; promoting peer support; individual conferencing; keeping dialogue journals; providing encouragement and support; and encouraging and guiding habits of reflective practice.

In sum, the function and role of the university supervisor is relatively ill-defined. Much of the research points to institutional, programmatic, and individual idiosyncrasies that drive the practices of supervisors. But it is Richardson-Koehler's (1988) challenge to reconceptualize the role that rings loud in our ears. Suggesting that supervisors attend to facilitation of the process and context for professional development rather than to supervising of practice may be most beneficial for you as preservice teacher.

Research Activities

As a start to becoming more cognizant about negotiations with the university supervisor, reflect on your own research and responses to the questions in the previous chapter. Like cooperating teachers, university supervisors have role expectations placed on them; similarly, the process of negotiating a role with them is complex. We reiterate two easily overlooked points made in the previous chapter: (1) you need to have some sense of the role and responsibilities of supervisors; and (2) you need to have some notions of what you want to negotiate with supervisors.

1. Talking with university or school-based supervisors and other teacher educators about the role of the person in the supervisory position is a useful place for you to begin your inquiry.
   a. What is the place of supervision in the teacher education program within which you are enrolled?
   b. What do you see as the benefit of working with a supervisor? What do you expect from the relationship? What do you expect to learn from working with the university supervisor? Are these expectations realistic given the various constraints placed upon you and him or her? What does the supervisor expect from you?
   c. What are the programmatic roles and responsibilities placed upon the supervisor? What kinds of demands and expectations do general university or school duties place

on the supervisor? What are the limitations on supervisors' time and energies, and how might these affect *their* interactions with you? How might this play out in their presence in classrooms? What are the multiple functions and roles of the university or school-based supervisor? How do these functions and roles play out in the way in which they work with preservice teachers? How do supervisors evaluate your participation in schools and classrooms?

d. What are the expectations for your practice held by other university teacher educators, and how do these affect your relationship with the supervisor? What advice do these other teacher educators give for optimizing field experiences? How do these notions fit in your picture of the process and the outcomes? How do other university teacher educators view the roles of the supervisor in relation to your developing practice?

e. How do cooperating teachers view the roles of university supervisors? How do school-based professionals differ in their perception of the roles and responsibilities of the supervisor?

2. Uncovering supervisors' personal theories about teaching may also be useful to you because it may enable you to make decisions about the potential for a productive, mutually beneficial relationship. It may also help you get a handle on how they will evaluate your participation in schools. But, more important, it is a chance to understand someone else's informal theories in relation to practice. You may want to directly inquire with them about their backgrounds and philosophies of teaching. Try obtaining some of the same kinds of information from them that we asked of you in the early chapters. One word of caution: the intent here is to help you *negotiate* roles—*not* for you to be chameleon-like and adopt what you know *they* may approve. The latter stance can be injurious to your professional development. The following are some questions to help you get a handle on the philosophies of university supervisors.

a. What are the supervisor's prominent beliefs about good teaching? How does the supervisor view the role of teachers? What are the prominent instructional strategies espoused by the supervisor? What are the supervisor's views of classroom management and disciplining students?

3. Consider the research findings in the *Links with Research*. Which research findings draw your interest? Why? Check out some of these citations and use them to converse with your supervisor.

a. How do these research findings jibe with the supervisor's perspectives? What does your supervisor think about Richardson-Koehler's (1988) suggestion to reconceptualize the role of supervisors?

Establishing Relationships with Others in the Learning Community

In Chapter 1 we distinguished between the processes of learning to teach and learning to be a teacher, suggesting that each is informed by different kinds of contexts, experiences, and perspectives. It is natural to want to focus your attention and energies inside the classroom on what takes place when you and the students (and your cooperating teacher) are engaged in teaching and learning. But that is only part—albeit a central part—of what being a teacher is all about, and the classroom is only part of the broader context in which you will work as a teacher. To help you in learning to be a teacher we invite and encourage you to move beyond the walls of the classroom to explore and come to know other dimensions of school life and others who comprise the school community. As you read on you will undoubtedly notice that this chapter is an extension of Chapter 7 in which we made clear the importance of understanding the school as a learning community and workplace.

You have a legitimate place in the school, and to move around the institution meeting people is potentially beneficial both to you and the students with whom you work. As a student, you were probably oblivious to many of the people and their functions within the building; being in school again for the first or second time is a good place to start to broaden your perspectives. One way to facilitate interaction with some members of the learning community is to carry out some of the research activities we have suggested.

You may feel awkward approaching people out of the blue, but with the assistance of your cooperating teacher and perhaps the principal, you can break the ice. For example, the principal and your cooperating teacher could draw up a list of individuals in the building and with whom you can engage. Or, you could meet faculty and staff on your own. You will find that most adults in the workplace will be willing to talk with you.

Apart from contributing to your professional knowledge about schools as workplaces there may be a pedagogical benefit to your interactions with professionals and other staff in the building. For example, as a teacher you may have need for students in your classes to do library work. Having had interactions with the library staff may facilitate the process. Or, you may want to familiarize yourself with the counselors and their program to better understand students and their needs. Special education professionals may also help you better understand the services and provisions for special needs students, especially if you have such pupils in your class. These professionals are usually available to give advice about instructional activities as well as emotional and physical needs. Talking with coaches may help you understand the "other lives" of students who are also athletes.

The noninstructional staff will present different perspectives on the students and learning community. Although you may not have direct need to interact with these people, do not neglect their potential for far-reaching assistance. Bus drivers, custodians, secretaries, maintenance persons, cafeteria and lunch room workers, and others each have perspectives on the children and teachers with whom you work. Developing professional relationships with these people may begin with inquiry about their roles within the school. Like most adults and students within learning communities, these people are likely to appreciate your interest in their presence and work.

As we said at the beginning of the chapter, your development as a teacher will continue to be influenced by the numerous and varied individuals with whom you interact in professional contexts. Your field experience is a prime opportunity for you to gain insights into the roles of others in the workplace and the contribution made by each member of a school community. Negotiating your own role as a new member of a learning community through the development of professional relationships with others is an extremely important task of your field experience. When you begin teaching (even as a preservice teacher) you become a member of a school community. You are not destined just to be a teacher in a classroom. The success of schools and the degree of students' learning are not just dependent on the work of teachers in classrooms; schools represent places where mutually dependent and interrelated groups of professionals and para-professionals work.

Learning about school culture and the norms and unwritten rules of the school primarily takes place through conversation with members of the learning community in places such as

- hallways
- staff rooms
- cafeteria kitchens
- maintenance workshops
- athletic and academic event sites
- dances and concerts
- parking lots
- over broom handles
- at photocopy machines

As you embark on a voyage of the school or learning community recognize that, although not all settings may seem inviting and not all people welcoming, it is important to become affiliated with the whole school community. By engaging in conversations you are beginning an ongoing process of negotiating relationships. In the following accounts, preservice teachers reflect on some of their interactions beyond the classrooms of their cooperating teachers and how those interactions informed both their immediate field experiences and their developing perspectives on teaching.

Mary, Rebekah, and Maurice value time spent observing in other teachers' classrooms. Such opportunities affirmed some of their beliefs about teaching, allowed them to observe diverse teaching styles and methods, contributed to their developing repertoires of strategies and ideas, and enabled them to identify potential sites for future field experiences. Ellen, Steven, and Colleen share some of their observations and learnings from interactions beyond the cooperating teachers' classroom walls. Maurice and Ellen point out some of the benefits derived from staff room contact. Steven and Colleen acknowledge the value of meeting other teachers.

As Colleen points out, other teachers are more than friendly faces in the school. They are key sources of knowledge about "how things work." In addition and perhaps most important, establishing contacts with other teachers is a first step toward breaking the barriers of isolationism. Sharing of ideas and materials might lead to other kinds of joint work such as team teaching, peer observations, collaborative planning, or ongoing reflective dialogue. In a sense, it is up to you as a new generation of teachers to challenge some of the traditional workplace norms, such as isolationism, by initiating or responding to cooperative ventures. Finally, we learn from some of Terry's and Carla's experiences with other members of the school community: librarians, custodians, the secretary, and cafeteria staff.

Narrative Accounts

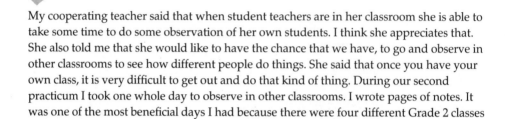

My cooperating teacher said that when student teachers are in her classroom she is able to take some time to do some observation of her own students. I think she appreciates that. She also told me that she would like to have the chance that we have, to go and observe in other classrooms to see how different people do things. She said that once you have your own class, it is very difficult to get out and do that kind of thing. During our second practicum I took one whole day to observe in other classrooms. I wrote pages of notes. It was one of the most beneficial days I had because there were four different Grade 2 classes in the school; I saw the same thing being taught in four different ways. (Mary Santos)

I especially enjoyed watching the four different math teachers and their ways of doing things. For instance, at the beginning of each class, Mike spends time individually with each student to talk about the assignments they turned in the day before. He uses this time to help them with problems he sees. Paul and Renee both go over the assignments by having each student one by one give the answer to a particular problem, giving the students credit if they get the correct answer. Jeff also spends time at the beginning of each class on the previous day's assignment, but he projects the answers with an overhead and lets the students correct them on their own. Each of these teachers seems quite effective, yet each uses varying methods. Out of the four teachers, I feel most comfortable with the way Mike does things, especially the way he presents lessons. (Rebekah Watson)

After spending four weeks in the classrooms of my cooperating teachers, I was very excited to observe Mrs. Hall's second grade classroom. I originally met her in the teachers' lounge the first day I was at the school and immediately recognized that she had a different attitude than the other teachers I had met. In general, she acted more "professionally" and was definitely more positive. Later, I spoke with the student teacher in her classroom and discovered that Mrs. Hall's class was run much differently than the class I was observing. Mrs. Hall's class was part of a program for gifted children. They used innovative teaching techniques, such as cooperative learning, and students were more able to work at their own pace than in other classrooms. I looked forward to observing further in this classroom.

I asked the vice principal if I could observe in Mrs. Hall's room. I soon entered the classroom and found the experience to be very helpful. In general, Mrs. Hall's teaching was very encouraging. I learned that it was possible to avoid all of the horrifying things that I had seen in the other classrooms. Although I had theories that those things were not necessary, I was able to see different techniques in practice with the same and similar children the other teachers had taught. My experience in this classroom helped me to regain confidence that there is hope for these children and the schools of the inner city. (Maurice Moroni)

I was fortunate to find a comfortable niche in the faculty structure. I spent one entire afternoon in the faculty room. I had a chance to visit with an assortment of the teachers who had become familiar with my face and found that they had watched and supported me all along. Gaylene, the art teacher, said, "The kids like you." Natalie, the gym teacher told me I had a reputation for holding my own against some of the tougher students. Bob, the vice principal, talked with me about discipline, his special area of expertise in the system. They all made it apparent that the faculty and staff are a team, and they could be counted on to help. (Ellen Findlay)

The highlight of today's teaching occurred outside the classroom on my way home. As I was preparing to leave the school, I stopped by the office to check my mailbox. As I was leaving the office, I ran into a faculty member named Ed. I have seen Ed on occasion around the building. (He teaches a wood block printing class.) I recall being introduced to Ed once in the Art Department here. What I do not remember, however, is telling Ed about my interest in printmaking, especially in the area of lithography. Well, he had not forgotten about me. As I was leaving the office, he stopped to ask me about the current print I was working on. I was a bit surprised that he knew I was in the process of completing a new print. I immediately traced back to the conversation we had a few weeks earlier.

Ed is quite the character—and not afraid to express himself. The students take to Ed well due to his unorthodox style of teaching and unusual but always interesting opinions. While Ed and I talked, he expressed an interest in my work. After a while, however, the conversation became geared more to philosophical statements about art as opposed to my work specifically. He was excited about showing me one of his prints hanging in the main office and wasted no time explaining the different technique he used in creating the piece. I found the time we spent together to be very enjoyable and, despite the tight schedule I faced, I did not want the conversation to end.

It is not often that one is given the opportunity to discuss art with an interested faculty member. Ed and I seemed to get on well. I look forward to our next meeting. It seems at times that it is more difficult to develop interpersonal relations with the working staff than it is with the student body—perhaps this is because of the tight schedule I am on. Regardless, today's encounter with Ed was both an enlightening and delightful experience. (Steven McMaster)

The introductory tour of the school was too brief. I was officially introduced to the librarian on the way to use the copy machine in the library. I later discovered that multiple copying for classroom use was supposed to be done at the main office. My cooperating teacher blithely disregarded this edict because the library was closer to her classroom. I disregarded it also, but I made it a point to refill the copier and get extra paper whenever I used it. I met the secretary this way because the paper was kept in the office. The nice thing about this was that the secretary also showed me a supply room and very patiently pointed out where each item was stored. I got a smile from her every day and some extra pencils too. I appreciated her helpfulness and brought her a small plant for "Secretary's Day." She was delighted by my small gesture of appreciation.

I literally stumbled upon the ditto machine when I went searching for something else. I did not even know that the building had one. Fortunately, it was being used by a first grade teacher. I introduced myself and confessed that I had not known about the location of the ditto machine. Like a mother hen she took me under her wing and demonstrated how to use the machine. She also explained all sorts of things about locating materials within the building and described the people in it. It was so nice to receive her friendly greeting in the hall throughout the rest of the term.

I met the other third grade teacher because my cooperating teacher introduced me to her at recess one day. She was wonderfully reassuring. When I took my class out for recess I talked further with her after she had remarked, "Student teaching can be overwhelming." I told her that I thought my cooperating teacher was wonderful and that I felt very lucky to have been placed in her class. She agreed with me and said, "After teaching for four years I have still not begun to approach the excellence of your cooperating teacher." She reminded me that my mentor had been in the field for 20 years. She also added that she had even visited the home of my cooperating teacher and that the entire second floor was devoted to teaching materials. She aspired to teach at such a high standard and even though she had family responsibilities she intended to strive in that direction. I recalled this conversation many times during the term to reestablish my perspective. I was awestruck by my mentor's giftedness and professionalism. She represented so beautifully what I hoped to become. I often wonder if I can achieve her level of expertise.

The other third grade class had already studied a unit that I was preparing to teach, and the teacher generously shared supplies and materials with me. When I thanked her she smiled and said, "That's what teachers do." I copied some information that I thought might be useful to her when I was researching the subject, and I left it in her mailbox. It was wonderful to talk to and work with her. (Colleen Presswood)

I have had many jobs in my life. Starting when I was twelve years old I worked with my dad in construction during holidays. I made good money for a twelve-year-old, and so I had very nice toys but not much free time to use them. My next afterschool job was as a sweeper in a junior high school. I quit during the summer to work in construction because I could make a lot more money, but during the school year, I went back to the sweeping job after school. I learned a lot about teachers and the behind the scenes activity in a school through this position. I saw a lot of cleaning favors going to teachers who respected custodians and treated them as equals rather than as "hired help." I saw, also, how the principal and other teachers would bad-mouth many of the teachers when they were not present. I really think now that I will try not to say anything disrespectful about other teachers. But, if I do, I will make sure the sweeper is not in the room.

Realizing the identity of "prime movers" in schools has also been an eye-opening experience for me. The people I refer to are not those proposing educational reform but those carrying out the reforms the best way they can. When I faced problems teaching a two-week unit plan I figured my cooperating teacher, principal, or vice principal would be my primary resources for assistance; however, the problems I faced were not dealt with by these busy people. Instead, they were solved by the school secretary, the custodian, and the media center director. For example, I was aware of the paper shortage and subsequent quotas that the school district placed upon the teachers, so I decided to print my handouts on both sides of the paper to minimize waste. Well, needless to say, I had problems with paper getting stuck in the copier when I ran it through the second time. What to do? Class was to begin in five minutes, and I needed to give the quiz I was running off. Who could I call on to get me out of this predicament? Yes, the school secretary, for she had dealt with this problem several times before and was probably the only one, next to the custodian and media center director, who knew how to get the paper out without ruining the machine. I began to realize that valuing my relationship with these people would be in my best interest; therefore, I began letting them know of my appreciation for the many things they did to insure learning occurred. (Terry Ingram)

One day a girl threw up in class. My cooperating teacher stopped mid-lesson to help the student, but I told her that I would help so that she could continue to teach. I cleaned up the girl and even managed to give her a hug through a few layers of paper toweling. I moved her desk away because it was in a group of four and her deskmates had become somewhat excited by the event. I continued cleaning her desk and books in a niche by the sink in the back of the room while my cooperating teacher taught. The janitor did not appear until several hours later. She was well armed with disinfectant, rubber gloves, bucket, and brush, but the job was done. She looked at me so strangely that I thought I had done something wrong. I quickly explained that I had only used soap and water, so she applied disinfectant and left. When my teacher realized that I had done the cleaning she patted my back with a smile and a shake of her head saying, "You didn't have to do that."

I always spoke to the janitor who came in after school. He seemed surprised and was quiet at first. One day I had given a lesson about the grain food group and the carpet had a small quantity of grain scattered over it. I apologized to him for the mess I had helped create, and he brightened as he assured me that it was no big deal. He deferentially asked if he should return later to vacuum when he saw me alone correcting papers. I assured him that the noise wouldn't bother me at all because I appreciated his work, and I offered to leave to make his job easier. He declined my offer and, for the rest of the term, we exchanged pleasantries as he started work. Later in the term I was surprised when the cooperating teacher mentioned that the janitor was doing a better job with the floor.

One class I was in had a science club two days a week. The students selected their own projects and work partners and wrote a list of their needed supplies for my teacher. One student elected to create dye from vegetables, and as he needed guidance and support, I helped him. I still don't know how my cooperating teacher kept up with supplying her students but, red cabbage in hand, Jermaine (a student) and I left class in search of a stove. The teachers' lounge was occupied that day, so we went to the cafeteria. This activity occurred after lunch, so the staff was still present. I asked permission to use the stove and received it with some officious hesitancy. We made sure that every trace of our presence was completely removed before we left. My cooperating teacher was surprised at the response I had received and indicated that permission was not necessary—she thought the staff were "showing off to a new person."

The project required several classes to complete, and I was pleased to see that the student's delight was contagious, affecting the cafeteria staff. We were met with smiles and pleasant inquiries regarding the project and that helped Jermaine articulate the process and goals of his project. I'm sure that my own efforts to establish a respectful rapport were appreciated by the staff. My student and I found someone to thank every time we left the room, and I greeted the staff every time we entered. I later noticed that our behavior differed somewhat from other faculty who "pulled rank" and entered and exited with an air of superiority. (Carla Preston)

For Reflection and Discussion

1. Rebekah observed four math teachers who each demonstrated different methods that appeared to be effective. Through observation she discovered her personal preference of method.
   a. How did Rebekah focus her observations to enrich her repertoire of teaching methods?
   b. How might Rebekah's observations influence her practice?
2. Maurice discovered a teacher whose practice differed a great deal from that of the cooperating teacher with whom he worked. His request to observe in this classroom was granted by the vice principal.
   a. How did Maurice's observations affect his beliefs about teaching?
   b. What factors may have motivated Maurice to initiate observation of a different teacher?
3. Ellen found a comfortable niche in the faculty structure of her cooperating school. During the afternoon spent in the faculty room she was able to "visit with" several faculty members, discovering that she had a support system.
   a. What did Ellen's afternoon in the faculty room reveal to her about the culture of the school?
   b. To what extent do the comments made by the other teachers illustrate the concept of schools as communities?
4. Steven describes his conversation about art with a faculty member as the highlight of his day. He notes that it seems more difficult to develop relationships with faculty than with students.
   a. To what does Steven attribute the difficulty of developing faculty relationships?
   b. In what ways might Steven's conversation with the art teacher have addressed his needs as a learner? as a teacher? as a new community member?
5. Casual contact with other teachers provided an opportunity for Colleen to engage in conversation with them.
   a. How did Colleen's accidental meeting with the first grade teacher enrich her perspectives of the school?
   b. What value did she find in conversations with the third grade teacher?
6. Terry entered his practice teaching with the perspective gained by his past work as an afterschool sweeper. He describes his recognition of the "prime movers" (as well as problem solvers) in schools as an eye-opening experience.

   a. How did Terry's custodial experience influence his decision to refrain from speaking disrespectfully about other teachers?

   b. How did the custodians respond when they were not treated as "the hired help?"

7. Carla discovered that preparation for lessons and conducting enrichment activities expand the boundaries of the classroom. Her work with and for students brought her into contact with various members of the school community.

   a. Why do you suppose the janitor reacted as she did when she discovered that the cleaning she was expecting to do had already been taken care of?

   b. What does the response of the cafeteria staff to Carla's request to use the facilities reveal about their regard for faculty? Might there be territorial issues involved in their response? What else might have been at the heart of their initial reaction?

   c. To what extent did Colleen's status as a "newcomer" allow her to interact with staff as she did? How could her lack of understanding of implicit job descriptions and status have had a negative impact upon her interactions?

Links with Research

The concept of the school as learning community is receiving attention in the literature on teacher education and development especially as it is linked with school improvement. The idea that more heads are better than one is catching on in schools as evidenced in efforts to increase peer interaction and collaboration in various formal and informal ways including

- professional development partnerships (mentoring, peer coaching, team teaching)
- classroom clustering arrangements
- school-based management and participatory decision making

These types of interactions are intended to challenge the traditional norms of isolationism in schools. (Refer to the *Links with Research* on Developing New Understandings of the School in Chapter 7 to review some of the literature in this area.)

    In some teacher preparation programs attempts to break down barriers of isolation and to foster collegiality are being made through a "whole school" approach to field experiences. In this approach, student teachers are placed in schools rather than in individual classrooms and perhaps work with several cooperating teachers in addition to spending time learning about the broader school context. In this way preservice teachers have opportunities not only to gain a better sense of the complexities of schools and teaching but also to become familiar with the wealth of resources and support available in the school. Such use of resources and support can ultimately inform classroom practice in important ways (Cole & Innes, 1991; McNay & Cole, 1993; Zeichner, 1992).

    Because the whole school concept is a recent structural and conceptual alternative to the traditional practicum, there is little available research describing the kind of experience such arrangements provide preservice teachers. In one report, however, a student teacher comments on how stimulating and energizing it was to work as part of a team and how much she appreciated not being isolated in her work and learning (Worth, 1990).

    In another whole school approach to the practicum project (McNay & Cole, 1993), student teachers were assigned to cooperating teachers as primary support personnel but spent up to half of their time observing and interacting with teachers and staff members in other parts of the school. All members of the school staff, professional and nonprofessional, were encouraged to explore ways of facilitating the student teachers' experiences. Various members of the school community offered their observations on the whole school approach, pointing out the many benefits to be derived not only for the student teachers but also for the entire school staff. One student teacher said:

> [Listening] to other student teachers not in this project, it was evident that very few were involved in P.A. [Professional Activity] Days, staff meetings, extracurricular activities, and meetings with the principal of their school. . . . The invitation to be involved in each of these areas, as well as the warmth that we felt in the schools reflected the "whole school" commitment (McNay & Cole, 1993, p. 123).

Another commented:

> By returning to the same school [for each practicum period], we were able to experience the school community. . . . And those of us who went back to observe or teach in the classrooms we were in before could see the progression and development of the students (McNay & Cole, 1993, p. 124).

Other teachers besides the cooperating teachers found professional satisfaction in their involvement with student teachers. Para-professionals reported that their participation broadened their involvement in the school and improved communication with the staff. The principal remarked:

> We have opened the doors to how adults . . . learn and grow and develop. . . . This [whole school approach] has given [the staff] one more impetus to look at themselves. . . . It's more than a preservice project. It's a staff development project (Cole & McNay, 1993, p. 125).

Although students, in a typical school day, interact with and are influenced by many more adults in the school than just their classroom teacher(s), until recently this reality received little overt recognition. It seems sensible to imagine that the people who are employed to facilitate student learning in different ways would pull together as a team to work toward that common purpose. Common sense, however, does not typically guide school practice. Turney, Eltis, Towler, and Wright (1985) point out the lack of awareness and use by teachers of the various computer, technical, and audiovisual resources within the school for facilitating teaching and learning. They also note teachers' lack of understanding of the various support-resource personnel roles in the school and their consequent failure to draw on these individuals for classroom-based support. The authors suggest that although many teachers are often critical of the lack of assistance provided by other staff members such as counselors, librarians, administrators, and other teachers, they themselves do little to appreciate the potential roles of such personnel, to seek out assistance, and to initiate collaborative work.

Turney, Eltis, Towler, and Wright (1985) suggest that teachers undertake four basic tasks to identify and mobilize human and other resources within the school:

- locate and determine the nature and accessibility of resources
- assess the relevance and usefulness of various resources in achieving educational objectives

- secure, organize, and coordinate required resources
- collaborate with support staff—teaching colleagues, school administrators, non-teaching personnel, and professional support personnel

Seeing yourself as an important and integral member of a learning community who works alongside and in tandem with other community members is an image worth cultivating, not only because of the meaning it gives to your own professional development but also because of the potential it holds for informing your work with students. Replacing the isolationist model with a persons-in-relation approach to teaching and being a teacher is a challenge that you, as a part of a new generation of teachers, will hopefully take up.

Research Activities

Each of the groups of professionals who work within learning communities has valuable perspectives about becoming teachers and working in schools. Given the complexity of teachers' work and responsibilities, we encourage you not only to interact with them and establish bases for relationships with them but also to tap into their knowledge about learning to teach.

1. Accessing the perspectives of school principals is likely to reveal some surprises as well as some expected points of view. Take time to get to know the administrators of the learning community and to understand their roles. By coming to new understandings of their various roles you will establish a foundation for developing relationships.
   a. Just as Matt did with Barnaby in Chapter 3, try shadowing for a day or so the principal/director and/or assistant principal/director of the institution. Observing the focus, scope, and intensity of their day-to-day work may help you understand the complexity of schools and the multiple demands placed on the roles of these individuals and the institution.
   b. Like teachers, much of the work of school administrators is out of sight from observing eyes. To uncover this aspect of their work try engaging them in conversations about these behind-the-scenes elements of their work such as

   - staffing
   - course and faculty scheduling
   - course offerings and curriculum development
   - student issues
   - evaluation of faculty performance
   - staff and faculty professional development
   - school improvement, development, or reform
   - financial concerns and budgetary matters
   - political and social issues
   - community relationships

2. The same approach as in example 1 might also be useful for understanding the work of counselors, librarians, special educators, and others within the learning community, especially, the noninstructional staff. Shadow several of these individuals, not only to

understand their places more fully but also to begin ongoing conversations about their work and their perceptions of issues, problems, and prospects within the setting. Together, you will likely establish a sound basis for relating to them. In a sense, these activities are represented by two questions: What work do these people perform? How is their work related to teaching and the work of teachers?

3. Many, if not all, of the individuals working in schools have probably observed preservice teachers pass through the building from time to time. If you are in a setting, such as a professional development school, in which many preservice and student teachers work, they are bound to have watched people like you struggle through the process of learning to teach. Engaging them in conversations about learning to become a teacher may further establish your temporary place in the learning environment. You might ask questions such as:

   a. What advice do you have for teachers-in-preparation? What are some of the ways in which preservice teachers can best capitalize on the resources of the community? Which professionals can facilitate preservice teachers' learning and help optimize the field experience? In what ways can you help student or preservice teachers get the most out of field experiences?

   b. In what ways does the advice support or contradict the perspectives of the university-based teacher educators? Why? What are their implicit beliefs about teaching and becoming a teacher?

4. Opportunities to observe in classrooms other than those to which you are assigned may be extended to you shortly after you arrive at your placement. Early in the term you may feel that you should devote your attention to "your" classroom, not only to familiarize yourself with the students but also to feel at home and to dispel the feeling of being a newcomer. If the opportunity to observe is offered to you make every effort to avail yourself of it. As the term progresses and your role in the classroom expands it may become impossible to "do it later." If an offer to observe elsewhere is not extended, ask about the possibility of it. Talk to the cooperating teacher about your desire to observe in other classrooms and ask for his or her suggestions regarding teachers that you could approach. Take descriptive notes while you are in the classroom and observing. Later on, add a section that includes your reflective response and impressions about what you observed. This record will be a valuable reference for you later in the term.

Establishing Relationships with Parents and the Community

Parents and the community exert both subtle and direct influences on schools and other learning communities by

- voting at elections, passing or rejecting increases in tax money for public schools
- participating in school functions such as concerts and athletic events
- participating both closely (for example, as assistant coaches) and loosely (for example, as transporters of their children) in many extracurricular activities
- serving on school district or board advisory and governing committees
- participating in parent-teacher committees and related home-school activities

- working as volunteers in schools, classrooms, and other learning communities, often running such volunteer programs
- visiting classrooms from time to time and participating as spectators in extracurricular activities and sports events
- meeting with teachers and principals in conferences

Parents are astute observers of the goings-on in and around schools as they deliver and meet children at school gates, read school and local newspapers, and participate in local debates about education. And, they also guide children's homework and project work around the kitchen table, perhaps while listening to their children's exploits of the day.

Teachers and other school professionals are also parents, and some may have children in the same building in which they work. Because of their proximity and easy access to teachers with whom you may be working, these parents may exert powerful and direct influences on your experience, perhaps without your even being aware. Some parents and community members have commercial or business connections with the school—they may even financially support some school-based activities such as sporting or musical events or supply special purpose equipment or services. Parents may have contributed and built special purpose furniture or playground equipment for the school. Finally, some parents and community members are likely to be politically active in areas related to formal education, participating in lobbying activities of various kinds and causes such as: regulation of textbooks and library or media materials; monitoring of curriculum; religious freedoms; and, school safety. They may also engage in censoring particular practices and activities, advocacy of particular fiscal measures; advocacy and introduction of projects and programs or curtailing of services.

Principals and teachers are often sensitive to parents' perceptions of their work, their classrooms, and their schools. Often this sensitivity, in the extreme, induces a subservience; parents are seen as either confounding the learning process, thwarting progress, or being unreasonably demanding. Whatever the context, reasonable or unreasonable, school administrators are likely to view parents as forces with which to be reckoned.

The chances are your presence in the learning community will not go unnoticed by parents, especially if you are placed in a small school, a school that has strong parent involvement, or are working within an institution in a small community. And, of course, many parents are likely to know about you—perhaps not by name—from their children. "The new teacher in class" is bound to be a topic of conversation, especially in families with young children. If you are proving to be a successful teacher or participant in the classroom, it is likely that parents will hear about you. Or, if you are different in dress, manner, style, focus, or energy students will tell stories about you around the dinner table. Conversely, if you have problems or idiosyncrasies that make you stand out, parents are sure to hear about them.

Because the presence of a preservice teacher in classrooms often results in more individualized and personalized attention for students, many parents are supportive of the kind of mentorship that occurs. Others, however, may criticize your lack of experience or see your presence as a distraction from the teacher's "real work," that of directly teaching *their* children. This latter position, we think, comes from relatively simplistic and uninformed beliefs about what learning and teaching is all about. (As future teachers and, perhaps, cooperating teachers working within a climate of fiscal restraint and large class sizes, this matter is important to resolve with the parents of the children you teach. After all, two adults in a classroom are likely to accomplish more than one!)

Almost since the inception of public schooling in North America a prevalent view among education professionals has been that *they* are the experts, and parents are inept at thinking about or facilitating children's learning. Parents who opt out of the public education system or private schools and choose to home-educate their children defy this view. These parents often have serious criticisms of public and private schools and the teachers who work therein. Although many of these criticisms are focused on moral issues, significant numbers reflect pedagogical and academic concerns. Since the early 1970s, parents who home-educate (commonly known as home schooling), and the concept of educating at home itself, have raised the hackles of many professional educators. But, the home education movement has provided clear evidence that some parents are able to facilitate children's learning and that parents have valuable insights into the needs, learnings, and academic performance of their children.

We raise the subject of home education because it provides an extreme example of the action of parents and the extent to which they can be involved in children's learning and academic development. We are not necessarily supporting the ideological perspectives of these families, but we are supporting the notion of parents' involvement in children's educational experiences. For too long many professional educators have not allowed parents to assume their rightful place in the education of their children—as partners in learning. The extreme example of home-educating parents helps to illustrate the importance of parent-school and parent-teacher relationships. Involvement of parents within the learning communities that *you* help create is not only highly beneficial to your own development as an emerging professional but also to the development of the children under your charge. We urge you to find ways to forge relationships with parents as well as encourage their direct involvement in your classrooms and schools.

In the following *Narrative Accounts* we hear about preservice teachers' experiences with parents. Renee tells of learning from parents—gaining additional insight to inform teaching and interactions with students. She also tells of the frustrations experienced by many teachers who attempt to establish strong communication links with parents. Her account reminds us of the importance of knowing situations and circumstances in more detail before making judgments about parents. Steve reminds us that communicating with parents effectively involves communicating respectfully and productively. Jane felt the unfair judgment of a parent. Her account illustrates the roles of parents as political authorities. The attitude of a parent toward her as student teacher had a profound effect on her self-esteem and professional identity. Claire made several observations that helped her think about strategies to use in communicating with parents, stressing the importance of working together with parents to help children realize their potential and achieve their goals.

Narrative Accounts

At 4:00 P.M. we started the first parent-teacher conferences. I thought it was so interesting to meet the kids' parents. Overall, I could see a lot of the parents in their children—it really gives a teacher added insight into a child. What I found really hard was saying negative things to a parent about a child. I guess you really need to find nice ways of saying negative things.

It saddened me to discover how many parents have an apparent lack of interest in their children's education. We held an open house at the beginning of the year, and only six parents came. There were parents who repeatedly missed conferences and did not return the teacher's phone calls or reply to notes sent home. I began to understand why children of these parents had such a disregard for education. There needs to be encouragement at home to reinforce what is learned at school. It seems unfair that some kids have parents who test them on spelling words, read stories aloud, and take trips to museums and so on, and others have parents who send their children to school without breakfast or lunch. Even the best teacher can't contend with a growling stomach. Also, sometimes kids come dragging into class looking like they are still half asleep; a teacher is not able to put students to bed at night in order to make sure that they are rested for the next day. (Renee Buscho)

In my encounters with parents, usually over discipline problems, I feel I handle myself well. My polite but candidly firm arguments seem to calm down even the most defensive parent. Also, I stress the need for the students to solve the problem. Instead of getting on my high horse, I am quite willing to admit my own fallibility. Whether it is that or my way with words, I have found parents easier to reason with than their children. After a couple of such meetings, I have been complimented on my conduct by members of the administration. (Steve Bruno)

Throughout the term I worked to establish and maintain parent communication. When I first began, I sent a note home to the parents explaining what we were doing in the reading groups and outlining some of my goals for the semester. Also included in this letter was an invitation to the parents to call whenever they had a question or concern. During Parents' Night at the school, Pam, my cooperating teacher, extended the same invitation to parents. I soon discovered, however, that although you may try to establish a system of communication, parents may choose to ignore it for a number of reasons.

Yesterday morning, Pam called me over to say that we needed to talk. She said that one of the parents who had a child in my reading group complained that the child was "always taught by the student teacher." In other words, because I am a student teacher the child is receiving an inadequate education. To make matters worse, the parent called the principal rather than Pam. The principal advised Pam to have me teach less because this was a parent who had "caused a lot of trouble in the past." Last year, this same parent had complained about a second grade teacher and had rallied many of the parents against her. Pam said, "In this town, the parents cannot only hurt you at school but they can run you out of town." Pam told me that we would switch reading groups after Thanksgiving to placate the parent. Also, she said that she would teach the rest of the day so that the student "would not run home and complain to Mom." Lastly, when filling out report cards for the reading groups, I was instructed not to say anything negative on the students' report cards.

Being asked to change reading groups especially bothered me because we were in the middle of making a newspaper. I was planning on having a few more weeks to complete it, now I had only a few days. This meant meeting with students during lunch break and completing much of the newspaper myself. I did not mind the work involved, I just felt strongly that children should experience as much of the process as possible. I asked Pam if the parents had complained about the quality of my instruction. Pam said that they had not. They just did not want a student teacher teaching their son. To be quite honest, I felt as if my dignity was in the toilet. So far this year, I have been told by the university supervisor, cooperating teacher, and principal that I am one of the best student teachers they have seen. And yet, because a parent complained, I am immediately "put in my place." What really upsets me is that this parent has never seen me teach; she just assumed that I would be ineffective. And what really hurts is that everyone is so scared of this parent, they are not even willing to back up a fellow teacher. (But then again, I am not a "real teacher" yet, so why should I be treated like one?) (Jane Atman)

On March 15, 1989, I attended my first parent-teacher conference, sitting on the teachers' side of the table. It was a very interesting experience. I made several observations. Mr. Fraligh only had with him at the conference his grade book and a copy of the paper on which the students are supposed to keep track of their assignments and grades received. Of course, most of the parents were interested in the present grade and whether their students could improve that grade before end of quarter (next week). Although Mr. Fraligh could do this adequately with only his grade book, I think parents would have liked to see some of what their child had done during the term.

When I am full-time teaching, I would like to keep a folder of various assignments or special projects the students have done so that I can show their parents when they come to parent-teacher conferences. Everyone likes to have accomplishments recognized even in small ways and, as a parent, I like to see the good work my children have done. I also would keep a data sheet on each student showing assignments, if they were completed, grade received, and tests and extra credit scores. Each parent would have access to this at parent-teacher conferences. They would know exactly where their child stood gradewise. With the help of a computer spreadsheet this would not be hard to accomplish once I had the basic demographic data entered.

I also noticed that most of the parents were concerned about their child's progress. They cared. One father mentioned that his son wants to become an aeronautical engineer. His son has a lot of potential as a leader and scholar if he would apply himself. He also likes athletics and is on the basketball team. His father is trying to show him that it is important to excel in academics if he wants to accomplish his career objective. "There is life after sports" was the message. I saw that this father cared a lot about the academic future of his son and wanted to help him. He also thanked us for doing our job. I wish that more parents came to the conferences, especially the ones whose children are not doing well in class academically. Attending this conference was so interesting and enlightening. I thought of ways that I could make this a good experience for parents and help them understand what goes on in my classes. (Claire Smith)

For Reflection and Discussion

1. Renee encounters students who arrive at school without eating breakfast or bringing a lunch. She also sees students who "come dragging into class looking like they are still half asleep."
   a. Does Renee need to make up for parents' apparent negligence before she can fulfill her teaching responsibilities?
   b. To what extent might Renee's vision of parental responsibility be viewed as "blaming the victim"? What might these parents (and children) be victims of?
2. Renee also discovered that parents provide information to teachers in two ways; explicitly by attending parent conferences and talking about family issues that may affect their child at school, and implicitly by not attending conferences or responding to communication from the teacher.
   a. Which type of communication should Renee rely on for information about her students? Why?
   b. To what extent is it appropriate to conclude that the parent's lack of communication with the teacher is explanation for a student's apparent disinterest?
3. Steve discovers that he is able to handle "encounters" with parents skillfully. He received compliments for his conduct with parents by members of the administration.
   a. Reread Steve's account. How does he describe the parents? How does he describe his approach to them? To what extent can his success be attributed to his assessment of the parent's position?
   b. What effect might his willingness to "admit my own fallibility" have upon the quality of his communication with parents?
4. On the threshold of becoming a classroom teacher, Jane found herself in the ironic position of having her student teaching experience curtailed by parental pressure. Her questioning of the cooperating teacher revealed that the issue was her status as "student teacher," not the quality of her teaching.
   a. How did Jane handle the situation to minimize damage to her self-esteem? In what ways could Jane have handled the situation differently? Was the response of the cooperating teacher appropriate? Why? Do you agree with the way the principal handled the complaint?
   b. How could this experience have influenced Jane's view of parents and their place in the education of their children? Why do you suppose the parent chose to complain to the principal rather than to Jane or the cooperating teacher?
   c. What does Jane's experience reveal about the power of one parent and the strength of the professional community within which she taught?

    d. How can you explain Jane's experience in light of the study conducted by Garcia and Farnsworth (1984)? (See the following *Links with Research* section.)

5. Claire's observation of parent-teacher conferences led her to think about elements she would include in them when she conducts them herself.

    a. What position do parents have in Claire's planning for conferences?

    b. Why does Claire want to share samples of student work with parents at conference time?

Links with Research

"If you had to choose between a thousand dollar raise and a written guarantee that you would never have to talk to a parent again I think I know what you would choose" (Sarason, 1982, p. 10). This remark opened a presentation to a large group of teachers. The uneasy laughter that followed, according to Sarason, reflects the frustration and dissatisfaction teachers experience over their interactions with parents. In spite of research and other literature advocating otherwise, teacher-parent and home-school communication in North American schools is limited.

There is considerable research to support parent involvement in schools (for example, Bronfenbrenner, 1974; Hess & Holloway, 1984; Lareau, 1989; Lombana, 1983; Phi Delta Kappan, 1980; Swap, 1990; Walberg, 1986). Among the numerous benefits to be derived from strong home-school links are improved homework habits, student achievement, and attitudes and behavior, as well as lower student absenteeism. Also, in a study of 66 elementary schools in a mid-southern state, Hoover-Dempsey, Bassler, and Brissie (1987) report a positive link between higher levels of teacher efficacy and parent involvement; that is, when parents were involved in conferences, home tutoring, and as volunteers in schools, and when teachers perceived them to be supportive, teachers' self-confidence and professional self-image increased. Teachers then believed in their abilities to teach, their students' abilities to learn, and in their own professionalism.

Stallworth, John, and Williams (1983) conducted a large scale, six-state, survey of attitudes toward parent involvement in schools. They compared attitudes of high ranking educational administrators with those of teacher educators, teachers, principals, and parents. There was a marked congruency across all groups in support of parent involvement in schools. All groups, however, reported parent involvement mainly in traditional (that is, non-decision-making) roles. Although parents indicated an interest in participation in curriculum and instruction or administrative decision making, their participation did not reflect this high level of interest. Stallworth, John, and Williams stress the importance of including in teacher preparation curriculum the topic of parent involvement.

As Turney, Eltis, Towler, and Wright (1985) and others (Houston & Houston, 1992; Williams, 1992) also point out, teacher education programs typically do not prepare teachers to work with parents and other nonprofessional community members. Little is done to help preservice teachers understand the environmental forces that affect students and the importance of developing positive attitudes toward working with parents. Consequently, insufficient attention is paid in preservice programs and beyond to the role of parents in formal education (see also, Williams & Stallworth, 1983; Williams, 1989). Williams' (1992) assessment is that, in spite of calls to pay attention to parent involvement in schools, particularly at the elementary level, most teacher preparation programs have not taken appropriate steps to respond. Nevertheless, Williams' challenge to teacher educators includes the exposure of preservice teachers to opportunities for the development of skills and appropriate attitudes for interacting and involving parents in the activities of learning communities. Similar and complementary recommendations were advocated by Stallworth, John, and Williams (1983), Houston and Houston (1992), and Epstein (1989).

Explorations of beginning teachers offer some insights into their preparedness to teach. In particular, two studies reveal their understandings of the home-school link. Houston, Marshall, and McDavid (1990) studied 250 first-year teachers. Two months into the school year the new teachers viewed parents as a minor problem (ranked ninth of 14), but by the tenth month, they viewed parents as fifth of 14 areas of concern, a change perhaps related to widening perspectives and experience. Research by Houston and Williamson (1990) involved 42 elementary teachers who were questioned about their formal program of teacher preparation one year after graduation. Nearly everyone had concerns about parents, and understandings about relations with parents were viewed as a serious programmatic omission. Despite such recognition, because of the pressures of teaching and the classroom, and because the major rewards of teaching are seen as resting in the development of students (Houston & Williamson, 1990), teachers are prone to overlook the importance of fostering the home-school link. Furthermore, for a number of reasons related to time pressures, teachers largely expect to interact with parents on their own terms and at the school. And, because the age gap between teachers and parents is increasing (the median age for teachers is over forty) teachers may be less inclined to bridge the communication gap with parents, especially when it may mean moving beyond the safety of the school environment (Houston & Houston, 1992).

Garcia and Farnsworth (1984) conducted a survey study of elementary school parents' and students' perceptions of student teachers. The majority of the 587 parents who responded had positive attitudes toward student teachers working with or teaching their children. Sixty-one percent were very satisfied and nearly 35 percent were moderately satisfied. Mainly, they saw student teachers as providing individual assistance to students and bringing new ideas to the classroom. Lack of teaching experience, interruption of the regular classroom teacher's plans, and lack of discipline techniques were concerns most commonly voiced. Because only slightly more than half the parents responded to this concern it seems to represent the feelings of a small percentage of the parents involved in the survey.

The isolation or alienation of parents from schools and teachers has been criticized, both for reasons related to teaching effectiveness and to parents' rights to be involved in the education of their children. Turney, Eltis, Towler, and Wright (1985) suggest that teachers who do not have strong working relationships with parents:

- lack knowledge and appreciation of students' home situations
- fail to foster parental interest, cooperation, and understanding
- fail to draw on available community resources to enhance their program
- are unresponsive to community needs, values, and aspirations

In a publication advocating greater school-home cooperation, Rich (1985) makes complementary observations.

The home education movement illustrates, in part, the extreme measures some parents take in response to the problems and confounding issues evident and perceived in public and private schools. Although many parents "exit" their children from schools in response to ideological differences associated with formal schooling, others do so as a direct result of expressed difficulties or problems associated with, for example:

- the conditions of schools and classrooms
- school requirements and curriculum
- administrators', principals', and teachers' actions
- academic standards
- the abusive and threatening behaviors of other students (Knowles, Marlow, & Muchmore, 1992)

In trying to resolve problems, many parents offer their services to teachers and schools (Knowles, 1989, 1991). Often, however, these parents are rebuffed and become adamant in their resolve to take the ultimate measure, that of teaching their children at home. This often reported rebuff is, we suspect, more because of teachers' unfamiliarity with working with parents than direct opposition to home education—even though many professional organizations and school boards have decried and actively opposed the operation of home schools (see, for example, National Association of Elementary School Principals, 1989–1990; National Education Association, 1988).

Parents who home-educate their children also share another perspective. Individual and family rationales for operating home schools often rest in parents' own experience of schools (Knowles, 1988, 1991). For example, home school parents involved in an in-depth ethnographic study had powerful memories of schools, teachers, and students emanating from their own attendance at schools, and these were often strongly negative. These parents were unwilling to have their own children subjected to the kinds of traumas associated with their own experiences in schools, and so, when the time came for their own children to attend school or when their school-attending children experienced difficulties, they immediately "exited" their children and took on the responsibility of educating them at home. Despite such negative responses to schools, many of these parents are willing to work with schools in some way (Knowles, 1989; Knowles, Mayberry, & Ray, 1991).

There is still another dimension to this extreme parental response to public schools. Although there have been numerous well-publicized court cases brought against home-educating parents (and in many of these, the decisions have been in the favor of parents), increasingly, school superintendents, principals, and teachers are seeking to work closely with parents. Although this trend was first initiated by court mandate, it often continues in the spirit of goodwill, at least in many school boards and districts (Knowles, 1989; Knowles, Marlow, & Muchmore, 1992). It is, we think, representative of the overall increased attention professional educators are beginning to give to all kinds of parents in diverse communities.

Some inquiries into reasons for the overall poor quality of home-school relations have focused on attitudinal barriers. Lombana (1983), for example, compared parents' and teachers' perceptions of one another, and several attitudinal barriers to communication were identified. Parents typically saw teachers as authority figures and, often because of their own negative experiences in school as students, were afraid of teachers. They also feared that any complaints would be taken out on their children and that they would be blamed for any problems their children might experience in school. Teachers and principals indicated that working with parents is the most frustrating part of their multiple roles and, although they want the support of parents, they have difficulty dealing with parents who disagree with them. Many educators in the study believed that parents lack expertise to make educational decisions. Also reported were the troublesome beliefs that low-income parents are not interested in their children's education and that middle-income parents overemphasize student achievement.

There is much wrong with the current status of home-school relations. One experienced teacher summarized the situation this way:

> The unfortunate truth is that parents stand in relation to the classroom as fathers once stood, and in many ways still stand, in relation to the delivery room. It is their job to pace nervously outside, to receive a few progress reports, to wave through the glass, to pay the bills and hand out cigars when the mess is all done. It's tidier that way, better for all concerned. . . . The challenge schools and teachers need to face is how to make the classroom, like the hospital, more inclusive and thus more humane (Keizer, 1988, p. 55).

Finally, in advocating greater involvement of parents in schools, Rich (1985) suggests:

> If teachers had to choose only one policy to stress . . . the most payoff for the most parents and students will come from teachers involving parents in helping their children in learning activities at home (Ibid., p. 15).

Even so, this statement reveals only one component of parent involvement. There are many more as Rich (1987a, 1987b) and Swap (1987, 1990) assert, and others, such as Lareau (1989), Grant and Sleeter (1986), Moles (1987), Epstein and Becker (1982), and Epstein (1987), verify.

You may realize that, because we did not present pertinent research findings, there is a dearth of research that directly explores the role of parents and community members in the formative experiences of teachers in preparation. You may also realize that the matter of preparation to work with parents is largely omitted from teacher preparation programs in North America. Thus, we suggest you make the development of understandings about parents, and the potential for communication with them and the community, an important focus of your professional preparation.

Research Activities

Parents can offer a great many insights into formal education and their *own* children's learning. Unless they have been educated at home by their parents, however, they are likely to have many, perhaps conflicting, experience-based views of schools and classrooms. Like you, they too have preconceptions about the role of teachers and schools. Some of them come to the junction of home and school with firm ideas about the optimum future experiences of school for *their* own children. Given that notions about schools and classrooms rest to some degree in past experiences, a useful place to begin learning about parents is to come to an understanding of *their* thoughts about school. You might want to begin by talking with friends who have school-age children, then branching out to others in the immediate school or community. Approach parents with the notion that you want to develop greater understandings of their needs and perspectives. A logical progression of research activities might start with trying to understand parents' experiences of school and learning. You might then move on to uncover their beliefs about education and how teaching and learning occur, expectations for their children, experiences associated with the home-school communication link and organizations that attempt to facilitate it, and ideas of ways to facilitate home-school connections and parent involvement in education.

1. Begin understanding parents by getting a sense of some of their experiences of schooling. You may want to purposely select a diverse group of parents who are racially, culturally, economically, and politically different from you and your experiences. (To help you frame this inquiry you might want to refer to Chapter 2, where we encouraged you to explore elements of your personal history, and Chapter 3 where we discussed interviewing and external information gathering.) Interview some parents to explore some of the topics suggested in the preceding paragraph beginning with their own experiences of school and learning.

2. Within the school in which you are working there is likely to be parent involvement (see Research Activity 3 in this section if there is heavy parent involvement). Explore the contribution that parents make to the school.

   a. In what ways are parents involved in the school? Are there formal and informal networks of parents who contribute to the ongoing affairs of the school? How do they contribute?

   b. What is the nature of the whole school communication with parents? In other words, how do the principal and administration typically communicate with parents? What are the occasions when administrators and parents meet?

   c. How do teachers communicate with parents? What are the occasions when teachers and parents meet? To what extent are parents involved in their children's learning? What do parents think about the levels of communication between school and home? How do parents view their relationship with the school and with teachers?

   d. What is the nature and extent of parents' interest in the public meetings of the school board? How does the board respond to parents? How is parent participation encouraged or discouraged?

3. Some schools emphasize, as an essential component of their philosophy and practice, direct, committed, and sustained parent involvement in classrooms with teachers and students. Sometimes parent involvement may go beyond the classroom, as in utilization of parents with special skills or expertise of special value to the school. Such participation may be contractual, the basis of admission and ongoing enrollment, and may range from an hour to a day or more per week. If the school in which you are placed is not oriented to intense parental involvement, try and locate one that is; uncover how such schools operate and the nature of parent involvement. Some appropriate questions to ask include

   a. What is the foundational philosophy of the school? What is the place and scope of parent involvement? What are the specific and direct benefits to the students? What kinds of assistance to classrooms and teachers do parents render?

   b. How is parent involvement organized? What are the organizational difficulties? What happens to students' enrollment if parents' commitments change? How do full-time working parents participate? How do single parents contribute? Are lower income students and families given equal access to schools that require parent involvement?

   c. What are administrators' and teachers' perspectives about parent involvement? What are parents' perspectives? Students' perspectives?

4. Most schools have parent-teacher organizations of some kind. In fact, there are several national organizations that promote parent involvement and the home-school connection, the most well known in the United States being the National Parent-Teacher Association (PTA), which has both state and local branches or chapters. In Canada most school boards have active parent-teacher organizations. Beginning with the context of the school in which you are placed explore the ways in which parent organizations contribute to schools and children's learning. Here are some questions to consider:

   a. Are there parent-teacher or home-school organizations within the site of your field experiences? What is the place of the PTA, or similar organization, within the school and district in which you are placed? What are their organizational structures? How do parents and teachers become involved? To what extent are teachers involved? How do these organizations define themselves?

   b. What are principals' and teachers' views of parent-teacher or home-school organizations? What do they say officially? privately? Specifically, how do school administrators frame home-school organizations' work in terms of goals and purposes of schools in general, and in the school in which you are placed, in particular? What freedoms are granted and what limitations are placed on these organizations within school boards or districts, and within individual schools? Why?

   c. What do the parent-teacher/home-school organizations' leadership say about their roles in the school? How is the leadership determined? Are schools ever served by more than one organization? If so, under what conditions? Who are their members? Whom do these organizations serve? Who participates? When do they formally meet and for what purpose? When? Where? How often?

5. Parents who are elected to school boards are likely to have run for the position of school board member based on some direct experiences, frustrations, or particular ambitions with respect to schools and learning. Follow some local newspaper stories about various members of the school board. Arrange a conversation with one of these parents.

   a. What are their political and educational agenda? How do they view parent involvement? How do they regard their contributions to the school board? To what extent are they involved in schools as typical parents? What is the nature of their contact with other parents in the school district or board?

6. The national associations of teachers' unions in North America—in Canada, the Canadian Teachers' Federation (CTF); in the United States, the National Education Association (NEA) and the American Federation of Teachers (AFT), as well as the provincial or state, and local chapters, may have literature on working with parents and perspectives about parents. Begin by talking with the local or school union representatives and begin to find out about the ways these organizations view the home-school link.

7. Rich (1987a, 1987b) has written about the home-school relationship, and some of this material is published by the National Education Association (NEA). Use this material as a beginning place and explore it and *other* publications, keeping in mind questions such as

a. What is the agenda of the authors and publishers? Are they likely to be the same? What are some of the political agenda? How do these publications take into account the diverse social, racial, economic, cultural, political, and locational needs and perspectives? To what extent do organizations such as these serve the white middle class? Lower income groups? To what extent do they serve culturally diverse groups of parents?

b. How is the notion of "parents as partners in the education process" conceived? What is the predominant view of parents in relation to teachers? Are there conflicting perspectives of parents presented in this literature? What is seen as the key to more productive relationships between parents and teachers?

c. What are the responsibilities of school administrators toward parents, the home-school link, and appropriate communication channels? What are the responsibilities of teachers? Parents? Students?

Summary

Our intent in this chapter was to raise awareness of some of the issues associated with developing professional relationships with those who work within learning communities. We turned first to university supervisors or school-based university representatives, because they are central to facilitating your development. Other professionals in the learning community were the next focus of attention; of these, principals and other teachers are potential and substantial sources of professional support. Not to be overlooked, however, are the nonteaching support staff. The relationships you develop with this group have potential to affect your practice in some surprising ways. Finally, we focused on developing relationships with parents and the community.

Having a sense of the potential and important relationships that can influence your emerging practice we now turn to those who are the foundation and purpose of your practice—students. Without developing sound relationships with students much that comes before and after is negated. We left this important topic to last, not because we see it as least important, but because we see attention to student relationships being much easier and more productive *once* other relationships are on sound footings.

Recommended Readings

Beck, L. G., & Murphy, J. (1993). *Understanding the principalship.* New York: Teachers College Press.

Berger, E. H. (1987). *Beyond the classroom: Parents as partners in education.* Columbus, OH: Merrill.

Bruckerhoff, C. E. (1991). *Between classes: Faculty life at Truman High.* New York: Teachers College Press.

Epstein, J. L. (1990). *School and family connections: Theory, research, and implications for integrating*

sociologies of education and family. New York: Haworth Press.

Epstein, J. L., & Becker, H. J. (1982). *Teacher reported practices of parent involvement: Problems and possibilities.* Baltimore, MD: Johns Hopkins University Press.

Frederick, E., & Shultz, J. (1983). *The counselor as gatekeeper.* New York: Academic Press.

Gitlin, A., & Smyth. J. (1989). *Teacher evaluation: Educative alternatives.* Barcombe, Lewes, East Sussex: Falmer Press.

Grant, C. A., & Sleeter, C. E. (1986). *After the school bell rings.* Philadelphia, PA: Falmer Press.

Kaplan, L. (Ed.). (1992). *Education and the family.* Boston: Allyn and Bacon.

Keizer, G. (1988). *No place but here: A teacher's vocation in a rural community.* New York: Penguin Books.

Kroth, R. L. (1984). *Communicating with parents of exceptional children: Improving parent-teacher relationships.* Denver, CO: Love.

Lareau, A. (1989). *Home advantage: Social class and parental intervention in elementary education.* Philadelphia, PA: Falmer Press.

Pierce, R. K. (1993). *What are we trying to teach them anyway? A father's focus on school reform.* San Francisco, CA: ICS Press.

Polakow, V. (1993). *Lives on the edge: Single mothers and their children in the other America.* Chicago: University of Chicago Press.

Swap, S. (1987). *Enhancing parent involvement in schools.* New York: Teachers College Press.

Swap, S. (1990). *Parent involvement and success for all children: What we know now.* Boston: Institute for Responsive Education.

Wolcott, H. (1973). *The man in the principal's office: An ethnography.* New York: Holt.

CHAPTER 10

Developing and Maintaining Relationships with Students

Will they like me? Will I like them? Will they see me as Teacher? Will they listen to me? Will I be able to relate to them and teach them? Will they learn from me? Will they respect me? Can I be their friend? Should I be their friend? How can I gain their respect, establish myself as teacher, and be a friend all at the same time? How will I introduce myself? Do I want to be called Ms.? How will it feel to be called Mr.? Will I be able to remember their names? What do they expect of me? How will I respond to those who demand special attention of me? What demands will they place on me? Will I be able to meet all their demands and expectations? What do they think of prospective teachers like me? Will they try to test me? When and how? What surprises are in store?

These and similar questions are probably floating in your mind awaiting impatiently for answers as you prepare to enter the classroom and school. And they will be especially relevant as you embark on your first field experiences.

Thus far in the book, we have followed a developmental progression. From an initial inward focus to facilitate understanding of the roles and responsibilities of teachers, we moved outward to the contexts of teachers' work and the cultures of schools and students, and then to the individuals who make up those contexts. And, throughout, we have centered on the importance of relationships. More specifically, we urged you to

- develop a clear sense of yourself as teacher by coming to grips with your classroom and nonclassroom roles
- develop reflexive practices
- find ways to understand the contexts in which you will begin to work
- develop professional relationships with experienced practitioners such as your cooperating teachers and others within the field experience

Here, we continue the developmental progression. Students are the largest and most important group of individuals with whom you will interact. They are the *raison d'être* of teaching, the source of teachers' pleasure and pain, anxiety and excitement, rewards and disappointments. They are the center, the focus, the pivotal piece in the puzzle of becoming a teacher. More than anything else, preservice teachers worry about how they will relate to and be received by students.

Many texts are devoted to understanding and working with students. Texts on curriculum, teaching methods, student discipline, classroom management, and child and adolescent psychology all approach the topic from different perspectives. The scope of relevant and related subject matter is great. In this chapter, we approach the subject of working with students from one angle, and then we only skim the surface of that broad area. We focus on elements associated with establishing, developing, and maintaining relationships with students. In particular, we consider the following:

- becoming acquainted with students and developing and negotiating productive working relationships with them in light of your obligations and responsibilities toward them
- dealing with student behavior
- maintaining productive classroom learning environments
- responding to individual needs and differences

The last three topics are the source of many of the difficulties that preservice teachers and, particularly, beginning teachers experience in the classroom. They are also areas that are difficult to address in the university setting and which seem to be infinitely more challenging in practice. Further, from our perspectives and experiences with preservice and beginning teachers and as reported in research, these issues are of most concern to those who have not developed a strong sense of themselves as teachers. Getting to know the students and presenting yourself as a teacher are two significant elements in the development of student-teacher relations. In other words, wrapped up in the presentation of one's teacher role identity are notions about what it means to deal with issues related to working with students. When individuals have little sense of their roles and responsibilities in the classroom and learning community, they are vulnerable to the ravages of poor relationships with students—difficulties dealing with student behavior and responding to individual needs and differences, and problems associated with classroom management.

Becoming Acquainted and Developing Relationships with Students

One problem you will probably encounter in your field placement, and likely throughout your teaching career, is dealing with preconceptions about students. At this point in your professional development the central question you are likely to have is a simple one, "Who are the students I am about to teach?" (Each year, as you progress in your career, it is tempting to answer this question based on your or others' interactions with pupils of previous years.) The answer you give, however, is likely to have profound consequences for your teaching, perhaps even the degree of your success in this early period of professional development. As you will recall from earlier chapters (especially Chapters 2 and 7) you are subject to several potent influences deriving from your own experiences of being a student as well as from more recent experiences such as talks with teachers and staff room conversations. Perhaps you also have a parent's perspective. As Robert, Jocelyn, and Kari recount in the narrative accounts that follow, it is important to try to remain open to and welcome the diversity that awaits you, and to form impressions about students through direct observation and interaction rather than from listening to the stories and opinions of others.

We have seen too many student teachers and others engaged in practica who, in dealing with the heavy pressures of school and university work, have bowed to the temptation to overlook the reason for their being in classrooms—students. Of those teachers in preparation who do not obtain teacher certification, some fall down on this particular point. They have been afraid to get to know their students individually or collectively, have "not had the time," or have not placed value on knowing students (not seeing it as necessary preparation to "delivering lessons and information" or facilitating students' growth). The last case is particularly troublesome. As incredible as it may seem, some prospective teachers—especially those at the secondary school level who believe that they teach subject matter, not pupils—hold this perspective strongly, relying on their long-held conceptions of students. They believe they already know all about students. To these individuals, students may be variously thought of as "just like me," "a bother," "problems," or "people needing straightening out." This last perspective, especially, is largely framed by conceptions of what it means to be a teacher. Unless prospective teachers who hold this view can reframe their perspectives, we recommend that they find other careers. (The chances are that many of the experienced teachers whom you observed who were not well liked or who seemed ineffective did not regard students as central in their professional lives and practice.) Having an understanding of students ensures an appropriate frame of mind for thinking about many of the other tasks that teachers engage in daily, particularly those related to curriculum development.

Given the importance of focusing on students, we want to remind you of the delicate balance between taking care of your own professional development and the development of the students with whom you are working. At one level, taking care of your own development will, ultimately, take care of your students—simply because you will be, in the end, a better teacher.

Despite how you go about it, coming to understand and developing relationships with students is *no* guarantee of your success in the classroom, but it will go a long way. Such understandings have to be followed up with coherent, relevant, and appropriate curriculum and learning processes and activities. Leila and Amy describe their initial uneasiness and the realizations they came to in the process of developing relationships with their students. Gary expresses his discomfort with the first impressions he made on the students. After a few weeks of teaching, Matt realized that he needed to make his teaching more relevant by getting to know the students better. Leila and Brian identify a number of important, yet unanticipated, concerns they needed to address. Milan, Francisco, Brad, and Rachel speak more directly to the issue of professional identity.

It is natural that some of you will be more comfortable with some age groups than with others. Teaching children of certain ages may present you with special problems. For example, it is not uncommon for some preservice and beginning teachers, those not long out of high school, to have difficulty establishing themselves as teachers with a class of high school students who do not differ from them a great deal in age or appearance. (If you are in a high school corridor and the hall monitors regularly try to shuffle you back to class you can be sure that students will see you as one of them.) Identifying oneself as a teacher is a dilemma most preservice and beginning teachers struggle to resolve—wanting to be perceived by the students as both a friend *and* a teacher or, as Milan puts it, being a "real person" and a teacher at the same time. Brad shares his experience of success in assuming both identities. Rachel extends the discussion on student-teacher relationships by expressing her view of a need for a high level of emotional bonding between teacher and pupil.

Rebekah and Trica share what they consider to be significant in establishing relationships with students, and Trica looks back on her progress toward understanding pupils. Matt concludes the section with a metaphoric reflection on student-teacher interactions and relationships.

Narrative Accounts

Once we started teaching at Stoney Brook, my biggest surprise was how wonderful the students are. When I went to high school over 20 years ago I saw few discipline problems and thought my fellow students well-behaved and considerate; however, as I told other people about my decision to re-enter college in order to become a high school teacher, I found people reacting with surprise and disappointment, feeling that I was entering a low status professional field. Many of these people would tell me that "the high schools of today are filled with disrespectful hoodlums who take drugs, vandalize property, and lack respect for teachers." Perhaps other high schools are inhabited by such "vermin," but I can testify that Stoney Brook High School is not. The students in all my classes have been intelligent and friendly, and the students in my English classes have been especially respectful and courteous. Why do you suppose all these horror stories circulate? (Robert Marigold)

Initially, I entered student teaching with much fear and apprehension. After getting some helpful hints and completing a micro-teaching lesson, my apprehension turned to excitement. I found myself with positive anxiety about teaching. I could hardly wait to meet my students and get started. These positive feelings became laced with fear again after talking to one of my two cooperating teachers.

One cooperating teacher spoke very negatively about the students—she had absolutely nothing positive to say. My feelings toward the other group of students I was to work with [from the other cooperating teacher's classes] remained positive, even though some of the same students were in both groups. Actually, the other cooperating teacher did not say anything negative or positive about students. She only told me about what they were studying and the overall difference in ability levels between the two classes.

After hearing the first teacher talk about her pupils to me and to other faculty members, in addition to hearing comments about these students from other teachers, I was convinced they were "animals." And every example the cooperating teacher pointed out in class seemed to prove her point; everything "bad" that they did was highlighted, and it became impossible for me to see anything good about them. Even when I saw something good, the cooperating teacher countered it with so many examples that I soon forgot the good things. Needless to say, I was terrified to teach the students.

As for my actual experience in the classroom, the only thing I would change is to have the cooperating teachers keep their personal feelings about the students to themselves. Otherwise, it sets us up. We, as student teachers, need to make up our own minds about the students. We do need some information on the students and courses (such as their working level in subject matter, what needs to be taught, what has been taught, and where they currently are in the curriculum) but not local gossip or other people's personal feelings about them. (Jocelyn Figuero)

It did not help that the "problem child" of the Math Department was assigned to my class; the math teachers were anxious to tell me all about her. Much of my apprehension and feelings about her were fueled by the anecdotes that flew around the Mathematics Department Office. Veteran teachers seemed to display an emotion akin to glee as they related tales to me during lunch time. Their motives were pure, I decided. They only wanted me to be prepared when I encountered this young woman; however, their "quotes" only fed the nightmares that I regularly had as [the period for] student teaching approached.

Mary is a truly bright girl. I knew this to be true because I had talked with her counselor and knew that she was one of the top students in the graduating class. My story telling friends of the lunch room frequently reiterated the fact that Mary was one of the most intelligent girls they had ever seen. Her creative writing shows an astonishing maturity and talent for a high school senior. (I had the opportunity to work with her on the school literary magazine later in the semester and was quite amazed at the depth of her work.)

I was assured by my almost-fellow colleagues that Mary's emotional development had not caught up with her intellectual powers. And, because these professionals all had so much more experience (an average of some 20 years), I believed them without question. My cooperating teacher did her best to encourage me, but her experience with Mary had also been less than positive. Mary had been in her class a couple of years earlier, and she felt that Mary's attitude had often been quite arrogant.

Easy students, I discovered, are a highly prized commodity among my almost-fellow colleagues. Easy students do not ask difficult questions; they accept everything their teachers tell them and believe in those things simply because their teachers tell them so. Because Jim was forever asking such involved questions, his name also was not greeted with a great deal of enthusiasm by many teachers in the Math Department. Other students also found Jim's incessant questions tiresome. Frequently, students became so exasperated with him that they would tell him to be quiet. Being the young, inexperienced educator that I was, I believed I would welcome such probing from an inquisitive student.

It was now that my almost-fellow colleagues began their gleeful telling of Mary and Jim anecdotes. I heard all about Mary's sullenness when she could not grasp a particular concept and Jim's penchant for asking the most impossible questions. I heard all about their respective intelligence and talents, their enduring romance. My collaborating teacher and I had several long talks about the situation. She told me that [their presence in the class] was ultimately my decision. If I felt that they would be too much to manage during this chaotic student teaching experience, she would approach the principal and inform him that we simply could not have Jim in our class. There were so many things to consider. On the one hand, I had a student who was known to be difficult to handle. Jim would not be an easy student. I was going to have Mary in my class, but was I willing to compound a potentially unfortunate situation by allowing her boyfriend to take part in the class and possibly exacerbate that situation? On the other hand, how could I turn away a student who assured everyone he just wanted to learn? After all, is that not what a teacher wants the most from students—a desire to learn?

On the first day of class I was more nervous about these two than anything else. Out of all of the things to worry about, I was scared of two kids. Repeatedly, I tried to tell myself that I was the person in the position of authority and that the situation would work itself out. I was the teacher. It did not help. I think the only other time in my life I have felt that panic was right before I walked down the aisle to be married. . . .

The school's senior prom [held later in the year] was surprisingly meaningful for me. So many of my students approached me and eagerly introduced their dates, boyfriends, and girlfriends. As I dragged my husband from young couple to young couple, I found myself smiling with excitement and feeling a warm acceptance I had never expected. This emotion was not only unanticipated but strangely important to me. One of the first couples we saw was Mary and Jim. Mary's smile was genuine, and I found myself really liking this young woman who had been such a frightening part of my initiation into teaching.

Since the conclusion of student teaching, I often think about the influence of Mary and Jim and the "peanut gallery." I sometimes think that my encounters with Mary and Jim might have been somewhat different if they had not been colored by others' impressions and feelings. In a profession where there seems to be little communication between colleagues, I hope that my future interactions with fellow teachers will be less about the troublesome students we share and more about how we can make our classrooms centers of learning. If I had never heard anything about Mary and Jim maybe we could have all become friends more quickly. (Kari Ralph)

At the beginning it was uncomfortable getting up in front of the class. I did not know how the students would react or what I should do if they "pulled something" on me. Then it dawned on me: to know me they will need to test me, the same way I have to try different things to get to know them. That realization helped me relax. It will take some time before I establish a rapport with the students. It will not happen overnight. I do not expect all the students to like me. I cannot like them all to the same degree. As long as we respect each other things will be fine. (Leila Muniroui)

Since the beginning of the year, I have learned with each passing day how to feel more comfortable with the children; however, I still am no expert. This is one thing I will have to work hard at. I really want to talk and be with the kids, but when I am, I sometimes freeze. I cannot think of anything appropriate to say. Conversations with the kids just do not flow. If the kids start to talk about home life or other events in their lives, I am at a loss for words. I'm always looking for something to say. I do not have the knack for igniting sparks when it comes to personal conversations. The kids do not seem to notice though. They just keep talking, and I just keep listening with my mouth closed. I would like to be able to talk to the children about anything, but I am awful at small talk. The children do not inhibit me in any way, but it is a problem. I am constantly trying to think of appropriate things to say.

   As the term progressed, I spent more time getting to know the children. At first I did not know how to approach them; after a little while, I just asked them what they were doing, and they would tell me. I also made sure that I paid attention to what they were doing. I tried to talk to all of the students every day even if it only meant saying a quick "hello." I also got to know the children by reading their journals, and by reading their journals I learned to strike up conversations. (Amy Schultz)

When I first got up to begin a unit on *The Grapes of Wrath,* I was more confident and better prepared than with previous units. I knew the students a little better. I began by giving the students a written and spoken introduction to the unit (which I did not do in the previous units). I laid down the ground rules: what was expected of each student; how I was to handle tardiness and absences; and policies about makeup work, grading, discipline, and so forth. This gave me some indication of how students respond to beginning of the year introductions with new teachers. And, that response was, "This is bullshit."

   Really, the students seemed to pay little attention. They were not talking, but they all seemed disinterested just the same. I cannot point to any direct behavior except that most of the students were slumped down in their seats, not even looking at the handout. Maybe I was trying to be too much of a "hard-ass"—setting myself up as a teacher who would not tolerate any misbehavior. I believe this to be partly true because my cooperating teacher, who was in the room, had made me very self-conscious about my lack of structure and discipline. I remember looking over at her while speaking. She gave me this nod that seemed to say, "That's right, you are doing well. Make those kids respect you." (Gary Purdue)

After experiencing several weeks of frustration, trying to design a lesson that would be both interesting and worthwhile, I decided to focus my thoughts on the students' experience in my classroom. Over the next few weeks, I spoke with as many of the students as I could on a one-to-one level to try to develop an understanding about their experience of school. After several conversations, it became clear that many of the students felt that school seemed irrelevant to their experience out of school. Moreover, they felt that they were continually offered material that gave them little room to think.

   I decided that it might be interesting to take one day a week and look at some of the great philosophers who mentally struggled with some crucial issues potentially relevant to the students. I introduced this weekly installment of philosophy by telling them that we were about to study a subject that has confused some of the brightest minds, and if they found it abhorrent, we would not have to look at it again. If, however, they enjoyed studying it, we could make it an ongoing part of the classroom culture. I began by distributing copies of Plato's "Allegory of the Cave" from Book Seven of *The Republic.*

As a class, we alternated reading Plato's text with taking time to address any confusion people might be experiencing with the issues presented. As it turned out, there was little confusion, and the students all seemed captivated by this way of looking at reality. After we got through the discussion, I asked them to see if they could draw any parallels between the world that Plato describes and the world as they experience it. As it turned out, many of the students wrote essays that made some complicated connections between Plato's allegory and the socio-political realities that exist in the world today.

After the first lesson was over, a number of the students came up to me to let me know how much they enjoyed being given the opportunity to think like that. In contemplating this lesson, I realize that the material was not presented in a way that separated me from them. Together, we looked at the work as fellow individuals who were curious about questions concerning what it means to be alone. I sensed that the students did not get the idea that I was in possession of the knowledge that may or may not be transmitted to them. Together we struggled with the issue; my role being a guide rather than the judging authority who is outside of their process.

There occurred a number of incidents, in addition to this one, that brought me into closer contact with the students. I also discovered that in order to be a better teacher, I needed to engage the students in a manner that allowed them to feel comfortable with what was going on in the classroom. I also learned that being a teacher meant being a learner. Much of what I learned cannot be articulated, but nonetheless, it seemed that every day in the classroom students would give me yet another opportunity to rethink my position on what it means to be human. (Matt Schlein)

The last thing in my mind when I started student teaching was that students would have crushes on me. [The possibility] just did not enter my mind. The boys react to me differently than the girls. Some act up all the time to get my attention, and others send their friends to ask me questions and report back to them. Girls seem to be somehow attracted to me too. They have started coming to class early and talk to me about their personal lives and their classes, or they simply comment about what I am wearing that day or about my jewelry. I don't quite understand why they are so interested in me and open up to me so easily. (Leila Muniroui)

I have an interesting situation occurring already. There is one student who has never had a father in the household. In fact, she has an extra mother. She has started to stick to me quite closely and is always trying to sit on my lap. I think she is just fascinated with having a man around. I am doing my best to support her but am uncomfortable with her sitting on my lap. I decided some time ago that her sitting on my lap was something I would not be able to allow. (Brian Forbes)

One of the major problems I had interacting with the children is that we became too comfortable together. I was not removed enough to be seen by them as "the teacher." I was a friend to my students more than I should have been. When I began the term, I wanted to be the "real" person, the friend. Now I want to get their respect first. When it came down to getting students to do what I needed them to do, it was just like a friend asking for something. With a friend, you always have the room to say "no." I felt like my students were saying "no" too much when in reality there really was not a choice. I think all teachers want their students to like them, but if this desire gets in the way of teaching then it becomes a problem. For me, it became a problem. I do not want to lose my role as the teacher. I am not going to become some terribly cold person, but I have to establish a healthy relationship with my students from the beginning. (Milan Kock)

One of the hardest things I had to overcome was not wanting to be a friend to my students. Before I began student teaching I reflected on my experience as a high school student. I was very fortunate to have had three teachers who, before now, I thought were my friends. Now that I look back on the situations, I realize that we did have a very special relationship but that it was a student-teacher relationship and *not* a friendship. They were my role models, they represented everything I wanted to be as an adult. They gave me direction, treated me as an up-and-coming adult, and helped me make some very important decisions. These actions can be classified as those of a friend, but the fine line between teacher and student was never broken.

I wanted students to like me. I realized very quickly that this was not going to work. Once I realized this and began not to worry about whether or not they liked me, my discipline skills improved. Consequently, the classroom atmosphere was much better, and I began to see a major change in the students. They began to respect me and treat me as their teacher, whereas before I was one of them. I feel they are now learning more. I still want to have the same kind of relationship with students that I had with my teachers, so I have tried to get to know them and their interests. At the same time, I have let my students get to know me. I also have been very involved in the activities my students are involved in by going to their games, their concerts, and other such activities they are involved in. (Francisco Perros)

Over the past term, I have become enthused about teaching middle-school-age youth. Because I have spent most of my time in the middle school classes, I have grown to like middle school students even more than the high school students. This to me is rather ironic as I was the last one to admit one and a half years ago that I would even be thinking about teaching middle school. This all started about five months ago.

On a couple of afternoons after school, I went up into the "eighth grade hallway," which is the place where the majority of the eighth grade students hang out between classes and during lunch break. The majority of these eighth graders had been in my general level music class the previous year, so I knew most of them by name. . . . Soon a certain rapport seemed to develop between me and the eighth graders, especially the guys, who seemed to enjoy visiting more so than the girls. I soon found myself talking to this group of about 20 guys after school almost every day. I almost always went to the cafeteria and ate lunch alone at a table or occasionally with another teacher. Soon after the chatting sessions with the eighth graders started, my daily lunch seclusion became a daily chatting session for the middle school. The guys, and sometimes the girls, would surround me and chat.

This, needless to say, was quite flattering at first. It is always nice to be considered cool or to be liked by the students.

Even so, I began to worry about the kind of relationship we were creating. I was worried that if I got too friendly with them, I would most certainly lose my credibility and authority as a teacher, and that could be devastating to my classroom teaching with these students. I was concerned about the personal contact with the kids. Teachers hear stories about other teachers being sued for different types of assaults on students, real or fictitious; I have maintained a certain distance from the students, even during these chat sessions. I also always try to chat with at least two or three of them together. It may seem silly, but it pays to be safe in these times of lawyers and lawsuits.

When the next semester came around, I found out that the principal wanted me to teach a general music class to the middle school as an activity period class. I agreed, thinking that it would be nice to see some of the eighth graders in class again, as I did not have any middle school classes at the time. It turned out that all of the 20 kids who signed up for music were eighth graders—all guys. I was really nervous. Could I still keep my teacher attitude and control after having so much contact with these guys on a more personal level? The first day, they all filed into class. We joked about being together in a class instead of in the hallway. Then, the bell rang. I asked for quiet and got it. I proceeded to go on with my lesson, with only the usual interruptions of chatting or general "guy talk." I was able to maintain the same kind of discipline that I had previously maintained.

I tried to figure what I did to make the jump from hallway friend to classroom teacher. I guess that I am in a teacher mode in class, with teacher language and nonverbal communication that signify that I am in charge. The kids responded to this and slipped into the student mode, just like they had the previous year when they did not know me outside of the classroom. I have come to a conclusion about two things: discipline can still be maintained in the classroom by a teacher, even though that teacher is a "chatting friend" in the hallway or at lunch, if the teacher maintains a definite mode of "teacher" in the classroom; and, a teacher can let his or her hair down with kids in middle school. They seem to be looking for this kind of personal attention or security from an adult and like it when they find it. (Brad Church)

It is important for children to be able to trust their teacher, to feel that they have an adult to turn to for emotional support. It has been told to me several times in university classes that a teacher should not get emotionally attached to students. Some professors seem to feel that if attachment occurs, a child will lose respect for the teacher and will only view the teacher as another "buddy." While I can see the validity of this argument, I find emotional detachment virtually impossible. Most preservice teachers pursued teaching because of an adoration of being and working with people. Why, then, are we being asked to act as emotionless robots, rather than as human beings who love and care? (Rachel Baab)

In the beginning Allan seemed a little wary of me. He appeared uncomfortable with the idea of having me for a teacher. I was actually quite worried that he would cause major disruptions in the class. I decided that I should try to get to know Allan better so that he could feel more comfortable in the classroom with me, and maybe then he would respect me a bit and not be as disruptive. I tried to make an effort to talk at least briefly with each student every day, and I felt I should definitely get to Allan. So, I would say "Hi" to him as he entered the classroom, and as I walked around while the students were working on their assignments, I would ask him how his work was coming and generally talk to him as much as I could without overdoing it.

Through this simple process, I found that Allan and I were becoming used to each other. One day Allan brought . . . "silly putty" [to class] and [his playing with it] became quite distracting to the other students. When I calmly asked him to put it away, he did. A bit later, he took it out again, and I told him that he needed to put it away since it was disrupting the class, and if he didn't, I would have to take it until the end of class. Again without argument he put it away, and it stayed away that time. Even though this was a small event, I felt great. It was no big deal to either one of us, and Allan did what I asked.

Allan still is noisy, and he still gets off task frequently; but to me we overcame uncomfortable, unsure feelings about one another and progressed to a very comfortable student-teacher relationship. We even like to talk together about the university basketball team or just, whatever. (Rebekah Watson)

"Hi, Color Lady." Our eyes met briefly while passing in the hall. He smiled warmly though he could not remember my name. "Hi, Color Lady." In a flash I had experienced the most rewarding moment of my two-week teaching unit on color in the most unpredictable way possible. When I realized this, I was concerned. I, who advocated attainment of student respect without concern for student approval, was uncomfortable with how much I had thrilled at the warmth in a student's eyes. I had developed a closer relationship in only two weeks with certain students than my cooperating teacher had established over the course of a term. Not that his approach was bad, it was very good—just different from mine. We each related better to different students.

Looking back at fall quarter, I remember how confused I was finding myself in a school setting, not as student, but as a teacher. Initially, I identified more with the students than the teachers. This gradually changed. Now I feel much more confident in the teacher role. I began with feelings of inadequacy and intimidation that midway through began to ease into confidence and enthusiasm. When my teaching competencies were questioned by my cooperating teacher I felt the feelings of inadequacy and intimidation might return. Although I have made good progress in mentally overcoming this discouraging experience, further field experience will help me tremendously. I need to put some successful teaching experiences behind me.

I still have a long way to go in understanding where the students are, although I am pleased to have taken a few steps in that direction. How specific instruction needs to be is still somewhat of a mystery to me. Art is not like other subjects. Too much restriction stifles creativity; not enough can discourage motivation, confuse students, and leave them ignorant of important concepts. (Trica Donald)

In many ways, my experience of moving from aimless confusion to some partial understanding of the school culture in the first few days at Colonial High is an excellent metaphor for my experience of teaching. In reading through my journal entries over the first few weeks I am struck by the nature of my comments. As I wrote about the students, I found that I often reduced them to some abstract amorphous group because I felt a certain distance between us. Although my experience in acting provided me with a number of invaluable skills, such as being comfortable speaking in front of people and understanding the manner in which to engage a group, it exacerbated the perceived gap between our worlds.

The constructs of the stage and the proscenium arch, which I was used to, lend themselves to the experience of the actor being distinct from the audience. While a skilled actor is able to communicate in a way that transcends the external barrier of actor and audience, the manner in which they accomplish this is through creating an intense focus on their words, expressions, and movements. Even though this manner of communication has certain distinct advantages, this style negates the possibility of active involvement on the part of the students. Moreover, this style is predicated on the idea that the teacher's skill is the overriding concern in establishing the means of communication.

As a student teacher, I found that I approached my lessons in this way. Instead of focusing on the learning environment for each of the individuals, I was focused on what was going on in an egocentric manner: were all the students paying attention to me; were they laughing at my jokes; and was my cooperating teacher impressed by the way I presented the material. This attitude was fostered by my teaching, at most, two days a week. As a result, I did not have to look at the students as individuals who were each approaching the subject matter in a unique manner. I could simply deliver the lesson I was teaching with a dramatic flair and not have to spend a great deal of time concerning myself with how the students were internalizing the lessons.

As the second semester began, I found that my strategy needed to change. While it was important that my lessons were conducted with enthusiasm and confidence, I found that in order for the lesson to be truly successful I needed to focus on what the individuals were experiencing. I also found that a deeper level of satisfaction occurred for both my students and me when we shared ideas. Teaching was transformed from a dramatic monologue to a means of sharing ideas. (Matt Schlein)

For Reflection and Discussion

1. Robert describes his surprise at discovering that the high school students he met were wonderful, courteous, and intelligent. The students were not the "drug taking hoodlums" that friends and acquaintances had warned him about.
   a. How would you answer Robert's question: "Why do you suppose such horror stories circulate?"
2. Jocelyn describes her positive anxiety toward teaching becoming tinged with fear after a cooperating teacher spoke negatively about the students that she was about to teach. She realized that the type of information she received influenced her feelings about the classes she taught. She felt more positive about the students when the cooperating teacher limited her comments to academic issues.
   a. What kinds of information about students do preservice teachers need before they begin to teach?

   b. Should new teachers review past records or start with a clean slate and form their own opinions about students? What are the possible benefits and drawbacks of each approach?

3. Kari describes the dynamic potential for one or two students to affect the classroom atmosphere. She relates that many teachers offered opinions about the students that colored her expectations and impaired her ability to be open. She believed, "without question," the voices of experienced teachers.
   a. How could Kari have distinguished for herself the difference between biased personal opinions and comments that could prove useful for understanding the students?
   b. To what extent might the advice offered by experienced teachers reflect elements of resignation or cynicism?

4. Leila realizes that students will test her in an effort to get to know her. She does not expect all of her students to like her but believes that "As long as we respect each other we will be fine."
   a. How is respect established? What elements constitute a respectful relationship?
   b. To what extent does testing by the students influence the formation of a relationship with them? To what extent may her assumption about mutual respect be productive? nonproductive?

5. Amy expresses difficulty in becoming comfortable with children. She attributes this to an inability to initiate conversation but notes that the children did not seem to notice.
   a. To what extent might adopting the role of teacher create difficulties in developing relationships with students?
   b. What steps did Amy take to increase her comfort in this area? What else might she do?

6. Gary observed that the body language of his students indicated disinterest in his authoritative introduction to a new unit of study. His cooperating teacher, however, encouraged this approach (having criticized Gary's previous lack of structure).
   a. How can Gary resolve the dilemma presented by such disparate feedback and feelings about his approach?
   b. Should Gary continue to refine his role or remain consistent and continue with the approach preferred by his cooperating teacher? Why?

7. After experiencing frustration in designing interesting lessons, Matt spoke individually with many students to understand "their experience of school." He found the students' perception to be that school was irrelevant and "gave them little room to think." In response to this, Matt invited the students to explore a work by Plato. When he reflected about the success of the approach he had used, Matt realized that his role as a guide and "fellow" questioner had not separated himself from them.
   a. How would you describe the relationship that developed between Matt and his students?
   b. Why is it significant to Matt that his presentation of the material had not "separated" him from his students? What caused the separation between himself and his students?
   c. Would this approach work (as well) in other content areas? Why, or why not?

8. Leila never considered the possibility that students would have crushes on her. She is also surprised by the attention she receives from girls. She observes that gender appears to determine the behavior of the students toward her.

   a. How might Leila address the issue of crushes? How do you account for Leila's popularity?

   b. How does student behavior inform Leila about the type of regard students have for her?

9. Brian encountered a student with two mothers and discovered that he had become a source of fascination to the student. Although the girl tries to sit in his lap he had decided that he would not allow this.

   a. Has Brian made a wise decision about the level of physical intimacy that he will allow? Why or why not?

   b. Should Brian make an exception in this case? Why or why not?

10. Milan recalls the difficulty he encountered by attempting to be a friend to his students. He wanted to be the "real" person, the friend. He found that there is always room to say "no" to a friend and his "students were saying 'no' too much when in reality there really was not a choice."

    a. How important is it to include aspects of friendliness in the teaching-learning process? Which aspects deserve emphasis?

    b. Must students like their teachers to learn from them? And, what does it mean to "be liked"?

    c. Can compassion and discipline be effectively combined? How and to what extent?

11. Prior to student teaching, Francisco recalled teachers whom she thought of as friends as well as role models.

    a. How did the experience of student teaching help Francisco refine and refocus her reflections about past teachers?

    b. What were the teacher actions that Francisco defined as friendly?

12. Brad was concerned that the casual relationship he had developed with students would interfere with his ability to teach them effectively.

    a. Why do you think students were attracted to Brad? What were the reasons he saw?

    b. How did Brad make the transition from lunchroom companion to classroom authority?

    c. Why do you think primarily male students were involved in Brad's group? What gender issues arise from this account?

13. Rachel finds "emotional detachment virtually impossible." It seems to her that people pursue teaching because of "adoration of being and working with people."

    a. How would you answer Rachel's question: "Why, then, are we being asked to act as emotionless robots, rather than as human beings who love and care?"

14. Rebekah describes the development of a relationship with a student who was initially wary of her. He disrupted a lesson she taught, and she felt relieved that the incident was a small one.

    a. What steps had Rebekah taken to minimize the escalation of disruptions by the student?

    b. To what extent did Rebekah's effort to address the comfort of the student affect her own?

15. Trica was surprised to discover how thrilled she was when a student greeted her warmly in the hall. She felt that this confirmed her belief that a positive student-teacher relationship would come naturally after respect was established. She felt that she had developed closer relationships in two weeks with some of the students than her cooperating teacher had established.

    a. Why did Trica regard student respect as more important than student approval?

    b. What part did Trica's position as student teacher play in her perception about the rapid development of close relationships? How appropriate is Trica's assumption about the closeness of relationships formed in two weeks?

16. Matt describes the evolution of his perspective about students. His journal revealed that he had initially written about them as "some abstract amorphous group" and his focus was upon himself as actor. His focus shifted after he had spent some time in the classroom, and he writes, "I found that in order for the lesson to be truly successful, I needed to focus on what the individuals were experiencing."

    a. To what extent do the elements of Matt's experience reflect the organization of topics in this text?

    b. How is Matt's experience reflected in the research on teachers' role identity formation? (See *Links with Research* in this section.)

    c. What is the potential of relationships with students to influence curricular, instructional, and other teacher practices?

Links with Research

In speaking of students' experience of the curriculum Erickson and Shultz (1992) write

> Virtually no research has been done that places student experience at the center of attention. We do not see student interests and their known and unknown fears. We do not see the mutual influence of students and teachers or see what the student or teacher thinks or cares about during the course of that mutual influence. If the student is visible at all in the research study he is usually viewed from the perspective of adult educators' interests and ways of seeing, that is, as failing, succeeding, motivated, mastering, unmotivated, responding, or having a misconception. Rarely is the perspective of the student herself explored (p. 467).

Given the centrality of students in classrooms and schools, the lack of attention in the research literature to how *they* experience education is ironical. The literature we draw on in this section illustrates the preceding quotation because it, too, focuses on the student-teacher relationship as experienced and viewed by teachers and teacher educators. The significance of student-teacher relationships in the developing practice of teachers is evident in these studies.

A study of university supervisors' perceptions of preservice teachers who failed student teaching points out how critical it is for preservice teachers to attend to students and their relationships with them (Knowles & Skrobola, 1992; see also, Knowles & Sudzina, 1991; Sudzina & Knowles, 1993). There was a general consensus among university supervisors in that study that most preservice teachers who fail are unable to determine and respond to students' needs and relate to students sufficiently well so as to engage their interest and participation. The supervisors reported that unsuccessful preservice teachers typically become preoccupied with themselves and their ability to "survive the semester," at the expense of students. This kind of detrimental self-absorption is explained and supported in research linking preservice teacher development with professional role identity (see Kagan, 1992).

Guillaume and Rudney (1991), reporting on a yearlong study of 19 preservice teachers' changing concerns, observed that developing and maintaining positive relationships with students remained a concern throughout the program and that satisfactory relationships in particular occupied a significant portion of preservice teachers' writings about their classroom experiences. Over time, these preservice teachers were able to do what the preservice teachers reported on earlier were not, that is, attend and respond to student diversity without being overwhelmed by it.

Feiman-Nemser and Floden (1986) discuss student-teacher relationships in terms of norms governing interactions. They assert that tension between themes of authority and friendship creates a fundamental ambiguity in how teachers view their roles and relate to students. This conflict is borne out time and again in the literature on beginning teacher development (for example, Bullough, 1989; Bullough, Knowles, & Crow, 1991; Cole, 1990a, 1990b; Thiessen, 1991).

Allison, a first-year teacher, was a participant in an in-depth study of student-teacher relationships and her emerging professional identity. Thiessen (1991) describes her as wanting "to be in control without taking or losing control, a difficult scale of power to balance" (p. 10). For Allison, the development of her identity as a teacher was integrally linked to the development of a healthy, productive relationship with her students. Unfortunately, in her first year there was a dramatic difference between the kind of relationships she anticipated having and the kind of relationships she experienced. Contextual factors and conditions beyond her control made it impossible for her to be the kind of teacher she wanted to be.

The significance of student-teacher relationships in beginning teacher development is also illustrated in another study (Cole, 1992). One beginning teacher experienced considerable difficulty in her first year until she was able to develop meaningful relationships with her students. The better she was able to get to know her students, the better she was able to meet their individual needs and differences, and the more confident and satisfied with her teaching she became. Another first-year teacher, primarily due to contextual factors beyond her control, was unable to form the kind of relationships with students she believed was integral to "good" teaching. A change in venue in her second year enabled her to form strong and meaningful relationships with students that resulted in a successful second year of teaching.

Research Activities

As you think about establishing relationships with students and defining your role within these relationships, it may be useful for you to consider three elements that comprise any relationship:

- the attributes and personal strengths that you bring to the relationship
- the nature of the relationship you hope to establish
- the individuals with whom you intend to enter a relationship

1. Starting with yourself, make a list of the qualities you bring to a relationship.
   a. What adjectives have friends or relatives used to describe you? (It might help to imagine that you are writing a personal advertisement, perhaps seeking suitable employment as a teacher.) What personal attributes would you include? How do you focus them, or, what is the common denominator of your attributes?

2. Think about teachers. Many factors are involved in negotiating a role for yourself as a teacher. List the attributes that you feel are important for teachers to have. Note the areas of intersection between your personal qualities (see exercise 1 in this section) and the qualities that you identified as important for teachers. The zone of intersection may help you identify qualities and behaviors that will be most comfortable for you to focus on as you begin to develop relationships with students.

3. How do others serve as mirrors for ourselves? As we interact with others, the role we adopt is often dependent upon the qualities of the relationship that we have with the other. Consider, then, how you have adopted roles in response to the roles of others (for example, the manner in which you relate to persons you admire, persons in authority, or persons for whom you have little respect).
   a. Think about and explore some of the relationships you have established and maintained with others, focusing on the roles you have played within those relationships and the ways in which you have sought to establish and maintain those relationships. For example, in friendships are you often the leader or initiator? Are you comfortable with following rather than leading when the relationship dictates a need for you to do this? Can you easily change roles within a relationship? Do you react to authoritarian styles with defiance, passivity, or both? How important is reciprocity in a relationship?
   b. Think about your responses within the context of developing relationships with students. What roles and qualities will it be important to keep in mind as you develop relationships with those individuals?

4. As Paley (1981, 1986, 1990) affirms, students are a never-ending source of joy, insight, and exasperation, and a focus of inquiry for teachers. In Chapter 7 we facilitated your focus on understanding students within the context of the learning community; in this chapter we refocus on students at a more individual level. Consider the following:
   a. As you observe and interact with students, consider how their values compare with your own. What are the fundamental ways in which their values are different? What roles do cultural backgrounds have in the apparent differences? It is important to recognize that some aspects of cultural differences will initially appear more prominent, but plan to move beyond those superficial or immediately recognizable differences. As you come to understand students in more depth concentrate on learning the importance of cultural identification to them.
   b. Observe students, carefully noting patterns of relationships, attributes, difficulties or needs, particular skills, and areas of interest. It may appear at times that you are looking into a mirror, seeing your experiences as a student reflected back at you and, at other times, that you are looking through a foggy window at blurred images of a person from a foreign culture. Each of these new perspectives, no matter how fuzzy, is useful to your understandings and for developing relationships.

5. As you know from experience and may find out quickly when in the field placement site, teachers earn or are assigned reputations—fairly or unfairly. Talking with students about their relations with teachers will likely reveal those reputations. Informal conversations in the teachers' lounge may also reveal them. Based on teacher and student talk seek out those teachers who are reputed to have extremely productive, congenial, and respectful relationships with students. You may also want to locate teachers who are known to have difficult or troublesome relationships with students. In so doing, be extremely mindful of the ethical implications of your inquiries. Consider exploring some of the following questions and inquiry activities (see also Chapter 3 for other ideas).

   a. Observing in these teachers' classrooms may be a good place to begin to understand the nature of teacher-pupil relationships. You may want to take note of the tone of the classrooms, teachers' presentations of themselves, teachers' interactions with students, and the kinds of teaching strategies and learning activities employed. A central question to guide your observations might be, "How do these teachers go about creating and maintaining productive and respectful relations with students?" (Keep in mind that the beginning of each year or term is likely to see the teacher working in overdrive toward these ends, and if you enter the classroom at the middle of the year or term, relationships are likely to be somewhat cemented.)

   b. Observe these same teachers in nonclassroom contexts within the learning community. How do they act similarly or differently from when in the classroom? What, then, are the various foci of their relationships with students?

   c. Engage in conversations with teachers about their relationships with students. How do they go about forging relationships? In their views, what is the key to developing and maintaining relationships? How is mutual respect developed? What are their beliefs about students? How do they go about trying to understand students and their individual differences? What is their central philosophy of teaching? What do they see as the relationship between teaching practices and relations with students? Are particular teaching methods or practices especially suitable for facilitation of productive and respectful relationships?

   d. Continue talking with students. What are students' perceptions of teachers? What do they see as the essential qualities in teachers for developing productive relationships with students? What are the ways that teachers, who do not have good relationships with pupils, act toward individual students and groups of students? What are the ways that teachers, who have good relationships with pupils, act toward individual students and groups of students? Why do some teachers develop productive relationships with some students and not others? Do teachers have particular skills, attributes, or interests that suit them to work with particular students?

6. Video and movie films also offer a rich source for exploring the teacher-student relationships within the context of classrooms (see *Video List*). After viewing some of the videos listed, consider the following questions.

   a. How might these portrayals influence students' thinking, if at all? In what ways are such portrayals of teacher-student relationships stereotypical? dysfunctional? atypical? What, if any, are the key elements of dysfunctional or nonproductive relationships? What kinds of relationships are presented as productive? How are the teachers presented in such relationships? How are students represented?

Dealing with Student Behaviors

Many new teachers see themselves as "nondisciplinarians." They view notions of "discipline" as representing a negative concept, one that is oppressive, is deprecating, denies students' freedoms, and intrudes into the responsibilities of teaching subject matter and developing learning opportunities for pupils. Actually, they are correct to a degree. In addition, young preservice teachers often state that their youthfulness prohibits them from taking traditional stances toward dealing with student behaviors (or disciplinary matters), a point that is also correct to a degree. Further, contemporary attitudes and notions of interacting with students (those which seek mutual respect, cooperation, and collaboration rather than control, coercion, and confrontation) are at odds with some of the traditional views of classroom and school discipline to which you may have been exposed as a student.

The matter of discipline is also a dreaded concept to many new teachers. That dread, however, is not unfounded. The research literature on learning to teach, particularly that which focuses on beginning teaching, provides ample evidence that issues of discipline (along with "classroom management"), however defined, press heavily on the experiences of new teachers. Keep in mind that the purpose of discussing this topic within the context of field experiences as represented in this book is *not* to treat it comprehensively or to develop potential solutions to various kinds of problems with student behavior. (There are many other texts that treat the topic in great detail, although our feeling is that such books may not be the best place to begin to form your own framework.) Our intent is to help you to think about issues related to student behavior through reading small slices of the experiences of others. Knowing that you are not alone with your concerns in this area can be comforting. Also, reading and thinking about the experiences of others and how they worked through or addressed problems related to student behavior may help you to anticipate and think more deeply about experiences or problems that may arise in your own situation. In addition, you may wish to challenge some of the views presented. To this end, the accounts are useful discussion stimulators.

Traditional textbooks dealing with issues of student discipline typically explore the interrelated nature of and boundaries between discipline and classroom management. They also tend to portray teachers as classroom managers or controllers of students. Teachers are said "to be in control," "to control or manage classrooms," and "to control students." In other words, the views of "teacher-as-manager," "teacher-as-controller," or "teacher as being in control" imply particular orientations to teaching and learning made without due regard to the development of the whole teacher. And, it may be that such an orientation is in conflict with your views about the nature of curriculum and instruction. Such orientations to the role of teacher, ones of ultimate classroom authority and power, are usually made with little close attention to long-term and emerging teacher development issues. (The patterns you develop early on are likely to be difficult to shake, for example.) Nor are they made with direct reference to intimate knowledge and understandings of students. In addition to the "teacher," it is the students and their cultures along with the contexts of the learning community, and the social, cultural, political, and historical milieu that help shape the tenor of classroom rules and mores.

Acceptance of principles for dealing with student behavior or discipline without consideration of the whole development of student and teacher has the potential to be confusing to all concerned. We urge you, then, to question the foundational principles and assumptions on which the advice and orientations to discipline (and classroom management) are based. In this vein, questions that continue to challenge us include

- What are the social consequences of traditional modes of thinking about teaching and student discipline?
- How does diversity within classrooms change perceptions of student discipline?
- What are the bases of cooperative and mutually respectful relationships?

These and many other questions may drive your critical exploration of issues of student discipline. And, with similar degrees of rigor, you should continue to question the assumptions that you bring to the classroom.

We suggest that you critically explore traditional textbooks on dealing with student behaviors (student discipline), as well as facilitation of productive learning environments (classroom management). In your exploration, work toward developing a set of coherent practices that are congruent with your conception of your identity as teacher and school professional, your orientation to thinking about curriculum and instruction, and your views of students (as well as parents and community). We see such formal representations of ways of dealing with students' diverse behaviors (discipline strategies) as being subservient to developing understandings about students and their diverse cultures and backgrounds. Ideally, this requires an alternative perspective on the place of field experiences in *your* preparation to teach. We hope this text is helping you to formulate such thinking.

We now turn to two issues. The first relates to common conceptions about developing relations with students; the second has to do with control. Both concepts are integrally related. "Don't smile until Christmas" is an often heard admonition to new teachers. It was such a common piece of advice to new teachers and a common theme in the writing of a group of beginning teachers that editor Kevin Ryan (1970) used it as a title for a book. What do people mean when they give this advice to newcomers?

Do the advice givers mean that the first half of the school year, from August to December, is a particularly difficult time for teachers and should be reflected in the way teachers interact with students? Do they mean that one's demeanor should be tough, rigid, unerringly placid, devoid of humor, and that one should be unsympathetic or unresponsive toward students? Do they mean that teaching is a humorless, unhappy activity? Do they mean that the five-month period is crucial for developing relationships with students and should be characterized by an unwillingness to engage in normal human interactions? Or, are they portraying an ideology that expresses relationships between students and teachers best characterized by heavy-handed, personal control (teacher over pupil), dour classroom demeanors, and atmospheres where the emphasis is exclusively on direct and directive teaching practices? The truth in the "Don't smile" advice is likely to be found in answers to all of the preceding questions. We think, however, that the notion is particularly insidious because it suggests that the manner in which adults go about establishing relationships with students is through manipulation and not through normal person-to-person, sensitive, and respectful interactions.

Traditional views of discipline in the classroom and school are based on principles of control. Teachers have absolute power over students and may denigrate the relationship to one of authoritarian action over subservience. This is not a useful construct with which to create healthy learning and living environments no matter how diluted the authoritarian action. We urge you to seek out ways to uncover how successful teachers, those who have meaningful professional relationships with students, choose *not* to use their ultimate authority in working with students. "What are the principles at the heart of these teachers' thinking and actions?" is a question well worth answering.

Some schools and school systems are potentially riddled with disrespect, and it filters throughout, flowing in many directions. In these systems, the manner in which teachers are treated by administrators is mirrored in the way teachers treat students. Teachers are disempowered by administrators; students are disempowered by teachers. This hierarchy of control can have devastating results. In recent years, calls for rethinking how schools operate have brought this matter into focus. Some schools have embarked upon site-based management governance strategies where teachers have greater input into the direction and operation of the school. Others have established "campaigns" to foster mutual respect within the whole learning community. Unless these efforts are accompanied by changes in the way administrators view their relationships with teachers, and the carrying out of their responsibilities, such campaigns may prove less than effective. Likewise, teachers must be willing to change their perspectives. Society is becoming more sensitive about the need for mutual respect of persons and individual differences—and schools need to be at the forefront of changes. <u>Our challenge to you, then, is to find ways to develop solid professional relationships with students characterized by sensitivity, understanding, and genuine interest in them.</u>

In the following accounts we hear from preservice teachers who grappled with some discipline issues. Their experiences as students shaped some of their perceptions about discipline and many of them held traditional orientations. Yet, they all attest to moves to challenge their own and others' thinking. Influenced by her own experiences as student, Leila expresses confusion over how to respond to students' off-task behavior. Amy compares her own experiences as a student with her cooperating teacher's approach to responding to students. Rachel describes a problem she had working with a small group of children and the disciplinary action she finally took. Rebecca found herself rethinking her approach to interacting with students when she was faced with a group of challenging students. Steve and Jane came to the realization that using punishment to solve problems was inappropriate and ineffective, and that they each need to consider alternative methods. Miles experiences disillusionment over having to deal with behavior problems and feels constrained by expectations that he assume authority over the students. Leila also is reluctant to assume a position of authority in her relationship with students.

Narrative Accounts

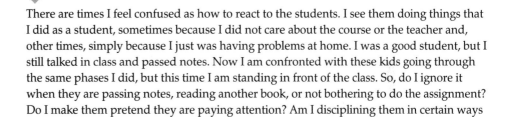

There are times I feel confused as how to react to the students. I see them doing things that I did as a student, sometimes because I did not care about the course or the teacher and, other times, simply because I just was having problems at home. I was a good student, but I still talked in class and passed notes. Now I am confronted with these kids going through the same phases I did, but this time I am standing in front of the class. So, do I ignore it when they are passing notes, reading another book, or not bothering to do the assignment? Do I make them pretend they are paying attention? Am I disciplining them in certain ways because they are doing what I am used to seeing in class? Are there right ways to deal with such school misconduct? (Leila Muniroui)

Most of the elementary teachers I had made me feel really awful about myself when I had done wrong. My cooperating teacher does not do that. She encourages the students to talk about what took place, asks them a series of questions, and then takes appropriate action. She looks at things objectively with the kids and can even have them laughing about what happened and also about themselves.

I can remember one day there was a little boy who was being obnoxious [during a lesson] and had to stay in for recess. He was not a grump about it. He had done something wrong, but my cooperating teacher did not string him up by his earlobe. This was because what he had done was nothing really major. His punishment fit his crime. He was able to walk away laughing at himself. I want to do that with my class. I want to be firm but, in the end, have the kids walking away with a better understanding of themselves and even laughing about what they have done. (Amy Schultz)

Problems of students' behaviors greatly tainted my view of the success of a lesson I taught in a small group setting. Although only six children participated in the activity, all but one posed a behavior problem. I falsely assumed that they would naturally be interested in the lesson and thus be cooperative; however, this was by far not the case. Of the six children, only one maintained an adequate level of attention and participation during the activity. Of the remaining five: one lay under a table, listless, the entire time; one wandered the hallway; one whispered songs and taunts into the tape recorder; and two beat up on each other.

I attempted every strategy I knew to restore the group to order. I asked them to refrain from whatever annoying activity they were carrying out at the moment. I tried to engage them through questions. I threatened them with being sent back to the classroom. I tried to ignore them. I informed them that they would soon be on their way to the principal's office. But all to no avail. Nearing a point of desperation and homicidal thoughts I yanked up the nearest child and quickly marched him back to the classroom. As the remaining students realized I would pursue my intentions, they began to behave in a slightly more civilized manner; and I was thus able to complete the activity. (Rachel Baab)

At the beginning of the semester, I was a pretty lax teacher. When things go well, I am pretty easygoing. When I started working with a math group consisting of nine slow learners, I had to set standards for myself and my students. It was no longer a case of just presenting the material and helping with the rough spots. I was no longer in a situation of calm. I had to assert control over these students from the moment class began; otherwise, they would try to run me down. They really tested me on where I stood as far as reprimanding them. It really made me stop and think about what I wanted from the students. I have always thought about what I could give them. Now it was time for me to consider what I wanted them to do for me. (Rebecca Buono)

I have instinctively reached for punishment strategies in response to problems. Although I am still grasping for answers, I have at least moved in my thinking. My realization on Friday was that my use of punishment was escalating problems rather than resolving them. There are alternative approaches. The next step is learning how to use them.

Later: I went into last week feeling very discouraged about teaching, but by week's end, I had perked up as I haltingly began to realize what was amiss. This jolt in my progress occurred after a few weeks of smooth sailing. I had slipped into a routine of repetitive lessons and heavy-handed management that was simply not sustainable. By not altering my strategies I was boring the kids and myself as well. As my enthusiasm waned, so did my ability to motivate. The resulting unruly classes revealed another problem, playing the drill sergeant takes a lot of energy. In the first few weeks, desperate for control, I had forcefully imposed orders to survive. By the last week it seemed that I was stamping out fires caused in part by the classroom monotony I introduced. Furthermore, martinets cause other problems—if you press too hard it begins to squeeze out the edges. In other words, some kids were actually provoked into misbehaving by such authoritarian practices. It seems I failed to heed my own earlier advice about democracy in the classroom. Repressive, teacher-centered classrooms are no fun to be in, for me or the students.

If I hope to make a career of teaching, I need to find satisfaction and enjoyment, or I will not last long. Prompted by the above mentioned problems, I have spent the last week working on solutions. Firstly, I have eased up on my style of class control. Although I cannot quite exactly explain what I am doing, the atmosphere in my room is much more pleasant. I am more tolerant of nondisruptive talking, and I am less severe in my reprimands. It is as if the confrontational sting has dissipated. Whatever the cause, it is relaxing as it takes less effort. (Steve Bruno)

Two weeks ago the cooperating teacher missed a day of school to go to an in-service [professional development] program. When the substitute teacher arrived, there was a note telling him that I was to teach the entire day. Though the morning was wonderful, the afternoon fell apart. The students shouted out answers inappropriately and did not listen. This caused me to become very tense and begin to "crack down." I took away their recess time. Rather than helping the problem this action made it worse. After thinking about the day I arrived at several conclusions. The students had sat quietly the entire morning; the activity of the afternoon was an exciting one, looking at travel brochures and writing a story about going on a trip. The nature of the lesson did not lend itself to the same atmosphere as the morning. Rather than "cracking down" on the class, I should have stopped and discussed with them what was happening, why, and how the behavior might be altered (if it really needed to be).

I think the basis of my tension was that I was afraid to let things get noisy and very active for fear I wouldn't be able to bring them back; however, I have resolved to experiment rather than always "rule with an iron fist." The students know that I am not equal in status to my cooperating teacher; however, they are aware that I am an important, respected member of the teaching staff. I want them to respect me just as I want the students to know I respect them. (Jane Atman)

My role as authority figure decreased yesterday and I am not sure how to take that. At the end of the period I assigned two readings for the next day and then went up to talk to five kids about problems in the class. As soon as I did the noise level went through the roof, and once again I had to yell for them to be quiet. I hate this job. It makes me feel really stupid. It feels like I put the kids below me, and I don't like doing that. I wish I could just sit and talk with them as equals. I am glad the weekend is almost here. I cannot believe I have to do this again next week. I cannot believe I am teaching British literature on Monday. I cannot believe it gets better. (Miles Coleman)

I want to be a teacher who maintains good discipline. I usually do, but it scares me whenever things start to get out of control. It is too easy to simply react. Being reactive is not what I want to do. My cooperating teacher says I have a voice of strong authority. I guess I do! Somehow I want to use my "voice of authority" to hold, not regain, authority. (Leila Muniroui)

▲

For Reflection and Discussion

1. Leila refers to her experience as a student as a basis for understanding the possible reasons behind the behaviors of her students. She admits to some confusion about how to react to the students because she remembers that she herself was a good student and indulged in talking in class and passing notes too. How should she answer the questions she poses for herself?
   a. Should she "make them pretend they are paying attention"? Why or why not? How might the relationship with her students be influenced if she ignores that behavior? addresses it?
2. Amy observed that her cooperating teacher handled discipline in a manner that was sensitive to students' self-esteem. Amy wants to be firm but "have the kids walking

away with a better understanding of themselves and even laughing about what they have done."

    a. How has Amy's prior experience as an elementary student influenced her perspective about discipline?

    b. To what extent is it possible to create consequences that elicit smiles? Is this an appropriate approach? Why or why not?

3. Contrary to her assumption that the students would be naturally interested and engaged in the lesson, Rachel "attempted every strategy" to restore her group of six students to order. Near desperation, she "yanked up the nearest child and quickly marched him back to the classroom." She was then able to complete the activity she had planned.

    a. To what extent might the students' unruly behavior have been the result of her indecisive responses to their actions or her relationship with them?

    b. What effect might Rachel's reaction have upon the tone of her relationship with the students? Was Rachel's response an appropriate one? Why? Why not?

    c. To what extent can Rachel's problem with her group be attributed to her assumption about the particular lesson?

4. Rebecca's work with "slow learners" caused her to consider issues of student behavior and discipline. She moved from thinking about what she could provide for her students to what she wanted her students to do for her.

    a. How might Rebecca's change of perspective influence her relationship with her students? How might it influence her professional development as a teacher?

    b. Does Rebecca view discipline as punishment or prevention? Why do you think so?

5. Steve recognized that the punishment he instinctively used caused an escalation rather than a resolution of the classroom problems he faced. He realized that he "had slipped into a routine of repetitive lessons and heavy-handed management that was simply not sustainable." His style provoked some students, and he found that "repressive, teacher-centered classrooms are no fun to be in, for me or my students."

    a. How did his resolve to employ alternative approaches affect the classroom atmosphere?

    b. Which element do you suppose Steve addressed first, his lesson delivery strategies or his "heavy-handed management?" Why?

    c. Are teacher-centered classrooms necessarily repressive? If not, why not? If so, to whom, teachers or students?

6. Jane was pleased to have the opportunity to teach for the entire day when the cooperating teacher was absent. The first part of the day went well but she writes that the afternoon "fell apart."

    a. What did Jane's reflection about the day reveal about the cause of the disintegration of the classroom atmosphere?

    b. What alternative to "cracking down" did Jane consider?

7. Miles felt that his authority decreased and writes that he yelled for quiet to restore order and felt stupid for doing it. He wishes that he could talk with students as equals.

    a. What is Miles conveying about himself (as teacher) to his students by yelling at them? What alternatives might he pursue in a situation like this?

    b. Should Miles attempt to sit and talk with his students as equals? Why or why not? What does it mean to be "equals"?

8. Leila wants to "maintain good discipline." She writes that it scares her when things appear to get "out of control" because it is then too easy to "simply react." She wants to use her "voice of authority" to hold rather than regain authority.

   a. Why is a reactive stance viewed negatively by Leila?

   b. How might Leila learn to use her voice as a tool to maintain good discipline?

   c. How might Guillaume and Rudney's (1991) study (see *Links with Research* in this section) shed some light on Leila's dilemma?

Links with Research

In the vast literature on preservice and beginning teacher development there is a pervasive and predominant focus on the phenomena of student discipline and classroom control. How much such a focus reflects preservice teachers' realities and how much reflects researchers' interpretation of these realities are open to question and consideration. Nevertheless, student discipline and classroom control are the subject of considerable study.

Several studies suggest that a socialization process takes place during student teaching that results in a shift in preservice teachers' thinking and practice toward more rigid and punitive attitudes and behavior (Hoy & Rees, 1977; Iannaccone, 1963; Jacobs, 1968; Lacey, 1977; Maxie, 1989; Silvernail & Costello, 1983; Walberg, Metzner, Todd, & Henry, 1968; Zeichner & Tabachnick, 1981). Crow (1991) explains this shift in terms of professional role identity. In her case study of Marilyn, Crow attributes Marilyn's ready acceptance of the school's conservative and mechanical discipline rules and procedures to her lack of sense of herself as classroom manager and lack of appropriate and relevant skills.

> Novice teachers may be more prone to adopt the custodial norms and values of the profession if they do not have firmly developed schema for being a classroom manager. Indeed, most people are more than willing to grab at any life raft of discipline procedures and policies if they believe they are sinking in an ocean of student unrest. . . . Searching for answers, the solutions are readily available from the experienced teachers and overseeing administration; indeed, new teachers are socialized quickly and are absorbed into the school system (p. 19).

Iannaccone (1963) is more specific about the kind of socialization that takes place in field experiences. He describes the overriding emphasis by cooperating teachers on preservice teachers' abilities to cover the curriculum and get through the lesson quickly; thus, in order to "succeed" in field experiences preservice teachers must develop strategies that have little to do with or preclude student learning. To teach successfully, according to this view, means, among other things, to "eliminate disruptive behavior by increasing doses of institutional pressures and sanctions to make the child conform to the organizational pattern of the room" (Ibid., p. 80).

Not all preservice and beginning teachers shift to a more custodial approach to interacting with students. As Tabachnick and Zeichner (1984) and Zeichner & Grant (1981) point out, cooperating teachers with less rigid control ideologies and preservice programs with a reflective inquiry focus exert influences on preservice teachers that are likely to result in more humanistic approaches.

For a variety of reasons, concern and anxiety over student discipline and classroom control are exhibited by student and beginning teachers. To conclude on an optimistic note, we refer again to Guillaume and Rudney's (1991) study of preservice teachers' changing concerns. Although discipline remained a primary concern for all preservice teachers throughout the preservice preparation program, the authors observed a distinct change in how student discipline was viewed. As the preservice teachers developed a trust in their own decisions and in themselves as teachers, they became less concerned with controlling students as a demonstration of their authority and more concerned with building relationships based on legitimate authority. Once again, the link between the developing self-image and successful teaching is illustrated.

Research Activities

1. What are some ways in which notions about dealing with student behaviors (student discipline) are conceptualized? This question could frame a series of discussions with many participants in the learning community. Beginning with students, you could talk in turn with teachers, other professionals and nonteaching staff within the building, school administrators, and board or district administrators. Having engaged these individuals you might consider talking with parents about their perspectives. Some questions that might assist you in framing conversations include
   - What is student discipline?
   - Are there policies intended to guide matters of student discipline? What are they?
   - Who is responsible for student discipline? Where? When? How?
   - What are the concerns and problems associated with matters of student discipline?
   - How and to what extent do matters of student discipline affect you? Why? When?
2. Teachers have reputations with students, and these reputations are likely to rest on teachers' conceptions and implementation of strategies of discipline as much as anything else. Talk with students about their observations of teachers' beliefs about discipline (the way teachers talk about it), teachers' actual strategies, and the outcomes of these various orientations. Simply listen to pupils' stories, perhaps asking to hear accounts of notorious student behavior and notorious teacher practices.
   a. What are students' assumptions about teachers (and their work) in the stories they tell?
3. To catch a glimpse of students' experiences with discipline practices (traditionally conceived) you may want to shadow a couple of students for a day or so (much as Matt did in Chapter 3), taking note of the ways in which students are treated by teachers. (Make sure you get permission from everyone concerned.) For example, note from the students' perspectives the varieties of ways teachers interact with them and influence their behavior.
   a. How do teachers deal with students' inappropriate behavior? In general? In specific instances? How do the students react?
4. Having talked with students or observed them, now turn your eyes and ears toward teachers. Uncover, through conversations, their beliefs and attitudes about dealing with student behavior. Through observations in their classrooms come to understandings about the match between theory or beliefs and practices, paying attention to and exploring those situations in which there are gaps. In addition, consider questions or foci such as

a. What are the stories about students (especially regarding disciplinary matters) that teachers tell in the lunch room and other places? On what kinds of issues do they focus? Why? From whose perspective do they tell these stories? What are the common themes? Is there any sense that their stories may be different from their practice? When? Why?

b. How do teachers say they think about issues of discipline? What role do students play in the development of discipline policies?

c. How do teachers implement their policies, rules, or concepts of discipline? To what extent do teachers' actions match their talk about discipline? Where are the gaps? How can those gaps be explained?

d. What discipline practices seem to be dysfunctional? What practices seem to work? How is mutual respect developed? Or, is it developed?

e. To what extent is the advice "Don't smile until Christmas" given? Under what circumstances is such advice given? What do teachers think about it as a rule of thumb? To what extent is the advice appropriate or inappropriate for new teachers?

Maintaining Productive Learning Environments

Teaching involves the facilitation of various learning processes and activities within a community made up of disparate individuals brought together for the purposes of learning. Although the teacher is also a learner, teaching is mainly for the benefit of students. Teachers' roles, therefore, are primarily cast in terms of fostering personal and intellectual growth within pupils. We now turn to elements of those roles and the environments in which they are played out.

When teachers feel that their roles and importance are questioned by students, they usually feel and express alarm. This tends to happen when teachers feel that their influence is reduced, their seniority, knowledge, or expertise belittled, their voices not heard or respected, or their guidance spurned. On such occasions, teachers are likely to feel as if the core of their professional existence in classrooms—their teacher role identity—is suspect and threatened. And, well it may be. At the heart of the matter of facilitating personal and intellectual growth is the presentation of self-as-teacher. Surrounding this presentation of self are many questions about learning from each other, developing mutual respect, engaging students in learning activities, encouraging and maintaining congenial relationships, and so on.

The issues of maintaining productive classroom learning environments (classroom management) and dealing with the behaviors of students (student discipline) are often focal in new teachers' thinking and present particular prospects and difficulties. Although we do not subscribe to stage theory explanations of teachers' professional development, the depiction of a period of intense challenge of teachers by students is aptly described by stage theorists as the period of "survival." For us, the term survival succinctly describes the state of being that often results when one's teacher role identity is intensely challenged; it also describes the goals and strategies that teachers employ at such times. Survival strategies are not designed with long-range learning purposes in mind; rather, they are the strategies used to merely get through the day-to-day crises and difficulties. They represent short-range perspectives used to alleviate the difficulties of the moment. Too often we see new teachers using coping strategies rather than approaches for facilitating the work of the learning environment and the relationships between the participants.

As you think about the complex tasks of teaching and creating and maintaining productive learning environments, there are several considerations to keep in mind:

- the ultimate purpose of the learning community
- the purpose of the activities underway
- the optimum contextual conditions necessary to progress toward immediate and long-range goals
- the minimum guidance required to facilitate students' participation in the learning community
- the extent to which your practices are consistent
- whether there are alternative ways of facilitating learning that develop mutual respect and consideration for all concerned

These points are useful to keep in mind as you examine every action that you engage in to maintain productive learning environments.

Each of the preservice teachers who have written accounts about maintaining productive learning environments witness traditional ways of thinking. The term "classroom management" is familiar to them, as is the practice of authoritarian strategies. Teachers and parents also use the term classroom management in many ways. Teachers are said to "manage classrooms" and "manage students," as if they were managing an office, a business, or an assembly line. Under such traditional views, teaching is seen as a technical activity, one reduced to a set of discrete functions, activities, and processes for which there are set procedures, skills, routines, and tests. These views are often tied to external constraints and limitations imposed on students and teachers by administrators and even by parents and the larger community. And students are also socialized into thinking in such ways.

Despite the preservice teachers' reliance on traditional ways of describing practices, and their long experience of such approaches, there is an impatience with traditional norms expressed and a searching for more appropriate strategies. There is also plenty of evidence of the power of classroom socialization and socialized expectations. Allen realizes how important classroom climate is to maintaining a productive learning environment. Renee realizes the complex considerations associated with setting up a classroom. Eva discovers another dimension to classroom environment—the physical arrangement of space. Mary and Leila discover the importance of consistency and clarity within learning contexts. Leila expresses her awareness of the need for more time and opportunity to experiment with different ideas and approaches to the creation of learning environments. Noelle also felt the importance of trying out other than traditional teacher-control strategies. Leona discovered the importance of finding both the students' pace and her own as a prerequisite to facilitating learning. A period of observation influenced Rachel's thinking about the long-term advantages of involving students in decision making about their own learning. Stacy, Debbie, and Sandra reflect self-doubt as a result of being overwhelmed by the complexity of "running a classroom." Finally, John struggles over the difficulty of maintaining positive relationships with students while experiencing disappointment over their behavior.

Narrative Accounts

Some of my most frustrating times in the classroom were when I was doing what I thought were some interesting things. The classroom was chaotic the day that I broke the students into groups to do some cooperative discovery work. When I had the "math gang" out in the hallway for multiplication work they tried to see just how much they could get away with. All of this was not bad, though. For the most part, the chaotic day was a pretty good learning experience for both the kids and me. I realized midway through the period that there was trouble in the hallway, that I had to structure what they are doing and provide enough good work for them to do so that they do not go off task and look for trouble.

I have come to realize that environment plays a big role in classroom management. I believe that issues of personal identity and discipline can be somewhat assuaged by providing an environment that is both beneficial and comfortable for the student and the teacher; a place that is conducive to cooperative learning, not driven by factors of guilt and anxiety; and a place where teachers and administrators alike realize that they are working with adolescents, not adults, who are growing up in an ever-increasingly diverse and troubled world. (Allen Montgomery)

Wow! The first day of school. I was and am so excited and a bit overwhelmed. It blows my mind how much a teacher needs to think through and organize before the students even step foot in the room. I think I am going to write down some of the planning that needs to be done so that, when it is my class, I will remember things that I will want to hang up: calendar, weather graph, days of school, money math, birthday cakes, and missing persons' graph. I want to make attendance cards and a job poster. I need to think about how I am going to have students hand in and pick up papers. I need to think about how I will have students organize their papers. I will have to think about how I am going to keep track of all the students' progress. I need to think of how I will hold the students accountable. I have to think of a grading system that is consistent. I have to think of how I want to arrange the desks and the lab areas. I have to think of what method I am going to use to get the students' attention. I think it is so important for a teacher to be organized from the first day. The sooner the kids know the routine, the smoother things run. (Renee Buscho)

Before starting the practicum, I took classroom management considerations for granted. I had only thought about basic classroom and school rules. I felt they would suffice. I never realized that the physical arrangement of the classroom played a substantial role in classroom management. (Eva Sendele)

From the two rooms I have observed, the students in Ms. Whineu's room (in which the rules are posted) are better behaved than those in Ms. Bardino's class (where the rules are not explained and the class is not well managed). In that class it takes us twice as long to accomplish something. Ms. Bardino has just started to implement some (specific) classroom management techniques and discipline strategies in the room. The students are confused because behavior that was once acceptable, no longer is. I think it is going to be difficult to have these new rules "stick." (Mary Mac)

I do not want teaching to be a battle between the students and the teacher, with the classroom as the battleground, nor do I view teaching in this way. I am much more conditioned [in my approaches to teaching] than I thought and have to keep an eye on every little thing I do—and ask myself the reason why.

I think that one needs to be consistent in practices used in the classroom. Consistency provides students with a degree of safety and security as to where they stand and what is expected of them. Yet, I find myself changing my strategies and methods all the time. This has been either because my previous strategy was not working or in order to try new ones to see how they work. I lack consistency in methods as well as objectives and goals in the classroom. The more I learn as time progresses, the more I define my objectives and the ways to achieve them. One other problem I have is that sometimes I realize a problem in my method, and after reflecting on it more, I think of other ways to go about it. But I have not had much time to develop these ideas more, which is frustrating. Twenty-four hours in a day has not been quite enough [time to do all I need to do]. (Leila Muniroui)

I have been struggling to gain control over the seventh period class. It is basically made up of good students who want to do well, so they listen and work hard; however, there are about five students who talk during the lesson and are great manipulators. They are also the leaders of the class. I came to the realization last week that I had to do something to change what the five were doing. The other students have also been waiting for me to take action.

At first, I was going to change the seating chart and separate the talkers but, as I thought more about it, I decided to try a different approach. I had read a lot about having students set the rules and consequences of breaking those rules. The conclusion I came to was that I would try having the students sit where they want to sit and, with my input, have them set the rules and consequences. The basis of my reasoning was that maybe by treating them as adults, they would act like adults. (They are juniors and seniors!) Anyway, as a class we decided that, indeed, to give everyone the opportunity to learn we needed people to be reasonably quiet during the lesson. As a consequence, for talking loudly I will give one warning, and after that, they will lose a point every time they speak out inappropriately. The students know I still reserve the right to change seats. If this strategy does not work, I will have to try plan three, whatever that is. (Noelle Frandsen)

When I first took over the classes, I made a big deal about learning each student's name and gave each one the opportunity to tell me about themselves. I found they wanted some personal help with math, so I worked hard to give them that help. Before I began to teach, I observed the classes extensively. I got the feeling that things were moving too fast for most of the students but that they were afraid to let that be known to the teacher. So, when I actually began to teach these kids, I showed them that I cared about whether or not they understood math. I purposely backtracked into the previous chapter and created some worksheets that would ensure a high percentage rate of success. I did that because some successful experiences in math are necessary in order to develop a good learning atmosphere and a good attitude about the subject. I think my tactics were rather successful.

My teaching experience started out on the right foot. All the students were coming from the same point as far as class management was concerned. They had been managed right into oblivion. No one dared move from his seat or speak out in class. No one dared to seek help or offer a comment; however, it did not take long to get most of the students to loosen up a bit and act like normal adolescent kids in school. I encouraged interaction while I taught. The situation remained in control, with people speaking in turn and only to me at first. But after a while, the students also began to talk among themselves. I encouraged this as long as the talk was about the work we were doing.

Students can help each other a lot if they are given the opportunity to do so. Students who understand can explain what they know to other students so that they may also understand. Students trust other students. The act of explaining reinforces the knowledge in the student who is doing the explaining. The student on the receiving end is often more receptive to another student and will ask questions in a way that the students understand, whereas the teacher may not. I move around the room while students work on assignments. This helps to maintain a higher number of students on task. Pacing also helps to relieve some anxiety and nervous energy that I tend to build up so easily. That release helps me to be a better teacher because I am more relaxed. I can also help students individually when I see that someone is having trouble with something. (Leona O'Halloran)

The strengths of using self-management as a strategy became evident to me through my observations. When pupils take an active part in developing the practical knowledge of how to educate themselves, they are in control of their own learning and can thus become able people when it comes to setting goals, monitoring work, and evaluating themselves. They do not find getting an education to be a hardship, for no one but themselves imposes tasks on them. They, at a very early age, are in control over what they learn, and their progress is made easily apparent through self-assessment. (Rachel Baab)

My ability to control the class is one of my foremost thoughts. At the beginning of the term I wanted to know how to do it. How do you manage a class? What do you do with a child who is causing problems? What if no one listens to you? My problem was that I wanted a formula. No such formula exists. There is no definite answer. None have the same experiences. Thinking about the responsibility of running a class intimidates me. The impact that a teacher has on the students is huge. Right now, I do not know if I have what it takes to fulfill the responsibility. We are told that certain things, like confidence, will come with experience; but what can I do my first few years without that experience? I can only hope that I will gain the confidence and experience necessary to make my first few years of teaching successful. (Stacy Lane)

Generally, the students do not take me seriously. I need to explore my feelings on the subject and clearly define in my mind what I expect the students to do, what behavior is not acceptable in my classroom, and how I will enforce my behavioral expectations. I need to develop a routine for activities so that students understand their responsibilities, know why they must follow through, and know how to evaluate themselves accordingly. Another gap in my teaching effectiveness is an openness to students' anxiety levels. Generally, I need to develop more observational capabilities to sense students individually and be more flexible within each lesson. I feel this will require more experience. (Debbie Martinez)

Regarding classroom management, I think that at times I have been my own worst enemy. I think I need to make up a list to review nightly so that my sense of purpose is perfectly clear to me. How else can I make it clear to students? My list would include class rules (be prompt, be polite, do your best work, and so on) and the reasons behind them; why English, French, and social studies are important to individuals; and my short-term and long-term goals. Anyone reading this is no doubt asking why I don't already have these things firmly in mind. The fact is that in calm, lucid moments I do, but I have a nasty habit of getting so caught up in what I am doing that I sometimes cannot see the forest for the trees. (Sandra Rene)

One particular area that brought some discomfort and anxiety to me was cheating. I had observed it before taking over the math classes. I gave the first two quizzes and tests the same way as my cooperating teacher. The only thing I did differently was to proctor more thoroughly during the test. The blatant cheating ended, but many students could not resist the temptation to look on their neighbor's paper. I was disappointed with these students' behavior but always tried to make our relationships positive and pleasant affairs. The anxiety came over having to stand in front of the room or sit at my desk in front of the room constantly on the lookout for cheating. (John Corporan)

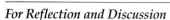

For Reflection and Discussion

1. Allen recognized that he could prevent problematic unfocused behavior by providing structure and "enough good work" for his students. He also realized that environment plays a "big role" in classroom management.
   a. Why is an environment "not driven by guilt and anxiety" important to Allen? How might an environment driven by guilt appear to an observer?
   b. What does Allen's ideal reveal about the type of relationship he hopes to establish with students?
   c. To what extent do decisions regarding the environment determine the tone of the relationship enjoyed by the students with their teacher?
2. Considering the many elements of classroom organization causes Renee to write, "It blows my mind how much a teacher needs to think through and organize before the students even step foot in the room."

    a. To what extent might Renee's teaching philosophy be revealed through her classroom organization decisions?

    b. What objectives should be considered when creating a plan for classroom organization?

3. Prior to her experience in the classroom Eva thought that basic rules would suffice for classroom management. She discovered that the physical arrangement of the classroom "played a substantial role in classroom management."

    a. What might the physical arrangement of the classroom reveal about the learning environment? How might the physical arrangement cause or alleviate problems in facilitating productive learning environments?

4. Mary observed two classrooms and attributed the "better" behavior of students in one classroom to the rules that were clearly posted. The second classroom lacked posted rules or explanations and took twice as along to accomplish tasks. Different classroom management and discipline strategies were to be implemented in the second classroom, and Mary writes that "the students are confused because behavior that was once acceptable, no longer is. I think it is going to be difficult to have these new rules stick."

    a. What other factors might be involved in the apparent differences between classrooms?

    b. Do you agree with Mary about the difficulty of establishing new rules? Why or why not? What does research say about this issue?

    c. Whose needs should take priority when strategies are implemented, the students' or the teacher's? Why?

5. Leila writes that she does not view teaching as a "battle between the students and the teacher." She discovers that she is more "conditioned" than she thought, so she closely analyzes her actions and motives.

    a. How might interactions with students have led Leila to an awareness of her "conditioning"?

    b. How has Leila's persistent self-reflection sensitized her to issues of learning environments?

    c. To what extent are students "conditioned" to view teachers as adversaries? Why might this occur?

6. Noelle handled disruptions in her classroom by involving all of the students in making decisions about classroom rules and consequences.

    a. Why did Noelle reject the option of imposing her own authority and solution? Do you agree with Noelle's decision? Why or why not?

    b. How might her decision to handle the problem with student input influence her relationship with students?

    c. How might the alternative approach of imposing authority have influenced the classroom climate?

7. Leona observed extensively before she began to teach. The assessment she made of the students' needs informed her approach to the lessons she prepared, and she felt successful. Leona taught her first lessons to students who "had been managed right into oblivion. No one dared move from his seat or speak out in class."

    a. Why did Leona focus on individual students initially?

    b. What steps did Leona take to change the classroom climate? What were her reasons for doing so? Do you agree with Leona's approach? Why or why not?

8. Rachel observed that students' "self-management" had several strengths; students did not "find education to be a hardship, for no one but themselves imposes tasks on them."

    a. To what extent is the classroom environment a product of the way in which instructional tasks are imposed?

    b. How might notions of personal empowerment affect the relationship between students and teachers?

9. "Control" of the classroom is one of Stacy's foremost thoughts. She did not receive the formula for control that she had hoped for because she found that none exists. Stacy expresses an anxiety familiar to beginners in many fields—confidence comes with experience, but how do you perform without it?

    a. To what extent might Stacy's anxiety be related to her unfamiliarity with the context of teaching?

    b. Is Stacy's concern unusual? What does research reveal about Stacy's concern?

10. Debbie felt that she was not taken seriously by the students. She decides that she needs to clarify her expectations for student behavior as well as develop sensitivity to individuals and their anxiety levels.

    a. Why does Debbie target student anxiety as something to which she should be sensitive? How might her awareness of student anxiety facilitate smoother activities?

    b. How might the absence of clear expectations affect the students' perceptions of Debbie's purpose?

    c. Why do you suppose Debbie included a need to "sense students individually" into her plan for improved management?

11. Sandra thinks that she is her own worst enemy regarding classroom management. She realizes that her sense of purpose must be "perfectly clear" to her before she can make it clear to her students. She has goals in mind but writes that she has "a nasty habit of getting so caught up in what I'm doing that I sometimes cannot see the forest for the trees."

    a. How can Sandra begin to plan for implementation of her goals while she is caught up in classroom activity?

    b. How might Doyle's (1977) research on classroom complexity help Sandra think about what she perceives as one of her shortcomings? (See *Links with Research* in this section.)

12. John observed students cheating in the math classroom prior to beginning his own teaching. He writes that he monitored students more closely during tests and felt anxious about being "constantly on the lookout for cheating."

    a. To what extent may student cheating be a result of classroom climate?

    b. How might John address the issue of cheating to reduce both its occurrence and his anxiety?

    c. To what extent may John's anxiety be the result of his feeling about students "pulling a fast one" on him?

Links with Research

Operationally, each classroom is organized and run according to an idiosyncratic rule system that is likely to be complex and ever-changing. With the beginning of each school year and an influx of new pupils, new dynamics and complexities develop as teacher and students systematically engage in what Bolster (1983) calls "a cue-exchanging process" to work out the rules of the classroom. "A mutually defined classroom culture emerges which, like all cultures, demands that participants conform to certain norms" (p. 297). Along with the stated rule system there usually resides an implicit set of conditions that emerge as teacher and pupils become more familiar with each other.

The classroom is in a constant state of flux with what Connelly and Clandinin (1984) call the "ebb and flow of the school year." On another dimension, the cyclical nature of the school year imposes unique constraints (Connelly & Clandinin, 1985b). Some of these classroom cycles (for example, holiday cycles, seasons, report card cycles) have a significant impact on the curricular and behavioral life of the classroom. For example, classroom activity often dramatically changes as report time approaches; the lightheartedness of holiday-related activities may give way to more serious academically oriented activity until the term is over, evaluations done, and report cards completed. Activities tied to day cycles and course cycles order the classroom character in other ways.

Personal rhythms also affect the character of the classroom as illustrated in Clandinin's account of her work with Stephanie (Clandinin, 1986; Clandinin & Connelly, 1986), Bullough's (1989) story of Kerry's first year, and Bullough, Knowles, and Crow's (1991) accounts of Nancy, Barbara, and other first-year teachers. Teachers' rhythms, in concert with the students' responses and anticipations, animate the life of the classroom so that it develops and exhibits a personality of its own with characteristic moods, feelings, attitudes, and energies. The individuality of the students and teacher unites in a collective force to breathe life into their classroom environment that then takes on a rhythm of its own.

Being in a classroom as a student teacher is like being a visitor or a guest in any group or community that has established cultural norms, rhythms, and practices. Though it is not always easy, to be part of the group it is necessary to identify and understand the structure of the group and the implicit rule system operating. In most cases, student teachers do not have opportunities to be part of the cue-exchanging process that determines the way things are done in classrooms. Unless preservice teachers like yourself are made aware of how and why the learning environment is structured the way it is, they can experience confusion and difficulty. And, if they are not sensitive at all to the importance of environment in the teaching-learning process, their difficulties are exacerbated. In Knowles and Skrobola's (1992) study, inattention to the context of instruction and the creation of environments conducive to academic, emotional, and social learning was the downfall of many who "failed" student teaching.

Doyle (1977) and Zeichner (1983) discuss the need for beginning teachers to learn the ecology of the classroom in order to succeed as teachers. In an intensive three-year study involving 58 preservice teachers, Doyle observed and analyzed the processes by which student teachers come to understand the classroom environment. He described the three features of the classroom that stood out most for student teachers as

- multidimensionality, the multiple purposes classrooms serve and the numerous, varied, and often unrelated activities that take place there
- simultaneity, the simultaneous occurrence of multiple events and unanticipated interruptions
- unpredictability, the sheer unpredictability of classroom events and activities

At times, the complexity of the learning environment was overwhelming for the student teachers in Doyle's (1977) study; yet, all attempted to cope by developing strategies to reduce the complexity. The less successful teachers, however, attempted to reduce complexity by ignoring it and thereby running into management problems. Those who were more successful were able to accept and understand the multidimensional, simultaneous, and unpredictable nature of classrooms, and develop strategies to help them adapt to the environmental demands.

Research Activities

1. Students and teachers come to classrooms or other learning environments with multiple agenda. Some students intend to learn; some intensely so and some in a less-focused manner. Others see the opportunity for socializing or engaging in less than socially acceptable behaviors. To play out their multiple agenda, teachers usually attempt to set standards of conduct. Explore students' perspectives of teachers' work in classrooms, specifically their attempts to facilitate productive learning environments. Some questions to consider include

   a. What are students' views of "productive learning environments"? How might they be similar to and different from the perspectives of teachers?

   b. What are students' views of teachers' efforts to facilitate or implement productive learning environments? (What do students think about the various ways teachers "manage" classrooms?) What are the stories they tell about teachers and their handling of classrooms full of students? Are teachers known for their "classroom management" styles and abilities? How do these styles and abilities influence students?

   c. What do students perceive as the extremes to which teachers go to organize classrooms and teaching-learning activities? What does a poorly managed classroom look like? a well-managed classroom? a classroom where productive learning is taking place? What kind of learning facilitation do students most appreciate? Why?

   d. How do students influence the classroom management styles of teachers?

2. Observe students in classrooms with the intention of uncovering potentially ineffective, ineffective, and dysfunctional "classroom management" strategies as used by teachers to encourage learning. Focus on teachers *only* as an aid to help you understand students' responses. Consider questions such as

   a. What issues need to be resolved in order for teachers to facilitate learning? Within the classroom and lesson context, what is the teacher's intent? How does the teacher attempt to facilitate learning?

   b. What teacher strategies seem to work? What does not work? Why? Under what conditions? What are the students' responses? To what extent are there strategies that appear to be effective but that are less than respectful to students? How do students respond? in public? in private? How do students shape the actions of the teacher?

3. Explore video representations of teachers trying to develop classroom learning environments (see *Video List*). Pay attention to how they represent teachers' "classroom management" strategies. Consider these representations in light of the questions posed in the previous two research activities.

Responding to Individual Needs and Differences

We need teachers who have more of a sense that they are working with young people than that they are teaching a subject. Some new teachers have lots of energy and strong academic backgrounds but have a hard time interacting with and relating to students, especially those who experience academic difficulties. My concern is that so much of their preservice [preparation] is academic and so little is based on relationships (Secondary school principal).

Teachers teach students, not academic subjects. That goes without saying. Or does it? If you think about it in today's increasingly diverse classrooms, this adage stands under a different light. To teach students rather than subject matter is a daunting challenge. It requires a considerable investment of time, energy, and emotion. To teach students rather than subject matter implies a holistic orientation to teaching and learning. Teaching the "whole child" requires a commitment to know each student as an individual and to facilitate each student's learning in an appropriately responsive way.

As you enter the field experience placement site preoccupied with so many thoughts, anxieties, concerns, and questions it will not be easy to look around at the sea of new faces and view them as anything but an amorphous group, perhaps even a formidable body. To see all students as individuals, each with characteristic needs and differences, is and will continue to be your challenge as a teacher. In that sea of faces is a range of academic abilities, backgrounds, and interests. Students with strengths in some academic or social areas are likely to experience difficulties in others. Some of those students come to school every day from nurturing and supportive home environments. Some do not. Some have poverty knocking on their door. Others have access to every foreseeable technological home appliance and toy that money can buy. Some have traveled the world. Some have not ventured past the boundaries of their neighborhoods. Some see the wearing of clothing and jewelry as an opportunity to make fashion statements. Others simply long to wear a freshly laundered or new garment to school. Students grow up in different conditions and contexts that have varying influences on their academic, psychological, and social development. They will manifest those influences in a variety of ways, sometimes in challenging and perhaps even threatening ways. Each of us has powerful defense mechanisms that come into play when we feel threatened or at risk, and some of those students will introduce you to theirs. And then, there are students who are academically bright, socially and psychologically well-adjusted, and who come from apparently stable and secure home environments. They, too, will need your individual attention.

Responding to individual differences is a pressing concern for new teachers. With everything else there is to know and do, the prospect of having to individualize instruction, or respond to individual differences, is overwhelming for many new teachers. In one sense, being overwhelmed is an appropriate response; in another, it is not. Given the purpose of your being in the classroom and learning community, how can you expect to achieve goals related to teaching and learning without knowing the learners?

Think about teaching and learning as nothing more than effective communication. If three different people were to engage you in conversation on the same topic, chances are you would respond differently to each one. You would intuitively pause for a quick assessment of each situation and respond accordingly. Depending on the persons, circumstances, and topic of conversation some interactions proceed more smoothly than others; some are plain "hard work." Is communication with students much different? Can you have the kind of meaningful and productive communication required in an educational context *without* considering the persons involved? So, rather than thinking about individualizing instruction, think about individualizing interactions which, in a sense, is a natural way of relating to individuals.

In the accounts that follow, several preservice teachers relate some of their experiences of responding to students' individual needs and differences. They express varying degrees of satisfaction with how the students' needs are being considered within the classroom context. Leila articulates a reality with which every teacher must deal—giving equal time and attention to all students. The rest of the preservice teachers give detailed accounts of individual students who presented particular challenges. In all cases, foremost in the preservice teachers' minds was the student's self-image. Ellen describes how she responded to a defiant and disruptive student. Portia recounts a story of a student whose learning difficulties were exacerbated by severe emotional trauma and reveals her frustration at the inadequacy of responses to his needs. Renee tells how she was able to keep in mind both her own needs and the needs of an overachieving student who challenged her. In a second account, Ellen relates a situation, involving an adolescent boy with severe reading and writing difficulties, in which she was faced with a moral dilemma. Paul reports how he successfully dealt with a hyperactive student who had alienated himself from classmates. And Dee Dee recounts her experience with a victim of sexual abuse.

Narrative Accounts

I notice myself paying more attention to students who are more mischievous or who respond more in class. I want to take more time with the shy and quiet ones in the classroom or the academically good students. It is not fair for me to focus so much on the ones who are potential management problems and, in the process, ignore the rest of the class. (Leila Muniroui)

Melissa. She looked tough right from the first day. She was tall and heavily built, especially for a seventh grader. She had me by several inches and at least ten, maybe twenty, pounds. But it was her expression more than her build that warned me to keep a wary eye on her. If I made eye contact with her, I received a jolt of defiance. She did not act up at first; perhaps she wanted to see how I would respond. After a day or two, she began moving seats when I had my attention somewhere else. It was distracting, but I made no move to correct her the first several times. I just watched. Then she began to talk, but always when I had my eye elsewhere. And, when I looked at her, she had a defiant stare and expression. Then the day came when she slouched in late—and moody. She talked out loud; I requested her to listen. She threw paper, but I did not directly see; so I had the whole class pick up papers from the littered floor. She scraped her seat around noisily and that brought a frown from me. Then she put her feet in the air on the back of the chair in front of her.

I was hesitant to approach her directly; I could tell from her glare that a polite request would not be honored. As I continued to talk, I had several helpful thoughts. I have had parenting classes where a method of getting a child to agree beforehand to consequences of actions is used. I also had the idea that perhaps the class was as tired of her disruptions as I was. I made a decision to react to the next disturbance she made. I did not have long to wait.

Having failed to draw me into a confrontation with little things, Melissa went all the way. She took off her shoe and advanced on another student as if to hit her in the head with it. Class stopped and, thank God, I was ready. I moved between them and backed her gently into her seat. "Class," I said calmly, "I have to handle this problem. Will you help me?" There was a chorus of muffled answers. Obviously some of them had felt the blow of her shoe and were not ready to face that—nor was I. "All I need you to do is to witness this." There was absolute quiet. I think they thought I was going to hit her. Instead, I asked her to agree that if she disrupted all of us again, she would move to a table in the back of the room and do an assignment. It took her a full minute to decide, as I and thirty interested students waited quietly for her answer. Finally it came, "Yes, I will." And, as all the others smiled, a smile slowly came to Melissa. There were no more disruptions from her.

One assignment was a paper on their positive skills and qualities. Melissa's started with, "I'm a good fighter. . . ." The theme continued with the fights she had won and how tough she was. I first thought to downgrade the paper for not being positive. Then, I checked into her background at the office and came away with the realization that she had learned to be tough in order to survive. I gave her a good grade and determined to teach her positive behavior by role modeling appropriate behaviors—not fighting. (Ellen Findlay)

Lenny is another student who keeps unfolding to me each day. Earlier in the school year, Lenny found his older brother dead—the brother had committed suicide. Lenny had difficulty in school even before this incident. On top of dealing with his brother's death, Lenny seems to be developmentally behind. He does not recognize all of the alphabet, his drawings are at the developmental level of a three-year-old, and he refuses to do any work. Yet, he is verbally engaging, possesses a wonderful imagination, and is probably extremely intelligent.

Lenny worked with the school counselor today. Upon returning, he shared with us a book he had made and called the "Happy Sad Book." In it he told, through dictation and illustrations, his story about days and things that made him happy and sad. The words and drawings focused on his brother's death, showing the coffin and a huge face with a huge frown. He talked about the feelings very openly, but he was tearing my heart out. How does a six-year-old boy deal with this? Lenny's mother has become emotionally paralyzed by the suicide and has little energy to deal with him. He has been tested for receiving special services but does not qualify. The cooperating teacher is beside herself too. She does not know what else to try. She does not feel equipped to handle all of this. Meanwhile, Lenny is not growing and learning in this classroom. (Portia Smith)

I have one boy who is smart, but he is such a perfectionist; and that gets in his way. He works very slowly, making sure everything is just so. If you try to rush him or encourage him not to worry about every mistake, he snaps into a tantrum. He has a very low frustration level. Anyway, today the work may have been too overwhelming for him, and he absolutely lost it. He pushed his papers off his desk, and sat under his desk and cried. Then he started pushing at other kids' work. He was really going to lose control. I tried my best to calm him. I gave him other work that I knew he could handle. He did calm down, but the incident scared me. How quickly he could snap! I don't know if it would help to move him down to a lower ability group. I know that he could handle the work in our group if he wasn't so hung up with being perfect. I know that his second grade teacher had a terrible time with him. They were just like fire and oil. She just increased his frustration level. I have to be so careful not to get him frustrated. I just hate feeling like I am walking on eggs with this child. I really think he is an intelligent kid, and I do like him a lot. But I don't want to be controlled by his tantrums. (Renee Buscho)

Chuck was well-groomed and handsome. He was always careful of the attention of other students, giving answers or causing disruptions to please the other students. I took the clues from his appearance and actions to mean that he was a bright and self-confident student. I was wrong. The first assignment was to make a list, and Chuck did not do it. The next assignment was three sentences that he did do, and which gave me my first clue. He managed to violate about twenty rules of grammar in those three sentences. But I was busy and did not attach too much importance, assuming he had just been careless and uninvolved. I began to notice that as soon as we finished with the teacher talk or class discussion and started the activity, some student, usually a girl, would move over by Chuck. On several occasions I moved them away, and on those days he did not turn in work. But he was warming to me in class, and getting interested and involved, almost in spite of himself. Then came the big assignment.

The students were to write a full page about themselves, emphasizing their positive qualities. I had lots going on and did not pay much attention to Chuck, who sat quietly by Steve and did his work. He handed in a full page, and the writing was neat. But when I read his account for grading purposes later in the day, something was amiss. For one thing, he referred to his black hair as brown, but I passed over that. Next he mentioned that his father was Italian—that did not go with his Spanish surname. The big clue did not come until I read Steve's paper. Steve had brown hair and an Italian father. Chuck had gotten his spelling, grammar, and a new personality by copying Steve's work.

I pondered the situation. It seemed convoluted, but somehow I was glad that he wanted to succeed, even if it meant cheating. I just could not fail him when he was obviously trying not to fail me, but neither could I ignore his plagiarism. I decided to lower him just one grade, from "A" to "B". I wanted to reward him for effort. I also had a talk with him, but carefully to avoid offense. I praised the neatness and correctness of his work. Then I casually said, "It is a good thing you were not sitting next to Amy, with her blond hair and blue eyes." He knew immediately what I was referring to and looked stricken, until I told him his grade.

I have learned from Chuck that the students can be valuable aids to each other when the classroom climate is cooperative and helpful. He cannot read or write as well as he wants to, and I plan to have a helper system that can give him the extra information he needs without damaging his pride. I have also decided that cheating indicates a desire to do well, which is preferable to an attitude of apathy. How ever I handle cheaters, it will be carefully to preserve, not stamp out, that desire to achieve. (Ellen Findlay)

Brett is the most disruptive student in either of the two world culture classes. He has fallen into a pattern of loud and obnoxious conduct, perhaps partly to compensate for the fact that he is not well-liked or accepted by most of his classmates. He has been on prescribed medication in the past for hyperactivity, but his parents recently took him off the medication. Brett's teachers have been asked to watch him for any changes in his behavior since he stopped his medication. The consensus is that his conduct has worsened, but my experience has been just the opposite.

One day, several weeks ago, Brett was totally out of control in class. He could not keep his mouth shut, stay in his chair, or keep from bothering his classmates for even a few seconds. After class I spoke with him about the problem I had with him that day, and he responded that he knew he was out of control, he had been that way all day, and he was sorry. Frankly, I did not know whether he was being sincere at the time, but I now think that he was. I told him that I was aware that the problem was not just him—that his classmates treated him poorly and that I did not think he should be treated that way. I said that I intended to do what I could to make sure that, at least in my classroom, everyone was treated with respect, including him. I asked him to try and help me by not giving his classmates any reasons to justify treating him badly. He agreed.

Since that conversation, while he is still the most disruptive student in the class, Brett's behavior has improved noticeably. He has not acted defiantly toward me once, and remarkably, he seems to be getting along somewhat better with his classmates. I have in fact gotten after some of the other boys in the class when I have heard them say unkind things toward Brett, and that seems to have become less frequent of late. His attitude toward school seems to have generally been that everyone, teachers included, was out to get him and that no one was on his side. One of his other teachers mentioned to me that, in a parent-teacher conference, his parents seemed to recognize and support that attitude. Perhaps it is not surprising, then, that Brett would respond positively to a teacher who was willing to stick up for him and view his position through his eyes. (Paul Colins)

She sparked my curiosity from the first time I met her. Without asking me my name or telling me hers, Barbara asked me if I would follow her to her desk. There, she pulled out a piece of paper and a red crayon, scribbled a red blob on the paper saying, "Here, this is what it looked like. Is this my period?" There was another student teacher in the room who had been in the classroom longer than me, and I told her about the incident. She looked at my supervising teacher and asked if it would be okay to share information about Barbara with me. With approval from the cooperating teacher the other student teacher began to tell me that Barbara comes from a "broken home" and that she was sexually molested by a family member. Even though I had some hesitations about being in a classroom with such a child—about how to act and so on—I was at the same time curious about her. I was interested in finding out if and how these acts against Barbara play out in her life as a student and if so, how this affected the dynamics of her relationships with teachers and classmates.

It did not take long, nor require any advanced level of psychological insight, to see the traces of the aftermath of Barbara's sexual experiences in her student life. Two areas in which the scars of her tragedy appear often are in her formal school work (particularly in written work and discussions) and during social time (mainly recess). At this point, in the eleventh week of student teaching, I am cautious about which questions I call on Barbara to answer, for often her answers or comments are "too advanced" (something to do with sex, the body, or her extreme dislike for someone) for the rest of the class. For example, in a social studies project, the students had to think of a personal goal they would like to work toward. They were given a few minutes to think of their goals and to share them if they wished to do so. Barbara's goal was to start her menstrual cycle, have sex, and have a baby. Wow! Another time the students were asked to write descriptions about objects I gave them. Barbara got a teddy bear, and in her description she wrote about how nice it is to be loved by it and hug it, especially after being hurt by her father.

Once I concluded that traces of Barbara's tragedy are present in her academic and social life at school, I began to observe how these indicators (her formal schoolwork and social talk during recess) affected her relationship with teachers and classmates. I know that I tend to keep Barbara's schoolwork separate from the others when they turn in assignments. It is a habit for me to automatically pick up her work out of my basket the second she puts it in. Knowing that she has a tendency to say what is on her mind (and often this is something sexual), as well as remembering how awkward I and perhaps other students felt when she read her personal goal, I felt it was a good idea to make sure her work is rated "G." (Dee Dee Edwards)

For Reflection and Discussion

1. Leila challenges herself to attend to the quiet and academically strong students rather than primarily to the more responsive or mischievous ones.
    a. How might Leila attend to the "quiet" students while remaining responsive to the assertive students?
2. Melissa's need for attention drew Ellen into a potentially difficult situation. Ellen observed the escalation of disruptions and Melissa's skill at avoiding detection but

decided to react to the next disturbance. Their confrontation ended with relief for everyone in the classroom.

   a. Why do you suppose Ellen decided to wait for yet another disturbance and then react to it?

   b. What do you think about Ellen's way of responding to Melissa's challenge?

   c. Ellen researched Melissa's background before she assigned a grade to her writing assignment. Should she have done this? Why or why not? How did Ellen's discovery influence the grade she assigned? Was her decision an appropriate one?

3. Portia worked with a young child whose brother committed suicide. The student was experiencing difficulty with school work, and his mother was too emotionally upset to help him. Testing revealed that he did not qualify for special services, and the cooperating teacher did "not feel equipped to handle all of this." Portia observed that the child was not growing or learning in the classroom.

   a. Should Portia take action to help Lenny learn and grow? Why or why not?

   b. Should Lenny be removed from his classroom until he exhibits a readiness to learn? Why or why not?

   c. What does Lenny need from his school and teachers? Can his needs be reasonably met by those closest to him at school?

4. Renee encountered a child with "a very low frustration level." She attributes his temper tantrums to his being a perfectionist. She was scared by how quickly he could snap. She felt that she was "walking on eggs" with him, but she did not want to be controlled by his tantrums.

   a. To what extent will Renee be able to avoid being controlled by his tantrums?

   b. Might there be other factors driving the student's behavior? Should Renee address the behavior of the student or the factors that appear to cause it?

5. Ellen taught a student with less developed writing skills. When he turned in a writing assignment she realized that he had copied from a neighbor. She decided that cheating indicated a desire to do well and resolved to carefully preserve the desire to achieve when she encountered it again.

   a. How might Ellen's handling of cheating influence her relationship with the students in a positive way? What might be the negative ramifications?

   b. How does the student's definition of success differ from Ellen's?

   c. How has the student accommodated himself to the type of rewards offered by the formal schooling system? What is the basis for the creation of this system? How do students, teachers, and preservice teachers fit into this system, and what part do they play in the creation of the values within it?

6. Paul decided to become an advocate for a student who had difficulty controlling his behavior. The student had been treated poorly by classmates, and Paul thought his behavior may have been in response to this. He asked the student to help him ensure that everyone in class would be treated with respect.

   a. How do you suppose the student felt when Paul told him that the problem was not all his fault?

   b. How was Paul able to adopt the student's perspective and "see his position through his eyes"?

7. A sexually abused student presents challenges within the classroom. The student's behavior drew Dee Dee's attention before the reasons for such behavior were disclosed. Because the student's "too advanced" responses caused Dee Dee (and possibly some of the students) to feel awkward, she decided to keep the student's written work separate from that of her classmates.

    a. In what other ways could Dee Dee have addressed the "inappropriate" responses of this student?

    b. What else could Dee Dee have done to protect other students from the sophisticated information the abused girl wanted to share without stigmatizing the victim?

    c. What are some of the more subtle behavioral clues that may indicate abuse?

Links with Research

Preservice and beginning teachers regularly talk of the importance of being able to respond to the diverse backgrounds, experiences, abilities, and interests of their soon to be students; yet, few understand or are prepared for the diversity that awaits them in many classrooms. The reality is that demographic differences between teachers and their students are increasing (Grant & Secada, 1990; Hodgkinson, 1988), and teachers are becoming increasingly frustrated by the numbers of students who come from physically, socially, emotionally, and financially stressed homes (Boyer, 1989). Traditionally, teachers have been prepared to work with middle class children from the dominant cultural group (Gollnick & Chinn, 1990; Lindsey, 1985). Lawless (1986, quoted in Ryan & Robinson, 1990) poignantly states the case:

> One-fourth of our school children are in families that live in or close to a culture of poverty. Many of them, and many others, live in families with varied (sometimes rural) life styles. Teachers come from the dominant and culturally-exclusive middle group in America. They are trained to become the rulers of their domains. They are oppressive to most children; they are intolerant of differences among children within even their own ethnic and cultural phylum; they are misled about the nature of learning and insist on a uniform structuring of subject matter for all their learners; and they confront their classroom situations expecting hostility. Imagine the helplessness that overpowers the children of the poor when they encounter the typically trained American public school teacher! (p. 1)

Recently, studies and programs have been initiated to address issues related to teaching culturally diverse learners. Larke (1990) involved 51 preservice teachers in a study of cultural sensitivity. The results of a questionnaire designed to measure attitudes, beliefs, and behavior toward culturally diverse children indicated that, although most of the preservice teachers realized that they would likely be working with culturally diverse students, only one fifth admitted a preference to do so. Almost one half reported being uncomfortable with people who spoke nonstandard English and felt that a student's spoken language should be corrected. Two thirds felt that students with learning difficulties related to cultural or language differences should be referred for testing; however, only 32 percent felt that the assessment procedures should be modified to take into account such differences. Finally, three quarters of the respondents did not object to the use of ethnic jokes, and one half reported that racial statements should often be ignored.

In another study, 24 preservice teachers were involved in a program designed to increase understanding and sensitivity toward minority students (Larke, Wiseman, & Bradley, 1990). The results of a pre-program questionnaire indicated that the majority of the preservice teachers had negative perceptions and/or poor attitudes about characteristics of minority students (for example, they would lack motivation, lack self-confidence, have low self-esteem, have academic problems, and come from poor homes). The results of these two studies find further support in research conducted by Ross and Smith (1992). Taken together, these studies (and other similar ones) lend discomforting support to Lawless' (1986) statement cited earlier (see, also, Ryan & Robinson, 1990). The recent emphasis in preservice preparation programs on preparing teachers for diversity comes none too soon (see for example, Cooper, Beare, & Thompson, 1990; Grant & Secada, 1990; Larke, Wiseman, & Bradley, 1990; Liston & Zeichner, 1990; Ross & Smith, 1992; Ryan & Robinson, 1990). (For additional work in the area of cultural diversity, revisit Chapter 7, *Links with Research,* on *Understanding Student Diversity and Culture.*)

Beyond cultural differences what does diversity mean? Paine (1988) explored prospective teachers' orientations toward diversity. Using questionnaires and interviews, Paine analyzed respondents' views on the meaning of diversity and the implications of that meaning for their thoughts about teaching. Paine's analysis led her to conclude that entering teacher education candidates' orientations toward diversity were often superficial; their ability to talk about student differences in thoughtful, comprehensive ways was often limited; and their thinking about its pedagogical implications was often problematic. The prospective teachers seemed to share the sense that student differences should be taken into account, but they were often unsure about how to think about those differences in terms of classroom practice. Their discussions of diversity were often contradictory. For example, although they felt that fairness was the key to successfully attending to student diversity, their projected mechanisms for dealing with diversity could often be judged to be inequitable.

Finally, Gomez and Comeaux (1990) report that preservice teachers found that failure to take into account individual needs and differences led to difficult to manage and uninterested students; however, rather than reexamine their teaching approaches, the preservice teachers involved in the study blamed the students for not fitting into the curriculum. In addition, they attributed low student performance to low socioeconomic status and family influences. They began endorsing, for those students, a curriculum with a life-skills orientation, that is, a program of study that would place them on a nonacademic learning track.

Research Activities

1. In Chapter 9, in the *Links with Research* section that focused on parents, we suggested that both teachers in preparation and experienced teachers need to adopt strategies for working more closely with parents. Some of the cited research showed that, mostly, teachers want to meet with parents on familiar ground—the school environment—and on their terms. To break this pattern of interaction there seem to be at least two options: meet parents in some neutral place; or, meet parents on their home ground—the family or neighborhood setting. To do this may require a fair amount of courage, especially for entering into urban settings that you know little about (and in some situations it might not be wise

to do so without having someone to guide you). But it will also allow you to develop some potentially productive perspectives on families and individual differences of students.

Develop strategies, therefore, that will take you into family homes, apartments, and community settings where you can observe firsthand the various contexts in which your students are rooted. In this way you might begin to appreciate the great diversity of backgrounds and the individual differences that children bring with them to the classroom. Moreover, parents are likely to feel different about such a teacher and reveal to you information that may help you understand the unique natures of your pupils, their children. In the book, *Small Victories,* by Freedman (1990), there are illustrations of what we are suggesting here.

2. One way to come to some understandings about how you might begin to address individual differences in your classroom is to talk with other professionals in the learning community. Inquire as to how *they* acknowledge, explore, comprehend, accommodate, and celebrate the vast array of students and their differences, both in the classroom and in other learning community settings. Do not limit your explorations to teachers, but talk with a range of professional and nonteaching staff. Some questions to get you started might include

   a. How is every individual treated with respect in the classroom? How do teachers come to understandings about individual students in their charge? Are any of those strategies potentially harmful to students who display extensive differences from most of the students?

   b. Are there potentially dysfunctional perspectives that teachers hold about the individual differences of students? What are they? Why are they dysfunctional?

   c. How do teachers respect and accommodate individual differences? (We use accommodate in the broadest sense to involve concepts such as acknowledge, explore, comprehend, involve, extend, and amplify.) How do they celebrate students' individual differences?

3. Explore some published accounts that explore teaching and either celebrate individual differences of and among students or illustrate teachers dealing with such differences. Accounts of the second kind may focus on either individuals or groups of students in learning contexts. See *Recommended Readings* in both this chapter and Chapter 7 for potentially useful accounts. The published work of Paley (1981, 1986, 1989, 1990), Hayden, (1981), Freedman (1990), Kidder, (1989), Kohl (1967), Kozol (1991), Mathews (1988), and Sorotnik (1992) are useful places to begin.

4. Video and movie films also offer a rich source for exploring how teachers are presented in regard to their response to students' individual differences. (See Video List.) Films such as *Stand and Deliver, Teachers, Dead Poets Society,* and *Sylvia,* focus closely on exploring teacher-student relationships founded on mutual respect and the teachers' response to individual differences.

   a. How are teachers represented? How are students represented? What kinds of relationships are presented as productive? In what ways are such portrayals of teacher-student relationships stereotypical? dysfunctional? atypical? useful?

   b. What are the key elements of teachers' successful responses to individual differences? How do students usually respond? To what extent do these portrayals represent some common experience? To what extent is their fictionalization useful for professional development? not useful?

Summary

As the period winds down, I have been pleasantly surprised that the kids have not been acting up. I was a little apprehensive. Apparently my fears were unfounded or based on rumor. This brings me to the next point—my growing fondness for the little dears. After those ugly early days where I was almost frightened of them, I now realize that it is in my relationships with all those boisterous, shy, bratty, charming youngsters that I have really grown. Over the years to come, there will be many more, but this first crowd will never be forgotten. In a way I will miss them. This thought struck me at field day as I rooted loudest for the very ones who pushed me the hardest. I like them. (Steve Bruno)

Such was Steve's recognition of one important element of his growth during a period of extended teacher preparation field experiences. Although the year-long experience resulted in some rough spots, he was able to step back and recognize how his relations with students had grown, even flourished at times. Thus, in the end, he felt he "was on the right track."

In presenting our perceptions and preservice teachers' experiences about negotiating relationships with students we have raised the matters of dealing with student behaviors (discipline), the facilitation of productive learning environments (classroom management), and the need to respond sensitively to individual needs and differences. Attention to each of these is essential for facilitating students' learning.

In Chapter 11 we focus on the general tenor of your field experiences. We want to help you to step back and recognize that both professional growth and the day-to-day, week-to-week, month-to-month experiences of schools and classrooms are most likely to witness ups and downs. Some have described the beginning period of teaching as a roller coaster, and in some ways it is an apt term. The period of practice as epitomized in field experiences is highly focused, extremely demanding, perhaps enervating but, most of all, extremely complex.

Recommended Readings

Armstrong, M. (1980) *Closely observed children: The diary of a primary classroom*. London: Writers and Readers Publishing Cooperative Society.

Axline, V. M. (1964). *Dibs in search of self*. New York: Ballantine Books.

Bossert, S. (1979). *Tasks and social relationships in classrooms*. Cambridge: Cambridge University Press.

Carini, P. F. (1982). *The school lives of seven children: A five year study*. Grand Forks, ND: University of North Dakota Press.

Chang, H. (1992). *Adolescent life and ethos: An ethnography of a U.S. high school*. Bristol, PA: Falmer Press.

Coleman, J. S. (1961). *The adolescent society*. New York: Free Press.

Coles, R. (1986). *The moral life of children: How children struggle with questions of moral choice in the United States and elsewhere*. Boston: Houghton Mifflin.

Coles, R. (1986). *The political life of children*. Boston: Atlantic Monthly Press.

Coles, R. (1990). *The spiritual life of children*. Boston: Houghton Mifflin.

Everhart, R. (1983). *Reading writing and resistance: Adolescence and labor in a junior high school*. Boston: Routledge and Kagan Paul.

Fine, M. (1993). *Framing dropouts: Notes on the politics of an urban high school.* New York: State University of New York Press.

Glenn, M. (1982). *Class dismissed: High school poems by Mel Glenn.* New York: Ticknor & Fields.

Glenn, M. (1986). *Class dismissed II: More high school poems.* New York: Ticknor & Fields.

Grant, C. A., & Sleeter, C. E. (1986). *After the school bell rings.* Philadelphia, PA: Falmer Press.

Hayden, T. L. (1980). *One child.* New York: G. P. Putnam's Sons.

Hayden, T. L. (1981). *Somebody else's kids.* New York: Avon Books.

Holt, J. (1964, 1982). *How children fail.* New York: Dell.

Holt, J. (1967, 1983). *How children learn.* New York: Dell.

Howe, Q., Jr. (1991). *Under running laughter.* New York: Free Press.

Hunter, L. (1992). *The diary of Latoya Hunter: My first year in junior high.* New York: Crown.

Jackson, P. W. (1990). *Life in classrooms.* New York: Teachers College Press.

Klass, C. P. (1986). *The autonomous child: Day care & the transmission of values.* London: Falmer Press.

Kohl, H. (1967). *Thirty-six children.* New York: New American Library.

Kohl, H. (1982). *Insight: The substance and rewards of teaching.* Menlo Park, CA: Addison-Wesley.

Kozol, J. (1991). *Savage Inequalities.* New York: Crown.

Lubeck, S. (1985). *Sandbox society: Early education in black & white America.* London: Falmer Press.

Mortimore, P., Sammons, P., Stoll, L., Lewis, D., & Ecob, R. (1988). *School matters.* Berkeley, CA: University of California Press.

Nieto, S. (1992). *Affirming diversity: The sociopolitical context of multicultural education.* White Plains, NY: Longman Publishing Group.

Paley, V. G. (1981). *Wally's stories.* Cambridge, MA: Harvard University Press.

Paley, V. G. (1986). *Mollie is three: Growing up in school.* Chicago: University of Chicago Press.

Paley, V. G. (1988). *Bad guys don't have birthdays: Fantasy play at four.* Chicago: University of Chicago Press.

Paley, V. G. (1990). *The boy who would be a helicopter: The uses of storytelling in the classroom.* Cambridge, MA: Harvard University Press.

Schoem, D. (Ed.). (1991). *Inside separate worlds: Life stories of young Blacks, Jews, and Latinos.* Ann Arbor, MI: University of Michigan Press.

Shaw, C. (1966). *Jack the roller: A delinquent boy's own story.* Chicago: University of Chicago Press.

Shuman, A. (1986). *Storytelling rights: The uses of oral and written texts by urban adolescents.* Cambridge, MA: Cambridge University Press.

Suransky, V. P. (1982). *The erosion of childhood.* Chicago: University of Chicago Press.

Troyna, B., & Hatcher, R. (1992). *Racism in children's lives: A study of mainly-white primary schools.* London, UK: Routledge.

Van Manen, M. (1986). *The tone of teaching.* Richmond Hill, Ontario: Scholastic—TAB Publications, Ltd.

Wigginton, E. (1985). *Sometimes a shining moment: The Foxfire experience.* Garden City, NY: Anchor Press/Doubleday.

Woods, P. (1990). *Teacher skills and strategies.* Bristol, PA: Falmer Press.

CHAPTER 11

Acknowledging the Complexity and Dealing with the Ups and Downs of Teaching

It seems like the further we are removed from something the less complex it appears, especially to the "untrained" or undiscerning eye. The actions associated with your reentering schools and classrooms bear some relationship to this observation, as does understanding your performance in classrooms with students. From the outside, teaching seems like an easy task. Once inside, however, you learn quickly that working in schools is precisely the opposite. Classrooms, which at one time seemed to you to be relatively simple environments, turn out to be complex ecosystems. And, as a prospective teacher participating in field experiences, you are trying to make sense of this complexity *and* your emerging practice.

Perhaps one of the keys to beginning to understand the complexity of schools, classrooms, and teaching is to *not* think about your actions as teacher as only having linear and sequential connections and consequences. Teaching is holistic in nature and consequence; it represents a web of interrelated thoughts, feelings, actions, interactions, contexts, and outcomes. Teaching is neither as simple as it appears through mass media nor as unidirectional as mandates placed on teachers and schools by governmental legislators or school district administrators seem to imply. And, the public's view of the scope and complexity of teachers' work is almost uniformly simplistic.

Because of the complexity of schools as learning communities and the overlapping roles and interactions of those who work and learn within their confines, it will at times be difficult for you to recognize your own success and professional growth let alone the success of the students with whom you work. This is especially so in large middle, junior, and high schools where students may be in the classrooms of up to six or seven teachers every day. Because your presence in the learning community is probably relatively short, the impact of your presence is likely to be difficult to gauge. In addition, you are faced with the difficulty of monitoring your own practices because, after all, unless you *feel* that your emerging practices are successful it is unlikely that you will be successful to a degree that meets *your* expectations. That is why it is important prior to entering field experiences for you to try to define the expectations that you and others place on yourself. (Using the tools described in Chapters 1 through 4 will help you make sense of your emerging practice.)

Given the complexity of learning communities, the diversity of students and neighborhoods, the interrelated roles of teachers and other professionals, the nature and goals of education, the purpose of field placements, and the potential for mismatches in placements and personnel, it is little wonder that some preservice teachers (albeit a small minority) experience serious difficulty. Achieving less than expected is bound to be disappointing. This is especially so for individuals who have firmly set their sights on becoming teachers, participated successfully in the university components of formal teacher preparation, and put considerable financial and other resources into becoming teachers. The reality is, though, that some preservice teachers find that once they are thoroughly immersed in the culture of schools and classrooms working with teachers and students, they are not temperamentally or otherwise suited to the multiple tasks and roles associated with teaching. And so, some individuals consider alternative careers or professions.

A normal teaching day, week, month, and year is like a roller coaster ride. While Kevin Ryan (1992) called the first year of teaching "The Roller Coaster Year" (the title of a book of essays by beginning teachers), it is by no means a characteristic exclusive to the early period of teaching. Even though the ups and downs of the roller coaster may eventually become less grueling, less pronounced, less definitive, less hair-raising, and less intimidating, teaching continues to be a challenging and unpredictable experience. Some say that the ride is just different after a while.

The scope of this chapter, therefore, is intended to help you prepare for and deal with some of the ups and downs of teaching and the complexities of understanding your emerging practices and roles in the classroom and school. In turn we provide contexts for acknowledging

- the scope and complexity of teaching
- teaching highs and lows
- professional growth in difficult and successful experiences
- failure

The categories are interrelated; teaching is a complex endeavor. The separation of integrally linked elements into categories is one way to try to make sense of that complexity.

Acknowledging the Scope and Complexity of Teaching

Consider yourself an artist for a moment, a person who works with the medium of paint on paper or canvas with the express purpose of conveying meanings or representations of emotions and feelings, objects, or social events and concepts. While traveling within a rural landscape, for example, you come upon a distant scene that triggers your artistic emotions. You decide to sit down and paint that which draws your attention. In the fashion of a realist (objectivist or representationalist) artist, and with a flick of your wrist, you use broad brush strokes to capture the essence of the scene framed by your eye—taking into consideration balance, forms, textures, colors, and hues. Even so, there are many ways and perspectives to view and represent the landscape that has taken your eye, and you have chosen one. In the sweeping strokes of color and texture layered upon the canvas you can either create loose representations or photographic, minutely detailed images. The choice is up to you. The first choice demands that you be artistically responsive to the totality of the viewed landscape; the second that you narrow your focus to elements within the landscape, perhaps a cliff, a group of trees, a stream, or even the rocks making up the cliff, the bark or leaves of a tree, the pebbles in the stream or the gently flowing eddies, for example. All these elements, and many more, are representative of the landscape; the closer you are to the objects of your representation the more detailed and complex they appear.

Even the artist as social critic exploring the political and social issues, and dilemmas of society, goes through a similar process of locating a focus and sifting through complex elements in order to define and simplify the topic. You often hear individuals, as they observe in art galleries, say how they could easily produce the works of the artist. But, place most people in front of the artist's easel with the artist's palette and the actions—let alone the finished product of the artist—become considerably more difficult to reproduce.

Being in schools is something like the experience of the artist framing a scene in preparation for producing objective art; the artist does not see every detail at once and chooses first a point to focus. Being in classrooms is also like being suddenly placed on the artist's stool in front of the easel. As we have mentioned before, it is much easier, indeed safer, to criticize schools and those who work in them from a distance. Suddenly being placed in the artist's chair demands a dramatically different perspective. Essentially, one of the purposes of this book is to help you make that transition—changing roles and places within classrooms and schools.

Like the experience of emerging artists searching for subject matter, the complexity of contexts in schools will emerge in proportion to your presence there. And, you will find that the scope and complexity of teachers' work appear different depending on the ideological perspective you take and develop. Being in a role of classroom leadership will test your understanding of the complexity of the contexts and tasks ahead of you. Even so, acknowledge that becoming a teacher is a developmental process and that the scope and complexity of teaching will unfold before you as you maintain a reflexive, inquiring perspective.

Aspiring artists often apprentice to successful, established artists. Like the emerging teacher, they place themselves in contexts where their vision can be challenged, gently cajoled, encouraged, and appropriate techniques and skills developed. They learn about artistic endeavor through exploring the thinking and practice of the mentor. By immersing themselves in the studio of the acclaimed artist they come to understand artistic vision, the ways of the artist, the complexity of the artist's work and thinking and, in the process, develop their own unique theories, perspectives, techniques, and artistic endeavors.

In the following narrative accounts the preservice teachers all agreed that the complexity and scope of teachers' work unfolded as they worked within the confines of their field placements. Jeannie acknowledges that a lack of opportunity to experience some of the many roles and activities of teachers contributes to her feelings of being ill-prepared to assume full responsibility for the classroom. Loraine, Dee Dee, and Diane are overcome by the sheer weight of time and energy, both indicators of the complexities of the work. They long for a balance between their personal and professional lives. Many student teachers who have serious difficulties in the classroom are overcommitted in their time and energies and are not able to do justice to the tasks associated with their professional development. (In thinking about this, recollect the suggestions we made in Chapter 6 about mediating fieldwork expectations of family and friends.) Beginning teachers also tend to underestimate the time and energy it takes to make that difficult transition to full-time teaching. Simplifying life outside school is one way of minimizing the stress of learning to teach. (We will further address this in Chapter 12.) For Terry, the role of teacher continually unfolded, revealing ever more complexity.

Narrative Accounts

Field experience has helped me learn more about the teaching part of being a teacher. I feel that I am still very unprepared for many other tasks that I will face. Outside of the classroom, jobs like parent conferences, report card evaluations, staff meetings, obtaining educational "extras" for the classroom (such as movies, maps, books of activity ideas, for example), and various other responsibilities are still a mystery to me. I do not think these things need to be taught in university classrooms, but they are issues that I would like to learn more about. Much of it will be learned when I am actually teaching on my own. This learning through experience will continue, even after my formal preparation is completed. (Jeannie Gore)

I have a four-page journal entry (my *only* journal entry) on the day I decided to abandon total dedication to teaching school. I had completely lost balance in my life between teaching and my other personal relationships and responsibilities. Even at those times when I was physically away from school, my mind was on school work or on the students in my classes. My first priority had to return to my family and then school would follow. My children deserved much more than they were getting from me. I also needed more sleep. Living on four hours sleep each night left me out of patience by 5:00 P.M. The obvious solution was more efficient time management. I tried to concentrate more during my preparation periods at school. I began to use those hours to prepare instead of socialize. I started to prepare lessons two weeks in advance. This gave me peace of mind, and I was able to give my undivided attention to my children after school. We got to be good friends again, and I felt better about myself and my organizational abilities. (Loraine Wilde)

Am I being productive? Well, I am taking care of me. I am being totally self-centered and enjoying every second of it—sleeping, exercising, reading teacher-type books (not lesson plan stuff), just sitting, and being quiet. I am afraid that I will not be able to find the energy to go back. Am I cut out for teaching if I am I so dead tired? I am sitting on the sofa, and I cannot budge. I am dead tired. I'm too tired to write; man am I exhausted! (Dee Dee Edwards)

It is very difficult to get enough sleep. I am really tired. I used to think if it were 8:00 P.M. I still had four hours of productive time left before sleep. Now it is 8:05 P.M., and if I closed my eyes, even for a long blink, I could end up not opening them until tomorrow or even next week sometime. This is all so much work. I am getting much more efficient though, and with any luck at all, I could be getting enough sleep and doing a decent job. I might even have time for a real bike ride, or a date, or even enough time to actually cook a meal (a real meal—I vaguely remember one). I don't get tired or worn out very often, and tomorrow I will be fine. But today, I want about a week off. One of the most incredible things about teaching is that even the most emotionally stable, happy, level-headed individual (in a time of quick depression it may be good to note my infallible strong points here) can experience more emotional change within one month than probably in the last three years (perhaps a slight exaggeration). Just think of what all this would do to someone who is even the slightest bit insecure or emotionally unstable!

There are so many things to work on to do a good job. It is kind of funny because, at a glimpse, or even a lot of glimpses, it could look like I am doing fine (sometimes). The list of things that I could do, or need to do, or have not done, or . . . is endless. Every time I hear people say, "You are doing a good job" and stuff like that, thoughts of all the mistakes and/or things I need to work on (billions of them) go screaming through my mind, and I wonder how long it will be before I really am free of them.

Before school started I remember being optimistic and idealistic about the upcoming months. I also remember being a bit nervous and afraid of not becoming a good teacher. I have a clear picture of a "not good" teacher, and I desperately want not to become one. Anyway, school started Monday morning, ready or not, and my mind has been a bit dazed ever since. . . .

When I think back, I remember when things could not have gone better and when they could not have been worse. Although I am not sure whether the better days came more often or not, I would like to think they did. So now school is here, and I find myself spending endless amounts of time grading, thinking of motivators, and trying to figure out how to deal with certain students and. . . . The year continues, carrying with it successes, failures, decisions, problems, frustrations, and satisfactions. Some moments are better than others. Some ideas are better than others. There are times I am prepared weeks in advance and other times only minutes ahead. Now the planning is almost over along with the entire year. (Diane Malone)

As I have had opportunities to teach, my attitudes about the amount of time, skill, and anxiety that goes into preparing an effective lesson have changed. Growing up, even in my collegiate career, I considered teaching to be a job that, after a few years, becomes an easy route to a paycheck. Indeed, there are teachers who perceive their occupation as such and put in a minimal amount of effort. But, as I have learned of the various methods of teaching and the different means of learning, I have discovered that teaching is a profession that requires not only skill but also a tremendous amount of time, patience, and intuition. For example, in preparing to teach a two-week unit plan about tobacco and alcohol, I found myself preparing a month in advance and still being left with loose ends at the last minute prior to actually teaching. My attitude concerning the difficulty of the teaching profession has obviously changed so that now I have more respect for those who have chosen to take upon themselves the awesome responsibility of being educator, facilitator, and *loci parentis*.

One of the initial attractions to the teaching profession was the idea of being able to attain tenure and not having to worry about being fired. I figured that it would be great to go to work where I would not have to be worried about getting a pink slip in my box. This perception of unlimited job security has been modified as I have had the opportunity to listen to teachers discuss their experiences with tenure. As I have spent time in schools I have realized the politics surrounding this policy. For example, I have learned that even though a person has tenure it does not mean that the administration and fellow teachers cannot make life unbearable, thereby forcing the tenured teacher to either move to another school in the district, consider the possibility of quitting, take an early retirement, or just simply endure to the end. I also learned that there are behaviors that I could be dismissed for, regardless of my tenure—behaviors that I could be sued for. More important to me, now, is maintaining a healthy rapport with everyone at the school in which I teach not only to attain tenure but also to ensure that I will enjoy getting up and going to work in the mornings. (Terry Ingram)

For Reflection and Discussion

1. Jeannie felt "unprepared" for "outside of the classroom" tasks associated with teaching. She identified procedures associated with report cards, parent conferences, and obtaining classroom materials as a "mystery"; however, she did not feel "these things need to be taught in university classrooms."
   a. Why do you suppose Jeannie concluded that such topics did not need to be addressed during the teacher education program at the university?
   b. What are some appropriate strategies for exploring the issues that Jeannie is concerned about?
2. Loraine "lost balance" between teaching and her other relationships and responsibilities. She found that even when she was away from school her mind was "on school work or the students in my classes."
   a. Why did she identify the problem as time management?
   b. What steps did she take to re-acquire a sense of balance in her life?
   c. Is there something about the nature of teachers' work that induces a preoccupation with it?
3. Dee Dee takes time out to care for herself. She questions whether she is "cut out" for teaching because she is "dead tired" much of the time. Dee Dee asked, "Am I being productive?"
   a. What do you think?

4. Diane describes the exhaustion and tumult of emotions she experiences while learning to be a teacher. She wonders how long it will be until her mind is free of the "billions" of thoughts about mistakes made and things to work on. She also wonders about the impact of such an experience on an insecure or unstable person.

   a. When you reread Diane's account, what evidence do you see of an emerging awareness of the scope of teaching?

   b. What does Diane's concern about the impact of the extended period of practice on the insecure or unstable person say about the importance of self-knowledge?

5. Experience quickly taught Terry that his assumption about teaching being an "easy route to a paycheck" was erroneous. He discovered that a "tremendous amount of time, patience, and intuition" were required besides the ability to assume multiple roles. His understanding about tenure also required some adjustment.

   a. How might his assumption about teaching as being "easy" have had an impact on his ability to handle the complexity of the profession?

Links with Research

There is an immediacy and complexity to classroom life that requires teachers to act and react spontaneously to environmental demands. Jackson (1968) estimates that teachers at work with students engage in as many as a thousand interpersonal transactions each teaching day in their various roles of teacher, "chairperson," "supply sergeant," "delegator," "time keeper," and "manager." To a beginning teacher, the facility with which experienced teachers respond to classroom complexity and the various roles and responsibilities they must assume seems overwhelming. As Zeichner and Gore (1990) maintain, because studies of preservice teacher socialization "have rarely taken into account the character and quality of institutions in which teacher education programs exist" (p. 336), there seems to be limited opportunity for preservice teachers to understand the complexity of learning to teach within the context of various institutional and programmatic demands and influences.

But, even for experienced teachers, coping with role complexity is a source of anxiety and frustration. Reflecting on her long career as a teacher, Sybil Shack (1965) addressed the issue of role complexity. After listing a full page of responsibilities teachers must carry out "in addition to teaching," she concludes:

> Undoubtedly most of these things are necessary and even important, but they bore into our teaching time. We need that time to prepare our lessons, to keep up with our academic disciplines, to help individual pupils, and merely to teach. We resent having to tunnel our way through the mounds of directives, reports, records, and accounts, which block our passage every day of the week and which reach mountainous heights at the beginning and end of the school term (p. 7).

In addressing this same phenomenon, Feiman-Nemser and Floden (1986) make a helpful distinction between the job of teaching and the work of teaching—the work of teaching being related to the realization of educational goals, and the job of teaching being related to the realization of organizational and bureaucratic goals. Because these often conflict with one another, the authors assert, teachers frequently find themselves in a position of having to deal with contradictory goals and behaviors, a source of stress, frustration, and burnout.

Freedman, Jackson, and Boles (1983) argue that coping with conflicting institutional demands and societal expectations is the primary source of teacher burnout.

Coping with role complexity and the numerous responsibilities associated with both the job and work of teaching is a major source of anxiety for beginning teachers. The preceding comments by preservice teachers are echoed by beginning teachers, especially in the early months of their first year as they shoulder the full impact of their new responsibilities and struggle to maintain a sense of balance in their lives (Cole, 1991; Cole & Knowles, 1992; Knowles, 1989, 1992; Thiessen, 1991). Usually in the first several months of teaching, beginning teachers are challenged to rethink high expectations of themselves and find ways of striking a balance between their personal and professional lives. As one beginning teacher discovered:

> It gets frustrating because you can't do it all. . . . You're pulled in all directions, . . . and that's hard to handle. I guess all teachers face this problem. I'm learning that it's impossible to be able to handle it all the first year. I have high expectations of myself so I've had to really try to make myself do other things in my life (Cole & Knowles, 1992, pp. 15–16.).

Research Activities

1. The multiple tasks that teachers perform are some indication of the scope and complexity of teachers' work. In exploring this subject, start with yourself and then move outward to others and their experiences.
   a. Make a list of the tasks that you think teachers perform.
   b. Sit down with experienced teachers and explore elements of their work. What are the multiple tasks teachers perform daily? weekly? monthly? yearly? What were the tasks that they completed today? What were the tasks that they worked on? What tasks did they begin? Where did the tasks originate? For what purpose? Were any of the tasks particularly rewarding? objectionable? How do they prioritize tasks?
   c. Repeat the exploration, using similar kinds of questions with new teachers, even other preservice teachers like yourself.
   d. Reexamine the lists that you generated in beginning this activity. Can you categorize the listed tasks? Is there any significance in the groupings? To what extent do you think these lists represent the complexity and scope of teachers' work? What do they or do they not tell about teachers' work?
2. Points of awareness about your emerging knowledge of the scope and complexity of teaching are likely to revolve around a number of obvious tasks. One of them, instructional activities and practices, for example, could provide you with opportunities for collecting considerable information. Here are some questions that barely begin to skim the surface of the topic. (To begin to find answers to these questions, spend some planning time with an experienced teacher, and ask him or her to talk aloud about their work *as* they are doing it. This "talk aloud" method is frequently used by researchers who are trying to understand teachers' thought processes. Although it may seem strange at first, it may prove to be an enlightening exercise.)
   a. How do experienced teachers plan? What is their thinking as they do so? How do they select curriculum foci, academic substance, activities, evaluation criteria, and so

on? What are some of the decisions they make quickly and with little hesitancy? How do teachers go about translating planning into instructional practice? What are the multiple decisions that teachers make as they go about implementing curriculum and instructional planning? What are some of the issues that teachers deal with moment by moment in the articulation of a formal lesson? What are the multiple tasks and activities associated with planning?

3. Cooperating teachers are in a position to facilitate your thinking about the complexity and scope of teaching. Have your cooperating teacher list experiences that *they* consider potentially useful, even essential, for expanding *your* conceptions of teachers' work. Endeavor to engage yourself in some of the experiences suggested noting how your conceptions of the scope and complexity of teaching have changed or been challenged.

4. University supervisors are likely to have advice about how you might facilitate your awareness of the complexity of teaching. Use the framework provided in exercise 3 as a place to begin taking advantage of their perceptions and insights.

Teaching Highs and Teaching Lows

As a child or an adolescent, did you ever visit a theme park and ride the roller coaster? Remember your experiences—the exuberance of living through the rides, surviving the physical and emotional highs and the deep, seemingly never-ending, gravity-accelerating troughs, the sensations and thoughts when your stomach came into your mouth, sometimes literally. That teachers have ups and downs in their teaching is a given. Too often, newcomers to classroom learning environments are likely to attribute these swings in success (and mood) as largely resting on *their* behaviors and practices. The reality is, however, that there are multiple factors likely to have an influence on the rate of success that you enjoy—or do not enjoy. The ups and downs of teaching are amplified by a host of factors, some of which you may understand, others of which may be beyond your immediate knowledge and control.

Teachers do not teach and work in vacuums. Schools are *not* disconnected from the world beyond. Schools and classrooms are microcosms of life and society, and as such, are full of struggles, disputes, obstacles, joys, successes, and failures. Classroom climates can be profoundly affected by

- the weather
- time of day
- events of the day (those preceding or impending)
- subsequent or preceding class periods (spent outside your classroom)
- interactions with teachers and other adults
- family events and circumstances
- athletic or social events
- interactions with other students

And to think that classrooms can and should *only* be fun places may well be one of the largest obstacles to every new teacher's ultimate success.

Many of the ups and downs of teaching will reflect the complex nature of teaching rather than the actions or attitudes of any individual teacher. Teachers are bound to be influenced by the larger, more pervasive social, political, and cultural circumstances as well as structural and administrative constraints resting in the learning community itself. Nevertheless, not to acknowledge that you, too, may have "up" and "down" days is as dysfunctional as a view of classroom as only "fun park." Further, feelings of being on an emotional roller coaster may have nothing directly to do with teaching itself. You and the students are greatly influenced by the surrounding world.

Contrary to the beliefs of some, teachers are "entitled" to have personal lives and emotional responses. Granting yourself permission to acknowledge these human attributes will also help you recognize some of the fluctuations and variations in classroom success. That is why we often recommend that first-year teachers do not unnecessarily complicate their lives. The fewer outside demands, constraints, distractions, and difficulties, the better new teachers will be able to handle the transition to full-time teaching and the emotional ups and downs of working with students in classrooms and other environments. Although this advice may appear to be patronizing to new teachers, we certainly do not intend it to be that way; nor do we mean to overlook the real and complicated lives that most of us live. Transitions are often difficult, especially when there are multiple ones to be made all at once. As a result, it is well recognized that for some individuals the beginning weeks, months, and even years of teaching can be very stressful.

In the following narratives, you will read preservice teachers' words describing the realization that fluctuations in their practices (and the students' responses to those practices) are *not* an indication of failure or disaster. To place oneself on a pedestal to "perform" consistently at some superhuman level is clearly dysfunctional, as some of the preservice teachers hint. Wanda experiences fluctuations in her attitudes toward working with adolescents. Paul highlights some high and low points of his student teaching experience citing his own feelings of insecurity as a major stumbling block. Renee reflects on some of the rewards of teaching that left her "feeling very high." Brian discovered that high points in his teaching increased when he used his own style to work with students. And, Steve likens his experience to an "emotional version of the stock market"—if he had read Ryan's (1992) book he may have referred to a roller coaster!

Narrative Accounts

At the end of my first week, I was asked to help another teacher whose mother had taken ill and had to go to the hospital. I gladly volunteered to teach this class for I saw it as an excellent opportunity. The class was a General Level Grade 10 class held last period on a Friday afternoon. Because I was a student teacher, another teacher was left in the classroom with me; however, this teacher could not assist me because he did not know the computer system we were using.

I was warned prior to teaching this class that it would be a challenge, and there were a few "snickers" here and there when teachers realized that a new student teacher would have to control this "rowdy" class. Anyhow, the class was very interesting to say the least. I was very firm with the students, but I found myself continually having to discipline them and to keep reminding them to do their work. I did not realize I was teaching this class until that day, therefore, I did not have time to prepare for it, which added extra stress. Needless to say, I felt the class was a disaster. I continually had to talk loudly so as to be heard, and as soon as one person settled down, somebody else would act up.

The next day, I seriously considered if I really wanted to teach teenagers. I was feeling quite down and could not understand why the cooperating teacher told me that I had done a good job because I actually "got them to do some work." This comment made me even more confused because I felt that it should not be a struggle to get students to do work. This class was more like a glorified baby-sitting job as opposed to an actual teaching position, and I did not have baby-sitting in mind when I planned for a teaching career.

When Sunday rolled around, I was feeling a little better, but I was becoming hesitant about teaching the class assigned to me. I prepared on the weekend and felt good about my lesson; however, I had never taught this class and was nervous that perhaps it would turn out to be like Friday's class.

Monday arrived and I was introduced to the assigned class. Fortunately, I was more than pleased with the outcomes. The students were terrific and wanted to learn. After that day, I began looking forward to teaching my regular classes and began to wonder how I could have let myself think that I did not want to teach teenagers.

I was on "cloud nine" until one particular student tested me. He became very distant toward me, and when I tried to help him, he acted totally uninterested. I was hurt by his actions and, again, began feeling somewhat confused about teaching adolescents. One day, I handed this student back a test that he had failed. On the test paper, I told him that I was willing to help him if he wanted to see me after class. I was almost assured that he would not remain after class; however, he surprised me by wanting my help. Again, I was very pleased, and as the week ended, I became reassured that I had chosen the right age group to teach. (Wanda Fillemanuosa)

The past two and one-half months of teaching have been an eye-opening, sometimes exciting, sometimes very discouraging experience. Personal considerations have made the task of being well-prepared, energetic, and forward thinking very difficult. At times, I have felt like I was barely hanging on by my fingernails. The positive aspects of my experiences so far are important. I have found that I enjoy teaching and working with teenagers, as I had hoped. I find the challenges I face to foster real learning and the growth of the whole individual exciting, interesting, and motivating. I am learning at least as much from my students as they are learning from me.

The biggest negatives I have experienced seem to come from my feelings of insecurity about whether I am meeting the needs and expectations of the school, the parents, the other teachers in the school (including my cooperating teacher, Rosetta—although she continues to be very supportive and encouraging), and even the kids. I am not overly concerned with being liked (in any event, I do not think that is a problem), but I do not want anyone to judge me a poor teacher. Because of these feelings of insecurity, my planning and preparation time has been difficult at times and, usually, inefficiently spent. Moreover, and more significantly, I find myself often making planning choices based on what I think other people expect rather than on what I think will contribute to what I want to accomplish with the students.

Classroom management is a concern for me. I am reluctant to really sit on my classes because I want to maintain a high energy level and a positive atmosphere. I do not want the class experience to be one of drudgery. Unfortunately, I let too many students get away with not participating in class on a fairly regular basis. In particular, in the third period class (which Rosetta considered her most difficult group) there are three boys who just do not want to do anything and several others who are glad to oblige them with distractions. I have tried several approaches and, so far, have found nothing that really motivates the whole class on a consistent basis. I need to think of ways to really get the nonparticipators actively involved.

Variety and creativity in class activities have become a big challenge for me lately, as well. Toward the beginning of the quarter, I was doing a lot more projects and activities intended to allow and encourage individual creativity and group participation. My experiences with those kinds of activities were somewhat disappointing, partly because I had high expectations that simply were not met. I have not consciously decided not to try similar projects in the future, but I have been reluctant to put any energy into planning them. This is an attitude problem that I need to overcome. For the rest of the year, my goals are clear—to find ways to involve everyone in the class on a consistent basis, and to redevelop some variety in class activities. Finally, I need and intend to inject just a bit more fun into the way I run the class. (Paul Colins)

Today was a fast and hectic day that left me feeling very "high." I feel like I finally got through to a "very hard to get through to" kid. He is a bright kid, but very confused. Unfortunately, his parents expect a lot from him, perhaps too much. They think he is a genius and let him and us know this. His parents want him to be working on special projects, but we have not been able to get him excited about anything. And then today, when I was just about to write the class newspaper, the boy came to my desk and saw the blank form and asked if he could do it. This was the first time he had taken initiative with anything. I was so excited. I said I thought it would be great if he did the newspaper. I helped him get organized, but he really did most of the work. It was great to see him excited about something. He worked very diligently on it. We discussed everything that we had done during the week. Then he planned the layout—the amount of space he was going to need for each topic. When he was all done, I photocopied it, and he presented it to the class. I know that he was very proud of himself, and I was proud to have helped him.

Teaching certainly can be very rewarding. It's days like these that make me sure that I want to be a teacher. I get some satisfaction in knowing that at least once during the course of the semester I stimulated a discussion, dried a tear, calmed a fear, explained a concept, boosted an ego, encouraged creativity, praised diligence, stopped a fight, lent an ear, brightened a day, maintained control, shared a song, told a story, sparked an imagination, offered encouragement, and helped some students learn to help themselves. (Renee Buscho)

Today was a learning experience for me. I obviously had a honeymoon the last four days. Last night at seminar meeting with other preservice teachers I had lots of positive things to say about my first four days. It is as if I jinxed myself. Today, I was really tired. I felt ineffective. I and the cooperating teacher each taught several discrete lessons during the day. My lessons on conflict resolution were long and boring. I did not have a feel for when to end; yet the kids seemed bored right from the start—very fidgety too. To cap it all off, my last lesson was at the end of the day. It really pounded. Dhanna said she would not have done anything differently and blamed the time of day and week for the partial downs of the lesson. I feel like I ended the week on a low note and that I do not really have the respect and support of the kids. I am feeling awkward in a place where, three days ago, I thought I would never feel awkward. I guess I have the weekend to regroup. Monday is a short day too. . . .

Today was an exciting day. As I have written previously, it seemed like somehow something had to change. I was not using my own style to work with the kids, and I think it was affecting both my effectiveness as a teacher and my relationships with them. Yesterday and today, I began to use my own quicker style of interaction, realizing that it does not necessarily disrupt the atmosphere of the classroom. It worked. I had more fun, the kids were having more fun, and I believe the kids were learning better also. I seemed to be more natural and at ease, and I was obviously more comfortable with what I was doing. Dhanna noticed too. It rounded out the week for me. (Brian Forbes)

What an emotional job. I am beginning to feel like an emotional version of the stock market, gaining and losing hundreds of points a week. By midweek, I was feeling roughly discouraged. I had had it with pubescent behavior. Not that anything in particular had gone wrong, rather it was as if I had reached my limit. My frayed nerves had lost all tolerance and patience. I was ready to quit, so ready that on Thursday I sneaked out early to find out about employment in another profession—or at least test the waters. (Steve Bruno)

For Reflection and Discussion

1. Wanda perceived her teaching of a particular class as a "disaster." She felt some confusion when her efforts were complimented by the supervising teacher because she "got them to do some work."
   a. To whom does Wanda attribute the successes and failures of her teaching? To what extent may her assessment be accurate?
   b. What effect may the amount of planning and preparation have had upon her perception of the quality of her teaching?
2. Paul notes that the experience of teaching yields mixed outcomes. The "highs" include his discovery that he enjoys teaching and finds the challenge to foster learning "exciting, interesting and motivating." He attributes the "lows" to feelings of insecurity about being viewed as a good teacher. He attributed the difficulty he encountered in planning lessons "based on what I think other people expect" to his concern with being viewed as a "good teacher." He also felt disappointed that the innovative lessons he presented at the beginning of the term did not meet his expectations.

    a. To what extent should Paul have disregarded the expectations of others and planned lessons according to his own goals?

    b. How might Paul have addressed the expectations of others as a way to reduce his anxieties? To what extent might Paul's concern about the expectations of others continue to influence his planning as an in-service teacher?

    c. To what extent might Paul's high expectations have affected his perception of success about the early class sessions? What other factors, other than his own expectations, might have contributed to the disappointing outcome of Paul's early lessons?

3. Excited when a "very hard to get through to kid" involved himself in the class newspaper, Renee writes that teaching can be rewarding and lists the many highlights of the term.

    a. Reread Renee's list of highlights. Which items has she included that might appear questionable to those unfamiliar with teaching?

4. Brian traces the rapid changes in his feelings from the first "honeymoon" days to disillusionment when he writes that he felt "awkward in a place where, three days ago, I thought I would never feel awkward." Later, he began to develop his own teaching style and noticed an increase in both his comfort and the feeling of fun experienced by himself and his students.

    a. What elements did Brian identify as contributing to his feelings of ineffectiveness?

    b. To what extent might Brian's feelings of ineffectiveness be related to his knowledge of students and classroom rhythms?

5. Steve feels "like an emotional version of the stock market, gaining and losing hundreds of points a week." His "frayed nerves had lost all tolerance and patience," and he felt so ready to quit that he tested the waters for other employment.

    a. To what extent should Steve base decisions about his career on emotional feelings?

    b. How might Steve address the emotional impact to avoid "frayed nerves?" How might Steve redistribute his emotional investment in teaching to accentuate the gains and minimize the negative impact?

Links with Research

The realization that learning to teach and becoming a teacher are *processes and not events* comes as a shock to most persons beginning the path toward becoming full-fledged teachers. Because emotional highs and lows do not figure into a view of teaching as a skill performance—first you learn how and then you go and do it—experiencing the emotional roller coaster ride that is a natural part of the process is often disconcerting. The process view, as represented in this book, reflects the complex and developmental nature of learning to teach and becoming a teacher. Inherent in this view is the understanding that development is multidimensional, encompassing skills acquisition, psychological and conceptual reorientation, and a variety of forms of knowledge growth including self-knowledge. The journey is not always smooth.

    The research cited throughout this book highlights various dimensions of the learning to teach process and addresses issues of preservice teacher development throughout the process. Previous *Links with Research* sections have focused on issues related to developing self-awareness and knowledge of others, learning about teaching and learning environments, and understanding interpersonal influences and relationships. In the narrative accounts you have just read, the preservice teachers make reference to many areas covered in previous chapters and *Links with Research* sections. In the context of this chapter, therefore, we transcend the *sources* of anxiety, frustration, joy, and excitement and focus on the affective dimension of preservice teachers' experiences. To help you make sense of this very real part of the learning to teach process, we look briefly at some of the ways that preservice and beginning teacher development is conceptualized in the research literature. From this, we hope you will gain an appreciation of the conceptual and psychological complexity of the process and, in so doing, gain some insight into the affective realm of the developmental process.

Teacher development has been characterized in a number of ways. Fuller and Bown (1975), for example, propose that new teachers progress through a series of concern-based stages beginning with actions based on self-centered concerns about survival to actions based on concerns about students and curricular issues. Ryan (1986) suggests that beginning teachers move through stages of "fantasy," "survival," "mastery," and "impact." Berliner (1988) describes teacher development in terms of conceptual progression from thinking like a novice and advanced beginner to being competent, proficient, and expert.

There are also varying perspectives on the kinds of knowledge that inform teacher development. Bullough, Knowles, and Crow (1991), Butt and Raymond (1987), Hunt, 1987, Knowles (1992), Knowles and Cole (in preparation), and Knowles and Holt-Reynolds (1991) consider teacher development to be rooted in the "personal," that is, informed by personal values, beliefs, and life and practical experiences. Clandinin (1986), and Connelly and Clandinin (1988) also focus on the personal nature of teacher development. They characterize teaching practice in terms of the development of personal practical knowledge. The development of pedagogical content knowledge is associated with the work of Shulman (1986, 1987) and Gudmundsottir (1990). Other studies have argued for a personal mode linked to broader contextual parameters (for example, Britzman, 1986; Ball & Goodson, 1985; Cole, 1990b, 1991, 1992; Goodson, 1981, 1992; Goodson & Cole (in press); Goodson & Walker, 1991; Zeichner & Grant, 1981; Zeichner & Tabachnick, 1981).

From an analysis of over 40 studies of learning to teach and existing models of teacher development, Kagan (1992) developed another way of explaining the process, one that is in line with what we have been proposing throughout the book. Kagan's model validates and helps to explain the learning to teach process as it is experienced, taking into account its complex and personal nature. According to Kagan, growth consists of at least five components:

- a developing awareness of initial and changing knowledge and beliefs about students and classrooms
- a reconstruction of idealized and inaccurate images of students and a reconstruction of early images of self as teacher
- a shift in attention to students and instruction upon resolution of one's own professional identity
- acquiring and becoming comfortable with standard classroom procedures
- growth in problem-solving skills

When and how development takes place depends on at least three factors:

- the novice teacher's biography or personal history (clarity of image of self as teacher and readiness to acknowledge and accept that beliefs and images are inaccurate)
- the configuration of the preservice teacher education program (including the amount of time spent in educational contexts)
- the contexts in which student and beginning teaching occur (nature of pupils, principal's beliefs, availability of materials, relationships with parents, and beliefs of and relations with other teachers)

Of particular importance are the relationship between preservice and cooperating teachers and the degree of autonomy afforded by a principal.

In short, Kagan (1992) acknowledges that "the practice of classroom teaching remains forever rooted in personality and experience and that learning to teach requires a journey into the deepest recesses of one's self-awareness, where failures, fears, and hopes are hidden" (pp. 164–165). This kind of acknowledgment validates the importance of attending to understanding the highs and lows in the early periods of learning to teach.

Research Activities

1. Assuming that you have kept a professional journal of your experiences in the learning community, especially of your classroom and teaching activities, and also assuming those records identify in some way high and low experiences, go back and analyze your writing in the fashion suggested in Chapters 2 and 3. Explore the circumstances around which you have acknowledged experiencing highs or lows.
   a. What does it mean to you to have highs and lows? What do the highs look like? the lows?
   b. Are there any circumstantial or contextual patterns? Are there cyclical periods? Do you have enough information to make judgments based on your accounts?
   c. As a result of exploring your journal, what new insights do you have about yourself? About the general nature of teaching?
   d. For future writing, what kinds of information do you need to include in your journal to help you identify the swings in your emotional responses? (Or, what information, observations, or perceptions might help you make a more complete record and help you come to more complete understandings about the nature of your highs and lows?)
2. Talk with your peers about their experiences of teaching. Ask them some of the same questions you asked yourself (see activity 1 in this section).
   a. Under what circumstances do your peers experience highs and lows? To what extent are your experiences similar? different? Why?
3. New and experienced teachers often talk about the phenomenon of the roller coaster experience. Ask them to elaborate.
   a. What are the stories that teachers tell in the faculty lounge about the roller coaster experience? To what extent is it recognized in public?
   b. What is a high? a low? When do they occur? Under what circumstances? How do teachers handle their feelings or responses? To what extent do they change their plans, actions, or practices? What are their assumptions about this phenomenon?

   c. What advice do teachers give you about handling highs and lows? How might such advice be useful? not useful?

4. Talk with students about their experiences in your classroom—as well as their experiences in the classrooms of others. There may be an individual or groups of students with whom you can comfortably examine this matter. Explore the extent to which *they* experience highs and lows (including the nature of the experiences) and the degree to which these feelings coincide or do not coincide with your own feelings. Also explore the extent to which they compensate or take advantage of these emotional swings, and the extent to which whole classes experience these swings.

Recognizing Difficulties and Successes in Experiences of Professional Growth

Feeling success and knowing success when you see it are important. Having a sense of the meaning of success will also help you recognize difficulties. More important, however, may be the ability to grow professionally from both successful and difficult experiences. Remember when you were a young child or an adolescent. Recollect how either adults remarked on or how you felt about the awkwardness associated with your growth spurts—sometimes adolescent bodies seem unsuited for activities intended by adolescent minds and those times are often difficult. Growing pains are inevitably an outcome of transitions or challenging experiences. Learning to teach embodies some of the elements associated with growth spurts. Difficulties are bound to occur. Although one of the subtle assumptions about working in classrooms is that "anyone can teach," nothing could be further from the truth. In a sense, this kind of attitude is dysfunctional.

As you begin teaching, the chances are that you have worked hard to establish an image of yourself as teacher, and we have urged you to pay close attention to this matter. One potential difficulty with this is that you expect to establish a high level of expertise overnight. Given a developmental perspective on your becoming a professional this perspective is unrealistic. It is one thing to aspire to "teach like an expert" and another to achieve such a state.

There is a considerable body of research that attempts to delineate the differences between experienced and novice teachers. One of the central themes in this work is the notion that experienced teachers think about teaching in much more complex ways than novices. Their teaching is informed by more information, more experience, and more insight into their own practice and the various contexts in which their work is situated. Obviously, for the most part, this is not due to chance. It comes about largely because of experience and systematic reflection on and analysis of that experience to determine appropriate and inappropriate courses of action (refer back to Figure 1.1, The Experiential Learning Spiral). After many years of teaching, experienced teachers come to know what constitutes success in the classroom. They know when students are learning, when their teaching is "right." They may not always be able to tell you why or how something works or does not, but they know. They have an intuitive response that is embedded in formal and informal theories about teaching and learning.

In many ways, success is individually defined. It is likely that, at this point, your notion of success in the classroom is only beginning to take shape. To help clarify your thinking we urge you to consider the following questions:

- What is success in the classroom?
- When are your emerging practices deemed successful by yourself or others?
- To what extent do the indications of success held by university- and site-based teacher educators overlap or contradict each other?
- Do any of the expected conditions of success contradict *your* thinking about practice in the classroom?
- To what extent are the responses of students to your teaching practices appropriate or inappropriate gauges of your performance?
- How might the impressions of cooperating teachers or other learning community professionals inform your emerging practice?

These are some of the many questions that might help you think about making sense of your classroom work. Before you can identify your successes in the classroom you must have some sense of what they look like. And further, those successes may be different from those of your peers, especially if you and those with whom you work acknowledge an individually determined developmental framework for becoming a teacher.

The flip side of success is failure. There will be times when your actions as a teacher will not be successful. And intense and accumulative difficulties that are not explored and corrected may lead to "failure" (the topic of the fourth section in this chapter). In this section, however, we imply that the circumstances in which you are unsuccessful indicate difficulties. By substituting "difficulties" for "success" we have modified the questions posed in the previous paragraph as a way to help you explore your thinking about the notion of difficulties:

- What are your difficulties in the classroom likely to look like? Can you foreshadow them and work toward preventing some of them? How?
- When are you likely to be seen by yourself or others as having difficulties?
- To what extent do the indications of difficulties held by university- and site-based teacher educators overlap or contradict each other?
- Do the conditions associated with your difficulties contradict or support *your* thinking about practice in the classroom?
- To what extent are the responses of students to your teaching practices appropriate or inappropriate gauges of your performance?
- How might the impressions of cooperating teachers or other learning community professionals inform your emerging practice?

Our insistence that learning to teach is a developmental process places on you almost exclusive responsibility for forming and framing the early period of your chosen career. Working with teacher educators based in the field and in the academy, you should be able to come to some firm decisions about appropriate goals and objectives for your professional development.[1] You should also be able to establish ways to access levels of success and indications of difficulties when working in field placements. In addition, if you have spent time making explicit *your* ideas of "good" or successful teaching through the various tools of self-analysis using autobiographical writing (introduced in Chapter 2), you will have a personal standard for success. And, by default, you will have parameters by which difficulties may be recognized. In addition, given the typical, traditional contexts into which many preservice teachers are placed, some of the teaching component of your experience is going to be based on meeting specific curricular goals and objectives within a specific time frame.[2] Meeting these goals and objectives, therefore, is one of many ways to learn about your practice and students' learning.

Although success or failure in teaching is much more than meeting sets of curricular goals and objectives, it is one gauge of your successful practices (or difficulties). Another way to measure your performance is through solicitation of feedback from students, teachers, administrators, and peers. Remember, also, formalized peer observations can play a useful part in self-assessment (refer to Chapter 4). And ongoing sensitivity and responsiveness to the students' actions and responses to your teaching will provide you with further evidence.

In the following accounts, many of the preservice teachers were initially exacting on themselves, placing high expectations on their performances in classrooms and schools. But, as they progressed, they were more able to gauge the moods of classrooms and groups of students, and to acknowledge success or difficulties in different ways. In a sense, they evidence learning to become more responsive. Perhaps as a function of time John became more comfortable with students. Jane acknowledges that as she grows in confidence, and with more experience, she expands the criteria for self-assessment. Like John, Amy gained confidence as she taught, and she brings a succinct view of success to the discussion. Brian's account witnesses growth in confidence proportional to responsibilities accepted. Coming to accept a different perspective on students' classroom behaviors is evidence of Eva's emerging perspective of her practice. Tony, like Debbie, is constantly reminded of the pressures and difficulties of teaching, acknowledging that becoming a teacher requires his full attention. In addition, Debbie talks about her anxieties and feelings of frustration and inadequacy, yet is able to also recognize that students seem comfortable and that her work appears to be effective. Steve is quick to criticize what he perceives to be his slow growth but, in the process, notes the subtlety of success—that it often comes in small increments. Diane simply begins an analysis of her work in the classroom whereas Miles questions his very presence in the classrooms of students, telling us on one hand that teaching "sucks" and on the other that growth simply did not come as fast as he expected. Finally, Jane tells of her specific effort to identify success in her classroom.

---

[1]   We do not intend to represent this activity as merely a rationalized technical pursuit. Rather, it ought to reflect the long-term, holistic perspective of ongoing professional development.

[2]   We are referring to curriculum designed as a set of rational, technical procedures (see, Eisner, 1985).

Narrative Accounts

As I began to get to know the students in the computer classes, and especially those in the fourth-fifth grade split class, I found that I was better able to communicate, and had more confidence in my capabilities. This must show, as the students seem to know when things are not going as planned. I learned that I need to plan presentations carefully but with enough freedom to use the mood and reactions of the class to my advantage. I think it is important to work with the class, not against them. If the students are in a jumpy mood and are losing interest, something needs to be done to pull them back together. . . . In a particular lesson, when I felt that some students were losing interest, I just had one student read the story and would ask another student if they could hear. At the end of the lesson, I played a song for them on the record player, and they immediately tuned back into the lesson. It is this combination of effective planning along with the ability to read the class and develop quick refocusing activities that I need to work on.

The more I teach, the stronger my self-confidence becomes—which makes me more comfortable. As I become more comfortable, my lessons become smoother, and the students pick up on this. If they enjoy the activity or lesson, they will let me know both by saying they liked it and by showing a further interest in the subject. All this I can store away in my memory and use to strengthen my lessons of the future. By reflecting upon my experiences I find the spots where I need to apply a little more effort and hone the areas in which I feel strong. (John Sill)

When I began student teaching, my list of goals and expectations was not as extensive as it is now. For example, for my first lesson, because I was so nervous, my goal was to simply hold the students' attention for the entire lesson. As the term progresses, however, I find myself becoming more and more critical of my teaching practices. Last week, I taught a math lesson on problem-solving. When the lesson was completed, I realized that I had not modeled thoroughly how to write a math story problem (one of their assignments). Instead, the lesson had focused on how to solve story problems. My means of evaluation did not meet the focus of my lesson. I was very disappointed in myself. In fact, I said to Mrs. Petrosky, "That is something I would have done as a [novice] preservice teacher." After I said this, I realized how much my expectations had grown. (Jane Atman)

As for my third lesson, I really had a blast! I was relaxed. I let the kids "take off." I found myself laughing at what the kids were saying. I felt like one of them. They had me grinning from ear to ear. After the lesson was through, I felt really good. I had a great time. (Amy Schultz)

My weeks have been much better. I really felt like I was in a slump a few weeks ago, although I have taken on much more responsibility and that has probably had a lot to do with how I am feeling about the job I am doing. I think I like to work [by having full responsibility for the day] because I am scared of having to be perfect in just doing a few things each day. I would rather run the whole day and make three good mistakes than run one third of the day and make one mistake. I feel more accomplished after doing the whole day. It seems to be a more realistic indicator of my skill and ability. (Brian Forbes)

In the child-care center the biggest learning experience and my greatest accomplishment surfaced when I gave the kids a lesson using the Language Experience Approach. I went into this lesson telling myself that I have to try to let the children dictate the lesson and that I should allow them to have as much freedom as possible when it came to discussions and rules of conduct (talking, wandering about, and so on). The children decided on a topic for their story. For the prewriting activity, I asked the children to think about the story topic, and when I asked them to simultaneously verbalize what they were thinking, they were very hesitant at first. One child said something that even sounded very restricted and choppy. I kept encouraging them to talk out and continued to do so when a child, who had something to say, raised his hand.

After a few minutes, every child was talking nonstop about the topic and their vocabulary and creativity seemed to increase incredibly. During this time I periodically prompted them to think more deeply about certain issues by asking them questions. At one point, a child started to crawl under the table he was sitting at. I immediately responded by starting to ask him if that was appropriate. I stopped mid-sentence when I realized that he remained on task and was very creative with what he was saying. So, I ended by muttering half under my breath that it was "okay" if it helped him to be creative. Shortly afterward, one girl got up and walked around while continuing to verbalize her thoughts. I also let her be. The fact that I was capable of allowing the children to be something other than those quiet kids I would have pictured in my "perfect classroom," was quite an accomplishment for me. (Eva Sendele)

My student teaching experience was generally not as smooth as I would have liked or as I had imagined it would be. For a number of reasons I found teaching to be much harder than expected. There is much more to developing lesson plans and content than I thought. Perhaps I tried too hard in this respect, trying to find lots of resources other than textbooks. In preparation for teaching history I have a real interest in reading what the historians who were living at the time had to say about a topic, but I simply do not have time to do this before every lesson. I think I will have to spend more time using the textbook as my source. I also have reams of college lecture notes that I can draw from at times. I also found just how much a person can perspire under pressure. I found myself very nervous teaching in front of other teachers and was not only especially nervous teaching in front of my supervisor but also in front of my peers. We had talked so much in seminar about good teachers and bad teachers that I kept thinking about how I was going to be viewed by my peers. The last time I taught there was no one there to observe me except the teacher (and he was busy talking to the aide), and I was not nearly as nervous.

Overall, I feel teaching activities have been much harder than I imagined and much more time-consuming. I find myself emotionally drained at the end of the day, and yet, I continue the process out of the hope that things will improve. (Tony Dehyle)

Lesson planning is still a difficulty. During the first term I spent copious amounts of time worrying, planning, preparing. In the second quarter I deliberately cut back on preparation time but had difficulty pinpointing content and focusing my presentation on those specifics. I felt preparation was a stop and go activity, a somewhat disjointed experience lacking personal satisfaction. Part of this was related to recurring doubts about student enthusiasm, my role as teacher, and taking responsibility for student motivation. My lack of adequate knowledge required extra preparation. These factors were basic flaws in my initial preparation and may have affected student motivation. Also, my lack of knowledge and experience of the particular subject matter inhibited my flexibility in answering questions, sharing personal experiences, throwing out thought-provoking questions, and stimulating deeper interest. I also need to incorporate specific anticipatory sets more often.

Generating quiz and test material was a frustrating experience. Simple quizzes and tests do not motivate students to put forth reasonable study efforts; yet, I am afraid of discouraging students. I have had no experience writing tests and evaluating written work, and I was overly concerned about judging question difficulty and whether the questions were appropriately stimulating and evaluative. Students' initial responses to my inquiry about the test were that the test was easier than they expected and that they thought it was reasonable. The subsequent grades, however, showed a wide range and some very low grades. I thought the quiz and text were very straightforward with relatively simple questions from published materials and lecture. I was afraid of students' reactions after the quiz and test, but there were no specific comments about unfairness and very little reaction at all. Students seemed to take responsibility for the grades they earned.

My personal experience overall was one of anxiety. Before and after class, I really felt apprehensive, uneasy, and overworked. During class—actually teaching, explaining, conducting activities—I did not feel as concerned and flustered. But these deep feelings of frustration and inadequacy, sometimes a feeling of unwillingness to follow through with this course, continue to disturb me. My cooperating teacher's comments have been encouraging. Generally, students' comments have been encouraging and positive when volunteered, and my performance level seems fairly effective and on task despite my lack of confidence. (Debbie Martinez)

I am learning what behaviors to ignore and what behaviors to stop as I get a feel for group dynamics and a sense of the mood of the class. It is hard to explain all that I am learning about kids, class control, and my own emotions and self-confidence, but it does seem to be jelling as things get smoother for me and for them. I also am able to plan a little further ahead. This is something that has long been urged upon me, that is, lessons where students do more for themselves and I am off center stage with less grading and active teaching to do.

I feel like such a slow study when it comes to learning new ways, but I have always been cautious about trying something new. I like to feel secure and well rehearsed before going on to the next phase. Now that I have been through some of the material once I am beginning to sense, but not quite grasp, how I might synthesize it into larger wholes. In the next few months I hope to be a bit more experimental. Yet it will probably be next year before this phase of subject matter growth really takes off. I feel impatient with my tardy growth in this area yet simply too pressed for time to act upon it.

Also, the feeling that my actual teaching is poor is slowly waning. I add on an element piece-by-piece and here and there so that I can say this is what I will cover today and logically lead them through it step-by-step, trying to have a variety of activities each lesson. (Steve Bruno)

Although my student teaching experience has been positive, there were some things with which I had problems. I could have been stricter. I was not consistent with all of my expectations. I was too lenient with my students at times. I probably allowed too much talking while I was talking. I also had some problems leading a good discussion. I found myself answering my own questions. Part of the problem was the rooms I was in. They were difficult to lead a discussion in because the seating arrangements were pretty set—each room was a laboratory. My subject matter was also part of the problem. Much of it was cut and dried; it did not lend itself well to a discussion. Another problem I had was that there were some students I never reached. They were usually absent a lot, and when they came, they did not participate very well. I never resolved the problem of the totally unmotivated student. I guess it is a problem for all teachers. I also had a hard time dealing with students with different ability levels. All of my classes had Grades 9 through 12 students in them. I am sure that some students were not challenged whereas others were overly challenged. For this reason, I used both applied and written evaluation techniques; I am not sure that it took care of the problem though. (Diane Cheins)

Although my cooperating teacher has only glowing accounts of my lesson plans and their enactment, I am still not settled and feel they are just not good enough. I have a responsibility to the kids not to bore them outright while trying to teach them a subject from the textbook (traditionally) that I think is boring. And another problem I have been having is trying to figure out exactly what they have been getting out of all this. I cannot tell. I am very removed from them, it seems, and that sucks. That is not what I am here for, and I know I have to change the rhythm of the class somehow. I have to try to get to their opinions. First, let them speak; let them learn from themselves. I have yet to have two kids talk about the subject matter back and forth in class. God, I feel like such a whiner, but this job is a bitch. There is a lot of pressure. It would be easy just to give up right now and say, "Okay, we are going to do the textbook every day." My cooperating teacher does this and he "takes nothing home with him at night." Looking back on this, it sounds as if I have been in the trenches or something. Truthfully, it has not been that bad; however, the lessons are just not good enough and the kids are not where I or they think they ought to be. (Miles Coleman)

Right now, I find I am having difficulty acknowledging success. In fact, I see most of my teaching as not being very good. For my own mental health, this is going to have to stop. By Thursday of each week, I am so down about my mistakes that I find myself growing very tense. To alleviate this, I have decided to identify at least one good thing that occurs during a lesson. For example, I am having my reading group write a play. Although the students are not behaving wonderfully, they are excited. And, more importantly, they are working together and making group decisions about their play. I heard one student remark, "I'm the skeleton. I don't have a costume." I was about to offer to bring one in for him when one of my students said, "Oh, I have one. You can borrow it." When I heard this, I felt incredibly warm inside. To me, the activity was fairly successful. (Jane Atman)

For Reflection and Discussion

1. John found that getting to know his students improved his ability to communicate with them and to respond to their needs. He noticed a connection between the amount of teaching he did and increased feelings of self-confidence.
   a. What impact did John's increased self-confidence have on his developing practice? How did John's growth in comfort affect his ability to reflect upon his practice?

2. Jane's list of criteria for self-assessment grew as the term progressed. She writes that "I find myself becoming more and more critical of my teaching practices."
   a. How might the frequency of Jane's successful lessons be influenced by her broadened criticism? To what extent are broadened criteria a result of improved practice?

3. Amy writes that she was relaxed when she presented a lesson and just "let the kids 'take off.'" She felt "like one of them" and was "grinning from ear to ear" during the lesson.
   a. What does letting students "take off" say about Amy's professional growth?
   b. To what extent might feeling "like one of them" be an appropriate indicator of Amy's success?

4. Brian feels a greater sense of accomplishment when he teaches for a whole day. He writes, "I am scared of having to be perfect in just doing a few things each day." Added teaching responsibility allowed Brian a "more realistic indicator of my skill and ability," or so he thought.
   a. To what extent does Brian's experience reflect his readiness to teach? How might he have been affected by the premature assignment of greater responsibilities?
   b. How did greater responsibility affect his fear of being perfect? To what extent do you agree with Brian's assessment that a greater "volume" of teaching provides a more realistic indicator of (developing) skill? Why?

5. As Eva used the Language Experience Approach she observed that the students changed as their engagement and creativity increased. She writes that it was an accomplishment for her to be "capable of allowing the children to be something other than those quiet kids I would have pictured in my 'perfect classroom.'"
   a. To what extent might Eva's awareness of her own preconceptions have contributed to her ability to respond positively to students? How might her ability to reflect-in-action indicate growth?

6. Tony found teaching much harder and much more time-consuming than he had imagined. Lesson planning is a challenge because there is not enough time to do all the research. He thinks he may need to rely more upon the textbook. Being observed by others also increased his nervousness; he felt most comfortable when he could teach without such scrutiny.
   a. To what extent might Tony's anxiety be due to the difference between his expectations and the realities of practice?
   b. Does Tony's thinking about using the textbook indicate his professional growth? Why or why not?

7. Developing assessment materials was a frustrating experience for Debbie. She notes that her lack of experience caused her to be overly concerned about evaluating written work. She felt most comfortable when teaching, but deep feelings of frustration and anxiety prevailed.

   a. Was Debbie's self-assessment realistic given the positive feedback she received? How might Debbie have developed self-assessment techniques that were sensitive to her own status as learner? To what extent should self-assessment include consideration of the feedback received from others?

8. Steve writes that it is hard to explain all that he has learned about kids, working in classrooms, his own emotions, and his self-confidence, but notices that things are smoother in the classroom. He exhibits self-awareness about his own learning pace and expresses some impatience with his "tardy growth in this area."

   a. To what extent might Steve's difficulty in explaining what he has learned be due to the context dependent nature of his knowledge?

   b. How might the increasing smoothness of lessons and Steve's ability to plan further ahead have affected his reflections about the pace of his growth? To what extent might his impatience with his own pace be a result of his increased awareness of the demands of teaching?

9. Diane reflects upon the difficulties she encountered. She attributes some of them to the physical space, others to the subject matter, and some to students of varying abilities and poor attendance.

   a. After identifying and sorting problems, what might be Diane's next step?

10. Miles feels critical of his lesson plans despite the cooperating teacher's praise. He feels removed from his students and wants to know what "they have been getting out of all this." He has yet to "have two kids talk about the subject matter back and forth in class" and feels that "the kids are not where I or they think they ought to be."

   a. In what ways might Miles' concerns reflect a successful assessment of items to be addressed?

   b. Has Miles identified for himself the areas of his own growth?

11. Jane writes, "I find I am having difficulty acknowledging success." She decides to address this for her own "mental health" and looks for "at least one good thing that occurs during a lesson."

   a. Is this a productive strategy? Why or why not?

   b. To what do you attribute Jane's difficulty in recognizing success? Why is it important to develop an ability to recognize success?

Links with Research

Experienced teachers know teaching in a way that novice teachers do not. Numerous studies comparing the thinking and action of novice and experienced teachers verify such a position (for example, Fogarty, Wang, & Creek, 1983; Housner & Griffey, 1983; Strahan, 1989). Through years of experience, teachers seem to develop an intuitive or sixth sense that tells them when an approach or situation is or is not working. Hunt (1976) calls this phenomenon the ability to "read and flex." Schön (1983) calls it "reflection-in-action." We also know it as "thinking on one's feet." For beginning teachers, observing the facility with which experienced teachers are able to improvise and modulate their teaching with such confidence and accuracy can sometimes be overwhelming and even discouraging. It looks so much easier than it really is.

Although this phenomenon of "just knowing" lies at the heart of experienced practice, few teachers can articulate the meaning behind it. And, because each teacher's practice is an expression of a personal way of knowing, each teacher has a personal standard or set of criteria to determine the "rightness" of a teaching situation (Cole, 1987, 1989). The development of a personal standard of rightness or success takes time. For beginning teachers, not being able to easily recognize success in the classroom or in their own development is a source of much frustration and confusion.

Ellwein, Graue, and Comfort (1990), as well as Borko, Lalik, and Tomchin (1987), report that student teachers' perceptions of unsuccessful lessons are often couched in terms of classroom management difficulties; whereas successful lessons are characterized as unique aspects of planning and instruction. Ellwein, Graue, and Comfort also noted that elementary preservice teachers were more inclined than secondary preservice teachers to attribute unsuccessful lessons to lack of self-confidence, nervousness, or being in a bad mood; whereas high school preservice teachers more often attributed lack of success to difficult subject matter. An alternative viewpoint is offered by the research of Brandt, Hayden, and Brophy (1975) who assert that preservice teachers tend to take credit for students' successes but not for their failures. Yet another perspective, one exactly contrary, is suggested by both Ames (1975) and Ross, Bierbrauer, and Polly (1974), where preservice teachers take blame for failures and attribute successes to students. These conflicting perspectives perhaps verify the idiosyncratic nature of learning to teach, and acknowledge that many influences play out in satisfactory and unsatisfactory encounters with students and classrooms.

In a case study analysis of four preservice teachers, Strahan (1990) identified three bases upon which the preservice teachers assessed their success in the classroom:

- confirmation of themselves as teachers
- affirmation of their status in their relationships with students
- students' progress in subject matter

McLaughlin (1988) conducted an intensive study of four preservice teachers' methods of self-evaluation and criteria of success. To varying extents, they tended to

- compare their behavior with their own intentions and teaching objectives
- use measured instruments or outside observers' judgments
- rely on feedback from students

The preservice teachers in that study, like most preservice teachers, relied primarily on externally determined criteria or standards. They had few personal standards by which to assess their own performance.

McLaughlin (1988) concludes with a set of recommendations to facilitate the development of skills and habits in, and appropriate attitudes toward, self-evaluation. They include

- providing opportunities for preservice teachers to engage in observation and analysis of classroom interaction
- encouraging the development of classroom routines so that preservice teachers can find out what works and why
- helping student teachers to prepare for uncertainty
- providing opportunities to articulate and challenge their values, beliefs, and educational goals.

Research Activities

1. Many emerging and new teachers find it difficult to acknowledge their successes. Perhaps it is easier to recognize failures or failure-like circumstances in their teaching because they are more obvious. If you botch a lesson *you* usually "really know it." Explore your journal entries, first looking for evidence of successes and, only afterward, looking for difficulties. Read the accounts carefully, paying attention to indications of:
   - experiences that felt good (or when you experienced something that you called "success") or represented difficulties
   - student success and growth (as evidenced, for example, in student workbooks, portfolios, and students' general enthusiasm or responses to you) or student outcomes that did not feel good
   - records of observations by and conversations with cooperating teachers and university supervisors
   - records of conferences, observations, and conversations with peers

   Use the medium of the student teaching or field experience seminars or "debriefings" to engage in discussions that fully explore your feelings about these issues within the context of the experiences of others. Explore the collective experiences of success. of difficulties.

2. Examine students' grades, workbooks, and portfolios. Note their progression and growth over the course of your teaching and working with them.
   a. What are their areas of common strength and success? What part in that may you have had? What are their areas of weakness and less than successful performance? To what extent, if any, do these areas reflect your work as teacher?

3. Look over your journal and other information about your teaching, including student work, and notes from conferences with peers, cooperating teachers, university supervisors, and so on.
   a. What do you see as obvious successes in your teaching? What appear to be the strengths in your teaching? What do others recognize as your strengths?
   b. To what extent, if at all, do your successes match or relate to your acknowledged strengths? How do you and others think you can capitalize on your strengths?
   c. What do you see as the indications of difficulties in your teaching? What do others recognize as being your difficulties? To what extent do these two categories overlap? Where do they overlap? Why? Why not?
   d. How do you and others think you can combat your difficulties?

Failure

You may wonder why we want to talk about the depressing topic of potential failure. We do so because we think it is important for you to understand the full scope of field experience outcomes. In becoming more aware of the ways in which potential failure is recognized, you may be better prepared to foster your own professional development in any direction necessary. Part of this discussion centers on the importance for some individuals to appropriately self-select *out* of programs of professional preparation. If you have strong doubts about continuing to participate in formal teacher preparation seek some professional assistance and counseling to help you sort out some of the issues. Also, explore your feelings in the spirit of inquiry that we have tried to convey and foster throughout the previous chapters of the book. This is simply another opportunity for you to be proactive about the direction of your future career, be it in schools or classrooms, or anywhere else. We urge you not to prolong the agony experienced when there are substantial mismatches between your idealized visions of practice and the realities of day-to-day classroom and school activities, achievements, or your effectiveness. Or, it may be that you experience real discomforts when working with students either because of poor relationships with them or inadequacies evident when dealing with subject matter or the facilitation of learning. If your feelings or experiences fall into any these categories, removing yourself from professional preparation may preserve your energies and integrity. It may also save a great number of students from being subjected to experiences that are at best conciliatory, patronizing, and noneducational (even mis-educational) and at worst dysfunctional and harmful.

A small percentage of preservice teachers fail to get passing grades to ensure either professional certification or graduation from programs of teacher preparation. (Professional certification and graduation from programs of teacher preparation are usually two different matters.) These individuals experience serious difficulties resting in unsatisfactory performance in any one or more of a variety of elements associated with becoming a teacher: contextual matters; professional identity concerns; curriculum and instructional issues; and past performance or personal histories (see *Links with Research* in this section). Such individuals may also be awarded grades considered so low for the field experience component of their program that they are failed by default—school boards and districts usually do not hire individuals with low grades in field experiences and student teaching.

Many teacher educators have "failure stories" to tell about preservice teachers engaging in field experiences. These are tales reminiscent of the "war stories" told by classroom teachers over coffee or lunch in school faculty rooms and cafeterias. Failure stories are usually framed in terms of student teachers who "did not make it." Often, in the stories, the contributing problem is couched in terms of what the preservice teacher could not accomplish in the period of practice. Sometimes, the cooperating teacher is implicated as being a contributing factor. Less frequently is responsibility attached to the teacher education program or field placement by way of, for example, the congruity between preservice teachers and the placement conditions and demands.

Because preparation programs do not usually have mechanisms to handle individuals who experience extreme difficulties and failure, the ultimate responsibility is on you. In the final analysis you are responsible for your professional development. We would expect that, for example, if on reading and interacting with the substance and spirit of this book you found yourself to be severely lacking in particular experiences, knowledge, or understandings, you will seek out mechanisms and experiences to rectify that lack of professional growth. Alternatively, if on the observations and consensus of informed others you do not evidence substantial professional development over the period of the professional preparation program we assume that *you* will take action—that *you* will take the initiative and attempt to propel your professional growth by seeking assistance of whatever kind is necessary. Such a view places preeminence on the notion that teachers' professional growth is idiosyncratic and is a developmental process; that each preservice teacher needs the freedom to progress in various ways at his or her own pace. We believe you have access to the tools, as represented in this book for example, to make such a judgment about yourself.

Failure is defined in the *Compact Edition of the Oxford English Dictionary* (1971) as "the fact of running exhausted or coming short, giving way under trial, . . . failing to effect one's purpose, want of success." Such a definition provides some clues about the usually taboo topic. Working in field placements is typically the first time many preservice teachers are seriously tested as they try on their new roles as nearly full-time teachers in the classroom. As might be expected, some of them come up short. Such individuals often cannot meet the sometimes unrealistic expectations that they and others have placed on them. They are overwhelmed by the intricacies of schools. They are burned by the pace, complexities, and circumstances of classroom life. They are overcome with the prospects and problems of facilitating learning within classrooms renowned to be rowdy.

Some preservice teachers are thrown headfirst into the murky waters of curriculum planning and development without substantial support to buoy them. Under such circumstances there are usually only two options—to sink or to swim. "You've simply got to get in there and do it" is a phrase often heard admonishing preservice teachers to greater heights of performance. Unfortunately, there are still many seasoned practitioners around who believe that, for the optimum development of prospective teachers like yourself, such options are appropriate. We think otherwise. "Leave preservice teachers in the classroom and let them settle the dust" is also frequently heard. These and many other rationales for extremely heavy workloads and experiences without close support and guidance are still often heard in the field. Examine the assumptions underlying these statements carefully and you are likely to find they are not true, especially when measured against the evidence of appropriate research.

For still other prospective teachers, noncompletion of student or practice teaching means they failed to meet their goals, their purpose for being in teacher education programs. Any way it is viewed, such failure is a difficult experience to bear.

> Most of us experience failure at some time in our lives. But usually it is in private and has little consequence. Clearly, the failure of a student teacher is public knowledge. Every pupil in the student teachers' classes knows about it. The cooperating teacher, the principal and the university supervisors know about it, as do peers and family. While student teaching peers may empathize, nonteaching friends and family often ask embarrassing questions and display no knowledge about the difficulties of teaching. To make matters worse, they often believe the adage: "Those who can, do; those who can't, teach (Knowles, 1988, p. 1).

To be labeled a "failure" in the most public sense is damning, embarrassing, humiliating, and potentially destructive, especially to one's sense of self, let alone one's planned professional career. To be sure, we can learn from our failures. Many of *our* most notable successes in the classroom or with individual or groups of children have been a hair's breadth from failure. Failure may only represent one normative viewpoint. And our views or the views of others with evaluative powers may sometimes be completely dichotomous from those views held by a preservice teacher whose circumstances are externally examined and labeled as inappropriate. Despite the trauma attached to the notion of failure, however, under certain conditions new directions and learning can be the creative outcomes of apparently devastating experiences.

Over the years we have had a number of experiences with preservice teachers who hovered in the margins of professional failure. One of those experiences was with Angela, at the time of student teaching, a thirty-eight-year-old, second-career, preservice teacher (see, Knowles, 1988, 1990, 1992; Knowles & Hoefler, 1989). We describe some of the elements of Angela's story as a way of exploring the fine line that separates success from failure.

In some ways the teacher preparation program in which Angela was a part did not adequately provide for her needs as a student of teaching or as one "practicing" the craft and methods of teaching while trying on the roles of "teacher" during the field placement. Although, intellectually, she grasped appropriate teaching methods and principles associated with the facilitation of classroom learning, she was not assigned the most secure and optimal place (in terms of the cooperating teachers or subject matter) in which to practice and develop her newfound skills and theoretical insights into teaching. Angela was assigned a junior high school classroom in which she was frightened—she was intimidated by the tall and large students—and with subject matter responsibilities that, because of evolving state Board of Education requirements, did not fit her academic preparation. In addition, her personality did not easily lend itself to the rigors and demands of teaching because, apart from other things, she found it difficult to assert herself.

Angela eventually maintained that her personal history provided no experiential basis for thinking about teaching and for acting like a teacher. Instead, it provided evidence of patterns of behavior inappropriate for working with large numbers of youngsters in confined classrooms. And, despite the strong theoretical and practical elements of her preparation, and her understanding of them and their relationship with each other, she found it incredibly difficult to modify her behaviors and present a more effective demeanor in the classroom. She was, however, very effective at working with small groups of students, and would do so productively while the majority of class members paid no attention to the assigned tasks of the class period. The faculty or staff of the teacher education program were not able to substantially help rectify her inadequacies and broaden her skills; nor was the program designed to assist or accommodate individuals like her. As a result, and despite innovative planning of individual lessons and units of work, Angela was unable to teach unruly students in ways that encouraged or facilitated group learning.

Those mentoring Angela in the school deemed her practices unsatisfactory for working in junior high school classrooms. In place of a letter grade indicating failure her transcript was simply labeled "Withdrawn from student teaching." Although many details have been omitted from this story, one of the points we wish to make is that attention to problems within field experience contexts must be expedient and to the point. And, knowing where help can be obtained, and when, may be an important thing for preservice teachers to know before they enter into field experiences. What is also significant in Angela's story is that she was "full of pluck," as one professor described her, and she turned a difficult situation into one of hope and bright prospect.

What did Angela do? She worked consistently and determinedly at understanding the dynamics of the immediate context of her placement as well as other contextual influences on her experiences. And she reconceptualized her professional goals:

1. She explored her feelings.
2. She talked with others, especially about the substance of her difficulties.
3. She explored her journal accounts.
4. She analyzed elements of her personal history and extended a formal written account of her experiences.
5. She challenged those who were critical of her.
6. She quietly wept with sympathetic peers, letting go of the anger and frustrations.
7. She raised myriad questions of all those that had been associated with her field experiences, especially her university supervisor.

In the end, she succeeded in developing a different, enlightened orientation to thinking about her role as a professional in education, making important decisions about her suitability of working with younger children and for being involved in the development of curriculum materials. Angela was one of the more resolute preservice teachers we have ever encountered. She was truly intent upon forging her professional development, in the end acknowledging that there were other careers in education for which she was better fitted apart from classroom teaching at the junior high school level.

Thus far we have defined failure as resting in situations in which an individual is either removed from the final field experience or does not pass provisional teacher certification or programmatic requirements for the successful completion of the student or practice teaching component of teacher preparation. Although not necessarily an appropriate term, it also refers to individuals who "counsel themselves out" of programs after recognizing that they are not suitable candidates for their anticipated profession. This latter application is problematic; therefore, we wish to convey the respect we have for individuals who take this often difficult line of action. As we said earlier, if you feel as though you are not suited to the profession, it is better to act on that feeling than inflict your dissatisfaction on children and yourself, no matter for how short or long a period.

Below, Renee, Harold, and Christopher recount elements of their painful experiences in schools and classrooms. Renee verifies the disastrous outcomes of expectations that were unrealistically high. When it became evident that she could not meet these personal goals Renee became paralyzed, eventually dropping out of student teaching. Harold had two opportunities at student teaching and was pulled from both of them by the university supervisor. Being strongly encouraged by family placed a considerable burden upon him. Harold represents many preservice teachers who seem to have questionable motives for becoming a teacher and unclear conceptions about the nature of teaching in the context of a diverse society. Christopher's experience in the field placement was equally devastating. Acknowledging the value of reflection on practice Christopher comes to important decisions about being prepared to teach and, despite failure in student teaching, comes away with the realization that following in a sister's footsteps was not necessarily appropriate.

Narrative Accounts

What I learned was not at all what I had expected. I had thought that I would figure out a way to bring to life all the wonderful theories I had studied. I had aimed to figure out a system for being so organized that the class would always run smoothly. I had aspired to use creative ideas to make every lesson interesting. I was determined to find a way to reach every student. What I actually discovered was that I had set too many high expectations, causing myself to burn out before I really got started. It was an extremely painful yet important lesson for me to learn. I naively plunged into student teaching expecting to accomplish goals that teachers with years of experience are still striving to attain. I was so disillusioned, I viewed not being perfect as failing. I had a lot to learn about my ideals, philosophies, and the realities of teaching. When I began to realize that I could not possibly live up to those expectations, I panicked. I became paralyzed. Something inside of me forced me to believe that it was better to not even attempt to teach rather than to risk teaching poorly. So, I painfully resigned as a student teacher, stifling my lifelong pursuit to become a teacher.

After I discontinued my student teaching, I was graciously given the opportunity to finish out the semester observing other teachers and their student teachers. I quickly noted that none of the teachers seemed to live up to all of the expectations that I had set for myself. I puzzled over why they did not seem to get discouraged or feel guilty about their performances, as I had. I began to wonder if I had been too harsh a self-critic. My observations forced me to reevaluate what was realistic to expect from a teacher. I compared my past performance to that of the student teachers whom I observed. The only significant difference that I noted was that they were not afraid to keep trying. I realized that if I was to ever teach that I would have to learn how to strive to accomplish my goals while simultaneously allowing myself to be satisfied with less than perfect results. (Renee Buscho)

This is very difficult. I have put my energies into becoming a teacher. My wife has been teaching for 15 years, and I've been part of her teaching—well, in all the planning and grading that she does at home. I've even helped her decorate her classroom and prepare for teaching at school. I enjoyed that. When I began to have serious problems with my new boss (the old one left after 9 years) my wife convinced me to do teacher training. I left a relatively secure job. I convinced my parents to provide a little support. My kids have been great (I've not had near as much time to spend with them lately) and have been mindful of my goals. My wife has been really supportive, encouraging me at every turn, especially when the university coursework seemed quite irrelevant to what was going on at the school. (She has even dreamed that we will be able to teach together somewhere.)

After two field placements, I'm in despair. Both have not worked out very well. Because of the major difficulties with Ms. Baird [the first cooperating teacher] I tried to examine what I was about. I still think her methods are not very good. My perspective about classroom management, for example, is better for kids in the long run. (The military stint that I did a long time ago was very good for me. It really taught me the value of strict behavior rules. Actually, I still think there ought to be a place for corporal punishment for kids who really need it.)

My second placement was just as difficult as far as classroom discipline issues were concerned. Bill, the cooperating teacher, was more in line with my thinking, but the kids were very tough. Even so, I managed to handle them. The real difficulty came with my relations with the students. I couldn't get them to do the work. Bill claimed that I didn't prepare well enough and that I needed to put more energies into how I was going to motivate them. I tried a couple of things, but it was very difficult. Kids have got to have more respect for the learning process. After all, learning is for them—not the teacher.

When I was pulled out of my second placement I was very angry at Bill. I'm not sure what he said about me. The other teachers were very sympathetic. The principal was not very understanding, and I think she was the main problem. She would not tell me the names of the parents who complained. I am very angry about this. Yes, I know that according to the cooperating teacher and the supervisor, I had serious problems in the classroom. But, I've invested a lot of money into this retraining and my wife is very angry at the university. She is also angry at me at times, although for the most part she is supportive. I don't know how to explain the situation to my kids. My parents think I've made a complete fool of myself. At this point I'm weighing my options. I don't know what to do. I'm beside myself. Do I insist on yet another placement? (Harold Longworth)

There are only a couple of things I really want to say at this point. I now recognize that there are many things working against my being a successful classroom teacher. I've just realized that, in some explicit ways, I am not suited to teaching small kids. Perhaps I might be better suited to the senior high school grade. I simply don't know at this point. My demeanor is too formal and stern, and although I've tried to change that, it's really off-putting to small kids. However, I simply did not like being around them—I guess they could tell. Kids are so perceptive!

The trauma of my experience could have been avoided if I had taken heed of the indications all along the way. I simply did not listen—or perhaps I was not sensitive to the observations of others. I simply needed a mechanism to help me be open to feedback, criticism, advice, and the more realistic observations of my peers. It's very easy to simply fool yourself that teaching is a career that anyone can do. It's not. I've had a lot of time these past weeks to reconsider my actions. At first I was going to take legal action—I even contacted a lawyer. Then, in a fit of despair and anger, I talked once more with one of the professors. She suggested that I take a considerable block of time to carefully reconsider my experience in the field. Yes, she used that "R" word, reflection. I had thought I had been reflective during the process, but now I don't think I was. I explored my writing (I used a journal to record my feelings about teaching) and was horrified to find myself as a terribly discontented person.

I now think the supervisor did the right thing by me. I only wish the teacher and others around me had really forced (well, perhaps, encouraged) me to be more open and to take the time to engage in serious discussions with me and others about the obvious gaps in my professional development. This has been a very, very, difficult learning experience. I feel like I've been backed up against a wall with a firing squad in front of me. But, the trigger hasn't been pulled—I've got a reprieve. I don't have to follow the footsteps of my older sister. (Christopher Yin)

For Reflection and Discussion

1. Renee resigned as a student teacher due to burnout caused by unrealistically high expectations for her practice. She writes "I had a lot to learn about my ideals, philosophies, and the realities of teaching."
   a. Toward what other aspects of teaching may Renee have held inappropriately high expectations? How might her sense of her own efficacy been influenced by such expectations?
2. Harold thinks about the two student teaching experiences that he was not allowed to finish. He maintains that his approach to teaching is sound, and he is angry because he has made substantial investments in his "retraining."
   a. Were Harold's reasons for becoming a teacher appropriate? How might the inappropriate aspects of his reasoning have influenced his performance?
   b. Should Harold seek yet another student teaching placement? What advice might you offer Harold about this?
3. Christopher attributed his failure in student teaching to a discomfort with "small kids," acknowledging that his personal style might be better suited to older students. He regrets not having taken heed of the indications of trouble and not being more open to feedback and criticism. He wished that others had "forced, (well, perhaps, encouraged) [him] to be more open." For Christopher, the reprieve is that he doesn't have to follow the footsteps of his older sister.
   a. Might Christopher experience greater success with a different age group? Why or why not?
   b. Christopher acknowledged being resistant to the feedback and criticism of others. How, then, might someone have encouraged more openness in his thinking about professional development?
   c. Christopher kept a journal during student teaching but realizes he was not reflective. What are the characteristics of meaningful reflection? Might critical reflection have helped him avoid the trauma of failure?
   d. How might the examination of motives for choosing a career have aided Christopher?

Links with Research

To fail at teaching, especially student or practice teaching, is a confounding experience (Ryan, 1986). Embarrassment and private ridicule, then, can profoundly affect those who fail (Knowles, 1988, 1992). Preservice teachers who fail often exit schools and teacher education programs in a fury, some threatening litigation as they go. Others, passively and embarrassingly, slink out the door, afraid of what their peers and professors think of them, quietly endorsing and encouraging the turning of backs toward the problem. Some remove themselves from programs a hair's breadth before the damning final grade is awarded (Knowles & Sudzina, 1991, 1992; Sudzina & Knowles, 1992).

Institutions have differing views of failure—some implied, others formalized. But, generally, failure in student teaching is not talked about. Although not openly recognized as a regular and consistent outcome of student or practice teaching, failure is assigned by institutions in two main ways: by assigning a low or failing grade or by requiring additional field experiences. Assigning a low or failing grade for student or practice teaching can often seal the fate of a potential new teacher because a low or failing grade is not acceptable for state or provincial certification (Knowles & Sudzina, 1991, 1992). Also, low grades limit job opportunities in tight job markets. Few institutions seem to assign failing grades to preservice teachers for the field components of their course work (Guyton & McIntyre, 1990; Knowles & Sudzina, 1991, 1992; Johnson & Yates, 1982). More often, they require additional student teaching assignments to raise a grade that would otherwise be regarded as "failure" by personnel directors of school districts and others who play central roles in the new teacher hiring process (Knowles & Sudzina, 1991, 1992).

Compared to other areas of teacher education research, there is little work available that focuses on failure in field experiences or student teaching (Guyton & McIntyre, 1990). Nevertheless, within the small body of research that directly addresses failure, numerous factors are cited as contributing to preservice teachers' poor performance in field settings. There are four clusters of factors. One cluster of factors relates to curriculum and instructional matters, and this is the area that has been given greatest attention in the relatively scant research:

- "reality shock" (Gaede, 1978) as experienced when preservice teachers find out what it is "really like" to be in the classroom (Knowles, 1988, 1992; Knowles & Hoefler, 1989; Schwab, 1989)
- lack of programmatic preparation for practice (Schwab, 1989)
- lack of instructional and motivational skills (Johnson & Yates, 1982; Knowles & Hoefler, 1989; Koehler, 1984; Pape & Dickens, 1990)
- inability to implement appropriate classroom management strategies (Johnson & Yates, 1982; Knowles, 1988; Knowles & Hoefler, 1989; Koehler, 1984; Pape & Dickens, 1990)
- inability to select and relate goals to objectives (Pape & Dickens, 1990)
- lack of awareness of available procedures, routines, and alternatives (*Ibid.*)
- problems developing evaluation procedures and setting criteria (*Ibid.*)
- inadequate image of students' characteristics and abilities (Knowles & Hoefler, 1989; Pape & Dickens, 1990)
- discipline problems (Knowles, 1988; Knowles & Hoefler, 1989; Martin, 1988; Pape & Dickens, 1990)

Many, if not most, of these factors are the same ones associated with the problems and difficulties that beginning teachers face (Bullough, 1989; Bullough & Knowles, 1991; Bullough, Knowles & Crow, 1991; Ryan, 1986; Veenman, 1984).

A second group of factors centers on preservice teachers' development of a sense of self as teacher:

- role conflict or the discrepancy between the idealized role and the role demanded by the reality of the teaching situation (Knowles, 1988, 1992; Knowles & Hoefler, 1989; Schwab, 1989)
- role ambiguity associated with little sense of how they want to act or, conversely, how they do not want to act in the classroom (Knowles, 1988, 1992; Knowles & Hoefler, 1989; Schwab, 1989)
- personality traits not conducive to optimal teaching and classroom leadership (Knowles, 1988, 1992; Knowles & Hoefler, 1989; Riner & Jones, 1990)

Like the previous group of factors, these are replicated in the experiences of beginning teachers whose very survival depends on their development of a resilient sense of self (Bullough, Knowles & Crow, 1991; Fuller & Bown, 1975; Knowles, 1992; Ryan, 1986).

Contextual factors make up the third group:

- isolation and lack of collegiality (Schwab, 1989) and inappropriate immediate role models as in the cooperating teacher (Knowles, 1988; Knowles & Hoefler, 1989)
- lack of understanding of the institutional culture as associated with one or a combination of: setting (for example, rural, urban and inner city, or suburban); orientation (public or private); philosophy (traditional or nontraditional, teacher-centered or student-centered); mismatch of grade level placement with preparation; and lack of confidence when dealing with the cognitive and social maturity levels of students (Knowles & Sudzina, 1991, 1992; Sudzina & Knowles, 1993).

Patterns of past performance and elements of personal histories are a fourth cluster of factors that may also contribute to individuals' inabilities to successfully master the expectations of classroom teaching during field placements:

- inconsistent levels of participation and performance in university course work (Pape & Dickens, 1990)
- an unwillingness to ask for help (*Ibid.*)
- a lack of time and resource management and role overload (Goodman, 1987; Pape & Dickens, 1990; Schwab, 1989)
- physical or mental dysfunction (Riner & Jones, 1990)
- previous difficulties in educational settings (Knowles, 1988)

Although failure in field experiences takes many different forms, it represents supervisors' perspectives of the performance of student teachers. As such, it may provide insights into the modes of supervision and the philosophies of supervisors (and cooperating teachers) as much as it does the practices of preservice teachers (Knowles & Skrobola, 1992). Nevertheless, the evidence is stacked against the favor of preservice teachers who do not apply themselves in serious, reflexive ways that demonstrate sensitive responses to students and considerable evidence that they have endeavored to come to understandings about the roles and responsibilities of teachers in the classrooms of schools within a diverse society.

Research Activities

In this section we focus on the extreme possibilities as far as your experiences in the field are concerned, acknowledging that some of you may feel like a failure, withdraw from field experiences and teacher preparation, or be given a failing grade.

1. Consider an exploration of self and others' perceptions of extreme difficulties and failure.
   a. In the context in which you are working, how do you define difficulties? How do you define success and failure? How do others define success and failure? To what extent does failure rest in noncompletion of personal and programmatic goals? How is failure evidenced?
   b. How do others perceive extreme difficulties? failure? success? How are you advised to handle extremely difficult experiences and potential trajectories for failure?
   c. To what extent may some of these notions about practice and performance be dysfunctional or less than helpful?
2. Explore the institutional mechanisms for ensuring that preservice teachers experience success.
   a. What advice do faculty and counselors give to preservice teachers who experience severe difficulties? What is the typical procedure in such cases? What strategies do faculty and others suggest for those who experience severe difficulties? What are the grading policies for dealing with preservice teachers who perform in the margins of acceptable practice or who fail?
3. The chances are some of your peers or teachers in the field placement site will know of someone who was given a failing grade for field experiences or student teaching. Try and locate such a person and explore his or her strategies for reorganizing thinking about the future. Try not to focus on anger or other highly emotional feelings but rather engage in discussion about the root causes, the context of the experience, and the potential actions that could have been taken to rectify inadequacies.
   a. What advice do these individuals have for others in remotely similar circumstances? To what extent is that advice useful? not useful? dysfunctional? How does their situation relate to yours? not relate?
4. Revisit the *Links with Research* section. Perhaps seek out some of the articles to read in their entirety. Talk or write about your responses to this small body of research about failure. Also, respond to particular research reports.

Summary

Within this chapter we have tried to present the full spectrum of preservice teachers' responses to field experiences. It has spanned the range of emotions, understandings, and levels of performance. We began by raising for discussion the recurring theme of complexity, this time in terms of understanding the scope of teaching and the roles of teachers. Moving on to the subject of teaching highs and lows, we presented observations and research that point to the value of acknowledging the swings and changes in teaching. Such feelings are typical of teachers' responses to the complex tasks associated with working with students within the confines of learning communities and classrooms. Through such experiences you are able to get some kind of handle on the degrees of your evolving professional identity and development. Growing from difficult and successful experiences alike is the hallmark of a reflexive teacher. Failure is not always easy to identify. But, when it is acknowledged, it brings with it often heartrending and perplexing feelings. We raised this topic for discussion because it is often not publicly acknowledged; however, by so doing, preservice teachers may be more able to facilitate their ongoing growth, taking what seem to be powerfully adverse circumstances and turning them into beneficial understandings about self.

Chapter 12 is the last in the book. It represents a culmination of our focus on professional development—although, as we have stated repeatedly, such development is an ongoing, negotiated process that will continue to the end of your teaching career and beyond. We see Chapter 12 as the most important chapter in the book; it represents the launching of a new phase of career development. Usually by the time preservice teachers complete their *final* field experiences they are ready to move on to full-time teaching. In preparation for that event we offer in Chapter 12 a set of perspectives that may continue to propel your professional development in productive ways.

Recommended Readings

Bullough, R. V., Jr. (1989). *First year teacher: A case study*. New York: Teachers College Press.

Bullough, R. V., Jr., Knowles, J. G., & Crow, N. A. (1991). *Emerging as a teacher*. London: Routledge, Chapman, & Hall.

Conroy, P. (1972). *The water is wide*. Boston: Houghton Mifflin.

Fletcher, R. (1990). *Walking trees: Teaching teachers in the New York City schools*. Portsmouth, NH: Heinemann.

Freedman S. G. (1990). *Small victories: The real world of a teacher, her students and their high school*. New York: Harper & Row.

Heck, S. F., & Williams, C. R. (1984). *The complex roles of the teacher: An ecological perspective*. New York: Teachers College Press.

Kane, P. R. (Ed.). (1991). *The first year of teaching: Real world stories from America's teachers*. Columbia University: Teachers College.

Ryan, K., Newman, K. K., Mager, G., Applegate, J., Lasley, T., Flora, R., & Johnston, J. (1980). *Biting the apple*. New York: Longman.

Ryan, K. (Ed.). (1970). *Don't smile until Christmas*. Chicago: University of Chicago Press.

Ryan, K. (Ed.). (1992). *The roller coaster year: Essays by and for beginning teachers*. Boston, MA: HarperCollins.

Shulman, J. H., & Colbert, J. A. (1987). *The mentor teacher casebook*. Oregon: ERIC Clearinghouse on Educational Management and Far West Laboratory for Educational Research and Development.

Shulman, J. H., & Colbert, J. A. (1988). *The intern teacher casebook*. Oregon: ERIC Clearinghouse on Educational Management, Far West Laboratory for Educational Research and Development and ERIC Clearinghouse on Teacher Education.

PART IV

Preparing for Future Teaching

This book will have failed to achieve its purpose if it does not kindle in your mind a strong desire to look forward to your future teaching practice. In the previous chapters we have encouraged you to explore the public and private elements of your experience. Part IV represents elements to consider in a complex kaleidoscope of meaning-making derived from prior personal experiences of school contexts and structures, groups and persons, relationships, and particular circumstances. Their order is not intended to convey a universal pathway to becoming a teacher. Rather it represents a pedagogy of field experience—ours. Together, however, the exploration of these elements isx of dubious benefit to your ongoing professional development as a teacher unless you find ways to make sense of them within the framework of future practice.

When hiking in the out-of-doors there is value in looking back on the path taken as a guide for planning the ongoing trek. Despite how you may feel—tired, exhausted, elated, or relieved—as you end the final (or one of many) field experience component of your formal teacher preparation program there may be a hesitancy to look back and take reflexive stock of your experience. But try not to hesitate. Take advantage of the momentum you are likely to have gained. By forging the meanings of those past experiences into the beginnings of a coherent whole you will likely move yourself forward to new heights of professional practice. With this purpose in mind we called the last chapter of the book, *Looking Back and Moving Forward*.

CHAPTER 12

Looking Back and Moving Forward

When you first entered schools for your formal field experiences some months or even years ago, you had in your mind particular conceptions of teachers, students, teaching, and learning. These conceptions were likely formed from long-held pre-conceptions as well as more recently informed notions generated from participation in university course work, adult life and work experiences, and perhaps, parenting. Coupled with these ideas about classrooms and schools you probably had both specific and general expectations for working in field settings as a preservice teacher. And, you went about working in field settings with the aim of achieving your own goals as well as satisfying some or all of the negotiated and unnegotiated expectations of others. Along with all this we invited you to explore your personal history to bring to the forefront of your thinking the origins and basic elements of your understandings about becoming a teacher. Does all this sound familiar? We hope so.

Weeks, months, or years later, after completing what seemed like myriad assignments and activities, you have concluded either the first or a set of field experiences. We assume that either you are ready to move on to more intensive elements of a formal teacher preparation program or you are finished with course work and professional requirements and are readying yourself for entry to schools as a probationary or provisionally certificated teacher (although in some states you may receive full certification).

Envisioning the scope of possible outcomes of working in field placements there are two polarized possibilities with infinite variations in between. One end of a continuum is represented by dramatic changes in your thinking, a total recon-ceptualization of the work and roles of teachers and the processes of learning. The other end is represented by solidified and unchanged perspectives. We cannot imagine how the latter extreme could be so because as individuals we are con-stantly responding to and interacting with stimuli and contexts that surround us and are changed by each interaction. The more likely case is that individuals main-tain some relatively stable perspectives, modified in detail only, and considerably broaden their thinking in other ways.

Then, there are those who see preservice teacher education as a circus event (maybe even a circus), and the only action required is to jump through a series of carefully placed hoops, some large, some small, and some flaming and emitting offensive, black smoke. These preservice teachers are not likely to extend their thinking much. For them, formal teacher preparation is wasted. Given the reciprocal nature of teaching and learning, and the potential for field experiences to be highly interactive and self-directed in the ways we have conceptualized in this book, we have strong objections to the hoop jumpers and performers becoming certificated classroom teachers. Fortunately, those who clear the hoops, unsinged yet unenlightened, are likely to represent a small minority.

In reality, we anticipate that most preservice teachers experience changes in thinking because of field experiences. Whether you have experienced a baptism or trial by fire, or a more developmentally synchronous growth is beside the point. Most important is that some kind of serious questioning of your earlier conceptions has occurred. No doubt you are asking many questions of yourself as you assess your learning and then articulate your position to others. Some of those questions might be

> *What have I figured out about myself as a result of the field experiences? Who am I as teacher now? Am I the same teacher I was before? How have my conceptions of teaching and learning changed? How would others who have witnessed my emerging practice describe how my thinking and practice have evolved? To what extent are my beliefs about teaching and my practices coherent and internally consistent? Can I articulate clearly to others my teaching persona as well as my conceptions of what it means to be a teacher?*

Given the pressures of day-to-day work in formal learning environments you may not have had sufficient time to sit back and take stock of your experiences and even ask, let alone answer, some of these "tough" questions. Reflection on your experiences in this phase of your formal development as a teacher is important because you are getting ready to move on. And, although you will continue to reflect on and analyze your teaching, it is important to bring closure to this period in your development and prepare for the next.

Making sense of your overall experience in the field requires much work on your part. We challenge you to be methodically critical about the state of your preparedness to teach in a way that motivates you to move forward in all aspects of your development. (We use "critical" to mean *careful, not unfavorable,* judgment.) You have begun a lifelong process of self-directed professional growth. Sustenance of this process will require your continued attention. Recollect the experiential learning spiral to which we have frequently made reference (see Figure 1.1).

In this chapter we continue to follow the natural progression of your development by shifting focus back to you. We urge you to consider those things most recently experienced and then move on to discuss preparation for the first year of teaching. We explore two processes:

- looking back on field experiences
- moving forward to the first year of teaching and ongoing professional growth

Looking Back on Field Experiences

You probably have had someone in the field tell you that field experiences are the most useful part of your preparation to become a teacher. We urge you to carefully consider this often repeated statement by questioning the underlying assumptions. The field experience component of teacher preparation programs is only the most valuable part of your development *if* you allow it to be a vehicle to refocus your thinking about becoming a teacher. What do we mean? Recollect Dewey's (1938) notion of the limited value of experience without reflection. Also recall the substance of Part II where we introduced a number of strategies and tools for exploring your developing practice in the field.

At this point, you have accumulated a considerable amount of information about yourself and your experiences:

- stories and journal writings
- lesson and unit plans
- observation notes
- critiques from formal evaluators, observers, and mentors (university supervisors and cooperating teachers)
- peer observation notes and insights from peers
- reflection papers
- professional development records and their summaries
- scholarly and reaction papers, and other assignments
- examples of student work and possibly their reactions to your teaching
- information resulting from exploring questions raised in the various *Research Activities*

Given the demands of working in schools you may not have had much opportunity to explore these materials since they were first produced (although they have surely influenced your development). You can turn to these items as you step back and reflect on your field experience.

Taken together, the documents you have acquired are a valuable source of information about your professional development. Think of them as artifacts of your professional life. Just as artifacts of personal histories and lives (personal belongings, old documents, financial and legal statements, trinket boxes and mementos, photo albums, birth and citizenship certificates and passports, diaries, and the like) tell stories of the past, so too will your documentation about your practice reveal the pathway, even some of the paving stones, of your professional development. In recommending this action we do not mean to infer that meaning-making only occurs at the conclusion of an experience. Obviously it does not. As we interact with the world around us we are constantly attaching meaning to those interactions. Here we are suggesting a process of reflection on collective rather than individual experiences.

Like the students you have taught, and as in your own experiences of learning other things, you have learned a great deal by "doing." (Again, recollect the spiral of experiential learning represented in Figure 1.1.) By engaging in professional practice you have begun to make sense of the theory-practice link. You also have refined, revised, and perhaps discarded some notions about teaching with which you entered the field placement. We urge you to take time to systematically explore and synthesize what you learned from field experiences. To illustrate what we mean, we present an example of how one preservice teacher made sense of her experiences in schools.

Writing served as a vehicle for Kate to respond to the question, "What did you learn about yourself during your field experiences?" As Kate indicates, she developed significant insights into herself and her emerging practice while raising many questions and concerns about general educational issues and particularly about her preparedness to teach.

A Preservice Teacher Looks Back

If someone had asked me a year ago how well I knew myself, my answer would have been smugly complacent. Casting modesty to the winds, I would have replied that, being an intelligent, well-educated, well-adjusted member of the middle class, I possessed the desirable characteristics of such an upbringing: tolerance, fairness, compassion, sensitivity to others, a sense of humor, a thirst for justice and truth, and, on the less desirable side, dull-gray patches of prejudice, a resistance to the suffering of fools, and a tendency toward looking at life through rose-colored glasses. My experiences in three different classrooms have shattered this placid, unattractive self-portrait. I have learned a little about children, more about teaching, and most about myself.

My first and third practice teaching placements were much alike; the children came from a variety of ethnic, socio-economic and educational backgrounds. After the first week, I was forced to face a truth about myself. I had made huge assumptions about education based on my own school years, and based *only* on my own school years. I learned that I had much to learn.

Tolerant? Compassionate? Sensitive to others? Fair? Until I spent time in this room, it would never have occurred to me to mix two colors of paint when the children were painting themselves, nor would I have set out pink, brown, and black shades for construction paper portraits. I had never noticed the plethora of shining white faces and angelic blond hair in my beloved illustrated collections of fairy tales. Fairy tales, actually, are a good example of my cultural awakening. I love fairy tales, and I had read Bruno Bettelheim's theories on the importance of reading such tales to children, how they answer various psychological needs in children and help them cope with fear and a sense of powerlessness. Thinking I was doing an enlightened job, I read fairy tales with the children. I asked them to act out scenes but change the situation so that they could use problem-solving, cooperative skills to resolve conflicts (that is, the ugly duckling confronts his or her tormentors, and asserts his or her right to live in the barnyard along with the other animals).

All very commendable, perhaps, in terms of learning and teaching strategies, but every tale I read was from the British Isles or Western Europe. It took an eight-year-old, a child recently arrived from China, to tell me, "We have that story too," to send me scuttling to the library, my white, Irish-Canadian, Protestant tail between my legs, to pore over fairy tales from Vietnam, the Punjab, Egypt, and Kenya. Sitting in that library in a child-sized rocking chair, I felt ashamed, but I learned. I learned how narrow my viewpoint had been, and I determined to do all I could to broaden it.

As a corollary to this experience, I also learned that I cannot expect all of my students to love and enjoy something simply because I do. My immediate response was to be annoyed, and then I reflected on that feeling. Was I angry because I wanted them to look to me as the authority on what is a good story; should they look to me to tell them what they should like? I realized I was being selfish. I wanted the children to like me, and agreeing with all my choices was an indication that they did. More important, however, is the fact that the children I teach be encouraged to think for themselves, to challenge standards, to question. I have learned that a child who disagrees is doing two things: expressing an independent, not necessarily a defiant, thought; and giving the teacher an opportunity to pursue what the child does like, which in turn is a chance to get to know the student better.

This seems relevant to me because of the broader implications for teachers. Do we welcome—as much of the literature suggests we should—critical, independent thinkers; or do we discourage them as disruptive nuisances? Do we want students who can run a machine, or do we want creative thinkers who can design a computer program that makes both operator and machine obsolete? I hope I have learned to celebrate when a child in my classroom says, "I disagree, and this is why."

Apart from a shock to my belief in my cultural broad-mindedness, I also had to ponder my beliefs about learning. I come from a background where my parents sat down each evening and helped me with my homework, helped me prepare for tests, and read aloud to me constantly. Aside from dyslexics, I believed that people who did not read were fundamentally lazy or had just missed a step along the way. I have learned that my view was ignorant and ill-informed. Children learn in so many ways. Some must hear, some must touch, some respond to phonics, some cannot make head or tail of it. Again, I learned I was extremely intolerant of those who did not learn the way I did. I got frustrated, annoyed—I thought of them, "You just are not trying!" Having witnessed the struggle of so many children just to decode a simple sentence, I have discovered how many other facets of my own learning style I must explore in order to help my students. Again, this has broad implications in the way teachers structure lessons to include the many different styles of learning there will be in each class.

I have learned two very positive things about myself. I have a deep respect for children as individuals, and I do see the world in a hopeful light. I am happy to say that my experiences practice teaching have only reinforced my love of children. Children fascinate me, and I am at my best with them. I try harder in every way. Having seen the casual and "them-and-us" way children are sometimes treated in schools, I have discovered that there is an advocate for children's rights within me. I have noted with bewilderment and disgust how many teachers use a "teacher voice" with kids as though they are a different species who need to be addressed as if they were inherently incapable of comprehension.

There is also a disquieting refusal to allow young children to express any perceived "negative" feelings. It seems adults have decided that childhood should be all lollipops and roses, and little children should not feel or express such things as anger, humiliation, loneliness, fear, or sadness. I was surprised at the horror I felt when an adult said to a child, "Are you in a bad mood? Well, we cannot have that. We must be cheerful. Happy up!" In my classroom, I will ask that child why he or she is in a bad mood, and maybe we will all learn something about coping with our feelings.

Finally, I learned that I am, in university-student parlance, "a keener." It used to be something to hide. I tried hard. I did well, but I did not allow myself to be seen to be trying. Confronted by the apathy, boredom, and sense of futility expressed by so many teachers as they down a coffee in the staff room, I have learned that if that is the alternative, I *want* to be a keener. I think teaching is very much a thing of which to be proud. I also find it exciting. The jaded cynicism I have felt in this [teacher education] faculty and in the schools has taught me that I am a positive, "up" person. I guess I have always known that. It's just that three stints of practice teaching have allowed me to stop hiding and rejoice in my status as a "keener." (Kate Cullen)

However you choose to do it, the task is to clarify, fine-tune, and begin to articulate a set of coherent beliefs and practices that celebrates the diversity of individuals and classrooms, and that seriously and reflexively considers the social, political, structural, and intellectual dimensions of and influences on classrooms and schools. A holistic perspective on your development, the development of students with whom you work, and the contexts in which you work will prepare you to maximize your potential as a teacher and learner. We invite you to listen further as other preservice teachers identify highlights of their learning from field experiences.

Eva, Susan, Terry, and Paulo experienced dramatic reconceptualizations of learning, teaching, and what it means to be a teacher. Paulo also reflects on the process by which his views were challenged and changed, and concludes with a challenge to himself for a career-long commitment to professional growth. Keri came away with a new appreciation for the multidimensional and demanding nature of teaching. Annie reflects on the overall impact of her field experiences on her development as a person—"one of those big 'grow-ups' in life." Besides confirming and extending some of their earlier views on teaching, Leona and Donna consider what they have yet to learn. Recognizing that there is still so much to learn about teaching and education was also a key learning for Kevin and Cynthia.

Narrative Accounts

If, before entering this semester, someone had asked me what I pictured my future classroom to be like, I would have equated "quietness" with learning and with a "good" classroom or "good" teacher. Through my experiences, I have learned otherwise. In three school settings—lunch and recess, class, and Child Care—I noticed that the children were most motivated and creative in their thoughts, words, and actions when they had freedom to converse with peers and to wander about. On the playground, conversations among children were often filled with excitement as they talked about the day, acted out an assignment, thought about a possible game, or invented an activity. When something was suggested or assigned, the children were less motivated and their products showed less effort, creativity, and thought. The same held true in the classroom and in Child Care. When children were given the opportunity to work in groups and come up with their own ideas and process, they were consistently innovative. (Eva Sendele)

My perception of teaching has changed dramatically over the last ten weeks. I started the quarter with the idea that education consisted of the dissemination of information and that a good teacher was one who was able to transmit information effectively. My philosophy of education, for now, is centered on the idea of stimulating and guiding students toward self-development by introducing them to concepts that are useful and meaningful to their lives. Qualities of a successful teacher that I now think are valuable are: being able to bring students and subject matter together in a way that has relevance to students' lives; remaining aware of and responsive to individual students' current levels of cognitive functioning when presenting new concepts; providing students opportunities for discovery; teaching quality rather than quantity whenever the choice is open; and, remaining intellectually approachable to students. (Susan Stewart)

At the beginning of this academic year I had some definite perceptions of what a teacher is or should be. Since that time, my definitions of what constitutes teaching and learning have changed. After being in school for what seems a lifetime, I have been exposed to primarily one teaching style—lecturing; therefore, prior to this year, my idea of education meant a teacher standing in front of the class, speaking for 50 minutes while students vigorously took notes. I remember my professor asking me at the conclusion of time spent in the elementary schools how I enjoyed it. I said, "It was enjoyable, even though I did not do any teaching." He then asked, "Did you interact with any of the students?" I responded, "Yes." He then assured me that I had taught. It was then that I realized that learning takes place, not only through lectures but through group work, observation, role playing, modeling, panel discussions, videos, field trips, and television. Indeed, learning is taking place during every waking hour of every day—perhaps even during sleeping hours as well.

Even though I am aware of various teaching methods, I have a lot of work to do to overcome preconceived ideas surrounding teaching and to develop a creative approach characterized by brainstorming ideas. I will use as many teaching methods as I can, not only to facilitate my students' learning but also to make my time spent as a teacher an enjoyable varied experience. (Terry Ingram)

I came into this program ready to begin teaching the first day. My attitude was: "Let me at them." I am glad for my sake, as well as the students', that I was not allowed to do that. I thought I knew all there was to know about teaching. It was so simple. You just take the book and go chapter by chapter. The course is already made up. Teachers just need to administer it. But then someone told me I could make up my own mind about what was taught and that I could even have a reason for doing it. This was a whole new concept to me. To think that I could have a say in what and how things are taught. There was nobody there to tell me how to do it. That seemed pretty good because I don't like to be told what to do anyway. But, then came the revelation that if nobody told me how to teach, I would have to figure it out for myself. That meant work. I would have to discover why I really wanted to be a teacher. I struggled with that and am still not totally sure of all my reasons. I would also have to decide how I would teach. Then, the barrage started.

Ideas, concepts, methods, and orientations began whizzing through my mind at an incredible rate, or so it seemed. I barely began to understand one concept when another came along. Soon I was enveloped in a cross fire of ricocheting orientations, some opposites, some overlapping. I could not even understand what use it was to study orientations to the curriculum, for example. My range of ideas about the substance of teaching crumbled, and I was forced to look at the orientations more closely to find out what I was even doing in a graduate level program. My first ideas of teaching were selfish—I just wanted a way to make money. The job would be more prestigious than being a construction worker! It would be easy work. Then my eyes began to open.

I went through a lot of changes. I entered the program sort of close-minded. I went from not accepting any ideas, to accepting all the ideas, to having to make a choice. As I deeply contemplated (for the first time) why I wanted to be a teacher, I was bombarded by so many new ideas. All the orientations [to teaching and curriculum that we studied] made sense, and I could see their worth. They were all developed by persons of great knowledge and understanding. Who was I to doubt their validity? But then I began to notice that they tended to conflict with each other and overlap, and I became totally confused and depressed. I had to iron out the contradictions within the different orientations. The faculty helped me work through this difficult time. Talking really helped. As I was better able to sort out what I really thought and felt about teaching I began not to worry so much. A lot of the pressure was taken off.

I learned that it is not enough to make a vague statement about your view of teaching (for example, "I want to be a teacher because I love kids and want to help them"). You must look more deeply into yourself and decide who and what you really are. Then you need to take a stand (leaving room for change and growth to occur). You must begin to make your own decisions based on facts, ideas, and experience. You need to develop a set of beliefs and then stand up for what you believe in so "that henceforth there will be no more children tossed to and fro, and carried about with every wind of doctrine." These ideas are perhaps the ones that affected me the most. I am learning to become more psychologically prepared to teach.

Teaching is more challenging than I thought at first. There are hundreds of ideas, teaching models, and concepts relevant to working in schools and classrooms. I was at first overwhelmed and disappointed. I was expecting to be told what was "right." I thought I would be taught "the best" methods and styles of teaching. Instead, I found a big, new world—expansive, limitless; a place where you never have to stop progressing and can continue to learn, grow, change, and progress. There are millions of ideas from which to pick and choose. It is like a big supermarket of concepts, orientations, tricks of the trade, and secrets to success.

I began to view teaching from a totally different outlook. It is a serious profession, not just a game or a fun job. The challenge is to be always in a state of flux, dissatisfied with the norm and always searching for ways to improve your teaching practice. I have no intention of or excuse for falling into a rut where I will become comfortable, complacent, apathetic, or stagnant. I surely do not know everything. I have a lifetime of learning ahead, and I must always be open to and respectful of the opinions of others. (Paulo Antonios)

I want to make a mathematical analogy about my experience. If all the theories are like points, all the readings are like lines, and the discussions are like planes, then teaching is truly a three dimensional work. It extracts all your wits, courage, knowledge, energy—everything—and tests you to the limit. I wish someone had told me that student teaching is a learning process so that I would have been prepared to accept risks and make mistakes and not feel so guilty when I did. Before student teaching I set certain expectations for myself, and when I did not meet those expectations, I . . . burdened myself with great pressure. I thought about the problem all the time and sometimes woke up in the middle of the night still thinking about students and work. I even began to doubt whether teaching was the right career choice for me. I was so occupied by the work that my family life was disrupted and, consequently, my whole family suffered. The teaching profession is much more demanding and strenuous than I expected. I hope that I will benefit from all the effort I put in and that this experience will ease some of the pain I am likely to have in the future. (Keri Hong)

As I reflect on the events of the past ten weeks I am pretty overwhelmed by what I have learned and experienced. I feel like a totally new person. It seems like an age has passed during this time. I have never been busier in my whole life, and in this space of time, never before has so much happened to me in such diverse ways. As I sit and ponder over these on the eve of the end of it all, I am a little overwhelmed and surprised that I made it through alive and with no major breakdowns. Also, I cannot believe the number of ideas and materials I've sifted through in all of my classes, my placement, and my personal life. I have arrived at another one of those big "grow-ups" in life, and it is interesting to re-establish my values and my philosophy of what I am about as a person. (Annie McGhie)

I came into the teacher education program with an open mind and not many concrete ideas of what teaching is or ought to be. The only part I had firm ideas about was instruction. I never pretended to know much else about teaching. Well, I still have some pretty firm ideas about instruction. I have not found that my ideas were off-base at all. In addition, I can say that I have done some other things that teachers do. I have learned about some of the administrative duties and hang-ups. I have learned how to chat with faculty. I have learned how to deal with a few parents. But that is about all. I cannot yet really say that I know the role of teacher in the public schools. (Leona O'Halloran)

I knew teaching would be hard work. But I thought it would be a little easier than it has turned out to be. I thought that I needed to take classes and practice and, then, I would be ready to go out and teach. I have found that it takes constant introspection and retrospection, in other words, reflection upon what I have learned, what I have done, and what it means for my future as a teacher. I learned not only where my strengths and weaknesses lie, and what I still need to learn but also that one can never really know everything. I found that the process of learning to teach does not end when I am handed my diploma. It ends when I stop teaching, or die, whichever comes first.

I have reaffirmed some of the notions I had at the beginning of the term, especially those referring to the teacher's role and ideal classroom tone. Some of them have been adjusted and filled out, but for the most part, my ideologies are the same. They have simply been subjected to a grand dose of reality for which I am very thankful. I learned to look critically at myself and what I am doing so that I can see what I need to change or learn to be a better professional. I am more polished and clearer about my abilities. As I move on, I will take with me on my journey toward teaching all the wonderful things I have experienced. (Donna Perez)

The conclusion of student teaching is the start of a new frontier. I have learned much, but there is much more to learn. I must continue to learn and grow or I will cease to be an effective teacher. I know some of my weaknesses and limitations, and I will learn of more. I have found some limits, expanded some limits, learned to deal with some, am working on others, and may always have difficulty with a few things no matter how hard I work on them. Whatever I do, I must never forget that I am teaching people, and the reason I am in the classroom is to help students and myself better ourselves. (Kevin Queen)

Working in the school placement has been a challenge. I confronted my previous opinions about schools and my feelings about being in a school. Some of the reality was a shock to me. I am working on reconciling my ideas with my experiences. I have seen that the school is not (and maybe cannot be) what I have imagined it should be. I intend to keep working on these problems. I am studying all the ideas about education that I can. I need to work with and study more the reality of situations. I do not feel as emotional about school as I did at the start.

I am not anywhere near reconciliation to being socialized as a teacher. I do not agree with all the ways of the education system. But I will try to find ways to work around the things I do not like. Before I can fully develop my own ideas, I need to more fully understand the "real world" of education. (Cynthia Hohnke)

For Reflection and Discussion

1. Eva once "equated 'quietness' with learning and with a 'good' classroom or 'good' teacher." She learned from experience with students that motivation and creativity increased with freedom to converse together and that "when something was suggested or assigned . . . products showed less effort, creativity, and thought."
   a. How do the teacher's roles and the tasks associated with each role differ in Eva's early and later notions about teaching?
   b. How might she have recognized the dampening effect on student participation inherent in her initial view?

2. Susan's perception of teaching "has changed dramatically." She initially regarded a good teacher as one who could "transmit information effectively." Later she discarded this notion in favor of one that emphasized students' self-development, discovery, and the relevance of subject matter to students' lives.

   a. Who was of primary consideration in Susan's first view? second view? What might have contributed to the evolution of her view?

   b. What new aspects of teaching was Susan able to consider because of her experience?

3. Terry's definition of teaching and learning changed from the formal lecture format experienced as a student to include a variety of interactions and experiences. He realized that he has a lot of work to do to overcome his preconceived ideas about teaching.

   a. How did conversation about his experience in the classroom facilitate the expansion of his ideas about teaching?

   b. How might Terry begin the work of challenging his preconceived ideas of teaching?

4. Paulo recalls that he "went through a lot of changes" learning about teaching. He began the program "sort of close-minded" and then became increasingly selective about accepting ideas presented. He asserts that "the challenge is to be always in a state of flux, dissatisfied with the norm and always searching for ways to improve your teaching practice."

   a. To what extent does Paulo's challenge represent a willingness to continue to undergo "a lot of changes?"

   b. To what extent is a "state of flux" sustainable? How might students respond to a teacher who is "always searching for ways to improve?"

5. Keri "burdened" herself in order to meet her own expectations. She wished someone had told her that student teaching was a learning process so that she was prepared "to accept risks and make mistakes and not feel guilty" when she did.

   a. How might Keri benefit from this realization as she begins teaching? To what extent should Keri regard inservice teaching as a learning experience?

6. Because of her intense learning experience Annie feels "like a totally new person." She describes it as "another one of those big 'grow-ups' in life" that allows an opportunity to reestablish her values and philosophy of what she is about as a person.

   a. Why might it be important for Annie to integrate her notions of teaching and learning with her own personal values and philosophy?

7. Having entered the teacher preparation program with an open mind, Leona recognizes that she has gained some experience in performing teachers' tasks. She concludes that "I cannot really say that I know the role of teacher in the public schools."

   a. How might Leona gain further understandings of the role of teacher?

8. Donna's notions about teaching were "subjected to a grand dose of reality." Experience in classrooms reaffirmed some of her notions and allowed her to adjust others. She also learned that "one can never really know everything" and that the learning process will end "when I stop teaching, or die, whichever comes first."

   a. To what extent might Donna's acceptance of herself as a lifelong learner contribute to her sense of self-confidence?

9. Kevin writes, "I must continue to learn and grow or I will cease to be an effective teacher. I know some of my weaknesses and limitations, and I will learn of others."

a. How might Kevin's acceptance of his own role as learner affect his emerging practice as a classroom teacher? In what ways might his perspective influence the stress level associated with first-year teaching?

10. Cynthia found working in the school to be a challenge. "The reality was a shock" that prompted her to begin "working on reconciling my ideas with my experiences." She feels a need to "more fully understand the 'real world' of education" so that she can develop her own ideas.

a. To what extent might Cynthia's response to "reality shock" be a useful one?

b. To what extent might Cynthia's study of the "real world" of education contribute to her socialization?

c. Because Cynthia is "not anywhere near being reconciled to being socialized as a teacher," what is her view of socialization? To what extent does socialization include becoming a member of the learning community? What does your view of socialization include?

Links with Research

There has been a gradual but substantial shift in recent years toward experiential or field-centered teacher preparation based on various interpretations of "reflective inquiry." Increasingly, emphasis is placed on the importance of attending to preservice teachers' personal understandings and on the contexts in which teaching and learning take place. Program reform in colleges and faculties of education throughout North America is illustrative of efforts to bridge the gap between campus and classroom. Teacher education reform efforts suggest a reconceptualization and restructuring of teacher education to better reflect the developmental nature of becoming a teacher, to more fully acknowledge the complexity and individuality of teaching practice, and to honor teaching as a profession (Bowman, 1991; Fullan & Connelly, 1987; Holmes Group, 1986).

Unfortunately, most efforts to bring about change are located either in schools of education *or* in the field (school-university partnership programs are an exception). Consequently, they lack intended continuity and coherence. For example, teachers leaving preservice programs that have been restructured to promote career-long inquiry and growth may begin teaching in schools that do not support and facilitate such practice, a situation that can be confusing and detrimental to new teachers (Bullough, Knowles, & Crow, 1991; Cole, 1990a; Zeichner & Liston, 1987).

The literature on beginning teacher development is filled with case studies and descriptions of beginning teachers' attempts to deal with the realities of classrooms and schools (Bullough, 1989; Bullough, Knowles, & Crow, 1991; Hoy & Rees, 1977; Lacey, 1977; Ryan, 1970, 1992; Ryan et al., 1980; Thiessen, 1991). The common thread running through studies and accounts that depict the traumatic nature of many beginning teachers' experiences is lack of ongoing assistance and support in the school. Even those who graduate from inquiry-based preservice programs, pedagogically and psychologically prepared to assume teaching responsibilities, experience difficulty when placed in school settings not conducive to their growth and development. Reality shock often zaps new teachers' enthusiasm and energy prompting them to change their "ideals" for "reals"; many decide to reconsider their career choice altogether (Bowman, 1991; Estes, Stansbury, & Long, 1990; Schlechty & Vance, 1983).

In one study (Cole, 1990a), four teachers who left their preservice program with clearly articulated personal theories of teaching and high ideals and aspirations had different experiences in their first year. One teacher was welcomed into a supportive environment compatible with her own philosophy of teaching—where she was given a realistic class assignment, where she felt sufficiently comfortable and confident to grow professionally, and where she was able to put into practice her beliefs and ideals. The other three experienced varying degrees of difficulty, frustration, disappointment, and success—all a function of the context in which they worked. In the beginning, they all tried to modify their situations to reflect their beliefs, a task which proved more difficult for some than others. With considerable effort, one teacher was able to approximate her image of teaching; another finally decided to become "more realistic" and conform to a style of teaching more compatible with her context than with her preference; and the third put in an exacting year, leaving at the end for a new start in another school.

Similarly, in other in-depth studies of first-year teachers who experienced a difficult first year (Bullough, 1989; Bullough & Knowles, 1990; Bullough, Knowles, & Crow, 1989, 1991; Thiessen, 1991), the workplace context was the identifying factor that made the difference between a survival or growth orientation to teaching. Fortunately, in the past few years, school systems have evidenced a surge of interest in the development of induction and support programs for new teachers (Ashton, 1992; Brooks, 1987; Burden, 1990; McNay & Cole, 1989; Cole & Watson, 1991a, 1991b, in press; Deal & Chatman, 1989; Griffin & Millies, 1987; Huling-Austin, Odell, Ishler, Kay, & Edelfelt, 1989).

In some cases, new teacher induction programs are primarily intended to socialize new teachers to the existing status quo culture of schools, systems, and the profession. In other cases, they are designed to "fill in the spaces or blanks" left by preservice programs, that is, to do what the preservice program "should have but did not do." Other schools and systems, though, are developing programs that express broader conceptions of instructional improvement and teacher development. In these cases, administrators and teachers are attentive to such things as class assignments and workloads, and to the technical, practical, psychosocial, and pedagogical needs and concerns of first-year teachers within the context of long-range teacher development and overall school improvement (Colbert & Wolff, 1992; Cole, 1991a, 1991b; Innes, 1991; Wildman, Magliaro, Niles, & Niles, 1992). As these studies show, welcoming teachers into supportive communities and facilitating their professional growth in a variety of ways has far-reaching benefits.

Research Activities

1. Sometimes the extent and complexity of your experiences in various field settings may feel overwhelming, especially as you reflect on all the various nuances of your learning and teaching. The chances are that you have had experiences that were contradictory and confusing as well as ones that were productive and beneficial to your professional development. Use the framework of the professional development summaries in Chapter 2 to explore your experiences and develop a statement similar to Kate's. Such a state-

ment will serve an important function at the time of formal interviews for teaching positions because it will reveal the essence of your professional identity and philosophy of teaching. It may even be a part of a professional portfolio.[1] Think about your learning over the course of field experiences. Like Kate, respond to the broad question:

What have you learned about yourself because of your field experiences? What are the major questions in your mind at this point in your career?

2. Using your professional development summaries to extend your thinking into future action may also be productive. This activity represents yet another way to pull together some of your learnings and professional development needs. Develop an extensive list identifying areas in which you have grown over the duration of the preparation program. Make a separate list of areas you want to learn about or pay attention to. Be as specific as you feel you need to be. Now make a list of your strengths and a separate list of areas that need further development. You now have two sets of parallel lists. Superimpose them on each other. What does this process reveal about your growth and development, the gaps in your development, and future self-directed professional development activities? Try placing the elements in order of priority for immediate, short-term, and long-term attention.

3. In the early chapters of this book (specifically Chapter 2) we encouraged you to write a personal history statement that explored elements of your experiences and thinking coming into formal preservice teacher education. Now is a potentially useful time to reacquaint yourself with that account. Also, dig out other personal documents that reveal your early thinking about being a teacher. Explore these documents—artifacts of your emerging practice—in some detail, noting areas, beliefs, or practices that have been challenged and reconceptualized because of the field experiences and intellectual activities associated with university course work. In preparation, consider reading "Shaping Pedagogies Through Personal Histories in Preservice Teacher Education" (Knowles & Holt-Reynolds, 1991) and relevant sections of *Writing to Grow* (Holly, 1989).

   a. What are the areas in which you have changed your thinking? Are you able to coherently and succinctly state your reconceptualizations? What areas or issues did you not change? What were the circumstances of change or that which promoted stability of thinking?

   b. What were the roles of particular individuals or relationships in the forming of your reconceptualizations?

4. Group discussions about the ways you and your peers have reconceptualized your thinking about teaching may be especially helpful. Having formally stated your reconceptions share with others these changes in your thinking and the experiences that promoted the changes.

   a. What are some of the common and major reconceptualizations you and your peers have made? Why?

   b. In what ways have others helped you form and eventually state your reconceptions? To what extent are reconceptions a shared outcome?

---

[1] For a sense of the potential place of portfolio usage for teachers, see Haertel, 1991; Bird, 1990; and Delandshere and Petrosky, 1992.

Moving Toward the First Year of Teaching and Ongoing Professional Growth

You are likely to experience a range of emotions as you leave behind the periods of field experience and prepare to teach either full- or part-time. Or, legitimately, you might decide to leave the notion of being a teacher behind you. Maybe you have decided to take a break and come back to teaching at a later point in your life. Whatever your course of action we hope that you will take with you many of the professional development tools and strategies that we have presented for consideration.

"Do you feel ready to teach full-time?" may well be one of the questions a principal asks as you interview for or inquire about a teaching position. Your answer is likely to express the joys found in teaching and working with students and a healthy optimism, as well as a hint of uncertainty. We wish to explore that uncertainty for a moment.

The traditions of the Maori people of Aotearoa New Zealand tell of a dead person's spirit journeying over hill and mountain to a place called Te Reinga (translated, the "Place of Leaping"), a windswept, rugged, tree- and brush-studded cliff at the northern-most tip of the country. There, the spirit leaps off, diving into the sea to a new beginning, a sea journey to the distant spirit world. The notion of a place of leaping, fits with our view of the transition from *preservice* teacher preparation and development to *inservice* professional development. Although we view teacher development as a continuing process, your move from the university to the field (this time as a provisionally certificated teacher), will be a sometimes difficult period of personal and professional transition.

For many, the first few weeks, months, and even years of life as a teacher are fraught with personal and professional trials. The move from campus to classroom often marks the beginning of a new period in teachers' personal as well as professional lives. It is a hectic time for those attempting to deal with myriad changes. Eagerness, excitement, apprehension, and uncertainty are but a few of the feelings new teachers experience as they anticipate their first teaching job. As you think about moving away from the safety and close support of peers and teacher educators to establish credibility in a particular learning community, be it formal school or another context, there are likely to be many questions on your mind. Some of these questions will be ones you have pondered for some time and for which you have partial or full answers; others will be new concerns:

- What level do I want to teach? Where do I want to teach? Where should I apply? How do I present myself in a resume?
- Will I get an opportunity to interview for a position? How should I present myself in person as "Teacher"? How do I go about interviewing the interviewers about the elements of the position and the learning community? Will I get a teaching position, and where?
- What kind of learning community best suits me? How will I know whether the learning community provides optimum contexts and opportunities for professional development?

- What is the philosophy of the school (or other learning community), and how does it play out in teachers' practice? What are the enduring problems and concerns of the learning community? For what is the school renowned? How do the faculty and staff get along?
- What are the classrooms like? What are the pupils like? What academic and other support is available to students and teachers? Is there a range of support services for students, and what are they? How do parents and the community interact with the learning community?
- Will there be other newcomers? How are newcomers regarded? To what extent are beginning teachers supported? Is there a formal induction program? Or, are there informal mechanisms for facilitating new teachers' development?
- Do I get a say in the formation of my teaching assignment? Is consideration given to my status as a first-year teacher? What is the principal's or director's view of first-year teachers and the process of becoming a full-fledged professional? What do other teachers think about professional development and the induction of new teachers into the learning community?
- How are new teachers evaluated, and what is the driving force or purpose of that evaluation? Who evaluates new teachers, and how?
- How is the school governed? What role do the faculty, staff, and students have in the governance structure? What are the expectations of the community for new teachers?

At this point, many of the preceding questions may seem premature. We pose them here to raise awareness of some key issues that need to be taken into account as you make decisions about work placement. As you have undoubtedly realized, most of the questions draw your attention to various aspects of the workplace context. We cannot stress enough how important it is to be mindful of contextual issues and we urge you, if at all possible, to make decisions heavily based on contextual factors. As we have indicated in the previous *Links with Research* section and elsewhere (see, for example, Chapter 7, *Links with Research* on *Developing New Understandings of the School*), the quality of beginning teachers' experiences in their first year of teaching is largely a function of the kind of context in which they work. Being in a supportive, facilitative environment can mean the difference between opting out of teaching, mere coping and survival, and professional growth.

Ideally, you will be hired sufficiently in advance of the beginning of school to have time to become oriented to your new setting and to do some initial preparation. We say "ideally" because most often new teachers receive last minute notification of employment and are catapulted into a new situation with no time for personal or professional preparation. It has been said that teaching is the only profession in which beginners are thrown into the profession with little or no formalized orientation and support but with expectations to perform on par with their experienced colleagues. The Darwinian "sink or swim" attitude has unfortunately prevailed in the teaching profession; little wonder that many new teachers decide to leave teaching in the early years.

On a more optimistic note, however, support for beginning teachers (similar to elements of the support Ruth describes in the following narrative) is becoming more commonplace. It is entirely legitimate, appropriate, and advisable, therefore, to inquire of your potential employers about the provision of such support. Also, because of your inquiry orientation to field experiences, your level of understanding of what it means to be a teacher, and your familiarity with the complexity of educational contexts, you are better prepared than many for what awaits you. You also have a clear idea of what you need to be thinking about to prepare for your first full-time position. You will undoubtedly recognize yourself in some of the accounts that follow.

Having completed her field experiences, Colleen still feels "pretty raw," especially when she thinks about the tremendous responsibility she is about to assume and the implicit trust children have in their teachers. Jodi is convinced of the importance of attention to work context, particularly of finding a setting consonant with her own views on teaching and education. She also articulates a commitment to reflective practice and continuing professional growth. In a similar vein, Colleen thinks about how she might continue to facilitate her professional growth. Dee Dee, also committed to continuing professional development, values experiential learning. Ellen, confident in her commitment to teaching, realizes that she needs to concentrate on job seeking skills.

Jane is uncertain about her readiness to be a full-time teacher. She decides to acquire additional experience as a substitute teacher and recounts some advantages and disadvantages of substitute teaching. It is important to note that, like being a student teacher, there is a big difference between teaching for a short time in someone else's classroom and being fully responsible for your own. Also, recall the distinction between teaching and being a teacher. As a substitute teacher you typically will have little opportunity to further your experience beyond the classroom unless you adopt the kind of inquiry approach you took to the field experience settings. If so, being a substitute teacher may provide you with interesting opportunities to further your insight into life in schools. Nevertheless, being a substitute teacher has certain disadvantages. Among them is the tendency to think short-term in planning and preparation, and in dealing with issues of student behavior and facilitation of student learning.

In the final narrative, Ruth gives careful thought to preparing for her first teaching job. She is excited that she is "finally going to be a teacher!"

Narrative Accounts

The response of the second-grade students to my first tries at teaching were positive and rewarding. The affection and trust that they so willingly gave me has rekindled my desire to be the best that I can be. It also caused some doubts to surface. I wonder how long I will wonder if I have the right stuff to be a teacher. How will I know? I once thought that a person should possess certain raw ingredients before attempting to become a teacher. I am not so sure about the ingredients, but I feel pretty raw. (Colleen Presswood)

I found through my observations that the attitude and personality of a teacher are the keys to the success of a classroom. It is essential that the teacher is able to create an atmosphere in the room that is conducive to learning. In order to develop into such a teacher, I believe first, that it is important for me to be open to learning continually. I must not only continue to learn about teaching methods and content matter but also persist in learning about children. In addition, I have observed the danger in being too proud and see the importance of being humble enough to ask questions and to accept correction and advice.

Second, I have recognized the importance of continually reflecting on what I am doing as a teacher. I must ask myself questions such as: Are my methods working? How are they affecting the children? What is my attitude toward the children? Am I allowing them to be individuals? Am I making the information relevant to their lives? As I do this, I hope to avoid developing ineffective or harmful teaching practices. Without such reflection, I have already discovered that I can quite easily do things in practice that I disagree with in theory.

Through my experience I have also become aware of qualities that I would look for when choosing a school in which to teach. Many of these qualities I observed at John F. Kennedy Open School. Perhaps most importantly, I would seek out a school that is child-centered and makes learning relevant to its students. The next important component would be the school's willingness to accept change and to adjust according to students' and teachers' needs. I would want the freedom to try new approaches in the classroom and not have to strictly adhere to a defined curriculum. A third characteristic that I would look for in a school would be good communication and unity among the staff. I would want to know that we were working toward the same goal, that of providing effective education for the students. (Jodi Johnson)

Working with my cooperating teacher helped me to realize the difficulty of balancing immediate classroom needs with personal and professional development needs. I wonder how I will be able to do it. I have a tentative list of periodical titles that I would like to subscribe to—but that's not adequate. Taking additional college courses might be a partial solution. Reading about the experiences of other teachers would be a good first step. Talking with experienced teachers who are willing to share would be even better. Opportunities to observe in others' classrooms would be a great help. (Colleen Presswood)

What am I doing at this point in my life? Not much. I am unemployed. Schools around the metropolitan area have started or will begin soon. This fact makes me a bit bothered because I would much rather be in a classroom growing into a better teacher day by day than sitting at home trying to think of ways to amuse myself. If I do not find something that approximates teaching pretty soon, I will consider this year a great loss. I need to teach so that I can learn. (Dee Dee Edwards)

With the quarter drawing to a close we are much closer to getting paid positions where we can [exhibit our acquired] skills and understandings. But, getting a job is in itself a skill. Time spent on the rudiments of resumes, curriculum vitae, and cover letters reminds us and provides us the opportunity to practice our job acquiring procedures. I've been offered jobs in the past, and I somehow assumed that teaching would be the same. I was offered the job at Southside, but I do not want an inner-city position far from my family. How will anyone in rural Fiji, my private utopia, even know about me? I realized I had better pay attention to the skills of job seeking. I have always equated teachers with the ones I had as a young student. It worried me that my liberal attitudes and criticisms of the school system would jeopardize me. But I am finding out that educators today tend to be of my age and orientation.

There are many educators and professors who have the same concerns I do over equality and opportunity in the classroom. I have encountered attitudes throughout the program that make me feel more comfortable about really getting a job and being in the milieu. In writing a statement of my philosophy and orientation I encountered the problem of telling my deep convictions—as opposed to telling what I think others want to hear. Through the last several university courses I am gaining an appreciation for the similarities in what we all want for the schools. I feel less like a reformer and challenger, and more like a willing member of a profession. I have realized that most teachers care a great deal about their students and their profession. The result of realizing that many others share my sentiments gives me the drive to express myself honestly and hope that my resume finds a receptive audience. It remains for me to get an active file in the placement center and scout the areas where I would like to live. I am quite confident that finding a job is only a matter of applying what we have learned. It is an exciting prospect to be able to market myself and make a move into the profession. (Ellen Findlay)

Well, according to the university and the state, I am now qualified to teach kindergarten through eighth grade. The prospect of teaching my own class is exciting and yet frightening. I need additional experiences with the different grades. Because of this and monetary demands, I have decided to be a substitute teacher for one semester. I want to outline what I hope to gain from this experience, and what I fear might happen.

Substitute teaching will give me the opportunity to teach many children of various ages, academic strengths, and weaknesses. It will also allow me to investigate how different teachers have set up their rooms and routines. It will allow me to fine-tune classroom management techniques. It is an exciting challenge for me to walk into a classroom on very short notice and do my best job of teaching. Along with this excitement, however, there is some trepidation on my part.

With the short notice that I will likely receive, I will not be given adequate planning time. I believe extensive planning is crucial to good teaching. My fear is that "winging it" will become a habit that will affect my future teaching career. Another fear is that I will excuse poor teaching techniques because, after all, "I'm just their substitute." I must constantly remind myself that any amount of poor teaching will affect the students.

I have already taken several steps to avoid the pitfalls of substitute teaching. For example, my briefcase is filled with educational activities for different age levels. If there are inadequate lesson plans left for me, these will help me [maintain continuity] of the students' education. But, I will need to think on my feet. Also, I have made a point of arriving an hour early to school when I am given enough notification. This extra time, not required by the school district, allows me to plan lessons and strategies. Lastly, I intend to keep a journal of each teaching experience—noting productive and nonproductive teaching techniques that I utilized during the day. This will allow me to keep tabs on my development. I think the best thing I can do, however, is to treat each student as a respected citizen who deserves my best no matter what. I am not just a baby-sitter passing out dittos. I am a professional hired to encourage the mental, physical, and emotional growth of children. . . .

I thought I would devote part of this journal account to overall impressions of my first few days of substitute teaching. I have "subbed" four times in four different schools, grades ranging from first through third. So far, I am surprised at my ability to relax in each classroom. Once the children file in, I introduce myself and lead classes effectively and with relatively few problems. It is interesting because the students treat me as a teacher. Also, the staff in the buildings are very supportive. Whenever I am on recess duty or in the office, I make it a point to introduce myself. In turn, people seem concerned about how I am doing.

What is most shocking for me is the variation among the schools. Although they are all elementary schools, they are surprisingly different. I assumed that the schools would be similar to the school where I did my student teaching. That school was not a community. In fact, the architecture of the building (it is arranged in interlocking octagons) supports the cliquish behavior that occurs there. I was pleased when I visited other schools and realized that creating and supporting a warm, professional community is possible. I witnessed people sharing ideas, team teaching, and demonstrating general politeness and concern for one another. I realized that, for me, a school's atmosphere is extremely important. It is something I will definitely investigate when I am job hunting. (Jane Atman)

Today, May 10, I received an offer to teach third grade from a small rural school district twenty miles northwest of home. I resisted the urge to jump at the offer and have scheduled a meeting with the principal on Monday the 14th. . . .

Today, Monday the 14th, I met the staff. I was really nervous, but they all seemed so friendly that the nervous feeling did not last. The principal was extremely helpful. She gave me the curriculum guide and . . . said, "This is what you must teach—how and in what order is up to you." I thought, "This is great—some freedom." But then I had a sudden sense of not knowing where to begin. The principal seemed to note my apprehension. She said she would introduce me to the other third grade teacher, who has agreed to be my "Guardian Angel." (This Guardian Angel program is to help teachers who are teaching a grade for the first time. I met my "GA" and observed her class.)

I decided to take the job, and the other third grade teacher and I planned to meet in three weeks to talk more. In the meantime, she gave me her phone number in case I have any questions that cannot wait. I am going to look over the curriculum guide and books before our next meeting. I am so glad I found a job before the summer starts. I now have a chance to prepare myself and my room, and plan for the coming year. I have already decided to work only part-time during the summer as a waitress so I will have time to get ready for the fall. . . .

The principal showed me the room in which I will teach. I will probably have 27 students. That means I can tentatively plan my room. Two weeks before school starts I am ready. My room is arranged, my first two weeks' lessons are planned (with moderate thoroughness), the first term's curriculum is roughly laid out, the bulletin boards are up, the classroom rules are tentatively laid out, and I have devised a provisional incentive plan. Now that I am ready, I am going on vacation for a week and a half. I am very excited to get started and finally feel capable. I hope to relax while I am on vacation and not to think too much about the coming year. I know I have done all I can to prepare, and I am ready. I also know unexpected things will come up, and I will deal with them the best I can.

I have a job, and I am finally going to be a teacher! (Ruth Lauer)

For Reflection and Discussion

1. The affectionate and trusting response of the students to Colleen's first teaching attempts provided inspiration as well as intimidation. She wonders if she has the "right stuff" to be a teacher and who will tell her if she does not.
   a. Why might evidence of trust from young students cause Colleen to question herself?
   b. To what extent might securing the trust of students indicate having "the right stuff?" What else might be indicated by students' easy acceptance of authority from an adult?

2. Jodi has established sets of criteria to evaluate the qualities of her own developing practice and the qualities she seeks in choosing the school in which she will teach.
   a. How useful might it be for Jodi to establish explicit criteria for choosing the school in which she will teach?
   b. To what extent do Jodi's needs mesh with the criteria she established for choosing the school in which she will work?

3. Colleen, in her second account, is concerned about balancing the need for professional growth with the daily demands of working in the classroom. She has identified several things that might help her do this.
   a. To what extent might it be useful to include planning for professional growth with plans for first-year teaching? What other ideas can you add to Colleen's list?

4. Dee Dee is a "bit bothered" because she is unemployed and schools are starting to open for the new school year. She writes that "I need to teach so that I can learn."
   a. What effect might a break before practice have upon Dee Dee's development as a teacher?
   b. What alternative ways might Dee Dee meet her need to teach?

5. Ellen recognizes that securing a teaching position requires skill. She worries that her liberal attitudes might jeopardize job opportunities. She also encounters the problem of expressing her "deep convictions" or "telling what I think others want to hear" when writing a personal philosophy statement. She decides to express herself honestly and hope that her resume finds a receptive audience.
   a. Do you agree with Ellen's decision? Why or why not?

6. Jane decided to be a substitute teacher in order to gain experience with different grades and to ease monetary demands. She thinks about the advantages and disadvantages of the position and prepares a briefcase full of educational activities. She learned something about the differences between schools that she will "definitely investigate when . . . job hunting."
   a. How might Jane explore schools as a potential staff member?
   b. What are some other advantages and disadvantages of being a substitute teacher?

7. Ruth "resisted the urge to jump at the offer" of a teaching position and met with the principal first. She was both pleased and apprehensive when the principal offered her the curriculum guide with "this is what you must teach—how and in what order is up to you." Her apprehension was eased when she met her "Guardian Angel," a same grade teacher who agreed to "help teachers who are teaching a grade for the first time."

   a. To what extent is the freedom presented to Ruth unusual? to be expected? What are your expectations about this aspect of beginning to teach?

   b. What effect might the Guardian Angel have upon Ruth's first year of teaching?

   c. Why might a mentor be called a Guardian Angel? What does this title imply about the kind of guidance that might be offered? What does the term imply about the context that the beginning teacher is entering? What might the title "Guardian Angel" imply about administrators' regard of teachers' professionalism?

Links with Research

It's stressful in the beginning. You're new and it takes time to settle. But once you start to settle in and become more comfortable and once you get to know people and team up with people you have things in common with, [sharing ideas and supporting one another] become just a natural way of doing things (Cole & Knowles, 1992, p. 10).

If I could give anyone advice in their first year of teaching it would be to find someone you know you can go to for answers that you know you'll be able to use. . . . I also meet with two other [beginning] teachers who are teaching in the same [subject] area. We talk about what is happening and how we're dealing with different things (Cole & Knowles, 1992, p. 13).

What you really need is just someone to talk to, someone to share ideas with, to talk about your children with to see if theirs are reacting the same way as yours, and just [to talk about] little problems with (Cole, 1991, p. 423).

In the early weeks and months of their teaching career, new teachers frequently feel ill at ease in their new positions. New surroundings, new colleagues, and so many new responsibilities can be disconcerting. Having many questions without a source for answers, and experiencing frequent bouts of self-doubt with no evident emotional support and encouragement can make for a difficult introduction to the teaching profession. Like the teachers cited at the beginning of this section, the turning point for many new teachers is finding one or more colleagues with whom to form mutually supportive relationships. Induction or support programs, which are being offered in many school systems, are intended to facilitate the formation of such relationships and thereby ease new teachers' transition to the school, system, and profession.

The goals of induction programs are

- to integrate beginning teachers into the school, system, and community
- to promote professional well-being and provide emotional support
- to assist with the ongoing development of knowledge, attitudes, and skills related to daily classroom teaching

- to promote the development of a philosophy of education, habits of reflective practice, and a commitment to continuing professional growth
- to encourage the retention of new teachers
- to encourage self-assessment (Cole & McNay, 1988; Huling-Austin, 1989; Odell, 1989).

One feature that distinguishes induction programs offered in Canada from those offered in some parts of the United States is an evaluation component. Some programs offered in the United States are competency-based with an emphasis on the development and mastery of technical skills; satisfactory performance is linked in some way to certification or re-employment. In Canada, induction programs are not explicitly linked to performance evaluation.

For the most part, teacher induction programs are linked with broader reform efforts supporting the view that becoming a teacher is a process of lifelong learning. Consequently, teacher education and development, which formally begin in a preservice preparation program, need to be continued beyond preservice through the early years and into experienced practice (Andrews, 1986, 1987; Fullan & Connelly, 1987; Huling-Austin, Odell, Ishler, Kay, & Edelfelt, 1989; Cole & Watson, 1991b). Implicit in this view is the recognition that the early years of teaching, especially the first, are formative and that beginning teachers have characteristic needs and concerns that must be addressed during this period to facilitate healthy professional development.

Although it is important not to generalize about what new teachers need and the kinds of experiences that may prove most helpful, research suggests that most novices need

- orientation information
- help and advice with technical and pedagogical aspects of teaching (including special assistance with organizing learning environments, responding to student behavior and individual differences, and reporting to parents)
- ideas and suggestions for curriculum
- emotional support and encouragement
- opportunities to establish a positive professional identity
- time and opportunity for ongoing reflection, observation, work with others, and self-assessment (Bullough, 1989; Bullough, Knowles, & Crow, 1991; Cole & Cathers, 1992; Odell, 1989; Veenman, 1984)

Research also shows that as new teachers develop through experience their needs and concerns change and vary so that certain kinds of assistance and support are more meaningful at certain times of the year. Hunt (1968), McNay and Cole (1989), and Cole and Cathers (1992) suggest that assistance and support for beginning teachers might more meaningfully be provided in four phases: (1) before school starts; (2) beginning-of-the-year orientation; (3) initial support and assistance during the early months; and (4) ongoing support and assistance beyond the early months. For example, assistance with setting up a classroom is likely to be more helpful prior to or at the beginning of school; whereas help with reporting to parents might be more appropriate later on. A focus on professional identity, emotional support, and self-assessment is, of course, an ongoing priority.

The kinds of activities designed to assist and support new teachers are many, diverse, and context-specific. Because of recent reform initiatives and the call for attention to the needs of beginning teachers, there is a plethora of literature on beginning teachers and their induction to the profession. Some journals have published special theme issues on teacher induction (for example, *Journal of Staff Development*, 1990, Vol. 11, No. 4; *Journal of Teacher Education*, 1986, Vol. 37, No. 1, 1992, Vol. 43, No. 3; *Orbit*, 1991, Vol. 22, No. 1). The Association of Teacher Educators has published a number of monographs related to new teacher induction: "Teacher Induction: A New Beginning" (Brooks, 1987); "Assisting the Beginning Teacher" (Huling-Austin, Odell, Ishler, Kay, & Edelfelt, 1989); "Mentoring: Developing Successful New Teachers" (Bey & Holmes, 1990); and, "Mentoring: Contemporary Principles and Issues" (Bey & Holmes, 1992). "Support for Beginning Teachers in Ontario: A Directory of Current Practices" (Cole, Cathers, & Watson, 1991) is a government publication in Ontario, Canada. A browse through any or all of these publications will give you a clear idea of the kind of support you might expect to receive as you begin your first year of teaching.

We conclude this section with a list of areas and issues that may be a useful guideline to understanding and assessing a school context. The following have been identified in the literature on teacher induction as important considerations for school administrators and others welcoming new teachers (Bullough, Knowles, & Crow, 1991; Cole, 1990a; Cole & McNay, 1988; Cole & Cathers, 1992; Hunt, 1968; NASSP Bulletin, 1968; Odell, 1989).

- teaching assignments—class size; composition; curricular demands; consistency with the level and subject area in which the teacher was prepared (attempts should be made to balance class assignments where possible and to avoid giving challenging teaching assignments to new teachers)
- room assignment—proximity; physical appearance; space (new teachers need a workplace to call their own; operating in and from a makeshift or temporary arrangement can interfere with establishing oneself as a "real" teacher; placing a new teacher in a portable classroom or remote area of the school can be isolating; classrooms clustered by grade level can aid informal interaction among new and experienced teachers)
- workload—teaching load; extracurricular duties; planning time (new teachers need more time for planning and preparation because they are doing everything for the first time; attention should be paid to extracurricular demands placed on new teachers)
- materials and resources (new teachers have a limited supply of basic resources and are likely to need help locating and acquiring materials)
- school culture (new teachers need sufficient opportunities to gain an understanding of the norms and routines of the school and become socialized to the school culture)
- climate (welcoming new teachers into a climate of caring and support engenders those qualities and behaviors)
- professional development—self-assessment; inquiry; collaborative work; long-term career planning (time and opportunity for new teachers to engage in professional development as part of their day-to-day practice will have long-term benefits for the entire community)

Research Activities

The worlds of beginning and experienced teachers as recorded in books provide a unique opportunity to explore your own preparation to teach. Using such books as a base, as a mirror, we encourage you to explore elements of your own professional development.

1. In preparation for full-time teaching there are a number of accounts about first-year teachers that you may find helpful. The *Recommended Readings* and *Links with Research* contain several examples, and you may want to draw on some of them: Bullough's (1989) *First Year Teacher: A Case Study;* Bullough, Knowles, and Crow's (1989) *Emerging as a Teacher;* Kane's (1991) *The First Year of Teaching;* Ryan's (1970, 1992) *Don't Smile Until Christmas* and *The Roller Coaster Year;* Ryan's et al. (1980) *Biting the Apple;* Walter's (1981) *So Where's My Apple: Diary of a First-year Teacher;* and, Kobrin's (1992) *In There with the Kids,* for instance, could form the basis for an exploration of beginning teachers. Try using your journal to make responses to these and other readings on beginning teachers and beginning teaching. Consider making critical as well as emotive responses to the perspectives presented. We suggest that your writing should *not* critique the articles or books but should focus on a discussion of the experiences of the beginning teachers. Explore, among other things, the contexts that influenced the teachers, paying attention to those that they could have potentially modified.

   a. What are the common elements of these beginning teachers' experiences? In what ways were they prepared or unprepared to teach? In what ways do these beginning teachers display a preparedness for the broader role of the work of teachers as opposed to the role associated with classroom work? What were their primary concerns?

   b. What were their responses to the successes and difficulties they experienced? What were the elements of their successes? What were the origins of their difficulties?

   c. In what ways did the beginning teachers' previous experiences and perspectives influence their thinking? To what extent did the beginning teachers attend to fostering their professional development? What are the central issues in the lives of these new teachers?

   d. What was most surprising about the accounts? To what extent were the beginning teachers complacent or active in thinking about issues of race, class, politics, and social issues?

   Consider sharing your writing with peers. As an alternative, write one or more formal responses to the readings (or to specific teachers' experiences), perhaps sharing them with beginning teachers or experienced teachers and using them as bases for discussion with peers.

2. Using the writing you have done in response to reading about beginning teachers (as in activity 1 in this section), take your thinking several steps further. Apply elements of the experiences of others to yourself. Some crucial questions to keep in mind include

   a. How can the experiences of other beginning teachers inform your thinking about teaching and your short- and long-term goals and strategies for professional development? How can their experiences help you shape your professional development?

   b. What are the pitfalls and prospects that you have to confront in your preparation for practice? Or, what are the contexts, situations, or circumstances to which you will need to pay close attention?

3. Consider your journal writing narratives (including autobiographical writing and other materials) as providing central information for consideration in the analysis of your professional development needs. Address perceived problems that you may have uncovered in your practice in the field. Having addressed areas that need attention, consider

ways in which you can capitalize on your strengths. Exchange your analysis with peers and others. Those who have observed your teaching—especially peer observers, cooperating teachers, and university supervisors—may have particularly insightful responses to your analysis.

   a. How do peers, cooperating teachers, and university supervisors react to your analysis? Why? What aspects of your thinking or practice do they support, contradict, or advise other courses of action or suggestions for professional development?

   b. How do beginning teachers and experienced teachers respond to your analysis? What issues do they support, contradict, or advise a different course of action? In what ways do beginning teachers' perspectives align with those of experienced teachers? Why? Why not?

4. Linking up with one or several beginning teachers may be beneficial to you (as well as to them). By now you will have many questions on your mind about the first year of full-time teaching. Try these questions out on teachers who are or who have just completed their first year. Perhaps more useful at first, however, may be *their* stories about the first year. Listen to their stories.

   a. What are the foci of their stories? What kinds of concerns and issues seem to take up a large part of their thinking? Why? How do they think about the theory-practice link? To what extent have they focused on long-term issues of professional development as opposed to the immediacy of short-term needs and problems? What are those issues and why have they been so focused or important to the teachers?

In light of our continued advice to make sense out of the theory-practice link and to think long-term about professional development, explore the ways in which these new teachers regard their own professional development. In addition, you could explore the following:

   b. How do the perspectives of the teachers compare to the perspectives we have espoused? Why might they be different? To what extent do their responses suggest a loss or maintenance of idealism?

   c. What are their long-term goals? How have these changed since their preservice preparation? over the course of their first year of teaching?

5. Explore elements of your preparedness to teach through the world of experienced teachers as also represented in books. For example, Palonsky's (1986) *900 Shows a Year: A Look at Teaching From a Teacher's Side of the Desk,* Freedman's (1990) *Small Victories: The Real World of a Teacher, Her Students, and Their High School,* and Kidder's (1989) *Among Schoolchildren* are a few recent publications that you could explore (perhaps again) now that you have views of practice different from those before your field placements. Some questions to explore include

   a. How does your preparedness to teach compare to the thinking and practices of these more experienced teachers? Where are the differences? To what extent are you prepared to deal with the contextual and circumstantial issues that these experienced teachers faced?

   b. In what kinds of circumstances do you find yourself at odds with the experienced teachers whose actions and practice are found in these texts? Why? What is the importance of this issue?

    c. Based on your field placement experiences, in what ways does the text representation of teachers' work (in these books) seem to exaggerate or gloss over the realities of everyday life in classrooms? What kinds of situations occurred in your field experience but not in these books? Why?

    d. What do other experienced teachers think about particular stories of practice as represented within these accounts? What are these teachers' reactions to the texts? Why? What are their opinions regarding the representation of practice?

6. As you move into the final phases of preparing to teach full-time, reconsider the advice you have received over the period of formal and initial preparation. Make a list of all the snippets of advice, perhaps categorizing them under headings such as personal issues, professional roles and professional identity issues, contextual elements, relational concerns, curriculum and instructional issues, and facilitation issues (management and discipline). Examine each piece of advice, noting its potential for contradiction with either your professional development foci or philosophy or orientation, making a statement as to why you should or should not heed the advice. Explore the underlying assumptions of the advice. Seek to establish a list that is internally consistent and coherent, deciding ways in which such advice can aid your ongoing growth.

Summary

Journeys to foreign lands, even to those places less than foreign, less than exotic, are always memorable. Whether those memories are imbedded in the preparation for journeying, the experiences of the journey itself, the fond or otherwise recollections of the event or the processes associated with it, or the anticipations of future journeys (continuing the previous journey or making a bold new one in a completely different direction), those memories are likely to influence your future actions. Journeys are usually significant events in the lives of travelers. Sometimes we are profoundly changed by brief excursions into a land or place until then unknown by us. A visit to a familiar environment under a different light or season may induce fresh appreciations and reveal new insights. Invariably, we are changed in some way. We become more sensitive to different peoples, traditions, and customs, to foods and cuisine, to climates and weather. We have learned. We have reconfigured part of our thinking. Sometimes we are profoundly affected as we have witnessed injustices, new expressions of joy and sorrow, impoverishment, refreshingly new literature and song, and simply lived in another place, trod in the pathways of others whom we may never know. And, the chances are that we have met and interacted with interesting, friendly and unfriendly people, individuals who are touched and untouched by our presence.

    Together, we have journeyed through your experience of working in classrooms and schools in one or more field settings. In this chapter we looked back on the journey of field experiences. We invited you to consider that which you have learned, been surprised about, and been challenged by. We illustrated and discussed how other preservice teachers reconceptualized their views of teaching and the roles of teachers. Our intent was to facilitate your pulling together the often disparate meanings of your experiences by sharing with you narrative accounts representing the experiences of others.

Journeys never end. They continue in our minds, as will the memories of your field experiences. Their impact will be great, sometimes profoundly so, in the early part of your full-time professional development. But, as time passes, and as you professionally grow in leaps and bounds, the first steps of a bold new journey will seem just as they are—first steps.

Just as looking back is important for configuring personal and professional growth, looking forward is a key to proactive participation in classrooms and other places of learning. As a new teacher with well-formed images of yourself as teacher, formed through extensive introspection, practice and theory testing, study, and inquiry, you will be more able to express your needs as a professional, making firm decisions about the kinds of context within you which you want to work, and shaping that chosen environment. Thus, coming to the end of the chapter and the book, we hope that you have discovered much about yourself as teacher and about the potentials of working in schools with other teachers, staff, parents, and of course, the *raison d'être*, the students with whom you will work.

Recommended Readings

Bey, T. M., & Holmes, C. T. (Eds.). (1990). *Mentoring: Developing successful new teachers.* Reston, VA. Association of Teacher Educators.

Bey, T. M., & Holmes, C. T. (Eds.). (1992). *Mentoring: Contemporary principles and issues.* Reston, VA: Association of Teacher Educators.

Britzman, D. P. (1991). *Practice makes practice: A critical study of learning to teach.* Albany, NY: State University of New York Press.

Bullough, R. V., Jr. (1989). *First year teacher: A case study.* New York: Teachers College Press.

Bullough, R. V., Jr., Knowles, J. G., & Crow, N. A. (1991). *Emerging as a teacher.* London: Routledge, Chapman, & Hall.

Conroy, P. (1972). *The water is wide.* Boston: Houghton Mifflin.

Diamond, C. T. P. (1991). *Teacher education as transformation.* Milton Keynes: Open University Press.

Dollase, R. (1992). *Voices of beginning teachers.* New York: Teachers College Press.

Fessler, R., & Christensen, J. C.. (1992). *The teacher career cycle: Understanding and guiding the professional development of teachers.* Boston, MA: Allyn & Bacon.

Gitlin, A. (1992). *Teachers' voices for school change.* New York: Teachers College Press.

Grumet, M. (1988). *Bitter milk.* Amherst, MA: The University of Massachusetts Press.

Hargreaves, A., & Fullan, M. G. (Eds.). (1992). *Understanding teacher development.* New York: Teachers College Press.

Huling-Austin, L., Odell, S. J., Ishler, P., Kay, R. S., & Edelfelt, R. A. (1989). *Assisting the beginning teacher.* Reston, VA: Association of Teacher Educators.

Jersild, A. T. (1955). *When teachers face themselves.* New York: Teachers College Press.

Kane, P. R. (Ed.). (1991). *The first year of teaching: Real world stories from America's teachers.* Columbia University: Teachers College.

Kobrin, D. (1992). *In there with the kids.* Boston, MA: Houghton Mifflin.

Kohl, H. (1984). *Growing minds: On becoming a teacher.* New York: Harper & Row.

Kowalski, T. J., Weaver, R. A., & Henson, K. T. (1990). *Case studies on teaching.* New York: Longman.

Kronowitz, E. L. (1992). *Beyond student teaching.* New York: Longman.

Lieberman, A., & Miller, L. (1992). *Teachers—Their world and their work.* New York: Teachers College Press.

Natkins, L. G. (1986). *Our last term: A teacher's diary.* Lanham, MD: University Press of America.

Nehring, J. (1989). *Why do we gotta do this stuff, Mr. Nehring?: Notes from a teacher's day in school*. New York: Fawcett.

Perl, S., & Wilson, N. (1986). *Through teachers' eyes: Portraits of writing teachers at work*. Portsmouth, NH: Heinemann.

Ryan, K. (Ed.). (1970). *Don't smile until Christmas*. Chicago: University of Chicago Press.

Ryan, K. (Ed.). (1992). *The roller coaster year: Essays by and for beginning teachers*. Boston, MA: HarperCollins.

Ryan, K., Newman, K. K., Mager, G., Applegate, J., Lasley, T., Flora, R., & Johnston, J. (1980). *Biting the apple*. New York: Longman.

Shulman, J. H. (1992). *Case methods in teacher education*. New York: Teachers College Press.

Shulman, J. H., & Colbert, J. A. (1987). *The mentor teacher casebook*. Oregon: ERIC Clearinghouse on Educational Management and Far West Laboratory for Educational Research and Development.

Shulman, J. H., & Colbert, J. A. (1988). *The intern teacher casebook*. Oregon: ERIC Clearinghouse on Educational Management, Far West Laboratory for Educational Research and Development and ERIC Clearinghouse on Teacher Education.

Van Manen, M. (1986). *The tone of teaching*. Richmond Hill, Ontario: Scholastic—TAB.

Walter, G. (1981). *So where's my apple?: Diary of a first-year teacher*. Prospect Heights, IL: Waveland.

References

Adler, R. B., & Towne, T. (1987). *Looking out, looking in.* New York: Holt, Rinehart, & Winston.

Aitken, J. L., & Mildon, D. (1991). The dynamic of personal knowledge and teacher education. *Curriculum Inquiry, 21*(2), 141–162.

Alverman, D. (1981). The possible value of dissonance in student teaching experiences. *Journal of Teacher Education, 32*(3), 24–25.

Ames, R. (1975). Teachers' attributions of responsibility: Some unexpected nondefensive effects. *Journal of Educational Psychology, 67,* 668–676.

Andrews, I. H. (1986, April). *An investigation of the academic paradigms underlying induction programmes in five countries.* Paper presented at the Annual Meeting of the American Educational Research Association, San Francisco, CA.

Andrews, I. H. (1987). Induction programs: Staff development opportunities for beginning and experienced teachers. In M. F. Wideen & I. Andrews (Eds.), *Staff development for school improvement.* Philadelphia, PA: Falmer Press.

Anthony, C. (Ed.). (1989). *Family portraits: Remembrances by twenty distinguished writers.* New York: Viking/Penguin Books.

Appleberry, M. (1976). What did you learn from student teaching? *Instructor, 85*(6), 38–40.

Applegate, J. (1986). Undergraduate students' perceptions of field experiences: Toward a framework for study. In J. D. Raths & L. G. Katz (Eds.), *Advances in teacher education, Volume 2* (pp. 21–38). Norwood, NJ: Ablex.

Applegate, J. H., & Lasley, T. J. (1982). Cooperating teachers' problems with preservice field experience students. *Journal of Teacher Education, 33*(2), 15–18.

Applegate, J. H., & Lasley, T. J. (1984). What cooperating teachers expect from preservice field experience teachers. *Teacher Education, 24,* 70–82.

Archambault, R. D. (Ed.). (1964). *John Dewey on education.* Chicago: University of Chicago Press.

Ashton, P. T. (Ed.). (1992). Theme: Induction and mentoring [Theme issue]. *Journal of Teacher Education, 43*(3).

Ashton-Warner, S. (1963). *Teacher.* New York: Simon & Schuster.

Ashton-Warner, S. (1972). *Spearpoint.* New York: Alfred A. Knopf.

Ball, S. J., & Goodson, I. F. (Eds.). (1985). *Teachers' lives and careers.* London: Falmer Press.

Barrows, L. (1979, April). *Power relationships in the student teaching triad.* Paper presented at the Annual Meeting of the American Educational Research Association, San Francisco, CA.

Baum, G. (1971). *Man becoming.* New York: Herder & Herder.

Becher, R., & Ade, W. (1982). The relationship of field placement characteristics and students' potential field performance abilities to clinical experience performance ratings. *Journal of Teacher Education, 33*(2), 24–30.

Berliner, D. C. (1988). Implications of studies on expertise in pedagogy for teacher education and evaluation. In *New directions for teacher assessment.* (Proceedings of the 1988 Educational Testing Service Invitational Conference, pp. 39–68). Princeton, NJ: Educational Testing Service.

Bey, T. M., & Holmes, C. T. (Eds.). (1992). *Mentoring: Contemporary principles & issues.* Association of Teacher Educators: Reston, VA.

Beynon, C. (1991). *Understanding the role of the cooperating teacher.* Unpublished manuscript, University of Western Ontario, Faculty of Education, London, Ontario.

Bird, T. (1990). The schoolteacher's portfolio: An essay on possibilities. In J. Millman and L. Darling-Hammond (Eds.), *The new handbook of teacher evaluation: Assessing elementary and secondary school teachers* (pp. 241-255). Newbury Park, CA: Sage.

Bird, T. (1991). *Making conversations about teaching and learning in an introductory teacher education course* (Craft Paper 91-2). East Lansing: Michigan State University, National Center for Research on Teacher Learning.

Blythe, R. (Ed.). (1989). *The pleasure of diaries: Four centuries of private writing.* New York: Pantheon Books.

Bogdan, R. C., & Biklen, S. K. (1992). *Qualitative research for education: An introduction to theory and methods.* Needham Heights, MA: Allyn & Bacon.

Bolster, A. S., Jr. (1983). Toward a more effective model of research on teaching. *Harvard Educational Review, 53*(3), 294-308.

Book, C., Beyers, J., & Freeman, D. (1983). Student expectations and teacher education traditions with which we can and cannot live. *Journal of Teacher Education, 34*(1), 9-13.

Booth, T., Fox, C., & Tubbs, P. (1992, April). *Enhancing the professional and cross-cultural knowledge of beginning teachers through an overseas practicum.* Paper presented at the Annual Meeting of the American Educational Research Association, San Francisco, CA.

Borko, H. (1985). Student teachers' planning and evaluations of reading lessons. In J. Niles & R. Lalik (Eds.), *Issues in literacy: A research perspective. Thirty-fourth yearbook of the National Reading Conference.* New York: National Reading Conference.

Borko, H. (1989). Research on learning to teach: Implications for graduate teacher preparation. In A. E. Woolfolk (Ed.), *Research perspectives on the graduate preparation of teachers* (pp. 69-87). Englewood Cliffs, NJ: Prentice-Hall.

Borko, H., Lalik, R., & Tomchin, E. (1987). Student teachers' understandings of successful teaching. *Teaching and Teacher Education, 3*, 77-90.

Boschee, F., Prescott, D. R., & Hein, D. (1978). Do cooperating teachers influence the educational philosophies of student teachers? *Journal of Teacher Education, 29*(2), 57-61.

Bowles, S., & Gintis, H. (1976). *Schooling in capitalist America: Educational reform and the contradictions of economic life.* New York: Basic Books.

Bowman, J. (1991). *Report to the College of Teachers on Teacher Education in British Columbia.* Vancouver, British Columbia: British Columbia College of Teachers.

Boyd, E., & Fales, A. W. (1983). Reflective learning: Key to learning from experience. *Journal of Humanistic Psychology, 23*(2), 99-117.

Boydell, D. (1991). Issues in teaching practice supervision research: A review of the literature. In L. Katz, *Advances in teacher education* (Vol. 4, pp. 137-151). Norwood, New Jersey: Ablex. (Reprinted from *Teaching & Teacher Education,* 1986, *2*(2), 115-125)

Boyer, E. (1989, May). What teachers say about children in America. *Educational Leadership,* 73-75.

Brandt, L. J., Hayden, M. E., & Brophy, J. E. (1975). Teachers' attitudes and ascription of causation. *Journal of Educational Psychology, 67,* 677-682.

Britzman, D. P. (1986). Cultural myths in the making of a teacher: Biography and social structure in education. *Harvard Educational Review, 56,* 442-456.

Britzman, D. P. (1991). *Practice makes practice: A critical study of learning to teach.* Albany, NY: State University of New York Press.

Brodbelt, S., & Wall, R. (1985, November). *Student teacher socialization: Role model influences.* Paper presented at the Eastern Education Research Association Conference, Virginia Beach, Virginia.

Bronfenbrenner, U. (1974). *Is early intervention effective? A report on longitudinal evaluations of preschool programs* (Vol. II). Washington, DC: U.S. Department of Health Education and Welfare.

Brooks, D. M. (Ed.). (1987). *Teacher induction: A new beginning.* Reston, VA: Association of Teacher Educators.

Brown, D., & Hoover, J. D. (1990). The degree to which student teachers report using instructional strategies valued by university faculty. *Action in Teacher Education, 12*(1), 20-23.

Buchmann, M. (1989, April) *Breaking from experience in teacher education: When is it necessary, how is it possible?* Paper presented at the Annual Meeting of the American Educational Research Association, San Francisco, CA.

Buchmann, M. (1990). Beyond the lonely choosing will: Professional development in teacher thinking. *Teachers College Record, 91*(4), 481-508.

Bullough, R. V., Jr. (1989). *First year teacher: A case study.* New York: Teachers College Press.

Bullough, R. V., Jr. (1990, April). *Personal history and teaching metaphors in preservice teacher education.* Paper presented at the Annual Meeting of the American Educational Research Association, Boston, MA.

Bullough, R. V., Jr. (1991). Exploring personal teaching metaphors in preservice teacher education. *Journal of Teacher Education, 42*(1), 43-51.

Bullough, R. V., Jr., & Knowles, J. G. (1990). Becoming a teacher: Struggles of a second-career beginning teacher. *International Journal of Qualitative Studies in Education, 3*(2), 101-112.

Bullough, R. V., Jr., & Knowles, J. G. (1991). Teaching and nurturing: Changing conceptions of self as teacher in a case study of becoming a teacher. *International Journal of Qualitative Studies in Education, 4*(1), 121–140.

Bullough, R. V. Jr., Knowles, J. G., & Crow N. A. (1989). Teacher self-concept and student culture in the first year of teaching. *Teachers College Press, 91*(2), 209-233.

Bullough, R. V., Jr., Knowles, J. G., & Crow, N. A. (1991). *Emerging as a teacher.* London: Routledge & Kagan Paul.

Bunting, C. (1988). Cooperating teachers and the changing views of teacher candidates. *Journal of Teacher Education, 39*(2), 42-46.

Burden, P. R. (Ed.). (1990). Teacher induction [Theme issue]. *Journal of Staff Development, 11*(4).

Butt, R. L., & Raymond, D. (1987). Arguments for using qualitative approaches in understanding teacher thinking: The case for biography. *Journal for Curriculum Theorizing, 7*(2), 62-93.

Butt, R., Raymond, D., McCue, G., & Yamagashi, L. (1992). Collaborative autobiography and the teacher's voice. In I. Goodson (Ed.), *Studying teachers' lives.* London: Routledge.

Calderhead, J., & Robson, M. (1991). Images of teaching: Student teachers' early conceptions of classroom practice. *Teaching and Teacher Education, 7,* 1-8.

Campbell, L. P., & Williamson, J. A. (1983). Supervising the student teacher: What is really involved? *NASSP Bulletin, 67*(465), 77-79.

Canning, C. (1990, April). *Reflection: Out on a limb. An intrapersonal process and the development of voice.* Paper presented at the Annual Meeting of the American Educational Research Association, Boston, MA.

Caruso, J. J. (1977). Phases in student teaching. *Young Children, 33*(1), 57-63.

Chang, H. (1992). *Adolescent life and ethos: An ethnography of a U.S. high school.* Bristol, PA: Falmer Press.

Clandinin, D. J. (1985). *Classroom practice: Teacher images in action.* London: Falmer Press.

Clandinin, D. J. (1986). *Classroom practice: Teacher images in action.* East Sussex: Falmer Press.

Clandinin, D. J., & Connelly, F. M. (1986). Rhythms in teaching: The narrative study of teachers' personal practical knowledge of classrooms. *Teaching and Teacher Education, 2*(4), 377-387.

Clandinin, D. J., & Connelly, F. M. (1987). Teachers' personal knowledge: What counts as 'personal' in studies of the personal. *Journal of Curriculum Studies, 19,* 487-500.

Clark, R. M. (1983). *Family life and school achievement: Why poor black children succeed or fail.* Chicago: University of Chicago Press.

Clark, R. M., & LaLonde, D. E. (1992). A case for department-based professional development sites for secondary teacher education. *Journal of Teacher Education, 43*(1), 35-41.

Colbert, J. A., & Wolff, D. E. (1992). Surviving in urban schools: A collaborative model for a beginning teacher support system. *Journal of Teacher Education, 43*(3), 193-199.

Cole, A. L. (1987). *Teachers' spontaneous adaptations: A mutual interpretation.* Unpublished doctoral dissertation, University of Toronto, Toronto, Ontario, Canada.

Cole, A. L. (1989). Personal signals in spontaneous teaching practice. *Journal of Qualitative Studies in Education, 29*(1), 25-39.

Cole, A. L. (1989, April). *Making explicit implicit theories of teaching: Starting points in preservice programs.* Paper presented at the Annual Meeting of the American Educational Research Association, San Francisco, CA.

Cole, A. L. (1990a). Personal theories of teaching: Development in the formative years. *The Alberta Journal of Educational Research, 36*(3), 203-222.

Cole, A. L. (1990b, April). *Teachers experienced knowledge: A continuing study.* Paper presented at the Annual Meeting of the American Educational Research Association, Boston, MA.

Cole, A. L. (1991a, June). *Four schools, four ways of doing things: A participatory approach to the development of school-based induction programs.* Paper presented at the at the Annual Conference of the Canadian Society for the Study of Education, Kingston, Ontario.

Cole, A. L. (1991b). Relationships in the workplace: Doing what comes naturally? *Teaching and Teacher Education, 7*(5/6), 415-426.

Cole, A. L. (1992). Teacher development in the workplace: Rethinking the appropriation of professional relationships. *Teachers College Record, 94*(2) 375-381.

Cole, A. L., & Cathers, P. (1992) *Supporting beginning teachers: A handbook for school administrators* Unpublished manuscript, Ontario Institute for Studies in Education, Toronto, Ontario.

Cole, A. L., Cathers, P., & Watson, N. (1991). *Support for beginning teachers in Ontario: A directory of current practices.* Toronto, Ontario: Teacher Education Council, Ontario.

Cole, A. L., & Innes, M. (1991, December). *The creation of caring communities: A whole school approach.* Paper presented at the Annual Conference of the Ontario Educational Research Council, Toronto, Ontario, Canada.

Cole, A. L., & Knowles, J. G. (1992, June). *Beginning teachers talk: Who listens? Who learns?.* Paper presented at the Annual Conference of the Canadian Society for the Study of Education, Charlottetown, Prince Edward Island.

Cole, A. L., & McNay, M. (1988). Induction programs in Ontario schools: Issues and possibilities. *Education Canada, 28,*(4), 4-11, 44-45.

Cole, A. L., & Sorrill, P.W. (1992). Being an associate teacher: A feather in one's cap? *Education Canada, 32*(3), 40-48.

Cole, A. L., & Watson, N. (Eds.). (1991a). *Support for Beginning Teachers: Renewal for All* [Special issue]. *Orbit, 22*(1).

Cole, A. L., & Watson, N. (1991b). *Support for beginning teachers: Ontario perspectives,* Toronto, Ontario: Teacher Education Council, Ontario.

Cole, A. L., & Watson, N. (in press). Beginning teacher development in Ontario: The ebb and flow of policy and practice. *Journal of Education Policy.*

Cole, M. (1985). "The tender trap?" Commitment and consciousness in entrants to teaching. In S. J. Ball & I. F. Goodson (Eds.), *Teachers' lives and careers* (pp. 89-104). London: Falmer Press.

Coleman, J. S., & Hoffer, T. (1987). *Public and private high schools: The impact of communities.* New York: Basic Books.

Comer, J. (1988). Educating poor minority children. *Scientific American, 259*(5), 42-48.

Compact Edition of the Oxford English Dictionary (1971). New York. Oxford University Press.

Connelly, F. M., & Clandinin, D. J. (1984). Personal practical knowledge at Bay Street School: Ritual, personal philosophy and image. In R. Halkes, & J. K. Olson (Eds.), *Teacher thinking: A new perspective on persisting problems in education.* Lisse: Swets & Zeitlinger, B. V.

Connelly, F. M., & Clandinin, D. J. (1985a). Personal practical knowledge and the modes of knowing: Relevance for teaching and learning. In E. Eisner (Ed.), *Learning and teaching the ways of knowing* (84th Yearbook of the National Society for the Study of Education, Part II, pp. 174-198). Chicago: University of Chicago Press.

Connelly, F. M., & Clandinin, D. J. (1985b). *The cyclic temporal structure of schooling.* Paper presented at a meeting of the Symposium on Classroom Studies of Teacher's Personal Practical Knowledge, Toronto, Ontario.

Connelly, F. M., & Clandinin, D. J. (1988). *Teachers as curriculum planners: Narratives of experience.* New York: Teachers College Press.

Cooper, A., Beare, P., & Thompson, J. (1990). Preparing teachers for diversity: A comparison of student teaching experiences in Minnesota and south Texas. *Action in Teacher Education, 12*(3), 1-4.

Copa, P. (1991). The beginning teacher as theory maker: Meanings for teacher education. In L. Katz (Ed.), *Advances in teacher education* (Vol. 4, pp. 105-133). Norwood, New Jersey: Ablex.

Copeland, W. (1978). Processes mediating the relationship between cooperating teacher behavior and student-teacher classroom performance. *Journal of Educational Psychology, 70,* 95-100.

Copeland, W. (1981). Clinical experiences in the education of teachers. *Journal of Education for Teaching, 7*(1), 3-16.

Copeland, W. (1986). The RITE framework for teacher education: Preservice applications. In J. Hoffman & S. Edwards (Eds.), *Reality and reform in teacher education* (pp. 25-44). New York: Random House.

Crow, N. A. (1987a, April). *Preservice teachers' biography: A case study.* Paper presented at the Annual Meeting of the Educational Research Association, Washington, DC.

Crow, N. A. (1987b). *Socialization within a teacher education program.* Unpublished doctoral dissertation, University of Utah, Salt Lake City, UT.

Crow, N. A. (1991, April). *Personal perspectives on classroom management.* Paper presented at the Annual Meeting of the American Educational Research Association, Chicago, IL.

Cruickshank, D. R. (1987). *Reflective teaching: The preparation of students of teaching.* Reston, VA: Association of Teacher Educators.

Cummins, J. (1986). Empowering minority students: A framework for intervention. *Harvard Educational Review, 56*(1), 18-36.

Deal, T. E., & Chatman, R. M. (1989). Learning the ropes alone: Socializing new teachers. *Action in Teacher Education, 9*(1),21-29.

Delandshere, G., & Petrosky, A. (1992, April). *Developing a high inference scheme to evaluate teacher knowledge.* Paper presented at the Annual Meeting of the American Educational Research Association, San Francisco, CA.

Dewey, J. (1933). *How we think: A restatement of the relation of reflective thinking to the educative process* (rev. ed.). Boston, MA: D. C. Heath.

Dewey, J. (1938). *Experience and education.* New York: Macmillan.

Deyhle, D. (1986). Break dancing and breaking out: Anglos, Utes, and Navajos in a border reservation high school. *Anthropology and Education, 17*(2), 111-127.

Dillard, A. (1987). *An American childhood.* New York: Harper & Row.

Disbrowe, H. B. (1984). *A schoolman's odyssey.* London: University of Western Ontario.

Doyle, W. (1977). Learning the classroom environment: An ecological analysis. *Journal of Teacher Education, 28*(6), 51-55.

Duckworth, E. (1986). Teaching as research. *Harvard Educational Review, 56*(4), 481-495.

Eckert, P. (1989). *Jocks & burnouts: Social categories and identity in the high school.* New York: Teachers College Press.

Eisenhart, M., Behm, L., & Romagnano, L. (1991). Learning to teach: Developing expertise or rite of passage? *Journal of Education for Teaching, 17*(1), 51-71.

Eisner, E. W. (1985). *The educational imagination* (2nd ed.). New York: Macmillan.

Elliott, J. (1991). *Action research for educational change.* Buckingham, UK: Open University Press.

Ellwein, M. C., Graue, M. E., & Comfort, R. E. (1990). Talking about instruction: Student teachers' reflections on success and failure in the classroom. *Journal of Teacher Education, 41*(5), 3-14.

Emans, R. (1983). Implementing the knowledge base: Redesigning the function of cooperating teachers and college supervisors. *Journal of Teacher Education, 34*(3), 14-18.

Epstein, J. L. (1987). Parent involvement: What research says to administrators. *Education and Urban Society, 19*(2), 119-136.

Epstein, J. L. (1989). *The home-school connection: Implications for teacher education.* Berkeley, CA: University of California.

Epstein, J. L., & Becker, H. J. (1982). *Teacher reported practices of parent involvement: Problems and possibilities.* Baltimore, MD: Johns Hopkins University Press.

Erickson, F., & Shultz, J. (1992). Students' experience of the curriculum. In P. W. Jackson (Ed.), *Handbook of research on curriculum.* New York: Macmillan.

Erickson, G. L., & MacKinnon, A. M. (1991). Seeing classrooms in new ways: On becoming a science teacher. In D. A. Schön (Ed.), *The reflective turn* (pp. 13-36). New York: Teachers College Press.

Estes, G., Stansbury, K., & Long, C. (1990). *Assessment component of the California New Teacher Project: First year report.* San Francisco, CA: Far West Laboratory for Educational Research and Development.

Feiman-Nemser, S. (1983). Learning to teach. In L. Shulman & G. Sykes (Eds.), *Handbook of Teaching and Policy* (pp. 150-170). New York: Longman.

Feiman-Nemser, S., & Buchmann, M. (1983). Pitfalls of experience in teacher preparation. *Teachers College Record, 87*(1), 53-65.

Feiman-Nemser, S., & Buchmann, M. (1987). When is student teaching teacher education? *Teaching & Teacher Education, 3*(4), 255-273.

Feiman-Nemser, S., & Floden, R. E. (1986). The cultures of teaching. In M. C. Wittrock (Ed.), *Handbook of Research on Teaching* (3rd ed) (pp. 505-526). New York: Macmillan.

Ferri, B., & Aglio, M. (1990). *I'm not alone: Teacher talk, teacher buddying.* Mississauga, Ontario: Peel Board of Education.

Florio-Ruane, S., & Lensmire, T. J. (1990). Transforming future teachers' ideas about writing instruction. *Journal of Curriculum Studies, 22,* 277-289.

Fogarty, J. L., Wang, M. C., & Creek, R. (1983). A descriptive study of novice and experienced teachers' interactive thoughts and actions. *Journal of Educational Research, 77*(1), pp. 22–32.

Freedman S. G. (1990). *Small victories: The real world of a teacher, her students and their high school.* New York: Harper & Row.

Freedman, S., Jackson, J., & Boles, K. (1983). Teaching: An "imperilled profession." In L. S. Shulman & G. Sykes (Eds.), *Handbook of teaching and policy* (pp. 261-299). New York: Longman.

Friebus, R. (1977). Agents of socialization involved in student teaching. *Journal of Educational Research, 70,* 263-268.

Fullan, M., & Connelly, M. (1987). *Teacher education in Ontario: Current practice and options for the future.* Position paper submitted to the Teacher Education Review Steering Committee. Toronto: Ministries of Education and Colleges and Universities.

Fuller, F. F., & Bown, O. H. (1975). Becoming a teacher. *Teacher education,* (74th Yearbook of the National Society for the Study of Education, Part II, pp. 25-52). Chicago: University of Chicago Press.

Fulwiler, T. (1987). *The Journal Book.* Portsmouth, NH: Boynton Cook.

Gaede, O. F. (1978). Reality shock: A problem among first-year teachers. *The Clearing House, 51*(8), 405-409.

Garcia, I. M., & Farnsworth, B. J. (1984). Student teachers: An appraisal by elementary students and their parents. *Education, 104*(4), 419-429.

Gipe, J. P., Duffy, C., & Richards, J. C. (1987). A comparison of two types of early field experiences. *Reading Improvement,* 254-265.

Gitlin, A., & Goldstein, S. (1987). A dialogical approach to understanding: Horizontal evaluation. *Educational Theory, 37*(1), 17-27.

Gitlin, A., & Smyth. J. (1989). *Teacher evaluation: Educative alternatives.* Barcombe, Lewes, East Sussex: Falmer Press.

Glover, M. K. (1992). *Two years: A teacher's memoir.* Portsmouth, NH: Heinemann.

Goetz, J. P., & LeCompte, M. D. (1984). *Ethnography and qualitative design in educational research.* Orlando, FL: Academic Press.

Goldhammer, R. (1969). *Clinical supervision: Special methods for the supervision of teachers.* New York: Holt, Rinehart, & Winston.

Gollnick, D., & Chinn, P. (1990). *Multicultural education in a pluralistic society* (3rd ed.). New York: Merrill/Macmillan.

Gomez, M. L. & Comeaux, M. A. (1990). *Start with the stone, not with the hole: Matching novice's needs with appropriate programs of induction.* National Center for Research on Teacher Education, East Lansing, MI. (ERIC Document Reproduction Service No. ED 327 541)

Goodlad, J. (1990). *Teachers for our nation's schools.* San Francisco: Jossey-Bass.

Goodman, J. (1983). The seminar's role in the education of student teachers: A case study. *Journal of Teacher Education, 34*(3), 44-49.

Goodman, J. (1987, April). *Key factors in becoming (or not becoming) an empowered elementary school teacher: A preliminary study of selected novices.* Paper presented at the Annual Meeting of the American Educational Research Association, Washington, DC.

Goodman, J. (1988). Constructing a practical philosophy of teaching: A study of preservice teachers' professional perspectives. *Teaching and Teacher Education, 4*(2), 121-137.

Goodson, I. F. (1981). Life histories and studies of schooling. *Interchange, 11*(4), 27–39.

Goodson, I. F. (Ed.). (1992). *Studying teachers' lives.* London: Routledge.

Goodson, I. F., & Cole, A. L. (in press). Teacher's professional knowledge: Constructing identity and community. *Teacher Education Quarterly.*

Goodson, I. F., & Walker, R. (1991). *Biography identity and schooling.* London: Falmer Press.

Grant, C. A., & Secada, W. G. (1990). Preparing teachers for diversity. In R. W. Houston (Ed.), *Handbook of research on teacher education* (pp. 403-422). New York: Macmillan.

Grant, C. A., & Sleeter, C. E. (1986). *After the school bell rings.* Philadelphia, PA: Falmer Press.

Griffin, G., & Millies, S. (Eds.). (1987). *The first years of teaching: Background papers and a proposal.* Chicago: University of Illinois at Chicago.

Griffin, G. A., Barnes, S., Hughes, R., O'Neal, S., Defino, M., Edwards, S., & Hukill, H. (1983). *Clinical preservice teacher education: Final report of a descriptive study.* Austin, TX: University of Texas, R & D Center for Teacher Education.

Grimmett, P. & Erickson, G. (Eds.). (1988). *Reflection in teacher education.* New York: Teachers College Press.

Grimmett, P. P., & Ratzlaff, H. C. (1986). Expectations for the cooperating teacher role. *Journal of Teacher Education, 37*(6), 41-50.

Gudmundsottir, S. (1990). Values in pedagogical context knowledge. *Journal of Teacher Education, 41*(3), 44-52.

Guillaume, A. M., & Rudney, G. L. (1991, April). *Changes in student teacher concerns: Growth toward independence.* Paper presented at the Annual Meeting of the American Educational Research Association, Chicago, IL.

Gunstone, R., & Northfield, J. (1987). *Constructivist views of teacher education.* Paper presented at the Annual Conference of the South Pacific Association of Teacher Education, Ballart, Victoria.

Guyton, E., & McIntyre, D. J. (1990). Student teaching and school experiences. In W. R. Houston (Ed.), *Handbook of research on teacher education* (pp. 514-534). New York: Macmillan.

Haertel, E. H. (1991). New forms of teacher assessment. In C. B. Cazden (Ed.), *Review of research in education*, Vol. 17, (pp. 3-29). Washington, DC: American Educational Research Association.

Halpern, D. (Ed.). (1989). *Our private lives: Journals, notebooks and diaries*. New York: Vintage Books.

Hargreaves, A. (1990). Cultures of teaching. In I. Goodson & S. Ball (Eds.), *Teachers' lives*. New York: Routledge.

Hargreaves, A. (1990, April). *Individualism and individuality: Reinterpreting the teacher culture*. Paper presented at the Annual Meeting of the American Educational Research Association, Boston, MA.

Hargreaves, A., & Dawe, R. (1991). Paths of professional development: Contrived collegiality, collaborative culture and the case of peer coaching. *Teaching and Teacher Education*, 6(3), 227-241.

Hayden, T. L. (1981). *Somebody else's kids*. New York: Avon.

Hess, R. D., & Holloway, S. D. (1984). Family and school as educational institutions. In R. D. Parke, R. M. Emde, H. P. McAdoo, & G. P. Sackett (Eds.), *Review of child development research: Vol. 7. The family* (pp. 179-222). Chicago: University of Chicago Press.

Hodgkinson, H. (1988). The right schools for the right kids. *Educational leadership*, 45(5), 10-14.

Hollingsworth, S. (1989). Prior beliefs and cognitive change in learning to teach. *American Educational Research Journal*, 26(2), 160-189.

Holly, M. L. (1989). *Writing to grow: Keeping a personal professional journal*. Portsmouth, NH: Heinemann.

Holmes Group. (1986). *Tomorrow's teachers: A report of the Holmes group*. East Lansing, MI: Holmes Group.

Holmes Group. (1990). *Tomorrow's schools: Principles for the design of professional development schools*. East Lansing, MI: Holmes Group.

Holt-Reynolds, D. (1992). Personal history-based beliefs as relevant prior knowledge in course work. *American Educational Research Journal*, 29(2), 325-349.

Hoover-Dempsey, K. V., Bassler, O. C., & Brissie, J. S. (1987). Parent involvement: Contributions of teacher efficacy, school socioeconomic status, and other school characteristics. *American Educational Research Journal*, 24,(3), 417-435.

Horwood, R. H. (1981). The relationship between associate teachers and student teachers: Images of the associate teacher. *Teacher Education, 19*, 74-83.

Housner, L. D., & Griffey, D. C. (1983, April). *Teacher cognition: Differences in planning and interactive decision making between experienced and inexperienced teachers*. Paper presented at the Annual Meeting of the American Educational Research Association, Montreal, Quebec.

Houston, W. R., & Houston, E. (1992). Needed: A new knowledge base in teacher education. In L. Kaplan (Ed.), *Education and the family* (pp. 255-265). Boston: Allyn & Bacon.

Houston, W. R., Marshall, & McDavid, (1990). *Perceptions of first year teachers of the assistance provided by experienced support teachers at the end of the year* (Study 90-92). Houston, TX: University of Houston.

Houston, W. R., & Williamson, J. L. (1990). *Perceptions of their preparation by 42 Texas elementary school teachers compared to their responses as student teachers*. Houston, TX: Texas Association of Teacher Educators.

Howey, K. R. (1977). Preservice teacher education: Lost in the shuffle? *Journal of Teacher Education, 28*, 26-28.

Hoy, W. K., & Rees, R. (1977). The bureaucratic socialization of student teachers. *Journal of Teacher Education, 28*(1), 23-26.

Hoy, W. K., & Woolfolk, A. E. (1990). Socialization of student teachers. *American Educational Research Journal, 27*, 279-300.

Huling-Austin, L. (1989). Beginning teacher assistance programs: An overview. In L. Huling-Austin, S. J. Odell, P. Ishler, R. S. Kay, & R. A. Edelfelt (Eds.). *Assisting the beginning teacher*. Reston, VA: Association of Teacher Educators.

Hull, R., Baker, R., Kyle J., & Good, R. (Eds.). (1982). *Research on student teaching: A question of transfer*. Eugene: University of Oregon, Division of Teacher Education. (ERIC Document Reproduction Service No. ED 233 561)

Hunt, D. E. (1976). Teacher adaptation: "Reading" and "Flexing" two students. *Journal of Teacher Education, 27*(3), 268–275.

Hunt, D. W. (1968). Teacher induction: An opportunity and a responsibility. *NASSP Bulletin, 52*, 130-135.

Hunt, D. W. (1987). *Beginning with ourselves: In theory, practice and human affairs*. Toronto, Ontario/Cambridge, MA: OISE Press/Brookline Books.

Hunt, D. W. (1991). *The renewal of personal energy.* Toronto, Ontario: OISE Press.

Hunter, L. (1992). *The diary of Latoya Hunter: My first year in junior high.* New York: Crown.

Iannaccone, L. (1963). Student teaching: A transitional stage in the making of a teacher. *Theory Into Practice, 11*(2), 73-80.

Innes, M. (1991). A whole-school approach to teacher induction. In A. Cole & N. Watson (Eds.), *Support for beginning teachers: Renewal for all* [Special issue]. *Orbit, 22*(1), 13.

Jackson, P. W. (1968). *Life in classrooms.* New York: Holt, Rinehart, & Winston.

Jackson, P. W. (1990). *Life in classrooms* (rev. ed.) New York: Teachers College Press.

Jacobs, E. (1968). Attitude change in teacher education: An inquiry into the role of attitudes in changing teacher behavior. *Journal of Teacher Education, 15,* 200-203.

Jervis, K. (1986). A teacher's quest for a child's questions. *Harvard Educational Review, 56*(2), 132-150.

Johnson, J. & Yates, J. (1982). *A national survey of student teaching programs.* De Kalb, IL: Northern Illinois University. (ERIC Document Reproduction Service No. ED 232 963)

Johnson, S. M. (1990). *Teachers at work: Achieving success in our schools.* New York: Basic Books.

Jones, G. (1991). *Crocus Hill notebook.* London, Ontario: Althouse Press.

Kagan, D. M. (1992). Professional growth among preservice and beginning teachers. *Review of Educational Research, 62*(2),129-169.

Kane, P. R. (Ed.). (1991). *The first year of teaching: Real world stories from America's teachers.* Columbia University: Teachers College.

Keizer, G. (1988). *No place but here.* New York: Penguin Books.

Kelleher, R., & Williams, L. (1986). Cross-cultural student teaching: An assessment of a Newfoundland Program. *Education Canada, 26*(2), 30–35.

Kelly, G. (1955). *The psychology of personal construct: A theory of personality* (Vol. 1). New York: Norton.

Kemmis, S. (1985). Action research and the politics of reflection. In D. Boud, R. Keogh, & D. Walker (Eds.), *Reflection: Turning experience into learning* (pp.139-163). London: Kogan Page.

Kidder, T. (1989). *Among schoolchildren.* Boston, MA: Houghton Mifflin.

King, J. R. (1991). Collaborative life history narratives: Heroes in reading teachers' tales. *Qualitative Studies in Education, 4*(1), 45-60.

Knowles, J. G. (1988). Parents' rationales and teaching methods for home schooling: The role of biography. *Education and Urban Society, 21*(1), 69-84.

Knowles, J. G. (1989). Cooperating with home school parents: A new agenda for public schools? *Urban Education, 23*(4), 392-411.

Knowles, J. G. (1990). "For whom the bell tolls": The failure of a student teacher and insights into self, teaching, and teacher education. Unpublished paper.

Knowles, J. G. (1991). Parents' rationales for operating home schools. *Journal of Contemporary Ethnography, 20*(2), 203-230.

Knowles, J. G. (1992). Models for understanding preservice and beginning teachers' biographies: Illustrations from case studies. In I. F. Goodson (Ed.), *Studying teachers' lives* (pp. 99-152). London: Routledge.

Knowles, J. G. (1993). Life-history accounts as mirrors: A practical avenue for the conceptualization of reflection in teacher education. In J. Calderhead & P. Gates (Eds.). *Conceptualizing reflection in teacher development* (pp. 70–92). London: Falmer Press.

Knowles, J. G., & Cole, A. L. (in preparation). Developing practice through field experiences. In *A knowledge base for teacher educators.* Washington, DC: American Association of Colleges of Teacher Education.

Knowles, J. G., & Hoefler, V. B. (1989). The student teacher who wouldn't go away: Learning from failure. *Journal of Experiential Education, 12*(2), 14-21.

Knowles, J. G., & Holt-Reynolds, D. (1991). Shaping pedagogies through personal histories in preservice teacher education. *Teachers College Record, 93*(1), 89-113.

Knowles, J. G., Marlow, S. E., & Muchmore, J. A. (1992). From pedagogy to ideology: Origins and phases of home education in the United States, 1979-1990. *American Journal of Education, 100*(2), 195-235.

Knowles, J. G., Mayberry, M., & Ray, B. (1991). *An Assessment of home schools in Nevada, Oregon, Utah, and Washington: Implications for public education and a vehicle for informed policy decisions.* Report to U.S. Department of Education, Washington, DC. (Grant No. R117E90220)

Knowles, J. G., & Skrobola, N. (1992, April). *We watched them "fail": University supervisors' perceptions of preservice teachers who "failed" student teaching.* Paper presented at the Annual Meeting of the American Educational Research Association, San Francisco, CA.

Knowles, J. G., & Sudzina, M. R. (1991, February). *"Failure" in student/practice teaching: A skeleton in the teacher education closet?* Paper presented at the Annual Meeting of the Association of Teacher Educators, Chicago, IL.

Knowles, J. G., & Sudzina, M. R. (1992, April). *Addressing "failure" in student teaching: Some practical and ethical issues.* Paper presented at the Annual Meeting of the American Educational Research Association, San Francisco, CA.

Knowles, J.G., & Sudzina, M.R. (1992, April). *Personal characteristics and contextual conditions of student teachers who "fail": Setting a course for understanding failure in teacher education.* Paper presented at the Annual Meeting of the American Educational Research Association, San Francisco, CA.

Kobrin, D. (1992). *In there with the kids.* Boston, MA: Houghton Mifflin.

Koehler, V. (1984, April). *University supervision of student teaching.* Paper presented at the Annual Meeting of the American Educational Research Association.

Kohl, H. (1967). *Thirty-six children.* New York: New American Library.

Kozol, J. (1991). *Savage inequalities.* New York: Crown.

Labosky, V. K. (1991, April). *Case studies of two teachers in a reflective teacher education program: How do you know?* Paper presented at the Annual Meeting of the Educational Research Association, Chicago, IL.

Lacey, C. (1977). *The socialization of teachers.* London: Metheun.

Lanier, J. E., & Little, J. W. (1986). Research on teacher education. In M. C. Wittrock, *Handbook of research on teaching* (pp. 527–569). New York: Macmillan.

Lareau, A. (1989). *Home advantage: Social class and parental intervention in elementary education.* Philadelphia, PA: Falmer Press.

Larke, P. J. (1990). Cultural diversity awareness inventory: Assessing the sensitivity of preservice teachers. *Action in Teacher Education, 12*(3), 23–29.

Larke, P. J., Wiseman, D., & Bradley, C. (1990). The minority mentorship project: Changing attitudes of preservice teachers for diverse classrooms. *Action in Teacher Education, 12*(3), 5-11.

Lasley, T. J., & Watras, J. (1991). Teacher education at the crossroads. In L. G. Katz and J. D. Rath (Eds.), *Advances in teacher education* (Vol. 4, pp. 1–19). Norwood, NJ: Ablex.

Laycock, M. R. (1991). Remembering Theressa: Please excuse my doing nothing; I was just an observer. *Teacher Education, 4*(1), 33-39.

Leslie, L. L. (1969). *Improving the student teaching experience through selective placements of students.* Final report of Grant No. OEG-8-9-540015-2019 (058), U.S. Department of Health Education and Welfare. (ERIC Document Reproduction Service No. ED 034 718)

Lindsey, A. (1985). Consensus or diversity? A grave dilemma in schooling. *Journal of Teacher Education, 36*(4), 31-36.

Liston, D. P., & Zeichner, K. M. (1987). Reflective teacher education and moral deliberation. *Journal of Teacher Education, 38*(6), 2-8.

Liston, D. P., & Zeichner, K. M. (1990). Teacher education and the social context of schooling: Issues for curriculum development. *American Educational Research Journal, 27*, 610-638.

Lombana, J. H. (1983). *Home school partnerships.* New York: Grune & Stratton.

Lortie, D. (1975). *Schoolteacher: A sociological study.* Chicago: University of Chicago Press.

Louden, W. (1991). *Understanding teaching: Continuity and change in teachers' knowledge.* New York: Teachers College Press.

MacKinnon, J. D. (1989a, June). *Relationships in the student teaching triad: Through the eyes of four student teachers.* Paper presented at the Annual Conference of the Canadian Society for the Study of Education, Quebec City, Quebec.

MacKinnon, J. D. (1989b). Living with conformity in student teaching. *The Alberta Journal of Educational Research, 35*(1), 2-19.

Macrorie, K. (1981). *Searching writing: The I-search paper.* Portsmouth, NH: Heinemann.

Mahan, J. M., & Lacefield, W. E. (1976, April). *Changes in preservice teachers' value orientations toward education during year-long, cluster, student teaching placements.* Paper presented at the Annual Meeting of the American Educational Research Association, San Francisco, CA.

Martin, D. (1988, April). *A study of the longitudinal development of more and less effective student teachers.* Paper presented at the Annual Meeting of the American Educational Research Association, New Orleans, LA.

Martin, R. E., & Wood, G. H. (1984). *Early field experiences: Unification of cooperating teachers' and teacher education students' diverse perspectives.* Paper presented at the Annual Meeting of the American Educational Research Association, New Orleans, LA.

Mathews, J. (1988). *Escalante: The best teacher in the world.* New York: Holt.

Maxie, A. P. (1989, March). *Student teachers' concerns and the student-teaching experience: Does experience make a difference?* Paper presented at the Annual Meeting of the American Educational Research Association, San Francisco, CA.

McDaniel, J. E. (1991, April). *Close encounters: How do student teachers make sense of the social foundations?* Paper presented at the Annual Meeting of the American Educational Research Association, Chicago, IL.

McDonald, J. P. (1986). Raising the teacher's voice and the ironic role of theory. *Harvard Educational Review, 56*(4), 355-378.

McGuire, M., & Guest, K. (1992, February). *Community field experience for preservice teachers.* Paper presented at the Annual Meeting of American Teacher Educators, Orlando, FL.

McIntyre, D., & Morris, W. (1980). Research on the student teaching triad. *Contemporary Education, 51*(4), 193-196.

McIntyre, D. J. (1983). *Field experiences in teacher education: From student to teacher.* Washington, DC: Foundation for Excellence in Teacher Education and the ERIC Clearinghouse on Teacher Education.

McLaren, P. (1986). *Schooling as a ritual performance: Towards a political economy of educational symbols and gestures.* London: Routledge & Kagan Paul.

McLaren, P. (1989). *Life in schools: An introduction to critical pedagogy in the foundations of education.* New York: Longman.

McLaughlin, H. J. (1988, February). *The reflection in the blackboard: Student teacher self-evaluation.* Paper presented at the Ethnography in Education conference, Philadelphia, PA.

McNay, M., & Cole, A. L. (1989). Induction programs in Ontario schools: Current views and directions for the future. *Education Canada. 29*(1), 9-15.

McNay, M., & Cole, A. L. (1993). A whole school approach to the practicum. *McGill Journal of Education, 28*(1), 115-131.

McNeely, S. R., & Mertz, N. T. (1990, April). *Cognitive constructs of preservice teachers: Research on how student teachers think about teaching.* Paper presented at the Annual Meeting of the American Educational Research Association, Boston, MA.

Metzger, M. T., & Fox, C. (1986). Two teachers of letters. *Harvard Educational Review, 56*(4), 349-354.

Moles, O. C. (1987). Who wants parent involvement? Interests, skills, and opportunities among parents and educators. *Education and Urban Society, 19*(2), 127-146.

Morris, J. E., & Morris, G. W. (1980). Stress in student teaching. *Action in Teacher Education, 2*(4), 57-62.

NASSP Bulletin. (1968, October). (National Association of Secondary School Principals). Alexandria, VA: Author.

National Association of Elementary School Principals (1989-1990). *Platform 1989-1990.* Alexandria, VA: Author.

National Education Association (1988, December 17-24). The 1988-1989 resolutions of the National Education Association. *NEA Today.*

Neill, A. S. (1960). *Summerhill: A radical approach to child rearing.* New York: Simon & Schuster.

Neira, C. (1988). Building 860. *Harvard Educational Review, 56*(3), 337-342.

Nias, J., Southworth, G. & Yeomans, R. (1989). *Staff relationships in the primary school: A study of organizational cultures.* London: Cassell.

Noffke, S. E., & Brennan, M. (1988, April). *The dimensions of reflection: A conceptual and contextual analysis.* Paper presented at the Annual Meeting of the American Educational Research Association, New Orleans, LA.

O'Connell Rust, F. (1988). How supervisors think about teaching. *Journal of Teacher Education, 39*(2), 56-64.

Odell, S. J. (1989). Developing support programs for beginning teachers. In L. Huling-Austin, S. J. Odell, P. Ishler, R. S. Kay, & R. A. Edelfelt (Eds.). *Assisting the beginning teacher* (pp. 19–38). Reston, VA: Association of Teacher Educators.

O'Neal, S. F. (1983). *Supervision of student teachers: Feedback and evaluation.* Austin: University of

Austin, R & D Center for Teacher Education. (ERIC Document Reproduction Service No. ED 240 106)

Paine, L. (1988, April). *Prospective teachers' orientations towards diversity.* Paper presented at the Annual Meeting of the American Educational Research Association, New Orleans, LA.

Paley, V. G. (1981). *Wally's stories.* Cambridge, MA: Harvard University Press.

Paley, V. G. (1986). *Mollie is three: Growing up in school.* Chicago: University of Chicago Press.

Paley, V. G. (1986). On listening to what the children say. *Harvard Educational Review, 56*(2), 122-131.

Paley, V. G. (1988). *Bad guys don't have birthdays: Fantasy play at four.* Chicago: University of Chicago Press.

Paley, V. G. (1989). *White teacher.* Cambridge, MA: Harvard University Press.

Paley, V. G. (1990). *The boy who would be a helicopter: The uses of storytelling in the classroom.* Cambridge, MA: Harvard University Press.

Palonsky, S. B. (1986). *900 shows a year.* New York: Random House.

Pape, S., & Dickens, J. (1990, February). *Learning the wisdom to teach.* Paper presented at the Annual Meeting of the Association of Teacher Educators, Las Vegas, NV.

Perry, I. (1988). A black student's reflection on public and private schools. *Harvard Educational Review, 56*(3), 332-336.

Peshkin, A. (1986). *God's choice: The total world of a fundamentalist Christian school.* Chicago: University of Chicago Press.

Peshkin, A. (1991). *The color of strangers, the color of friends: The play of ethnicity in school and community.* Chicago: University of Chicago Press.

Phi Delta Kappan. (1980). *Why do some urban schools succeed?* Bloomington, IN: Author.

Pigge, F. L., & Marso, R. N. (1989, March). *A longitudinal assessment of the affective impact of preservice training on prospective teachers.* Paper presented at the Annual Meeting of the American Educational Research Association, San Francisco, CA.

Poirier, C. F. (1992). A student teacher's voice: Reflections on power. *Journal of Education for Teaching, 18*(1), 85-91.

Pritchard, E. F. (1974). *Matching student teachers with cooperating teachers: A review of the literature.*

(ERIC Document Reproduction Service No. ED 087 759)

Progoff, I. (1975). *At a journal workshop.* New York: Dialogue House Library.

Rich, D. (1985). *The forgotten factor in school success— The family.* Washington, DC: Home School Institute.

Rich, D. (1987a). *Teachers and parents: An adult to adult approach.* Washington, DC: National Education Association Press.

Rich, D. (1987b). *Schools and families: Issues and actions.* Washington, DC: National Education Association Press.

Richardson-Koehler, V. (1988). Barriers to the effective supervision of student teaching: A field study. *Journal of Teacher Education, 39*(2), 28-34.

Riner, P., & Jones, W. P. (1990, February). *The reality of failure: Two case studies in teaching.* Paper presented at the Annual Meeting of the Association of Teacher Educators, Las Vegas, NV.

Rosenholtz, S. J. (1987). Workplace conditions of teacher quality and commitment: Implications for the design of teacher induction programs. In G. A. Griffin & S. Millies (Eds.), *The first years of teaching: Background papers and a proposal.* Chicago, IL: University of Illinois at Chicago.

Rosenholtz, S. J. (1989). *Teachers' workplace: The social organization of schools.* New York: Longman.

Ross, D. D., & Smith, W. (1992). Understanding preservice teachers' perspectives on diversity. *Journal of Teacher Education, 43*(2), 94-103.

Ross, E. W. (1987). Teacher perspective development: A study of preservice social studies teachers. *Theory and Research in Social Education, 15*(4), 225-243.

Ross, E. W., Cornett, J. W., & McCutcheon, G. (1992). *Teacher personal theorizing: Connecting curriculum practice theory and research.* Albany, NY: State University of New York Press.

Ross, L., Bierbrauer, G., & Polly, S. (1974). The impact of the student teaching experience on the development of teacher perspectives. *Journal of Teacher Education, 35*(6), 28-36.

Russell, T., Munby, H., Spafford, C., & Johnston, P. (1988). Learning the professional knowledge of teaching: Metaphors, puzzles, and the theory-practice relationship. In P. Grimmett & G. Erickson (Eds.), *Reflection in teacher education* (pp. 67-89). New York: Teachers College Press.

Ryan, K. (Ed.). (1970). *Don't smile until Christmas.* Chicago: University of Chicago Press.

Ryan, K. (1986). *The induction of new teachers.* Bloomington, IN: Phi Delta Kappan Educational Foundation.

Ryan, K. (Ed.). (1992). *The roller coaster year: Essays by and for beginning teachers.* Boston, MA: HarperCollins.

Ryan, K., Newman, K. K., Mager, G., Applegate, J., Lasley, T., Flora, R., & Johnston, J. (1980). *Biting the apple.* New York: Longman.

Ryan, P. M., & Robinson, K. S. (1990, March). *Enhancing the preservice teacher's contextual understanding about their learners.* Paper presented at the Annual Meeting of the American Association of Colleges for Teacher Education, Chicago, IL.

Sacks, S. R., & Harrington, G. (1982, April). *Student to teacher: The process of role transition.* Paper presented at the Annual Meeting of the American Educational Research Association, New York.

Sapon-Shevin, M. (1991). As we teach, we change our students and ourselves. *Teaching Education, 4*(1), 63-67.

Sarason, S. B. (1982). *The culture of the school and the problem of change.* Boston: Allyn & Bacon.

Saunders, S. (1991). Reflections on my educational experiences as an African-American. *Teaching Education, 4*(1), 41-48.

Schlechty, P., & Vance, V. (1983). Recruitment, selection and retention: The shape of the teaching force. *Elementary School Journal, 83,* 469-487.

Schnur, J. O., Kersh M. E., & Slick, G. A. (1992, February). *A paradigm for student teaching abroad.* Paper presented at the Annual Meeting of the Association of Teacher Educators, Orlando, FL.

Schoem, D. (Ed.). (1991). *Inside separate worlds: Life stories of young Blacks, Jews, and Latinos.* Ann Arbor, MI: University of Michigan Press.

Schofield, J. W. (1989). *Black and white in school: Trust, tension, or tolerance?* New York: Teachers College Press.

Schön, D. A. (1983). *The reflective practitioner: How professionals think in action.* New York: Basic Books.

Schön, D. A. (1987). *Educating the reflective practitioner.* San Francisco, CA: Jossey-Bass.

Schön, D. A. (1988). Coaching reflective teaching. In P. Grimmett & G. Erickson (Eds.), *Reflection in teacher education* (pp. 19-30). New York: Teachers College Press.

Schön, D. A. (Ed.). (1991). *The reflective turn: Case studies in and on educational practice.* New York: Teachers College Press.

Schumer, B., & Knowles, J. G. (1991, April). *A case study of second-career and traditional student teachers' beliefs about pupil control.* Paper presented at the Annual Meeting of the American Educational Research Association, Chicago, IL.

Schwab, R. (1989, March). *Stress and the intern teacher: An exploratory study.* Paper presented at the Annual Meeting of the American Educational Research Association, San Francisco, CA.

Shack, S. (1965). *Armed with a primer: A Canadian teacher looks at children, schools, and parents.* Toronto, Ontario: McClelland & Stewart.

Shapiro, B. L. (1991). A collaborative approach to help novice science teachers reflect on changes in their construction of the role of science teacher. *Alberta Journal of Educational research, 37,* 119-132.

Shulman, L. S. (1986). Those who understand: Knowledge growth in teaching. *Educational Researcher, 15,* 4-14.

Shulman, L. S. (1987). Knowledge and teaching: Foundations of the new reform. *Harvard Educational Review, 57*(1), 1-22.

Sikes, P., & Aspinwall, K. (1990, April). *Time to reflect: Biographical study, personal insight and professional development.* Paper presented at the Annual Meeting of the American Educational Research Association, Boston, MA.

Silvernail, D. L., & Costello, M. H. (1983). The impact of student teaching and internship programs on preservice teachers' pupil control perspectives, anxiety levels, and teaching concerns. *Journal of Teacher Education, 34*(4), 32-36.

Solnicki, J. (1992). *The real me is gonna be a shock.* Toronto, Ontario: Lester.

Spradley, J. P., (1979). *The ethnographic interview.* New York: Holt, Rinehart, & Winston.

Stallworth, J. T., & Williams, D. L., Jr. (1983). *A survey of school administrators and policy makers: Executive summary of the final report. Parent involvement in education project.* Austin, TX: Southwest Educational Development Laboratory.

Staton, J., Shuy, R. W., Peyton, J. K., & Reed, L. (1988). *Dialogue journal communication: Classroom, linguistic, social and cognitive views.* Norwood, NJ: Ablex.

Steinitz, V. A., & Soloman, E. R. (1986). *Starting out: Class and community in the lives of working class youth.* Philadelphia, PA: Temple University Press.

Stout, C. (1982). Why cooperating teachers accept students. *Journal of Teacher Education, 33*(6), 22-24.

Strahan, D. (1989). Experienced and novice teachers' reflections on instruction: An analysis of semantic ordered trees. *Teaching and Teacher Education, 5,* 53-67.

Strahan, D. (1990, April). *A developmental analysis of preservice teachers' orientations toward themselves, their students, and their subject matter.* Paper presented at the at the Annual Meeting of the American Educational Research Association, Boston, MA.

Stuart, J. L. (1949). *The thread that runs so true.* New York: Charles Scribner's Sons.

Sudzina, M., & Knowles. J. G. (1993). Personal, professional and contextual circumstances of student teachers who "fail": Setting a course for understanding failure in teacher education. *Journal of Teacher Education, 44*(4), 254–262.

Swap, S. (1987). *Enhancing parent involvement in schools.* New York: Teachers College Press.

Swap, S. (1990). *Parent involvement and success for all children: What we know now.* Boston: Institute for Responsive Education.

Tabachnick, B. R., & Zeichner, K. M. (1984) The impact of the student teaching experience on the development of teacher perspectives. *Journal of Teacher Education, 15*(6), 28-36.

Thiessen, D. (1991, April). *Student-teacher relationships and the emerging professional identity of a first year teacher.* Paper presented at the Annual Meeting of the American Educational Research Association, Chicago, IL.

Tittle, C. K. (1974). *Student teaching: Attitude and research bases for change in school and university.* Metuchen, NJ: Scarecrow Press.

Turney, C., Eltis, K. J., Towler, J., & Wright, R. (1985). *A new basis for teacher education: The practicum curriculum.* Sydney, Australia: Sydmac Academic Press.

Veenman, S. (1984). Perceived problems of beginning teachers. *Review of Educational Research, 54,* 143-178.

Walberg, H. L. (1986). Home environment and school learning: Some quantitative models and research synthesis. In R. J. Griffore & R. P. Boger (Eds.), *Child rearing in the home and school* (pp. 104-120). New York: Plenum.

Walberg, H. L., Metzner, S., Todd, R., & Henry, P. (1968). Effects of tutoring and practice teaching on self-concepts and attitudes in education students. *Journal of Teacher Education, 19,* 283-291.

Watts, D. (1987). Student teaching. In M. Haberman & J. M. Backus (Eds.), *Advances in teacher education* (Vol. 3, pp. 151-167). Norwood, NJ: Ablex.

Wear, D., & Hawthorne, R. (1991). No matter how you slice it . . . emotional spaces between teachers and students. *Teaching Education, 4*(1), 123-132.

Weinstein, C. S. (1988). Preservice teachers' expectations about the first year of teaching. *Teaching and Teacher Education, 4*(1), 31-40.

Weinstein, C. S. (1989). Teacher education students' preconceptions of teaching. *Journal of Teacher Education, 40*(2), 53-60.

Weinstein, C. S. (1990). Prospective elementary teachers' beliefs about teaching: Implications for teacher education. *Teaching and Teacher Education, 6,* 279-290.

Westerback, M. E. (1982). Studies on attitude toward teaching science and anxiety about science in preservice elementary teachers. *Journal of Research in Science Teaching, 19*(7), 603-616.

Wildman, T. M., Magliaro, S. G., Niles, R. A., & Niles, J. A. (1992). Teacher mentoring: An analysis of roles, activities, and conditions. *Journal of Teacher Education, 43*(3), 205-213.

Williams, D. L. (1989). *Attitudes toward parent involvement and implications for teacher education.* Berkeley, CA: University of California.

Williams, D. L. (1992). Parental involvement teacher preparation: Challenges to teacher education. In L. Kaplan (Ed.), *Education and the family* (pp. 243-254). Boston: Allyn & Bacon.

Williams, D. L., & Stallworth, J. T. (1983). *Parent involvement and elementary school teacher training.* Austin, TX: Southwest Educational Development Laboratory.

Witherell, C., & Makler, A. (1989, March). *Giving each other reason: Building a community of inquirers through collaborative teacher education.* Paper presented at the Annual Meeting of the American Educational Research Association, San Francisco, CA.

Witherell, C., & Noddings, N. (Eds.). (1991). *Stories lives tell: Narrative and dialogue in education.* New York: Teachers College Press.

Woods, P. (1986). *Inside schools*. London: Routledge & Kagan Paul.

Worth, K. (1990, April). *The Wheelock/Brookline collaborative: The internship program*. Paper presented at the Annual Meeting of the American Educational Research Association, Boston, MA.

Wright, B. (1959). Identification and becoming a teacher. *Elementary School Journal, 59*(7), 361–374.

Wright, B., & Tuska, S. (1967). The childhood romance theory of teacher development. *School Review, 25*, 123–154.

Wright, B., & Tuska, S. (1968). From dream to life in the psychology of becoming a teacher. *School Review, 27*(3), 253–293.

Zahorik, J. A. (1988). The observing–conferencing role of university supervisors. *Journal of Teacher Education, 39*(2), 9-16.

Zeichner, K. M. (1980). Myths and realities: Field based experiences in preservice teacher education. *Journal of Teacher Education, 31*(6), 45-46.

Zeichner, K. M. (1983). Individual and institutional factors related to the socialization of beginning teachers. In G. Griffin & H. Hukill (Eds.), *First years of teaching: What are the pertinent issues?* (pp. 1–60). Austin, TX: University of Texas, Research & Development Center for Teacher Education.

Zeichner, K. M. (1990). Changing directions in the practicum: Looking ahead to the 1990's. *Journal of Education for Teaching, 16*(2), 105-132.

Zeichner, K. M. (1992). Rethinking the practicum in the professional development school partnership. *Journal of Teacher Education, 43*(4), 296-307.

Zeichner, K. M., & Gore, J. M. (1990). Teacher socialization. In W. R. Houston (Ed.), *Handbook of research on teacher education* (pp. 329-348). New York: Macmillan.

Zeichner, K. M., & Grant, C. A. (1981). Biography and social structure in the socialization of student teachers: A re-examination of the pupil control ideologies of student teachers. *Journal of Education for Teaching, 7*(3), 298-314.

Zeichner, K. M., & Liston, D. P. (1987). Teaching student teachers to reflect. *Harvard Educational Review, 57*(1), 23-48.

Zeichner, K. M., & Tabachnick, B. (1981). Are the effects of university teacher education "washed out" by school experience? *Journal of Teacher Education, 32*(3), 7-11.

Zeichner, K. M., & Teitelbaum, K. (1982). Personalized and inquiry oriented teacher education: An analysis of two approaches to the development of curriculum for field-based experiences. *Journal of Education for Teaching, 8*(2), 95-117.

Zevin, J. (1974, April). *In the cooperating teacher's image: Convergence of social studies student teachers' behavior patterns with cooperating teachers' behavior patterns*. Paper presented at the Annual Meeting of the American Educational Research Association, Chicago. (ERIC Document Reproduction Service No. ED 087 781)

Zimpher, N., deVoss, G., & Nott, D. (1980). A closer look at university student teacher supervision. *Journal of Teacher Education, 31*(4), 11-15.

Zitlow, C. S. (1986). A search for images: Inquiry with preservice teachers. (ERIC Document Reproduction Service No. ED 284 211)

Bibliography

Agar, M. H. (1980). *The professional stranger: An informal introduction to ethnography.* Orlando, FL: Academic Press.

Aptekar, L. (1988). *Street children of Cali.* Durham: Duke University Press.

Armstrong, M. (1980) *Closely observed children: The diary of a primary classroom.* London: Writers and Readers Publishing Cooperative Society.

Ashton-Warner, S. (1963). *Teacher.* New York: Simon & Schuster.

Ashton-Warner, S. (1972). *Spearpoint.* New York: Alfred A. Knopf.

Axline, V. M. (1964). *Dibs in search of self.* New York: Ballantine Books.

Ball, S. J., & Goodson, I. F. (1985). *Teachers' lives and careers.* London: Falmer Press.

Barker, R. G., & Gump, P. V. (1964). *Big school, small school.* Stanford, CA: Stanford University Press.

Beck, L. G., & Murphey, J. (1993). *Understanding the principalship.* New York: Teachers College Press.

Berger, E. H. (1987). *Beyond the classroom: Parents as partners in education.* Columbus, OH: Merrill.

Bey, T. M., & Holmes, C. T. (Eds.). (1990). *Mentoring: Developing successful new teachers.* Reston, VA. Association of Teacher Educators.

Bey, T. M., & Holmes, C. T. (Eds.). (1992). *Mentoring: Contemporary principles and issues.* Reston, VA: Association of Teacher Educators.

Bissex, G. L., & Bullock, R. H. (1987). *Seeing for ourselves.* Portsmouth, NH: Heinemann.

Bogdan, R. C., & Biklen, S. K. (1992). *Qualitative research for education: An introduction to theory and methods.* Needham Heights, MA: Allyn & Bacon.

Bossert, S. (1979). *Tasks and social relationships in classrooms.* Cambridge: Cambridge University Press.

Brause, R. S., & Smayher, J. S. (1991). *Search and research: What the inquiring teacher needs to know.* London: Falmer Press.

Britzman, D. P. (1991). *Practice makes practice: A critical study of learning to teach.* Albany, NY: State University of New York Press.

Bruckerhoff, C. E. (1991). *Between classes: Faculty life at Truman High.* New York: Teachers College Press.

Bullough, R. V., Jr. (1989). *First year teacher: A case study.* New York: Teachers College Press.

Bullough, R. V., Jr., Knowles, J. G., & Crow, N. A. (1991). *Emerging as a teacher.* London: Routledge, Chapman, & Hall.

Cangelosi, J. S. (1988). *Classroom management strategies.* White Plains, NY: Longman.

Carini, P. F. (1979). *The art of seeing and the visibility of the person.* Grand Forks, ND: University of North Dakota Press.

Carini, P. F. (1982). *The school lives of seven children: A five year study.* Grand Forks, ND: University of North Dakota Press.

Chang, H. (1992). *Adolescent life and ethos: An ethnography of a U.S. high school.* Bristol, PA: Falmer Press.

Clandinin, D. J. (1986). *Classroom practice: Teacher images in action.* East Sussex: Falmer Press.

Clark, R. M. (1983). *Family life and school achievement: Why poor black children succeed or fail.* Chicago: University of Chicago Press.

Clift, R. T., & Evertson, C. M. (1992). *Focal points: Qualitative inquiries into teaching and teacher education.* Washington, DC: ERIC Clearinghouse on Teacher Education.

Cohen, R. M. (1991). *A lifetime of teaching: Portraits of five veteran high school teachers.* New York: Teachers College Press.

Coleman, J. S. (1961). *The adolescent society.* New York: Free Press.

Coles, R. (1986). *The moral life of children: How children struggle with questions of moral choice in the United States and elsewhere.* Boston: Houghton Mifflin.

Connelly, F. M., & Clandinin, D. J. (1988). *Teachers as curriculum planners*. New York: Teachers College Press.

Conroy, P. (1972). *The water is wide*. Boston: Houghton Mifflin.

Cottle, T. (1973). *The voices of school: Educational issues through personal accounts*. Boston: Little Brown.

Cusick, P. (1972). *Inside high school*. New York: Holt, Rinehart, & Winston.

Daiker, D. A., & Morenberg, M. (1990). *The writing teacher as researcher: Essays in the theory and practice of class-based research*. Portsmouth, NH: Boynton Cook.

Davies, B. (1982). *Life in the classroom and playground*. Boston: Routledge & Kagan Paul.

Dennison, George. (1969). *The lives of children: The story of the First Street school*. New York: Random House.

Diamond, C. T. P. (1991). *Teacher education as transformation*. Milton Keynes/Philadelphia: Open University Press.

Dichter, S. (1989). *Teachers: Straight talk from the trenches*. Los Angeles: Contemporary Books.

Dillard, A. (1987). *An American childhood*. New York: Harper & Row.

Disbrowe, H. B. (1984). *A schoolman's odyssey*. London, Ontario: University of Western Ontario.

Dollase, R. (1992). *Voices of beginning teachers*. New York: Teachers College Press.

Dworkin, A. G. (1987). *Teacher burnout in the public schools: Structural causes and consequences for children*. Albany, NY: State University of New York Press.

Eckert, P. (1989). *Jocks & burnouts: Social categories and identity in the high school*. New York Teachers College Press.

Eddy, E. M. (1969). *Becoming a teacher*. New York: Teachers College Press.

Epstein, J. L. (1990). *School and family connections: Theory, research, and implications for integrating sociologies of education and family*. New York: Haworth Press.

Epstein, J. L., & Becker, H. J. (1982). *Teacher reported practices of parent involvement: Problems and possibilities*. Baltimore, MD: Johns Hopkins University Press.

Everhart, R. (1983). *Reading writing and resistance: Adolescence and labor on a junior high school*. Boston: Routledge & Kagan Paul.

Fedullo, M. (1992). *Light of the feather*. New York: William Morrow.

Ferri, B., & Aglio, M. (1990). *I'm not alone: Teacher talk, teacher buddying*. Mississauga, Ontario: Peel Board of Education.

Fletcher, R. (1990). *Walking trees: Teaching teachers in the New York City schools*. Portsmouth, NH: Heinemann.

Fosnot, C. T. (1989). *Enquiring teachers enquiring learners: A constructivist approach for teaching*. New York: Teachers College Press.

Frederick, E., & Shultz, J. (1983). *The counselor as gatekeeper*. New York: Academic Press.

Freedman S. G. (1990). *Small victories: The real world of a teacher, her students and their high school*. New York: Harper & Row.

Froyen, L. A. (1993). *Classroom management: Empowering teacher-leaders* (2nd ed.). New York: Merrill/Macmillan.

Fulwiler, T. (1987). *The Journal Book*. Portsmouth, NH: Boynton Cook.

Giroux, H. A., & Simon, R. I. (1989). *Popular culture, schooling, and everyday life*. Toronto: Ontario Institute for Studies in Education Press.

Gitlin, A. (1992). *Teachers' voices for school change*. New York: Teachers College Press.

Gitlin, A., & Goldstein, S. (1987). A dialogical approach to understanding: Horizontal evaluation. *Educational Theory*, 37(1), 17-27.

Gitlin, A., & Smyth. J. (1989). *Teacher evaluation: Educative alternatives*. Barcombe, Lewes, East Sussex: Falmer Press.

Glenn, M. (1982). *Class dismissed: High school poems by Mel Glenn*. New York: Ticknor & Fields.

Glenn, M. (1986). *Class dismissed II: More high school poems*. New York: Ticknor & Fields.

Glover, M. K. (1992). *Two years: A teacher's memoir*. Portsmouth, NH: Heinemann.

Goetz, J. P., & LeCompte, M. D. (1984). *Ethnography and qualitative design in educational research*. Orlando, FL: Academic Press.

Good, T. L., & Brophy, J. E. (1991). *Looking in classrooms* (5th ed.). New York: HarperCollins Publishers.

Goodson, I. F., & Walker, R. (1991). *Biography, identity and schooling episodes in educational research*. London: Falmer Press.

Goswami, D., & Stillman, P. R. (1987). *Reclaiming the classroom*. Upper Montclair, NJ: Boynton Cook.

Grant, C. A., & Sleeter, C. E. (1986). *After the school bell rings*. Philadelphia, PA: Falmer Press.

Greenstein, J. (1983). *What the children taught me.* Chicago: University of Chicago Press.

Grumet, M. (1988). *Bitter milk.* Amherst, MA: University of Massachusetts Press.

Hammersley, M. (1990). *Classroom ethnography.* Toronto, Ontario: OISE Press.

Hargreaves, A., & Fullan, M. G. (Eds.). (1992). *Understanding teacher development.* New York: Teachers College Press.

Hayden, T. L. (1980). *One child.* New York: G.P. Putnam's Sons.

Hayden, T. L. (1981). *Somebody else's kids.* New York: Avon Books.

Heck, S. F., & Williams, C. R. (1984). *The complex roles of the teacher: An ecological perspective.* New York: Teachers College Press.

Holt, J. (1964, 1982). *How children fail.* New York: Dell.

Holt, J. (1967, 1983). *How children learn .* New York: Dell.

Howe, Q., Jr. (1991). *Under running laughter.* New York: Free Press.

Huling-Austin, L. (1989). Beginning teacher assistance programs: An overview. In L. Huling-Austin, S. J. Odell, P. Ishler, R. S. Kay, & R. A. Edelfelt (Eds.). *Assisting the beginning teacher.* Reston, VA: Association of Teacher Educators.

Hunt, D. E. (1987). *Beginning with ourselves: In theory, practice and human affairs.* Cambridge, MA/Toronto, Ontario: Brookline Books/OISE Press.

Hunt, D. E. (1991). *The renewal of personal energy.* Toronto, Ontario: OISE Press.

Hunter, L. (1992). *The diary of Latoya Hunter: My first year in junior high.* New York: Crown.

Jackson, P. W. (1990). *Life in classrooms* (rev. ed.). New York: Teachers College Press

Jersild, A. T. (1955). *When teachers face themselves.* New York: Teachers College Press.

Johnson, S. M. (1990). *Teachers at work: Achieving success in our schools.* New York: Basic Books/HarperCollins.

Jones, G. (1991). *Crocus Hill notebook.* London, Ontario: Althouse Press.

Kane, P. R. (Ed.). (1991). *The first year of teaching: Real world stories from America's teachers.* Columbia University: Teachers College.

Kaplan, L. (Ed.). (1992). *Education and the family.* Boston: Allyn & Bacon.

Keizer, G. (1988). *No place but here: A teacher's vocation in a rural community.* New York: Penguin Books.

Kidder, T. (1989). *Among schoolchildren.* Boston, MA: Houghton Mifflin.

Kincheloe, J. L. (1991). *Teachers as researchers: Qualitative inquiry as a path to empowerment.* London: Falmer Press.

Kobrin, D. (1992). *In there with the kids: Teaching in today's classrooms.* Boston: Houghton Mifflin.

Kohl, H. (1967). *Thirty-six children.* New York: New American Library.

Kohl, H. (1982). *Insight: The substance and rewards of teaching.* Menlo Park, CA: Addison-Weslsy.

Kohl, H. (1984). *Growing minds: On becoming a teacher.* New York: Harper & Row.

Kotlowitz, A. (1991). *There are no children here: The story of two boys growing up in the other America.* New York: Doubleday.

Kottak, C. P. (Ed.). (1982). *Researching American culture: A guide for student anthropologists.* Ann Arbor, MI: University of Michigan Press.

Kowalski, T. J., Weaver, R. A., & Henson, K. T. (1990). *Case studies on teaching.* New York: Longman.

Kozol, J. (1967). *Death at an early age.* New York: New American Library.

Kozol, J. (1988). *Rachel and her children: Homeless families in America.* New York: Crown.

Kozol, J. (1991). *Savage inequalities.* New York: Crown.

Kronowitz, E. L. (1992). *Beyond student teaching.* New York: Longman.

Kroth, R. L. (1984). *Communicating with parents of exceptional children: Improving parent-teacher relationships.* Denver, CO:Love.

Lareau, A. (1989). *Home advantage: Social class and parental intervention in elementary education.* Philadelphia, PA: Falmer Press.

Lieberman, A., & Miller, L. (1992). *Teachers—Their world and their work.* New York: Teachers College Press.

Lortie, Dan C. (1975). *Schoolteacher: A sociological study.* Chicago: University of Chicago Press.

Louden, W. (1991). *Understanding teaching: Continuity and change in teachers' knowledge.* New York: Teachers College Press.

Lubeck, S. (1985). *Sandbox society: Early education in black & white America.* London: Falmer Press.

Lytle, S. L., & Cochran-Smith, M. (1992). Teacher research as a way of knowing. *Harvard Educational Research, 62*(4), 447-474.

Macrorie, K. (1984). *20 teachers*. New York: Oxford University Press.

Mathews, J. (1988). *Escalante: The best teacher in the world*. New York: Henry Holt.

McLaren, P. (1989). *Life in schools: An introduction to critical pedagogy in the foundations of education*. New York: Longman.

Mohr, M. M., & Maclean, M. S. (1987). *Working together: A guide for teacher-researchers*. Urbana, IL: National Council of Teachers of English.

Mortimore, P., Sammons, P., Stoll, L., Lewis, D., & Ecob, R. (1988). *School matters*. Berkeley CA: University of California Press.

Natkins, L. G. (1986). *Our last term: A teacher's diary*. Lanham, MD: University Press of America.

Nehring, J. (1989). *Why do we gotta do this stuff, Mr. Nehring?: Notes from a teacher's day in school*. New York: Fawcett.

Neill, A. S. (1960). *Summerhill: A radical approach to child rearing*. New York: Simon & Schuster.

Newman, J. M. (1989). *Finding our own way: Teachers exploring their assumptions*. Portsmouth, NH: Heinemann.

Nias J., & Groundwater-Smith, S. (1988). *The enquiring teacher*. London: Falmer Press.

Nias, J., Southworth, G, & Yeomans, R. (1989). *Staff relationships in the primary school: A study of organizational cultures*. London: Cassell.

Oja, S. N., & Smulyan, L. (1989). *Collaborative action research: A developmental approach*. Philadelphia, PA: Falmer Press.

Paley, V. G. (1981). *Wally's stories*. Cambridge, MA: Harvard University Press.

Paley, V. G. (1986). *Mollie is three: Growing up in school*. Chicago: University of Chicago Press.

Paley, V. G. (1988). *Bad guys don't have birthdays: Fantasy play at four*. Chicago: University of Chicago Press.

Paley, V. G. (1990). *The boy who would be a helicopter: The uses of storytelling in the classroom*. Cambridge, MA: Harvard University Press.

Palonsky, S. B. (1986). *900 shows a year*. New York: Random House.

Perl, S., & Wilson, N. (1986). *Through teachers' eyes: Portraits of writing teachers at work*. Portsmouth, NH: Heinemann Educational Books.

Perrone, V. (1991). *A letter to teachers*. San Francisco, CA: Jossey-Bass.

Peshkin, A. (1986). *God's choice: The total world of a fundamentalist Christian school*. Chicago: University of Chicago Press.

Peshkin, A. (1991). *The color of strangers, the color of friends: The play of ethnicity in school and community*. Chicago: University of Chicago Press.

Posner, G. J. (1989). *Field experience: methods of reflective teaching*. New York: Longman.

Progoff, I. (1975). *At a journal workshop*. New York: Dialogue House Library.

Roe, B. D., Ross, E. P., & Burns, P. C. (1989). *Student teaching and field experiences handbook*. New York: Macmillan.

Ross, E. W., Cornett, J. W., & McCutcheon, G. (Eds.). *Teacher personal theorizing: Connecting curriculum practice, theory, and research*. (1992). Albany, NY: State University of New York Press.

Rosenholtz, S. J. (1989). *Teachers' workplace: The social organization of schools*. White Plains, NY: Longman.

Russell, T., & Munby, H. (Eds.). (1992). *Teachers and teaching: From classroom to reflection*. Bristol, PA: Falmer Press.

Ryan, K. (Ed.). (1970). *Don't smile until Christmas*. Chicago: University of Chicago Press.

Ryan, K. (Ed.). (1992). *The roller coaster year: Essays by and for beginning teachers*. Boston, MA: HarperCollins.

Ryan, K., Newman, K. K., Mager, G., Applegate, J., Lasley, T., Flora, R., & Johnston, J. (1980). *Biting the apple*. New York: Longman.

Schoem, D. (Ed.). (1991). *Inside separate worlds: Life stories of young Blacks, Jews, and Latinos*. Ann Arbor, MI: University of Michigan Press.

Schofield, J. W. (1989). *Black and white in school: Trust, tension, or tolerance*. New York: Teachers College Press.

Schubert, W. H., & Ayers, W. C. (1992). *Teacher lore: Learning from our own experience*. New York: Longman.

Shack, S. (1965). *Armed with a primer: A Canadian teacher looks at children, schools, and parents*. Toronto, Ontario: McClelland & Stewart.

Shaw, Clifford. (1966). *Jack the roller: A delinquent boy's own story*. Chicago: University of Chicago Press.

Shulman, J. H. (1992). *Case methods in teacher education*. New York: Teachers College Press.

Shulman, J. H., & Colbert, J. A. (1987). *The mentor teacher casebook.* Oregon: ERIC Clearinghouse on Educational Management and Far West Laboratory for Educational Research and Development.

Shulman, J. H., & Colbert, J. A. (1988). *The intern teacher casebook.* Oregon: ERIC Clearinghouse on Educational Management, Far West Laboratory for Educational Research and Development and ERIC Clearinghouse on Teacher Education.

Shuman, A. (1986). *Storytelling rights: The uses of oral and written texts by urban adolescents.* Cambridge, MA: Cambridge University Press.

Spindler, G. (1982). *Doing the ethnography of schooling: Educational anthropology in action.* New York: CBS College.

Spindler, G., & Spindler, L. (Eds.). (1987). *Interpretive ethnography of education: At home and abroad.* Hillsdale, NJ: Lawrence Erlbaum.

Spradley, J. P. (1979). *The ethnographic interview.* New York: Holt, Rinehart, & Winston.

Spradley, J. P. (1980). *Participant observation.* New York: Holt, Rinehart, & Winston.

Staton, J., Shuy, R. W., Peyton, J. K., & Reed, L. (1988). *Dialogue journal communication: Classroom, linguistic, social and cognitive views.* Norwood, NJ: Ablex.

Steffy, B. E. (1989). *Career stages of classroom teachers.* Lancaster, PA: Ablex.

Stuart, Jesse. (1949). *The thread that runs so true.* New York: Charles Scribner's Sons.

Swap, S. (1987). *Enhancing parent involvement in schools.* New York: Teachers College Press.

Swap, S. (1990). *Parent involvement and success for all children: What we know now.* Boston: Institute for Responsive Education.

Van Manen, M. (1986). *The tone of teaching.* Richmond Hill, Ontario: Scholastic—TAB.

Walter, G. (1981). *So where's my apple?: Diary of a first-year teacher.* Prospect Heights, IL: Waveland.

Webb, J. (1990). *Children learning at home.* London: Falmer Press.

Welker, R. (1992) *The teacher as expert: A theoretical and historical examination.* Albany, NY: State University of New York Press.

Wigginton, E. (1985). *Sometimes a shining moment: The Foxfire experience.* Garden City, NY: Anchor Press/Doubleday.

Witherell, C., Noddings N. (1991). *Stories lives tell: Narrative and dialogue in education.* New York: Teachers College Press.

Wolcott, H. (1973). *The man in the principal's office: An ethnography.* New York: Holt.

Wood, D. R. (1992). Teaching narratives: A source for faculty development and evaluation. *Harvard Educational Review, 62*(4), 535-550.

Woods, P. (1986). *Inside schools.* London: Routledge & Kagan Paul.

Yee, S. M. (1990). *Careers in the classroom: When teaching is more than a job.* New York: Teachers College Press.

Video List

Azoff, I., & Linson, A. (Producers), & Heckerling, A. (Director). (1982). *Fast times at Ridgemont High* [Video]. USA: Universal City Studios.

Berman, P. S. (Producer), & Brooks, R. (Director). (1955). *Blackboard jungle* [Video]. USA: Loew's.

Black. T., & Thomas, M. (Producers), & Miller, R. (Director). (1992). *Kid 'n play: Class act* [Video]. USA: Warner Bros.

Brodek, T. H. (Producer), & Cain, C. (Director). (1987). *The principal* [Video]. USA: Tri-Star Pictures.

Clavell, J. (Producer & Director). (1967). *To Sir with love* [Video]. UK: Columbia (British) Productions.

Deutsch, S. (Producer), & Chapman, M. (Director). (1983). *All the right moves* [Video]. USA: Twentieth Century Fox.

DiNovi, D. (Producer), & Lehman, M. (Director). (1991). *Heathers* [Video]. USA: New World Pictures.

Dupont, R., & Clark, B. (Producers), & Clark, B. (Director). (1983). *A Christmas story* [Video]. USA: Metro-Goldwyn-Mayer.

Eisenstock, A., & Mintz, L. (Producers), & Amateau, R. (Director). (1983). *High school USA* [Video]. USA: Karl Lorimar Home Video.

Evans, B.A., Gideon, R., & Scheinman, A. (Producers), & Reiner, R. (Director). (1986). *Stand by me* [Video]. USA: Columbia Pictures.

Fryer, R. (Producer), & Neame, R. (Director). (1969). *The prime of Miss Jean Brodie* [Video]. England: Fox.

Gilbert, L. (Director). (1983). *Educating Rita* [Video]. UK: Good Times Home Video.

Green, H. (Producer), & Hughes, J. (Director). (1984). *Sixteen candles* [Video]. USA: Universal Studios.

Haft, S., Junger-Witt, P., & Thomas, T. (Producers), & Weir, P. (Director). (1989). *Dead poet's society* [Video]. USA: Touchstone Pictures.

Harvey, R., & Stern, S. (Producers), & Moyle, A. (Director). (1990). *Pump up the volume* [Video]. USA: New Line Cinema.

Hertzog, L. (Producer), & Narrizano, S. (Director). (1977). *Why shoot the teacher?* [Video]. CAN: Quarter Films.

Hughes, J., & Tonen, N. (Producers), & Hughes, J. (Director). (1985). *The breakfast club* [Video]. USA: Universal City Studios.

Hughes, J. (Producer), & Deutch, H. (Director). (1987). *Some kind of wonderful* [Video]. USA: Paramount Pictures.

Ikin, B. (Producer), & Campion, J. (Director). (1990). *An angel at my table* [Video]. NZ: Fine Line Features.

Krane, J. D. (Producer), & Gordon, K. (Director). (1988). *The chocolate war* [Video]. USA: Forum Home Video.

Malle, L. (Director). (1987). *Au revoir les enfants* [Video]. France: Orion Pictures.

Milloy, R. (Producer), & Hook, H. (Director). (1990). *Lord of the flies* [Video]. USA: Castle Rock Entertainment.

Musca, T. (Producer), & Menendez, R. (Director). (1987). *Stand and deliver* [Video]. Warner Brothers.

Peters, J., & Guber, P. (Producers), & Becker, H. (Director). (1985). *Vision quest* [Video]. USA: Warner Brothers.

Pillsbury, S., & Sanford, M. (Producers), & Hunter, T. (Director). (1986). *The river's edge* [Video]. USA: Nelson Entertainment/RCA/Columbia.

Platt, P. (Producer), & Crowe, C. (Director). (1989). *Say anything* [Video]. USA: Twentieth Century Fox.

Reitman, I., & Grazer, B. (Producers), & Reitman, I. (Director). (1990). *Kindergarten cop* [Video]. USA: Universal City Studios.

Reynolds, D. (Producer), & Firth, M. (Director). (1986). *Sylvia* [Video]. USA: CBS/Twentieth Century Fox.

Ronsin, C., & Star (Producers), & Attias, D. (Director). (1993). *The graduation* [Video]. USA: World Vision Home Video.

Rudin, S., & Rajski, P. (Producers), & Foster, J. (Director). (1991). *Little man Tate* [Video]. USA: Orion Pictures.

Russo, A. (Producer), & Hiller, A. (Director). (1984). *Teachers* [Video]. USA: United Artists.

Saville, V. (Producer), & Wood, S. (Director). (1939). *Goodbye, Mr. Chips* [Video]. USA: Warner Brothers.

Schuler, L. (Producer), & Deutch, H. (Director). (1986). *Pretty in pink* [Video]. USA: Paramount Pictures.

Schultz, M. (Director). (1975). *Cooley High* [Video]. USA: Orion Home Video.

Sellers, A., & Winitsky, A. (Producers), & Ritt, M. (Director). (1990). *Stanley & Iris* [Video]. USA: Metro-Goldwyn-Mayer.

Shapiro, G., & West, H. (Producers), & Reiner, C. (Director). (1987). *Summer school* [Video]. USA: Paramount Pictures.

Sugarman, B., & Palmer, P. (Producers), & Haines, R. (Director). (1986). *Children of a lesser god* [Video]. USA: Paramount Pictures.

Truffant, F. (Director). (1959 film, 1981 video). *The 400 blows* [Video]. France: Les Films du Carrosse.

Twain, N. (Producer), & Avildsen, J.G. (Director). (1989). *Lean on me* [Video]. USA: Warner Brothers.

Warner, J.L. (Producer), & Cukor, G. (Director). (1964). *My fair lady* [Video]. USA: Warner Brothers.

Author Index

Subject Index

Preservice Teacher Index

ISBN 0-02-365371-X